MW00838231

Discrete
Location Theory

Discrete Location Theory

Edited by

PITU B. MIRCHANDANI
Systems and Industrial Engineering Department
The University of Arizona
Tucson, Arizona

RICHARD L. FRANCIS
Department of Industrial and Systems Engineering
University of Florida
Gainesville, Florida

A Wiley-Interscience Publication
John Wiley & Sons, Inc.
New York / Chichester / Brisbane / Toronto / Singapore

Library of Congress Cataloging in Publication Data:

Discrete location theory / edited by Pitu B. Mirchandani, Richard L.
  Francis.
       p.   cm.--(Wiley-Interscience series in discrete mathematics
  and optimization)
    "A Wiley-Interscience publication."
    Includes bibliographies and index.
    ISBN 0-471-89233-5
    1. Industries--Location--Mathematical models.   I. Mirchandani,
  Pitu B.   II. Francis, R. L.   III. Series.
  T57.6.D565   1989
  338.6'042--dc20   89-34350
                                                           CIP

Printed in the United States of America

10 9 8 7 6 5 4 3 2 1

Contributors

RAJAN BATTA
Department of Industrial Engineering
State University of New York at Buffalo
Buffalo, NY 14260

ODED BERMAN
College of Management
University of Massachusetts
Boston, MA 02125

RAINER E. BURKARD
Institute for Mathematics
Technical University Graz
A-8010 Graz, Austria

SAMUEL S. CHIU
Engineering-Economic Systems
 Department
Stanford University
Stanford, CA 94305

GERARD CORNUEJOLS
Graduate School of Industrial
 Administration
Carnegie Mellon University
Pittsburgh, PA 15213

RICHARD L. FRANCIS
Department of Industrial and Systems
 Engineering
University of Florida
Gainesville, FL 32611

S. LOUIS HAKIMI
Department of Electrical Engineering
 and Computer Science
University of California
Davis, CA 95616

GABRIEL Y. HANDLER
Graduate School of Business
 Administration
Tel Aviv University
Ramat Aviv, Tel Aviv, Israel

PIERRE HANSEN
RUTCOR
Rutgers University
New Brunswick, NJ 08903

SØREN KRUSE JACOBSEN
The Institute of Mathematical Statistics
 and Operations Research
The Technical University of Denmark
DK-2800 Lyngby, Denmark

ANTOON KOLEN
Department of Quantitative Economics
University of Limburg
6200 MD Maastricht, The Netherlands

JAKOB KRARUP
DIKU, Department of Computer
 Science
University of Copenhagen
DK-2100 Copenhagen, Denmark

RICHARD C. LARSON
Operations Research Center
Massachusetts Institute of Technology
Cambridge, MA 02139

T. J. LOWE
College of Business Administration
University of Iowa
Iowa City, IA 52242

THOMAS L. MAGNANTI
Sloan School of Management
Massachusetts Institute of Technology
Cambridge, MA 02139

PITU B. MIRCHANDANI
Systems and Industrial Engineering
  Department
The University of Arizona
Tucson, AZ 85721

GEORGE L. NEMHAUSER
Department of Industrial and Systems
  Engineering
Georgia Institute of Technology
Atlanta, GA 30332-0440

AMEDEO R. ODONI
Operations Research Center
Massachusetts Institute of Technology
Cambridge, MA 02139

PETER M. PRUZAN
DASY, Institute of Computer and
  Systems Sciences
Copenhagen Business School
Copenhagen, Denmark

ARIE TAMIR
Department of Statistics
Tel Aviv University
Ramat Aviv, Tel Aviv, Israel

B. C. TANSEL
Department of Industrial Engineering
Bilkent University
Bilkent 06533, Ankara, Turkey

JACQUES-FRANÇOIS THISSE
Center for Operations Research and
  Econometrics
Université Catholique de Louvain
1348 Louvain-la-Neuve, Belgium

RICHARD E. WENDELL
The Joseph M. Katz Graduate School
  of Business
University of Pittsburgh
Pittsburgh, PA 15260

LAURENCE A. WOLSEY
Center for Operations Research and
  Econometrics
Université Catholique de Louvain
1348 Louvain-la-Neuve, Belgium

RICHARD T. WONG
Krannert Graduate School of
  Management
Purdue University
West Lafayette, IN 47907

Preface

To the best of our recollection, it was at the October 1981 ORSA/TIMS meeting in Houston, Texas, that we first discussed the idea of editing a state-of-the-art book on discrete location theory, with the thought that this field had reached a stage of maturity where a standard reference text would be welcomed. We approached our publisher, John Wiley and Sons, as well as several potential authors who were among the foremost authorities on various aspects of location theory, with the idea of publishing a text like this one. Everyone we talked to was encouraging, and all the authors we invited made commitments to contribute to this volume. Before we knew it our idea took root, and we were signing contracts with our publisher. Now, after innumerable delays and unforeseen circumstances, we feel, perhaps immodestly, that the idea has blossomed into this rather good book. We thank the contributing authors, and our publisher, for making this book possible.

Discrete location theory is, of course, theory for solving discrete location problems. As an introduction to such problems, consider the "Hi & Lois" cartoon. Note that the home under consideration is a good location, in the sense that the travel distance between it and a nearest hospital, restaurant, and school (not to mention a golf course) is negligible. As we shall see in subsequent chapters, travel distance, or travel cost, appears in many location problems, either in the objective function, or in the constraints, of an optimization model of a problem. Further, in the cartoon, we imagine that either the clients being shown this home will choose it or they will not; in this sense they have a discrete "zero-one" (binary) decision problem. The clients will, of course, be very interested in the cost of the house and lot,

and we shall see subsequently that such a cost, often treated as a fixed cost, is included in many location models. Thus, in several important ways, the cartoon illustrates aspects of the discrete location problems which are to come in this book. We hasten to add that most of the problems in this book are quantifiable ones encountered by companies or organizations of some sort, and not by a family buying a home.

Since we cannot claim, of course, that everyone who appreciates the cartoon will also appreciate our book, let us try to identify the potential readership of our book. There are basically two types of readers who may be interested in this book. Those who know little or nothing about location theory, but are quite knowledgeable about the mathematical concepts of operations research and related fields, should find this the ideal book to learn about discrete location theory—enough to initiate research on the subject, or to use known location models and algorithms for solving some problems of interest. The second type of reader who may be interested in this book includes those who know some special aspects of location theory, which they have learned, for example, from a course in industrial engineering, operations research, management science, computer science or geography, or those who are faced with a location problem in transportation systems analysis, design of urban service systems, computer/communication systems planning, and so on. They will find this book useful for further understanding the underlying mathematical structure, and possibly, for developing appropriate algorithms for solving location problems of special interest to them. The book may also interest readers who know little about location theory or the mathematical concepts of operations research, but they will require considerable supplementary reading and literature review if they wish to get much from the book apart from the material in Chapter 1 and some introductory material in the other chapters.

For whom is a book such as ours useful? We believe it may be useful for industrial engineers, systems analysts, computer scientists, and transportation/urban planners in industry, research laboratories, consulting companies, planning agencies, and others who wish to study and apply OR-based approaches to the problems of locating facilities or locatable entities (e.g., items, activities, warehouses, service centers, departments or machines within a facility, a silicon junction on an electronic chip, a chip on a wafer, a processor in a computer network, data files within a distributed data base, etc.) on a discrete (or discretizable) set of points to optimize a given objective. Our book should also be useful for researchers and academics (such as the authors of this book) who are interested in developing models, methods, and algorithms for problems such as those above. Finally, our book should be useful for graduate and advanced undergraduate students in Computer Science, Industrial Engineering, Management Science, Mathematics, Operations Research, Systems Engineering, and other related fields who are conducting or initiating research in discrete location theory.

Our book can be used for a one- or two-semester course in advanced location theory for university students. The tree diagram below shows the recommended precedences for reading the chapters.

A one-semester course can be obtained by going through all the chapters, but not covering thoroughly all the parts of each chapter, or by covering a selected subset of the chapters in order, such as Chapters 1, 2, 3, 4, 7, 9, and 12. The prerequisites for such a course consist mostly of a good understanding of OR-optimization methods such as linear programming and combinatorial optimization and, mainly for Chapter 12, a course in queueing theory or stochastic processes. Also, a one-semester course can be offered as an advanced graduate seminar covering five or six selected chapters of interest to the instructor and the student, including Chapter 1, since most chapters are largely self-contained. Finally, those who wish to learn or teach every detail of the book can cover in two semesters all the chapters of the book in the order they are written.

Not all of the subjects in location theory are treated comprehensively in this book. We have purposely omitted the vast topic of planar location problems (some results on competitive locations in the plane appear in Chapter 10) since that material is available in other recent texts, and, frankly, because we believe discrete location theory is more useful. We have also omitted most of the new (as of this writing) and exciting results on probabilistic analysis of location algorithms; although some probabilistic analysis of the quadratic assignment problem occurs in Chapter 9, and some remarks are made on the probabilistic analysis of the p-median and the uncapacitated facility location problems in Chapters 2 and 3, respectively. Many of the probabilistic results appeared after we were well underway with this book, and it would have been a major undertaking to have them included as a separate chapter.

It would be a Herculean task to name and thank every individual who contributed towards this final product, a book on the shelf. Even if we tried to do so we would undoubtedly (and unintentionally) omit important contributors. Therefore, on behalf of all the contributing authors, we wish to thank the pioneers in the field of location theory, our professional colleagues who gave us comments on our papers and on earlier drafts of the chapters, the external reviewers who diligently refereed several chapters,

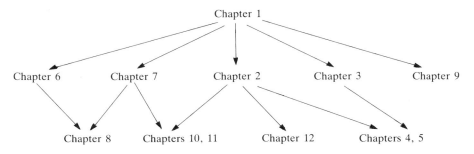

and funding agencies, industrial technical groups and academic departments who have supported our research on location theory. Editor Pitu Mirchandani particularly wishes to acknowledge the Electrical, Computer, and Systems Engineering Department at Rensselaer Polytechnic Institute where much of this book was edited. Finally, we wish to thank our patient Wiley-Interscience editor Maria Taylor and editorial supervisor Bob Hilbert, and those unsung heroines and heros, our secretaries, who spent hours typing, retyping, copying, and mailing the various drafts of the chapters.

PITU B. MIRCHANDANI
RICHARD L. FRANCIS

Tucson, Arizona
Gainesville, Florida

Contents

Discrete
Location Theory

1

Ingredients of Locational Analysis

Jakob Krarup
DIKU, Department of Computer Science
University of Copenhagen
Copenhagen, Denmark

Peter M. Pruzan
DASY, Institute of Computer and Systems Sciences
Copenhagen Business School
Copenhagen, Denmark

1.1. INTRODUCTION

The pervasive theme throughout all of the ensuing chapters is the notion of *optimal choice within a spatial context*. Examples of such choices include the location of factories, warehouses, schools, oil drills, hospitals, and machines and departments within a production facility, as well as the design of computer backboards and water, energy, transportation and information networks. As the location of any physical object whatsoever can be claimed to represent the solution to a location problem, this theme is certainly not a new one. As long as history records, people in some way or other have "formulated" problems as to how objects or facilities should be placed in relation to other facilities and the clients to serve/be served by them and have proceeded to "solve" them, to make *locational decisions* so to speak. Such decisions have typically been based upon consideration of physical, economic, social, aesthetic, military, environmental or political factors such as available building sites, distances, transportation routes, markets, investments, freight and handling costs, geographically dispersed organizations, competitors, enemies, proximity to recreative areas, and public opinion.

From a historical perspective, however, it is only relatively recently that the intellectual process underlying the prescription of choice of a locational decision has focussed upon the design and utilization of *symbolic models*. These are the models that we design, study, analyze, and evaluate in the ensuing chapters of the book.

The emphasis in the book is on optimal locational decisions. This calls for a distinction between *descriptive* and *normative* (or prescriptive) location models. Economists and geographers traditionally employ the former when they attempt to describe or explain observable socio-economical phenomena such as patterns of industrial location, labor migration, urban conglomeration, the development of transportation networks, inter- and intra-regional resource development, and price structures. Furthermore, their analyses typically presume that the objects to be located can be placed *anywhere*, that is, within a context of *continuous* space.

Our aim is different. It is to advocate principles and to recommend tools for investigating locational decision problems via normative models. The ultimate goal is to provide decision-makers with quantitative tools for finding good solutions to realistic locational decision problems.

The families of problems explored in the sequel, the terminology, the formulation of the problems in terms of optimization and the algorithmic approaches employed all have their roots within *operations research, industrial engineering, management science*, and *computer science*. This is not to say that the forementioned economists and geographers, to say nothing of practitioners such as regional- and town-planners, and architects have not made and do not, within their own traditions, make contributions to the formulation and solution of locational decision problems. Rather, their intellectual and procedural frameworks for approaching such problems may lead to their neglecting or suppressing the *discrete optimization* framework which we consider to be so fundamental.

On the other hand, we do not assert that our approach represents an "ideal"; as will be seen in Section 1.4, there are some significant aspects of locational decision-making which, for all intents and purposes, are ignored in the literature, an indication perhaps of the magnitude of the communication gap between the "locationists" (the authors of this book) and those faced with the responsibility of making locational decisions in practice.

The word "discrete" appearing in the title of this book has not as yet been accounted for. As will be further elaborated upon in Section 1.4, reasonable analyses of most realistic locational decision problems lead to the formulation of such problems in so-called *discrete space*, where the objects to be located can only be placed at a finite number of potential sites selected via some prior analyses. The significance of the finite location set, the *inherent indivisibilities* characterizing the objects to be located, and therefore the *discrete* or combinatorial nature of locational decision problems were not fully recognized until the late 1950s. Accordingly, *discrete location theory*, steeped in a *framework of a discrete optimization*, covers a period of development which only spans about three decades.

The literature is nevertheless huge and rapidly growing. Among the myriads of formulations considered, however, only four of these: the *p-median problem, the p-center problem, the uncapacitated facility location problem*, and *the quadratic assignment problem*—at times referred to as *prototype location problems*—have played a particularly dominant role. These models, which deservedly occupy a substantial proportion of the subsequent chapters, and despite the seeming simplicity of their underlying assumptions, have provided important, quantitative bases for the investigation of numerous practical locational decision problems. They have been used both as optimization models in their own right or have been employed as subroutines in more integrated models.

1.1.1. Chapter Outline

Due to the large number of extensions available, each of the four prototype problems referred to above can be viewed as the foremost member of a *family* of location problems. The extensive Section 1.2 is devoted to these four families. To avoid gluttony and distress, this four-dish main course will be served in easily digestable portions. We commence by introducing some concepts related to general networks. Examples of p-median problems including the network version and the more general "bipartite" version are then considered in Section 1.2.1. Following the same line, p-center problems are discussed in Section 1.2.2 before we proceed to the uncapacitated facility location problem which resembles the p-median problem but possesses other attractive properties. We sketch the so-called *set covering problem* as a special case of the uncapacitated facility location problem, although, perhaps, the collection of such problems may in itself constitute a family of location problems. As the first three families share several common features, we provide a unifying formulation framework in Section 1.2.4. An integer programming formulation of a hybrid model which combines features of the *p*-median and the uncapacitated facility location problems, the so-called *p-uncapacitated facility location problem* is given in Section 1.2.5. The final prototype problem, the quadratic assignment problem, which has a different flavor than the models previously considered, appears in Section 1.2.6. Here the problem scenario includes mutual interaction among the facilities to be located and their attendant costs.

Whereas certain properties of the problems considered along the way are briefly accounted for, no specific computational techniques are devised for their solution. Solely for pedagogical reasons we solve the small problems appearing in this chapter by complete enumeration; that is, we evaluate all possible solutions and pick the best. However, due to the large number of feasible solutions characterizing realistic locational decision problems, complete enumeration simply forbids itself in practice. Accordingly, more sophisticated methods have been developed and constitute the substance of the remainder of this book. Section 1.3 sets the stage for the ensuing chapters by introducing fundamentals of *computational complexity*, a conceptual framework commonly used in characterizing problems and algorithms devised for their solution.

Bearing the ultimate goal of the present book in mind, we feel that modeling principles should not be ignored. Section 1.4 contains far from all that can be said about formulation of realistic locational decision problems. However, it attempts to discuss some of the major characteristics of realistic problems, and how they can and should affect the model building phase.

Chapter 1 is largely self-contained. To emphasize its introductory character, we have deliberately chosen not to frustrate the reader with bibliographical references in the body of the text. Indeed there are lots of papers and other books that the interested reader may wish to consult. As a first step in this direction we have in the concluding Section 1.5 provided a collection of selected references together with some historical notes. Additional references are given at the end of each of the subsequent chapters.

1.2. FOUR FAMILIES OF LOCATION PROBLEMS

The *undirected network* $N = (V, A)$ shown in Figure 1.1 consists of a set $V = (v_a, v_b, \ldots, v_h)$ of 8 *nodes* and a prescribed set $A = ([v_a, v_b]$ or $[v_b, v_a], [v_a, v_c]$ or $[v_c, v_a], \ldots, [v_g, v_h]$ or $[v_h, v_g])$ of 12 *unordered* pairs of *distinct* nodes of V. Each pair, for example $[v_a, v_b]$ or $[v_b, v_a]$ of nodes in A is an *arc* in N. With each arc $[v_i, v_j]$ is associated a positive real number $\alpha(v_i, v_j)$ called the *length* of that arc. Thus, $\alpha(v_d, v_h) = \alpha(v_h, v_d) = 8$ is referred to as the length of arc $[v_d, v_h]$ no matter whether it is interpreted as

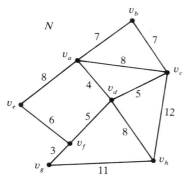

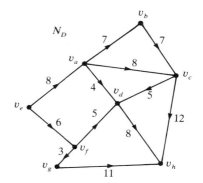

Figure 1.1. An undirected network.   Figure 1.2. A directed network.

"there are 8 miles between v_d and v_h" or "the travel time between v_d and v_h is 8 minutes" or "the price of shipping one unit from v_d to v_h along arc $[v_d, v_h]$ is \$8."

Arcs are at times passable in one direction only (one-way streets, valves, etc.). This feature is visualized in Figure 1.2. An arc of a *directed network* is an ordered pair of distinct vertices. As a consequence, since $[v_h, v_d]$ is not an arc in the directed network N_D in Figure 1.2, $\alpha(v_h, v_d)$ is undefined and $\alpha(v_d, v_h)$ is no longer the travel time *between* v_d and v_h, but, rather, it is the travel time *from* v_d to v_h.

Since we will deal mostly with undirected networks in this chapter, let us return to the undirected network N in Figure 1.1 to define a few additional concepts. Informally, a *path* between v_c and v_f in N is a sequence of arcs, for example $[v_c, v_a]$, $[v_a, v_d]$, $[v_d, v_f]$, which connect nodes v_c and v_f. In a more convenient notation this sequence can be written as $(c-a-d-f)$. In general, the length of a path is the sum of the lengths of its constituent arcs; for this particular path the length equals $\alpha(v_c, v_a) + \alpha(v_a, v_d) + \alpha(v_d, v_f) = 8 + 4 + 5 = 17$. It appears, however, that there are several distinct paths between v_c and v_f. Other such paths include, for example, $(c-h-d-f)$ of length 25, $(c-b-a-c-d-f)$ of length 32, and $(c-d-f)$ of length 10. A path connecting a node with itself and consisting of at least three arcs is called a *cycle*. The path $(c-b-a-c-d-f)$ is seen to include the cycle $(c-b-a-c)$. For a pair of nodes in a network we are, however, primarily interested in a *shortest path*, that is, a path of minimum length connecting the two nodes (we ask for *a* shortest path rather than *the* shortest path since uniqueness is not required). Since all arc lengths are assumed positive we can thus restrict ourselves to search for a shortest path among cycle-free paths. Clearly, if all distinct, cycle-free paths connecting v_c and v_f are considered, (c, d, f) is a shortest path and, in this case also, *the* shortest one.

A shortest path between nodes v_i and v_j in a network N will henceforth be denoted by $P[v_i, v_j]$; its length is $d(v_i, v_j)$ also referred to as the *distance* between v_i and v_j.

By definition, all arc lengths are positive; hence, the distance between two distinct nodes will also be positive. Furthermore, the definition of a network does not allow for arcs connecting a node with itself. Yet, it is at times practical to consider the distance from a node to itself; in this chapter we define such a distance to be zero.

The network N in Figure 1.1 is repeated in Figure 1.3, now accompanied by the symmetric (8×8)-matrix D of distances between any of the $\binom{8}{2} = 28$ pairs of distinct nodes in N, with the eight zeros in the main diagonal representing the distance between each node and itself.

1.2.1.   *p*-Median Problems

Assume now that each of the eight nodes in N corresponds to a client, and that the ith client has a fixed demand of w_i units (per time period) for a certain commodity, which is independent of the location of the facility that fulfills it. Furthermore, assume that each node is a potential location site for a facility which (per time period) can produce any amount of the desired commodity and ship it along the roads represented by the arcs of N. All facilities are operated by a single company having complete control over the number of facilities to be opened, and their locations. Each delivery of goods is assumed to require a single trip between a single facility and a single client, for example, to occupy a full truckload. Although the *p*-median model easily extends to oriented networks and round-trips (see Chapter 2), it does not apply to scenarios where a single tour serves several demands, or, alternatively, demands are not served in a coordinated fashion (e.g., car pools and trip-chaining).

While facilities and clients belong to the "real-world" as opposed to their representation by nodes in networks or indices in other models, this distinction need not be rigorously maintained in the accompanying text. Unless ambiguities may arise, we shall thus use "client f" or "facility g"

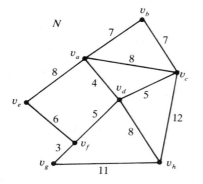

Figure 1.3. Network N with distance matrix D.

$$
D
\begin{array}{c|cccccccc}
 & v_a & v_b & v_c & v_d & v_e & v_f & v_g & v_h \\
\hline
v_a & 0 & 7 & 8 & 4 & 8 & 9 & 12 & 12 \\
v_b & 7 & 0 & 7 & 11 & 15 & 16 & 19 & 19 \\
v_c & 8 & 7 & 0 & 5 & 16 & 10 & 13 & 12 \\
v_d & 4 & 11 & 5 & 0 & 11 & 5 & 8 & 8 \\
v_e & 8 & 15 & 16 & 11 & 0 & 6 & 9 & 19 \\
v_f & 9 & 16 & 10 & 5 & 6 & 0 & 3 & 13 \\
v_g & 12 & 19 & 13 & 8 & 9 & 3 & 0 & 11 \\
v_h & 12 & 19 & 12 & 8 & 19 & 13 & 11 & 0 \\
\end{array}
$$

equivalently with "a client located at or represented by node v_f" or "a facility placed at location v_g."

To obtain the first discrete location model, we embark with a very transparent cost structure. Let $c_{ij} = w_i d(v_i, v_j)$ be the total cost incurred if all of the w_i units demanded by client i are supplied by facility j.

Assume for the moment that all clients have unity demand, that is, all $w_i = 1$. Thus $c_{ij} = w_i d(v_i, v_j)$ is simply the distance between locations (nodes) v_i and v_j. In the present case the (8×8)-matrix $C = (c_{ij})$ then becomes identical to D in Figure 1.3.

Facilities can be either closed or open (established). Facility j is called *closed* if no facility is placed at location v_j and hence no clients can be served from that potential location. *Open* or *established* means the opposite and, unless otherwise stated, open facilities are *uncapacitated* in the sense that they can supply any number of clients.

For a given value of p specified by the company, the so-called *p-median problem* is to establish p facilities in p of the potential locations and to supply each client from a subset of the established facilities such that the demands of all clients are met and such that the total costs thereby incurred are minimized.

The p-median problem is a prototype formulation that reflects many realistic locational decision problems. It is frequently employed to serve as the starting point for deliberating in cases where, for example, due to other strategic considerations, it has been decided to establish a predetermined number of new facilities to serve new markets or to modify an existing facility structure so as to have exactly p new and/or existing facilities. Even though the requirement "exactly p facilities" may happen to be rather rigorous, it is our experience that in practical applications p is frequently treated as a parameter permitting valuable insights.

To avoid perpetual repetitions of the words "the" and "problem" whenever a specific problem is mentioned we shall throughout the chapter replace problem names by appropriate abbreviations. Thus, *the p-median problem* is henceforth referred to as *p-MP*.

Only the nodes of N are considered as potential location sites for the facilities to be established. Suppose an optimal solution is known. Is it conceivable that an even better solution exists if we extend the finite set of potential location sites by regarding any point on any arc of N as a potential location site? As will be shown in Chapter 2, the well-known *node optimality property* settles this conjecture in the negative by asserting that p-MP, defined with respect to this extended set of potential location sites, has an optimal solution where all established facilities are located at nodes of N. It can in this context be noted that the subset of p nodes corresponding to established facilities in an optimal solution to p-MP is referred to as a *p-median set* (or simply a *median* for $p = 1$).

p-MP itself is an example of a *problem type*, that is, an example of a general question to be answered, usually in terms of assigning specific values to a set of *variables* such that the resulting solution satisfies certain properties. Algorithms for solving a well-defined problem can be proposed regardless of the specific values of the problem's *parameters*; for p-MP they consist of p, the number of rows and columns in C, and each individual c_{ij}. Whenever all such parameter values are specified, we talk of a *data instance* or just an *instance* of the corresponding problem.

Suppose that $p = 3$ and that three facilities have been located at nodes v_b, v_g, v_h, respectively. Consider a client located at v_f. The total cost of supplying all of its demand from each of these facilities is seen to be 16, 3 and 13, respectively. In terms of costs, nothing is gained from supplying that client from two or more facilities; the optimal choice is simply to supply all of its demand from a single facility, in this case the facility located at v_g.

For a client located at v_d, these costs are 11, 8, and 8. In this case the least cost of supplying the client is obtained by serving it either from both v_g and v_h or exclusively from v_g or v_h. Once again, however, nothing is gained from supplying the client from more than a single facility. The same arguments apply for any other client and—since each facility is assumed to have unlimited capacity—for any other pattern of open and closed facilities.

However trivial this observation may seem, the fact that we only have to consider solutions where every client is supplied by a single facility, plays a significant role for the appreciation of the problem as well as for the algorithms developed for its solution. It is customary in this context to say that p-MP possesses the *Single-Assignment Property*.

Whenever cost or distance matrices are used in the sequel, we will assume each *client* to be represented by a *row* and each *potential facility* by a *column*. We can thus view the sets of row and column indices as the *client location set* and the *facility location set*, respectively. As long as C is symmetric, this distinction may seem irrelevant, but shortly we shall encounter situations where C is non-symmetric or not even a square matrix.

For a given C, and upon specifying the number p of facilities to be established, we have a complete data instance of p-MP. For $p = 1$ and with C taken as the matrix in Figure 1.3, the total cost of serving all clients from a single facility is equal to the sum of all entries in the corresponding column. These sums are given in the following table.

Facility located at	v_a	v_b	v_c	v_d	v_e	v_f	v_g	v_h
Total cost	60	94	71	52	84	62	75	94

Thus, an optimal solution to 1-MP (or to p-MP, $p = 1$) is to locate a facility at node v_d. This node is then the median of network N.

For $p = 2$ there are $\binom{8}{2} = 28$ distinct pairs of nodes where two facilities can be located. Suppose that facilities are established at nodes v_c and v_d. To minimize the total cost, how then should the shipments of commodities to the eight clients be arranged?

The Single-Assignment Property provides the answer: each client is supplied only from that open facility for which the corresponding c_{ij} is smallest. In other words, we consider only the submatrix of C consisting of columns v_c and v_d and pick the smallest entry (underlined below) from each row, to give us the following costs:

	v_c	v_d	Distance to closest facility
v_a	8	<u>4</u>	4
v_b	<u>7</u>	11	7
v_c	<u>0</u>	5	0
v_d	5	<u>0</u>	0
v_e	16	<u>11</u>	11
v_f	10	<u>5</u>	5
v_g	13	<u>8</u>	8
v_h	12	<u>8</u>	8

Total cost = 43

Whereas the instance of 1-MP was *solved to optimality by complete enumeration* (all *feasible* solutions were listed and the corresponding total costs were evaluated), a similar approach for 2-MP would involve evaluation and comparison of 28 feasible solutions. To avoid this tedious task we shall leave it to the reader to verify that $\{v_d, v_f\}$, with total cost 37, is in fact the 2-median set sought.

p-MP: *The Weighted Case*
For the previous instance of p-MP, all clients were assumed to have unity demand. This assumption was expressed in the model by letting $w_a = w_b = \cdots = 1$.

In general, w_i is referred to as the *weight* associated with node v_i and may represent, for example, a certain demand of a single client, an aggregation of demands of several clients, or the population of a city. We use the adjective *unweighted* to characterize instances where all weights are equal as above; otherwise such instances are called *weighted*. Some problem types allow for unweighted data instances only whereas others—including p-MP— can accommodate both cases.

The now familiar network N in Figure 1.3 reappears in Figure 1.4, now with individual weights, $w_a, \ldots, w_h$ (the circled numbers), associated with each node. The cost of supplying client a from facility f is the weight w_a (= demand) of client a multiplied by the distance $d(v_a, v_f)$ (see Figure 1.3) between nodes v_a and v_f. If two or more facilities were established, the minimal cost of supplying client a would be $w_a d(v_a, v_k)$ where v_k is the closest open facility. Thus, the single assignment property still applies and we can appropriately define c_{ij}, the total cost of supplying all of client i's

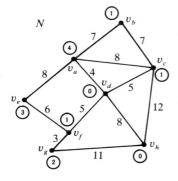

w_i	v_a	v_b	v_c	v_d	v_e	v_f	v_g	v_h
v_a	4	0	28	32	16	32	36	48	48
v_b	1	7	0	7	11	15	16	19	19
v_c	1	8	7	0	5	16	10	13	12
v_d	0	0	0	0	0	0	0	0	0
v_e	3	24	45	48	33	0	18	27	57
v_f	1	9	16	10	5	6	0	3	13
v_g	2	24	38	26	16	18	6	0	22
v_h	0	0	0	0	0	0	0	0	0

Figure 1.4. A weighted network and the corresponding cost matrix C with $c_{ij} = w_i d(v_i, v_j)$.

demand from facility j, by $c_{ij} = w_i d(v_i, v_j)$. Note that this is equivalent to assuming that, once again, all clients have unity (unweighted) demand where we simply replace the original $C = \{d_{ij}\}$ matrix of Figure 1.3 by a new, non-symmetric matrix $C = \{w_i d(v_i, v_j)\}$. The full C-matrix, together with the vector $w = (w_a, \ldots, w_h)$ of weights are shown in Figure 1.4. With the eight nodes of N as both the facility and the client location set, p-MP is now to select p nodes and assign each client to the closest of these such that the sum of the corresponding weighted distances is minimized.

For $p = 1$, the 1-median can easily be determined by complete enumeration. For each of the eight feasible solutions, the total costs associated with it is the sum of the entries in the corresponding column of the C-matrix. These sums appear below.

Facility located at	v_a	v_b	v_c	v_d	v_e	v_f	v_g	v_h
Total cost	72	134	123	86	87	86	110	171

In comparison with the unweighted case, it is not surprising that the 1-median no longer remains at node v_d but moves to the heavily-weighted node v_a. Similarly the 2-median set, previously found to be $\{v_d, v_f\}$, now becomes $\{v_a, v_f\}$ with total cost 39.

Some node weights have deliberately been chosen as zeros. Consequently, rows v_d and v_h in the resulting cost matrix C consists solely of zeros and these rows might just as well have been discarded. This illustrates that p-MP retains its full flavor even if C is not a square matrix. This simple observation leads us to the next generalization of p-MP.

Let v_i, v_j, v_k be any triple of nodes of some network N. As per our definition, shortest distances possess the following three properties:

$$\textit{Nonnegativity}: \quad d(v_i, v_j) > 0 \quad \text{for} \quad v_i \neq v_j \,,$$
$$d(v_i, v_j) = 0 \quad \text{for} \quad v_i = v_j \,,$$
$$\textit{Symmetry}: \quad d(v_i, v_j) = d(v_j, v_i) \,,$$
$$\textit{Triangle inequality}: \quad d(v_i, v_j) \leq d(v_i, v_k) + d(v_k, v_j) \,.$$

In realistic locational decision problems amenable for modeling by p-MP, however, the c_{ij} need not be interrelated such that they possess these properties. For example, a node v_i may represent a zone or some other geographical region and the cost of serving the region from a facility located within it will not be zero; that is, $c(v_i, v_j) > 0$. In fact, depending on the region's road network and the location of the facility, it may be less costly to serve the region represented by v_i from another region. In addition, there may exist one-way roads or other road restrictions such that neither symmetry nor the triangle inequality holds. In general, the c_{ij} may reflect a cost structure which in no natural way associates with the concept of distance. Furthermore, it occurs frequently that the client location set does not coincide with the facility location set, nor do these two sets necessarily have the same cardinality.

A conclusion is that C in principle can be any $(m \times n)$-matrix, where m and n are the number of clients and potential locations, respectively, and where each c_{ij} can be any real number. It may also be concluded that while C for a given weighted network is uniquely determined, we cannot always construct a network, weighted or unweighted, which, via calculations of shortest path distances, leads to a given C-matrix.

We close the presentation of p-MP by a modest example completely disentangled from any specific network. It is then shown that we need only consider instances of p-MP where all c_{ij} are nonnegative. Finally, a general graphical representation of p-MP is provided via the concept of *bipartite networks*.

Consider an instance of p-MP: $p = 2$, $m = 4$, $n = 3$, and

$$\begin{array}{c} \\ 1 \\ 2 \\ 3 \\ 4 \end{array} \begin{pmatrix} 1 & 2 & 3 \\ 7 & 5 & \infty \\ -2 & \infty & -4 \\ \infty & -1 & -5 \\ \infty & 0 & 2 \end{pmatrix} = C$$

where column j, $j = 1, 2, 3$ corresponds to the jth potential facility. For the three feasible solutions we obtain

Facilities located at	(1, 2)	(1, 3)	(2, 3)
Total cost	2	0	−4

If a constant β_i is added to all entries in the ith row then the total cost for each feasible solution will be increased by β_i. An optimal solution will therefore remain optimal.

For each i, choose, for example, $\beta_i = -\min\{0, \min_j c_{ij}\}$ and increase all c_{ij} by β_i. Matrix C then becomes

$$\begin{Bmatrix} 7 & 5 & \infty \\ 2 & \infty & 0 \\ \infty & 4 & 0 \\ \infty & 0 & 2 \end{Bmatrix} \quad \begin{aligned} \beta_1 &= 0 \\ \beta_2 &= 4 \\ \beta_3 &= 5 \\ \beta_4 &= 0 \end{aligned}$$

and the total cost for each feasible solution will be increased by $\beta_1 + \beta_2 + \beta_3 + \beta_4 = 9$.

Since the optimal location of the p facilities is insensitive to such transformations, we can without loss of generality assume all data to be nonnegative.

A *bipartite network* $N_B = (V, A) = (I \cup J, A)$ is a network where the nodes are partitioned into two subsets I and J and where each arc connects a node in I with a node in J.

A bipartite network N_B with arc lengths representing costs, permits a completely general representation of p-MP. Since $c_{ij} = \infty$ supposedly says that facility j cannot supply client i—the direct transportation route $P[i, j]$ may for some reason be blocked—we need only include arcs $[i, j]$ corresponding to finite values of c_{ij}. Figure 1.5 is self-explanatory (note that arc lengths equal to zero are allowed) in showing how an instance of p-MP is represented on a bipartite network.

1.2.2. *p*-Center Problems

The *p-center problem*, abbreviated by p-CP, differs significantly from p-MP in several respects, primarily with respect to the criterion used for assessing

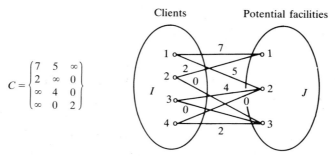

Figure 1.5. A cost matrix C and the corresponding bipartite network N_B.

the quality of a feasible solution. Whereas p-MP is a *minisum* problem, p-CP has a *minimax* objective: Open p facilities and assign each client to exactly one of them such that the *maximum distance* (unweighted case) or the *maximum weighted distance* from any open facility to any of the clients assigned to it is a minimum. An optimum location of just one facility is called a *1-center* or just a *center*, and when $p > 1$ facilities are to be located, the optimal locations constitute a *p-center set*.

Such a minimax objective function occurs frequently in formulations of locational decision problems for emergency services such as police, fire and ambulance services. A common criterion for the effectiveness of such service coverage is that any demand point may be reached from the facility nearest it within a given weighted distance, time or cost. The weight characterizing a demand point may be interpreted as a scaling constant for that demand point (for example, the value of time for clients at that demand point) which allows one to compare client demands at different locations. The weights could, for example, transform distances to times. For a given number of emergency facilities to be located, the optimal value of the problem's objective function represents a lower bound for this criterion.

An additional factor that distinguishes p-CP from p-MP is that the node optimality property does not apply. For example, if a single facility is to serve just two clients of equal weight and if the location set is not constrained to be either of the two nodes representing these clients, but also includes any point on the arc connecting them, then the center sought obviously is the midpoint of that arc.

For simplicity, however, in this chapter we restrict the location set to be either the node set of the network considered or one of the node sets defining a bipartite network. Moreover, to facilitate the comparison of the solutions to p-CP and p-MP, we return to the same series of modest-sized examples as were used to introduce p-MP.

Consider the instance of p-CP defined by $p = 1$, $w_a = w_b = \cdots = w_h = 1$ (the unweighted case), and with the distance matrix D as shown in Figure 1.3 for a single facility located at some node of N, the maximal distance for such a feasible solution is found as the largest element in the corresponding column of D. Hence, the following table is obtained:

Facility located at	v_a	v_b	v_c	v_d	v_e	v_f	v_g	v_h
Maximal distance	12	19	16	11	19	16	19	19

The center is thus node v_d, which coincidently was also the median.

For the placement of two facilities there are $\binom{8}{2} = 28$ distinct possibilities. If, for example, node set $\{v_f, v_g\}$ is selected, to compute the maximal distance, we consider the corresponding columns, take the smallest entry in each row and record the largest such distance:

	v_f	v_g	Distance to the closest facility
v_a	9	12	9
v_b	16	19	16
v_c	10	13	10
v_d	5	8	5
v_e	6	9	6
v_f	0	3	0
v_g	3	0	0
v_h	13	11	11

Maximal distance = 16

If all 28 feasible locations are considered explicitly or implicitly, we will find that the 2-center set is $\{v_a, v_d\}$ with $d(v_a, v_e) = d(v_d, v_g) = d(v_d, v_h) = 8$ as the minimax distance.

We have previously found $\{v_d, v_f\}$ to be the 2-median set of the undirected network N which demonstrates that the p-median set and the p-center set do not, in general, coincide. Similarly, there is no reason to believe that a 1-center is necessarily a member of a 2-center set, just as a 1-median is not in general contained in a 2-median set.

If individual weights are associated with the clients, we encounter the weighted p-CP where the objective obviously is to minimize the maximum weighted distance. Similarly, the bipartite network version of p-CP parallels that of p-MP to such an extent that further comments can be postponed until Section 1.2.4 where both problems are revisited.

The only type of *algorithm* used so far for solving specific instances of p-MP or p-CP has been complete enumeration: Evaluate all feasible solutions and pick the best. Since the number of feasible solutions for virtually all instances of problems encountered in practice is "huge," we remark to our readers that our use of complete enumeration is solely for pedagogical purposes and in no way implies that such an approach is advocated in general. In fact one major justification of this book is the availability of other algorithmic approaches!

1.2.3. Uncapacitated Facility Location Problems

Let $J = \{1, \ldots, n\}$ be a finite set of n possible sites for establishing new facilities or redimensioning already existing facilities. The *uncapacitated facility location problem* (UFLP) deals with the supply of a single commodity (or standard product-mix) from a subset of these potential facility locations to a set $I = \{1, \ldots, m\}$ of m clients with prescribed demands for the commodity. Facilities are assumed to have unlimited capacity such that in principle any facility can satisfy all demands. For given costs associated with the facilities and the transportation routes from potential facility sites to clients, we seek a minimum cost production/transportation plan (in terms of the number of facilities established, their locations, and the amount shipped from each facility to each client) satisfying all demands.

Like the last and most general version of p-MP considered, UFLP can be viewed as a location problem for which the underlying network is bipartite. Two features distinguish UFLP from p-MP: (1) a nonnegative *fixed cost* is associated with each potential facility site and this fixed cost is incurred only if a facility is actually placed at that site, and (2) the number of facilities to be located is *not* prespecified.

The bipartite network in Figure 1.5 is reproduced in Figure 1.6. Furthermore, a fixed cost is associated with each of the three facility sites. If facilities are opened at sites $\{1, 2\}$ of the set J, then the fixed cost will be $f_1 + f_2 = 13$. As was done for p-MP, we assign each client i to that open facility j for which the total (variable) cost c_{ij} of supplying all of client i's demand is minimal. Hence, clients 1, 3, 4 will be assigned to facility 2 at cost $c_{12} + c_{32} + c_{42} = 5 + 4 + 0 = 9$ while client 2 will be supplied from facility 1 at cost $c_{21} = 2$. Note that the sum of the total fixed and variable costs is $13 + (9 + 2) = 24$.

Excluding the case where no facilities are established, there are $2^3 - 1$ different combinations of open and closed facilities. Total costs for each of these are:

Open facility sites	Fixed costs, f_j	Variable costs	Total costs
$\{1\}$	3	∞	∞
$\{2\}$	10	∞	∞
$\{3\}$	6	∞	∞
$\{1, \quad 2\}$	$3 + 10$	11	24
$\{1, \qquad 3\}$	$3 + \quad 6$	9	<u>18</u>
$\{2, \quad 3\}$	$10 + 6$	5	21
$\{1, \quad 2, \quad 3\}$	$3 + 10 + 6$	5	24

A (unique) optimal solution is thus to establish facilities at sites $\{1, 3\}$.

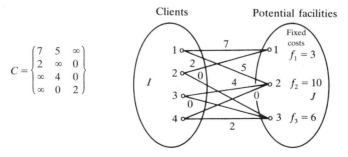

$$C = \begin{pmatrix} 7 & 5 & \infty \\ 2 & \infty & 0 \\ \infty & 4 & 0 \\ \infty & 0 & 2 \end{pmatrix}$$

Figure 1.6. A data instance for UFLP.

So-called *split assignments* occur whenever some clients are supplied by two or more facilities. As was the case for p-MP, it is evident that nothing is gained in terms of total costs by permitting split assignments in solutions to UFLP.

While most well-defined problems bear unambiguous names, UFLP has been dealt with in the literature under a wide variety of different titles, usually composed of an adjective (uncapacited, simple, optimal) and a noun (plant, warehouse, facility, site), followed by the word location. Allowing omission of the adjective, we have, among the possible combinations, seen ten or so of these used so far. Further confusion arises if "economies-of-scale" or "fixed-cost discrete space location-allocation" and such phrases are incorporated for describing the problem. While discussing this matter of names, it may be considered unfortunate that UFLP includes the adjective "uncapacitated"; both of the previous families of location problems, the p-median and p-center problems, also assume that the facilities to be located have unlimited capacities. The adjective, however, is included to distinguish UFLP from the family of "capacitated" location problems (see Chapter 4).

Judging from the literature, no other model of a locational decision problem has received so much attention. We postulate that the major reason is that despite (or perhaps due to) its transparent structure, it has contributed to the formulation and solution of a multitude of complex planning problems. We have personally utilized UFLP formulations as the basis for providing proposals for decisions with respect to the number, size, design, location, and service patterns for such widely varied "facilities" as high-schools, hospitals, silos, slaughterhouses, electronic components, warehouses, and production facilities.

Covering Problems
Consider an instance of UFLP, say, $m = 5$, $n = 4$, where all c_{ij} are either zero or infinite:

$$f_j: \quad 2 \quad 6 \quad 3 \quad 8$$

$$C = \begin{Bmatrix} 0 & 0 & 0 & \infty \\ \infty & 0 & \infty & 0 \\ \infty & 0 & 0 & 0 \\ 0 & \infty & \infty & 0 \\ 0 & \infty & 0 & \infty \end{Bmatrix}$$

and let A be a (5×4)-matrix $\{a_{ij}\}$ defined as

$$a_{ij} = \begin{cases} 1, & \text{for } c_{ij} = 0 \\ 0, & \text{for } c_{ij} = \infty, \end{cases}$$

whereby A becomes

$$A = \left\{ \begin{matrix} 1 & 1 & 1 & 0 \\ 0 & 1 & 0 & 1 \\ 0 & 1 & 1 & 1 \\ 1 & 0 & 0 & 1 \\ 1 & 0 & 1 & 0 \end{matrix} \right\}.$$

If a facility is established at location j at cost f_j it can either serve client i at no cost ($c_{ij} = 0$) or it cannot serve that client ($c_{ij} = \infty$ indicates that transportation route $P[i, j]$ is blocked). In terms of A we introduce a slightly different terminology by saying that a facility j, if established, *covers* all clients i for which $a_{ij} = 1$. Furthermore, a subset Q of column indices, $Q \subseteq J = \{1, \ldots, n\}$, defines a *cover* of the set $I = \{1, \ldots, m\}$ of row indices if $\Sigma_{j \in Q} a_{ij} \geq 1$ for all i. The cost of a cover Q is $\Sigma_{j \in Q} f_j$ and the *weighted set cover problem* (SET COVER) is to find a cover of minimum cost.

For the particular data instance shown, an optimal cover is seen to be $\{1, 2\}$ of cost $2 + 6 = 8$.

If all fixed costs equal 1, we refer to the corresponding SET COVER as *unweighted*. In this case an optimal cover is simply a cover of minimum cardinality. For the given data instance so modified, optimal covers are $\{1, 2\}$, $\{1, 4\}$, and $\{3, 4\}$.

SET COVER relates in a natural way to certain location problems involving distance constraints. We will use our network N of Figure 1.3 to illustrate this aspect. Assume that we want to determine the minimum number of facilities and their locations such that the distance between a facility and any client assigned to it does *not* exceed 8. The resulting A-matrix defined for all i, j as $a_{ij} = 1$ for $d(v_i, v_j) \leq 8$, or $a_{ij} = 0$ otherwise, is shown in Figure 1.7. An optimal solution in this case (but certainly not in

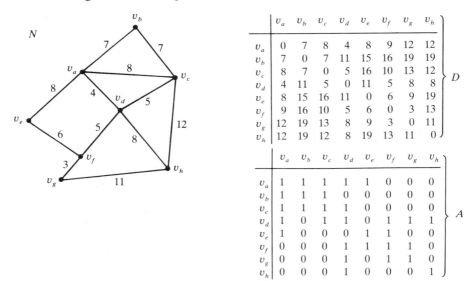

Figure 1.7. An instance of SET COVER: $a_{ij} = 1$ for $d(v_i, v_j) \leq 8$ or 0 otherwise.

general) is rather conspicuous: no single facility can cover all clients, while the pair $\{v_a, v_d\}$ covers all.

SET COVER provides a basis for analyzing problems which can be interpreted as now best to locate a subset of nodes in a network such that all nodes of that network are covered. SET COVER is also an adequate model for analyzing a wide variety of other discrete optimization problems. As can be seen in Chapters 6–8, it appears that studies of covering problems within the context of cycle-free networks, or *trees*, have proven to be particularly fruitful. Such cycle-free networks arise sometimes, and in a natural way in practice, as models for locational decision problems, and they lead to computationally much more tractable problems than do cyclic networks.

1.2.4. Concise Formulations of p-MP, p-CP, and UFLP

Having digested the foregoing small examples, the reader has hopefully grasped the main ideas of the models presented and will possibly have some impression as to each model's versatility and potential as a tool for decision-making in practice.

We now consider p-MP, p-CP, and UFLP in their most general forms, where the underlying network is bipartite, and provide concise, symbolic formulations of each of these models within a common framework.

The constituents of p-MP, p-CP, and UFLP are included in the following list:

m: the finite number of clients, indexed by i, $i \in I = \{1, \ldots, m\}$,

n: the finite number of sites for potential facilities, indexed by j, $j \in J = \{1, \ldots, n\}$,

p: the number of facilities to be opened or established, $1 \le p \le n$.

While the final location pattern of the facilities to be established is to be decided upon, the locations of the m clients are assumed known and invariant. These clients have prespecified demands for a common good which in principle can be provided by any potential facility.

For the jth potential facility define

f_j: the fixed cost of establishing facility j.

For each of the mn facility-client pairs, define

c_{ij}: The total variable cost of serving all of client i's demand from facility j.

The "cost" c_{ij} may include measures of the distance from client i to facility j as well as of the time or cost of serving client i from facility j. For example, the c_{ij} may be interpreted as $c_{ij} = w_i(h_j + t_{ij})$ where

w_i: the number of units demanded by client i,

h_j: the per unit cost of operating facility j (including variable production and administrative costs, etc.), and

t_{ij}: the transportation cost of shipping one unit to client i from facility j.

Cost t_{ij} may also be interpreted as $t_{ij} = d_{ij}$ where d_{ij}, as in the introductory sections, is defined by

d_{ij}: the physical distance (or its time or monetary equivalent) of a shortest path from client i to facility j.

Then, for $h_j = 0$, c_{ij} reduces to $c_{ij} = w_i d_{ij}$. Thus, c_{ij} captures the various notions of distance, time, and variable costs referred to so far.

With c_{ij} so defined, we can, without loss of generality, assume all clients to have unity demand. Furthermore, for each of the three problems, no capacity constraints are imposed on the number of clients that each potential facility can serve. Finally, without loss of generality, all data are assumed nonnegative.

As will be explained shortly, we can conveniently express the locational decisions to be made in terms of

Q: $Q \subseteq J$, a subset of potential facilities to be opened and from which all clients are to be served. The cardinality of Q is denoted by $|Q|$.

Conceptually, an approach to solving each of the three problems can then be said to involve two phases:

(1) a *location phase* which determines Q and
(2) an *allocation phase* in which each client is assigned to exactly one open facility and hence is assumed to receive all of its demand from that facility

such that a certain objective function is minimized. In *algorithms* for solving such problems to optimality, these two phases cannot, in general, be separated from one another but may be carried out simultaneously. The conceptual decomposition into two phases is suggested solely to facilitate comprehension of the ensuing compact formulations.

p-MP, Data Instance: $m, n, p, C = \{c_{ij}\}$. Open p facilities and assign each client to exactly one of them such that the total variable cost is minimized. For Q given, an assignment minimizing total variable cost can be determined "by inspection:" Client i is assigned to an established facility corresponding to the smallest c_{ij} (up to ties), that is, to facility j such that $\min_{j \in Q} c_{ij}$. Upon assigning all clients in this manner, the resulting total variable cost becomes $\Sigma_{i \in I} \min_{j \in Q} c_{ij}$. Hence, the problem becomes

p-MP:
$$\min_{Q \subseteq J, |Q| = p} \left\{ \sum_{i \in I} \min_{j \in Q} c_{ij} \right\}.$$

p-CP, Data Instance: $m, n, p, C = \{c_{ij}\}$. Open p facilities and assign each client to exactly one of them such that the maximum variable cost of serving any client is a minimum. Suppose Q is known. We can then do no better than assigning the ith client to that open facility from which the cost c_{ij} is a minimum, that is, to facility j such that $\min_{j \in Q} c_{ij}$, where ties are resolved arbitrarily. Upon assigning all clients in this manner, the resulting maximum cost becomes $\max_{i \in I} \{\min_{j \in Q} c_{ij}\}$. Hence, we obtain the formulation:

p-CP:
$$\min_{Q \subseteq J, |Q| = p} \{\max_{i \in I} \{\min_{j \in Q} c_{ij}\}\}.$$

UFLP, Data Instance: $m, n, C = \{c_{ij}\}, f = (f_i)$. Open a subset $Q \subseteq J$ of facilities and assign each client to exactly one of them such that the sum of the fixed and the variable costs is minimized. That is,

UFLP:
$$\min_{Q \subseteq J} \left\{ \sum_{j \in Q} f_j + \sum_{i \in I} \min_{j \in Q} c_{ij} \right\}.$$

Note that the number of facilities established is not prespecified, but rather it is determined by the solution.

1.2.5. The p-Uncapacitated Facility Location Problem

Besides the compact "combinatorial formulations" just presented, most of the problems considered so far are amenable for formulation as *integer linear programming problems* where each of the integer variables are restricted to be either 0 or 1. We present here such a formulation for the so-called *p-uncapacitated facility location problem* (p-UFLP) which is among the problems discussed in-depth in Chapter 3. Viewed against p-MP and UFLP as examples of "pure" prototype location problems, p-UFLP is a *hybrid* model in the sense that it combines certain features of both p-MP and UFLP and includes p-MP as a special case. p-UFLP can be viewed as an extension of p-MP in that fixed costs like those encountered in UFLP are associated with the potential facilities. Alternatively, p-UFLP is similar to UFLP with the additional constraint that the number of facilities to be established is prespecified as p. Therefore, a data instance of p-UFLP consists of positive integers m, n, p, the n-vector $f = (f_1, \ldots, f_n)$ and the $(m \times n)$-matrix C.

We introduce the $n + mn$ variables

$$x_j: \quad x_j = \begin{cases} 1, & \text{if facility } j \text{ is established} \\ 0, & \text{otherwise} \end{cases}$$

$$y_{ij}: \quad y_{ij} = \begin{cases} 1, & \text{if client } i \text{ receives all of its supply from facility } j \\ 0, & \text{otherwise.} \end{cases}$$

p-UFLP can now be stated as the following $(0, 1)$ integer program with linear constraints:

$$\min \sum_{j \in J} f_j x_j + \sum_{i \in I} \sum_{j \in J} c_{ij} y_{ij} , \tag{1.2.1}$$

$$\sum_{j \in J} y_{ij} = 1 , \quad \text{all } i , \tag{1.2.2}$$

$$x_j - y_{ij} \geq 0 , \quad \text{all } i, j , \tag{1.2.3}$$

$$\sum_{j \in J} x_j = p , \tag{1.2.4}$$

$$x_j \in (0, 1) , \quad \text{all } j ; \quad y_{ij} \in (0, 1) , \quad \text{all } i, j . \tag{1.2.5}$$

Constraint (1.2.2) assures that all demands are met and (1.2.3) guarantees that no client is supplied from a facility unless that facility is actually established since the fixed cost will otherwise not be paid. If $f_j = 0$, all j, p-UFLP reduces to p-MP. Similarly, UFLP is obtained if the requirement (1.2.4) that exactly p facilities be established is ignored.

p-Active Uncapacitated Facility Location Problem
A facility has hitherto been regarded as either closed or open but, as will be demonstrated shortly, under certain circumstances a refinement of the notion of "open" is needed.

Assume (x_j, y_{ij}), all i, j, is a feasible solution to p-UFLP. Unless certain assumptions are made as to the values of the fixed costs f_j and the variable costs c_{ij}, there is absolutely no reason to believe that some $x_j = 1$ (facility j is open) necessarily implies the existence of some i for which $y_{ij} = 1$, that is the open facility supplies at least one client. To this end we say that an open facility $(x_j = 1)$ is either *active* $(\Sigma_i \, y_{ij} > 0)$ or *passive* $(\Sigma_i \, y_{ij} = 0)$. Obviously this distinction is needed to clarify what exactly is meant by requiring $\Sigma_j \, x_j = p$. Do we permit feasible solutions involving passive facilities or should all of the p open facilities in any feasible solution necessarily be active?

Consider a hypothetical situation where a management requests a least cost plan for establishing, say five facilities and where the solution of a corresponding 5-MP results in only three active facilities. Such a solution most probably indicates that either or both of the following explanations are relevant: (1) management did not have good foresight when it chose the strategic parameter "5"; (2) the 5-MP formulation is a poor representation of management's perception of the decision problem at hand and the focus upon "costs" alone may be inadequate; other criteria may also be of importance. We will not attempt to delve more deeply into such reflections here. It suffices to note that the subject of multiple criteria locational analysis deservedly is receiving increasing attention as is evident from the discussion in Section 1.4.

In contrast to most of the material presented so far, we note that the formulation below is rather new.

For p-MP in a general network (or p-UFLP with $I = J = V$, the node set of network N) where all demand weights are positive and all distances are nonnegative with $d(v_i, v_i) = 0$ for all i, there will always be a client at distance 0 from any facility location thus preventing the occurrence of passive facilities. On the other hand, as will be exemplified shortly, if no particular limitations as to the composition of a data instance of p-UFLP are imposed, passive facilities can certainly occur in an optimal solution.

The *p-active uncapacitated facility location problem*, (p-ACTIVE), the problem of locating p active facilities serving all clients with least cost is obtained with minor modifications of p-UFLP. For all j, "active" is the requirement that $x_j = 1$ implies $\Sigma_i y_{ij} \geq 1$; hence, the additional constraints can be stated as

$$-x_j + \sum_{i \in I} y_{ij} \geq 0, \qquad \text{all } j.$$

Note that $p \leq m$ is a necessary condition for the existence of feasible solutions to p-ACTIVE.

Following conventional terminology, since p-UFLP evolves from removing or *relaxing* some constraints defining the set of feasible solutions to p-ACTIVE, we say that p-UFLP is a *relaxation* of p-ACTIVE.

Besides illustrating new features of p-ACTIVE, the following example summarizes much of the material covered so far in Section 1.2.

Consider the following instance of UFLP: $m = 6$, $n = 5$, and f, C are defined by

Facility locations		1	2	3	4	5
Fixed costs		12	5	3	7	9
Clients	1	2	3	6	7	1
	2	0	5	8	4	12
	3	11	6	14	5	8
	4	19	18	21	16	13
	5	3	9	8	7	10
	6	4	7	9	6	0

Based on this data, five instances of p-MP, p-CP, p-UFLP, and p-ACTIVE are generated by letting p assume all values within the range $1 \le p \le 5$ and by ignoring the fixed costs when p-MP is considered.

The entire collection of instances of the five problems considered have been solved by complete enumeration. All $2^5 - 1$ possible distinct solutions in terms of open facilities are listed in Figure 1.8 with columns labeled (1)–(12) for ease of reference.

(1)	(2)	(3)	(4)	(5)	(6)	(7)	(8)	(9)	(10)	(11)	(12)
p	Open facilities	Σf	Σc	$\Sigma f + \Sigma c$	$c_{\max}$	p-MP	p-CP	UFLP	p-UFLP	A: Active P: Passive ·: Closed	p-AC-TIVE
1	1	12	39	51	19	1			1	A····	1
	2	5	48	53	18					·A···	
	3	3	66	69	21					··A··	
	4	7	45	52	16					···A·	
	5	9	44	53	13	1				····A	
2	12	17	33	50	18					AA···	
	1 3	15	39	54	19					A·P··	
	1 4	19	30	49	16					A··A·	
	1 5	21	25	46	13	2	2	*	2	A···A	2
	23	8	47	55	18					·AA··	
	2 4	12	41	53	16					·A·A·	
	2 5	14	34	48	13		2			·A··A	
	34	10	44	54	16					··AA·	
	3 5	12	38	50	13		2			··A·A	
	45	16	30	46	13		2	*	2	···AA	2
3	123	20	33	53	18					AAP··	
	12 4	24	30	54	16					AP·A·	
	12 5	26	23	49	13		3		3	AA··A	3
	1 34	22	30	52	16					A·PA·	
	1 3 5	24	29	53	13		3			A·P·A	
	1 45	28	22	50	13	3	3			A··AA	
	234	15	41	56	16					·APA·	
	23 5	17	33	50	13		3			·AA·A	
	2 45	21	30	51	13		3			·P·AA	
	345	19	30	49	13		3		3	··PAA	
4	1234	27	30	57	16					APPA·	[5]
	123 5	29	23	52	13		4		4	AAP·A	[5]
	12 45	33	22	55	13	4	4			AP·AA	[2]
	1 345	31	22	53	13	4	4			A·PAA	[5]
	2345	24	30	54	13		4			·PPAA	4[2]
5	12345	36	22	58	13	5	5		5	APPAA	5[7]

Figure 1.8. Instances of p-MP, p-CP, UFLP, p-UFLP, and p-ACTIVE solved by complete enumeration.

The fixed and the variable costs associated with each solution appear in columns (3) and (4), respectively. Thus, (4) records the objective function values of p-MP and (5) does the same for UFLP, p-UFLP, and p-ACTIVE. "c_{max}" in column (6) is a short notation for $\max_{(i, j)} \{c_{ij} x_{ij}\}$ and represents the objective function values of p-CP. For each subset of open facilities, both (4) and (6) are based on the assumption that each client is assigned to the "nearest" open facility. Column (11) displays the resulting pattern of closed ($\cdot$), active (A), and passive (P) facilities and substantiates the point that passive facilities can indeed occur in feasible solutions to p-MP, p-CP, and p-UFLP.

Optimal solutions to the five problems considered are recorded in columns (7)–(10) and (12). For $p = 1, \ldots, 5$, column (7) indicates optimal solutions to p-MP, that is, solutions minimizing Σc for the corresponding value of p. Based on (6) the same is shown in (8) for p-CP. It is seen that p-medians are uniquely determined for $p \neq 4$ and that the proportion of p-centers in relation to the corresponding number of feasible solutions increases substantially for increasing values of p.

UFLP has two distinct optimal solutions marked by asterisks in (9); both minimize $\Sigma f + \Sigma c$ in column (5). Column (5) also houses the objective function values for p-UFLP from which the entries in (10) are derived. The asterisks in (9) are meant to emphasize that p is not prespecified in an instance of UFLP but results from the problem solution. Here, two facilities are opened in both optimal solutions to UFLP; these solutions obviously also solve p-UFLP for $p = 2$.

Column (12) calls for an additional comment. Since p-UFLP is a relaxation of p-ACTIVE, an optimal solution to p-UFLP which also satisfies the constraints requiring all open facilities to be active must also be an optimal solution to p-ACTIVE. This observation, valid for relaxations in general, provides us, as shown in (12), with optimal solutions to p-ACTIVE for $p = 1, 2$ and also for $p = 3$ where one of the optimal solutions in (10) involves active facilities only.

All of the solutions listed for $p \geq 4$ include one or two passive facilities. Without plunging into details, we assert that the smallest *incremental cost* of changing the first such solution from (APPA $\cdot$) to (AAAA $\cdot$) is 5, recorded as [5] in column (12). The other figures shown in brackets [ ] are to be interpreted analogously. Thus, the optimal solution to p-ACTIVE, $p = 4$, is a solution minimizing $\Sigma f + \Sigma c$ in column (5) *plus* the corresponding increments [ ] in (12); in other words the solution is to open facilities 2, 3, 4, 5.

For $p = 5$, not much of a choice is left for the decision-maker. The number of ways in which the six clients can be assigned to the five facilities so that they all become active is, however, far from negligible. We assert that an optimal (but not unique) solution in terms of y_{ij} is to make $y_{12} = y_{21} = y_{34} = y_{45} = y_{53} = y_{65} = 1$ and all other $y_{ij} = 0$, with resultant total cost $= 58 + [7] = 65$.

1.2.6. Quadratic Assignment Problem (QAP)

Architects and engineers are frequently facing problems involving the optimal design of a structure's layout, subject to certain conditions. To determine the number of buildings, the shape, location and orientation of each of these on the ground(s) and the mutual placement of the individual functions within the buildings, is a typical example.

The *layout planning problem* has for years attracted the attention of building planners (architects, industrial engineers) and operations researchers. We will study a special case of this problem, formulated below as the *Quadratic Assignment Problem (QAP)*, the fourth and final prototype location problem to be considered in this introductory chapter.

Suppose that we are in the process of designing the layout of a university department which is to house four functions or operational units, $a-d$:

a: administrative personnel,
b: canteen, recreational facilities,
c: scientific staff,
d: computer, library, etc.

Due to limited budgets the decision-maker cannot afford to erect a fancy new building appealing to his/her aesthetic tastes but will have to accept the ground floor of an existing building available for this purpose and capable of accommodating the four units $a-d$.

The existing building with four equally sized areas 1, 2, 3, 4 and with the open space between areas 3 and 4 occupied by elevators and stairs is shown in Figure 1.9. The accompanying symmetric *distance matrix* $A = \{a_{ij}\}$ expresses the so-called *rectangular distance* between each pair of areas. Assume that each area can house exactly one of the four units. Now, the problem is to assign each unit to an area such that the resulting layout in some well-defined sense becomes optimal. In fact, several criteria for assessing such a layout might be contemplated. We shall resort here to one of the more straightforward criteria and, in this context, the most commonly used "measure of performance."

Assume that the four units $(a-d)$ to be located are represented by nodes v_a, v_b, v_c, v_d of network N of Figure 1.10 with *connection matrix* $B = \{b_{ij}\}$, with $b_{ij} = b_{ji}$ equal to the length $\alpha(v_i, v_j)$ of arc $[v_i, v_j]$ if such an arc exists,

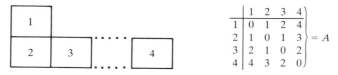

Figure 1.9. First part of an instance of QAP with distance matrix A.

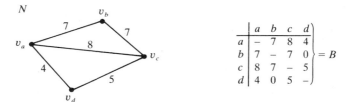

Figure 1.10. Second part of an instance of QAP with connection matrix B.

otherwise, $b_{ij} = 0$. The elements in the main diagonal of B remain undefined (–). B is called the connection matrix because, for example, $b_{bc} = b_{cb} = 7$ units is assumed to capture all aspects of "connection" between "staff" and "canteen" accumulated over all coffee breaks, lunches, leisure hours, and the like. Although methods to obtain specific numbers such as those given in Figure 1.10 can give rise to endless debates, we take the existence of such numbers for granted and trust that the decision-maker provides and interprets each b_{ij} appropriately.

If units c and d are assigned to areas 2 and 4, respectively, then the corresponding contribution to the objective function will be $b_{cd}a_{24}$, the product of the connection between units a and d and the distance between areas 2 and 4. With all four units placed, the value of the objective function is determined as the sum of $\binom{4}{2} = 6$ such individual contributions, and a layout minimizing that sum is regarded as optimal.

We invite the reader to join us in solving the instance of the QAP consisting of the matrices A (Figure 1.9) and B (Figure 1.10) by complete enumeration, which in the present case will involve evaluation of $4! = 24$ distinct layouts. Such an exercise offers insight but not much fun and it can safely be said that only readers with a particularly well-developed penchant for number crunching should ever attempt a similar approach if just one or two more units were to be located; quantities $5!, 6!, \ldots$ grow rapidly. Excerpts of the 24 layouts are listed in Figure 1.11. Having completed the computations for Figure 1.11, and reconsulting Figures 1.9–1.10, the reader should hardly be surprised that an optimal layout, in terms of minimizing the quantity "Σ conn. $\times$ dist." in the right-hand column in Figure 1.11, is to assign units $\{b, a, c, d\}$ to areas $\{1, 2, 3, 4\}$, respectively.

Note that in contrast to the families of prototype problem formulations considered so far, the notions of "client" and "facility" are not explicitly employed in QAP. Each object to be located provides/receives connection to/from other objects and, thus, can be viewed both as a client and a facility.

The layout problem considered has been referred to as "QAP." Whereas the *assignment* aspect is quite obvious, how does the term *quadratic* come in?

Units located at areas 1 2 3 4	Distances associated with units pairs					Σ conn. $\times$ dist.
	(a, b)	(a, c)	(a, d)	(b, c)	(c, d)	
a b c d	1	2	4	1	2	56
a b d c	1	4	2	3	2	78
a c b d	2	1	4	1	3	60
a c d b	4	1	2	3	1	70
a d b c	2	4	1	2	3	79
a d c b	4	2	1	2	1	67
b a c d	1	1	3	2	2	51
b a d c	1	3	1	4	2	73
$\vdots$	$\vdots$	$\vdots$	$\vdots$	$\vdots$	$\vdots$	$\vdots$
d c a b	2	1	2	3	1	
d c b a	2	3	4	1	1	66
Connection between units	7	8	4	7	5	

Figure 1.11. An instance of QAP solved by complete enumeration

Assume, in the general case that a set $M = \{1, \ldots, m\}$ of m equally-sized units are to be located at a set $N = \{1, \ldots, n\}$ of $n \geq m$ areas each of which can house at most one unit. Let matrices A, B be interpreted as before, and let the $m \times n$ decision variables x_{is}, $i \in M$, $s \in N$ be defined as: $x_{is} = 1$ if unit i is located at area s; otherwise, $x_{is} = 0$. If a pair $\{i, j\}$ of units are assigned to areas $\{s, t\}$, respectively, then the contribution to the objective function is $b_{ij}a_{st}$ which, with the decision variables introduced, can be expressed by the *quadratic* term $x_{is}x_{jt}b_{ij}a_{st}$. A 0–1 programming problem formulation of QAP is then

$$\min z = \sum_{i \in M} \sum_{j \in M} \sum_{s \in N} \sum_{t \in N} x_{is}x_{jt}b_{ij}a_{st}$$

such that

$$\sum_{s \in N} x_{is} = 1, \quad \text{all } i \text{ (each unit must be located)},$$

$$\sum_{i \in M} x_{is} \leq 1, \quad \text{all } s \text{ (at most one unit in each area)},$$

$$x_{is} \in (0, 1), \quad \text{all } i, s.$$

Conceptually, the two cases $m = n$ and $m < n$ are not distinct. For $m < n$ we can extend the set of units by including $(n - m)$ new units, each having zero connection with all other units. The addition of the $(n - m)$ "dummy" objects as described will not affect the objective function. Thus, without loss of generality, we can assume $m = n$ and simplify the formulation accordingly. Now, given two $n \times n$ matrices, A and B, a feasible placement is conveniently expressed in terms of a permutation φ of the n integers in the set $N = \{1, \ldots, n\}$. That is, if unit i is assigned to area $\varphi(i)$, for all i, the QAP can be expressed as:

$$\text{QAP: } \min_{\varphi} \sum_{i \in N} \sum_{j \in N} b_{ij} a_{\varphi(i)\varphi(j)}$$

Although, as has been argued, the two cases, $m = n$ and $m < n$ are conceptually equivalent, from a practitioner's point of view these two cases may well represent two different situations.

With the "straightforward" interpretation of a QAP in mind (for example, the assignment of operational units to locations within a building), $m = n$ means that the building is designed to house exactly the n units in its free locations; of course, there may be other locations in the building, but they are regarded as inadmissible in this context, as was exemplified in Figure 1.9, perhaps because they are reserved for other purposes.

The $m < n$-case is relevant when none or only some information is available as to the exact shape of the building. Suppose the set N of locations is the set of points with integral coordinates in a three-dimensional space and that the objective is to find the most compact arrangement of units in terms of minimizing $\Sigma \Sigma b_{ij} a_{\varphi(i)\varphi(j)}$. The resulting permutation may give some indications of how an appropriate building should be designed.

The problem considered so far is the so-called *Koopmans–Beckmann* variant of the more general QAP: Given a set $N = \{1, \ldots, n\}$ of n integers and n^4 coefficients, d_{ijst}, find a permutation φ which minimizes $\Sigma_{i \in N} \Sigma_{j \in N} d_{ij\varphi(i)\varphi(j)}$. This formulation permits a more general treatment of the "costs" associated with a layout. The Koopmans–Beckmann formulation implicitly assumes that the connection from one unit to another is independent of the locations of the units and that the costs vary linearly with distance. This may certainly not be the case in some situations.

Even the more general formulation may be criticized for its naivety. One reason is that QAP implicitly assumes that all units have identical area demands, while in fact many problems are characterized by the various units having different area demands. Another reason is that the connection data required for QAP are not readily available, and require considerable subjective estimates.

This naturally leads to the following questions. Should a layout be based upon current data or should it be based upon future expectations as to turnover, technology, cost levels, and organizational developments? Will the future production process, technology, and organization, result in the same division into units as in the current situation? Although many of these questions are equally applicable to the previously presented prototype location problems, they appear to be particularly pertinent in the case of QAP.

Despite these criticisms, QAP has served as the starting point for several practical approaches to layout planning. In addition to finding optimal layouts and/or analyzing alternative building designs, other applications of the QAP model—far from the traditional domain of architects, building planners, and industrial engineers—have also been encountered. Backboard wiring problems, arrangement of electrical components in printed circuits, and arrangement of printed circuits themselves are among the better known examples within electrical engineering. Other applications include planning of a presidential election campaign, arranging wedding guests around a table, scheduling parallel machines with change-over costs, and the design of typewriter keyboards. Personally, we have also encountered the problem in relation to finding the chronological order of 38 Babylonian texts and in setting up a model analyzing the movement of governmental institutions from Stockholm to a number of other Swedish cities.

Before ending the discussion on QAP we shall briefly mention its widely studied variant, the *Quadratic Bottleneck Problem* (QBP). The only distinction between QAP and QBP is the objective function: QBP is to determine a layout such that the largest $b_{ij}a_{st}$ (using the same notation as for QAP) becomes as small as possible. With this minimax objective, QBP is thus related to QAP as p-CP is to p-MP.

1.3. COMPUTATIONAL ASPECTS: ENUMERATION AND COMPLEXITY

Bearing in mind that the overall objective of this book is to provide insights and tools which can contribute to the solution of locational decision problems in practice, all of the normative models presented are inextricably bound to the development of algorithms for their solution. An even stronger statement is that a model is treated in depth only if operational algorithms exist for providing quantitative solutions to (noncontrived) data instances conforming to the model's structure. The term "operational" implies empirically tested, known to possess provably true properties, and works well in practice. Thus, theoretical discussions will primarily be motivated by algorithmic considerations as well as by their potential contributions to insight and understanding.

Based on the prototype problems considered in this chapter, the aim of this section is to review the terminology and the main concepts used to characterize algorithms and to account for their properties. In addition we address the following issue. From a computational viewpoint, how *difficult* is it to solve such problems to optimality?

1.3.1. Enumeration

The reader, possibly exhausted from solving problems by *complete enumeration*, has gained the following experience with respect to such an approach. For a given instance of some problem, the total effort invested in its solution consists of a fixed amount (to grasp the idea of what has to be done) plus a variable amount proportional to the number of feasible solutions to be evaluated. Disregarding the fixed amount, the question as to the difficulty of solving problems to optimality can then be rephrased as: For a given optimization problem called, say, OPT and the *family of all data instances* of a well-defined *length* (say, measured in terms of m and n specifying the number of clients and potential locations, respectively), what is the number of feasible solutions? Let $F1(OPT)$ denote the number sought. We commence the evaluation with three problems having the same number of feasible solutions.

> *p-MP, p-CP, p-UFLP.* For given p there are $\binom{n}{p}$ distinct location patterns of open and closed facilities. Since not all open facilities necessarily need be active, we can in principle assign each of the m clients to any open facility. Hence, $F1(p\text{-MP}) = F1(p\text{-CP}) = F1(p\text{-UFLP}) = \binom{n}{p}p^{m}$.
>
> *UFLP.* Since p is not prespecified, the answer is immediately at hand: $F1(\text{UFLP}) = n^{m}$.
>
> *p-ACTIVE.* For each of the $\binom{n}{p}$ distinct patterns of open and closed facilities, let $T(p, m)$ denote the number of feasible assignments whereby the p open facilities may be assigned to the m clients, $p \le m$, such that each open facility is active. Then $F1(p\text{-ACTIVE}) = \binom{n}{p}T(p, m)$, where it can be shown that
>
> $$T(p, m) = \sum_{j=1}^{p} (-1)^{p+j}\binom{p}{j} j^{m}$$
>
> *QAP, QBP.* For the family of all instances where m units are to be located at m out of n areas, $n \ge m$, we obtain
>
> $$F1(\text{QAP}) = F1(\text{QBP}) = \binom{n}{m}m!$$

Note that for a given *instance* of p-MP, p-CP, or p-UFLP and a given pattern of open and closed facilities among the $\binom{n}{p}$ such patterns, all of the p^{m} distinct assignments of clients to open facilities need not be *explicitly* evaluated. The small examples in the previous sections show that each of the p^{m} assignments in fact are *implicitly* evaluated as each client is assigned to the "nearest" open facility. This remark also stresses the distinction between "a family of instances of a well-defined length" and a specific "instance" viewed as a member of a family.

Based on the last remark, for a given *instance* of some OPT, $F2(OPT)$ is defined as the number of distinct location patterns of open and closed facilities and, hence, the number of feasible solutions that need be explicitly evaluated in a complete enumeration approach.

All of the above results are displayed in Figure 1.12. The $2^{n} - 1$ entry for $F2(\text{ULP})$ excludes the possibility that all facilities are closed. $F2(p\text{-}$

OPT	p-MP, p-CP, p-UFLP	UFLP	p-ACTIVE	QAP, QBP
$F1(OPT)$	$\binom{n}{p} p^m$	n^m	$\binom{n}{p}\sum_{j=1}^{p}(-1)^{p+j}\binom{p}{j} j^m$	$\binom{n}{m} m!$
$F2(OPT)$	$\binom{n}{p}$	$2^n - 1$		

Figure 1.12. Numbers of feasible solutions to various problems. The figures in the bottom row are based on the assumption that clients, wherever relevant, are assigned to the "nearest" open facility.

ACTIVE) is undefined since an assignment of clients to the "nearest" open facility need not imply that all open facilities become active. Moreover, there is no obvious way of defining $F2(QAP)$ and $F2(QBP)$.

Even for moderate values of m and n, all of the numbers listed are virtually astronomical. As an example, suppose that the layout design of a hospital involves just 20 units to be located at 20 areas, then $F1(QAP) = 20! = 2,432,902,008,176,610,000 \approx 2 \times 10^{18}$. Even on the fastest computer available, an approach based on complete, explicit enumeration would require an exorbitant amount of time, here, on the order of thousands of years.

In assessing the computational complexity of some problem, just counting the number of feasible solutions, however, may be quite misleading. Suppose 100 lottery tickets, each marked by distinct numbers among $1, \ldots, 100$ are spread in a completely disorganized way on a table. A deck of the 100 lottery tickets in which they appear in ascending order $1, 2, \ldots, 100$ is but one ordering of the deck out of the 100! distinct arrangements of such a deck. The task of searching for the proverbial needle in a haystack is negligible in comparison to the task of searching for a single item out of 100! Yet, it takes but a matter of minutes for anyone to sort the lottery tickets as specified.

Likewise, there are a wealth of nontrivial optimization problems and corresponding large-scale data instances for which cleverly designed algorithms can identify an optimal solution in matters of seconds. On the other hand, there are also optimization problems for which the largest instance that can be solved to optimality by the "best" algorithm available is surprisingly small. Why is this so?

The theory of computational complexity, the subject of the following section, is not as yet fully developed to give conclusive answers. It does, however, provide certain clues and, as a by-product, a conceptual framework for further algorithmic analyses.

1.3.2. The Computational Complexity of Locational Decision Problems

In the following we provide a series of characterizations of the prototype problems studied in terms of *computational complexity*. Since excellent textbooks and expository articles on the theory of $\mathcal{NP}$-completeness are available, we shall resort to intuitively appealing definitions of the classes $\mathcal{P}$ and $\mathcal{NP}$, sufficient for conveying our main message: Each of the prototype problems is termed $\mathcal{NP}$-*hard*, and the so-called *decision problem* related to it is $\mathcal{NP}$-*complete*.

First, a word about the distinction between polynomial and exponential time-bounded algorithms. For our purposes, we can consider *algorithms* as step-by-step procedures for solving problems in a finite computing time for all data instances. It is practical and commonly accepted to characterize algorithms by a measure related to their so-called time complexity function. For a given problem type OPT, a family of data instances of a given size q corresponding to a given input length, and a specific algorithm, Ω, we denote the *time complexity function* of the algorithm by $f_\Omega(q)$ where $f_\Omega(q)$ expresses the largest amount of time required for solving the problem for an arbitrary data instance of that size.

Obviously, $f_\Omega(q)$ depends on both the computer used, and the encoding scheme employed for the algorithm and the data instance, but neither of the two has any significant effect on the assessment of the algorithm. Roughly, $f_\Omega(q)$ expresses the maximum number of elementary steps, such as additions, multiplications, and comparisons performed by the algorithm to solve any instance of size q.

To characterize the *order* of $f_\Omega(q)$, we say that $f_\Omega(q)$ is $O(g(q))$ whenever there exists some constant α such that $|f_\Omega(q)| \leq \alpha|g(q)|$ for all q, $q = 1, 2, 3, \ldots$. We then refer to the algorithm Ω as an $O(g(q))$ algorithm for OPT. An algorithm Ω with time complexity function $f_\Omega(q)$ is called *polynomial* (*time-bounded*) or *good* or *fast* or *efficient* if $f_\Omega(q)$ is $O(g(q))$, $q = 1, 2, \ldots$, and if $g(q)$ is some polynomial of the input length q. If $f_\Omega(q)$ cannot be so bounded, the algorithm Ω is called *exponential*. Since this definition involves "all data instances," we can alternatively say that an algorithm is either polynomial or exponential in the *worst* (most time-consuming) *case*. A problem for which a polynomial algorithm exists is occasionally referred to as *well solved*.

To exemplify this notation, for some problem OPT, algorithm Ω, and for $q = 1, 2, \ldots$, assume $f_\Omega(q) = 7q^5 + 3q^2 + \log q$. For $g(q) = q^5$, $|f_\Omega(g)| \leq 10g(q)$, hence, Ω is an $O(q^5)$—and therefore polynomial—algorithm for OPT.

In the remainder of this section we illustrate the major concepts of computational complexity in regard to the uncapacitated facility location problem, UFLP.

For OPT = UFLP, a "data instance of length q" has no obvious meaning since a data instance m, n, C, f consists (at most) of $1 + 1 + mn + n$ numbers. However, we can define $q = \max\{m, n\}$ whereby the length of any data instance will be, at most, a polynomial of second order in q. Since the product of two polynomials is a polynomial, any algorithm which is $O(h(q))$ for some polynomial h of $q = \max\{m, n\}$ would also be polynomial time-bounded for the family of all instances of UFLP defined by given values of m, n. In this manner we can characterize an approximate algorithm (a concept to be explained shortly) for the $m = n$ case of QAP as "an $O(n^3)$ algorithm" where n is the number of units to be located at the n areas available whereas the length of a data instance is of the order n^2 (n itself plus two ($n \times n$) matrices representing connections and distances, respectively).

In contrast to the optimization problems discussed so far, we shall refer to a *decision problem* π as one with only two possible solutions, either the answer "yes" or the answer "no." As an example, a decision problem $\pi(\text{UFLP})$ related to UFLP is: for a given instance m, n, C, f and a given *threshold value* k, does UFLP have a solution of value at most k?

The formal theory of $\mathcal{NP}$-completeness is based on the concept of deterministic and nondeterministic Turing machines, designed to provide yes/no answers to decision problems posed in terms of *language recognition*. For a given alphabet and "language," an input consisting of a finite *string* of symbols from the alphabet is accepted by the machine (that is, solves the decision problem) if and only if it belongs to the language.

We will consider a string as a *data instance* and a language as a *problem type* or as the *set of all its feasible instances*. A decision problem to check the feasibility of a data instance for a given problem type is said to belong to the class $\mathcal{P}$ if feasibility *or* infeasibility of any data instance can be determined, by some algorithm, in polynomial time on a digital computer, idealized to accept input of arbitrary length. Thus, $\pi(\text{UFLP}) \in \mathcal{P}$ if, for any given m, n, C, f, k, we can in polynomial time either confirm or refute its membership in the set of feasible instances. Actually, it is not known whether $\pi(\text{UFLP})$ belongs to $\mathcal{P}$ or not.

It does however, as will be demonstrated shortly, belong to the (wider?) class $\mathcal{NP}$ which can be characterized as follows. For a given *instance* γ of a decision problem its feasibility implies the existence of an appropriate *structure* δ associated with γ. If the length of δ (the encoding of the desired structure) is bounded by some polynomial in the length of γ, and if for given (γ, δ) we can *affirm the feasibility* of δ in polynomial time on a digital computer, then this decision problem is said to belong to the class $\mathcal{NP}$.

For $\pi(\text{UFLP})$ we consider an instance γ defined by m, n, C, f, k. Clearly γ is feasible if we can assign values 0 or 1 to all x_j, y_{ij} variables in the integer programming formulation of UFLP such that all constraints are satisfied and such that the value of the objective function does not exceed k. Here the structure δ associated with γ is a 0–1 vector with $n + mn$ elements representing the values of the $n + mn$ variables x_j, y_{ij}. Then a binary encoding of δ is of length $n + mn$ which is of the same order as the length of γ. To affirm the feasibility of δ, that is, to verify that δ satisfies the constraints and that the objective function does not exceed k, requires computations of the order $n + mn$. Since both conditions for its membership are met, $\pi(\text{UFLP}) \in \mathcal{NP}$ as asserted.

If for any data instance of a decision problem π', we can construct in polynomial time a data instance of a decision problem π such that the instance of π' is feasible if and only if the instance of π is feasible, then π' is said to be *polynomially transformable* to π; we will use the notation $\pi' \propto \pi$ for this. Thus, $\pi' \propto \pi$ implies that π' can be viewed as a special case of π and, consequently, π is at least as difficult to solve as π'. If $\pi' \propto \pi$ for all $\pi' \in \mathcal{NP}$ then any problem belonging to the class $\mathcal{NP}$ can be viewed as a special case of π which is then called $\mathcal{NP}$-*hard*. Finally π is called $\mathcal{NP}$-*complete* if π is $\mathcal{NP}$-hard and $\pi \in \mathcal{NP}$. It can be shown that if some $\pi' \propto \pi$, π belongs to $\mathcal{NP}$ and π' is $\mathcal{NP}$-complete, then π is also $\mathcal{NP}$-complete.

Based upon the underlying theory, in terms of language recognition, the $\mathcal{NP}$-*completeness of* 21 *decision problems including* π(SET COVER) was proven in 1972 (cf. the collection of references in Section 1.5). If for a given instance m, n, A, f, k of π(SET COVER), we define an instance of π(UFLP) by $c_{ij} = \infty$ if $a_{ij} = 0$ and $c_{ij} = 0$ if $a_{ij} = 1$, then the answer to π(SET COVER) will be positive if and only if the answer to the question: "Does this instance of π(UFLP) have a solution of value at most k?" is positive. Since we have just shown π(UFLP) is in $\mathcal{NP}$ and since the transformation π(SET COVER) to π(UFLP) is polynomial (in this case linear) in mn then π(UFLP) is $\mathcal{NP}$-complete.

Optimization Problems versus Decision Problems

Our primary concern in this section is to study the computational tractability of certain locational decision problems formulated as *optimization* problems, whereas our temporary interest in decision problems was merely because key concepts like $\mathcal{NP}$-completeness and $\mathcal{NP}$-hardness are only defined with respect to these. What remains in order to characterize the computational complexity of UFLP itself is to elaborate upon the connection between a given optimization problem and *some* related decision problem. For a given minimization problem OPT, the most direct way of deriving a related decision problem π_0(OPT) is to introduce a *threshold* k and ask the question: "Does OPT have a feasible solution of value at most k?". If π_0(OPT)—which for given OPT and given k is uniquely defined—possesses the property of $\mathcal{NP}$-completeness and if this property is retained upon certain simplifications of π_0(OPT), then alternative decision problems π_1(OPT), π_2(OPT), ... possessing that property can be formulated. In order to characterize the computational complexity of optimization problems, a π(OPT) related to a given OPT is usually chosen as the most "simplified" version, that is, "simplified" as long as its complexity remains unaltered.

For any instance of a decision problem $\pi \in \mathcal{P}$ answers can be provided in polynomial time to both the question "is this instance feasible" and the complementary question "is this instance infeasible," (also referred to as the *complement* of the given decision problem). For $\pi \in \mathcal{NP}$, however, a similar symmetry between a problem and its complement is not known to exist since in general for a given instance only the *feasibility* of an associated structure can be *affirmed* in polynomial time. Actually, no complement of any $\mathcal{NP}$-complete problem is known to belong to $\mathcal{NP}$.

In general, an instance of a given OPT cannot be optimally solved in polynomial time by solving a sequence of some related $\pi(\text{OPT})$ for varying thresholds. The assertion is true even for an optimization problem OPT whose corresponding decision problem $\pi(\text{OPT}) \in \mathcal{P}$. Although the infeasibility, as well as the feasibility, of an instance of $\pi(\text{OPT})$ can be determined in polynomial time, the number of such instances to be solved will not in general be bounded by some polynomial in the length of the input.

We are thus unable to prove formally that UFLP is $\mathcal{NP}$-complete or $\mathcal{NP}$-hard, whereas the following argument provides at least a reasonable characterization of its computational complexity. Evidently, while the converse is not true, an optimal solution of some OPT will solve a related decision problem $\pi(\text{OPT})$ as well. Furthermore, if OPT is solvable in polynomial time then so is $\pi(\text{OPT})$. In addition, if $\pi(\text{OPT})$ is known to be $\mathcal{NP}$-hard, then any decision problem in $\mathcal{NP}$ is solvable in polynomial time and $\mathcal{P} = \mathcal{NP}$. Since $\mathcal{NP}$-hardness is defined only with respect to decision problems, then *the corresponding optimization problems* can be called *$\mathcal{NP}$-hard* in the sense that the existence of polynomial algorithms for their solution would imply $\mathcal{P} = \mathcal{NP}$.

The conclusion then is that $\pi(\text{UFLP})$ is $\mathcal{NP}$-complete and that the corresponding optimization problem, UFLP itself, is $\mathcal{NP}$-hard. It is relatively straightforward, but beyond the scope of this chapter, to verify that the same applies for p-MP, p-CP, p-UFLP, p-ACTIVE, QAP, and QBP. For all the problems mentioned, however, there exist special cases for which polynomial algorithms can be devised. As an example, each member of the subfamily of instances m, n, C, f, max $\{m, n\} < 3$ of UFLP is solvable in polynomial time.

Although the theory of computational complexity has provided useful complexity measures of decision problems via the definition of classes $\mathcal{P}$ and $\mathcal{NP}$, followed up by concepts like $\mathcal{NP}$-completeness and $\mathcal{NP}$-hardness, the fact that some instances of $\mathcal{NP}$-hard optimization problems (occurring in practice or generated randomly but not necessarily in the "worst-case" situations underlying complexity analysis) are computationally more demanding than others is still a constant source of dissatisfaction. To illustrate this aspect, let $t(\text{OPT})$ be a rough measure of the largest instances of OPT that can be solved to optimality by the "best" algorithm known within a "reasonable" amount of computer time. For the $m = n$ case of QAP, $t(\text{QAP})$ is approximately 20 whereas $t(\text{ULP})$ taken as max $\{m, n\}$ is about 200. For other $\mathcal{NP}$-hard optimization problems, $t(\text{OPT})$ can approach several thousands.

There is thus a strong need for further refinements of complexity measures. A not very sophisticated but rather useful notion is that of *empirical complexity* (EC). For some OPT, let EC(OPT) denote the ratio $t(OPT)/T(OPT)$ where $T(OPT)$ is a measure of the largest instances of OPT solvable by complete enumeration given that we evaluate at most a prescribed number, say 1 million, of feasible solutions. For QAP with $m = n$, $F1(OPT)$ in Figure 1.12 reduces to $n!$ Since $1,000,000 \approx 10!$, $T(QAP) \approx 10$, and, therefore, $EC(QAP) \approx 20/10 = 2$. For UFLP, the pertinent entry in Figure 1.12 is $F2(UFLP) = 2^n - 1$. Since $1,000,000 \approx 2^{20}$, $T(UFLP) \approx 20$, and $EC(UFLP) \approx 200/20 = 10$. Straightforward as it is, this EC-measure is likely to be spurned by concerned theorists, but it does nevertheless provide an intuitively appealing distinction between the real hard QAP and the somewhat easier UFLP.

Exact Algorithms versus Approximate Algorithms

For all of the location problems considered, with QAP as the most illustrative in this context, there is, at times, a substantial gap between the dimensions of a realistic problem and the computational effort required of the best existing algorithm giving an *exact* optimal solution. Thus, proven optimality cannot always be hoped for in cases where no known *exact algorithm* is computationally capable of handling a given instance. We are then compelled to resort to some *approximate algorithm*.

Throughout the book exact and approximate algorithms will be discussed in parallel. Theorists have previously ranked approximate algorithms as "second class members." This is no longer so; on the contrary, such approaches have enjoyed much fruitful research over the past decade.

For a given data dependent set S of feasible solutions to an optimization (minimization) problem and a given, real-valued, data dependent objective function $g(x)$, our algorithms will be required to find either x^0 such that $z^0 = g(x^0) = \min \{ g(x): x \in S \}$ or some "reasonable" solution. For a given problem type and *for all data instances*, assume that the algorithm terminates after a finite computing time with a solution x' and the corresponding value $z' = g(x')$ of the objective function. If $x' \in S$ and $g(x') = z^0$, the algorithm is called an *exact algorithm*; otherwise, it is an *approximate algorithm*. If $x' \in S' \supseteq S$ and $z' \leq z^0$, some of the constraints are *relaxed* and x' need not be feasible with respect to the original set S, then this approximation algorithm is said to solve a *relaxation* of the original problem. The word "relaxation" refers to the reduced constraint set. Finally, if $x' \in S$ and $z' \geq z^0$, the approximation algorithm is a *heuristic*. A heuristic is thus an algorithm producing feasible solutions for all data instances without guaranteeing optimality.

The distinction between exact and approximate algorithms for a given optimization problem raises the fundamental question: How should approximate algorithms for solving optimization problems be assessed?

Apart from empirical investigations, possibly guided by a decision-maker's opinion about the solutions proposed, there are basically two distinct approaches, worst-case analyses and probabilistic analyses. Upon defining an appropriate measure for a solution's deviation from optimality, the aim of *worst-case analyses* of approximate algorithms for a given problem type is to devise bounds for the maximum deviation and, if possible, to provide data instances to demonstrate that no better bounds exist. *Probabilistic analyses*, on the other hand, must be based on certain assumptions as to how the problem data are distributed. A measure of the "deviation" from optimality is then a random variable. Results provided via probabilistic analysis might be the probability that a data instance drawn at random satisfies some property, for example, that the solution obtained is within a prespecified percentage of optimality.

Probabilistic analyses also deal with algorithms' *average-case behavior*, and, although more difficult, they may be—at least from a practitioner's point of view—more pertinent than worst-case analyses. The most striking example is the Simplex algorithm for linear programming for which highly contrived data instances, generated by twisting a hypercube, have been constructed to demonstrate its exponential behavior in the worst case. Nevertheless, the Simplex algorithm is recognized as working exceedingly well in practice.

1.4. ISSUES OF PROBLEM FORMULATION

Having emphasized the notion of choice in a discrete spatial context, we now proceed to discuss several of the major characteristics of most realistic locational decision problems and how they can and should affect the transformation of such problems into operational models. We remark that such critical discussions play only a secondary role in the ensuing chapters as major emphasis is placed upon analytical and computational aspects.

There is a plethora of ways of classifying normative models. With particular reference to the models within our scope of interest, significant keywords for classifying according to objectives include: *single criterion* (for example, the minimization of the total cost associated with a locational decision); *multicriteria* (simultaneous optimization of several incommensurable objectives such as minimizing the maximal travel distance and minimizing the total travel cost); and *vector optimization* (determination of nondominated solutions to a multicriteria problem (see Section 1.4.2).

We can furthermore classify a model as *capacitated* as opposed to *uncapacitated* where the former term may refer to upper bounds on the number of units that each facility can produce and ship per time period, or upper bounds on the number of units that can be transported along certain routes. At times we must also distinguish between *one-product* (single-commodity) models where different products are represented by a surrogate, aggregated product, and *multiproduct* (multicommodity) models where several products share certain common facilities but cannot be reasonably aggregated. Models are called *multiperiod* or *dynamic* (as opposed to *static*) if the time element is explicitly represented; such models may be used to analyze realistic decision problems where not only the location and size of facilities, but also questions regarding "when" to establish them are of importance. Models are referred to as *stochastic* (as opposed to *deterministic*) when some parameter values are given by probability distributions. The title of the present book indicates that we focus upon *discrete* models rather than their *continuous* or *planar* counterparts comprising, for example, a nondenumerable location set such as the continuum consisting of any point in a plane.

Based on the keywords above, all of the models presented so far can be characterized as *single-criterion, uncapacitated, one-product, static, deterministic, discrete optimization* problems.

The purpose of the above characterization is twofold. First, consider for example UFLP, the uncapacitated facility location problem. If "uncapacitated" is replaced by "capacitated" we arrive at a model which is but one of the many extensions of UFLP studied. The same applies for the multiproduct, the multiperiod, the stochastic, and the planar versions of UFLP. Similar extensions of the other prototype problems have also been investigated. Secondly, the list of keywords is to some extent used to structure the remainder of this concluding section which addresses general modeling aspects of discrete locational decision problems.

1.4.1. The Strategic Aspect of Locational Decisions

Generally speaking, locational decision problems focus upon *strategic* rather than tactical matters, for example, where to place factories or schools rather than how to steer the day-to-day deliveries from factories to warehouses and retail outlets or how to route school buses. That is, the emphasis is placed upon *planning* and *design* problems rather than on operational problems.

For this reason, such locational decision problem formulations employ surrogate measures to describe the operational aspects; for example, some measure of distance may be employed to determine the "cost" of providing services from a facility to a client instead of attempting to model in some detail the routing of service vehicles and the associated costs. Nevertheless, in some contexts—for example, where the distribution aspects are so dominating—it may be appropriate to consider integrated location and distribution problems at the cost of greatly increased problem complexity and data collection/processing costs.

It should be noted that in practice a locational decision problem can seldom be considered in isolation from other strategic decisions. Nevertheless, it is seldom that the interfaces between locational decisions and other such decisions, for example, regarding choice of technology, organizational development, strategic marketing plans, and long-range planning in general, are integrated within the context of models of locational decisions. Instead, the results of the analyses of such models must implicitly be assumed to be evaluated together with the results of other strategic analyses, where such evaluation is performed externally to the locational decision model.

To exemplify the importance of such interfaces, consider briefly how questions of design and technology can be of utmost importance for long-term locational decisions. Depending on the time span and/or the potential size or location of the facilities being considered, it may be relevant to consider alternative technologies, modeled for example by different functional relationships between capacities, production, and costs. Nevertheless, it is the exception rather than the rule that such design considerations are explicitly considered in locational decision models.

1.4.2. Measures of Performance: Single Criterion or Multicriteria?

Reflection as to the strategic nature of most locational decision problems also leads to consideration of the appropriateness of the objective functions employed in the prototype formulations. These are usually of a rather simplistic nature, such as "minimize total costs" or "minimize the maximal distance between any facility-client pair". Today, there is an increasing interest in the ability to operationalize the handling of more complex criteria, particularly as regards decisions concerning the location of public facilities.

Furthermore, we have tacitly regarded facilities to be located as "friendly" in the sense that "closeness" throughout has been viewed as an attractive property. Certainly, location theory does also encompass the counterpart: location of so-called *obnoxious* facilities, where one frequently used criterion is to maximize the minimum distance between a facility and its closest client. Disregarding its workers and subcontractors, who else likes an obnoxious nuclear power plant in their backyard? Note that even a friendly facility may well become obnoxious unless "closeness" is taken with a grain of salt. For example, optimal closeness to a noisy elementary school is "reachable within a few minutes of walking" rather than "next door."

Relatively little is known as to the rationale employed by managers and politicians when they make locational decisions. In fact, empirical investigation on companies' motives for making (and, even more importantly, for *not* making) locational decisions indicates that in many cases, the "rational" criteria employed to measure performance in the most widely used prototype models may be rather poor surrogate measures for the decision-makers' real, but rather unclear, motives.

As was demonstrated in Section 1.2, most of the models presented employ either a *minisum* criterion or a *minimax* criterion. Neither of these criteria alone, however, capture all essential elements of a location problem where it is important to consider both the total "costs" of serving clients as well as the service provided to those clients who are located far away from a facility. The minisum criterion alone may result in solutions which are unacceptable from the point of view of the service level for the clients who end up being located far away. On the other hand, the minimax criterion if used alone may lead to very costly service systems.

Some attempts have been made to alleviate the above deficiencies using *bicriteria* models (that is, models incorporating two criteria such as minisum and minimax). A well-known example is the development of algorithms for identifying the so-called *cent-dian* or *medi-center* of a network, where these terms refer to locations which minimize the convex combination of median and center criteria.

Another example is a set of algorithmic modules designed for the investigation of a hybrid problem which can be stated roughly as follows. For selected values of a parameter λ, $0 \le \lambda \le 1$, and for all values of p within a prespecified range $p' \le p \le p''$, determine the location of p facilities such that each client is assigned to one of these and such that the convex combination

$$\lambda \text{ (minisum criterion of UFLP)} + (1 - \lambda)(\text{minimax criterion of } p\text{-CP})$$

is minimized.

Special cases of this hybrid model include:

p-MP: $\lambda = 1$, $p' = p'' = p$, all fixed costs $= 0$
p-CP: $\lambda = 0$, $p' = p'' = p$
UFLP: $\lambda = 1$, $p' = 1$, $p'' = n$
p-UFLP: $\lambda = 1$, $p' = p'' = p$.

As it unites, so to speak, several prototype models, we refer to this uni-location model as UNILOC.

Within the context of "measures of performance," UNILOC can be viewed as one of several steps on the road from single criterion models to models for *multiple criteria decision making* (MCDM). Such models contribute to the analysis of decision-makers' preferences in a multidimensional criteria space where these criteria may either be quantifiable (for example, costs and physical distances) or nonquantifiable (for example, the aesthetic value of a layout).

Often the criteria involved tend to be conflicting: the improvement of one objective can be accomplished only at the expense of another. As an illustration, suppose that two populated areas at a given distance from each other are to be served by a single hospital. Where should it be located? Formulated in terms of 1-MP, an optimal solution (the 1-median) is to locate the hospital at the more populated area. From a minimax point of view, however, the optimal solution (the 1-center) is to locate at the midpoint between the two areas. Neither of these two solutions are optimal with respect to both criteria so which one, if any, should actually be chosen by the decision-maker?

This and similar questions are inherent in MCDM. The crux of the difficulty in answering such questions is that the concept of optimality loses its significance for models involving two or more criteria. Suppose that a realistic locational decision problem is modeled in terms of minimizing k real-valued criterion functions $f_i(x)$, $i = 1, \ldots, k$ subject to certain constraints. Ideally, we seek a feasible solution x which minimizes the *vector-valued function* $[f_1(x), \ldots, f_k(x)]$. Now, whereas an optimal solution to a single criterion optimization problem is unambiguously defined, there is no general definition of the minimum of a vector-valued function. If each of the k criteria is minimized separately, we arrive at a solution often referred to as the *ideal* or *utopia point*. As the word indicates, the decision-maker's wildest expectations are likely to be exceeded but the ideal point which concurrently minimizes the k criteria is normally infeasible.

Rather than optimality, a far more operational concept within an MCDM context is that of efficiency. For a pair (x, y) of feasible solutions we say that y *dominates* x if $f_i(y) \leq f_i(x)$, for all i, and if strict inequality holds for at least one i. A feasible solution which is not dominated by any other feasible solution is called *efficient*. Without dwelling on details, we note that although UNILOC essentially embeds the minisum and minimax criteria within a framework of traditional optimization, parametric solutions in (λ, p) of UNILOC provide solutions which are "efficient" with respect to the two criteria.

Admittedly, the minisum and minimax criteria employed in the prototype models of Section 1.2 are intuitively appealing. In practice, however, such criteria must often be supplemented by additional criteria, either within the confines of the models used or in the form of supplementary information to be considered outside the model. It is not our intent here to attempt to answer the question of how best to balance what should be explicitly included in a locational decision model, and what should be treated with other means of analysis. In fact, it can be forcefully argued that, rationally speaking, there are no criteria for the selection of criteria.

In conclusion we conjecture that multicriteria models, used in an interactive manner, are likely to play a more dominant role in locational decision making in the future.

1.4.3. The "Size" of Facilities and Clients

When discussing a locational decision, facilities are usually characterized by their capacities, areas, designs, productive efficiencies, product costs as functions of quantities produced, the technologies employed, and so on. In contrast to this observable behavior, such characteristics usually are treated only rudimentarily in many locational decision models.

For example, in most formulations reported in the literature, the notion of *facility size* is essentially ignored and facilities are implicitly assumed to be points in space as are the sites where they may be located. A notable exception is the case of those location problems with spatial interactions which, like QAP in Section 1.2.6, deal with the relative location of departments, or the like, of unequal size, each of which is to deliver predetermined quantities of goods or services to each other. Here the "size" of the departments will typically be crucial for the layout design. This "capacity" aspect will also be considered within the context of the multi-period location models of Chapter 4.

At first glance, it may appear reasonable to assume that, within the confines of the strategic planning problem being considered, it is appropriate to neglect area considerations and to let the capacity of the facilities be indirectly determined via the determination of the optimal throughput per time period. Nevertheless, and with reference to the previous remarks on the influence of technology, "size" may be a very important factor in that different technologies characterized by their productive capabilities and costs may be appropriate for different production levels.

Clients too are typically represented by discrete points in space, for example as nodes on a road network, each of which is characterized by a demand, perhaps by demand over time. In fact, the notion of a client is far more complicated and may affect a locational decision in many more ways than a perusal of the literature would imply. As an illustration of this potential effect, consider how the notion of a "point client" affects the representation of distance, and thereby also of costs, in a discrete locational model.

How are the distance data generated? Intuitively, one is led to think of using road kilometers or the like. But then the question arises, what in fact do the points represent? Are they given precise locations or do they represent, for example, a centroid of a more or less homogeneous area? Is the area a community or other such arbitrary district considered as an entity solely for historical administrative reasons? Presumably it is the former in the case of a point representing a possible location of a facility such as a factory, warehouse or school, and often the latter in the case of a "client" having a demand for goods/services. To digress briefly upon this latter concept, a client often represents an *aggregation* of many individuals, households, shops or the like. This is clearly the case in public facility location problems where some measure of the service provided to the clients or the total cost of providing the service is to be optimized. In such cases (these are by far the most common as opposed to the case where a client has a precise, point-like location), it is far from clear what distance actually should be. Measuring road kilometers, for example, from a potential facility location to a point assumed to represent the demand for a product or service in a region may give an inaccurate representation of the relevant distance. The same applies for other types of travel measures such as travel time or travel costs. It can be shown that the effect of such aggregation can produce substantial errors in the solutions to some locational decision problems and that solutions based upon aggregated data are open to extensive manipulation, dependent upon the aggregation procedures employed.

On the other hand, due to the statistical law of large numbers, the more aggregated the client representation the more accurate are our estimates of the aggregated clients' demands. In addition, the number of clients and therefore the computational demands, will be reduced.

The question arises then on what is the *optimal degree of aggregation* where accuracy of representation, goodness of solution, and computational effort are relevant measures of performance. Note that this question in itself constitutes a challenging multicriteria decision problem!

1.4.4. Distances between Facilities and Clients

Closely related to the above discussion on the "size" of facilities and clients is the notion of "distances" between facilities and clients. In general, the prototype formulations considered in this book all presume the availability of (or the ability to generate as required) the *shortest path distances* between all relevant "points," that is, between each possible facility-client pair and, for those problems where spatial interactions between facilities is important, between each possible facility-facility pair.

For discrete points on a plane, approximate shortest distances can be computed on the basis of points' coordinates and a given metric, for examples the Euclidean metric and the rectilinear metric. When the distances between points can be calculated by the use of a simple formula based on a metric, there may be considerable savings in computer storage requirement. This is in contrast to explicitly computing the distances on a network, when an underlying network is predefined. Here an algorithm is needed to compute the shortest distances on the network. Although polynomial algorithms are available to determine these shortest distances, the requirement to generate and *store* all the shortest path distances may place a rather large demand upon computer storage capacity. Thus, the use of explicit network distances limits the size of the problem formulation amenable to solution. Once again, the modeler faces a "balancing" decision between the two options available: (1) to seek greater accuracy and realism in the distances employed at the cost of increased computational effort and perhaps the requirement that the number of aggregated "points" must be limited, or (2) to accept reduced accuracy and realism when generating the distances while reaping the benefits of reduced computational costs and more accurate (less aggregated) representations of clients and/or with a greater number of potential facility locations.

1.4.5. The Single-Product Assumption

The prototype formulations considered in Section 1.2 all assume that different products or services can be *aggregated* into equivalent units. This *single-product* assumption may be reasonable whenever the production and transportation processes are not significantly different for different products and when the strategic aspect dominates.

On the other hand, when there are significant economies-of-scale in production or distribution or when the distribution component of the locational decision problem is dominating, it may appear necessary to model the multiproduct aspects of the decision problem at the expense of greatly increased data collection and computational demands. However, even in such cases before concluding that a multiproduct formulation should be utilized, consideration should be given on whether the existing products and technologies may be replaced in the long run. Uncertainties here may lead to the choice of a single-product formulation even though the existing structural aspects may indicate a multiproduct approach.

It appears from the remainder of this book that the single-product assumption is particularly significant for center and covering problems when the underlying network is a tree (see Chapters 6–8). Via a transformation provided in Chapter 2, many of the other locational decision problems considered can, in a fairly straightforward way, be generalized to accommodate the multiproduct aspect.

1.4.6.   The Allocation of Clients to Facilities

Most discrete location models assume some simple rule for determining which clients are to be served by which facilities. For example, in formulations which do not presume the existence of constraints on the capacity of the facilities or the transportation network, clients are usually assumed to be served by that facility which is located "nearest" (typically in terms of distance, time or cost) to them, which then leads to what may be called single-assignment rules. Disregarding QAP, all of the prototype problems discussed in Section 1.2 exhibit such a feature. In fact, however, single-assignment may be an oversimplification and there may exist several reasons why other more complicated allocation rules should be considered. One such reason is closely related to the notion, just discussed, of a single, aggregated product. If the problem at hand involves several products and several kinds of services to be provided and not all products and services are available at each facility (for example, to take advantage of economies-of-scale or due to the design of existing facilities), then the single-assignment assumption cannot be maintained. Furthermore, even if all such products/ services are assumed to be potentially available at each facility, considerations of distribution economics may lead to the allocation of the clients to several facilities. Other reasons might have to do with market considerations (for example, traditional ties between specific facilities and clients), and legal or contractual considerations (for example, labor agreements or rules regulating interstate commerce).

There are other scenarios where the single-assignment assumption is not valid. For example, when the closest facility to a given client is busy, the second closest or some other facility may end up serving that client. Thus, the assignment of a client depends on the state of the system. Some of these aspects are discussed in Chapter 2 (where the state of the system changes due to changes in travel costs) and Chapter 12 (where the state of the system depends on the congestion in the service facilities).

When the probability of being served by the closest facility from a given demand point is not 1, but rather depends on how close are the other facilities, we have the models of Chapter 10. Here, we find that demands from that point get distributed among the facilities, where, of course, the closest facility receives the largest fraction of the demands. Such behavioral assumptions are common in describing locational patterns of housing and industries in geographical and urban planning literature. Here again we do not have the Single-Assignment Property. Some of these issues are discussed in detail in Chapter 10.

1.4.7. Single versus Competing Firms

Most models discussed so far implicitly assume that a single firm or agency is locating the facilities and its concern is the minimization of a cost related to either the client's cost or the cost for providing the services to the client. However, in many situations competing firms locate these facilities. In such cases a criterion of performance for each of the firms may be to maximize its (market) share of the client's demands that it serves. Here consumer behavior may be to go to the closest facility (the single assignment assumption) or may be to "most likely" go to the closest facility (here the probability or frequency of going to the closest facility depends on the relative locations of the other facilities). It is only recently that significant modeling effort has been expended to the locational decisions for competitive facilities. Chapter 10 discusses normative optimization approaches for each of two competing firms where each firm knows exactly how many facilities it wishes to establish. Chapter 11, on the other hand, studies the location equilibria that result when each of the two firms are locating a single facility.

1.4.8. Static, Deterministic Models

Much work on locational analysis emphasizes *static* rather than *dynamic* or *multiperiod* formulations and *deterministic* rather than *probabilistic* formulations. This does not necessarily reflect a belief amongst either location analysts or decision-makers that the environment in a locational decision context is subject to but few and small changes over time and that the data are so reliable that it is reasonable to ignore uncertainties. Just the opposite is true. However, attempting to introduce directly stochastic and dynamic elements may lead to a degree of refinement which far exceeds the other levels of abstraction employed, and which cannot be supported by the data available. Furthermore, static deterministic models are easier for decision-makers to understand whereas it is more difficult to validate stochastic/ dynamic formulations. Finally, for even the most simple prototype stochastic/dynamic formulations, there is a relative dearth of efficient algorithms. It is therefore sometimes more relevant to tackle strategic locational questions by considering representative years and varying scenarios rather than by detailed dynamic/probabilistic analyses.

On the other hand, this book is by no means limited to static, deterministic models. Some static probabilistic models are discussed in Chapter 2, whereas some dynamic/stochastic ones are described in Chapter 12. In some contexts, it is quite reasonable to employ multiperiod formulations like those described in Chapter 4. For example, if plans are to be made for the number, sizes, and locations of new schools, and if reasonably reliable demographic data and prognoses are available, then a multiperiod formulation may be able to provide far more insight into the temporal interplay of supply and demand, and lead to better decisions than static formulations.

1.4.9. Continuous versus Discrete Formulations

We began this chapter by stating simply that "reasonable analyses of most realistic locational decision problems lead to the formulation of such problems in discrete space." By now the reader is presumably so skeptical as to what "reasonable analyses" are and so unwilling to take for granted any assumptions regarding problem formulation, that it is fitting to conclude our critical discourse by returning to the question: when is a discrete formulation more appropriate than a continuous one? Both options are frequently available to practitioners and the following issues are often crucial when a choice is to be made: (a) Is the transportation network so well developed in the region being considered and so free from barriers that a continuous formulation is reasonable? (b) Is there a relatively small set of identifiable, facility sites so that a discrete formulation is reasonable? (c) Are the optimal solutions to a continuous formulation readily transferable to a set of possible locations without resulting in serious errors in the measure(s) of performance used to evaluate solutions? (d) Are there considerable computational simplifications obtainable via either a discrete or a continuous formulation?

Although the answers to such questions may be ambiguous, and although the analyst will often have considerable flexiblility in his/her choice, our experience from practice indicates that these answers most often lead to the choice of a discrete representation. The major reasons are that in most cases decision-makers consider a discrete representation to be a more realistic and a more accurate portrayal of the problem at hand, and that continuous formulations appear to be relatively difficult to solve. There do not even appear to exist well-documented, operational algorithms (or even adequate problem formulations in some cases) for several broad classes of simple continuous location problems as opposed to the corresponding tried-and-tested algorithms for discrete formulations. The major difficulty in solving the continuous problems appears to be intimately related to the notion of distance. The very fact that the objects may be located anywhere in the space considered often makes it hard to show that iterative procedures will converge and good bounds cannot be established for guiding various search procedures. The "freedom" provided by planar formulations permits very simple computational procedures for solving problems involving only one facility but complicates the development of operational algorithms for the multifacility case. Often it can be shown that such problems are characterized by objective functions that are not "well-behaved" in an optimality context.

1.4.10. A Normative Approach to Locational Decisions

Many locational decision models—and virtually all of those considered in this book—are characterized by their *normative* or prescriptive approach to the problem of choice based upon the use of optimization methods. Alternative approaches could be the use of simulation or consequence analyses attempting to provide answers to a limited number of "what if" questions. Optimization, however, permits valid comparisons between analyses based on different assumptions and therefore contributes to model validation as well. Furthermore, postoptimal analyses usually provide greater insight into the structural relationships underlying the location problem at hand than normally can be achieved via consequence analyses. Optimization routines can also be employed to "filter" unattractive solutions from further consideration. Finally, solutions obtained by such routines may provide the starting point for more detailed investigations of factors not directly represented in the model, such as additional criteria, organizational constraints and the like.

In spite of the existing arsenal of exact and approximate algorithms for solving various normative locational decision models, it is our belief that the above considerations together with the increasing interest in multicriteria analyses will lead to much greater emphasis upon interactive search procedures. More specifically, we refer to systems allowing for interaction among the decision-maker, the analyst, and the computer, and which not only employ various notions of multicriteria analyses but also, directly or indirectly, reflect the interfaces between locational decisions and other strategic decisions. The "visual interactive modeling" concept may prove to be useful for developing such a system, where the decision-maker visually interacts with the computer, using computer graphics, for model development and evaluation of alternatives.

1.4.11. Where Do We Go from Here?

Highlighting a handful of conceptually simple and yet very versatile models, this chapter has attempted to identify some of the major ingredients of locational analyses. To claim that our discussion on problem formulation should enable the reader to act as a perfect model builder of a realistic locational decision problem would be indeed a bold statement. Endless series of books and papers substantiating the fact that model building invariably is a tight-rope walk—and hence an art—have already appeared and more will follow. Being less ambitious, we can express the hope that the reader has appreciated the flavor of the "meta problem of optimal problem formulation."

In conclusion, it is our belief that it is not at present possible to devise a standard according to which the appropriateness of alternative formulations of locational decision problems can be characterized. From a behavioral point of view one would desire, in general, that a model should be a "reasonable" or "accurate" representation of reality. In that way it will, presumably, be considered to be realistic by the managers, politicians, and, in general, decision-makers who may base their decisions upon the model. On the other hand, there may be quite a price to be paid for more "realism," in the form of more complicated models, the need for considerably more data and data processing, and the requirement for more demanding algorithms. From a decision point of view, it is not a model's "realism," but its ability to lead to "good" decisions that is vital!

1.5. NOTES AND BIBLIOGRAPHY

General

For historical reasons we can appropriately commence with the classic:

A. Weber, *Über den Standort der Industrien*. (In German), Tübingen, 1909; Engl. Transl.: *Theory of the Location of Industries* (C. J. Friedrich, ed. and transl.), Chicago University Press, Chicago, Illinois, 1929.

Weber's ideas are widely recognized as basis for substantial parts of subsequent location theory.

Very extensive bibliographies on normative approaches to solving locational decision problems include:

W. Domschke and A. Drexl, *Location and Layout Planning*: *An International Bibliography*, *Lecture Notes in Economics and Mathematical Systems*, Vol. 238. Springer-Verlag, Berlin and Heidelberg, 1985.

R. L. Francis and J. M. Goldstein, "Location Theory: A Selective Bibliography." *Operations Research* 22, 400–410 (1974).

A. C. Lea, *Location-Allocation Systems*: *An Annotated Bibliography*, Discuss. Pap. No. 13. Department of Geography, University of Toronto, Toronto, Canada, 1973.

To substantiate the characterization "very extensive" used above, we note that the 1985 bibliography compiled by Domschke and Drexl contains well over 1500 entries. In comparison, the bibliography provided in this section is quite modest. A selected bibliography containing about 75 references on locational models and concentrating on research published between 1981 and 1985 is the following by Wong:

R. T. Wong, "Location and Network Design" in *Combinatorial Optimization: Annotated Bibliographies* (M. O'hEigeartaigh, J. K. Lenstra, and A. H. G. Rinnooy Kan, eds.), Wiley, New York, 1985.

As to other previous textbooks on location theory, the following three deserve special mention as forerunners of this book:

R. L. Francis and J. A. White, *Facility Layout and Location: An Analytical Approach*, Prentice-Hall, Englewood Cliffs, New Jersey, 1974.

G. Y. Handler and P. B. Mirchandani, *Location in Networks: Theory and Algorithms*, M.I.T. Press, Cambridge, Massachusetts, 1979.

S. K. Jacobsen and P. M. Pruzan, *Lokalisering—modeller og løsningsmetoder*. (In Danish), Studentlitteratur, Lund, Sweden, 1978.

Newer books in this area are:

W. Domschke and A. Drexl, *Logistik: Standorte*. (In German), R. Oldenbourg Verlag GmbH, Munich, West Germany, 1985.

R. F. Love, J. G. Morris, and G. O. Wesolowsky, *Facilities Location: Models and Methods*, North-Holland, New York, 1988.

J.-F. Thisse and H. G. Zoller, eds., *Locational Analysis of Public Facilities*, North-Holland, Amsterdam, 1983.

The first emphasizes location problems on networks, the second planar location models, and the third, an edited book, contains material on both planar and discrete location models, including several topics discussed in this book.

General interest surveys providing additional background for the material covered in Chapter 1 include:

R. L. Francis, L. F. McGinnis, and J. A. White, "Locational Analysis." *European Journal of Operational Research* **12**, 220–252 (1983).

P. Hansen, D. Peeters, and J.-F. Thisse, "Public Facility Location: A Selective Survey" in *Locational Analysis of Public Facilities* (J.-F. Thisse and H. G. Zoller, eds.). North-Holland, Amsterdam, 1983.

The Four Prototype Formulations

The 1-median problem in a plane is a generalization of a problem posed, purely as a problem in geometry, by Fermat in the early 1600s: "Given three points in a plane, find a fourth point such that the sum of its distances to the three given points is as small as possible." Geometrical solutions were provided around 1640, the weighted case was studied in 1750, and Weber utilized this model in 1909 to determine the optimal location of a factory serving a single client and with two distinct sources for its raw material. Note that the 1-median problem in a plane is frequently referred to as the Weber problem.

Presumably, the shortest paper ever published in our field is:

J. J. Sylvester, "A Question in the Geometry of Situation." *Quarterly Journal of Pure and Applied Mathematics* **1**, 79 (1857).

The full text reads: "It is desired to find the least circle which shall contain a given system of points in a plane." We believe Sylvester's $1\frac{1}{2}$ line brain teaser to be the earliest instance of a p-center problem encountered in the literature, here the unweighted 1-CP with Euclidean distances.

Disregarding such seminal works, however, all of the four prototype problems, p-MP, p-CP, UFLP, and QAP, entered the stage in their present form in the period 1957–1964. As far as the origins of p-MP and p-CP in a network are concerned, the key references are:

L. K. Hua and others, "Application of Mathematical Methods to Wheat Harvesting." *Chinese Mathematics* **2**, 77–91 (1962).

S. L. Hakimi, "Optimal Locations of Switching Centers and the Absolute Centers and Medians of a Graph." *Operations Research* **12**, 450–459 (1964).

Recent surveys with particular emphasis on p-MP and p-CP are:

J. Krarup and P. M. Pruzan, "Selected Families of Location Problems." *Annals of Discrete Mathematics* **5**, 327–387 (1979).

B. C. Tansel, R. L. Francis, and T. J. Lowe, "Location on Networks: A Survey." *Management Science* **29**, 482–511 (1983).

The corresponding single-facility versions, and other single-facility problems on networks are discussed in the following survey paper:

P. Hansen, M. Labbé, D. Peeters, and J.-F. Thisse, *Single Facility Location on Networks*, Research Report 5-85-AFOSR, Rutgers University, New Brunswick, New Jersey, 1985.

UFLP, the uncapacitated facility location problem, also known as the simple plant location problem, is the subject of

J. Krarup and P. M. Pruzan, "The Simple Plant Location Problem: Survey and Synthesis." *European Journal of Operational Research* **12**, 36–81 (1983).

Among the aims of that expository article is to shed more light over the early and somewhat obscure history of UFLP. In spite of some detective work, the "who was first" question has found no decisive answer as yet; it seems that this problem has been formulated independently by

M. L. Balinski and P. Wolfe, *On Benders Decomposition and a Plant Location Problem*, W. P. ARO-27. Mathematica Inc., Princeton, New Jersey, 1963.

A. A. Kuehn and M. J. Hamburger, "A Heuristic Program for Locating Warehouses." *Management Science* **9**, 643–666 (1963).

A. S. Manne, "Plant Location Under Economies-of-Scale." *Management Science* **11**, 213–235 (1964).

J. F. Stollsteimer, "A Working Model for Plant Numbers and Locations." *Journal of Farm Economics* **45**, 631–645 (1963).

Whereas the UFLP literature exhibits several incorrect references in this respect, nobody seems to question that the first formulation of QAP should be attributed to

T. C. Koopmans and M. J. Beckmann, "Assignment Problems and the Location of Economic Activities." *Econometrica* **25**, 53–76 (1957).

Another central paper in this context is the often cited

L. Steinberg, "The Backboard Wiring Problem: A Placement Algorithm." *SIAM Review* **3**, 37–50 (1961).

Much subsequent QAP-literature is due to R. E. Burkard who has also authored a recent survey:

R. E. Burkard, "Quadratic Assignment Problems." *European Journal of Operational Research* **15**, 283–289 (1984).

Hybrid Models

The literature on analyses of exact and approximate algorithms has witnessed an explosive growth over the last decade. Because of its tremendous catalytic effect, the following paper on the hybrid model *p*-UFLP should not be neglected:

G. Cornuéjols, M. L. Fisher, and G. L. Nemhauser, "Location of Bank Accounts to Optimize Float: An Analytic Study of Exact and Approximate Algorithms." *Management Science* **23**, 789–810 (1977).

p-Active was introduced along with the hybrid model UNILOC in:

J. Krarup and P. M. Pruzan, "UNILOC—A Uni-Location Model." *Regional Science and Urban Economics* **12**, 547–578 (1982).

Studies of convex combinations of medians and centers were initiated in the mid 1970s by Halpern (who coined the term cent-dian) and by Handler (who suggested the notion of a medi-center). For the case where a single facility is to be located on a tree network, there is a strong resemblance between the results achieved by these two authors. The two main references are:

J. Halpern, "The Location of a Center-Median Convex Combination on an Undirected Tree." *Journal of Regional Science* **16**, 237–245 (1976).

G. Y. Handler, *Minimax Network Location*: *Theory and Algorithms*, Tech. Rept. No. 107. OR Center and FTL-R74-4, Flight Transportation Laboratory, Massachussetts Institute of Technology, Cambridge, 1974.

Multiple Criteria Decision Making

Among the wealth of publications available in this field we have found the following book on the general area of multiple criteria decision making particularly interesting:

M. Zeleny, *Multiple Criteria Decision Making*, McGraw-Hill, New York, 1982.

The following paper reviews multicriteria facility location problems

C. S. ReVelle, J. L. Cohon, and D. Shobrys, "Multiple Objectives in Facility Location: A Review" in *Lecture Notes in Economics and Mathematical Systems*, Vol. 190 (M. Beckmann and A. P. Künzi, eds.), pp. 321–337. Springer-Verlag, Berlin, 1981.

Although containing very little on location models per se, the following survey article on multiobjective transportation network design discusses several issues pertaining to locational decisions and contains several references on related multiobjective problems on routing and network design:

J. Current and H. Min, "Multiobjective Design of Transportation Networks: Taxonomy and Annotation." *European Journal of Operational Research* **26**, 187–201 (1986).

Computational Complexity

An excellent general book in this area is the Lanchester Prize Winner:

M. R. Garey and D. S. Johnson, *Computers and Intractability*: *A Guide to the Theory of $\mathcal{NP}$-completeness*, Freeman, San Francisco, 1979.

Among the first results related to $\mathcal{NP}$-completeness of location problems is that II(SET COVER) is $\mathcal{NP}$-complete, which is due to

R. M. Karp, "Reducibility among Combinatorial Problems" in *Complexity of Computer Computations* (R. E. Miller and J. W. Thatcher, eds.), pp. 85–103. Plenum, New York, 1972.

$\mathcal{NP}$-completeness proofs of p-MP and p-CP are given in

O. Kariv and S. L. Hakimi, "An Algorithmic Approach to Network Location Problems." *SIAM Journal on Applied Mathematics* **37**, 513–560 (1979).

N. Megiddo and K. J. Supowit, "On the Complexity of Some Common Geometric Location Problems." *SIAM Journal on Computing* **13**, 182–196 (1984).

C. H. Papadimitriou, "Worst-Case and Probabilistic Analysis of a Geometric Location Problem," *SIAM Journal on Computing* **10**, 542–557 (1981).

The first paper considers the network versions of these problems; the latter two deal with planar versions.

The notion of empirical complexity was suggested in 1978 by N. Christofides in a lecture delivered at the First International Symposium on Locational Decisions, Banff, Canada.

A subject not treated extensively in the book but of significant recent interest is the probabilistic analysis of deterministic locational decision models and algorithms. It is briefly mentioned in Chapter 2, some basic results are reviewed in Chapter 3, and some results on QAP are discussed in detail in Chapter 9. In addition, we refer the reader to the Papadimitriou (1981) reference given above for a probabilistic analysis of two heuristics for p-MP problem on the Euclidean plane. Also of note are the following references:

S. Ahn, C. Cooper, G. Cornuéjols, and A. Frieze, "Probabilistic Analysis of a Relaxation for the K-Median Problem." *Mathematics of Operations Research* **13**, 1–31 (1988).

M. L. Fisher and D. S. Hochbaum, "Probabilistic Analysis of the Planar K-Median Problem." *Mathematics of Operations Research* **5**, 27–34 (1980).

V. Lifschitz and B. Pittel, "The Worst and the Most Probable Performance of a Class of Set-Covering Algorithms." *SIAM Journal on Computing* **12**, 329–346 (1983).

The first two papers also consider p-MP on the Euclidean plane, but the comprehensive article by Ahn et al. includes, in addition, the probabilistic analysis of the network version of the problem. A probabilistic analysis of SET COVER is provided by Lifschitz and Pittel, the last reference given above.

Finally, recall that we ended our Section 1.3.2 on the computational complexity of locational decision problems with reference to the average behavior of the Simplex algorithm for linear programming. The proof that on the average the Simplex algorithm behaves in polynomial manner is given in the following seminal papers:

K. H. Borgwardt, "The Average Number of Steps Required by the Simplex Method Is Polynomial." *Mathematics of Operations Research* **7**, 441–462 (1982).

S. Smale, "On the Average Number of Steps of the Simplex Method of Linear Programming." *Mathematical Programming* **27**, 241–262 (1983).

Also, the June 1986 special issue of the journal *Mathematical Programming* (Volume 35, Number 2) focuses on probabilistic analysis of the Simplex method and contains papers by several other authors.

Problem Formulation, Discrete Location Theory
The first direct statement as to the relevance of a discrete optimization framework for analyzing locational decisions can be traced back to:

T. C. Koopmans, *Three Essays on the State of Economic Science*, McGraw-Hill, New York, 1957.

The following excerpt from Koopmans' book (p. 154) can appropriately end this chapter:

> . . . without recognizing indivisibilities—in the human person, in residences, plants, equipment and in transportation—urban location problems down to the smallest village cannot be understood. [ ] One may conclude from these observations that, in regard to the allocation problem raised by indivisible commodities, with or without locational distinctions, theoretical analysis still has not yet absorbed and digested the simplest facts establishable by the most casual observation.

2

The p-Median Problem and Generalizations

Pitu B. Mirchandani

Systems and Industrial Engineering Department
The University of Arizona
Tucson, Arizona

2.1. INTRODUCTION

The *p-median problem* is a special case in the class of *minisum locational problems*. Since this chapter deals with the "*p*-median problem" as well as its generalizations, it will be useful for readers to realize how these problems are abstracted from the general class of minisum locational (decision) problems. Therefore, we will first define a class of minisum locational problems that is general enough to deal with a large number of real-life locational decisions. We will introduce this class within the context of locating facilities for physical distribution, but the resulting locational models may be applied in a wide variety of application areas. Some of these application areas will be briefly discussed later.

Let $N = (V, A)$ be the underlying transportation network for distributing commodities from facilities to demand points, where V is the node set and A is the arc set. We will assume that the demands occur only on the node set $V = \{v_1, v_2, \ldots, v_m\}$.

Let $c_k(x_j, v_i)$ be the unit cost of transporting commodity k from point x_j (for example, where a facility may be located) to node v_i (where a demand may occur). At the moment we will defer the discussion on how this cost may be obtained, but for now we will assume we know these costs for all x_j and v_i and all (say) K commodities k, $k = 1, 2, \ldots, K$.

Suppose we have m demand points, $v_1, v_2, \ldots, v_m$, and only one facility at some point x_0. Then the total transportation cost of physically distributing all the commodities to the demand points is

$$TC(x_0) = \sum_{k=1}^{K} \sum_{i=1}^{m} w_{ki} c_k(x_0, v_1) \qquad (2.1.1)$$

where the "weight" w_{ki} is proportional to the demand for commodity k at node v_i. Now suppose we have several (say, p) facilities at the set of points $X_p = \{x_1, x_2, \ldots, x_p\}$. A demand at v_i could be serviced by any of these facilities. However, for obvious rational reasons we will assume that commodity k will be delivered to node v_i from that facility for which the transportation cost for delivering that commodity is lowest. Hence, the total transportation cost in this scenario is

$$TC(X_p) = \sum_{k=1}^{K} \sum_{i=1}^{m} w_{ki} \min \{c_k(x_j, v_i): x_j \in X_p\} . \qquad (2.1.2)$$

When there are two or more facilities that are equally "closest" in terms of transportation cost, then an arbitrary choice of any one of them will not alter the transportation cost given by (2.1.2).

Of course, there are real-life situations where the "closest" facility will not serve a given demand point, for example, when contractual agreements are involved, or when the same commodity is available at a *cheaper* price from some "further" facility such that the lower price more than offsets the additional transportation cost from the "further" facility. The latter situation may be covered by our model by including the prices of the commodities at the various facilities within the "transportation cost." That is, we can replace $c_k(x_j, v_i)$ in (2.1.2) by $c'_k(x_j, v_i)$ where

$$c'_k(x_j, v_i) = c_k(x_j, v_i) + p_{kj} \qquad (2.1.3)$$

and where p_{kj} is the price of commodity k at facility at x_j. However, we must point out that an implicit assumption in many of the minisum locational models that have appeared in the literature is that the price of commodity k is equal at each of the facilities. This assumption is often dictated by the problem scenario. For example, in the so-called "public sector locational problems," the cost borne by the "users" is only the transportation cost; the price of each commodity (often a public service such as fire protection) is "free." Fortunately, as we will show later in Section 2.2.4, the use of expression (2.1.3) for the transportation cost does not significantly affect the theoretical results and the algorithms for the median-type locational decision problems discussed in this chapter—as long as p_{kj} does not change by relocating the facility within the neighborhood of x_j.

Note that the total transportation costs given in (2.1.1) and (2.1.2) are obtained by *summing* component transportation costs (for each commodity and each demand point). Locations X_p (or x_0 for the single facility case) that minimize this *sum*, which gives the total transportation cost, are called "minisum" locations. The associated decision problem of determining the minisum locations is called a "minisum locational decision problem."

The class of locational problems that minimize only the transportation costs is a small subset of minisum locational problems. A related class of minisum locational problems includes the "fixed cost" of establishing facilities. An example of a scenario for such problems is to establish one or more facilities, say p facilities where p is also a decision variable, so that the sum of transportation costs and the "fixed costs" of establishing facilities is minimized. The "fixed cost" for each facility includes the cost due to construction of the facility as well as the maintenance/operating cost of the facility.

To obtain an expression for the total cost by summing transportation costs and fixed costs, we must take care to not sum "apples" with "oranges." Transportation costs are usually periodic costs (for example, annual, monthly, or daily costs). Thus, fixed costs must also be defined and computed with respect to the same period. For example, if we are considering annual transportation costs, then the fixed cost, say $f_j(x_j)$, for establishing a facility at x_j includes the annual capitalization cost due to the construction of the facility (obtainable from the construction cost, the depreciation or the lifetime of the facility, and the interest rate) and the annual maintenance/operating cost of the facility. The total distribution cost in this scenario is

$$DC(X_p) = TC(X_p) + \sum_{j=1}^{p} f_j(x_j) . \tag{2.1.4}$$

The problem of determining locations $X_p = \{x_1, x_2, \ldots, x_p\}$, p variable, to minimize $DC(X_p)$ is also a minisum locational decision problem. The p-median problem and its generalizations discussed in this chapter are special cases of the minisum locational problems associated with the cost functions (or optimization criteria) given by (2.1.2) and (2.1.4).

2.1.1. The Classical *p*-Median Problem

Although formal treatment of locational decisions may be attributed to Weber (1909), various locational decision problems have appeared as hypothetical mathematical exercises in the last two to three centuries. Thus it is not certain who first formalized minisum locational problems. Nevertheless Weber does indeed discuss minisum locational problems on a *plane* within the context of real-life locational decisions. However, focusing on *discrete* location models (we argue in Chapter 1 that most real-life problems are more appropriately handled in a discrete space), the impetus for the formal treatment of discrete minisum locational decision problems must be attributed to Kuehn and Hamburger (1963), Hakimi (1964), Manne (1964) and Balinski (1965). (See the excellent survey by Krarup and Pruzan (1983) on the uncapacitated facility location problem, which includes the origins of that problem.) Among those referred to above, it was Hakimi who coined the term "*p*-median" and introduced the *p*-median problem. The earliest reference for the *p*-median problem on a network appears to be Hua et al. (1962) who gave an algorithm to find the 1-median on a tree network.

The locational decision problem introduced by Hakimi considered only one commodity, that is $k = 1$, and assumed that the cost $c_1(x, y) = c(x, y)$ was proportional to the deterministic travel distance $d(x, y)$ between points x and y. The cost function (2.1.2) then becomes $F(X_p)$ where

$$F(X_p) = \sum_{i=1}^{m} w_i \min \{d(x_j, v_j): x_j \in X_p\} , \tag{2.1.5}$$

and w_i is the demand for the single commodity at node v_i. We refer to the p locations that minimize $F(X_p)$ as the classical p-medians or, simply, the p-medians. (Actually, Hakimi differentiated between *absolute p-medians* and *vertex p-medians*, but showed that the set of vertex p-medians includes a set of absolute p-medians by his "Node Optimality Theorem," a theorem which we will discuss later and which has proven to be very significant for various p-median type of locational models. Therefore, the distinction between the sets of absolute and vertex p-medians is unimportant here, and, hence, we call the optimal locations in this scenario as, simply, the p-medians.) We refer to the associated decision problem as the *classical p-median problem* in view of the various generalizations that have appeared since Hakimi's initial work. Also, since Hakimi's work, numerous publications and reports have appeared where the theoretical underpinnings and the complexity of the classical p-median problem (as well as some of its generalizations) have been discussed. This chapter surveys and synthesizes the state-of-the-art of the p-median problem and its generalizations.

2.1.2. The Uncapacitated Facility Location Problem

The *uncapacitated facility location problem* (UFL problem) will be discussed extensively in Chapter 3. We only present it here to indicate how it is also a special case of a minisum locational decision problem and how it relates to the classical p-median problem. This relationship is exploited in Section 2.4.2 where we develop algorithms to solve p-median problems.

When we are dealing with a single commodity (that is, $K = 1$), the cost function (2.1.4) becomes

$$U(X_p) = \sum_{i=1}^{m} w_i \min \{c(x_j, v_i): x_j \in X_p\} + \sum_{j=1}^{p} f_j(x_j). \qquad (2.1.6)$$

The problem of determining the X_p, p variable, that minimizes $U(X_p)$ is called the uncapacitated facility location problem.

Because of the location specific fixed cost $f_j(x_j)$ associated with each site x_j, the UFL problem is usually formulated such that X_p is restricted to be chosen from a given finite set of feasible sites, which we may call "vertices" without loss of generality. Hence, as in the p-median problem, we are looking for a subset of "vertices" which minimize the given cost function.

2.1.3. Generalizations

Although researchers have paid much attention to the p-median and UFL problems, it is surprising that generalizations of these problems which account for various real-life considerations have not been studied much. Perhaps this is partly due to the fact that good techniques for the classical p-median and UFL problems have not been available (until recently) and the problems are simple, well-defined, and challenging enough to have attracted many researchers. Also, perhaps the dearth of published studies on generalizations of the classical models may be due to the fact that developed solution approaches for the generalizations may not have been sufficiently elegant to have motivated the associated researchers to publish them.

Nevertheless, few researchers have studied some generalizations, at least up to the point of problem formulation. Handler and Mirchandani (1979) give an extensive discussion of the *p*-median problem, its literature review and its algorithmic state-of-the-art as of 1979. (In some respects this chapter may be considered an update of Chapter 2 of that text.) Included in their exposition is a list of various natural generalizations that may occur along the lines which consider (i) deterministic versus probabilistic demands and costs, (ii) nonoriented versus oriented networks, and (iii) various transportation cost measures. In the next section we will briefly review their generalizations, as well as present some new ones that result from the consideration of additional real-life issues.

We have already introduced one generalization at the beginning of this chapter when we used a subscript *k* to denote commodity *k*. The classical *p*-median and UFL problems have always considered only one commodity. We allow for multiple commodities in our formulation. For example, the *p*-median problem for multiple commodities, say the *multiple commodity p-median problem*, is to determine the optimal locations X_p^* that minimize

$$F_b(X_p) = \sum_{k=1}^{K} \sum_{i=1}^{m} w_{ki} \min \{d_k(x_j, v_i): x_j \in X_p\} \qquad (2.1.7)$$

where $d_k(x, y)$ is the travel distance required for transporting commodity *k* from *x* to *y*. This and other generalizations are formally formulated in the next section.

To introduce various *p*-median type problems, one can *either* start with the classical *p*-median model and keep relaxing assumptions or adding complexities to obtain more and more general models (the "generalization" process) *or* start with a rather general model and keep restricting assumptions or making simplifications to obtain simpler and simpler models (the "specialization" process). Note that we introduced the *p*-median and UFL problems as special cases of minisum locational problems. However, for clarity of exposition and pedagogical reasons, we will formulate our generalizations by "building-up" from the classical *p*-median model. The directions we will consider in our generalization process will include the consideration of: (i) probabilistic demands and costs; (ii) multiple commodities and multiple objectives; and (iii) multiattributed nonlinear transportation costs. Then, in summarizing, we will show how each model is a special case of a minisum locational problem.

Before concluding this section, we remind the reader that one could easily think of a very large number of generalizations, corresponding to the very large number of real-life issues in locational decisions. Of course, due to the lack of space as well as lack of inclination, we will not include all these generalizations here. Instead, we will include only a small subset which we feel is important to warrant inclusion and mostly for which there are available solution techniques. Bear in mind that this text is to report the state-of-the-art and not to list unsolved (but formulated) locational problems.

One important property of the problems formulated in the next section is that optimal locations are either *shown* or *assumed* to be among a finite set of points or vertices. This reduces the problem, from an optimization problem over an infinite set of points to a finite "combinatorial" problem— where one seeks to find the *p* best locations among a set of *n* sites—and, thus, considerably decreases the computational effort needed to determine the optimal locations.

Whether the problem scenario *assumes* or *requires* that one must select *p* best among *n* *given* sites, or whether from theory it is *known* that the best sites must be among the finite set of nodes of an underlying network, the algorithms to determine the *p* best locations are the same. Being already familiar with the introductory material on the *p*-median problem in Chapter 1, readers interested in solution techniques for the problem may refer to Section 2.4 for computational methods for the *p*-median problem in a general discrete space characterized by a distance or a cost matrix, and to Section 2.3 for graph-theoretic approaches to the 1- and 2-median problems on *tree* networks.

However, to further appreciate the robustness and the applicability of the *p*-median *model*, readers are referred to Section 2.2 which discusses various generalizations in the problem scenario which still result in the *node-optimality property* and the use of the various *p*-median solution techniques, especially the Nested-Dual Algorithm of Section 2.4.2. In particular, generalizations considered include (1) oriented networks, (2) discretely distributed probabilistic demands and costs, (3) multiple commodities, and (4) multiattributed nonlinear transportation costs.

2.2. GENERALIZATIONS OF THE *p*-MEDIAN PROBLEM

We have already defined the classical *p*-median problem by (2.1.5). Exploiting properties of the optimal solution (especially the "node-optimality property" proven in Section 2.2.4) one may formulate the problem as a mathematical programming problem. We will rely heavily on mathematical programming formulations of the *p*-median problem in Section 2.4, which includes a discussion of computational methods for the problem. In this section we will formulate, in the definitional sense as (2.1.5), generalizations of the *p*-median problem. We will also point out or prove properties of the associated optimal solutions.

In the first few succeeding subsections we will explicitly assume an underlying network (for example, a transportation network if the context of the problem is physical distribution). Later, we will point out that even median problems on planes are treated in a "discrete fashion" in most applications. This restricts facility locations to discrete sites and results in similar problem formulations.

For convenience, and for a better exposition, we will use the following notation resulting from our assumption that the "closest" facility serves each demand point:

$$C_k(X_p, v_i) = \min \{c_k(x_j, v_i): x_j \in X_p\} \tag{2.2.1}$$

$$D(X_p, v_i) = \min \{d(x_j, v_i): x_j \in X_p\} . \tag{2.2.2}$$

That is, $C_k(X_p, v_i)$ is the transportation cost for commodity k from the "closest" of the facilities in X_p to the demand v_i. By "closest" we mean here the one for which the transportation cost is the least. Likewise, $D(X_p, v_i)$ is the smallest distance of the distances from each facility in X_p to the demand point v_i. Note now the cost function $F(X_p)$ for the classical p-median problem may be written as

$$F(X_p) = \sum_{i=1}^{m} w_i D(X_p, v_i) . \tag{2.2.3}$$

2.2.1. Oriented versus Nonoriented Networks

When a network is *oriented*, $d(x, y)$ is not necessarily equal to $d(y, x)$. In most real transportation networks $d(x, y)$ is rarely equal to $d(y, x)$. This is not only due to one-way streets but also due to some two-way arcs having different traffic capacities in the two directions. Thus, in our context, by an "oriented" network we shall mean a network where the properties (e.g., travel time) of the flows in the two directions of each arc are not necessarily equal.

When the transportation costs associated with a facility are principally due to travel *from* the facility *to* the demand points (for example, from fire stations to fire incidents) we will call the facility an *out-facility*. When the transportation costs are due to travel *from* the demand points *to* the facility (for example from emergency medical incidents to emergency clinics) we will refer to the corresponding facility as an *in-facility*.

When the network is nonoriented, $d(x, y) = d(y, x)$. Then, for a given set of demand weights, there is no difference between the optimal locations of in-facilities and out-facilities. Hence, as far as nonoriented networks are concerned, there is no ambiguity (in regard to the direction of flow) when one refers to $d(x, y)$ as the distance between x and y, or as the distance from x to y, or as the distance from y to x.

However, for oriented networks the optimal locations for in-facilities and out-facilities need not be the same. Thus, corresponding to the classical p-medians in nonoriented networks we have the following definitions for medians on oriented networks.

Definition 2.1. A set of points X_p^* is a set of *p*-inmedians of the given network N if for every X_p in N

$$F^-(X_p^*) \le F^-(X_p)$$

where

$$F^-(X_p) = \sum_{i=1}^{m} w_i D(v_i, X_p) \qquad (2.2.4)$$

and

$$D(v_i, X_p) = \min \{d(v_i, x_j): x_j \in X_p\} .$$

Definition 2.2. A set of points X_p^* is a set of *p*-outmedians of the given network N if for every X_p in N

$$F^+(X_p^*) \le F^+(X_p)$$

and

$$F^+(X_p) = \sum_{i=1}^{m} w_i D(X_p, v_i) . \qquad (2.2.5)$$

Handler and Mirchandani (1979) point out that the underlying network must have some connectivity properties for *p*-inmedians and *p*-outmedians to exist (see Exercise 2.1). We emphasize again that if the given network is nonoriented, there is no distinction between *p*-inmedians and *p*-outmedians; we call the associated optimal locations as, simply, *p*-medians.

Finally, consider the problem of locating ambulances and clinics for an emergency medical service system. Suppose we wish to locate p^+ ambulances and p^- emergency medical clinics. If our sole criterion was to minimize average travel distance, then we would locate the ambulances and clinics at sets of points $X_{p^+}^*$ and $Z_{p^-}^*$, respectively, where for all sets X_{p^+} and Z_{p^-} on the network,

$$F(X_{p^+}^*, Z_{p^-}^*) \le F(X_{p^+}, Z_{p^-})$$

where

$$F(X_{p^+}, Z_{p^-}) = \sum_{i=1}^{m} w_i[D(X_{p^+}, v_i) + D(v_i, Z_{p^-})] . \qquad (2.2.6)$$

Let us refer to $\{X_{p^+}^*, Z_{p^-}^*\}$ as the p^+*out-p^- in medians* of the given network. Simple arguments will convince the reader that (i) when the given network is nonoriented, the $X_{p^+}^*$ are the p^+-medians and $Z_{p^-}^*$ the p^--medians, and

(ii) when the given network is oriented, the $X^*_{p^+}$ are the p^+-outmedians and the $Z^*_{p^-}$ the p^--inmedians. Note that there are at most $p^+ + p^-$ points in the set $\{X^*_{p^+}, Z^*_{p^-}\}$.

If in the above scenario the problem dictates that $p^- = p^+ = p$ and at each selected site we must have an in-facility and an out-facility, then there are exactly p sites to be selected. When the network is nonoriented, it is easy to show that the optimal p sites are at the p-medians. However, for an oriented network, the optimal p sites are, in general, neither at the p-inmedians nor at the p-outmedians. We thus define the "p-medians of an oriented network" as a special case of the following definition.

Definition 2.3. A set of points X^*_p is a set of p-medians of the given network N if for every X_p in N,

$$F(X^*_p, X^*_p) \leq F(X_p, X_p)$$

where $F(X_p, X_p)$ is defined by (2.2.6). The given network can be either oriented or nonoriented.

The theoretical and algorithmic developments for the p-median problem reported in the literature *usually* assume an underlying nonoriented network. Fortunately, many of these developments are not significantly affected when the underlying network is oriented. The major reason for this is that the node optimality property for the optimal locations also holds when the network is oriented if it holds for the corresponding problem on nonoriented networks (see Exercise 2.2). Nevertheless, some developments only hold for nonoriented networks, especially most of the graph-theoretic results. In the meantime, although we will present the generalizations in Sections 2.2.2–2.2.5 mostly within the context of nonoriented networks, readers should bear in mind that there are corresponding definitions and results when the underlying network is oriented.

2.2.2. Probabilistic Transportation Costs and Demands

The transportation cost associated with travel from one point to another is not deterministic in many applications. For example, if the transportation cost was measured in terms of travel time (e.g., as in emergency service systems applications), then this cost is often not deterministic. Random fluctuations in traffic density, cyclic (hourly, daily, weekly, and seasonal) changes in volume of traffic, and weather conditions all make this cost probabilistic.

Let us generalize our notation and let $d(x, y)$ denote any measure or attribute proportional to the distance from x to y. Likewise let α_{ij} be a measure or attribute proportional to the length of arc $[i, j]$. For example, $d(x, y)$ and α_{ij} may denote travel distances in problems where the distance attribute is of sole concern in the cost function, denote travel times when time attribute is of sole concern, and so on. Generically, we will refer to $d(x, y)$ and α_{ij} as a travel distance and an arc length, respectively. We are now allowing them to be random variables. We refer to the underlying network as a *probabilistic network*.

Suppose we are given an algorithm that determines the *p*-medians in a deterministic network. Can it be argued that when the network is probabilistic, the optimal locations are obtained by using the expected values of α_{ij}, denoted by, say, $\bar{\alpha}_{ij}$, for the link weights and determining the *p*-medians of the resulting deterministic "average network"? The answer to this question is "No!". This is because the use of the expected values $\bar{\alpha}_{ij}$ does not account for the fact that different travel routes may be used between a facility and a demand point for different "states of the network," as opposed to the use of only the route having the minimum expected travel distance. This is especially relevant if the "traveler" (or, in general, the "router," the person making the routing decision) knows the state of the network at all times and thus chooses the shortest path during each state. Example 2.1 below illustrates this idea.

Example 2.1. Consider the nonoriented network shown in Figure 2.1. Arcs [1, 3], [2, 3], [2, 4], and [3, 4] have deterministic travel times of 5, 1, 5, and 4, respectively. Arc [1, 2] has a 0.6 probability of having a travel time of 1 unit and 0.4 probability of having a travel time of 16 units. The expected travel time $\bar{\alpha}_{12}$ on arc [1, 2] is 7 units. Associating with each arc, a weight equal to its expected travel time places the 1-median of the resulting deterministic average network at node v_3, and the associated expected travel time to the demands as $3\frac{1}{3}$ units. However, if the facility is located at node v_2, and the router knows the state of the network at all times, the time to respond to an incident at v_1 is either 1 or 6 units (via node v_3 when travel

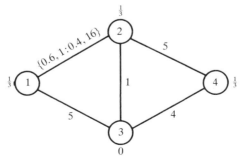

Figure 2.1. A probabilistic nonoriented network. Arc [1, 2] has a 0.6 probability of 1 unit in travel time and a 0.4 probability of 16 units in travel time. Nodes v_1, v_2, v_4 have demands of $\frac{1}{3}$ each and node v_3 has zero demand.

time of $[1, 2]$ is 16). Thus the expected travel time from v_2 to v_1 is 3 units $[(0.6 \times 1) + (0.4 \times 6) = 3.0]$. Therefore the expected travel time to the demands when the facility is at v_2 is $2\frac{2}{3}$ units (calculated from $0.6[(\frac{1}{3} \times 1) + (0 \times 1) + (\frac{1}{3} \times 5)] + 0.4[(\frac{1}{3} \times 6) + (0 \times 1) + (\frac{1}{3} \times 5)])$, better than the expected travel time when the facility is at v_3. In fact, in this particular example, v_2 is the optimal location that minimizes the average travel time to the demands. ○

Notice that when the deterministic weight $\bar{\alpha}_{12} = 7$ was used for arc $[1, 2]$, the route from v_1 to v_2 with the shortest expected travel time was from v_1 to v_3 to v_2 (that is, on arcs $[1, 3]$ and $[3, 2]$ in sequence). However, when the router knows the state of the network at all times, the expected travel time from v_1 to v_2 denoted by, say, $\bar{d}(1, 2)$, is 3.

Query 2.1. Will the 1-median be at node v_2 if we used $\bar{\alpha}_{12} = 3$ in our average network? For any general network, will the 1-median of the deterministic network resulting from fixing the weight of arc $[i, j]$ at $\bar{d}(i, j)$ give the optimal location that minimizes the expected travel time, or any other travel attribute that $d(x, y)$ represents?

After a little thought, the reader should realize that the correct responses are affirmative to the questions raised in the above query.

In view of Example 2.1 and Query 2.1, can we say that the *p*-medians of the deterministic network obtained by using expected values $\bar{d}(i, j)$ for arc weights α_{ij} are always the optimal p locations that minimize the expected travel time? The answer is still "No." This is because the use of $\bar{d}(i, j)$ does not account for the case where different facilities may serve a particular demand point in different "states of the network." This is especially possible when the router knows the state of the network at all times and chooses the closest facility for each state of the network. Example 2.2 (given later) will illustrate this idea. Mathematically, the reason why the use of $\bar{d}(i, j)$ does not work is as follows. Let $\bar{D}(X_p, y) = E[D(X_p, y)]$, where $E[z]$ denotes the expectation of any random variable z. Then, because the minimum operator is nonlinear, $\bar{D}(X_p, y)$ is not generally equal to $\min \{\bar{d}(x_j, y) : x_j \in X_p\}$. The use of $\bar{d}(i, j)$ for the deterministic weight α_{ij} and the finding of the *p*-medians in the resulting deterministic network assumes they are always equal. Nevertheless, in some scenarios (for example, when the router has only the probabilistic knowledge available to him and chooses the facility with the closest expected distance) the use of $\bar{d}(i, j)$ does give the optimal locations.

Let us formalize some of the concepts developed in this subsection. Consider the problem of determining the set of p optimal locations on a probabilistic network N that minimizes the expected travel distance. The optimal locations are X_p^* in N if for all X_p in N

$$\bar{F}(X_p^*) \le \bar{F}(X_p)$$

where

$$\bar{F}(X_p) = E\left[\sum_{i=1}^{m} w_i D(X_p, v_i)\right].$$ (2.2.7)

Note that $\bar{F}(X_p)$ is the expected travel distance for location set X_p. The optimal locations X_p^* have been referred to as the "expected *p*-medians" by Mirchandani and Odoni (1979a). Observe that the expected *p*-medians are the classical *p*-medians when we consider the deterministic network as a very special case of a probabilistic network (that is, by allowing each arc length to take on a specified value with probability 1 and other values with probability zero). Thus, in this chapter, we refer to the optimal locations X_p^* as, simply, the *p*-medians of the given network; the "given" network could be deterministic (special case) or probabilistic (general case). When the network is probabilistic we refer to the associated problem as the *p-median problem on a probabilistic network*.

Similarly, as for existence conditions for *p*-medians on oriented deterministic networks, Handler and Mirchandani (1979) give conditions for the existence of *p*-medians on probabilistic networks, both oriented and nonoriented.

What can we say about the location of various *p*-medians defined on probabilistic networks? It turns out that under two quite general and reasonable assumptions it can be shown that at least one set of *p*-medians exist on the nodes of the network. This "node optimality property" is proven in full generality in Section 2.2.4.

To state these assumptions we need to introduce some additional notation. Let random variable $\tilde{l}$ represent the probabilistic aspects of the network and let N^l denote the state of the network when $\tilde{l} = l$. Let $N^{\Sigma l}$ denote the set of all possible network states. Finally, let α_{ij}^l be the weight (denoting some travel attribute α) of arc $[i, j]$ in state N^l.

The first assumption is called the "Arc Homogeneity Assumption."

Assumption 2.1: Arc Homogeneity Assumption. The value of any travel attribute α in traveling a fraction θ of arc $[i, j]$ in state N^l is given by $\theta \alpha_{ij}^l$ for all possible N^l in $N^{\Sigma l}$.

For example, if α denotes travel time, Assumption 2.1 implies that the speed of travel of any given arc is uniform in any given state N^l. Note that we allow the speed of travel to vary among the arcs and the speed of travel on a given arc to change as the state of the network changes. Generally, the network may be defined or constructed so that this assumption holds.

The other assumption that we need, to make the *p*-median problems on probabilistic networks meaningful, especially when the random variable $\tilde{l}$

represents a temporal stochastic process, regards the router's knowledge of the state of the network.

Assumption 2.2.   The router knows the exact state of the network at all times. Moreover, the time intervals between changes in the state of the network are much longer than trip times on the network.

Assumption 2.2 implies that travelers in the system know of all the routes available to them, and each traveler chooses the shortest route at the time of traveling. Moreover, this route continues to be the shortest throughout the trip. Although Assumption 2.2 idealizes the system in some scenarios, it is a good approximation of the system as long as the state of the network does not change significantly during a trip. This is a valid assumption or approximation in most locational decision problems. For example, in physical distribution problems the router often selects a route (presumably based on current cost) at the time of starting the trip and keeps to that route during the trip; the cost incurred to the router is usually a pre-set contractual cost. At another trip starting time, the router may select another route if its cost became cheaper.

Query 2.2.   If in Example 2.1 the travelers do not know the exact state of system at all times, but know only its probabilistic description (i.e., the travel time on arc [1, 2] is 1 with probability 0.6 and 16 with probability 0.4), then where should a facility be located to minimize the expected travel time? Assume here that each traveler is rational and will choose that route with the smallest expected travel time.

Under Assumptions 2.1 and 2.2 we can show that the "node optimality property" also holds for the *p*-medians of probabilistic networks. Assumption 2.2 is not *necessary*, but rather it is *sufficient* for the node optimality property to hold. Instead of Assumption 2.2 we may assume that the router has only a probabilistic description of the network and based on that he chooses facilities and paths that minimize expected travel distances. Here also the node optimality property holds; the resultant problem is simply the classical *p*-median problem on a deterministic network with arc weights $\bar{\alpha}_{ij}$ (recall Query 2.2).

For the case when the underlying random variable $\tilde{l}$ is a continuous or mixed random variable, the mathematical or computational manipulation of associated probability density functions to determine the *p*-medians becomes rather cumbersome for large *p* or *m*. However, assuming or approximating $\tilde{l}$ to be discrete with a finite number of possible outcomes somewhat reduces this difficulty. Furthermore, it may be argued that in many scenarios it is very appropriate to do so because discrete probability distributions can easily fit any finite set of data measurements. In the subsequent developments we will assume that $\tilde{l}$ is discrete over a finite range.

This assumption, that $\tilde{l}$ is discrete over a finite range, implies that the network can have a finite number of possible states, say S of them, each occurring with a nonzero probability. Let the network states be denoted by $N^1, N^2, \ldots, N^S$ with probabilities of occurrence $P_1, P_2, \ldots, P_S$, respectively. Then the cost function $\bar{F}(X_p)$ for the *p*-median on nonoriented probabilistic networks, given by (2.2.7), can be written as

$$\bar{F}(X_p) = \sum_{l=1}^{S} P_l \sum_{i=1}^{m} w_i D^l(X_p, v_i) \qquad (2.2.8)$$

where

$$D^l(X_p, v_i) = \min \{d^l(x_j, v_i): x_j \in X_p\},$$

and $d^l(x_j, v_i)$ is the shortest travel distance from x_j and v_i when the network is in state N^l. Here the expectation operator is replaced by a weighted sum.

Example 2.2.   Consider the 10-node, 3-state network (Figure 2.2) of Handler and Mirchandani (1979) where each state is equally probable. The set of 2-medians X_p^* of the network is $\{D, F\}$ which gives an expected travel time of 0.865 units. Observe that we have *different service districts* for different states when the two facilities are located at D and F. For instance, in state 2, node I is served by the facility at D and in states 1 and 3 by the facility at F.

In comparison, if the travel time matrices are averaged first and the 2-medians are determined from the average travel time matrix, then I and B

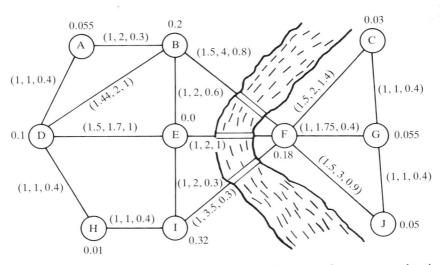

Figure 2.2. A ten-node, three-state example. The three numbers on each arc correspond to the travel times in the three states.

will be selected as the optimal locations. The use of an average travel time matrix implicitly assumes *fixed service districts*. The expected travel time for $\{I, B\}$ is 0.895 units. On the other hand, if the arc travel times are averaged first and the 2-medians are obtained for the resultant "average network," then I and F would be selected. The expected travel time becomes 0.905 units. Now, not only do we implicitly assume fixed service districts, but we also assume *fixed routes* from each facility to each demand node. In contrast, our probabilistic network model allows each demand node to be served by the optimal facility in each state, using the shortest travel time route in that state. ○

Consider now the *demands* generated at the nodes. In most of the literature on locational problems these demands are implicitly assumed to be deterministic. However, demands could have hourly, daily, and seasonal variations. For example, in locational decisions for fire-fighting units, it is well known that the distribution of population in an urban environment shifts around during any typical day and, hence, the spatial pattern for fire incidents (the demands) also varies during the day.

Actually, when defining the various median problems on deterministic networks we have allowed for the case where only the demands w_i are independently random while the transportation costs are deterministic. In this case, the cost $\bar{F}(X_p)$, given by (2.2.7), becomes

$$\bar{F}(X_p) = \sum_{i=1}^{m} \bar{w}_i D(X_p, v_i) \tag{2.2.9}$$

where $\bar{w}_i$ is the average demand at node v_i. This cost function is identical to that of the classical p-median problem, the $F(X_p)$ given by (2.2.3); here we use average weights $\bar{w}_i$ instead of the fixed deterministic weights w_i. Thus the p-medians of the deterministic "average network"—obtained by using the expected value $\bar{w}_i$ for the weight of node v_i—give the optimal locations that minimize the expected travel distance.

Now let us consider the case when *both* the demands and the transportation costs are probabilistic. Here again let us assume, or approximate, the underlying random variable to be discrete. Thus one network state differs from another in the weight of at least one arc or at least one node. The corresponding cost function for the p-median problem becomes

$$\bar{F}(X_p) = \sum_{l=1}^{s} P_l \sum_{i=1}^{m} w_i^l D^l(X_p, v_i) \tag{2.2.10}$$

where w_i^l is the demand at node v_i in network state N^l. Here again the node optimality property holds. (This p-median problem is a special case of the problem for Theorem 2.1, proven in Section 2.2.4.) Hence one looks for a p-node subset for the optimal p sites to minimize $\bar{F}(X_p)$ given by (2.2.10).

Computational methods to determine the optimal p-node subset are given in Section 2.4.

It turns out that a probabilistic network where node and arc weights have discrete probability distributions can be looked on as a "multidimensional network." The concept of multidimensional networks plays an important role in multiple commodity location problems. Hence we defer further discussion on p-medians on a probabilistic network with random node and arc weights until we define multidimensional networks in the succeeding subsection.

2.2.3. Multidimensional Networks and Multiple Commodities

In this subsection we present a generalization of the modeling framework so that "multiple dimensions" may be considered. In fact, within this generalization one can consider the problems of determining optimal facility locations when

  i. the travel costs and demands are stochastic,
  ii. multiple services or commodities are considered, or
  iii. multiple "median-type" objectives are present.

The underlying network within this framework will be referred to as a "Multidimensional Network" (MN).

To illustrate the concept of MN and its application to modelling the three problems posed above, consider a hypothetical problem of locating p fire-fighting units in a region with an underlying transportation network. When the transportation costs and the demands for fire-fighting services are stochastic (in the sense they are probabilistic and time-varying), then we have an example of the first type of problem. We have already introduced this problem in the last subsection.

Now, instead of facilities only housing fire-fighting units suppose they also need to house other emergency response units, such as ambulances and police response units. In this case we wish to locate p facilities to provide multiple services. It is clear that for each service there will generally be a different demand pattern and different transportation costs. (The transportation cost, as a function of travel time, is probably different for emergency medical services than for fire-fighting services and so on). Also, within each type of service there may be different classes of services incurring different transportation costs, for example, a 1-alarm fire versus a 2-alarm fire, a heart-attack victim versus a burn victim. Furthermore, as before, these demands and costs may be stochastic. We refer to the problem of locating p such emergency facilities to minimize the expected transportation cost as the "p-median problem on probabilistic multidimensional networks."

Finally, consider the multiobjective problem where for each objective the network weights (i.e., the costs and demands) are different. For example, one could visualize several decision-makers, perhaps one for each type of service, who view the network differently. This is an instance of the third type of problem and will be referred to as the "multiobjective *p*-median problem."

To define the above problems formally, let us introduce some terminology and notation. When the demand weight at any node $v_i \in V$ is a K-vector $\mathbf{w}_i = (w_{1i}, w_{2i}, \ldots, w_{Ki})$, and the travel distance between any two points x and y on N is a K-vector $\mathbf{d}(x, y) = (d_1(x, y), d_2(x, y), \ldots, d_K(x, y))$ we refer to the network as a *multidimensional network* (MN) with K the number of "*dimensions*." If the vectors are not deterministic then the network will be referred to as a *probabilistic multidimensional network* (PMN). For the moment we will still assume that our objective is to minimize the expected travel distance (or some other travel attribute that is proportional to the travel distance). Then, the *multidimensional p-median problem* on network N is to find a set of locations X_p^* such that for all X_p in N

$$\bar{F}(X_p^*) \le \bar{F}(X_p)$$

where

$$\bar{F}(X_p) = E\left[\sum_{i=1}^{m} \mathbf{w}_i \cdot \mathbf{D}(X_p, v_i) \right] \qquad (2.2.11)$$

$$\mathbf{D}(X_p, v_i) = (D_1(X_p, v_i), D_2(X_p, v_i), \ldots, D_K(X_p, v_i)), \qquad (2.2.12)$$

and $\cdot$ is the operator for the dot product of two vectors. We then have the following definition.

Definition 2.4. A set of points X_p which minimizes $\bar{F}(X_p)$ given by (2.2.11) is a set of *multidimensional p-medians*.

The multidimensional *p*-medians will be referred to as, simply, the *p*-medians when the context is clear.

Now consider the case when the probability distribution describing the random vectors $\mathbf{w}_i$ and $\mathbf{D}(X_p, v_i)$ is assumed *discrete* with a finite number S of outcomes. The cost function (2.2.11) can now be written as

$$\bar{F}(X_p) = \sum_{l=1}^{S} P_l \sum_{i=1}^{m} \mathbf{w}_i^l \cdot \mathbf{D}^l(X_p, v_i) \qquad (2.2.13)$$

where $\mathbf{w}_i^l$ and $\mathbf{D}^l(X_p, v_i)$ are the demand and cost vectors, respectively, when the network is in state N^l.

Consider the special cases of (2.2.13) and (2.2.11). When the random vectors $\mathbf{w}_i$ and $\mathbf{D}(X_p, v_i)$ are uncorrelated then (2.2.13), or (2.2.11), may be written as (say) $\bar{F}_a(X_p)$ where

$$\bar{F}_a(X_p) = \sum_{i=1}^m \bar{\mathbf{w}}_i \cdot \bar{\mathbf{D}}(X_p, v_i) = \sum_{i=1}^m \sum_{k=1}^K \bar{w}_{ki} \bar{D}_k(X_p, v_i), \qquad (2.2.14)$$

and where $\bar{\mathbf{w}}_i$ and $\bar{\mathbf{D}}(X_p, v_i)$ are the expected values of $\mathbf{w}_i$ and $\mathbf{D}(X_p, v_i)$, respectively, and $\bar{w}_{ki}$ and $\bar{D}_k(X_p, v_i)$ are the kth components of these expected vectors.

When we have only one network state, which occurs with probability 1 (i.e., when the network is deterministic), cost function (2.2.13), or (2.2.11), becomes

$$\bar{F}_b(X_p) = \sum_{i=1}^m \mathbf{w}_i \cdot \mathbf{D}(X_p, v_i) = \sum_{i=1}^m \sum_{k=1}^K w_{ki} D_k(X_p, v_i). \qquad (2.2.15)$$

When we have only one service (or commodity), cost function (2.2.13) becomes

$$\bar{F}_c(X_p) = \sum_{l=1}^S P_l \sum_{i=1}^m w_i^l D^l(X_p, v_i) \qquad (2.2.16)$$

where w_i^l and $D^l(X_p, v_i)$ are the demands and costs, respectively, when the network is in state N^l. Note that cost functions $\bar{F}_a(X_p)$, $\bar{F}_b(X_p)$, and $\bar{F}_c(X_p)$ are essentially the same, where in $\bar{F}_a(X_p)$ and $\bar{F}_b(X_p)$ index k represents different services (or commodities) while the corresponding index l in $\bar{F}_c(X_p)$ represents different network states. Such cost functions may exist in other applications, for example, if one wants to locate p "chutes" (e.g., mail-chutes) in a large multistory building to minimize some travel costs. Here index l in $\bar{F}_c(X_p)$ would represent the different stories, while P_l, w_i^l, and $D^l(X_p, v_i)$ would denote, respectively, the population, demand distribution, and travel costs on story l. Other examples where a multidimensional framework is useful are (1) in the location of copies of K distinct files in a computer/information network (e.g., Kollias and Hatzopolous, 1981) and (2) for locating hierarchical facilities where a "higher level" facility can serve a wider range of demands (see Section 2.5.3 for further discussion on this application).

When we have only one network state and only one service (or commodity), cost function (2.2.13) becomes the classical p-median cost function (on deterministic networks), originally introduced by Hakimi (1964, 1965).

Observe that cost function $\bar{F}_c(X_p)$ is the same as $\bar{F}(X_p)$ given by (2.2.10). Locations that minimize $\bar{F}_c(X_p)$, or $\bar{F}(X_p)$, were defined in the last subsection as the p-medians of a probabilistic network. Although the cost functions are essentially the same as $\bar{F}_c(X_p)$, we have the *multicommodity* interpretations of the objective function, as modeled by $\bar{F}_a(X_p)$ when the probabilities have been averaged out, or by $\underline{F}_b(X_p)$ when the network is deterministic. In this chapter we refer to the optimal locations for the more general problem associated with $\bar{F}(X_p)$ given by (2.2.11) or (2.2.13) as the *p-medians on PMN*, while the special cases as modeled by $\underline{F}_a(X_p)$, $\underline{F}_b(X_p)$, or $\bar{F}_c(X_p)$ as the *p-medians on MN*. We will see in Section 2.2.4 that the "node optimality property" still holds for the various *p*-medians defined above.

Finally, let us briefly formulate the multiobjective *p*-median problem. Suppose the *k*th objective (for example, for the *k*th service) is

$$F_k(X_p) = \sum_{i=1}^{m} w_{ki} d_k(X_p, v_i), \quad k = 1, 2, \ldots, K. \tag{2.2.17}$$

One method to generate some *nondominated* locations is to optimize various positive linear combinations of the multiple objectives; the resultant solutions belong to the *nondominated set* of solutions. Suppose the linear combination is given by (say) $\underline{F}(X_p, \boldsymbol{\pi})$ where

$$\underline{F}(X_p, \boldsymbol{\pi}) = \sum_{k=1}^{K} \pi_k F_k(X_p), \tag{2.2.18}$$

and where $\Sigma_{k=1}^{K} \pi_k = 1$. Note the similarity between objective $\underline{F}(X_p, \boldsymbol{\pi})$ given by (2.2.18) and $\bar{F}_c(X_p)$ given by (2.2.16). The weights π_k are similar to the probabilities P_l in (2.2.16). Hence the X_p that minimizes $\bar{F}_c(X_p)$ can be interpreted as a nondominated solution to a multiobjective location problem. The determination of the *p*-medians on multidimensional networks, from the minimization of $\underline{F}(X_p, \boldsymbol{\pi})$ for various $\boldsymbol{\pi}$, yields a subset of the set of nondominated locations.

2.2.4. Multiattributed Nonlinear Transportation Costs

In the introduction of this chapter we let $c_k(x_j, v_i)$ be the unit cost of transporting commodity k from x_j to v_i. However, in our definitions of the various medians on deterministic and probabilistic networks we minimized an expected cost that was proportional to the distance traveled. That is, it was assumed that $c_k(x_j, v_i)$ was a *linear* function of $d_k(x_j, v_i)$.

There are many real-life scenarios where the transportation cost is not a linear function of travel distance. For example, it has been observed that the utility function for travel time is generally nonlinear in emergency service systems (e.g., see Keeney, 1973; Ruffel-Smith, 1970). Likewise, concave transportation cost functions often occur in physical distribution problems where each successive mile (or minute) of travel is no more costly than its predecessor. Thus, one generalization of the models presented earlier is to allow $c_k(x, y)$ to be any function (linear or nonlinear) of the travel distance $d_k(x, y)$ between x and y.

A further generalization can be made if one observes travel behavior of commuters on a transportation network; here route choices are usually based on more than one travel attribute. Travel time as well as travel distance are two important attributes in this choice. Thus, now, associated with every arc $[i, j]$ we have a set of r weights for *each* commodity denoting various values of the attributes of concern (such as distance, time, energy, and so on). Let us denote these weights by a vector $\boldsymbol{\alpha}_{ijk}$ for the commodity k. In keeping with our generalized treatment, we will, of course, allow $\boldsymbol{\alpha}_{ijk}$ to be random.

Before defining a median-type objective function and associated optimal set of locations with such multiattributed nonlinear travel costs, the router's travel behavior must be clearly specified. What does one mean by an optimal path in such networks? How does a router select a facility? We will say that Assumption 2.2 still holds here and that the router chooses the (optimal) facility and (optimal) path which minimize the expected travel cost. Then, associated with the trip for transporting commodity k from the facility at point x_j to point v_i via the optimal path is the travel cost $c_{ki}(\mathbf{d}_k^{l^*}(x_j, v_i))$ where $\mathbf{d}_k^{l^*}(x_j, v_i)$ is the vector of travel attributes along the optimal path *in state* N^l. Note that we are subscripting the cost $c(\cdot)$ with the index i to allow for the cost to be demand location specific; there is no reason to assume that demands at any point v_i always have the same cost function as the demands at any other point.

If the router has the choice of p facilities at X_p, we will assume that he chooses the facility with least travel cost and we will let the corresponding travel cost be denoted by $c_{ki}(\mathbf{D}_k^{l^*}(X_p, v_i))$.

The optimal p locations that minimize the expected transportation cost, which we refer to as the "generalized *p*-medians," are defined by the following.

Definition 2.5. A set of points X_p^* is a set of *generalized p-medians* of the given network N if for every X_p in N

$$\bar{F}_g(X_p^*) \le \bar{F}_g(X_p)$$

where

$$\bar{F}_g(X_p) = \sum_{l=1}^{S} P_l \sum_{i=1}^{m} \mathbf{w}_i^l \cdot \mathbf{c}_i(\mathbf{D}^{l^*}(X_p, v_i)), \qquad (2.2.19)$$

and where vector $\mathbf{c}_i(\mathbf{D})$ has the components $c_{1i}(\mathbf{D}_1), c_{2i}(\mathbf{D}_1), \ldots, c_{Ki}(\mathbf{D}_K)$. It appears that the subscripts and superscripts of the cost function $\bar{F}_g(X_p)$ given by (2.2.19) are rather cumbersome. But that is the price one has to pay for generalizations. All the *p*-medians (*p*-outmedians in the case of oriented networks) defined so far are special cases of the generalized *p*-medians. When $\mathbf{c}(\mathbf{d}(x, y))$ is linear and single attributed we have the multidimensional *p*-medians. These, in turn, define *p*-medians on probabilistic networks when each "dimension" represents a state of the network, and multicommodity *p*-medians when each "dimension" represents a commodity. Further, by assuming only one state and one commodity we have the definition of the classical *p*-medians on deterministic networks.

For the sake of completeness, we present and prove a very general version of a theorem stating the *node optimality property*. Less general cases have been proven before by Hakimi (1964), Handler and Mirchandani (1979), and others; the proofs are usually simpler and less cumbersome. In any case, the basic notion that is pursued in all these proofs is rather straightforward and simple: the cost function is *concave* with respect to the distance *x* that a facility is from a node on an arc and, hence, the minimum of the cost function is attained at an extreme point, i.e., at one of the nodes of the arc.

To prove the node optimality property, we need to state some basic facts derivable from properties of convex and concave functions.

Fact 2.1.   A linear function is concave (and also convex).

Fact 2.2.   Multiplying a concave (convex) function by a nonnegative number yields a concave (convex) function.

Fact 2.3.   The sum of concave (convex) functions is concave (convex).

Fact 2.4.   If $c(\mathbf{d})$ is a concave function of vector $\mathbf{d}$ and components of $\mathbf{d}$ are linear functions of θ, then $c(\mathbf{d}(\theta))$ is concave in θ.

Fact 2.5.   If $f_i(\theta)$ are concave functions of θ for all $i \in I$, then $f(\theta) = \min_{i \in I} \{ f_i(\theta) \}$ is concave in θ.

Fact 2.6.   If $f(\theta)$ is a concave function defined on the closed interval $0 \le \theta \le 1$ then $\min_{0 \le \theta \le 1} f(\theta) = \min_{\theta \in \{0, 1\}} f(\theta)$.

Using the above facts we find that if the transportation costs $c_{ki}(\mathbf{d}_k)$ are concave in the travel attributes $\mathbf{d}_k$ then a set of generalized *p*-medians exists on the node set of the given network. We state this in the following theorem.

Theorem 2.1.   *When the transportation cost functions for the travel attributes are concave, then there exists at least one p-node subset of V which is a set of generalized p-medians of the given network.*

We refer to the property of the optimal locations due to Theorem 2.1 as the *node optimality property* of the (generalized) *p*-medians. The proof of Theorem 2.1 is given below. In the proof we use the notation $\mathbf{d}_k^{l^*}(x, v_q, v_i)$

to denote the vector of travel attributes on the optimal path (for commodity k) from point x on arc $[q, t]$ to point $v_i \in V$ via $v_q \in V$ and not via $v_t \in V$ (when the network is in state l).

Proof of Theorem 2.1. Let the set of generalized *p*-medians be located at a set of points $X_p = \{x_1, x_2, \ldots, x_p\}$. Let the point x_r be on arc $[q, t]$ and let

$$\theta = \frac{\text{length of arc from } v_q \text{ to } x_r \text{ in } N^l}{\text{length of arc } [q, t] \text{ in } N^l}, \quad 0 \le \theta \le 1 \text{ for all } N^l \text{ in } N^{\Sigma l}.$$

Note that this fraction θ is independent of the state of the network, N^l, because of the Arc Homogeneity Assumption (Assumption 2.1).

In any state N^l and for delivery of any commodity k, the node set V may be partitioned into two subsets V_{rk}^l and $\bar{V}_{rk}^l$ where

$$V_{rk}^l \equiv \text{set of nodes for which } x_r \text{ is optimal}$$
$$(\text{``closest'' in terms of travel cost})$$

$$\bar{V}_{rk}^l \equiv V - V_{rk}^l .$$

Hence the cost function $\bar{F}_g(X_p)$ given by (2.2.19) may be written as

$$\bar{F}_g(X_p) = \sum_{l=1}^{S} P_l \sum_{k=1}^{K} \left[\sum_{v_i \in V_{rk}^l} w_{ki}^l c_{ki}(\mathbf{d}_k^{l^*}(x_r, v_i)) + \sum_{v_i \in \bar{V}_{rk}^l} w_{ki}^l c_{ki}(\mathbf{D}_k^{l^*}(X_p, v_i)) \right].$$
$$(2.2.20)$$

Since x_r is on $[q, t]$, by definition of the optimal path, the first term on the right-hand side of (2.2.20) can be written as

$$w_{ki}^l c_{ki}(\mathbf{d}_k^{l^*}(x_r, v_i)) = \min \{ w_{ki}^l c_{ki}(\mathbf{d}_k^{l^*}(x_r, v_q, v_i)), w_{ki}^l c_{ki}(\mathbf{d}_k^{l^*}(x_r, v_t, v_i)) \} .$$
$$(2.2.21)$$

From the Arc Homogeneity Assumption (Assumption 2.1) the components of $\mathbf{d}_k^{l^*}(x_r, v_q, v_i)$ and $\mathbf{d}_k^{l^*}(x_r, v_t, v_i)$ are linear functions of θ. Hence, from Fact 2.4 the component costs $c_{ki}(\mathbf{d}_k^{l^*}(x_r, v_q, v_i))$ and $c_{ki}(\mathbf{d}_k^{l^*}(x_r, v_t, v_i))$ are concave functions of θ. Then, from Fact 2.2 the weighted costs $w_{ki}^l c_{ki}(\mathbf{d}_k^{l^*}(x_r, v_q, v_i))$ and $w_{ki}^l c_{ki}(\mathbf{d}_k(x_r, v_t, v_i))$ are also concave in θ. From (2.2.21) and Fact 2.5 $w_{ki}^l c_{ki}(\mathbf{d}_k^{l^*}(x_r, v_i))$ is concave in θ. Hence, by Fact 2.3 the first term on the right-hand side of (2.2.20) is concave in θ. Since the second term is independent of θ, $\bar{F}_g(X_p)$ given by (2.2.20) is concave in θ.

Finally, from Fact 2.6 we see that $\bar{F}_g(X_p)$ is minimal at either $\theta = 0$ or $\theta = 1$. That is, the cost is not increased if x_r is replaced in X_p by the appropriate node, v_q or v_t. Since x_r was selected as any one of the generalized *p*-medians, the proof can be repeated for $r = 1, 2, \ldots, p$.

Hence, at least one p-node subset in the given network is a set of generalized p-medians. $\square$

Theorem 2.1 is quite general. As special cases, we have the node optimality property for the classical p-medians on nonoriented networks, the p-medians on nonoriented probabilistic networks, the p-medians on nonoriented multidimensional networks, and the p-outmedians on corresponding oriented networks. Interchanging the variables X_p and v_i in the definitions and proofs, we have the node optimality property for the p-inmedians on corresponding oriented networks.

As we did in earlier subsections, we can think of problem scenarios where the optimal locations are generalized p-medians of an oriented probabilistic network, or even *generalized p^+out-p^-in medians* of any given network. Here too, if the transportation costs are concave in the travel attributes, then there exists at least one node subset which is a set of optimal locations. We leave it to the reader to generalize the results in these directions (see Exercise 2.3).

Before concluding this subsection, we refer to our earlier discussion, in the introduction, on prices of each commodity at various facility sites. We defined $c'_k(x_r, v_i)$, given by (2.1.3), as the "transportation cost" which includes the price p_{kr} of commodity k at the facility at location x_r. Let us assume that this price does not change if we allow the facility at x_r to be relocated at a site in the neighborhood of x_r. In particular, if x_r is in the interior of arc $[q, t]$, we allow it to be anywhere on $[q, t]$ without affecting the price p_{kr} (which may, for example, be the production cost for a manufacturing facility). Hence, if $c_k(x_r, v_i)$ is concave in the travel attributes $\mathbf{d}_k(x_r, v_i)$, then so is $c'_k(x_r, v_i)$ concave in the neighborhood of x_r, since all we are adding is a constant term independent of position of x_r (i.e., independent of θ in the proof of Theorem 2.1). Therefore, in this case the node optimality property of the optimal locations also holds. In fact, the property holds if the cost has *any* fixed component that is independent of the position x_r but may be dependent on commodity k and demand location v_i.

2.2.5. Node Restricted Facilities

Often the p-median problem is formulated as follows. Given a set of m demand points and a set of n potential sites, at what p sites among the site set must facilities be located to minimize the average transportation cost to the demand points? We are given the demand weight, if any, at each demand point and, through a *distance matrix*, we are given unit transportation costs from each potential site to each demand point.

Notice that there is no mention of any transportation network. Presumably, the transportation costs are computed from pre-selected optimal routes from point to point. If the transportation cost is directly proportional to the travel distance then the optimal route between the two points is the shortest distance route. In fact, in the literature on computational methods for the *p*-median problem, authors often use travel distances (and, therefore, the distance matrix) to compute travel costs in illustrations and applications.

Suppose there is an underlying network connecting the *m* demand points and the *n* potential sites. Without loss of genarality, the "node" set of the network may now include the potential sites as well as the demand points. Now, if the transportation costs are not concave in travel distance, then node locations are not necessarily optimal (see Theorem 2.1). But, if we *require* that the *p* facilities *must* be located among the given *n* sites, then by definition the node set must contain the optimal set of *p* locations. Thus, in this version of the *p*-median problem we do not need the node optimality property to decrease the number of alternatives to evaluate for finding the *p*-medians. Our requirements restrict locations to a subset of the nodes. We call the associated problem the *node-restricted p-median problem*.

Observe that, if in actuality there is no restriction on where each facility may be located, but there is an underlying transportation network and the transportation costs are concave in travel distances, then by the node optimality property, the solution to the node-restricted *p*-median problem also solves the unrestricted problem. If the transportation costs are not concave, then the restricted problem does not necessarily solve the unrestricted problem.

On the other hand, if we must select *p* best sites among *n given* sites, whether or not there is an underlying transportation network, then the problem is, by definition, the restricted one and its solution gives the *p* optimal sites. The restricted scenario is not unreasonable in many real-life locational decision problems. For example, a company may have available to it (by purchase or rent) only *n* sites on which to build warehouses for distribution. Also, in planar locational problems, a region is often partitioned into *n* zones (or districts, or reporting areas, or sectors, etc.) and demands are assumed to occur at the zone centroids. That is, continuous demand distributions are approximated by discrete distributions. The *p*-median problem in such scenarios is to select *p* zones (out of *n* zones) in which to establish facilities, given interzonal distances or travel costs.

Most computational methods developed for the *p*-median problem are "combinatorial" in nature—they choose *p* best sites among *n* given sites. Thus, these methods give the optimal solution for the node-restricted *p*-median problems and the *p*-median problems with concave transportation costs. The reader should keep in mind that when the transportation costs are not concave in travel distances, these methods may not give optimal solutions but rather give approximate ones.

2.3. THE 1- AND 2-MEDIAN PROBLEMS ON TREE NETWORKS

The problem of locating one or two facilities to minimize the average transportation cost is relatively easy; algorithms whose effort is polynomial in *n* (the number of available sites) can be constructed in a straightforward manner. However, the effort increases exponentially when the number of facilities (p) or the number of available sites (n) increases. In fact, it has been shown that the p-median problem is $\mathcal{NP}$-hard (see, e.g., Kariv and Hakimi, 1979; Garey and Johnson, 1979). Nevertheless, *good* algorithms are available which solve "moderate" size problems in a reasonable time. Section 2.4 discusses some of the more successful algorithms.

A special case of the p-median problem arises when the problem has an underlying network with a tree structure. Efficient polynomial-time graph-theoretic algorithms have been developed for the case of single-attributed linear transportation cost functions (e.g., when we have to minimize expected travel distance). The efficiency of the algorithms is due primarily to the general convexity properties of tree networks (see, e.g., Dearing, Francis, and Lowe, 1976).

In this section we will discuss the problems of finding 1- and 2-medians on various (deterministic, probabilistic, and multidimensional) nonoriented tree networks. Besides providing some interesting graph-theoretic concepts, the results presented here should also provide the reader some insight into the p-median problem on general networks. Tree network algorithms may be applied to general networks if (i) the problem can be decomposed into subproblems on tree networks (for example, as in the p-center problem of Chapter 7) or (ii) if the network has a few cycles and the algorithm can be modified for "nearly" acyclic networks (many rural networks in a bounded region are nearly acyclic).

2.3.1. Some Definitions and Notation

$T = (V, A)$ denotes a nonoriented tree. To eliminate trivial cases, we shall assume that there exist at least two nodes with positive demands. For any subtree T_1 of T we let $w(T_1)$, and/or $w(V_1)$ if node set (say) V_1 of T_1 is specified, denote the total weight of the nodes in T_1.

Let $P[x, y]$ denote the unique path between x and y, $P(x, y)$ a path through x and y and $P[x, y)$ a path from x and through y. (Similarly, $P(x, y]$ stands for a path through x ending at y.) For instance, consider the network shown in Figure 2.3. In this network, $P[x, y]$ is the path from x through z to y, i.e., path x–z–y, consisting of arcs $[x, z]$ and $[z, y]$; $P[x, y)$ can be either the path x–z–y–v_8 or the path x–z–y–v_9; $P(x, y)$ is any path which contains path x–z–y, for example, v_1–x–z–y–v_8.

Let x_1, x_2 be two points of T, we define $F_2(x_1, x_2)$ as the total weighted distance (which is the average distance if weights w_i denote fractions of total demand) from x_1 and x_2 to the nodes;

$$F_2(x_1, x_2) = \sum_{i=1}^{m} w_i D(\{x_1, x_2\}, v_i) \tag{2.3.1}$$

where

$$D(\{x_1, x_2\}, v_i) = \min\left(d(x_1, v_i), d(x_2, v_i)\right).$$

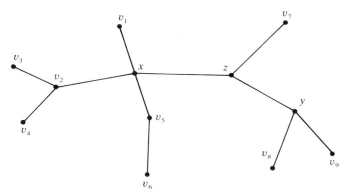

Figure 2.3. Illustration of $P[x, y]$, $P[x, y)$, and $P(x, y)$.

A set of 2-medians of T consists of two points, μ_1, μ_2 in T such that for all x_1, x_2 in T,

$$F_2(\mu_1, \mu_2) \leq F_2(x_1, x_2).$$

To determine a pair $\{\mu_1, \mu_2\}$, it suffices to minimize $F_2(x_1, x_2)$ over the nodes of T due to our node optimality property. (In this section we will assume that all nodes are available sites for facility locations, i.e., $m = n$).

A set of 2-medians of a probabilistic or a multidimensional tree T consists of two points μ_1, μ_2 in T such that for all x_1, x_2 in T,

$$\bar{F}_2(\mu_1, \mu_2) \leq \bar{F}_2(x_1, x_2)$$

where

$$\bar{F}_2(x_1, x_2) = \sum_{l=1}^{S} P_l \sum_{i=1}^{m} w_i^l D^l(\{x_1, x_2\}, v_i). \qquad (2.3.2)$$

Again, because of the node optimality property, it suffices to consider the minimization problem of $\bar{F}_2(x_1, x_2)$ only over the nodes of T.

Finally, for the 1-median problems we have the cost functions: (i) in the deterministic case

$$F_1(x) = \sum_{i=1}^{m} w_i d(x, v_i), \qquad (2.3.3)$$

and (ii) in the probabilistic or multidimensional cases

$$\bar{F}_1(x) = \sum_{l=1}^{S} P_l \sum_{i=1}^{m} w_i^l d^l(x, v_i). \qquad (2.3.4)$$

2.3.2. The 1-Median Problem

In this section, we first present Goldman's (1971) *Majority Algorithm* for the 1-median problem on deterministic trees. We then discuss the 1-median problem on probabilistic trees and show the applicability of Goldman's algorithm for this case.

Goldman's algorithm is based on the two lemmas given below. Let T_1 and T_2 be two subtrees corresponding to some partition $\{V_1, V_2\}$ where T_k contains V_k, $k = 1, 2$. Let this partition be described by the deletion of some arc $[v_1, v_2]$ in A, where $v_k \in V_k$, $k = 1, 2$. Let μ be a 1-median of T.

Lemma 2.1 (Goldman, 1971). $\mu \in V_1 \leftrightarrow w(V_1) \geq w(V_2)$.

Lemma 2.2 (Goldman, 1971).   *If* $w(V_1) \geq w(V_2)$ *then finding a 1-median of* T *is equivalent to finding a 1-median for* T_1 *except that* $w(v_1)$ *is replaced by* $w(v_1) + w(V_2)$.

As a consequence of these two lemmas, we have the following efficient algorithm whose complexity is $O(m)$.

Algorithm 2.1   *Majority Algorithm* (Goldman, 1971)

Step 1: If T consists of a single node then *stop*; that node is the 1-median.
Step 2: Search for an end-node v_i. If $w(v_i) \geq w(V)/2$ go to *Step 4*, otherwise go to *Step 3*.
Step 3: Let v_j be the adjacent node of v_i. Modify T by deleting v_i and the arc $[i, j]$ and incrementing $w(v_j)$ by $w(v_i)$. Then return to *Step 1*.
Step 4: *Stop*; v_i is a 1-median.

Let us now consider the 1-median problem on probabilistic tree networks where *only* the arc weights are random. The 1-median for each state of the network is at the same location, since arc lengths do not enter into the Majority Algorithm. This location is, in fact, the 1-median of the probabilistic tree. Note that the cost function defined by (2.3.4) can be written as

$$\bar{F}_1(x) = \sum_{i=1}^{m} w_i \bar{d}(x, v_i) \ .$$

The expected distance $\bar{d}(x, v_i)$ is, in fact, equal to the sum of expected arc lengths on the path $P[x, v_i]$ since a path between two points on a tree network is *unique*. Hence, the problem becomes a 1-median problem on the deterministic tree obtained by using, for each arc length, an expected value instead of the probability distribution. Thus Algorithm 2.1 now becomes applicable, where, after all, the lengths do not enter into the determination of the 1-median. Note, however, that arc lengths are necessary to compute the *value* for $\bar{F}_1(\mu)$.

Finally, let us study the multidimensional case, or the probabilistic case with *both* arc and node weights random. Observe that we can write $\bar{F}_1(x)$, defined by (2.3.4), as

$$\bar{F}_1(x, \mathbf{P}) = \sum_{l=1}^{s} P_l F^l(x)$$

where $\mathbf{P} = (P_1, P_2, \ldots, P_S)$ are given probabilities, and $F^l(x)$ is the 1-median cost function in each (deterministic) "dimension",

$$F^l(x) = \sum_{i=1}^{m} w_i^l d^l(x, v_i) .$$

Let M_l be the set of 1-medians in dimension l and let M_{Ul} be the set of all such 1-medians;

$$M_{Ul} = \bigcup_l M_l .$$

Let T^* (a subtree) be the union of all the paths between all pairs of 1-medians in M_{Ul};

$$T^* = \bigcup_{x, y \in M_{Ul}} P[x, y] .$$

Furthermore, let $M(\mathbf{P})$ be the set of (multidimensional) 1-medians that minimize $\bar{F}_1(x, \mathbf{P})$ and let M be the set of (multidimensional) 1-medians for all P

$$M = \bigcup_{\text{all } \mathbf{P}} M(\mathbf{P}) .$$

Then we can show (we leave the proof as Exercise 2.4) the following theorem.

Theorem 2.2 (Oudjit, 1981).   *T^* contains M.*

In other words, T^* localizes the set of all multidimensional 1-medians of T. We refer to T^* as the *localization subtree* for these 1-medians. Furthermore, by the node optimality property, we know at least one of these 1-medians exists at a node. Therefore, if V^* denotes the node set of T^*, then the following corollary follows.

Corollary to Theorem 2.2.   *At least one 1-median exists in V^*.*

The implication of the above corollary is that once we have determined the *localization node set* V^*, we need only to examine its elements to find the 1-median of the given multidimensional tree T. Note that T^* and V^* are

easily obtained by means of the very efficient Majority Algorithm to find the
1-medians of the various dimensions.

Example 2.3. Consider the multidimensional tree T with three states T^1,
T^2, and T^3 shown in Figure 2.4. Nodes v_5, v_6, and v_{10} are the 1-medians for
the three network states, T^1, T^2, and T^3, respectively. The figure exhibits
the localization subtree T^*. Due to the corollary of Theorem 2.2 we can
state that a multidimensional 1-median is in $V^* = \{v_5, v_{10}, v_6, v_2\}$. ○

We mentioned earlier that the convexity of the 1-median cost function
allowed us to obtain an efficient algorithm like the Majority Algorithm for
the deterministic case (and, even for the case where only arc lengths are
random). However, we do not have such an algorithm for the multidimensional case. We can only find T^* efficiently in this case. Figure 2.5 illustrates
how the cost functions vary over a tree. For the multidimensional case the
cost function is not necessarily convex over the subtree T^* (see Exercise
2.5). Since problem scenarios may arise where T^* could be the complete
given tree, finding the multidimensional 1-median by evaluating every node
in T^* may require considerably more effort compared to finding the classical
1-median using the Majority Algorithm.

Before concluding this subsection, let us briefly discuss the multiobjective
1-median problem. Recall that (see equations (2.2.17) and (2.2.18) in

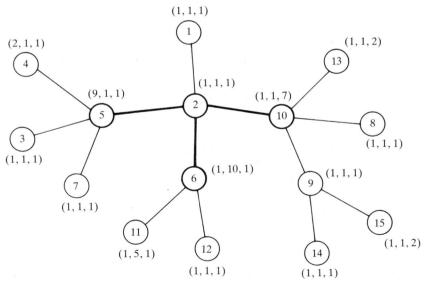

Figure 2.4. Illustration of a localization subtree T^* (shown in bold) of a multidimensional tree
with three states. (The numbers beside each node represent the node weights. Travel cost on
each arc is unity.)

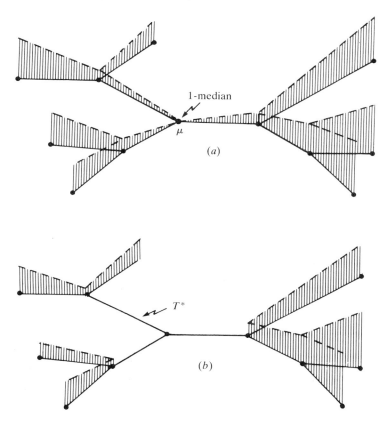

Figure 2.5. (*a*) Convexity of cost function $\bar{F}_1(x)$ for a probabilistic tree with only arc weights random. (Height over tree indicates function value.) (*b*) Function $\bar{F}_1(x, \mathbf{P})$ for the multidimensional tree. This function may have several local minima over T^*.

Section 2.2.3) *some* nondominated solutions are obtained by finding for all $\mathbf{P}$ the 1-medians for cost function $\bar{F}_1(x, \mathbf{P})$. However, we can state a stronger result for the tree case. If E denotes the set of *all* nondominated solutions, then we have the following.

Theorem 2.3 (Oudjit, 1981). T^* *contains* E.

In general, T^* is not identical to E; T^* can have points which are not in E.

2.3.3. The 2-Median Problem on Deterministic Tree Networks

Even though we know that there exists a pair of nodes which is a set of 2-medians on a tree, how does one find such a pair? Several approaches are possible, utilizing enumeration, graph theoretic, or mathematical programming techniques. Three such methods are briefly presented below, two of which solve the problem quite efficiently, especially the "arc-deletion" method. We then derive a new property (Theorem 2.4) which relates the 2-median locations to the 1-median and improves the arc-deletion algorithm.

1. *Enumeration Method.* One way of finding the set of 2-medians of a tree is the naive approach of exhaustive enumeration; this requires $O(\binom{m}{2} 2m) \approx O(m^3)$ operations. Here the cost function value is evaluated for every pair of nodes as candidate 2-medians and the two nodes which give the minimum value are chosen as the 2-medians.

2. *Arc-Deletion Method.* A second method of finding 2-medians of a tree is to consider arc-deletions. An arc-deletion partitions the tree T into two subtrees T_1 and T_2 and corresponding node subsets V_1 and V_2. Since we have $(m-1)$ arcs we have $(m-1)$ partitions. For each arc deletion we determine, using Algorithm 2.1, a 1-median, μ', in T_1 and a 1-median, μ'', in T_2, performing a total of $O(m)$ operations. For every arc-deletion we must also compute $F_2(\mu', \mu'')$, where

$$F_2(\mu', \mu'') = \sum_{v_i \in V_1} w_i d(\mu', v_i) + \sum_{v_i \in V_2} w_i d(\mu'', v_i) ;$$

the $\{\mu', \mu''\}$ which gives the minimum $F_2(\mu', \mu'')$ is a set of 2-medians. The computation of $F_2(\mu', \mu'')$ requires an additional $O(m)$ operations when the distance matrix is given. Thus for all $(m-1)$ arc-deletions we perform a total of $O(m^2)$ operations. When the distance matrix is not given the complexity is still $O(m^2)$ since the computation of the distance matrix of a tree requires $O(m^2)$ operations.

In comparing the arc-deletion method with the enumeration method note that in the enumeration method we *located* the facilities first and then *allocated* the demands to the facilities; whereas in the arc-deletion method we allocated first and then located the facilities. This illustrates one case in which an "allocate first, locate second" approach is superior to a "locate first, allocate second" approach in location-allocation problems.

3. *Algorithm of Kariv and Hakimi* (1979). Kariv and Hakimi have presented a dynamic programming type algorithm for the *p*-median problem on trees. The complexity of their algorithm is $O(p^2 m^2)$. Hence, for the 2-median case the algorithm would require $O(4m^2) = O(m^2)$ operations, resulting in no improvement over the arc-deletion method. Besides, the algorithm of Kariv and Hakimi is considerably more complicated to program, and explain, as compared to the arc-deletion method.

We now derive some properties satisfied by $\{\mu, \mu_1, \mu_2\}$, where μ is a 1-median of T and $\{\mu_1, \mu_2\}$ is a set of 2-medians of T. We need some additional notation before presenting these properties. Consider T as "rooted" at μ. Let $V_\mu = \{v_1, v_2, \ldots, v_f\}$ ($f \geq 1$ is the degree of μ) be the set of immediate successors of μ. Let T_{v_j} be the subtree of T rooted at v_j when arc $[\mu, v_j]$ is deleted. Figure 2.6 illustrates this notation.

Given two facilities at $\{\mu_1, \mu_2\}$, the facility at μ_1 services a demand at v_i if $d(\mu_1, v_i) < d(\mu_2, v_i)$. Therefore location set $\{\mu_1, \mu_2\}$ *implicitly partitions* the node set into two subsets, say V_1 and V_2, where nodes in V_1, we say, "are serviced by (the facility at) μ_1" and nodes in V_2 "are serviced by μ_2." (Any node equidistant from μ_1 and μ_2 can be arbitrarily included in either V_1 or V_2.) In contrast, an arc-deletion *explicitly partitions* the tree, and, hence, the node set.

Theorem 2.4. $\mu \in P[\mu_1, \mu_2]$.

Proof (By contradiction). Assume the contrary, that is $\mu \notin P[\mu_1, \mu_2]$. Therefore $\{\mu_1, \mu_2\} \in T_{v_j}$ for some $v_j \in V_\mu$, with μ_2 servicing (say) $T_2 \subset T_{v_j}$, and μ_1 servicing $T_1 = T - T_2$ (see Figure 2.7). Then

$$w(T - T_{v_j}) \geq w(T_{v_j}) > w(T_{v_j} - T_2)$$

where the first inequality is implied by Lemma 2.1. But $w(T - T_{v_j}) > w(T_{v_j} - T_2)$ implies, also because of Lemma 2.1, that the 1-median μ_1 of T_1 cannot be in T_{v_j}; this results in a contradiction. $\square$

As a consequence of Theorem 2.4, we have the following two corollaries.

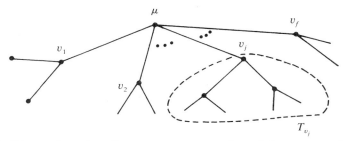

Figure 2.6. T is rooted at a 1-median μ. $v_1, v_2, \ldots, v_f$ are immediate successors of μ. T_{v_j} is the subtree of T rooted at v_j when arc $[\mu, v_j]$ is deleted.

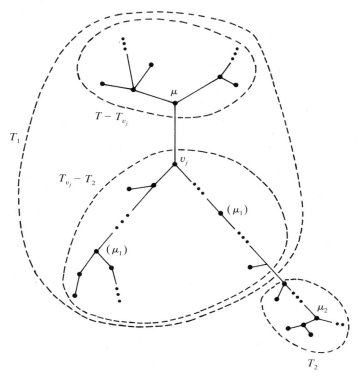

Figure 2.7. Illustration of the proof of Theorem 2.4. Location set $\{\mu_1, \mu_2\}$ partitions the tree T into T_1 and T_2. If $\mu \not\in P[\mu_1, \mu_2]$, two cases are possible for $\mu_1 \in T_{v_j} - T_2$: (i) $\mu_1 \in P[v_j, \mu_2]$; (ii) $\mu_1 \not\in P[v_j, \mu_2]$.

Corollary A of Theorem 2.4. $\mu_1 \not\in P[\mu, \mu_2) - \{\mu\}$.

A similar result (Corollary B of Theorem 2.5) is stated in the next subsection for probabilistic trees. The second corollary is applicable when the tree T possesses two or more distinct 1-medians.

Corollary B of Theorem 2.4. *Suppose μ, μ' in V are two distinct 1-medians of T. If $\{\mu_1, \mu_2\}$ is a set of 2-medians of T, then*

$$P[\mu, \mu'] \subset P[\mu_1, \mu_2].$$

In other words, the second corollary states that if a tree has two distinct nodes μ and μ' as 1-medians then the path between μ and μ' is contained in the path between every pair of 2-medians. If μ and μ' are two adjacent nodes, then deleting arc $[\mu, \mu']$ disconnects T into two subtrees T_μ and $T_{\mu'}$ and each one of these subtrees must contain one of the 2-medians.

From Theorem 2.4 and its corollaries, the set of 2-medians, $\{\mu_1, \mu_2\}$, cannot be on any single T_{v_j}. Similar, though somewhat weaker, properties are derived in the next subsection for probabilistic tree networks.

A straightforward application of the above results improves the search for 2-medians in the arc-deletion method. For every arc deleted in T_{v_j} we now know one candidate 2-median must lie in the disconnected subtree of T_{v_j}, that does not contain μ, and the other in some T_{v_i}, $i \neq j$, or on μ. It would benefit our search if we knew in which T_{v_j} we should consider arc-deletions and in which other T_{v_i}, $i \neq j$, should we expect the other 2-median. The properties given below, which are stated without proof (see Exercises 2.6 and 2.7), are useful for localizing the 2-medians $\{\mu_1, \mu_2\}$.

Property 2.1.   Given any solution $\{\mu_1, \mu_2\}$, there exists an optimal allocation such that exactly one of the 2-medians serves at most one subtree $T_1 \subseteq T_{v_j}$, for some v_j in V_μ.

The following property states that when one of the 2-medians serves a subtree T_1 in some T_{v_i}, then the other will be localized either in one of the remaining subtrees T_{v_r}, $r \neq i$, that has the largest weight, or at the 1-median. Note that if $|V_\mu| = f = 1$, then T_{v_r} is empty and, hence, we define $w(T_{v_r})$ to be zero.

Property 2.2.   When μ_1 serves $T_1 \subseteq T_{v_i}$, for some v_i in V_μ, then μ_2 belongs to $T_{v_r} \cup \{\mu\}$, where $w(T_{v_r}) = \max \{w(T_{v_j}): v_j \in V_\mu - v_i\}$.

Two properties follow directly from Property 2.2. We define T_{v_1} and T_{v_2}, respectively, as the first and the second largest subtrees in $\{T_{v_j}: v_j \in V_\mu\}$. That is,

$$w(T_{v_1}) = \max_{v_j \in V_\mu} w(T_{v_j})$$

and

$$w(T_{v_2}) = \max_{v_j \in V_\mu - v_1} w(T_{v_j}).$$

Property 2.3.   One of the 2-medians belongs to $T_{v_1} \cup \{\mu\}$.

Property 2.4.   If μ_1 serves only subtree $T_1 \subseteq T_{v_1}$, then $\mu_2 \in T_{v_2} \cup \{\mu\}$.

The first property localizes one of the 2-medians either at the 1-median or in the largest subtree T_{v_1}. The second states that when one of the 2-medians serves only a subtree in T_{v_1}, then the other 2-median is either at the 1-median or in the second largest subtree T_{v_2}.

In summary, the above properties localize one of the 2-medians, μ_1, in $T_{v_1} \cup \{\mu\}$; and when μ_1 does not serve the 1-median μ they localize μ_2 in $T_{v_2} \cup \{\mu\}$. The next logical step would be to examine the localization of μ_2 for the case when μ_1 in $T_{v_1} \cup \{\mu\}$ does serve m. However, it is not obvious how one can efficiently characterize T_{v_j} such that μ_2 is in T_{v_j}. Simple examples show that μ_2 could belong to any subtree T_{v_j}, $v_j \in V_\mu - v_1$, when μ_1 serves m.

Mirchandani and Oudjit (1980) present the *Improved Arc-Deletion Method*, where, as a consequence of the preceding theorems, corollaries, and properties, only candidate arcs are considered for deletion to determine the optimal partition $\{T_1, T_2\}$. In an example given by them, Algorithm 2.1 was called 36 times in the arc-deletion procedure but was used only 9 times in the improved arc-deletion algorithm. More importantly, in the first procedure the cost function was computed 36 times (once for each arc-deletion) while in the improved method it was computed only 3 times (for each *selected* arc-deletion). This would result in considerable saving in computational effort if the distance matrix is not given. Although the complexity of the improved version is also $O(m^2)$ it is quite likely that the computational time would be substantially reduced for most problems; in the worst case it would be the same.

2.3.4. The 2-Median Problem on Probabilistic and Multidimensional Tree Networks

Now let T be a probabilistic tree network where only the arc weights are random. At first glance it may seem that Theorem 2.4 for deterministic trees will also hold for such probabilistic trees; that is, $\mu \in P[\mu_1, \mu_2]$. Unfortunately, this result does not always hold for the probabilistic case. The following counterexample shows this.

Counterexample. Consider the probabilistic tree shown in Figure 2.8; we have two states T^1 and T^2 each occurring with probability 0.5. Enumeration gives us the locations of μ, μ_1 and μ_2 as shown in the figure. Note that in this example $\mu \not\in P[\mu_1, \mu_2]$ and μ is serviced by facility at μ_1 in state T^1 and by the facility at μ_2 in state T^2.

Nevertheless, we can prove a result analogous to Theorem 2.4 for the case when the 1-median site is served by one of the 2-medians for *all* the states of the network. However, we first need to prove two lemmas for deterministic trees. Let us define $F_{T_j}(x)$ for all x in a deterministic tree T by

$$F_{T_j}(x) = \sum_{v_i \in T_j} w_i d(x, v_i)$$

for any subtree T_j. The first lemma can be proved similarly as Theorem 2.4, but we use different arguments here to illustrate the importance of convexity properties of tree networks.

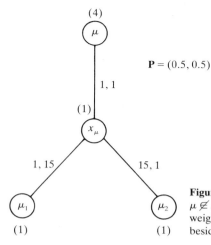

$P = (0.5, 0.5)$

Figure 2.8. Example of a probabilistic tree for which $\mu \notin P[\mu_1, \mu_2]$. The numbers beside each arc are the arc weights in state T^1 and T^2, respectively. The number beside each node is the node weight.

Lemma 2.3. *Let T_2 be any subtree of some T_{v_j}, $v_j \in V_\mu$, with $w(T_2) > 0$. Then 1-medians of subtree $T_1 = T - T_2$ cannot be in T_{v_j}.*

Proof (By contradiction).   Suppose a 1-median of T_1 is at y^* in $T_1 \cap T_{v_j}$. Consider any point x on $P[y^*, \mu]$. Due to convexity of $F_{T_1}(\cdot)$ (Dearing et al., 1976), $F_{T_1}(x)$ is a nondecreasing function of $d(x, y^*)$ and, hence

$$F_{T_1}(y^*) \le F_{T_1}(x) \le F_{T_1}(\mu) . \tag{2.3.5}$$

In particular, if we let $x = v_j$ in (2.3.5) we have

$$F_{T_1}(v_j) \le F_{T_1}(\mu) . \tag{2.3.6}$$

Adding $F_{T_2}(\mu)$ to both sides of (2.3.6) we obtain

$$F_{T_1}(v_j) + F_{T_2}(\mu) \le F_{T_1}(\mu) + F_{T_2}(\mu) = F_1(\mu) \tag{2.3.7}$$

Since $F_{T_2}(\mu) = F_{T_2}(v_j) + w(T_2)d(\mu, v_j)$ and $F_1(v_j) = F_{T_1}(v_j) + F_{T_2}(v_j)$, the left-hand side of (2.3.7) becomes

$$F_{T_1}(v_j) + F_{T_2}(\mu) = F_1(v_j) + w(T_2)d(\mu, v_j) > F_1(v_j) , \tag{2.3.8}$$

and the strict inequality in (2.3.8) follows from the fact $w(T_2)d(\mu, v_j) > 0$. From inequalities (2.3.7) and (2.3.8) we have

$$F_1(v_j) < F_1(\mu) ,$$

which contradicts the definition of μ. $\square$

Lemma 2.4. *Let T_1, T_2 be two disjoint subtrees containing the node-set V; T_1 contains μ, and T_2, with $w(T_2) > 0$, is a subtree of some T_{v_j}, $v_j \in V_\mu$. Then for all x in T_{v_j}*

$$F_{T_1}(\mu) < F_{T_1}(x) .$$

Proof. Let y^* be the 1-median of T_1. From Lemma 2.3, $\{\mu, v_j\} \subseteq P[y^*, x]$. Due to convexity of $F_{T_1}(\cdot)$ we have

$$F_{T_1}(y^*) \le F_{T_1}(\mu) \le F_{T_1}(v_j) \le F_{T_1}(x) . \qquad (2.3.9)$$

In fact, the middle inequality in (2.3.9) is strict because $F_{T_1}(\mu) = F_{T_1}(v_j)$ implies that

$$F_{T_1}(\mu) + F_{T_2}(\mu) = F_{T_1}(v_j) + F_{T_2}(\mu) = F_{T_1}(v_j) + F_{T_2}(v_j) + w(T_2)d(\mu, v_j)$$

which means

$$F_1(\mu) = F_1(v_j) + w(T_2)d(\mu, v_j) > F_1(v_j) ,$$

and this contradicts the definitoin of μ. Therefore (2.3.9) becomes

$$F_{T_1}(\mu) < F_{T_1}(v_j) \le F_{T_1}(x) . \qquad \square$$

We can now prove the result analogous to Theorem 2.4 for the case of probabilistic tree networks with random arc weights.

Theorem 2.5. *If μ is serviced by μ_1 for all the states of T, then $\mu \in P[\mu_1, \mu_2]$.*

Proof (By contradiction). Assume the contrary that $\mu \notin P[\mu_1, \mu_2]$. Therefore $\{\mu_1, \mu_2\} \in T_{v_j}$, for some $v_j \in V_\mu$. By hypothesis, μ_1 serves μ for all the states of the network and therefore $d^l(\mu, \mu_1) \le d^l(\mu, \mu_2)$, for $l = 1, 2, \ldots, S$. Let x_μ be the closest point in $P[\mu_1, \mu_2]$ to μ. (Note that x_μ is a node and could also be μ_1.) Therefore all the partitions (say) Q^l, $l = 1, 2, \ldots, S$ (corresponding to the states of T) occur between x_μ and μ_2. Let T_l and $\bar{T}_l$ be the two subtrees of T generated by partition Q^l, where T_l contains $\{\mu, x_\mu, \mu_1\}$ (see Figure 2.9). From Lemma 2.4 we have

$$F_{T_l}(\mu) < F_{T_l}(\mu_1) , \quad l = 1, 2, \ldots, S .$$

Therefore, since all P_l are positive,

$$\sum_{l=1}^{S} P_l F_{T_l}(\mu) < \sum_{l=1}^{S} P_l F_{T_l}(\mu_1) . \qquad (2.3.10)$$

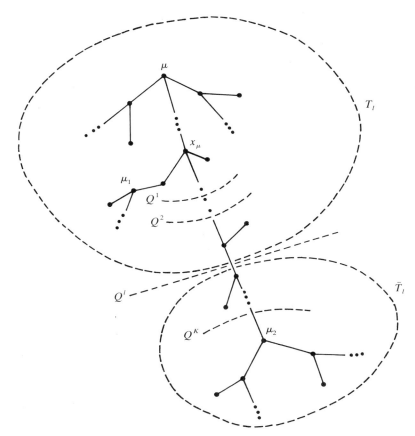

Figure 2.9. Illustration for the proof of Theorem 2.5. For any state T^l, $l = 1, \ldots, K$, we have two subtrees $\bar{T}_l$ and T_l, served by μ_1 and μ_2, respectively. If μ is served by μ_1 for all the states then all the partitions $Q^1, Q^2, \ldots, Q^K$ are between x_μ and μ_2.

Adding to both sides of (2.3.10) the quantity $\Sigma_{l=1}^S P_l F_{\bar{T}_l}(\mu_2)$, we obtain

$$\sum_{l=1}^S P_l F_{T_l}(\mu) + \sum_{l=1}^S P_l F_{\bar{T}_l}(\mu_2) < \sum_{l=1}^S P_l F_{T_l}(\mu_1) + \sum_{l=1}^S P_l F_{\bar{T}_l}(\mu_2) .$$

$$(2.3.11)$$

Note that the right-hand side of (2.3.11) is equal to $\bar{F}_2(\mu_1, \mu_2)$ by definition. Let $\bar{I}(\mu, \mu_2)$ denote the left-hand side of (2.3.11). Now

$$\bar{F}_2(\mu, \mu_2) \le \bar{I}(\mu, \mu_2) \tag{2.3.12}$$

because $\bar{F}_2(\mu, \mu_2)$ is the cost function value for locations $\{\mu, \mu_2\}$ with partitions that are optimal for those locations, while $\bar{I}(\mu, \mu_2)$ is also the cost function value for the same locations, but with partitions which are optimal to $\{\mu_1, \mu_2\}$ and not to $\{\mu, \mu_2\}$. Therefore, from (2.3.11) and (2.3.12)

$$\bar{F}_2(\mu, \mu_2) < \bar{F}_2(\mu_1, \mu_2),$$

and this contradicts the definition of μ_1, μ_2 as the 2-medians of T. $\quad\square$

Note that Theorem 2.4, for deterministic trees, turns out to be a special case of Theorem 2.5 when we let $S = 1$. Also, as a consequence of Theorem 2.5, the following corollary says that a 2-median μ_1 cannot lie on the path from μ through μ_2, whether or not μ is always served by the same 2-median (see Exercise 2.8).

Corollary to Theorem 2.5. $\quad \mu_1 \not\subseteq P[\mu, \mu_2) - \{\mu\}$.

Recall that in the counterexample presented in the beginning of this section we noted that the 2-median locations $\{\mu_1, \mu_2\}$ had a property that the 1-median μ is serviced by the facility at μ_1 in state T^1 and by the facility μ_2 in state T^2. This observation and Theorem 2.5 results in the following generalization of Theorem 2.4 to the probabilistic case.

Theorem 2.6. *Either* $\mu \in P[\mu_1, \mu_2]$ *or there exists* $z_\mu \in P[\mu, \mu_1) \cap P[\mu, \mu_2)$, $z_\mu \neq \mu$, *such that* z_μ *is serviced by* μ_1 *in some states and is serviced by* μ_2 *in the other states.*

As a consequence of this theorem, we see that if μ is not on the path between μ_1 and μ_2 as in the deterministic case, then we can find at least two different states of the network for which μ is serviced by the facility at μ_1 in one of these states and serviced by the facility at μ_2 in the other state. We leave the proof of this theorem to the reader (see Exercise 2.9).

Selective Enumeration Algorithm. Note first that an arc-deletion method does not work in the case of finding 2-medians on probabilistic networks because facility locations do not necessarily partition the network. In an arc-deletion method we assume that a deleted arc will not be traveled when demands are serviced by the closest facility. However, in the case of probabilistic networks, the facility serving a particular demand depends on the state of the network and, hence, each arc may be used at least once. In other words the allocation of demands to facilities may change with the state of the network. Nevertheless, the naive approach of *exhaustive* enumeration will always work. However, as a consequence of the corollary to Theorem 2.5 and Theorem 2.6 we can be *selective* in our enumerations to decrease the computational effort.

In an exhaustive enumeration scheme one needs to compute $\bar{F}_2(v_i, v_j)$ for every $m(m-1)/2$ possible pairs $\{v_i, v_j\} \in V$. As a consequence of the corollary to Theorem 2.5 we can disregard any pair $\{v_i, v_j\}$ such that $v_i \in P[\mu, v_j] - \{\mu\}$ or $v_j \in P[\mu, v_i] - \{\mu\}$. As a consequence of Theorem 2.6 we can further disregard any pair $\{v_i, v_j\}$ such that $\mu \in P[v_i, v_j]$ and μ is serviced by only one of v_i, v_j for all states of the network. Note that from the distance matrices for the various states, it is straightforward to determine whether μ is serviced by only one of v_i, v_j by comparing distances $d^l(\mu, v_i)$ and $d^l(\mu, v_j)$ for all states T^l, $l = 1, 2, \ldots, S$. An illustration of a selective enumeration approach is given by Mirchandani and Oudjit (1980). Although in the worst case such an approach requires the same number of operations as an exhaustive enumeration, in general it requires fewer enumerations.

Finally, let us briefly consider the 2-median problem on a multidimensional tree (e.g., when both arc weights and node weights are random). Let T be a multidimensional tree and T^* the localization subtree for its 1-medians. Using similar proofs as before, we can show the following relationships among μ, μ_1, μ_2, and T^*.

Theorem 2.7. *If μ_1 serves all points in T^* for all dimensions, then*

$$P[\mu_1, \mu_2] \cap T^* \neq \varphi \, .$$

Corollary A to Theorem 2.7

$$\mu_1 \not\subseteq P[T^*, \mu_2) - T^*$$

where $P[T^*, \mu_2)$ is any path from z_μ through μ_2, and z_μ is the closest node in T^* to μ_2.

Corollary B to Theorem 2.7

$$\mu_1 \not\subseteq P[\mu, \mu_2) - \{\mu\} \, .$$

Using the above results, an algorithm similar to the selective enumeration method just described will improve any exhaustive enumeration scheme.

2.4. ALGORITHMS FOR THE *p*-MEDIAN PROBLEM IN DISCRETE SPACE

Most algorithm development effort, of various researchers, for the *p*-median types of problems has focused on the classical *p*-median problem or on the problem of selecting *p* sites among *n* given sites to minimize the total transportation cost. The developed algorithms are, by problem definition, combinatorial in nature. Fortunately, such algorithms apply to most of the *p*-median problem generalizations formulated in this chapter. A situation where no *p*-node subset is optimal can happen only when the transportation cost function is *not* concave in travel attributes and facility siting is *unrestricted* (see Section 2.2.5). For the cases when the transportation costs are concave, or when the facility locations are restricted to be among given sites, the node optimality property holds and an optimal set of locations exists on the node set. The algorithms discussed in this chapter apply only to these cases—where only a finite discrete set is examined for possible location points.

The approaches in solving the *p*-median problem can be classified into five categories: (1) enumeration, (2) graph-theoretic, (3) heuristic, (4) primal-based mathematical programming, and (5) dual-based mathematical programming. Enumerating all possible solutions to determine the optimal solution is of course a naive approach, and for large networks the required computational effort is unwieldly. However, for locating one or two facilities, or when the network is small, the enumeration approach does, in fact, solve the problem quite easily.

Graph-theoretic approaches take advantage of the underlying network structure to determine the *p*-medians. Some of thes approaches are very efficient when the underlying network is a tree, as we saw in the last section. On the other hand, heuristic procedures, which rely on intuitive trial-and-error methods but cannot guarantee an optimal solution, can be applied to any general network structure. Heuristic procedures are especially useful when a "good" but not necessarily an "optimal" solution is required.

The mathematical programming approaches are based on an integer programming formulation of the *p*-median problem. Because of the availability of several integer programming computer routines and the large theoretical base in mathematical programming, these approaches have attracted wide attention and have proved to be rather successful for general networks. We will focus, in Section 2.4.2, on the mathematical programming based *nested-dual* approach that may, perhaps, be the best method available to solve the *p*-median problem exactly.

Handler and Mirchandani (1979) discuss the state of the art, circa 1979, on the computational methods for the *p*-median problem. In particular, they present various heuristic and mathematical programming approaches for problems with large *p*. The heuristics discussed include (i) the "node partitioning" scheme of Maranzana (1964), (ii) the "greedy" or the "myopic" approach of Kuehn and Hamburger (1963), (iii) the "node-substitution" procedure of Teitz and Bart (1968), and (iv) several heuristic branch-and-bound schemes. The mathematical programming approaches discussed include (i) the linear programming relaxation of ReVelle and Swain (1970), (ii) the branch-and-bound algorithms of Khumawala (1972) and others, (iii) the Dantzig–Wolfe decomposition of Garfinkel, Neebe, and

Rao (1974), (iv) the variable upper bounding scheme of Schrage (1975), (v) the Lagrangian relaxations of Diehr (1972), Narula, Ogbu, and Samuelsson (1977), and Cornuejols, Fisher, and Nemhauser (1977), and (iv) the linear programming dual of Erlenkotter (1978). We will not present these approaches in this chapter but will refer to some of them as they relate to the "nested-dual" method presented later. Readers are referred to Handler and Mirchandani (1979) for conceptual and concise discussions of the various approaches, and, of course, the original sources for detailed discussions. Readers note also that some of these approaches are discussed in other chapters of this book, specifically Chapters 3, 4, and 5.

2.4.1. Integer Programming Formulation

Let us first examine the cost function $\bar{F}_g(X_p)$, given by (2.2.20) for the generalized *p*-median problem. This can be written as

$$\bar{F}_g(X_p) = \sum_{l=1}^{S} \sum_{i=1}^{m} \sum_{k=1}^{K} P_l w_{ki}^l C_{ki}^l(X_p, v_i) \tag{2.4.1}$$

where $C_{ki}^l(X_p, v_i)$ is the cost of transporting commodity k in state N^l from the optimal facility in X_p to demand point v_i via the optimal path in state N^l. Thus, by definition of an optimal path and an optimal facility,

$$C_{ki}^l(X_p, v_i) = \min_{x_j \in X_p} c_{ki}^l(x_j, v_i) . \tag{2.4.2}$$

Let us denote $c_{ki}^l(x_j, v_i)$ by c_{kij}^l. Thus our cost function can now be written as

$$\bar{F}_g(X_p) = \sum_{l=1}^{S} \sum_{i=1}^{m} \sum_{k=1}^{K} P_l w_{ki}^l \min_j (c_{kij}^l) . \tag{2.4.3}$$

If we let decision variable x_{ijkl} be defined by

$$x_{ijkl} = \begin{cases} 1, & \text{if the demands at } v_i \text{ for commodity } k \text{ are served by} \\ & \text{facility at } v_j \text{ when the network is in state } N^l \\ 0, & \text{otherwise}, \end{cases}$$

then the transportation cost for given decisions is

$$\bar{F}_g(x_{ijkl}) = \sum_{l=1}^{S} \sum_{k=1}^{K} \sum_{i=1}^{m} \sum_{j=1}^{m} P_l w_{kij}^l c_{kij}^l x_{ijkl} . \tag{2.4.4}$$

Minimizing the above cost function $\bar{F}_g(x_{ijkl})$ with appropriate constraints on x_{ijkl} gives us a mathematical programming formulation for the generalized *p*-median problem (see Exercise 2.10).

For illustrative purposes, and better exposition of the procedure to solve the problem, we present below a slightly less general formulation which does not include the index l. In the particular formulation, index k will denote a "dimension," which represents a "network state" in single commodity problems on probabilistic networks *or* a "commodity" in multicommodity problems on deterministic networks. (Inclusion of both indices k and l allows us to consider problems with probabilistic states *and* multiple commodities. Inclusion of additional indices is straightforward in this formulation.)

Within the framework of the formulation given below, for the multicommodity problem interpretation, the π_k are all unity and the other symbols are as described before. For the probabilistic network interpretation, π_k is the probability of state N^k, w_{ki} is the demand for the given single commodity at v_i in state N^k, and c_{kij} is the cost of transporting the given commodity from v_j to v_i in state N^k. There is also a multiobjective interpretation; the solution of the program for all π yields a set of nondominated solutions for the multiobjective p-median problem (see expressions (2.2.17) and (2.2.18) and related discussion).

In the formulation given below, the index set $I = \{1, 2, \ldots, m\}$ will be associated with the demand points, and the demand points will be denoted by v_i, $i \in I$. Likewise, index set $J = \{1, 2, \ldots, n\}$ with the potential sites, denoted by v_j, $j \in J$. When there is an underlying network in the problem scenario, the v_i and v_j may be referred to as nodes in such a network. If all nodes are potential sites as well as demand points then $m = n$.

The decision variables in the formulation are defined by

$$y_j = \begin{cases} 1, & \text{if a facility is established at } v_j \\ 0, & \text{otherwise}, \end{cases}$$

and

$$x_{ijk} = \begin{cases} 1, & \text{if the demands at } v_i \text{ are serviced by a facility at} \\ & v_j, \text{ when the network is in dimension } k \\ 0, & \text{otherwise}. \end{cases}$$

Now consider the following mathematical programming problem:

(P1) $$\sum_{k=1}^{K} \sum_{i=1}^{m} \sum_{j=1}^{n} \pi_k w_{ki} c_{kij} x_{ijk} \qquad (2.4.5)$$

subject to

$$\sum_{j=1}^{n} x_{ijk} = 1, \qquad i \in I; k = 1, 2, \ldots, K, \qquad (2.4.6)$$

$$y_j \geq x_{ijk}, \qquad i \in I; j \in J; k = 1, 2, \ldots K, \qquad (2.4.7)$$

$$\sum_{j=1}^{n} y_j = p \, , \qquad\qquad (2.4.8)$$

$$x_{ijk} \in \{0, 1\} \, , \quad i \in I; \; j \in J; \; k = 1, 2, \ldots, K \, , \qquad (2.4.9)$$

$$y_j \in \{0, 1\} \, , \quad j \in J \, . \qquad\qquad (2.4.10)$$

Constraint (2.4.6) assures that demands at each v_i are fully assigned in each dimension k; constraint (2.4.7) insures that node v_i can be serviced only by established facilities; and (2.4.8) restricts the number of facilities to p. (We should note in the above formulation that constraint (2.4.9) may be relaxed to $x_{ijk} \geq 0$ without loss of optimality. However, since at optimality x_{ijk} can be 0 or 1, the x_{ijk} may be restricted as 0–1 variables.)

Note that problem **P1** includes most of the *p*-median problems formulated earlier. Also note that the minimization will assure that each demand point is served by the optimal facility, via an optimal path, and thus allows us to eliminate the "min" operator in the cost-function (2.4.3).

Now consider the following transformation for **P1**. Let (here h is just a composite index which depends on indices i and k),

$$x_{jh} = x_{ijk}$$
$$\qquad\qquad (2.4.11)$$
$$d_{jh} = \pi_k w_{ki} c_{kij}$$

where $h = i + m(k-1); \; i \in I; \; k = 1, 2, \ldots, K; \; j \in J$. We can rewrite **P1** as

(P2) minimize $\displaystyle\sum_{j=1}^{n} \sum_{h=1}^{mK} d_{jh} x_{jh}$ $\qquad\qquad (2.4.12)$

subject to

$$\sum_{j=1}^{n} x_{jh} = 1 \, , \quad h = 1, 2, \ldots, mK \, ,$$
$$\qquad\qquad (2.4.13)$$

$$y_j \geq x_{jh} \, , \qquad j \in J; \; h = 1, 2, \ldots, mK \, , \qquad (2.4.14)$$

$$\sum_{j=1}^{n} y_j = p \qquad\qquad (2.4.15)$$

$$x_{jh} \in \{0, 1\} \, , \quad j \in J; \; h = 1, 2, \ldots, mK \, , \qquad (2.4.16)$$

$$y_j \in \{0, 1\} \, , \quad j \in J \, . \qquad\qquad (2.4.17)$$

Observe that **P1** and **P2** will both have the same optimal solution value. With the above transformation we can map any optimal solution for **P2** into an optimal solution for **P1** and vice-versa. Thus solving **P2** is equivalent to solving **P1**.

Observe that **P2** closely resembles the classical *p*-median problem, and existing *p*-median algorithms may be modified to solve it. The index set *J* still represents the set of possible facility locations. The index set for *h*, $\{1, 2, \ldots, mK\}$, in **P2** can be viewed as the set of "customers" in the various dimensions of the network. That is, each *h* corresponds to a demand node, say $v(h)$, and a dimension, say, dimension $k(h)$. Figure 2.10 illustrates a geometrical interpretation of the transformation.

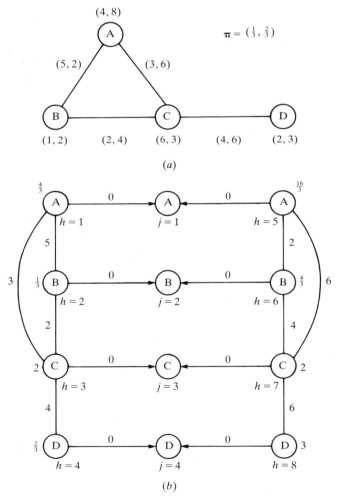

Figure 2.10. A geometrical interpretation of the transformation. (*a*) The original network where $k = 2$ dimensions, and points $i, j = 1, 2, 3, 4$ correspond to nodes *A*, *B*, *C*, *D*, respectively. (*b*) The transformed network where $j = 1, 2, 3, 4$ are the potential sites and $h = 1, \ldots, 8$ are the demand points.

Unlike in the classical *p*-median problem, the cost d_{jh} for **P2** does not correspond to the transportation cost component from v_j to v_h but rather the transportation cost component from v_j to $v(h)$ *in dimension* $k(h)$. Except for this minor difference in interpretation, the two problems are mathematically identical. Thus, any *p*-median solution technique can be applied to solve **P2**.

2.4.2.   Solution Techniques for the Integer Programming Formulation

Linear programming (LP) relaxations have been somewhat successful in solving the *p*-median problem optimally (e.g., ReVelle and Swain, 1970; Schrage, 1975). That is, when the integer requirements (2.4.16) and (2.4.17) are relaxed to

$$1 \geq x_{jh} \geq 0, \quad j \in J; h = 1, 2, \ldots, mK \qquad (2.4.18)$$

$$1 \geq y_j \geq 0, \quad j \in J, \qquad (2.4.19)$$

the solution of the resultant linear program quite frequently gives integer $(0, 1)$ values. It can be shown that the LP relaxation *always* gives an optimal solution for the class of simple networks consisting of *line networks* (a line network consists of a single simple path), *single cycle networks*, or a forest having these components (Oudjit, 1981). However, integer solutions cannot be guaranteed for general networks.

Researchers have focused recently on dual-based techniques for minisum location problems, which have proved to be quite successful. Cornuejols et al. (1977) introduced a two-phase approach for generating and verifying near-optimal solutions for both the *p*-median and the uncapacitated facility location (UFL) problems.* A greedy-interchange heuristic generates good upper bounds for the optimal solution value. A Lagrangian relaxation, obtained by dualizing with respect to the assignment constraints (2.4.13), provides sharp lower bounds for the optimal solution value. Narula et al. (1977) also successfully used the same Lagrangian relaxation approach for generating lower bounds for the *p*-median problem.

Bilde and Krarup (1977) and Erlenkotter (1978) developed a very efficient dual-based procedure for the UFL problem. The method solves a dual problem that is equivalent to the Lagrangian relaxation mentioned above. However, Erlenkotter's method, DUALOC, solves the dual problem with a heuristic ascent and adjustment procedure instead of the subgradient approach used by Cornuejols et al. and Narula et al. Through the "complementary slackness conditions," the dual solution frequently gives an optimal solution to the UFL problem (e.g., Geoffrion, 1974). Otherwise, a branch-and-bound procedure is used to search for an optimal solution. Computational results with Erlenkotter's procedure indicate that it is perhaps the most efficient technique available for solving the UFL problem.

*Dual-based approaches to the UFL problem are discussed in detail in Chapter 3.

Galvão (1980) modified Erlenkotter's dual-based approach to solve the *p*-median problem. His procedure is equivalent to applying the heuristic ascent procedure to the dual problem obtained by relaxing the assignment constraints (2.4.13) and the *p*-median constraint (2.4.15). The lower bounds generated by the dual problem are then used in a branch-and-bound solution procedure.

Mavrides (1979) developed another dual approach for solving the *p*-median problem. He used a Lagrangian relaxation obtained by dualizing only the *p*-median constraint (2.4.15). The resulting Lagrangian subproblem is

$$(\textbf{SP}(f)) \quad L(f) = \text{minimize} \sum_{j=1}^{n} \sum_{h=1}^{mK} d_{jh} x_{jh} + f\left(\sum_{j=1}^{n} y_j - p\right) \qquad (2.4.20)$$

$$\text{subject to } (2.4.13), (2.4.14), (2.4.16), \text{ and } (2.4.17)$$

where *f* is the dual variable corresponding to (2.4.15).

In comparison, the objective of the UFL problem is (recall (2.1.6) and let $w_h c(x_j, v_h) = d_{jh}$; see also Chapter 3)

$$\text{minimize} \sum_{j=1}^{n} \sum_{h=1}^{mK} d_{jh} x_{jh} + \sum_{j=1}^{n} f_j y_j \qquad (2.4.21)$$

where f_j is the fixed cost of establishing a facility at v_j. Since the number of facilities to be established is not constrained in the UFL problem, it does not have a constraint like (2.4.15). Hence notice that the Lagrangian subproblem $\textbf{SP}(f)$ is a UFL problem with cost of establishing facilities being *f* for all facility sites $v_j, j \in J$.

The corresponding Lagrangian dual problem for (2.4.20) is

$$(\textbf{D}) \qquad\qquad \underset{f}{\text{maximize}}\ L(f) . \qquad (2.4.22)$$

Mavrides solves problem **D** with a special heuristic search technique. In fact, his procedure generates solutions of the *p*-median problem for *all possible* values of *p*. Computational results with some real-world problems seem to indicate that the procedure is very frequently successful in generating solutions for all values of *p*. However, because the technique for finding the values for *f* is heuristic, this success cannot be guaranteed.

Weaver and Church (1983) have recently published a dual approach to solve the *p*-median problem on multidimensional networks. They solve the multidimensional formulation **P1**, given by (2.4.5)–(2.4.10), directly and not the transformed problem **P2**. They dualize with respect to the assignment constraints (2.4.6) and give a subgradient optimization method to solve the dual. This approach is essentially a generalization of the procedures used by Narula et al. (1977) and Cornuejols et al. (1977). Their reported computational times, for various values of p, on a 30-node three-state problem appear to be quite good: 1.28–9.57 s on an IBM 360/65.

We present below another approach to solve the p-median problem or the transformed version of the multidimensional p-median problem. Consider the problem $\mathbf{SP}(f)$ defined by (2.4.20), where f is a scalar dual variable. As we observed earlier, $\mathbf{SP}(f)$ is a UFL problem. Hence, Erlenkotter's technique can be used to solve it. However, there remains the problem of determining an f, say $f(p)$, that gives the optimal locations for a *specified* p. Such an $f(p)$ may be found by solving the Lagrangian dual problem $\mathbf{D}$ defined by (2.4.22).

In the algorithm given below we use a subgradient type approach to determine $f(p)$. The procedure generates a sequence of fixed costs f_t, $t = 1, 2, \ldots$, (index t refers to an iteration count) so that $\mathbf{SP}(f_t)$ is an approximation of $\mathbf{SP}(f(p))$.

Let $z(s)$ be defined by

$$z(s) = \text{minimum} \sum_{j=1}^{n} \sum_{h=1}^{mK} d_{jh} x_{jh}$$

$$\text{subject to} \sum_{j=1}^{n} y_j = s$$

and constraints (2.4.13), (2.4.14), (2.4.16), and (2.4.17).

A global subgradient (say) g for $z(s)$ at $s = p$ is a real number satisfying

$$z(s) \geq z(p) + (s - p)g \qquad (2.4.23)$$

It has been shown by Geoffrion (1971, 1974) that if there is no duality gap between **P2** and **D** (that is, if the optimal solution values for these two problems are equal) then each optimal solution $f(p)$ of **D** is the negative of a global subgradient of $z(s)$ at $s = p$. Thus, geometrically, finding the $f(p)$ that solves the dual, for a given set $\mathbf{x} \equiv \{x_{jh}\}$ and $\mathbf{y} \equiv \{y_j\}$, turns out to be the determination of the slope at $s = p$ of a line that supports $z'(s)$, where $z'(s)$ is the convexified version of $z(s)$ (Geoffrion, 1974). Figure 2.11 illustrates the two functions $z(s)$ and $z'(s)$ and the linear support of $z'(s)$ at $s = p$. Note that $f = 0$ in (2.4.20) results in a facility being located at each of the n sites and $f = M$ (a large number) results in only one facility being located at the 1-median; this is geometrically consistent with subgradient $-f(n)$ at $s = n$ being zero and subgradient $-f(1)$ at $s = 1$ being very large.

We use this geometric interpretation to update the values of f_t in our algorithm. (The resultant f_t are used in the UFL problems $\mathbf{SP}(f_t)$ which are solved by Erlenkotter's technique.) The algorithm and the procedure to generate the f_t are as follows.

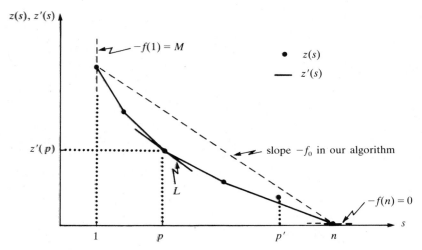

Figure 2.11. Illustration of $z(s)$ and $z'(s)$. $z'(s)$ is continuous and convex, while $z(s)$ is discrete. The slope of the subgradient L of $z'(s)$ at $s = p$ is the negative of $f(p)$. In this example there is a duality gap at $s = p'$.

Algorithm 2.2   *Nested-Dual Algorithm*

Step 0: Initialization
  Set $q = 1$.
  Set $r = n$.
  Set $f_0 = \dfrac{z(q) - z(r)}{r - q} = \dfrac{z(1)}{n - 1}$.

Step 1: Iteration t
  Solve **SP**(f_t) by Erlenkotter's technique (or any other UFL algorithm) and let the solution be $\mathbf{x}(t)$, $\mathbf{y}(t)$.

Step 2: Termination test

  Let $\displaystyle\sum_{j=1}^{n} y_j(t) = p_t$ ($=$ number of facilities opened).

  If $p_t = p$ or $z(p_t) + (p_t - p)f_t = z(r) + (r - p)f_t = z(q) + (q - p)f_t$ then STOP.

Step 3: Update

  Update f_t by $f_{t+1} = \dfrac{z(q) - z(r)}{(r - q)}$

  where if $p_t < p$, p_t replaces q, and if $p_t > p$, p_t replaces r; then go to *Step 1*.

Observe that, to initialize, we use for f_0 the negative of the slope between points $\{1, z(1)\}$ and $\{n, z(n)\}$. Note that when the algorithm terminates with $p_t = p$ we have an optimal solution to the p-median problem due to the "complementary slackness conditions." When it terminates with $p_t \neq p$, then the optimal dual objective function value $z'(p)$ is only a lower bound on the optimal objective function value $z(p)$. The difference between $z'(p)$ and $z(p)$ is the duality gap of the problem relaxation. An upper bound on $z(p)$ can be generated by some heuristic technique such as greedy-interchange (see Cornuejols et al., 1977). Computational experience, however, shows that the algorithm usually terminates with $p_t = p$.

Close inspection of the algorithm reveals that it is equivalent to applying the dual simplex method to the linear programming formulation of **D** (Mirchandani, Oudjit, and Wong, 1985). At each step of the dual simplex method, the most violated inequality is generated by solving the UFL subproblem **SP**(f_t). The equivalence with the dual simplex method also shows that the nested-dual algorithm computes an optimal solution to the dual problem **D** (see (2.4.22)). Therefore, even when we only have a lower bound $z'(p)$ on the optimal cost function value $z(p)$, the bound should be fairly tight. It is well known (e.g., Geoffrion, 1974) that the lower bound provided by a Lagrangian relaxation is at least as good as the one provided by the LP relaxation of the original integer program. Moreover, since the Lagrangian dual subproblems in this procedure are UFL problems, they do not always satisfy the "integrality property" (see Geoffrion, 1974). Thus the bounds given by this Lagrangian relaxation could be *stronger* than the LP relaxation bounds.

The standard arguments concerning finite termination of the simplex method guarantees that Algorithm 2.2 terminates in a finite number of steps. However, the following stronger convergence property can be obtained by examining the special structure of the problem (Mirchandani et al., 1985).

Property 2.5. Algorithm 2.2 requires at most $(n - 1)$ iterations (executions of Step 1) before terminating.

Let us summarize in a global perspective the solution approach presented above. The problem is first dualized with respect to the p-median constraint using a dual variable f. The dual UFL subproblems are then solved using the dual-based procedure of Erlenkotter. Furthermore, the procedure to update f to determine (when there is no duality gap) $f(p)$, the optimal value of f, is equivalent to the dual simplex. Thus the method is referred to as the "nested-dual" approach for the p-median problem.

Some computational experience by this method has been reported (Mirchandani et al., 1985). On multidimensional problems with four dimensions ($K = 4$) and 33 nodes ($m, n = 33$) computation times on an IBM 370/3033 (with FORTRAN IV and G compiler) have been between 0.107 s and 1.09 s.

Considering that an IBM 370/3033 is 5–6 times faster than an IBM 360/65, these times appear to be about 1.5–2 times faster than those reported for the direct dual method of Weaver and Church (1983) (i.e., when the multidimensional problem **P1** is solved directly by subgradient optimization of its dual.

Computation times on large-scale single-dimension deterministic *p*-median problems have also been very good. Times* (on an IBM 370/3033, with FORTRAN IV and H compiler) of 0.3–3.62 s for 100-node problems, 0.35–6.32 s for 150-node problems, and 3.15–15.78 s for 200-node problems have been obtained by Mirchandani et al. A duality gap was encountered for about 5% of the randomly generated test problems. Table 2.1(a) gives a summary of the computational experience on the 200-node problem and Table 2.1(b) gives some examples of the p_t sequences generated by Algorithm 2.2.

Algorithm 2.2 compares quite favorably with other *p*-median procedures. The routine is significantly faster and comparable in accuracy to Cornuejols et al.'s (1977) Lagrangian relaxation-based method for computing lower bounds. It is much faster than Galvão's (1980) algorithm.

TABLE 2.1(a)   Computational Experience for the 200-Node Problem

p	No. of Iterations	CPU Time* (s)	*p*	No. of Iterations	CPU Time* (s)
5	5	6.78	80	7	4.41
10	4	15.78	100	8	3.63
20	4	12.70	120	9	3.73
30	6	9.25	140	7	3.23
40	7	11.28	160	6	3.15
50	6	11.82	180	8	3.43
60	8	15.09**	190	9	3.59
			195	10	3.76

*The times are on IBM 370/3033, using FORTRAN IV and H Compiler.
**No solution for any value of f (duality gap).

TABLE 2.1(b)   Some p_t Sequences for the 200-Node Problem

p	p_t Sequence	CPU Time (s)
5	23, 6, 3, 4, 5	6.78
40	23, 76, 44, 32, 36, 41, 40	11.28
60	23, 76, 44, 58, 67, 62, 61, 61	15.09**
120	23, 76, 136, 104, 119, 127, 123, 121, 120	3.73

**No solution for any value of f (duality gap).

*The computation times exclude the set-up time needed to create a sorted cost (or distance) matrix.

Algorithm 2.2 can also be used to solve p-median problems for multiple values of p. For these types of problems, the algorithm can exploit the obvious efficiency of reusing the iterations for previous values of p. For example, referring to Table 2.1(b), if the problem has already been solved for $p = 40$ then for $p = 60$ (or more generally for any $45 \leq p \leq 75$) we do not have to go through the first three iterations (i.e., $p_1 = 23$, $p_2 = 76$, $p_3 = 44$) since they can be reused from the results for $p = 40$. (Note that the computational results reported, for example in Table 2.1(a), *do not* take advantage of this fact; for each value of p, the problem has been solved without using results from the previously solved problems with other values of p.)

Finally, we note that the efficiency of Algorithm 2.2 is highly dependent on the efficiency of solving the UFL subproblems. A slower procedure than Erlenkotter's DUALOC would give longer times. Fortunately, improvements to Erlenkotter's routine (see Van Roy and Erlenkotter, 1982, and Chapter 4) can increase DUALOC's speed by a factor of three for difficult problems. This could make Algorithm 2.2 even faster, and it should be able to solve very large-scale p-median problems without excessive computational effort.

2.5. FURTHER REMARKS AND NOTES

Introductory treatments of the p-median problem on a network have already appeared in several texts on graph theory and applications (e.g., Frank and Frisch, 1971; Francis and White, 1974; Christofides, 1975; Minieka, 1978; Larson and Odoni, 1981). A more extensive treatment on the problem is given by Handler and Mirchandani (1979) and in some ways this chapter may be considered an update of the material on the p-median problem presented in that text. The recent survey article by Tansel, Francis, and Lowe (1983) briefly reviews some further work on the problem. The reader is referred to Handler and Mirchandani, and Tansel et al. for the most complete bibliographies on the p-median problem.

Sections 2.1 and 2.2 of this chapter are based largely on extensions of the models developed by the author in his doctoral dissertation (Mirchandani, 1975) and in the Handler–Mirchandani text. Section 2.3 reflects the authors significant collaboration with his doctoral student Aissa Oudjit. Some additional material on the 1- and 2-median problem on trees is presented by Mirchandani and Oudjit (1980) and Oudjit (1981).

In Section 2.4 we only briefly reviewed the various methods available to solve p-median problems; somewhat more detailed descriptions are given by Handler and Mirchandani (1979) and, of course, much more detailed descriptions are given in the original sources. We did discuss in detail the nested-dual approach, which may perhaps be the best available method to solve the problem. Section 2.4 is largely based on the author's collaborative work reported by Mirchandani et al. (1985). Christofides and Beasley (1982) use a similar Lagrangian relaxation but utilize a different approach to update the fixed-cost dual variable f_t.

There are other generalizations and modifications of the *p*-median problem that have appeared in the literature but have not been discussed in this chapter. Handler and Mirchandani and Tansel et al. review some of them. At the risk of doing injustice to the researchers/authors who have developed/presented the corresponding models we only very briefly review below some other generalizations that have appeared. We will end the chapter with a list of actual and potential applications of the discrete *p*-median problem.

2.5.1. Constrained *p*-Median Problems

In some problem scenarios there are additional constraints on the locational decision. Thus, several constrained versions of the *p*-median problem have appeared in the literature. We discuss some of them below.

Capacitated Facilities. Each facility may have a limitation on how much demand it can serve. Levy (1967) showed that the node optimality property still holds for this case. The analogous *capacitated UFL problem* has been extensively studied; some recent references are Van Roy (1981) and Jacobsen (1983). Relevance of capacitated facilities for locational decisions over a time horizon is discussed in Chapter 4.

Capacitated Flows. The amount of goods or service that can flow over any arc in the underlying network may be restricted to below a given capacity. Hakimi and Maheshwari (1972) and Wendell and Hurter (1973) prove the node optimality property for this case.

Distance Constraints. The objective of a locational decision may be to minimize the average travel distance subject to the requirement that "the closest facility to each demand point must be within a specified distance from the demand point." This constraint prevents an optimization solution being formed that makes some demands to be "too far" from every facility. Analogously, for "obnoxious" facilities we may want to either minimize the average distance subject to each demand being greater than a specified distance, or maximize average distance subject to each demand being less than a specified distance. These and other distance-constrained *p*-median problems are reviewed by Moon and Chaudhry (1984).

Implementation Constraints. In some locational decision problems, due to economic, political, societal, or other reasons, we may have constraints that do not permit the *p* facilities to be established at the optimal *p* sites. Instead, it may be specified that "only p' ($p' < p$) facilities may be located at *new* sites given existing $p - p'$ facilities," or "any p^* of the existing facilities may be *relocated*" or "certain *particular sites* must have a facility each" or some other implementation constraint. Hillsman (1979) discusses how various implementation constraints may be included in a unified computer code. Mirchandani and Reilly (1987) report how these constraints arise in fire station location decisions. Mirchandani and Odoni's (1979b) proof of the node optimality property for the *new* and *supporting p-medians* also applies to these situations.

2.5.2.   Spatially Continuous and Stochastic Demands

In all of the p-median problem generalizations presented so far, it has been assumed that demands are independently generated at discrete points, or at nodes of an underlying network.

Continuous Arc Demands. One generalization is to also allow demands to be generated continuously on the arcs of the network. Handler and Mirchandani (1979) formulate the problem of finding the corresponding p-medians. They give an exact algorithm to determine the 1-median of a *tree* and an approximate method for the 1-median on a network. Chiu (1987) gives an exact method for the 1-median, and Cavalier and Sherali (1986) and Sherali and Nordai (1988) study the corresponding 1- and 2-median problems for the special case where the demand distribution on each arc is uniform. Minieka (1978) implicitly considers arc demands by introducing the "general absolute median" as a point that minimizes the total distance from it to all the arcs of the network.

Spatial Nodes. Another generalization of the p-median problem is to include in the objective function, explicitly or implicitly, the "intranodal" travel costs. As we mentioned earlier, demands are usually assumed to originate at point nodes. If a node represents a zone with a finite area then the average travel cost is affected by intrazonal travel. Hillsman and Rhoda (1978), Goodchild (1979), and Casillas (1987) have studied the errors introduced from aggregating m' demand points to m ($m < m'$) demand nodes in the classical p-median problem. Mirchandani and Reilly (1986) discuss generalized p-median type locational decisions which minimize average travel cost (where the cost is nonlinear in travel distance) to spatially random demands within zones, or, as they say it, to demands within "*spatial nodes*." (We note that in the extreme case where the demand is continuously distributed over a plane and the objective is to find the location of p facilities to minimize the average travel cost to the demands we have the generalization of the classical Weber problem—but this is no longer within the scope of *discrete* location theory.)

Spatially Stochastic Demands. Our probabilistic network model (see Section 2.2.2) allows for the nodal demands to be probabilistically discrete and correlated. However, models have appeared that deal with probabilistically continuous demands. Frank (1966, 1967) assumes that the uncertainty in demand at any node can be modeled by a continuous distribution and determines an optimal location that maximizes the probability that the expected travel distance is below a given threshold λ. Carbone (1974) considers the analogous problem of maximizing this threshold subject to the constraint that the corresponding probability (that the expected travel distance is less than the threshold) is smaller than a specified α. Carbone uses a chance-constrained mathematical programming approach to determine the optimal p-locations. Jucker and Carlson (1976) have considered versions of the UFL problems where there are uncertainties in prices, costs, and demands; their objective is the maximization of a linear combination of the mean and the variance of profit. They examine a class of such problems where each demand point is optimally served by only one facility and develop branch-and-bound solution procedures (see, e.g., Efroymson and Ray, 1966; Khumawala, 1972) where the subproblems are simple and are solved analytically.

Frank, Carbone, Jucker, and Carlson all utilize the central limit theorem to approximate the distribution of the mean distance with a normal distribution function. Their models are inherently nonlinear and, hence, they use nonlinear optimization techniques to solve the resultant problems.

2.5.3. Hierarchical Median Problems

In some problem scenarios the locational decision problem involves siting several types of facilities (e.g., health centers, hospitals, clinics) servicing various types of demands (e.g., heart-attack victims, pregnancies, common colds, flu, etc.). Here there is a hierarchy of facilities; a higher level facility can serve the same types of demands as a lower level facility, plus more. The objective of the hierarchical median-type facility location problem is to locate p_k facilities of type k ($k = 1, 2, \ldots, K$, when there are K hierarchical levels) to minimize the average travel cost. Narula (1984) gives a classification of hierarchical median-type problems.

In a more general setting, a type k facility serves a subset of demand types, say I_k, where these sets need not be hierarchical with respect to k; that is, $I_k \not\supseteq I_{k-1}$. After a little thought, the reader should be able to observe the "multidimensional" aspect of these problems of locating different demand-specific facilities. Jagannathan et al. (1986) apply a nested-dual type approach for locating two ($K = 2$) types of facilities.

2.5.4. Temporally Stochastic Demands and Queues

Until now we have assumed that the closest facility (or, more generally, the "optimal" facility if the travel cost is probabilistic and nonlinear) is always available to serve a particular demand point. That is, we have neglected the possibility that this facility may be busy when the demand occurs. The probabilistic network model of Section 2.2.2 allows for temporally stochastic demands when there are no queues; that is, each facility has sufficient capacity to handle all the required demands appropriately. However, if demands are lost or if demands queue up when a facility is busy, then explicit consideration of queues may be important in the locational decision. Chapter 12 discusses median-type location problems in the presence of queues.

2.5.5. Probabilistic and Worst-Case Analyses

The p-median problem is NP-hard (Garey and Johnson, 1979; Kariv and Hakimi, 1979). However, researchers have developed efficient heuristics for *special* cases of the p-median problem and analyzed their computational complexity. When the m ($= n$) demand points (and sites) are distributed over a plane and the travel costs are proportional to the Euclidean distances, Papadimitriou (1981) shows that the resultant problem is NP-hard but develops a heuristic that is shown to be, from a probabilistic analysis, asymtotically optimal if $\log(m)/m < p/m < 1/\log(m)$. Fisher and Hochbaum (1980) conduct a probabilistic analysis of an aggregation heuristic for the same problem and show it to be asymptotically optimal if $p/m < \log(m)/m$. Ahn, Cooper, Cornuéjols, and Frieze (1988) provide probabilistic analyses for some p-median problems on special networks and trees.

2.5.6. Applications of the p-Median Problem

Exposition of a mathematical model is not complete without a discussion on how the model may be useful. The last chapter discussed model formulation in general and indicated that even though most locational decision models are based on idealization and simplification of real-world phenomena the solution of a model can provide (1) a good *initial solution* to start a detailed analysis of a locational decision, or (2) a *benchmark* to compare and evaluate alternative locational sets, or (3) a *building block* for more complicated locational models and analyses. With this in view, the p-median model indeed has many applications. This final section will briefly indicate, without references, some actual and some potential applications of the discrete p-median model.

Handler and Mirchandani (1979) list several potential applications of the p-median model—for locational decisions in emergency service systems (e.g., police, fire, emergency medical services), in computer communication networks (e.g., location of data files), in distribution problems (e.g., location of industrial plants, warehouses, garages), in military applications, in the public sector (location of governmental agencies, shopping centers), in financial application (location of bank accounts and lock boxes), and to locate mailboxes and bus stops.

A recent large scale application of the *p*-median model is due to Anderson and Chelst (1986). Within the framework of a decision support system, they embedded a procedure, similar to the nested-dual algorithm, which found the optimal *p* locations for "outlets" to geographically distribute goods or services. In particular, they discussed its actual utilization in the automotive industry. Given a data set, obtained from historical trade data, census-type data, and market surveys, which defined the geographical distribution of demand points, they were able to provide the decision-maker with locations for new car dealerships that would minimize the average distance (or any other measure given by the "distance" matrix) to the closest dealership. Their system was particularly user friendly in that the market information, as well as other data such as maps and locations for present and proposed dealerships, was displayed on high resolution computer color graphics. This allowed the decision-maker to use the result of the locational analyses truly as a guide, a benchmark, or an initial solution—as it should be and as we recommend that all abstract or idealized mathematical models be. With the graphics display and the analyses, the decision-maker was able to easily "see" the effect of moving a dealership to a new location, or establishing *p* new locations, or the "cost" for not being at the optimal locations, and so on. The sizes of problems reported by Anderson and Chelst ranged between 338 and 532 demand nodes and between 5 and 24 dealerships. They also report the actual use of their system to reconfigure networks of bank branches in existing markets, and to design new networks in new markets.

The *p*-median model, having a well-defined mathematical programming structure, has also been useful in the academic arena. In particular, the model has been used by computer scientists and mathematical programmers for studies on computational complexity of algorithms. Statisticians have used the *p*-median problem structure for cluster analysis (see Chapter 3).

Finally, observe that in the nested-dual approach of Section 2.4.2, the UFL problem was a subproblem in the solution procedure. Because the subproblem was well solvable, the nested-dual approach was rather successful in solving the *p*-median problem. Likewise, the *p*-median problem turns out to be a subproblem in many approaches for several discrete optimization problems (e.g., manpower scheduling, routing and location of service vehicles, hierarchical facility design, network design, etc.). Efficient solution approaches for the *p*-median problem may be usefully applied to solve such discrete optimization problems.

ACKNOWLEDGMENTS

The author wishes to acknowledge the support provided by the Electrical, Computer, and Systems Engineering Department at Rensselaer Polytechnic Institute, Troy, New York, where this chapter was written. Comments and suggestions of the two reviewers are also well appreciated.

EXERCISES

2.1 Give an example of a network where a set of 3-inmedians exists but no 1-inmedian.

2.2 Prove that at least one set of p-inmedians exists on the nodes in a strongly connected oriented network.

2.3 We define an oriented network where cost of flow in one direction of an arc is not necessarily equal to the cost of flow in the other direction. Prove that a set of p^+out-p^-in medians of the oriented network exists on the node set. Assume that the network is strongly connected.

2.4 Prove Theorem 2.2.

2.5 Construct an example of a 1-median problem on a multidimensional tree network where the cost function is *not* convex over the localization subtree T^* for the problem.

2.6 Prove Property 2.1.

2.7 Prove Properties 2.2–2.4.

2.8 Prove the corollary to Theorem 2.5, that

$$\mu_1 \not\subseteq P[\mu, \mu_2) - \{\mu\} \,.$$

2.9 Prove Theorem 2.6.

2.10 Formulate the generalized p-median problem given by (2.2.19) as a linear integer program minimizing objective (2.4.4). Argue that the solution will minimize $\bar{F}_g(X_p)$ as defined by (2.2.19) or (2.4.3).

REFERENCES

Ahn, S., C. Cooper, G. Cornuéjols, and A. Frieze (1988). "Probabilistic Analysis of a Relaxation for the k-Median Problem." *Mathematics of Operations Research* **13**, 1–31.
Anderson, J. A., and K. Chelst (1986). *Computer Graphics and Optimal Location: Improved Retail Network Analysis*, Tech. Rep. Urban Science Applications, Inc., Detroit, Michigan

(revised version of paper presented at the TIMS XXVI International Meeting, Copenhagen, Denmark, June, 1984).

Balinski, M. L. (1965). "Integer Programming: Methods, Uses, Computation." *Management Science* **12**, 253–313.

Bilde, O., and J. Krarup (1977). "Sharp Lower Bounds and Efficient Algorithms for the Simple Plant Location Problem." *Annals of Discrete Mathematics* **1**, 79–97.

Carbone, R. (1974). "Public Facilities Location under Stochastic Demand." *INFOR* **12**, 261–270.

Casillas, P. (1987). "Data Aggregation and the *p*-Median Problem in Continuous Space," In *Spatial Analysis and Location-Allocation Models* (A. Ghosh and G. Rushton, eds.), pp. 327–344. Van Nostrand-Reinhold, New York.

Cavalier, T. M., and H. D. Sherali (1986). "Network Location Problems with Continuous Link Demands: *p*-Medians on a Chain, 2-Medians on a Tree." *European Journal of Operational Research* **23**, 246–255.

Chiu, S. S. (1987). "The Minisum Location on an Undirected Network with Continuous Link Demands." *Computers and Operations Research* **14**, 369–383.

Christofides, N. (1975). *Graph Theory: An Algorithmic Approach*. Academic Press, London.

Christofides, N., and J. E. Beasley (1982). "A Tree Search Algorithm for the *p*-Median Problem." *European Journal of Operational Research* **10**, 196–204.

Cornuejols, G., M. L. Fisher, and G. L. Nemhauser (1977). "Location of Bank Accounts to Optimize Float: An Analytic Study of Exact and Approximate Algorithms." *Management Science* **23**, 789–810.

Dearing, P. M., R. L. Francis, and T. J. Lowe (1976). "Convex Location Problems on Tree Networks." *Operations Research* **24**, 628–641.

Diehr, G. (1972). *An Algorithm for the p-Median Problem*, Working Paper No. 191. Western Management Science Institute, University of California, Los Angeles.

Efroymson, M. A., and T. L. Ray (1966). "A Branch-Bound Algorithm for Plant Location." *Operations Research* **14** 361–368.

Erlenkotter, D. (1978). "A Dual-Based Procedure for Uncapacitated Facility Location." *Operations Research* **26**, 992–1009.

Fisher, M. L., and D. S. Hochbaum (1980). "Probabilistic Analysis of the Planer *K*-Median Problem." *Mathematics of Operations Research* **5**, 27–34.

Francis, R. L., and J. A. White (1974). *Facility Layout and Locations: An Analytical Approach*. Prentice-Hall, Englewood Cliffs, New Jersey.

Frank, H. (1966). "Optimum Locations on a Graph with Probabilistic Demands." *Operations Research* **14**, 409–421.

Frank, H. (1967). "Optimum Locations on Graphs with Correlated Normal Demands." *Operations Research* **15**, 552–557.

Frank, H., and I. T. Frisch (1971). *Communication, Transmission and Transportation Networks*. Addison-Wesley, Reading, Massachusetts.

Galvão, R. D. (1980). "A Dual-Bounded Algorithm for the *p*-Median Problem." *Operations Research* **28**, 1112–1121.

Garey, M. R., and D. S. Johnson (1979). *Computers and Intractability: A Guide to the Theory of NP-Completeness*. Freeman, San Francisco, California.

Garfinkel, R. S., A. W. Neebe, and M. R. Rao (1974). "An Algorithm for the *M*-Median Plant Location Problem." *Transportation Science* **8**, 217–236.

Geoffrion, A. M. (1971). "Duality in Nonlinear Programming: A Simplified Applications-Oriented Development." *SIAM Review* **13**, 1–37.

Geoffrion, A. M. (1974). "Lagrangian Relaxation for Integer Programming." *Mathematical Programming Study* **2**, 82–114.

Goldman, A. J. (1971). "Optimal Center Location in Simple Networks." *Transportation Science* **5**, 212–221.

Goodchild, M. F. (1979). "The Aggregation Problem in Location-Allocation." *Geographical Analysis* **11**, 240–255.

Hakimi, S. L. (1964). "Optimum Locations of Switching Centers and the Absolute Centers and Medians of a Graph." *Operations Research* **12**, 450–459.

Hakimi, S. L. (1965). "Optimum Distribution of Switching Centers in a Communication Network and Some Related Graph Theoretic Problems." *Operations Research* **13**, 462–475.

Hakimi, S. L., and S. N. Maheshwari (1972). "Optimum Locations of Centers in Networks." *Operations Research* **20**, 967–973.

Handler, G. Y., and P. B. Mirchandani (1979). *Location on Networks: Theory and Algorithms.* MIT Press, Cambridge, Massachusetts.

Hillsman, E. L. (1979). *A System for Location-Allocation Analysis.* Ph.D. Dissertation, Department of Geography, University of Iowa, Iowa City.

Hillsman, E. L., and R. Rhoda (1978). "Errors in Measuring Distances from Populations to Service Centers." *Annals of the Regional Science Association* **12**, 74–88.

Hua, L. K. and others (1962). "Applications of Mathematical Methods to Wheat Harvesting." *Chinese Mathematics* **2**, 77–91.

Jacobsen, S. K. (1983). "Heuristics for the Capacitated Plant Location Model." *European Journal of Operational Research* **12**, 253–261.

Jagannathan R., P. G. Krishnakumar, P. B. Mirchandani, and R. T. Wong (1986). *A Nested-Dual Approach to the Generalized Hierarchical Location Model*, Working Paper No. 8601. Operations Research and Statistics Program, Rensselaer Polytechnic Institute, Troy, New York.

Jucker, J. V., and R. C. Carlson (1976). "The Simple Plant-Location Problem under Uncertainty." *Operations Research* **24**, 1045–1055.

Kariv, O., and S. L. Hakimi (1979). "An Algorithmic Approach to Network Location Problems. Part 2. The *p*-Median." *SIAM Journal on Applied Mathematics* **37**, 539–560.

Keeney, R. L. (1973). "A Utility Function for the Response Times of Engines and Ladders to Fires." *Journal of Urban Analysis* **1**, 209–222.

Khumawala, B. M. (1972). "An Efficient Branch and Bound Algorithm for the Warehouse Location Problem." *Management Science* **18**, B718–B731.

Kollias, J. G., and M. Hatzopoulos (1981). "Allocation of Copies of *s* Distinct Files in an Information Network." *Information Systems* **6**, 201–204.

Krarup, J., and P. M. Pruzan (1983). "The Simple Plant Location Problem: Survey and Synthesis." *European Journal of Operational Research* **12**, 36–81.

Kuehn, A. A., and M. J. Hamburger (1963). "A Heuristic Program for Locating Warehouses." *Management Science* **9**, 643–666.

Larson, R. C., and A. R. Odoni (1981). *Urban Operations Research*, Prentice-Hall, Englewood Cliffs, New Jersey.

Levy, J. (1967). "An Extended Theorem for Location on a Network." *Operational Research Quarterly* **18**, 433–442.

Manne, A. (1964). "Plant Location under Economics of Scale—Decentralization and Computation." *Management Science* **11**, 213–235.

Maranzana, F. E. (1964). "On the Location of Supply Points to Minimize Transport Costs." *Operational Research Quarterly* **15**, 261–270.

Mavrides, L. (1979). "An Indirect Method for the Generalized *k*-Median Problem Applied to Lock-Box Location." *Management Science* **25**, 990–996.

Minieka, E. (1978). *Optimization Algorithm for Networks and Graphics*. Dekker, New York.

Mirchandani, P. B. (1975). *Analysis of Stochastic Networks in Emergency Service Systems*, IRP-TR-15-75. Operations Research Center, Massachusetts Institute of Technology, Cambridge.

Mirchandani, P. B., and A. R. Odoni (1979a). "Location of Medians on Stochastic Networks." *Transportation Science* **13**, 85–97.

Mirchandani, P. B., and A. R. Odoni (1979b). "Locating New Passenger Facilities on a Transportation Network." *Transportation Research* **13**, 113–122.

Mirchandani, P. B., and A. Oudjit (1980). "Localizing 2-Medians on Probabilistic and Deterministic Tree Networks." *Networks* **10**, 329–350.

Mirchandani, P. B., A. Oudjit, and R. Wong (1985). "Multidimensional Extensions and a Nested Dual Approach for the *m*-Median Problem." *European Journal of Operational Research* **21**, 121–137.

Mirchandani, P. B., and J. M. Reilly (1986). "Spatial Nodes in Discrete Location Problems." *Annals of Operations Research* **6**, 203–222.

Mirchandani, P. B., and J. M. Reilly (1987). "Spatial Distribution Design for Fire Fighting Units." In *Spatial Analysis and Location-Allocation Models* (A. Ghosh and G. Rushton, eds.), pp. 186–223. Van Nostrand-Reinhold, New York.

Moon, D. I., and S. S. Chaudhry (1984). "An Analysis of Network Location Problems with Distance Constraints." *Management Science* **30**, 290–307.

Narula, S. C. (1984). "Hierarchical Location-Allocation Problems: A Classification Scheme." *European Journal of Operational Research* **15**, 93–99.

Narula, S. C., U. I. Ogbu, and H. M. Samuelsson (1977). "An Algorithm for the *p*-Median Problem." *Operations Research* **25**, 709–712.

Oudjit, A. (1981). *Median Locations on Deterministic and Probabilistic Multidimensional Networks*. Ph.D. Dissertation, Rensselaer Polytechnic Institute, Troy, New York.

Papadimitriou, C. H. (1981). "Worst-Case and Probabilistic Analysis of a Geometric Location Problem." *SIAM Journal on Computing* **10**, 542–557.

ReVelle, C., and R. W. Swain (1970). "Central Facilities Location." *Geographical Analysis* **2**, 30–42.

Ruffell-Smith, H. P. (1970). "Time to Die from Injuries Received in Road Traffic Accidents." *Injury* **2**, 99–102.

Schrage, L. (1975). "Implicit Representation of Variable Upper Bounds in Linear Programming." *Mathematical Programming Study* **4**, 118–132.

Sherali, H. D., and F. L. Nordai (1988). "A Capacitated, Balanced, 2-Median Problem on a Tree Network with a Continuum of Link Demands." *Transportation Science* **22**, 70–73.

Tansel, B. C., R. L. Francis, and T. J. Lowe (1983). "Location on Networks: A Survey." *Management Science* **29**, 482–511.

Teitz, M. B., and P. Bart (1968). "Heuristic Methods for Estimating the Generalized Vertex Median of a Weighted Graph." *Operations Research* **16**, 955–961.

Van Roy, T. J. (1981). "Cross Decomposition for Mixed Integer Programming with Application to Facility Location." In *Operational Research '81* (J. P. Brans, ed.), pp. 579–587. North-Holland Publ., Amsterdam.

Van Roy, T. J., and D. Erlenkotter (1982). "Dual-Based Procedure for Dynamic Facility Location." *Management Science* **28**, 1091–1105.

Weaver, J.R., and R. L. Church (1983). "Computational Procedures of Location Problems on Stochastic Networks." *Transportation Science* **17**, 168–180.

Weber, A. (1909). "Über den Standort der Industrien. Tübingen; Engl. Transl.: *Theory of Location of Industries* (C. J. Friedrich, ed. and transl.), Chicago University Press, Chicago, Illinois, 1929.

Wendell, R. E., and A. P. Hurter (1973). "Optimal Locations on a Network." *Transportation Science* **7**, 18–33.

3

The Uncapacitated Facility Location Problem

Gerard Cornuejols
Graduate School of Industrial Administration
Carnegie Mellon University
Pittsburgh, Pennsylvania

George L. Nemhauser
Department of Industrial and Systems Engineering
Georgia Institute of Technology
Atlanta, Georgia

Laurence A. Wolsey
Center for Operations Research and Econometrics
Université Catholique de Louvain
Louvain-la-Neuve, Belgium

3.1. FORMULATION AND APPLICATIONS

A locational decision problem of great practical importance is to choose the location of facilities, such as industrial plants or warehouses, to minimize the cost (or maximize the profit) of satisfying the demand for some commodity. In general there are fixed costs for locating the facilities and transportation costs for distributing the commodities between the facilities and the clients. This problem has been extensively studied in the literature and is commonly referred to as the *plant location problem*, or *facility location problem*. When each potential facility has a capacity, which is the maximum demand that it can supply, the problem is called the *capacitated facility location problem*. When capacity limitations are not required, we have the *simple* or *uncapacitated facility location problem*, or, for short, the *UFL problem*.

The mathematical formulation of these problems as integer programs has proven very fruitful in the derivation of solution methods. To formalize the UFL problem, we consider a set of clients $I = \{1, \ldots, m\}$ with a given demand for a single commodity, and a set of sites $J = \{1, \ldots, n\}$ where facilities can be located. In the literature it has been traditional to use the phrase "facility j is open" to mean that a facility is actually established at site j. Let f_j be the given fixed cost of opening facility j and assume there is a known profit c_{ij} that is made by satisfying the demand of client i from facility j. Typically, c_{ij} is a function of the production costs at facility j, the transportation costs from facility j to client i, the demand of client i and the selling price to client i. For example, $c_{ij} = d_i(p_i - q_j - t_{ij})$ where d_i is the demand, p_i the price per unit, q_j the production cost per unit and t_{ij} the transportation cost per unit.

The UFL problem is to open a subset of facilities in order to maximize total profit, given that all demand has to be satisfied. An instance of the problem is specified by integers m and n, an $m \times n$ matrix $C = \{c_{ij}\}$ and a $1 \times n$ matrix $f = \{f_j\}$. Note that there is no loss of generality in assuming $f_j \geq 0$ for all $j \in J$ since if $f_k < 0$ every optimal solution contains facility k.

For any given set S of open facilities, it is optimal to serve client i from a facility j for which c_{ij} is maximum over $j \in S$. Thus, given S, the profit is $z(S) = \Sigma_{i \in I} \max_{j \in S} c_{ij} - \Sigma_{j \in S} f_j$. The problem is to find a set S that yields the maximum profit Z, that is $Z = \max_{S \subseteq J} z(S)$. This can be viewed as a combinatorial formulation of the problem.

An integer linear programming formulation is obtained by introducing the following variables. Let $x_j = 1$ if facility j is open and $x_j = 0$ otherwise; $y_{ij} = 1$ if the demand of client i is satisfied from facility j and $y_{ij} = 0$ otherwise. The integer program is

$$Z = \max \sum_{i \in I} \sum_{j \in J} c_{ij} y_{ij} - \sum_{j \in J} f_j x_j \qquad (3.1.1)$$

$$\sum_{j \in J} y_{ij} = 1 \qquad \text{all } i \in I \qquad (3.1.2)$$

$$y_{ij} \leq x_j \qquad \text{all } i \in I, j \in J \qquad (3.1.3)$$

$$x_j, y_{ij} \in \{0, 1\} \qquad \text{all } i \in I, j \in J . \qquad (3.1.4)$$

The constraints (3.1.2) guarantee that the demand of every client is satisfied, whereas (3.1.3) guarantees that the clients are supplied only from open facilities.

Note that because of (3.1.2) if c_{ij} is replaced by $c'_{ij} = c_{ij} + c_i$ for all $j \in J$, then the profit of each feasible solution is changed by c_i. Hence we can add a constant to any row of matrix C and the set of optimal decisions remains the same. In particular, the selling price of the commodity to client i is a constant added to row i. Therefore, only the costs (production, transportation and fixed operating costs) are relevant for the decision. This is why in the literature the UFL problem is often presented as

$$\min \sum_{i \in I} \sum_{j \in J} d_{ij} y_{ij} + \sum_{j \in J} f_j x_j \qquad (3.1.1')$$

subject to (3.1.2)–(3.1.4) where d_{ij} is the cost (production plus transportation) of serving client i from facility j. This formulation is mathematically equivalent to (3.1.1)–(3.1.4) since (3.1.1') becomes $-(3.1.1)$ by setting $c_{ij} = -d_{ij}$. In other words, costs can simply be regarded as negative profits.

In the integer program (3.1.1)–(3.1.4), the x_j are the strategic variables. Once a set of x_j that satisfy (3.1.4) are specified, it is simple to determine a set of y_{ij} that solves the integer program for the fixed x_j. Even if we drop the integrality requirement on the y_{ij}, an optimal set of y_{ij} is given by $y_{ij^*} = 1$ and $y_{ij} = 0$, $j \neq j^*$ where $c_{ij^*} = \max \{c_{ij} : x_j = 1, j \in J\}$. Thus (3.1.4) can be replaced by

$$x_j \in \{0, 1\} , \qquad y_{ij} \geq 0 \qquad \text{all } i \in I, j \in J . \qquad (3.1.4')$$

The formulation (3.1.1)–(3.1.3), (3.1.4') is a mixed integer linear program.

An integer linear program equivalent to (3.1.1)–(3.1.4) is obtained by replacing the constraints (3.1.3) by the more compact set of constraints

$$\sum_{i \in I} y_{ij} \leq m x_j \qquad \text{all } j \in J . \qquad (3.1.3')$$

To see that (3.1.3) can be replaced by (3.1.3′), note that when $x_j = 0$ both (3.1.3) and (3.1.3′) imply $y_{ij} = 0$ for all $i \in I$, and when $x_j = 1$ both (3.1.3) and (3.1.3′) are satisfied for all choices of y_{ij} that satisfy the constraints (3.1.2). However, the two formulations are equivalent only for 0–1 values of the variables x_j. For each j, (3.1.3′) is obtained by summing (3.1.3) over all $i \in I$; hence any solution to (3.1.2), (3.1.3) is also a solution to (3.1.2) and (3.1.3′). But the converse is false when $0 < x_j < 1$; that is, the feasible region defined by (3.1.2), (3.1.3′), and

$$0 \le x_j \le 1, \ y_{ij} \ge 0 \qquad \text{all } i \in I, j \in J \tag{3.1.5}$$

strictly contains the region defined by (3.1.2), (3.1.3), and (3.1.5).

In the UFL problem, the number of facilities that are open in an optimal solution is not specified; it is determined by a solution of (3.1.1)–(3.1.4). From a practitioner's standpoint, it might be useful to consider a formulation where the number p of open facilities is a parameter of the problem. This is realized by adding one of the following constraints to the program (3.1.1)–(3.1.4):

$$\sum_{j \in J} x_j = p \tag{3.1.6}$$

or

$$\sum_{j \in J} x_j \le p \tag{3.1.7}$$

where p is some given integer, $1 \le p \le n$. The formulation (3.1.1)–(3.1.4), (3.1.6) is called the *p-facility location problem*. When $f_j = 0$ for all $j \in J$, (3.1.1)–(3.1.4), (3.1.6) is known as the *p-median problem*. This model is the topic of Chapter 2.

In addition to the classical interpretation of the UFL problem given above, the mathematical model (3.1.1)–(3.1.4) has several other applications. We conclude this section by giving two such applications. First we interpret (3.1.1)–(3.1.4) as a bank account location problem (see Cornuejols, Fisher, Nemhauser, 1977b). The second example occurs in clustering analysis (see Mulvey and Crowder, 1979). Other applications arise in lock-box location (Kraus, Janssen, and McAdams, 1970), location of offshore drilling platforms (Balas and Padberg, 1976), economic lot sizing (Krarup and Bilde, 1977), machine scheduling and information retrieval (Hansen and Kaufman, 1972), portfolio management (Beck and Mulvey, 1982) and the design of communication networks, (Mirzain, 1985). The formulation (3.1.1)–(3.1.4) also arises as a subproblem in several contexts, such as some problems in network design, vehicle routing and, of course, location theory when additional constraints, such as capacity constraints, are present.

3.1.1. A Bank Account Location Problem

The number of days required to clear a check drawn on a bank in city j depends on the city i in which the check is cashed. Thus, to maximize its available funds a company that pays bills to clients in various locations may find it advantageous to maintain accounts in several strategically located banks. It would then pay bills to clients in city i from a bank in city j that had the largest clearing time. The economic significance to large corporations of such a strategy is discussed in an article in Businessweek (1974).

To formalize the problem of selecting an optimal set of account locations, let $I = \{1, \ldots, m\}$ be the set of client locations, $J = \{1, \ldots, n\}$ the set of potential account locations, f_j the fixed cost of maintaining an account in city j, d_i the dollar volume of checks paid in city i, and φ_{ij} the number of days (translated into monetary value) to clear a check issued in city j and cashed in city i. All this information is assumed to be known and $c_{ij} = d_i \varphi_{ij}$ represents the value of paying clients in city i from an account in city j. Let $x_j = 1$ if an account is maintained in city j, and $x_j = 0$ otherwise; $y_{ij} = 1$ if clients in city i are paid from account j, and $y_{ij} = 0$ otherwise. Then the account location problem can be stated as (3.1.1)–(3.1.4).

Besides delaying payments for as long as possible, corporations also want to collect funds due to them as quickly as possible. This can be done by situating check collection centers or "lock-boxes" at optimal locations. Since (3.1.1) and (3.1.1') are mathematically equivalent, (3.1.1)–(3.1.4) is also a model for the *lock-box problem*.

3.1.2. A Clustering Problem

Cluster analysis consists of partitioning objects into classes, known as clusters, in such a way that the elements within a cluster have a high degree of natural association among themselves while the clusters are relatively distinct from one another. Cluster analysis is used in biology, psychology, medicine, artificial intelligence, pattern recognition, marketing research, automatic classification, statistics, and other areas.

Let $I = \{1, \ldots, m\}$ be the set of objects to be clustered. The clustering is done around objects that "represent" the clusters. Let $J = \{1, \ldots, n\}$ be the set of eligible "cluster representatives." In many applications $J = I$. However, in some applications $|J| < |I|$, that is, only objects with certain characteristics can qualify as representatives (e.g., survey papers and books in the automatic classification of technical material in some field). In other cases $|I| < |J|$, (e.g., in the automatic classification of technical material, an alternative to the above policy is to represent a cluster by a list of key words. This list does not need to match exactly that of any single paper in the cluster).

The clustering problem is defined relative to a matrix of parameters c_{ij} that represent the similarity between objects i and j. For example c_{ij} could be the number of common key words associated with technical papers i and j. Anderberg (1973) gives several ways of calculating the similarity matrix C. In many applications there are no natural fixed charges; rather, the constraint (3.1.6) is added to the formulation (3.1.1)–(3.1.4) and the problem is solved as a p-median problem. As an alternative, artificial fixed charges can be introduced and then the problem is solved as a UFL problem.

3.2. BRIEF HISTORICAL OVERVIEW

There is a vast literature on the UFL problem. Krarup and Pruzan (1983) give an up-to-date survey. We will not repeat their effort here. However, to set the stage for the ensuing sections, we will mention the main solution approaches and cite some basic references.

The first approaches were heuristic. One of the earliest of these is due to Kuehn and Hamburger (1963). Their heuristic approach is actually designed for a wider class of location problems. It consists of two routines. The first routine opens facilities sequentially in an order that maximizes the increase of the objective function value at each step. It stops when adding a new facility would decrease the value. Kuehn and Hamburger called it the "add routine"; in the modern literature such a procedure is called a *greedy heuristic* because of its appetite for maximum improvement at each step. Their second routine is the "bump and shift routine." It eliminates (bumps) any facility that has become uneconomical because of the presence of other facilities chosen subsequently by the greedy heuristic. Then, starting from this feasible solution, it considers interchanging an open facility with a closed facility. Such a pairwise interchange is performed if it improves the current feasible solution and the procedure stops when a solution has been found that cannot be improved by such interchanges. In the remainder of this chapter, the shifting procedure will be referred to as an *interchange heuristic*.

The greedy and interchange heuristics are the basis of numerous approximation algorithms. They can, of course, be helpful in exact algorithms that require feasible initial solutions or use feasible solutions in other ways (Spielberg, 1969b; Hansen and Kaufman, 1972). However, when a heuristic is used to obtain a final solution, it is very important to have an upper bound as well so that the user can be confident that the heuristic solution value is not too far from the optimal value. Cornuejols et al. (1977b) gave such bounds for the greedy and interchange heuristics, both *a priori* worst-case bounds and *a posteriori* bounds on a particular solution constructed by the heuristic. These heuristic approaches are discussed in more detail in Section 3.5. In Section 3.9, we mention that some of the heuristic results can be generalized to the maximization of submodular set functions (see Nemhauser, Wolsey, and Fisher, 1978).

General solution techniques for finding optimal solutions to integer programs have been specialized to the UFL problem. The mixed integer linear programming formulation can be solved by Benders decomposition (see Benders, 1962). This approach was proposed by Balinski and Wolfe (1963) and appears to have been the first attempt to solve the UFL problem to optimality. The computational experiments were discouraging (see Balinski, 1965), and this method was abandoned until recently. Magnanti and Wong (1981) develop techniques to accelerate the convergence of Benders decomposition. They generate "strong" cuts from the set of feasible Benders cuts and by so doing they are able to reduce the number of integer programs to be solved. Nemhauser and Wolsey (1981) consider the Benders cuts in the more general framework of maximizing a submodular set function.

Branch-and-bound algorithms for the UFL problem use the fact that it is not necessary to constrain the variables y_{ij} to be integral. Branching is done on a binary enumeration tree with respect to the variables x_j. Bounds are obtained from one of the two linear programming relaxations, (3.1.1), (3.1.2), (3.1.5), and (3.1.3) or (3.1.3′). The earlier algorithms used the linear program with (3.1.3′), which we call the *weak linear programming relaxation*. Efroymson and Ray (1966) showed that this linear program can be solved analytically so that the bound at each node of the enumeration tree could be computed very quickly in constant time. Improvements to Efroymson and Ray's algorithm were made by Spielberg (1969a) and Khumawala (1972). However, the bounds obtained from the weak linear programming relaxation are generally not sufficiently strong to curtail the enumeration adequately.

As we observed previously, the constraints (3.1.3) imply (3.1.3′) but not the converse. The linear programming relaxation that uses (3.1.3) is called the *strong linear programming relaxation* (SLPR). ReVelle and Swain (1970), among others, observed that SLPR is so effective that its solution is very often integral. Thus a branch-and-bound algorithm that uses SLPR to compute bounds is very likely to perform well in the sense that very little (if any) enumeration will be required. However, because of its size, it is not efficient to solve SLPR directly by the simplex method.

Much of the recent research on the UFL problem has involved the development of special purpose algorithms for solving SLPR. Marsten (1972) used parametric linear programming and a special implementation of the simplex method. Garfinkel, Neebe, and Rao (1974) used Dantzig–Wolfe decomposition. Schrage (1975) devised a generalized simplex method to treat the variable upper bounds (3.1.3). Guignard and Spielberg (1977) suggested a version of the simplex method that pivots only to integral vertices of the polytope of feasible solutions to (3.1.2), (3.1.3), and (3.1.6). Cornuejols and Thizy (1982b) used a primal subgradient algorithm.

Dual algorithms or algorithms that solve the dual of the SLPR have the advantage that upper bounds are obtained from any dual feasible solution.

Thus a sufficiently good bound may be obtained to fathom a node of the enumeration tree prior to solving the dual to optimality. Duality, as it relates to the UFL problem, is discussed in Section 3.4.

Bilde and Krarup (1977) and Erlenkotter (1978) used heuristic methods to obtain a near-optimal solution of the dual. Erlenkotter went a step further by using the complementarity slackness conditions of linear programming to improve this bound. His procedure was so effective that in 45 out of the 48 problems that he tested, optimality was reached at the first node of the branch-and-bound algorithm. His DUALOC code appears to outperform all existing algorithms.

A Lagrangian dual of the formulation (3.1.1)–(3.1.4), proposed by Geoffrion (1974), is obtained by weighting the constraints (3.1.2) by multipliers and placing them in the objective function. It can be solved using subgradient optimization (see Held, Wolfe, and Crowder, 1974) or a projection method (Conn and Cornuejols, 1987). The Lagrangian approach can also be used for the p-median location problem. Some computational results with subgradient methods are reported by Narula, Ogbu, and Samuelsson (1977), Cornuejols et al. (1977b) and Mulvey and Crowder (1979). Krarup and Pruzan (1983) mention a different Lagrangian dual obtained when constraints (3.1.3) (instead of (3.1.2)) are weighted by multipliers and placed in the objective function.

In Section 3.6, we present and relate some of the methods for solving SLPR.

3.3. COMPUTATIONAL COMPLEXITY

An algorithm is said to be a *polynomial-time algorithm* for problem P, if for all instances of P (possible data sets), the computing time of the algorithm can be bounded by a polynomial function of the data size. If L measures the data size and k is the order of the polynomial, we say that the computing time of the algorithm is $O(L^k)$. Sometimes it is more convenient to express the computing time as a function of basic data parameters, such as the dimension of a matrix or the number of nodes in a graph. Then, but only then, is it assumed that all arithmetric operations and comparisons are performed in unit time.

A fundamental theoretical question, also of some practical importance, is whether a given combinatorial optimization problem can be solved by some polynomial-time algorithm. Denote by $\mathscr{P}$ the class of problems that can be solved in polynomial-time, that is by some polynomial-time algorithm. For most combinatorial optimization problems of practical interest, the question—"Are they in $\mathscr{P}$?"— has not been answered. A significant step was made by Cook (1971) and Karp (1972), who introduced the notion of $\mathscr{NP}$-*complete* problems. This is a class of combinatorial problems that are equivalent in the sense that either all or none of these problems can be solved by a polynomial-time algorithm.

At present no polynomial-time algorithm is known for solving any NP-complete problem and it has been widely conjectured that none exists. A problem is said to be $\mathcal{NP}$-*hard* if the existence of a polynomial-time algorithm to solve it would imply that all NP-complete problems can be solved by a polynomial-time algorithm. Thus to show that a problem (P) is $\mathcal{NP}$-hard it suffices to find a polynomial transformation that reduces a known $\mathcal{NP}$-complete problem, (see, e.g., the comprehensive list given by Garey and Johnson, 1979), to the problem (P).

Theorem 3.1. *The UFL problem is $\mathcal{NP}$-hard.*

Proof. First we need to introduce the *node cover problem*. Given a graph G and an integer k, does there exist a subset of k nodes of G that cover all the arcs of G? (Node v is said to *cover* arc e if v is an endpoint of e.) The node cover problem is $\mathcal{NP}$-complete (see Karp, 1972, or Garey and Johnson, 1979).

We now reduce the node cover problem to the UFL problem. Consider a graph $G = (V, E)$ with node set V and arc set E. Construct an instance of the UFL problem with the set of potential facilities $J = V$ and set of clients $I = E$. Let $c_{ij} = 2$ if $v_j \in V$ is an endpoint of $e_i \in E$ and let $c_{ij} = 0$ otherwise. Also let $f_j = 1$ for all $v_j \in V$. This transformation is polynomial in the size of the graph. A small example of the transformation is shown in Figure 3.1.

An instance of the UFL problem defined in this way consists of covering all the arcs of the graph G with the minimum number of nodes. Thus an optimal solution of the UFL problem provides the answer to the node cover problem. This proves that the UFL problem is $\mathcal{NP}$-hard. (In the example, $x_1 = x_3 = x_4 = 1$, $x_j = 0$ otherwise, is an optimal solution to the instance of UFL. Hence three nodes are needed to cover all of the arcs of G.) $\square$

A polynomial transformation that reduces a known $\mathcal{NP}$-hard problem to a problem (Q) shows that (Q) is also *NP*-hard. An immediate corollary of Theorem 3.1 is that the p-facility location problem is $\mathcal{NP}$-hard since solving it for every $p = 1, \ldots, n$ provides a solution to the UFL problem.

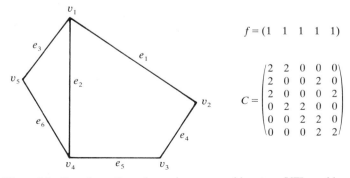

Figure 3.1. Transformation of a node cover problem to a UFL problem.

Although the UFL problem is $\mathcal{NP}$-hard, some special cases can be solved in polynomial-time. Kolen (1983) has shown that the UFL problem is solvable in time $O(r^3)$ when the problem is defined on a tree with r nodes, and some other assumptions are imposed. These are:

   i. the clients as well as the facilities are located at nodes of the tree;

   ii. a positive length is associated with each edge of the tree;

   iii. d_{ij} is the length of the path between nodes i and j.

Kolen solves the formulation $(3.1.1')$, $(3.1.2)$–$(3.1.4)$ and also shows that SLPR always has an integral optimal solution in this case.

Another interesting case of the UFL problem that can be solved in polynomial time was discovered by Krarup and Bilde (1977). The conditions required by Krarup and Bilde generalize those obtained when a classical economic lot size problem is formulated as a UFL problem. In this problem too, it is very significant that SLPR always has an integral optimal solution.

Finally, Bárány, Edmonds, and Wolsey (1986) have given a polynomial-time algorithm for a tree partitioning problem that contains both the problems of Kolen and of Krarup and Bilde. These problems are described and studied in Section 3.8.

3.4. DUALITY

Suppose we are given a feasible solution to the UFL problem that is claimed to be optimal or nearly optimal (within a specified absolute or relative tolerance). We know of only two ways to verify this claim.

   a. *Enumeration.* Compare, perhaps implicitly, the value of this feasible solution to all others, and

   b. *Bounding.* Determine an upper bound on the optimal value of all feasible solutions that is sharp enough to verify the claim.

Enumeration is useful algorithmically only when it can be done implicitly. Generally, this means that the enumerative approach, as in a branch-and-bound algorithm, uses upper bounds to curtail the enumeration. Conversely, an algorithm whose primary thrust is bounding may need to resort to some enumeration to verify the claim.

The point is that good upper bounds, as well as good feasible solutions, are crucial in solving the UFL problem, as for that matter, any hard combinatorial optimization problem. We will see, however, that the UFL problem has many features that make it a relatively easy $\mathcal{NP}$-hard problem.

Duality plays a key role in the determination of upper bounds. The dual of the strong linear programming relaxation given by $(3.1.1)$–$(3.1.3)$, $(3.1.5)$ is

$$W = \min \sum_{i \in I} u_i + \sum_{j \in J} t_j \tag{3.4.1}$$

$$u_i + w_{ij} \geq c_{ij} \qquad \text{all } i \in I, j \in J \tag{3.4.2}$$

$$-\sum_{i \in I} w_{ij} + t_j \geq -f_j \qquad \text{all } j \in J \tag{3.4.3}$$

$$w_{ij}, t_j \geq 0 \qquad \text{all } i \in I, j \in J. \tag{3.4.4}$$

We can eliminate variables and constraints from this formulation by noting that:

a. Because of (3.4.1), we would like to make t_j as small as possible. Thus, for given w_{ij}, (3.4.3) and (3.4.4) imply that $t_j = (\sum_{i \in I} w_{ij} - f_j)^+$ where $(\alpha)^+ = \max(0, \alpha)$;

b. Hence, for given u_i, to make t_j as small as possible, we would like to make w_{ij} as small as possible. Thus (3.4.2) and (3.4.4) imply that $w_{ij} = (c_{ij} - u_i)^+$ so that

$$t_j = \left[\sum_{i \in I} (c_{ij} - u_i)^+ - f_j \right]^+ \qquad \text{all } j \in J. \tag{3.4.5}$$

If we think of u_i as the price of the ith client, we can interpret t_j as the profits from the jth facility relative to these prices.

Substituting (3.4.5) into (3.4.1) yields the condensed dual

$$W = \min_u \left\{ \sum_{i \in I} u_i + \sum_{j \in J} \left[\sum_{i \in I} (c_{ij} - u_i)^+ - f_j \right]^+ \right\}. \tag{3.4.6}$$

The first term in (3.4.6) is the value of the clients and the second term is the value of the facilities. The dual problem (3.4.6) is to determine values or prices for the clients to minimize the total value of the resources.

If $\sum_{i \in I} [(c_{ij} - u_i)^+ - f_j]^+ > 0$, then there is a k such that $c_{kj} - u_k > 0$. Hence if u_k is increased by a small amount, then t_j will be decreased by the same amount so that the objective function (3.4.6) does not increase. Hence there is an optimal solution with $\sum_{i \in I} (c_{ij} - u_i)^+ - f_j \leq 0$ for all $j \in J$. Also if $u_i > \max_{j \in J} c_{ij}$, then u_i can be decreased without increasing the objective function (3.4.6). These observations yield a second condensed dual

$$W = \min_u \sum_{i \in I} u_i \tag{3.4.7}$$

$$\sum_{i \in I} (c_{ij} - u_i)^+ - f_j \leq 0 \qquad \text{all } j \in J \tag{3.4.8}$$

$$u_i \leq \max_{j \in J} c_{ij} \qquad \text{all } i \in I. \tag{3.4.9}$$

Although both condensed dual formulations are nonlinear, they are important because they contain only m variables, $u = (u_1, u_2, \ldots, u_m)$. Furthermore, since u is unconstrained in (3.4.6), by duality, we obtain an upper bound on the primal objective function given by

$$W(u) = \sum_{i \in I} u_i + \sum_{j \in J} \left[\sum_{i \in I} (c_{ij} - u_i)^+ - f_j \right]^+ . \tag{3.4.10}$$

When (3.4.8) holds, the upper bound reduces to

$$W(u) = \sum_{i \in I} u_i . \tag{3.4.11}$$

A Lagrangian dual of (3.1.1)–(3.1.4) is obtained by weighting the constraints (3.1.2) by multipliers u_i and placing them in the objective function. Let

$$L(u) = \max \left[\sum_{i \in I} \sum_{j \in J} c_{ij} y_{ij} - \sum_{j \in J} f_j x_j + \sum_{i \in I} u_i \left(1 - \sum_{j \in J} y_{ij} \right) \right] \tag{3.4.12}$$

subject to (3.1.3) and (3.1.4).

Frequently, a Lagrangian dual provides a tighter upper bound than a linear programming dual. However, this is not the case here.

Proposition 3.1. $L(u) = W(u)$ *for all* u.

Proof. $L(u) = \max \sum_{i \in I} \sum_{j \in J} (c_{ij} - u_i) y_{ij} - \sum_{j \in J} f_j x_j + \sum_{i \in I} u_i$ subject to (3.1.3) and (3.1.4). Hence

$$y_{ij} = \begin{cases} x_j , & \text{if } c_{ij} - u_i > 0 \\ 0 , & \text{if } c_{ij} - u_i < 0 \\ 0 \ \text{ or } \ x_j , & \text{if } c_{ij} - u_i = 0 . \end{cases} \tag{3.4.13}$$

Thus

$$L(u) = \max_{x_j \in \{0, 1\}} \sum_{j \in J} \left[\sum_{i \in I} (c_{ij} - u_i)^+ - f_j \right] x_j + \sum_{i \in I} u_i .$$

Hence

$$x_j = \begin{cases} 1 , & \text{if } \sum_{i \in I} (c_{ij} - u_i)^+ - f_j > 0 \\ 0 , & \text{if } \sum_{i \in I} (c_{ij} - u_i)^+ - f_j < 0 \\ 0 \ \text{ or } \ 1 , & \text{otherwise} . \end{cases} \tag{3.4.14}$$

Thus

$$L(u) = \sum_{j \in J} t_j + \sum_{i \in I} u_i = W(u)$$

where t_j is given by (3.4.5). $\square$

An immediate consequence of Proposition 3.1 is the following.

Corollary 3.1. $L = \min_u L(u) = W.$

When u satisfies the constraints (3.4.8), the solution (3.4.14) satisfies the complementarity conditions

$$\left(\sum_{i \in I} (c_{ij} - u_i)^+ - f_j \right) x_j = 0 \qquad \text{all } j \in J. \tag{3.4.15}$$

Equation (3.4.15) suggests that if u satisfies (3.4.8), then $x_j = 0$ unless $\sum_{i \in I} (c_{ij} - u_i)^+ - f_j = 0$. In other words, to find a good primal solution, we should only consider opening those facilities for which $\sum_{i \in I} (c_{ij} - u_i)^+ - f_j = 0$.

The results of this section will be used in the next two sections in the development of solution techniques for the UFL problem.

3.5. HEURISTICS

The combinatorial formulation of the UFL problem $\max_{S \subseteq J} z(S)$, where $z(S) = \sum_{i \in I} \max_{j \in S} c_{ij} - \sum_{j \in S} f_j$ can be viewed as a condensed, nonlinear primal that depends only on the values of the sets $S \subseteq J$. Based on this observation numerous authors have proposed heuristics that iterate on the set S of open locations and avoid an explicit integer programming formulation. Primal heuristics of this type are described in Section 3.5.1 and a dual descent heuristic is given in Section 3.5.2.

3.5.1. Primal Heuristics

The *greedy heuristic* starts with no facilities open. Given a set of S of open facilities, the greedy heuristic adds to S that facility $j \notin S$ whose incremental value $\rho_j(S) = z(S \cup \{j\}) - z(S)$ is as large as possible, and is positive. If no such facility exists, it stops with the set S of open facilities. Formally, the procedure is stated as follows:

Initialization: $S^0 = \emptyset$, $\rho_j(\emptyset) = \sum_{i \in I} c_{ij} - f_j$, $t = 1$.

Iteration t: Find $j_t = \arg\max_{j \notin S^{t-1}} \rho_j(S^{t-1})$. If $\rho_{j_t}(S^{t-1}) \leq 0$, stop. The set S^{t-1} is the greedy solution with value $Z^G = z(S^{t-1})$ if $t > 1$. If $t = 1$, the greedy solution is $S^1 = \{j_1\}$. (Note that when $t = 1$, some facility must be opened since $S = \emptyset$ is not feasible). If $\rho_{j_t}(S^{t-1}) > 0$, $S^t = S^{t-1} \cup \{j_t\}$. Set $t \leftarrow t + 1$.

The greedy heuristic requires at most n iterations and each iteration requires $O(nm)$ calculations. Thus the overall running time is $O(n^2m)$.

Example 3.1. We will use the following small example to introduce and motivate the ideas developed subsequently. Real-world problems are typically much larger (e.g., $m = n = 100$). Consider the instance of the UFL problem defined by the data:

$$m = 4, \qquad n = 6, \qquad f = (3 \ \ 2 \ \ 2 \ \ 2 \ \ 3 \ \ 3)$$

and

$$C = \begin{bmatrix} 6 & 6 & 8 & 6 & 0 & 6 \\ 6 & 8 & 6 & 0 & 6 & 6 \\ 5 & 0 & 3 & 6 & 3 & 0 \\ 2 & 3 & 0 & 2 & 4 & 4 \end{bmatrix}.$$

Applying the greedy heuristic to the example yields

Iteration 1: $(\rho_1(\emptyset), \ldots, \rho_6(\emptyset)) = (16, 15, 15, 12, 10, 13)$.

$$\text{Hence } j_1 = 1 \quad \text{and} \quad S^1 = \{1\} .$$

Iteration 2: $(\rho_2(\{1\}), \ldots, \rho_6(\{1\})) = (1, 0, -1, -1, -1)$.

$$\text{Hence } j_2 = 2 \quad \text{and} \quad S^2 = \{1, 2\} .$$

Iteration 3: $(\rho_3(\{1, 2\}), \ldots, \rho_6(\{1, 2\})) = (0, -1, -2, -2)$.

The set S^2 of value $Z^G = z(S^2) = 17$ is the greedy solution.   ○

We can now use (3.4.10) to obtain upper bounds on the values of the feasible solutions produced by the greedy heuristic. In fact, such an upper bound can be associated with any $S \subseteq J$.
Define

$$\bar{u}_i(S) = \max_{j \in S} c_{ij} \qquad \text{all } i \in I . \tag{3.5.1}$$

Note that

$$z(S) = \sum_{i \in I} \bar{u}_i(S) - \sum_{j \in S} f_j \tag{3.5.2}$$

and

$$\rho_j(S) = \sum_{i \in I} [c_{ij} - \bar{u}_i(S)]^+ - f_j \qquad \text{all } j \notin S .$$

Thus, from (3.4.10)

$$W(\bar{u}(S)) = \sum_{i \in I} \bar{u}_i(S) + \sum_{j \notin S} [\rho_j(S)]^+$$

since $c_{ij} - \bar{u}_i(S) \leq 0$ for all $i \in I$ and $j \in S$.

In particular if S^G is the final set chosen by the greedy heuristic then, by the stopping criterion, $\rho_j(S^G) \leq 0$, $j \notin S^G$, so that $W(\bar{u}(S^G)) = \Sigma_{i \in I} \bar{u}_i(S^G)$. Hence by (3.5.2), the greedy solution S^G deviates from optimality by at most $\Sigma_{j \in S^G} f_j$. This suggests that it will yield a small error when the fixed costs are small in comparison to the profits. Furthermore, we may obtain a better bound by considering all of the sets produced by the greedy algorithm. Let $\bar{u}_i^0 = \min_{j \in J} c_{ij}$ all $i \in I$ and $\bar{u}^k = \bar{u}(S^k)$, $k = 1, \ldots, t - 1$. Define a dual greedy value by $W^G = \min_k W(\bar{u}^k)$. For Example 3.1, $\bar{u}^0 = (0 \ \ 0 \ \ 0 \ \ 0)$, $W(\bar{u}^0) = \Sigma_{j \in J} \rho_j(\emptyset) = 81$, $\bar{u}^1 = (6 \ \ 6 \ \ 5 \ \ 2)$, $W(\bar{u}^1) = \Sigma_{i \in I} \bar{u}_i^1 + 1 = 20$, $\bar{u}^2 = (6 \ \ 8 \ \ 5 \ \ 3)$ and $W(\bar{u}^2) = \Sigma_{i \in I} \bar{u}_i^2 = 22$. Hence $W^G = 20$.

The bound we have given so far is an *a posteriori* bound for a particular instance of the UFL problem. In fact, a general relationship between Z^G and W^G that *a priori* applies to all instances of the UFL problem is given by the following.

Theorem 3.2 (Cornuejols et al., 1977b). *Let* $R = \Sigma_{i \in I} \min_{j \in J} c_{ij} - \Sigma_{j \in J} f_j$ *and e be the base of the natural logarithm. Then*

$$Z^G \geq \left(\frac{e-1}{e}\right) W^G + \left(\frac{1}{e}\right) R .$$

A proof of Theorem 3.2 that uses linear programming duality is given by Fisher, Nemhauser, and Wolsey (1978).

For the *p*-median problem with $c_{ij} \geq 0$ for all i and j, we have $R \geq 0$. Thus we achieve a simple data independent statement of Theorem 3.2.

Corollary 3.2 (Cornuejols et al. 1977b). *For the p-median problem with* $c_{ij} \geq 0$ *for all i and j,*

$$\frac{Z^G}{W^G} \geq \frac{e-1}{e} \cong 0.63 .$$

There are families of p-median problems for which this bound is achieved asymptotically. Furthermore, since $Z^G \leq Z \leq W \leq W^G$

$$\max \left\{ \frac{Z^G}{Z}, \frac{Z}{W}, \frac{W}{W^G} \right\} \geq \left(\frac{e-1}{e} \right)^{1/3} \cong 0.86 \, .$$

There are several variations and generalizations of the greedy heuristic for which bounds similar to those of Theorem 3.2 and Corollary 3.2 are known (see Cornuejols et al., 1977b; Nemhauser, Wolsey, and Fisher 1978). For example, we can begin with all facilities open and at each iteration close a facility that gives the largest improvement in the objective function so long as such a facility exists. A generalization of the greedy heuristic is to start with the family consisting of all sets of cardinality k, for some fixed k, and to apply greedy to each of these ($\binom{n}{k}$) initial sets separately; we then choose the best of the resulting ($\binom{n}{k}$) solutions.

None of these variations or generalizations, however, improve the worst-case bound of the greedy heuristic. In fact, what is remarkable about the bound on the greedy heuristic is not its value, but that no polynomial-time procedure of any degree whatsoever is known for p-median problems that have a better worst-case performance.

The salient feature of the greedy heuristic is that the maximum possible improvement is made at each step. If this is not done, worst-case performance deteriorates, even if a broader choice of improvements is considered.

An example of such a heuristic is *generalized interchange* (see Nemhauser et al., 1978). Here we begin with an arbitrary set S^0. Given S^{t-1}, at iteration t we select any set S^t such that $z(S^t) > z(S^{t-1})$, $|S^t \backslash S^{t-1}| \leq 1$ and $|S^{t-1} \backslash S^t| \leq 1$ or stop if no such S^t exists. Thus, at each iteration, we are allowed to open a facility, close a facility or do both so long as an improvement is made.

The worst-case bound of *generalized interchange* is weaker than that of greedy. For example, under the conditions of Corollary 3.2, this heuristic can guarantee only to find a solution of value at least half of the optimum value. Of course, by starting with a greedy solution, the bounds of Theorem 3.2 and Corollary 3.2 are obtained. Nevertheless, they are not strengthened by applying generalized interchange. On the other hand, greedy followed by generalized interchange seems to give good empirical performance (see Hansen and Kaufman, 1972; Cornuejols et al., 1977b).

The dual solution $\bar{u}(S)$ given by (3.5.1) yields a bound on the value of the primal solution S. Conversely, given a dual solution that satisfies (3.4.8), the complementarity conditions (3.4.15) suggest considering a primal solution in which $x_j = 0$ if $\sum_{i \in I} (c_{ij} - u_i)^+ - f_j < 0$.

Define set

$$J(u) = \left\{ j : \sum_{i \in I} (c_{ij} - u_i)^+ - f_j = 0 \right\} .$$

An optimal solution with $x_j = 0$ for $j \notin J(u)$ is obtained by solving

$$\max_{S \subseteq J(u)} \left\{ \sum_{i \in I} \max_{j \in S} c_{ij} - \sum_{j \in S} f_j \right\},$$

but this problem may not be much easier to solve than the original problem. Instead, we take any minimal set $K(u) \subseteq J(u)$ that satisfies

$$\max_{j \in K(u)} c_{ij} = \max_{j \in J(u)} c_{ij} \qquad \text{all } i \in I. \tag{3.5.3}$$

Proposition 3.2. *Given a u that satisfies* (3.4.8) *and* $u_i \leq \max_{j \in J(u)} c_{ij}$ *all* $i \in I$, *and a primal solution* $K(u)$ *defined by* (3.5.3), *let* $k_i = |\{ j \in K(u): c_{ij} > u_i \}|$. *If* $k_i \leq 1$ *all* $i \in I$, *then* $K(u)$ *is an optimal set of open facilities.*

Proof

$$z(K(u)) = \sum_{i \in I} \max_{j \in K(u)} c_{ij} - \sum_{j \in K(u)} f_j.$$

If $k_i = 0$

$$\max_{j \in K(u)} c_{ij} = u_i = u_i + \sum_{j \in K(u)} (c_{ij} - u_i)^+$$

and if $k_i = 1$

$$\max_{j \in K(u)} c_{ij} = u_i + \sum_{j \in K(u)} (c_{ij} - u_i)^+.$$

Hence, if $k_i \leq 1$ all $i \in I$,

$$z(K(u)) = \sum_{i \in I} \sum_{j \in K(u)} (c_{ij} - u_i)^+ - \sum_{j \in K(u)} f_j + \sum_{i \in I} u_i$$

$$= \sum_{j \in K(u)} \left(\sum_{i \in I} (c_{ij} - u_i)^+ - f_j \right) + \sum_{i \in I} u_i$$

$$= \sum_{i \in I} u_i = W(u) \qquad \text{by (3.4.11).} \quad \square$$

Example 3.2. In the problem of Example 3.1, with $u = (6 \quad 6 \quad 4 \quad 3)$, we obtain $J(u) = K(u) = \{2, 3, 4\}$ and $(k_1, k_2, k_3, k_4) = (1, 1, 1, 0)$. Hence these are optimal primal and dual solutions of value $\sum_{i \in I} u_i = 19$. $\bigcirc$

While Proposition 3.2 may permit us to recognize an optimal solution, it is limited to those cases in which $\min_u W(u) = Z$ and even then it is still necessary to find an appropriate u and $K(u)$.

3.5.2. Dual Descent

Dual descent is a heuristic that begins with a u satisfying (3.4.8) and then attempts to decrease the u_i one at a time while maintaining (3.4.8) (see Erlenkotter, 1978; Bilde and Krarup, 1977). It is surprisingly effective, but not fail safe, in finding a u that satisfies the conditions of Proposition 3.2. This descent approach, with some embellishments, is the inner loop of Erlenkotter's DUALOC algorithm. The basic descent method proceeds as follows.

Begin with $u_i^0 = \max_{j \in J} c_{ij}$ all $i \in I$. Cycle through the indices $i \in I$ attempting to decrease u_i while satisfying the constraints (3.4.8). If u_i cannot be decreased, then consider u_{i+1}. If u_i can be decreased, then decrease it to $\max \{c_{ij}: c_{ij} < u_i\}$ if this change satisfies (3.4.8). If not, then decrease u_i to the minimum value allowed by (3.4.8). When all of the u_i are blocked from further decreases, the procedure terminates. The reason for decreasing u_i only to the next smaller c_{ij}, rather than to the smallest permissible value, is to keep the k_i of Proposition 3.2 as small as possible.

Example 3.3. Applying dual descent to the problem of Example 3.1 yields the results shown in Table 3.1. For the first four steps, each of the u_i is decreased to the second max in the row. Now u_1 is considered again, but cannot be decreased because the constraints (3.4.8) for $j = 3$ would be violated. Similarly, a decrease of u_2 would violate (3.4.8) for $j = 2$. However, u_3 can be decreased; but it is decreased only to 4 because (3.4.8) becomes active for $j = 4$ when $u_3 = 4$. Finally u_4 cannot be decreased because of (3.4.8) for $j = 2$. This completes the dual descent with $u = (6 \quad 6 \quad 4 \quad 3)$ and $W(u) = \Sigma_{i \in I} u_i = 19$. Now, as noted above, $J(u) = K(u) = \{2, 3, 4\}$ and we also obtain a primal solution of value 19. $\bigcirc$

A possible improvement of dual descent, which is more likely to produce a primal and dual pair for which Proposition 3.2 applies, is obtained by modifying the order in which the u_i are considered as candidates to decrease. In particular, rather than just cycling through the u_i, let $Q_i(u) =$

TABLE 3.1   Dual Descent Results for Example 3.3

Step	u^T				$f_j - \sum_{i \in I} (c_{ij} - u_i)^+$					
0	8	8	6	4	3	2	2	2	3	3
1	6	8	6	4	3	2	0	2	3	3
2	6	6	6	4	3	0	0	2	3	3
3	6	6	5	4	3	0	0	1	3	3
4	6	6	5	3	3	0	0	1	2	2
5	6	6	4	3	2	0	0	0	2	2

$\{j: c_{ij} - u_i \geq 0\}$. Then if u_i is decreased and descent terminates, $k_i \leq |Q_i(u)|$. Hence we choose u_s next if $|Q_s(u)| \leq |Q_i(u)|$ for all $i \in I$.

Suppose dual descent terminates with the dual solution u^* and we determine a primal solution given by $K(u^*)$ such that Proposition 3.2 fails to verify optimality. Then there exists an i such that $k_i > 1$. By increasing u_i to its previous value and reapplying dual descent, it may be possible to improve the dual solution further.

We have sketched the basic ideas of the dual descent procedure. An example in which it does not find an optimal solution is given by

$$f = (2 \quad 2 \quad 2), \qquad C = \begin{bmatrix} 0 & 2 & 2 \\ 2 & 0 & 2 \\ 2 & 2 & 0 \end{bmatrix}. \tag{3.5.4}$$

In this instance, beginning with $u^0 = (2 \quad 2 \quad 2)$, dual descent terminates with $u = (0 \quad 2 \quad 2)$, which is not optimal. Moreover, the usual embellishments do not give an optimal solution either. An optimal u is $(1 \quad 1 \quad 1)$ yielding $W = 3$ and $Z = 2$. Nevertheless, dual descent has performed extremely well on the problems that Erlenkotter and others have considered. Erlenkotter reports that in 45 of 48 problems tested, the heuristic found an optimal solution. To provide the capability of finding an optimal solution and proving optimality, the heuristic is imbedded in a branch-and-bound algorithm. The whole procedure is called DUALOC. Given its simplicity, speed, and availability, DUALOC may be the most efficient way to solve the UFL problem. However, it may perform poorly on hard problems in which the heuristic bound is not as good as the linear programming bound. Thus, one is motivated to develop efficient algorithms for solving the strong linear programming relaxation. This is the subject of the next section.

3.6. ALGORITHMS AND REFORMULATIONS OF THE STRONG LINEAR PROGRAMMING RELAXATION

The strong linear programming relaxation SLPR of the UFL problem is

$$Z_{LP} = \max \sum_{i \in I} \sum_{j \in J} c_{ij} y_{ij} - \sum_{j \in J} f_j x_j \tag{3.6.1}$$

$$\sum_{j \in J} y_{ij} = 1 \qquad \text{all } i \in I \tag{3.6.2}$$

$$y_{ij} - x_j \leq 0 \qquad \text{all } i \in I, j \in J \tag{3.6.3}$$

$$y_{ij} \geq 0, x_j \geq 0 \qquad \text{all } i \in I, j \in J. \tag{3.6.4}$$

The polyhedron of feasible solutions to (3.6.2), (3.6.3) and (3.6.4) has fractional extreme points when $|I| \geq 3$ and $|J| \geq 3$. In the example given by (3.5.4), the unique optimal solution to SLPR is $x_j = 1/2$ for $j = 1, 2, 3$, $y_{ij} = 1/2$ for $i \neq j$, and $y_{ij} = 0$ for $i = j$. The fractional extreme points of this polyhedron are characterized in the next section. However, for reasons that are barely understood, *very frequently, SLPR has an optimal integral solution*. This observation is supported by results in the literature on random problems and some applications. Thus, an efficient method for solving SLPR will also be an efficient method for solving many instances of the UFL problem. Even when SLPR has a fractional optimal solution, its optimal value generally provides a very good upper bound on the optimal value of UFL so that a branch-and-bound algorithm should terminate rapidly.

On the basis of these remarks, one might conclude that the UFL problem can be solved in a straightforward manner using SLPR and a standard mixed integer programming package. However, this is not true because of the large number of constraints (3.6.3). For example, an instance of the UFL problem with $m = n = 100$ has more than 10,000 constraints. Hence, any approach to the UFL problem that uses the SLPR must be capable of solving very large linear programs.

In this section, we consider several approaches for solving very large structured linear programs. We begin the section by briefly mentioning two direct approaches to eliminating the difficulty caused by the large number of constraints (3.6.3). Then we will apply some well-known reformulations and algorithms including Lagrangian duality and subgradient optimization, Dantzig–Wolfe decomposition, Benders decomposition, and subgradient optimization on the primal. Connections among those approaches will be noted. We consider also a reformulation that involves the aggregation and disaggregation of clients so that the matrix C reduces to a useful canonical form. Finally, we mention a projection method.

3.6.1. Direct Approaches

The constraints $y_{ij} \leq x_j$ are generalizations of simple upper bound constraints in which the upper bounds themselves are variables. It is well known how to handle fixed upper bound constraints in the simplex method without expanding the dimension of the basis to include them. Schrage (1975) has generalized this idea to incorporate variable upper bounds and has reported computational results obtained by applying the method to SLPR.

An alternative is to generate the constraints $y_{ij} \leq x_j$ as cuts only when they are violated in an optimal solution to the weak linear programming relaxation. This idea has been tested by Morris (1978). In the example of the last section, an optimal solution to the weak linear programming relaxation is $x_2 = x_3 = x_4 = x_5 = 1/4$ and $y_{13} = y_{22} = y_{34} = y_{45} = 1$. We could then add the four violated variable upper bound constraints and continue to solve the linear program.

The direct approaches are primal methods. Dual methods however, may be superior for two reasons. First, if SLPR is incorporated in a branch-and-bound algorithm, it may not be necessary to solve SLPR to optimality at every node of the enumeration tree, since at some of the nodes, a dual feasible solution may suffice to bound the subproblem. Second, as we have already shown in the last section, one may easily generate an integral primal solution from a given dual solution.

3.6.2. Lagrangian Duality and Subgradient Optimization

The Lagrangian $L(u)$ of (3.4.12) forms the basis of a subgradient algorithm for solving the dual of SLPR. The subgradient algorithm solves the problem $\min_u L(u)$.

The function $L(u)$ given by (3.4.12) is the maximum of a finite number of linear functions. Therefore $L(u)$ is piecewise linear and convex. Subgradient optimization (Held et al., 1974) has proved to be a useful method for minimizing unconstrained piecewise linear convex functions. This approach is a generalization of the gradient method for minimizing smooth, nonlinear convex functions. Since gradients do not exist at nondifferentiable points of $L(u)$, the gradient direction is replaced by a "subgradient direction," which is explained below.

Given u^t, an iteration of the subgradient algorithm generates a new dual solution by the formula

$$u^{t+1} = u^t - \gamma^t \partial L(u^t) \tag{3.6.5}$$

where $\partial L(u^t)$ is a subgradient at u^t and γ^t is the stepsize. If $\partial L(u^t) = 0$, then u^t is an optimal dual solution.

Suppose

$$L(u) = \sum_{i \in I} \sum_{j \in J} c_{ij} y_{ij}^* - \sum_{j \in J} f_j x_j^* + \sum_{i \in I} u_i \left(1 - \sum_{j \in J} y_{ij}^*\right)$$

where $\{x_j^*, y_{ij}^*\}$ are defined by (3.4.13) and (3.4.14). If the $\{y_{ij}^*\}$ are unique then

$$\partial L(u)_i = 1 - \sum_{j \in J} y_{ij}^* \qquad \text{all } i \in I \tag{3.6.6}$$

is the gradient of $L(u)$ at u. However, if the $\{y_{ij}^*\}$ are not unique, then any direction given by (3.6.6) or convex combinations of such directions is a subgradient direction. Although a step in a subgradient direction does not guarantee a decrease in $L(u)$, it can be proved that with an appropriate choice of stepsize, the iterates given by (3.6.5) converge to an optimal solution (Polyak, 1969). Cornuejols et al. (1977b) have reported computational results on solving the Lagrangian dual by subgradient optimization.

Example 3.4. For the problem of Example 3.1, if we start with $u^0 = (8 \quad 8 \quad 6 \quad 4)$, then $L(u^0) = 26$ and $\partial L(u) = (1 \quad 1 \quad 1 \quad 1)$. With a stepsize of $\gamma^0 = 2$, we obtain $u^1 = (6 \quad 6 \quad 4 \quad 2)$ and $L(u^1) = 19$. With $u = u^1$, the solution (3.4.13), (3.4.14) is not unique; however, the optimal solution $x_2 = x_4 = 1$, $x_j = 0$ otherwise, and $y_{12} = y_{22} = y_{34} = y_{42} = 1$, $y_{ij} = 0$ otherwise, yields $\partial L(u^1) = (0 \quad 0 \quad 0 \quad 0)$ and verifies the optimality of u^1. ○

3.6.3. Dantzig–Wolfe Decomposition

For all nonempty $R \subseteq I$, let $\lambda_j^R = 1$ if facility j serves only these clients in the set R and $\lambda_j^R = 0$ otherwise. If $\lambda_j^R = 1$, facility j yields a profit of $\Sigma_{i \in R} c_{ij} - f_j$. Thus the UFL problem can be reformulated as the integer program

$$Z = \max \sum_{j \in J} \sum_{R \subseteq I} \left(\sum_{i \in R} c_{ij} - f_j \right) \lambda_j^R \qquad (3.6.7)$$

$$\sum_{j \in J} \sum_{R \ni i} \lambda_j^R = 1 \qquad \text{all } i \in I \qquad (3.6.8)$$

$$\sum_{R \subseteq I} \lambda_j^R \leq 1 \qquad \text{all } j \in J \qquad (3.6.9)$$

$$\lambda_j^R \in \{0, 1\} \qquad \text{all } R \subseteq I, j \in J . \qquad (3.6.10)$$

The equations (3.6.8) state that each client is served by exactly one facility and the inequalities (3.6.9) state that each facility can serve only one set of clients.

We consider the linear programming relaxation of this integer program obtained by replacing (3.6.10) by

$$\lambda_j^R \geq 0 \qquad \text{all } R \subseteq I, j \in J . \qquad (3.6.11)$$

Proposition 3.3. *Let $\bar{Z}$ be the optimal value of the linear program (3.6.7), (3.6.8), (3.6.9), and (3.6.11). Then $\bar{Z} = Z_{LP}$.*

Proof. Apply Dantzig–Wolfe decomposition to the linear program (3.6.1)–(3.6.4) with master constraints (3.6.2) and subproblem constraints (3.6.3), (3.6.4), and $x_j \leq 1$ all $j \in J$. Substituting the subproblem extreme points into (3.6.2) yields (3.6.8), and (3.6.9) are the convexity constraints for the subproblems. □

Some simplifications can be made in the integer program (3.6.7)–(3.6.10) and its linear programming relaxation. First observe that the constraints (3.6.9) are unnecessary. To see this, suppose $\lambda_j^R = \lambda_j^{R'} = 1$ where $R \neq R'$. If $R \cap R' \neq \emptyset$, then (3.6.8) will be violated. If $R \cap R' = \emptyset$, then since $f_j \geq 0$, we have

$$\sum_{i \in R \cup R'} c_{ij} - f_j \geq \sum_{i \in R} c_{ij} - f_j + \sum_{i \in R'} c_{ij} - f_j \,.$$

Hence the alternate solution with $\lambda_j^{R \cup R'} = 1$ and $\lambda_j^R = \lambda_j^{R'} = 0$ is at least as good.

A further simplification is obtained by noting that if $\sum_{i \in R} c_{ij} - f_j > \sum_{i \in R} c_{ik} - f_k$, then $\lambda_k^R = 0$ in every optimal solution. Hence for each R, we need only one variable, say λ_R, whose profit is given by

$$d_R = \max_{j \in J} \left(\sum_{i \in R} c_{ij} - f_j \right).$$

Thus we can restate the integer program as

$$Z = \max \sum_{R \subseteq I} d_R \lambda_R$$

$$\sum_{R \ni i} \lambda_R = 1 \qquad \text{all } i \in I \qquad\qquad (3.6.12)$$

$$\lambda_R \in \{0, 1\} \qquad \text{all } R \subseteq I \,.$$

This formulation has 2^{m-1} variables and m constraints. Since n does not enter into the size of this formulation, for fixed m, it can be solved in polynomial-time.

The linear program obtained from (3.6.12) by replacing the integrality requirement by $\lambda_R \geq 0$ all $R \subseteq I$, can be solved by column generation. Suppose we begin with m columns, say those for $R = \{i\}$, $i = 1, \ldots, m$. Then the primal solution is $\lambda_R^0 = 1$ for $R = \{i\}$, $i = 1, \ldots, m$, and the dual solution is $u_i^0 = \max_{j \in J} (c_{ij} - f_j)$ all $i \in I$.

We now need to see if any of the nonbasic columns have a positive price. This can be done at iteration p by solving, for each $j \in J$, the subproblem

$$t_j^p = \max \sum_{i \in I} (c_{ij} - u_i^p) y_{ij} - f_j x_j \,,$$

subject to (3.1.3) and (3.1.4), since $\sum_{i \in R} (c_{ij} - u_i^p) - f_j$ is the price of variable λ_j^R. The solution of the subproblem is $t_j^p = (\sum_{i \in I} (c_{ij} - u_i^p)^+ - f_j)^+$. If $t_j^p = 0$ all $j \in J$ then the current solution is optimal. For each k such that $t_k^p > 0$, let R_k be any set satisfying $\{i : c_{ik} - u_i^p > 0\} \subseteq R_k \subseteq \{i : c_{ik} - u_i^p \geq 0\}$. We now add to the linear program variables λ_{R_k} for all k such that $t_k^p > 0$.

Garfinkel et al. (1974) have obtained computational experience with this type of algorithm.

An important feature of this approach is that both lower and upper bounds on Z_{LP} are obtained at each iteration. By primal feasibility, $Z_{LP} \geq \sum_{i \in I} u_i^p$; and from (3.4.12) we see that $Z_{LP} \leq \sum_{j \in J} t_j^p + \sum_{i \in I} u_i^p = W(u^p)$. Moreover, as well as obviously being a primal method, it also can be viewed as a dual method and compared with the method that uses Lagrangian duality and subgradient optimization. Here the u_i at each iteration are determined by solving a linear program, while in the previous method the dual variables are determined by moving in the direction of a subgradient of the function $L(u)$.

Example 3.5. Considering again the problem of Example 3.1. Suppose we start with an initial basis consisting of the four unit columns $R_i = \{i\}$, $i = 1, \ldots, 4$ with objective coefficients $d_{R_1} = d_{R_2} = 6$, $d_{R_3} = 4$, and $d_{R_4} = 1$. This yields the dual solution $u^0 = (6 \quad 6 \quad 4 \quad 1)$. Solving the subproblems, we obtain $t^0 = (0 \quad 2 \quad 0 \quad 1 \quad 0 \quad 0)$ and thus $17 \leq Z_{LP} \leq 20$. We generate two new columns $R_5 = \{1 \quad 2 \quad 4\}$ and $R_6 = \{3 \quad 4\}$ with objective coefficients $d_5 = 15$ and $d_6 = 6$. The next master linear program yields the primal solution $\lambda^1_{R_5} = \lambda^1_{R_3} = 1$, $\lambda^1_{R_i} = 0$ otherwise and the dual solution $u^1 = (6 \quad 6 \quad 4 \quad 3)$. Now $t^1_j = 0$ all $j \in J$ so that the primal has been solved. In terms of the original variables, we have $x_2 = x_4 = 1$, $x_j = 0$ otherwise. ○

3.6.4. Primal Subgradient Algorithm

For a given x, the profit from the ith client is

$$V_i(x) = \max \sum_{j \in J} c_{ij} y_{ij}$$

$$\sum_{j \in J} y_{ij} = 1$$

$$y_{ij} \leq x_j \qquad \text{all } j \in J \tag{3.6.13}$$

$$y_{ij} \geq 0 \qquad \text{all } j \in J.$$

It is known from the theory of parametric linear programming that the function $V_i(x)$ is piecewise linear and concave. Hence we can formulate SLPR as the maximization of a piecewise linear concave function subject to simple constraints. In particular,

$$Z_{LP} = \max \sum_{i \in I} V_i(x) - \sum_{j \in J} f_j x_j$$

$$0 \leq x_j \leq 1 \qquad \text{all } j \in J. \tag{3.6.14}$$

Technically, (3.6.14) also requires the constraint $\sum_{j \in J} x_j \geq 1$, but this constraint can be omitted by adding a suitably large constant to any row of the profit matrix C. In the remainder of this chapter, we assume that $\sum_{j \in J} x_j \geq 1$ is satisfied by every optimal solution to (3.6.14).

The formulation given by (3.6.14) can be solved by subgradient optimization. Let $\partial Z(x)_j$ be the jth component of a subgradient of the objective function at x. We have $\partial Z(x)_j = \Sigma_{i \in I} \partial V_i(x)_j - f_j$ where $\partial V_i(x)_j$ is the jth component of a subgradient of $V_i(x)$.

To obtain a closed form expression for $\partial V_i(x)_j$, we consider the linear program (3.6.13), which can be solved by a greedy method. In particular, suppose $c_{ij_1} \geq c_{ij_2} \geq \ldots \geq c_{ij_n}$ and define p_i by $\Sigma_{k=1}^{p_i-1} x_{j_k} < 1 \leq \Sigma_{k=1}^{p_i} x_{j_k}$. Then an optimal solution to (3.6.13) is given by $y_{ij_k} = x_{j_k}$ for $k = 1, \ldots, p_i - 1$, $y_{ij_{p_i}} = 1 - \Sigma_{k=1}^{p_i-1} x_{j_k}$, and $y_{ij_k} = 0$ otherwise. Thus we can make $\partial V_i(x)_j = (c_{ij} - c_{ij_{p_i}})^+$ and

$$\partial Z(x)_j = \sum_{i \in I} (c_{ij} - c_{ij_{p_i}})^+ - f_j \qquad \text{all } j \in J. \qquad (3.6.15)$$

Given x^t, an iteration of the subgradient algorithm generates a new point $x^{t+1} = x^t + \gamma^t \partial Z(x^t)$. If x^{t+1} does not lie in the cube $0 \leq x_j \leq 1$, all $j \in J$, and therefore violates some of the constraints of (3.6.14), we modify it by simply projecting it on the cube, that is, we replace x_j^{t+1} by 0 if $x_j^{t+1} < 0$ and by 1 if $x_j^{t+1} > 1$.

Cornuejols and Thizy (1982b) report some computational experience in solving (3.6.14) by a subgradient algorithm.

Example 3.6. The results of attempting to solve (3.6.14) by subgradient optimization for our example are summarized in Table 3.2. An optimal solution to SLPR is obtained at iteration 3, but the expression (3.6.15) for the subgradient is not adequate to verify optimality. ○

3.6.5. Benders Decomposition

We can state (3.6.14) as

$$Z_{LP} = \max \sum_{i \in I} V_i - \sum_{j \in J} f_j x_j$$

$$V_i \leq V_i(x) \qquad \text{all } i \in I$$

$$\text{and all feasible } x \qquad (3.6.16)$$

$$0 \leq x_j \leq 1 \qquad \text{all } j \in J.$$

Now we observe that

TABLE 3.2 Subgradient Iterations for Example 3.6

Iteration	x						V(x)				$Z_{LP}(x)$	$\partial Z(x)$						Step-size
0	0	1	1	1	1	0	8	8	6	4	17	−3	−2	−2	−2	−3	−3	1/4
1	0	1/2	1/2	1/2	1/4	0	7	7	9/2	3	71/4	−1	1	0	1	−1	−1	1/4
2	0	3/4	1/2	3/4	0	0	7	15/2	21/4	11/4	37/2	−1	1	0	1	−1	−1	1/4
3	0	1	1/2	1	0	0	7	8	6	3	19	−3	−2	0	−2	−2	−2	

$$V_i(x) = \min u_i + \sum_{j \in J} x_j w_{ij}$$

$$u_i + w_{ij} \geq c_{ij} \qquad \text{all } j \in J \qquad (3.6.17)$$

$$w_{ij} \geq 0$$

since (3.6.17) is the dual of (3.6.13). We have $w_{ij} = (c_{ij} - u_i)^+$ so that

$$V_i(x) = \min \left[u_i + \sum_{j \in J} x_j (c_{ij} - u_i)^+ \right] \qquad (3.6.18)$$

The right-hand side of (3.6.18) is a piecewise linear function of u_i and the function changes slope when $u_i = c_{ij}$ for some j. Hence the minimum is attained when $u_i = c_{ik}$ for some $k \in J$. Hence

$$V_i(x) = \min_{k \in J} \left[c_{ik} + \sum_{j \in J} x_j (c_{ij} - c_{ik})^+ \right]$$

and (3.6.16) can be stated as the linear program

$$Z_{LP} = \max \sum_{i \in I} V_i - \sum_{j \in J} f_j x_j$$

$$V_i - \sum_{j \in J} x_j (c_{ij} - c_{ik})^+ \leq c_{ik} \qquad \text{all } i \in I, k \in J \qquad (3.6.19)$$

$$0 \leq x_j \leq 1 .$$

This is precisely the linear program that arises when applying Benders decomposition to SLPR. Although we have *mn* constraints of the form (3.6.19), we can think of these as cutting planes and generate them only as they are needed.

In particular, suppose we have only a proper subset of the constraints (3.6.19). We solve the relaxed linear program and determine an optimal solution (x^q, V^q). Now we use x^q in (3.6.13) to determine $V_i(x^q)$ all $i \in I$. If

$$V_i(x^q) \leq V_i^q \qquad \text{all } i \in I , \qquad (3.6.20)$$

then (x^q, V^q) satisfies all of the constraints (3.6.19) and x^q is an optimal solution. If not, each i for which (3.6.20) is violated specifies a violated constraint of the form (3.6.19). These are added to the linear program and we continue.

Example 3.7. In the problem of Example 3.1, we begin with the constraints (3.6.19) determined by the second maximum in each row, that is $V_1 - 2x_3 \leq 6$, $V_2 - 2x_2 \leq 6$, $V_3 - x_4 \leq 5$, and $V_4 \leq 4$. A solution to the linear program is

$V^1 = (6 \quad 8 \quad 5 \quad 4)$ and $x^1 = (0 \quad 1 \quad 0 \quad 0 \quad 0 \quad 0)$. Then by solving (3.6.13) we obtain $V(x^1) = (6 \quad 8 \quad 0 \quad 3)$ and generate the constraints

$$V_3 - 5x_1 - 3x_3 - 6x_4 - 3x_5 \leq 0$$
$$V_4 \qquad\qquad\quad - x_5 - x_6 \leq 3 .$$

Now we obtain the solution $V^2 = (6 \quad 8 \quad 6 \quad 3)$ and $x^2 = (0 \quad 1 \quad 0 \quad 1 \quad 0 \quad 0)$. Since $V(x^2) = (6 \quad 8 \quad 6 \quad 3)$, all of the constraints of (3.6.19) are satisfied and x^2 is an optimal solution.   ○

Magnanti and Wong (1981) have used a variation of this approach and have developed stronger inequalities in an attempt to accelerate the convergence of the algorithm.

3.6.6.   Canonical Reduction

We now present a formulation that involves the disaggregation and aggregation of clients (see Cornuejols, Nemhauser, and Wolsey, 1980). The *aggregation* of two clients i_1 and i_2 means to replace clients i_1 and i_2 by a single client i such that

$$c_{ij} = c_{i_1 j} + c_{i_2 j} \qquad \text{all } j \in J . \tag{3.6.21}$$

The *disaggregation* of clients i into two clients i_1 and i_2 means to replace i by two clients i_1 and i_2 such that (3.6.21) holds. While aggregation is uniquely defined, disaggregation is not.

In general, aggregation yields an underestimation of profit and disaggregation overestimates. This is true, because if (3.6.21) is satisfied the greedy solution to the linear program (3.6.13) implies $V_i(x) \leq V_{i_1}(x) + V_{i_2}(x)$ for all x with $0 \leq x_j \leq 1$. We say that aggregation or disaggregation is *valid* when

$$V_i(x) = V_{i_1}(x) + V_{i_2}(x) \tag{3.6.22}$$

for all x with $0 \leq x_j \leq 1$.

For $k \in I$, let $s_k = (s_k(1), s_k(2), \ldots, s_k(n))$ be any permutation of $\{1, 2, \ldots, n\}$ such that $c_{ks_k(1)} \geq c_{ks_k(2)} \geq \ldots \geq c_{ks_k(n)}$.

Proposition 3.4.   *For $i_1, i_2 \in I$, if there exist s_{i_1} and s_{i_2} such that $s_{i_1(j)} = s_{i_2(j)}$, $j = 1, \ldots, n$, then (3.6.21) is a valid aggregation of rows i_1 and i_2.*

Proof.   If $s_{i_1(j)} = s_{i_2(j)}$ for all j, and rows i_1 and i_2 are aggregated by (3.6.21), then $s_{i(j)} = s_{i_1(j)} = s_{i_2(j)}$, $j = 1, \ldots, n$. Thus the greedy solution to (3.6.13) implies that (3.6.22) holds.   □

As a consequence, we obtain the following corollary.

Corollary 3.3. *If row $i \in I$ is disaggregated into rows i_1 and i_2 and (3.6.21) is satisfied and there exist s_i, s_{i_1}, and s_{i_2} such that $s_{i(j)} = s_{i_1(j)} = s_{i_2(j)}$ for all j, then the disaggregation is valid.*

The following proposition shows how any row with at least two unequal elements can be disaggregated.

Proposition 3.5. *Suppose $c_{is_i(1)} \geq \cdots \geq c_{is_i(p-1)} > c_{is_i(p)} \geq \cdots \geq c_{is_i(n)}$. Then for $j = 1, \ldots, p - 1$,*

$$c_{i_1 s_{i_1}(j)} = c_{is_i(p)} \quad \text{and} \quad c_{i_2 s_{i_2}(j)} = c_{is_i(j)} - c_{is_i(p)}$$

and for $j = p, \ldots, n$,

$$c_{i_1 s_{i_1}(j)} = c_{is_i(j)} \quad \text{and} \quad c_{i_2 s_{i_2}(j)} = 0$$

is a valid disaggregation of row i.

Proof.   The condition of Corollary 3.3 holds. $\square$

We can apply Proposition 3.5 recursively to disaggregate a row i into at most n rows, $i_1, \ldots, i_n$ with the following properties:

   i. $c_{i_t j} \in \{0, r_{i_t}\}$ for $t = 1, \ldots, n$;
   ii. $r_{i_t} > 0$ for $t > 1$;
   iii. $c_{i_1 j} = r_{i_1}$ for $j = 1, \ldots, n$;
   iv. $c_{i_t j} = 0$ implies $c_{i_{t+1} j} = 0$ for $t = 2, \ldots, n - 1$.

To do this, suppose $c_{is_i(q)} = \cdots = c_{is_i(n)}$ for some $q \leq n$. Apply Proposition 3.5 with $p = q$. This yields

$$c_{i_1 s_{i_1}(j)} = \quad c_{is_i(q)}, \qquad\qquad j = 1, \ldots, n$$

$$c_{i_2 s_{i_2}(j)} = \begin{cases} c_{is_i(j)} - c_{is_i(q)}, & j = 1, \ldots, q - 1 \\ 0, & j = q, \ldots, n. \end{cases}$$

Row i_1 is in the desired form and if $c_{is_i(j)} = c_{is_i(j+1)}$, $j = 1, \ldots, q - 2$, so is row i_2. Otherwise let l be the largest value of j for which $c_{is_i(l-1)} > c_{is_i(l)}$.

Now apply Proposition 3.5 with $p = l$ to disaggregate row i_2. Here we refer to the two new rows as i_2 and i_3. Thus

$$c_{i_2 s_{i_2}(j)} = \begin{cases} c_{is_i(l)} - c_{is_i(q)}, & j = 1, \dots, q-1 \\ 0, & j = q, \dots, n \end{cases}$$

$$c_{i_3 s_{i_3}(j)} = \begin{cases} c_{is_i(j)} - c_{is_i(l)}, & j = 1, \dots, l-1 \\ 0, & j = l, \dots, n. \end{cases}$$

Row i_2 is now in the desired form and we now disaggregate row i_3 if necessary. Since at each step, the row to be disaggregated has at least one more zero than the previous row, the procedure takes at most $n - 1$ steps and yields at most n rows each having the desired property.

Example 3.8. Consider

$$(c_{i1} \quad c_{i2} \quad c_{i3} \quad c_{i4}) = (4 \quad 2 \quad 2 \quad -1).$$

We obtain

$$(c_{i_1 1} \quad c_{c_{i_1} 2} \quad c_{i_1 3} \quad c_{i_1 4}) = (-1 \quad -1 \quad -1 \quad -1)$$

and

$$(c_{i_2 1} \quad c_{i_2 2} \quad c_{i_2 3} \quad c_{i_2 4}) = (5 \quad 3 \quad 3 \quad 0).$$

Disaggregating row i_2 yields $(3 \quad 3 \quad 3 \quad 0)$ and $(2 \quad 0 \quad 0 \quad 0)$. Thus a client represented by the row $(4 \quad 2 \quad 2 \quad -1)$ can be replaced by three equivalent clients, $(-1 \quad -1 \quad -1 \quad -1)$, $(3 \quad 3 \quad 3 \quad 0)$, and $(2 \quad 0 \quad 0 \quad 0)$. ○

Suppose each of the clients $i \in I$ is disaggregated in this way. Now we may obtain pairs of clients say i_t and k_l such that for $j \in J$, $c_{i,j} \neq 0$ if and only if $c_{k_l j} \neq 0$. By Proposition 3.4, these two clients can be aggregated into a single client with profit $c_{i,j} + c_{k_l j}$ for $j \in T$ and 0 profit for $j \notin T$. Finally, a client whose profit is constant for all $j \in J$ can be eliminated from the problem since this client produces the same profit for all feasible x.

To summarize this procedure, we can transform the matrix C into an equivalent *canonical* matrix R containing at most $\min(m(n-1), 2^n - 2)$ rows. Each row of R represents a set $T \subset J$, $T \neq \emptyset$, and there is a profit r_T for all $j \in T$ and a profit of zero for $j \notin T$.

For the problem of Example 3.1,

$$R = \begin{bmatrix} 6 & 6 & 6 & 6 & 0 & 6 \\ 0 & 0 & 2 & 0 & 0 & 0 \\ 6 & 6 & 6 & 0 & 6 & 6 \\ 0 & 2 & 0 & 0 & 0 & 0 \\ 3 & 0 & 3 & 3 & 3 & 0 \\ 2 & 0 & 0 & 2 & 0 & 0 \\ 0 & 0 & 0 & 1 & 0 & 0 \\ 2 & 2 & 0 & 2 & 2 & 2 \\ 0 & 1 & 0 & 0 & 1 & 1 \\ 0 & 0 & 0 & 0 & 1 & 1 \end{bmatrix} \begin{array}{l} \left.\rule{0pt}{2.2ex}\right\} client\ 1 \\ \left.\rule{0pt}{2.2ex}\right\} client\ 2 \\ \left.\rule{0pt}{3.3ex}\right\} client\ 3 \\ \left.\rule{0pt}{3.3ex}\right\} client\ 4 \end{array}$$

We will now use this transformation to obtain a reformulation of SLPR. Given x, $0 \le x_j \le 1$ all $j \in J$, the profit from the client represented by the set T is

$$V_T(x) = r_T \left[\min \left(\sum_{j \in T} x_j, 1 \right) \right] = r_T - r_T \left(1 - \sum_{j \in T} x_j \right)^+ .$$

If $\sum_{j \in T} x_j \ge 1$, we say that the client represented by the set T is fully served. The quantity $\pi_T = (1 - \sum_{j \in T} x_j)^+$ is the fraction of client T not served. Thus

$$V_T(x) = r_T - \min (r_T \pi_T)$$

$$\pi_T \ge 1 - \sum_{j \in T} x_j , \qquad \pi_T \ge 0 .$$

Let $\mathscr{T}$ be the collection of subsets of J that are represented in the profit matrix R. Then

$$Z_{LP} = \sum_{T \in \mathscr{T}} r_T - \min \left(\sum_{T \in \mathscr{T}} r_T \pi_T + \sum_{j \in J} f_j x_j \right)$$

$$\pi_T + \sum_{j \in T} x_j \ge 1 \qquad \text{all } T \in \mathscr{T} \tag{3.6.23}$$

$$\pi_T \ge 0 , \quad x_j \ge 0 \qquad \text{all } T \in \mathscr{T} , \quad \text{all } j \in J .$$

The dual of (3.6.23) is

$$Z_{LP}^* = -\max \sum_{T \in \mathscr{T}} u_T$$

$$\sum_{T \ni j} u_T \le f_j \qquad \text{all } j \in J \tag{3.6.24}$$

$$0 \le u_T \le r_T \qquad \text{all } T \in \mathscr{T} .$$

The linear program (3.6.24) has at most $m(n-1)$ variables and n constraints plus upper bounds on the variables. It is the most compact linear programming formulation we know and has the structure of the linear programming relaxation of a set packing problem. In our example, see the matrix R given above, there are only 10 variables and 6 constraints other than upper bounds. In comparison, the original linear programming formulation of SLPR, (3.6.1)–(3.6.4), has 32 variables and 28 constraints. In experimenting with some k-median problems, Cornuejols et al. (1980) have observed that when the simplex method (with upper bounds treated implicitly) is applied to the various linear programming formulations, the formulation (3.6.24) was by far the best in terms of simplex pivots and running time. Simao and Thizy (1986) have tested an efficient implementation of the simplex algorithm for this formulation. In addition, the formulation (3.6.24) provides a nice interpretation for the dual descent heuristic given in Section 3.5. We leave this for the reader to verify.

3.6.7. A Projection Method

In practice, dual methods have outperformed primal methods for UFL. We have already mentioned three such dual approaches: dual descent applied to (3.4.10), subgradient optimization applied to the Lagrangian relaxation (3.4.12) and a simplex algorithm applied to (3.6.24).

Another possibility is to solve (3.4.10) using techniques of unconstrained nonlinear nondifferentiable optimization. Rewrite (3.4.10) as

$$W(u) = \sum_{i \in I} u_i + \sum_{j=1}^{n} S_j^+(u)$$

where $S_j(u) = \sum_{i=1}^{m} (c_{ij} - u_i)^+ - f_j$. The piecewise linear convex function $W(u)$ is nondifferentiable at all points u such that either

i. $S_j(u) = 0$ for some $j \in J$ or
ii. $c_{ij} = u_i$ for some $i \in I$ with $S_j(u) \geq 0$.

Let $J_0(u) = \{j \in J : S_j(u) = 0\}$ and $I_0(u) = \{i \in I : c_{ij} = u_i$ for some $i \in I$ with $S_j(u) \geq 0\}$. Define a "base gradient" of W as follows

$$g(u) = e + \sum_{j:\, S_j(u) > 0} \tilde{\nabla} S_j(u)$$

where

$$e = \begin{pmatrix} 1 \\ \cdot \\ \cdot \\ \cdot \\ 1 \end{pmatrix} \quad \text{and} \quad \tilde{\nabla} S_j(u) = \begin{pmatrix} s_1^j \\ \cdot \\ \cdot \\ \cdot \\ s_m^j \end{pmatrix}$$

$$s_i^j = \begin{cases} -1, & \text{if } c_{ij} \geq u_i \\ 0, & \text{otherwise} . \end{cases}$$

Note that $g(u)$ is a uniquely defined subgradient of W. Conn and Cornuejols (1987) show that u^* minimizes W if and only if there exist scalars λ_j^* and μ_i^* such that

$$g(u^*) = \sum_{j \in J_0(u^*)} \lambda_j^* \tilde{\nabla} S_j(u^*) - \sum_{i \in I_0(u^*)} \mu_i^* e_i$$

where $-1 \leq \lambda_j^* \leq 0$ and

$$0 \leq \mu_i^* \leq |\{ j \in J : c_{ij} = u_i \text{ and } S_j(u^*) > 0| - \sum_{j \in J_0(u^*): c_{ij} = u_i} \lambda_j^*.$$

In the above optimality conditions, e_i denotes the ith unit vector. The result is constructive in the sense that, when these conditions are not satisfied, it is relatively straightforward to obtain a descent direction for W. More specifically, the procedure works as follows. First try to obtain a descent direction by projecting $-g(u)$ orthogonally into the space defined by $S_j(u) = 0$ for $j \in J_0(u)$ and u_i unchanged for $i \in I_0(u)$. A descent direction is obtained when such a projection is nonzero. When the projection is zero, it follows that $g(u)$ can be expressed as a linear combination of the vectors $\tilde{\nabla} S_j(u)$ for $j \in J_0(u)$ and e_i for $i \in I_0(u)$. Thus, the effect of dropping a *single* activity is easily determined. This either finds a descent direction or establishes the required optimality conditions.

Example 3.9. Let us solve the problem of Example 3.1 by the projection method, starting from u^0 defined by $u_i^0 = \max_{j \in J} c_{ij}$. So $u^0 = \begin{pmatrix} 8 \\ 8 \\ 6 \\ 4 \end{pmatrix}$. As $S_j(u^0) < 0$ for all $j \in J$, we have $g(u^0) = \begin{pmatrix} 1 \\ 1 \\ 1 \\ 1 \end{pmatrix}$. The line search along this direction yields $u^1 = \begin{pmatrix} 6 \\ 6 \\ 4 \\ 2 \end{pmatrix}$. Now $S_1(u^1) = -2$, $S_2(u^1) = 1$, $S_3(u^1) = S_4(u^1) = 0$, and $S_5(u^1) = S_6(u^1) = -1$. So $W(u^1) = 19$, $J_0(u^1) = \{3, 4\}$, and $I_0(u^1) = \{1, 2, 4\}$. Note that $g(u^1) = \begin{pmatrix} 0 \\ 0 \\ 1 \\ 0 \end{pmatrix} = -\tilde{\nabla} S_4(u^1) - e_1 - e_4$ satisfies the optimality conditions. Therefore u^1 is optimum. By complementary slackness, $S_j(u^*) < 0$ implies $x_j^* = 0$ and $S_j(u^*) > 0$ implies $x_j^* = 1$. So, here, $x_1 = x_5 = x_6 = 0$ and $x_2 = 1$. Furthermore, the multiplier of $\tilde{\nabla} S_j(u^*)$ for $j \in J_0(u^*)$ in the optimality conditions is in fact the optimal value of x_j^*, up to the sign. Therefore, here $x_3 = 0$ and $x_4 = 1$ as $\tilde{\nabla} S_3(u^1)$ has a coefficient of 0 and $\tilde{\nabla} S_4(u^1)$ has a coefficient of -1 in the expression of $g(u^1)$. ○

Conn and Cornuejols also show how the projection method can be extended when the primal formulation includes side constraints. For example, SLPR can be strengthened by the addition of cutting planes.

3.6.8. Summary

Two types of decompositions have been considered in this section. Lagrangian duality and Dantzig–Wolfe decomposition assign prices to the clients and for a fixed set of prices, the problem decomposes into n independent, simple problems for the facilities. The two methods differ only in their schemes for adjusting prices. Benders decomposition and the formulation of Section 3.6.4 choose a facilities vector x and for a given x, the problem decomposes into independent, simple problems for the clients. The two methods differ only in their schemes for adjusting x.

Any method for solving the UFL problem that uses exact or approximate solutions of SLPR as a subroutine, must be imbedded into a branch-and-bound algorithm. One approach is to solve SLPR by a special purpose algorithm. Another approach is to use a general purpose mixed-integer programming (MIP) system.

Among the special purpose algorithms, DUALOC, which uses approximate dual solutions to SLPR, is a strong candidate. It is generally available as a FORTRAN program, is very fast on most problems, and is not limited by size unless quite a lot of enumeration is necessary.

Difficult instances of the UFL problem may require the capability of finding optimal solutions of SLPR in order to curtail the enumerative phase of the algorithm. In this case, solving the Lagrangian dual by subgradient optimization provides an easily programmable and a relatively fast algorithm. Another method worth considering is the linear programming formulation (3.6.24), which has a significant advantage in size over the other linear programming formulations and can be solved directly by the simplex method for instances that are not too large. Schrage's (1975) adaptation of the simplex method to handle generalized upper bounds is still another possibility.

If we choose to use a general purpose MIP system, the original formulation (3.1.1)–(3.1.4), the Benders formulation with $x_j \in \{0, 1\}$ for all $j \in J$, and the canonical formulation (3.6.23) with $x_j \in \{0, 1\}$ are candidates. However, each of these formulations is limited by problem size since they involve $O(mn)$ constraints and/or variables. The formulation (3.6.24), which is the dual of (3.6.23) is the most compact linear programming formulation, but to use it in a conventional MIP system would require a modification that permits branching on fractional dual variables.

The main advantage of using a general MIP system is that additional constraints create no difficulties, as they may for special purpose codes. There is work in progress in MIP systems that will be capable of working with the weak linear programming relaxation and will generate violated variable upper bound constraints as needed (see Martin and Schrage, 1985; Van Roy and Wolsey, 1986.) Codes of this type should make it feasible to solve medium-sized instances of the UFL problem as general mixed integer programs.

3.7. POLYHEDRAL RESULTS

In this section, we study the polytope of feasible solutions to the SLPR
constraints

$$
\begin{cases}
\displaystyle\sum_{j=1}^{n} y_{ij} = 1 & i = 1, \ldots, m \\[2mm]
0 \le y_{ij} \le x_j \le 1, & i = 1, \ldots, m \quad \text{and} \quad j = 1, \ldots, n,
\end{cases}
\tag{3.7.1}
$$

and the polytope defined by the convex hull of integral solutions to (3.7.1).

3.7.1. The SLPR Polytope

Let $Q_{m,n}$ be the polytope of feasible solutions to (3.7.1). When $m \le 2$ or
$n \le 2$, it has been shown by Mukendi (1975), Krarup and Pruzan (1983),
and Cho, Johnson, Padberg, and Rao (1983a) that all the extreme points of
(3.7.1) are integral. In fact, the constraint matrix is totally unimodular in
that case. However, for values as small as $m = n = 3$, $Q_{m,n}$ has fractional
extreme points. For example, when $C = \begin{bmatrix} 0 & 1 & 1 \\ 1 & 0 & 1 \\ 1 & 1 & 0 \end{bmatrix}$ and $f_j = 1$ for $j = 1, 2, 3$, we
have remarked previously that $x_j = 1/2$ for $j = 1, 2, 3$ and $y_{ij} = 1/2$ for $i \ne j$,
$y_{ij} = 0$ for $i = j$ is the unique optimal solution.

The fractional extreme points of $Q_{m,n}$ are completely characterized by the
next theorem. For a given fractional solution (x, y) of (3.7.1) let $J_1 = \{ j \in J : 0 < x_j < 1 \}$ and $I_1 = \{ i \in I : y_{ij} = 0$ or x_j for all j and y_{ij} is fractional for at
least one $j \}$. Let $a_{ij} = 1$ if $y_{ij} > 0$, and 0 otherwise, and denote by A the
$|I_1| \times |J_1|$ matrix whose elements are a_{ij} for $i \in I_1$, $j \in J_1$.

Theorem 3.3 (Cornuejols et al., 1977a). *A fractional solution (x, y) of
(3.7.1) is an extreme point of $Q_{m,n}$ if and only if*

   i. $x_j = \max_{i \in I} y_{ij}$ *for all $j \in J_1$*
   ii. *for each $i \in I$, there is at most one $j \in J$ with $0 < y_{ij} < x_j$*
   iii. *the rank of A equals $|J_1|$.*

The three conditions of this theorem are easily verified for the example
given above.

Since $Q_{m,n}$ has many fractional extreme points, the type of objective
function that is optimized over this polyhedron must play an important role
in the attainment of integral optimal solutions. Frequently, $C = \{c_{ij}\}$ is
defined over a network with the property that the further node v_i is from
node v_j in the network the smaller is c_{ij}. (For example, if $v_{i'}$ is on the
shortest path from v_i to v_j in the network then $c_{ij} \le c_{i'j}$.) This property is

important in showing that SLPR always has an integral optimal solution for tree networks (see Section 3.8). A similar result is known for the p-median problem defined on a path (Wong, Ward, Oudjit, and Lemke, 1984). However, for more general networks, appropriate conditions on C for attaining an integral optimal solution are not known.

In some cases SLPR often has fractional optimal solutions. An example is the linear programming relaxation of the set covering problem. The set covering problem is the special case of the UFL problem where $C = \{c_{ij}\}$ is a general 0, 1 matrix and $f_j = 1$ all $j \in J$. (The set covering problem is treated extensively in Chapter 6.)

Some valid inequalities for the UFL problem that are violated by fractional extreme points of $Q_{m,n}$ are given in the following theorem.

Theorem 3.4 (Cho, Padberg, and Rao, 1983b). *Let B be a $k \times k$ nonsingular 0, 1 matrix such that $B^{-1}e \geq 0$, where e is a column vector of ones. Index the rows and columns of B by $I_k \subseteq I$ and $J_k \subseteq J$ where $|I_k| = |J_k| = k$. Then*

$$\sum_{i \in I_k} \sum_{j \in J_k} b_{ij} y_{ij} - \sum_{j \in J_k} x_j \leq |k - e^T B^{-1} e|$$

is a valid inequality for the UFL problem. It cuts off at least one fractional extreme point of $Q_{m,n}$ if $e^T B^{-1} e$ is not integral.

For example, if $B = \begin{bmatrix} 0 & 1 & 1 \\ 1 & 0 & 1 \\ 1 & 1 & 0 \end{bmatrix}$ we generate the constraint $y_{12} + y_{13} + y_{21} + y_{23} + y_{31} + y_{32} - x_1 - x_2 - x_3 \leq 1$, which cuts off the fractional extreme point given in the beginning of this section.

Moreover, it is easy to show that the family of valid inequalities defined in Theorem 3.4 cuts off all the fractional extreme points of $Q_{m,n}$. However, in general, new fractional extreme points arise.

3.7.2. The UFL Polytope

Let $P_{m,n}$ be the polytope defined as the convex hull of the integer solutions to the system (3.7.1). Thus the extreme points of $P_{m,n}$ are the feasible solutions to the UFL problem. Here we consider the valid inequalities for $P_{m,n}$ that define facets. To explain these results, we need some definitions from linear algebra and polyhedral theory.

A set of $k + 1$ points $w^0, w^1, \ldots, w^k$ is *affinely independent* if the k vectors $w^1 - w^0, w^2 - w^0, \ldots, w^k - w^0$ are linearly independent. A polytope has *dimension k* if it contains $k + 1$ affinely independent points but not more. An *affine space* is the intersection of hyperplanes. The smallest affine space which contains a polytope P is called its *affine hull*. The polytope $P_{m,n}$ has dimension $mn + n - m$ and affine hull given by $\{(x, y) \in \mathcal{R}^n \times \mathcal{R}^{mn} : \sum_{j=1}^n y_{ij} = 1$ for $i = 1, \ldots, m\}$.

A *face* of a polytope P is a set $F = P \cap \{x: ax = b\}$ where $ax \le b$ is satisfied by every $x \in P$ and $ax < b$ for at least one $x \in P$. The inequality $ax \le b$ is said to *define* the face F. Any face of a polytope is itself a polytope. When its dimension is one less than that of the polytope P, the face F is called a *facet*. To describe the polytope P by a linear system, it suffices to have a description of its affine hull and one defining inequality for each facet of P.

If such a description of $P_{m,n}$ were known then, in principle, the UFL problem could be solved as a linear program. Cho et al. (1983a) give a complete description of $P_{m,n}$ when $n \le 3$ or $m \le 3$. However, when $n \ge 4$ and $m \ge 4$, a complete linear system defining $p_{m,n}$ is not known explicitly. Even if one were, only relevant portions of it need be used to solve an instance of the UFL problem. That is, some of the facets of $P_{m,n}$ can be used as cutting planes in the spirit of Padberg and Hong's (1980) and Grötschel's (1980) work on the traveling salesman problem.

Whatever the algorithmic use of a partial linear description of $P_{m,n}$, the first step is to identify some of its facets.

Theorem 3.5. *The following inequalities define distinct facets of $P_{m,n}$.*

   i. $y_{ij} \le x_j$ for all $i \in I, j \in J$,
   ii. $y_{ij} \ge 0$ for all $i \in I, j \in J$,
   iii $x_j \le 1$ for all $j \in J$.

These facets are called the *elementary* facets of $P_{m,n}$. The next theorem provides a necessary and sufficient condition for an inequality with coefficients of 0 or 1 to define a facet of $P_{m,n}$.

Assume that $I' \subseteq I$ and $J' \subseteq J$ are two nonempty sets and that $B = (b_{ij})$, $i \in I', j \in J'$ is a 0, 1 matrix with no zero row. Consider the inequality

$$\sum_{i \in I'} \sum_{j \in J'} b_{ij} y_{ij} - \sum_{j \in J'} x_j \le r. \tag{3.7.2}$$

Define the graph G as follows. It has a node associated with each variable y_{ij}, $i \in I, j \in J$, and $x_j, j \in J$. We will use the same notation for a node and its associated variable. For all $i \in I$ and $j \in J$, the node y_{ij} is joined by an arc to the node x_j and to every node y_{ik} for $k \ne j$.

Let N' be the set of nodes $\{y_{ij}: i \in I', j \in J'\} \cup \{x_j: j \in J'\}$ and let G' be the subgraph of G induced by the node set N'. Given a graph H we denote by $\alpha(H)$ the maximum size of a stable set in H (a *stable set* is a set of mutually nonadjacent nodes). Finally, an arc e of H is *critical* if $\alpha(H - e) > \alpha(H)$, where $H - e$ denotes the graph obtained from H by removing the arc e.

Theorem 3.6 (Cornuejols and Thizy, 1982a). *The inequality* (3.7.2) *is a facet of $P_{m,n}$ if and only if the following set of conditions is satisfied.*

   i. $r = \alpha(G') - |J|$,

  ii. G' is connected,

 iii. for every $i \in I'$, $j \in J'$ such that $b_{ij} = 1$, the arc (x_j, y_{ij}) is critical,

 iv. for every $j,k \in J'$, there exists a sequence of critical arcs $(y_{i_1 j}, y_{i_1 l_1})$, $(y_{i_2 l_1}, y_{i_2 l_2}), \ldots, (y_{i_{s-1} l_{s-2}}, y_{i_{s-1} l_{s-1}})$, $(y_{i_s l_{s-1}}, y_{i_s k})$.

  v. for every $i \in I$, $j \in J$ such that $y_{ij} \notin N'$, the inequality $\alpha(G') < \alpha(G'')$ is strict, where G'' denotes the subgraph of G induced by $N' \cup \{y_{ij}\}$.

These necessary and sufficient conditions can be used to prove the next theorem, which provides constructively a large class of facets for the UFL problem.

For $2 \le t \le l \le n$, define $B^{lt} = (b^{lt}_{ij})$ as a matrix with $\binom{l}{t}$ rows and l columns whose rows consist of all distinct 0, 1 vectors with t ones and $l - t$ zeros.

Theorem 3.7 (Cornuejols and Thizy, 1982a). *For any pair of integers l and t such that $2 \le t \le l \le n$ and $\binom{l}{t} \le m$, and any sets $I' \subseteq I$, $J' \subseteq J$ such that $|I'| = \binom{l}{t}$ and $|J'| = l$, the inequality*

$$\sum_{i \in I'} \sum_{j \in J'} b^{lt}_{ij} y_{ij} - \sum_{j \in J'} x_j \le \binom{l}{t} + t - l - 1$$

defines a facet of $P_{m,n}$.

For example, take $t = 2$, $l = 3$, $B^{23} = \begin{bmatrix} 0 & 1 & 1 \\ 1 & 0 & 1 \\ 1 & 1 & 0 \end{bmatrix}$, and $I' = J' = \{1, 2, 3\}$. According to Theorem 3.7 we obtain the facet

$$y_{12} + y_{13} + y_{21} + y_{23} + y_{31} + y_{32} - x_1 - x_2 - x_3 \le 1,$$

which is identical to the valid inequality of Theorem 3.4 that we obtained above with $B = B^{23}$.

Additional results on facets of the UFL polytope are given by Guignard (1980), Cornuejols and Thizy (1982a), and Cho et al. (1983a, b).

Besides the study of facets, information about the adjacency of extreme points of an integer polytope can have useful algorithmic implications. Two extreme points are *adjacent* if they are joined by an *edge* of the polytope, that is, a face of dimension one. It was observed by Trubin (1969) and, in a different form, by Balas and Padberg (1972) that every edge of $P_{m,n}$ is also an edge of $Q_{m,n}$. Therefore, in theory, one can solve the UFL problem by applying the simplex algorithm to SLPR with the additional stipulation that a pivot to a new extreme point is allowed only when this new extreme point is integral. Unfortunately, it is not known how to implement such a pivoting rule efficiently. In particular, cycling may become a problem. Nevertheless, this approach has been tried in practice. Some computational experience is reported by Guignard and Spielberg (1977).

More generally, Trubin (1969) shows that any two integral extreme points of $Q_{m,n}$ belongs to a face of $Q_{m,n}$ all of whose extreme points are integral.

3.8. POLYNOMIALLY SOLVABLE CASES

Formally, by a special case of the UFL problem, we mean a problem of the form (3.1.1)–(3.1.4) all of whose instances are described by a subfamily of objective functions (C, f). In this section, we consider two special cases that have the following significant properties.

1. SLPR always has an integral optimal solution
2. The problem can be solved in polynomial-time by a combinatorial algorithm.

3.8.1. The Economic Lot Size Problem

There is a demand d_i in period i, $i = 1, \ldots, n$. The fixed cost of producing in period j is $f_j \geq 0$. The variable production cost is p_j. The variable storage and backorder costs are $c_j^+ \geq 0$ and $c_j^- \geq 0$, respectively. Let y_{ij} represent the fraction of the demand of period i produced in period j, and $x_j = 1$ if and only if there is production in period j. Then the UFL formulation can be used to minimize production cost where

$$c_{ij} = -(p_j + c_j^+ + \cdots + c_{i-1}^+)d_i \qquad if\ i \geq j$$

and

$$c_{ij} = -(p_j + c_j^- + \cdots + c_{i+1}^-)d_i \qquad if\ i < j.$$

3.8.2. The Tree Location Problem

Let $G = (V, E)$ be a graph with node set V and arc set E and suppose that G is a *tree*, (that is, there is a unique path in G between each pair of nodes). Here the nodes represent both clients and facilities. The cost of opening the jth facility is $f_j \geq 0$ all $v_j \in V$. Associated with each arc $e \in E$, there is a given nonnegative distance. The distance d_{ij} between any pair of nodes v_i and v_j is the sum of the edge distances along the unique path between v_i and v_j for all $v_i, v_j \in V$. There is also a nonnegative weight w_i associated with each node v_i. Let $c_{ij} = -w_i d_{ij}$, $v_i, v_j \in V$, $i \neq j$, and $c_{ii} = 0$ all $v_i \in V$.

The induced subgraph of G generated by $V_j \subseteq V$ is the graph $G_j = (V_j, E_j)$ where $E_j = \{e \in E : \text{both end nodes of } e \text{ are in } V_j\}$. G_j is said to be a *subtree* of G if G_j itself is a tree.

Theorem 3.8 (Kolen, 1983).   *There is an optimal solution to the tree location problem in which the set of open facilities $S \subseteq V$ is such that for each $v_j \in S$, $V_j = \{v_i \in V: \text{node } v_i \text{ is served by node } v_j\}$ induces a subtree. Moreover, this solution is also optimal to the linear programming relaxation of the tree network problem.*

A similar result applies to the lot sizing problem. Consider the tree $G = (V, E)$ where $V = \{v_1, v_2, \ldots, v_n\}$ and $E = \{(v_i, v_{i+1}): i = 1, \ldots, n - 1\}$. Here G is simply a path from node v_1 to node v_n so that $V' \subset V$ is a subtree or a path if and only if $V' = \{v_i, v_{i+1}, \ldots, v_k\}$ for some i and $k, 1 \le i \le n$ and $k \ge i$.

Theorem 3.9 (Krarup and Bilde, 1977).   *There is an optimal solution to the lot sizing problem in which the set of periods having positive production $S \subseteq V$ is such that for each $j \in S$, $V_j = \{v_i \in V: \text{period } i \text{ is served by production in period } j\}$ induces a path. Moreover, this solution is also optimal to the linear programming relaxation of the tree network problem.*

The fact that an optimal solution to these problems induces subtrees that partition V is not surprising. In the tree location problem, suppose that node v_i is on the path joining nodes v_j and v_k and node v_j serves node v_k but not node v_i, that is, v_j does not induce a subtree. Suppose node v_i is served by node $v_{j'} \ne v_j$. Then the cost from this part of the solution is $d_{jk} + f_j + d_{j'i} + f_{j'}$. If instead, node v_i is served by node v_j, the cost is $d_{ji} + d_{jk} + f_j + f_{j'}$.

Thus if $d_{ji} \le d_{j'i}$, then v_j can serve v_i and all nodes after v_i that are being served by $v_{j'}$ without increasing the cost. Otherwise $d_{ji} > d_{j'i}$, which implies

$$d_{jk} = d_{ji} + d_{ik} > d_{j'i} + d_{ik} = d_{j'k} \, .$$

This inequality implies that the solution in which $v_{j'}$ serves v_k and only nodes after v_k that are currently being served by v_j costs less than the original. A recursive application of this argument proves the first statement of Theorem 3.8.

A similar argument proves this result for the economic lot sizing problem. Both of these results suggest that the ability to partition the solution into subtrees is crucial and leads us to consider the following generalization.

3.8.3.   The Tree Partitioning Problem

Given a tree graph $G = (V, E)$ and a node by node matrix with elements γ_{ij} all $v_i, v_j \in V$, let the weight of a subtree $G_j = (V_j, E_j)$ be $w(G_j) = \max_{v_k \in V_j} (\Sigma_{v_i \in V_j} \gamma_{ik})$. Find a partition of G into subtrees such that the sum of the weights over all subtrees in the solution is maximum.

To model the lot sizing problem as a tree partitioning problem we take

$$\gamma_{jj} = -(f_j + p_j d_j)$$

$$\gamma_{ij} = -(p_j + c_j^+ + \cdots + c_{i-1}^+)d_i \qquad if \; i > j$$

$$\gamma_{ij} = -(p_j + c_j^- + \cdots + c_{i+1}^-)d_i \qquad if \; i < j .$$

To model the tree location problem as a tree partitioning problem we take $\gamma_{jj} = -f_j$ and $\gamma_{ij} = -w_i d_{ij}$ if $i \neq j$.

We now formulate the tree partitioning problem as an integer program in a manner that establishes its connection to the UFL problem. If $v_{j*} \in V_j$ is such that $\arg \max_{v_k \in V_j} (\Sigma_{v_i \in V_j} \gamma_{ik}) = v_{j*}$, we say that v_{j*} is the root of subtree G_j. Let $y_{ij} = 1$ if $v_i \in V$ is in a subtree rooted at v_j and $y_{ij} = 0$ otherwise. Then the tree partitioning problem can be formulated as

$$\max \sum_i \sum_j \gamma_{ij} y_{ij} \tag{3.8.1}$$

$$\sum_j y_{ij} = 1 \qquad \text{all } v_i \in V \tag{3.8.2}$$

$$y_{ij} - y_{i'j} \leq 0 \qquad \begin{array}{l} \text{all } v_i, v_{i'}, v_j \in V \text{ such that } v_{i'} \\ \text{precedes } v_i \text{ on a path from } v_j \text{ to } v_i \end{array} \tag{3.8.3}$$

$$y_{ij} \in \{0, 1\} \qquad \text{all } v_i, v_j \in V . \tag{3.8.4}$$

Constraint (3.8.3) guarantees that if v_j is the root of a tree that contains v_i then the tree must also contain $v_{i'}$. Constraint (3.8.2) guarantees that each node must be in exactly one tree.

The linear programming relaxation of this integer program is obtained by replacing (3.8.4) by

$$y_{ij} \geq 0 \qquad \text{all } v_i, v_j \in V . \tag{3.8.5}$$

Theorem 3.10. (Bárány et al., 1986). *The polyhedron defined by* (3.8.2), (3.8.3), (3.8.5) *has only integral extreme points. Hence for any objective function* (3.8.1), *the solution to the linear programming relaxation is integral.*

This model for the tree partitioning problem resembles the model (3.1.1)–(3.1.4) for the UFL problem if we think of the y_{jj} as x_j and replace (3.8.3) by (3.1.3). In fact, we can represent solutions of (3.1.1)–(3.1.4) as a collection of subtrees that partition a graph G, but unfortunately G is not necessarily a tree. In the graph of Figure 3.2, V_1 represents the set of clients and V_2 the set of facilities. A solution to the problem is a set of subtrees, each of which is rooted at a node in V_2. The arcs from the root of a tree to nodes in V_1 show the clients being served by the facility that corresponds to the root. A node in V_2 that is not a root corresponds to an unused facility.

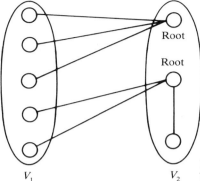

Figure 3.2. Subtrees representing the solution of a
UFL problem.

V_1 V_2

We set $\gamma_{ij} = c_{ij}$ for $v_i \in V_1$ and $v_j \in V_2$. To eliminate the possibility of nodes in V_1 being roots we set $\gamma_{jj} = -M$ for $v_j \in V_1$ (M is a large positive number) and to represent the fixed costs we set $\gamma_{jj} = -f_j$ for $v_j \in V_2$. Finally to accomodate unused facilities we set $\gamma_{jk} = 0$ if v_j and v_k are in V_2.

We close this section by giving an $O(|V^2|)$ dynamic programming algorithm for solving the tree partitioning problem. Another very general dynamic programming algorithm for location problems on trees is given by Megiddo, Zemel, and Hakimi (1983).

Given the tree $G = (V, E)$ we choose an arbitrary root node r. This induces a partial order on V. For all $v \in V$, let $V(v) = \{u : v$ is on the unique path between r and $u\}$ and $S(v) = \{u : u \in V(v)$ and $(v, u) \in E\}$. Let T_v be the tree induced by $V(v)$ and $g(v)$ be the maximum weight of a partition for the tree T_v.

The idea of the algorithm is to calculate $g(r)$ recursively by determining $g(v)$ from $\{g(u)\}$ for all $u \in S(v)$. To develop the general recursion equations, we need another function. Let $g_u(v)$ be the maximum weight of a partition of T_v when v is served by node u. If $u \notin V(v)$, then $g_u(v)$ includes the terms γ_{uw} for all $w \in V(v)$ that are served by u.

Then

$$g(v) = \max_{u \in V(v)} g_u(v) . \tag{3.8.6}$$

Now suppose we are given $g_u(w)$ for all $w \in S(v)$ and all $u \in V$. The calculation of $g_u(v)$ divides into two cases as shown in Figure 3.3. If $u \notin V(v)$ or $u = v$, and u serves v, then $w \in S(u)$ is either served by u or some node in $V(w)$ because of the tree structure. Thus w is served by u when v is served by u if and only if $g_u(w) > g(w)$. Hence

$$g_u(v) = \gamma_{vu} + \sum_{w \in S(v)} \max \{ g_u(w), g(w) \} . \tag{3.8.7}$$

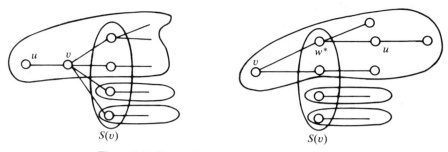

Figure 3.3. Illustration for the computation of $g_u(v)$.

If $u \in V(v) \backslash \{v\}$ serves v, then the tree structure implies that the node $w^* \in S(v)$ on the path joining v and u must also be served by u. Hence

$$g_u(v) = \gamma_{vu} + \sum_{w \in S(v) \backslash \{w^*\}} \max \{g_u(w), g(w)\} + g_u(w^*) . \qquad (3.8.8)$$

A node $v \in V$ is said to be a *leaf* of T_r if $S(v) = \emptyset$. The recursion is begun with the leaves. For all leaves $v \in V$, we have

$$g(v) = g_v(v) = \gamma_{vv} \quad \text{and} \quad g_u(v) = \gamma_{vu} \quad \text{for } u \neq v . \qquad (3.8.9)$$

Example 3.10. We consider the UFL problem on the tree network of Figure 3.4. The number on the arcs are the d_{ij} and the pair of numbers adjacent to the nodes are (w_i, f_i) all $v_i \in V$. Let $\gamma_{jj} = -f_j$ all $v_j \in V$ and $\gamma_{ij} = -w_i d_{ij}$ all $v_i \neq v_j \in V$. Hence we obtain the matrix

$$\gamma = \begin{bmatrix} -7 & -4 & -3 & -7 & -6 \\ -8 & -4 & -14 & -6 & -4 \\ -6 & -14 & -11 & -20 & -18 \\ -7 & -3 & -10 & -6 & -5 \\ -12 & -4 & -18 & -10 & -8 \end{bmatrix} .$$

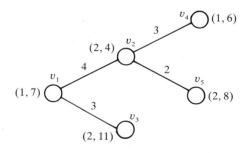

Figure 3.4. Tree network for Example 3.10.

For the leaves v_3, v_4 and v_5, the bottom three rows of the matrix γ give g_u (see (3.8.9)).

For node v_2, (3.8.7) and (3.8.8) yield

$$g_1(2) = \gamma_{21} + \max\{g_1(4), g(4)\} + \max\{g_1(5), g(5)\}$$
$$= -8 + \max(-7, -6) + \max(-12, -8) = -22$$
$$g_2(2) = -4 + \max(-3, -6) + \max(-4, -8) = -11$$
$$g_3(2) = -14 + \max(-10, -6) + \max(-18, -8) = -28$$
$$g_4(2) = \gamma_{24} + \max\{g_4(5), g(5)\} + g(4)$$
$$= -6 + max\{-10, -8\} + (-6) = -20$$
$$g_5(2) = -4 + \max\{-5, -6\} + (-8) = -17.$$

Hence

$$g(2) = \max\{g_2(2), g_4(2), g_5(2)\} = \max\{-11, -20, -17\} = g_2(2) = -11.$$

For node v_1 we obtain

$$g_1(1) = -7 + \max\{-22, -11\} + \max\{-6, -11\} = -24$$
$$g_2(1) = -4 + \max\{-14, -11\} + (-11) = -26$$
$$g_3(1) = -3 + \max\{-28, -11\} + (-11) = -25$$
$$g_4(1) = -7 + \max\{-20, -11\} + (-20) = -38$$
$$g_5(1) = -6 + \max\{-18, -11\} + (-17) = -34.$$

Hence $g(1) = g_1(1) = -24$, where $g_1(1) = \gamma_{11} + g(2) + g_1(3)$.

Thus node v_1 serves itself and node v_3. Since $g(2) = g_2(2) = \gamma_{22} + g_2(4) + g_2(5)$, node v_2 serves itself and nodes v_4 and v_5. $\bigcirc$

3.9. SUBMODULARITY

As defined at the outset of this chapter, the UFL is the combinatorial optimization problem $\max_{S \subseteq J} z(S)$ where

$$z(S) = \sum_{i=1}^{m} \max_{j \in S} c_{ij} - \sum_{j \in S} f_j \tag{3.9.1}$$

is the profit made when the set S of facilities is open. A very important property of the set function z is its submodularity. A function w defined on the subsets of a finite set J is *submodular* if

$$w(S \cup \{k\}) - w(S) \le w(R \cup \{k\}) - w(R) \qquad \text{for all} \quad k \notin S$$
$$\text{and} \quad R \subseteq S \subseteq J\backslash\{k\} .$$

The fact that the profit function z is submodular was observed by Spielberg (1969a), Babayev (1974), Frieze (1974) and Fisher et al. (1978). It means that the additional profit that can be made by opening a facility in location k when a set S is already open in other locations is a nonincreasing function of S with respect to set inclusion. The larger S, the smaller the profit of establishing a new facility. This is proved formally in the next theorem.

Theorem 3.11. *The profit function z given by (3.9.1) is submodular.*

Proof. Let $R \subseteq S \subseteq J\backslash\{k\}$. For all $i = 1, \ldots, m$

$$\max_{j \in S \cup \{k\}} c_{ij} - \max_{j \in S} c_{ij} = \max (0, c_{ik} - \max_{j \in S} c_{ij})$$
$$\le \max (0, c_{ik} - \max_{j \in R} c_{ij}) = \max_{j \in R \cup \{k\}} c_{ij} - \max_{j \in R} c_{ij}$$

where the inequality follows from $\max_{j \in S} c_{ij} \ge \max_{j \in R} c_{ij}$.
By summing these inequalities for all i, we obtain

$$\sum_{i=1}^{m} \max_{j \in S \cup \{k\}} c_{ij} - \sum_{i=1}^{m} \max_{j \in S} c_{ij} \le \sum_{i=1}^{m} \max_{j \in R \cup \{k\}} c_{ij} - \sum_{i=1}^{m} \max_{j \in R} c_{ij} .$$

Hence

$$z(S \cup \{k\}) - z(S) \le z(R \cup \{k\}) - z(R) . \qquad \square$$

Thus the UFL problem is a special case of the problem

$$\max_{S \subseteq J} \{ z(S) \colon z \text{ submodular} \} . \tag{3.9.2}$$

We can apply the greedy and interchange heuristics to (3.9.2). We can formulate (3.9.2) as an integer program and many of the results that we have given for the UFL problem extend to (3.9.2) and, in particular, to the capacitated location problem, which is another special case of (3.9.2). We will not elaborate on these results here, but refer the interested reader to Fisher et al. (1978), Nemhauser and Wolsey (1978, 1981), Nemhauser et al. (1978), Cornuejols et al. (1980), and Conforti and Cornuejols (1984).

3.10. PROBABILISTIC RESULTS

In Section 3.4 the point was made that good feasible solutions as well as good upper bounds are crucial in solving the UFL problem. Accordingly, the algorithmic tools presented in this chapter focused on heuristics (Section 3.5) and on the solution of SLPR (Section 3.6). The computational experience accumulated over the years on this problem has shown that several algorithms produce very good lower and upper bounds. Can these observations be explained formally? The first formal probabilistic analysis of a location algorithm was performed by Fisher and Hochbaum (1980). Their main result is for the p-median problem, but it is also useful for the UFL problem.

This type of analysis requires that we assume an underlying probability distribution of problem instances. Since these assumptions can be somewhat arbitrary, different models can emerge, each giving a different insight. To illustrate the approach, we will consider one specific model, the so-called Euclidean model.

Here n points, $x_1, \ldots, x_n$, are chosen independently and uniformly at random in the unit square $[0, 1]^2$. Denote by $\|x_i - x_j\|$ the Euclidean distance between points x_i and x_j, and let f be a fixed cost. The *Euclidean UFL* problem is to choose $S \subseteq \{x_1, \ldots, x_n\}$, $S \neq \emptyset$, such that $\Sigma_{x_i \notin S} \min_{x_j \in S} \|x_i - x_j\| + f|S|$ is minimum.

The results of Fisher and Hochbaum were improved by Papadimitriou (1981). Papadimitriou's paper is about the p-median problem but his results can also be applied to the Euclidean UFL problem defined above. We will state them for this problem. Assume that

$$\text{for some } \varepsilon > 0, \qquad n^{-(1/2)+\varepsilon} \leq f \leq n^{1-\varepsilon}. \tag{3.10.1}$$

Theorem 3.12 (Papadimitriou, 1981). *Under assumption* (3.10.1), *the optimum value of the Euclidean UFL problem is*

$$Z \sim (0.986612\ldots)f^{1/3}n^{2/3} \qquad \text{almost surely.}$$

Equivalently, this theorem states that, for any $\alpha > 0$,

$$\Pr\left[1 - \alpha \leq \frac{Z}{(0.986612\ldots)f^{1/3}n^{2/3}} \leq 1 + \alpha\right] \to 1 \qquad \text{as } n \to \infty.$$

Papadimitriou also proposes the following heuristic.

a. Let $K = (0.328871\ldots)f^{-2/3}n^{2/3}$.
b. Tile the plane with hexagons $H_1, \ldots$ each of area $1/K$. Choose those hexagons H_j for which $H_j \subset [0, 1]^2$. Let the set of their centers be $H = \{h_1, \ldots, h_p\}, p \leq K$.
c. Define the set $S = \{s_1, \ldots, s_p\}$ of open facilities as follows. For $j = 1, \ldots, p$, let $s_j \in \{x_1, \ldots, x_n\}$ be a point such that $\|s_j - h_j\| \leq \|x_i - h_j\|$ for all $i = 1, \ldots, n$.
d. $Z^H = \Sigma_{x_i \notin S} \min_{x_j \in S} \|x_i - x_j\| + f|S|$.

Theorem 3.13 (Papadimitriou, 1981). *Under assumption* (3.10.1), *the value* z^H *of the solution produced by the heuristic for the Euclidean UFL problem is*

$$Z^H \sim (0.986612...) f^{1/3} n^{2/3} \qquad \text{almost surely .}$$

In other words, Theorems 3.12 and 3.13 assert that the error $(Z^H - Z)$ made by using the heuristic is of an order smaller than the optimal value Z, that is

$$\frac{Z^H - Z}{Z} \to 0 \qquad \text{as } n \to \infty .$$

The bound W provided by the SLPR can be analyzed in a similar fashion.

Theorem 3.14 (Ahn, Cooper, Cornuejols, and Frieze, 1988). *Under assumption* (3.10.1), *the value of the SLPR for the Euclidean UFL problem is*

$$W \sim (0.984745...) f^{1/3} n^{2/3} \qquad \text{almost surely .}$$

Corollary 3.4. $(Z - W)/Z \sim 0.00189...$ *almost surely.*

The probabilistic results obtained for this model have some interesting consequences. If we insist on obtaining and verifying an optimum solution, any branch and bound algorithm where the branching is done on the variables x_j and the bounding is based on the SLPR, will almost surely enumerate an exponential number of subproblems before it can produce an optimum solution. On the other hand, a very good solution and a proof that the solution is within two tenths of one percent of the optimum can almost surely be found very quickly (details are given by Ahn et al., 1988).

Of course, the quality of the bound W depends heavily on the probabilistic assumptions. The results given earlier in this section hold for the Euclidean model with uniform demand. It turns out that these probabilistic results are quite robust to changes in the demand assumption but very sensitive to the Euclidean assumption. A radically different model assumes that the c_{ij} are i.i.d. in some interval, say $[0, 1]$. This model is known as the *uniform cost model*. Note that here, contrary to the Euclidean model, the c_{ij} do not satisfy the triangle inequality. For this model, SLPR is a poor relaxation of the UFL problem, as shown by the following theorem.

Theorem 3.15 (Ahn et al. 1988). *Under assumption* (3.10.1), $(Z - W)/Z \sim 0.5$ *almost surely for the uniform cost model.*

For the problem instances reported in the literature, the c_{ij} are often related to transportation costs and such costs usually satisfy the triangle inequality. Clearly, the uniform cost model is not representative of such problem instances and, therefore, it is not surprising that big duality gaps have not been reported in the literature.

ACKNOWLEDGEMENT

This work was supported in part by National Science Foundation grants ECS-8005350, ECS-8307473, ECS-8205425, DDM-8719128, and ECS-8901495.

EXERCISES

3.1 Sometimes a p-median problem can be solved by removing the condition $\sum_{j \in J} x_j = p$, introducing an artificial fixed charge of $f_j = f$ for each $j \in J$, and solving the resulting UFL problem for different value of f until a value f^* is found for which an optimal solution of the UFL problem has p open facilities.

    (a) Show that this method does not always work by giving an instance of a 2-median problem for which no value of f provides an optimal solution with two open facilities in the associated UFL problem.

    (b) For each $n \geq 3$, find an integer m and an $m \times n$ matric C such that the instance of the UFL problem defined by C and $f_j = f$ for $j = 1, \ldots, n$, has only two possible optimal solutions when f varies: when $f < f^*$, there is a unique optimal solution and it has one open facility; when $f > f^*$ there is a unique optimal solution and it has $n - 1$ open facilities; when $f = f^*$, both of these solutions are optimum.

3.2 The set covering problem is defined as follows and is known to be $\mathscr{NP}$-hard. Given a finite set E and a family of subsets $A_i \subseteq E$, $i = 1, \ldots, q$, find a subfamily $\{A_i\}_{i \in H}$, where $H \subseteq \{1, \ldots, q\}$ such that $\cup_{i \in H} A_i = E$ and $|H|$ is minimum. Show that the UFL problem is $\mathscr{NP}$-hard by a polynomial transformation of the set covering problem.

3.3 The strong linear programming relaxation of the p-facility location problem is given by (3.1.1)–(3.1.3), (3.1.5), (3.1.6).

    (a) Write its dual.

    (b) Write a condensed dual similar to (3.4.6).

    (c) Write a condensed dual similar to (3.4.7)–(3.4.9).

    (d) Write a Lagrangian dual similar to (3.4.12).

(e) Can you prove a proposition similar to Proposition 3.1 for the p-facility location problem?

3.4 Consider an instance of the UFL problem where the optimum value W of SLPR equals the optimum value Z of UFL. Let u be a dual solution satisfying (3.4.8), (3.4.9). Define $J(u) = \{j: \sum_{i \in I}(c_{ij} - u_i)^+ - f_j = 0\}$ and, for any set $K(u) \subseteq J(u)$, let $k_i = |\{j \in K(u): c_{ij} > u_i\}|$. Show that a necessary condition for u to be an optimal dual solution is that there exists a set $K(u) \subseteq J(u)$ such that $k_i \leq 1$ for all $i \in I$.

3.5 Consider the greedy algorithm applied to the p-facility location problem. Show that, if $\rho_j(S') = \rho_j(\emptyset)$ for $t = 1, \ldots, p-1$ and all $j \in J - S'$, then the greedy algorithm is optimum.

3.6 Let $j_1, \ldots, j_p$ be a solution obtained by applying the greedy algorithm to the p-facility location problem, and let A be an optimum solution. Denote by $S^t = \{j_1, \ldots, j_t\}$ the partial greedy solution obtained at iteration t. Show that, if $\rho_{j_t}(S^{t-1}) = \rho_{j_t}(S^{t-1} \cup A)$ for all $t = 1, \ldots, p$, then the greedy algorithm is optimum.

3.7 Consider the instance of the UFL problem defined by $m = 5$, $n = 8$, $f_j = 2$ for $j = 1, \ldots, 8$, and

$$C = \begin{bmatrix} 3 & 6 & 3 & 5 & 6 & 4 & 3 & 0 \\ 4 & 4 & 5 & 3 & 5 & 2 & 0 & 5 \\ 4 & 3 & 4 & 3 & 4 & 0 & 4 & 5 \\ 5 & 3 & 4 & 6 & 0 & 4 & 6 & 3 \\ 5 & 5 & 4 & 0 & 3 & 6 & 5 & 3 \end{bmatrix}.$$

(a) Use the greedy heuristic to find a solution. Give the greedy value Z^G and the dual greedy value W^G.

(b) Give the value W' of the weak linear programming relaxation.

(c) Apply the dual descent procedure, cycling through the indices i. Give the value $W(u)$ found by this procedure. Is the set $K(u)$ given by (3.5.3) an optimal set of open facilities for this problem instance?

3.8 Let P denote the set of nine integral points in the square $0 \leq x \leq 2$, $0 \leq y \leq 2$. For any point $j \in P$, let x_j and y_j be its coordinates. Consider the instance of the UFL problem defined by $m = n = 9$, $f_j = 2$ for all $j \in P$, and $c_{ij} = -|x_i - x_j| - |y_i - y_j|$ for all $i, j \in P$.

(a) Use the greedy heuristic to find values Z^G and W^G.

(b) Apply the variation of the dual descent procedure based on the sets $Q_i(u)$. Is the set $K(u)$ given by (3.5.3) an optimal set of open facilities for this problem instance?

3.9 Find an instance of the UFL problem having the following properties: (i) $Z = W$; (ii) c_{ij} is integer for every $i \in I$, $j \in J$, and f_j is integer for every $j \in J$; (iii) any optimum dual solution $(u_1, \ldots, u_m)$ has at least one fractional coordinate u_i. Can the dual descent procedure solve the SLPR for this problem instance?

3.10 Consider the instance of the UFL problem defined in Exercise 3.7.

(a) Starting from the point u^0 defined by $u_i^0 = \max_{j=1, \ldots, 8} c_{ij}$, perform two iterations of the subgradient algorithm applied to the Lagrangian dual. Take $\gamma^0 = 1.2$ and $\gamma^1 = 0.4$ as the respective step sizes.

(b) Solve the problem using the Dantzig–Wolfe approach. Start with $R_i = \{i\}$, $i = 1, \ldots, 5$ and, in the iterative step, take $R_k = \{i: c_{ik} - u_j^p > 0\}$ whenever there is a tie for the choice of R_k.

(c) Starting from the point $x^0 = (0\ 0\ 0\ 0\ 1\ 1\ 1\ 1)$, perform three iterations of the primal subgradient algorithm using the step sizes $\gamma^0 = \gamma^1 = 1/4$ and $\gamma^2 = 1/16$.

(d) Solve the problem using Benders decomposition. Start from the five constraints (3.6.19), one for each i, determined by the index k such that c_{ik} is the second maximum c_{ij}. Then choose an optimal solution x^1 to this linear program which is not identically zero.

(e) Solve the problem using the projection method.

3.11 Let p and q be two positive integers and consider a $p \times q$ matrix A with elements $a_{ij} = 0$ or 1 for all $i = 1, \ldots, p$ and $j = 1, \ldots, q$. Let b be a p-vector and c be a q-vector. Given any set S of columns of A, let $I(S) = \{i: a_{ij} = 1$ for at least one $j \in S\}$. We define the following problem. Find a set S of columns of A which maximizes $\sum_{i \in I(S)} b_i - \sum_{j \in S} c_j$.

(a) Formulate this problem as an integer program.

(b) How does this relate to the canonical formulation (3.6.23)?

3.12 (a) Show that the constraint matrix of the UFL problem is totally unimodular when $m \leq 2$.

(b) Show that it is totally unimodular when $n \leq 2$.

3.13 (a) Show that the conditions (i)–(iii) of Theorem 3.3 are necessary.

(b) Prove Theorem 3.4.

3.14 Prove Theorem 3.5.

3.15 Show that the inequality of Theorem 3.7 satisfies all the conditions of Theorem 3.6.

3.16 Prove Theorem 3.9.

3.17 **(a)** Prove that, if a set function w is submodular and nondecreasing, then

$$w(T) \le w(S) + \sum_{j \in T-S} \rho_j(S) \qquad \text{for all } S, T.$$

(b) Consider a p-median problem with $c_{ij} \ge 0$. Let ρ_t be the increase in the profit value achieved at the tth step of the greedy heuristic, $t = 1, \ldots, p$. Show that the optimal solution Z of the p-median problem satisfies

$$Z \le \sum_{t=1}^{k-1} \rho_t + p\rho_k \qquad \text{for } k = 1, \ldots, p.$$

(c) Use the inequalities found in **(b)** and the fact that the greedy value is $Z^G = \Sigma_{t=1}^p \rho_t$ to prove that

$$\frac{Z^G}{Z} \ge 1 - \left(\frac{p-1}{p}\right)^p.$$

REFERENCES

Ahn, S., C. Cooper, G. Cornuejols, and A. M. Frieze (1988). "Probabilistic Analysis of a Relaxation for the k-Median Problem," *Mathematics of Operations Research* **13**, 1–31.

Anderberg, M. R. (1973). *Cluster Analysis for Applications*. Academic Press, New York.

Babayev, D. A. (1974). "Comments on a Note of Frieze." *Mathematical Programming* **7**, 249–252.

Balas, E., and M. W. Padberg (1972). "On the Set Covering Problem." *Operations Research* **20**, 1152–1161.

Balas, E., and M. W. Padberg (1976). "Set Partitioning: A Survey." *SIAM Review* **18**, 710–760.

Balinski, M. L. (1965). "Integer Programming: Methods, Uses, Computation." *Management Science* **12**, 253–313.

Balinski, M. L., and P. Wolfe (1963). *On Benders Decomposition and a Plant Location Problem*, Working Paper ARO-27. Mathematica, Inc., Princeton, New Jersey.

Bárány I., J. Edmonds, and L. A. Wolsey (1986). "Packing and Covering a Tree by Subtrees." *Combinatorica* **6**, 245–257.

Beck, M. P., and J. M. Mulvey (1982). *Constructing Optimal Index Funds*, Rep. EES-82-1. School of Engineering and Applied Science, Princeton University, Princeton, New Jersey.

Benders, J. F. (1962). "Partitioning Procedures for Solving Mixed Variables Programming Problems." *Numerische Mathematik* **4**, 238–252.

Bilde, O., and J. Krarup (1977). "Sharp Lower Bounds and Efficient Algorithms for the Simple Plant Location Problem." *Annals of Discrete Mathematics* **1**, 79–97.

Businessweek (1974). "Making Millions by Stretching the Float." November 23, pp. 89–90.

Cho, D. C., E. L. Johnson, M. W., Padberg, and M. R. Rao (1983a). "On the Uncapacitated Plant Location Problem. I. Valid Inequalities and Facets." *Mathematics of Operations Research* **8**, 579–589.

Cho, D. C., M. W. Padberg, and M. R. Rao (1983b). "On the Uncapacitated Plant Location Problem. II. Facets and Lifting Theorems." *Mathematics of Operations Research* **8**, 590–612.

Conforti, M., and G. Cornuejols (1984). "Submodular Set Functions, Matroids and the Greedy Algorithm: Tight Worst-Case Bounds and Some Generalizations of the Rado-Edmonds Theorem." *Discrete Applied Mathematics* **7**, 251–274.

Conn, A. R., and G. Cornuejols (1987). *A Projection Method for the Uncapacitated Facility Location Problem*, CS-87-19. Computer Science Department, University of Waterloo, to apppear in *Mathematical Programming*.

Cook, S. A. (1971). "The Complexity of Theorem-Proving Procedures." *Proceedings of the Third Annual ACM Symposium on the Theory of Computing*, pp. 151–158.

Cornuejols, G., and J. M. Thizy (1982a). "Some Facets of the Simple Plant Location Polytope." *Mathematical Programming* **23**, 50–74.

Cornuejols, G., and J. M. Thizy (1982b). "A Primal Approach to the Simple Plant Location Problem." *SIAM Journal on Algebraic and Discrete Methods* **3**, 504–510.

Cornuejols, G., M. L. Fisher, and G. L. Nemhauser (1977a). "On the Uncapacitated Location Problem." *Annals of Discrete Mathematics* **1**, 163–177.

Cornuejols, G., M. L. Fisher, and G. L. Nemhauser (1977b). "Location of Bank Accounts to Optimize Float: An Analytic Study of Exact and Approximate Algorithms." *Management Science* **23**, 789–810.

Cornuejols, G., G. L. Nemhauser, and L. A. Wolsey (1980). "A Canonical Representation of Simple Plant Location Problems and Its Applications." *SIAM Journal on Algebraic and Discrete Methods* **1**, 261–272.

Efroymson, M. A., and T. L. Ray (1966). "A Branch and Bound Algorithm for Plant Location." *Operations Research* **14**, 361–368.

Erlenkotter, D. (1978). "A Dual-Based Procedure for Uncapacitated Facility Location." *Operations Research* **26**, 992–1009.

Fisher, M. L., and D. S. Hochbaum (1980). "Probabilistic Analysis of the Planar K-Median Problem." *Mathematics of Operations Research* **5**, 27–34.

Fisher, M. L., G. L. Nemhauser, and L. A. Wolsey (1978). "An Analysis of Approximations for Maximizing Submodular Set Functions. II." *Mathematical Programming Study* **8**, 73–87.

Frieze, A. M. (1974). "A Cost Function Property for Plant Location Problems." *Mathematical Programming* **7**, 245–248.

Garey, M. R., and D. S. Johnson (1979). *Computers and Intractability: A Guide to the Theory of $\mathcal{NP}$-Completeness*. Freeman, San Francisco, California.

Garfinkel, R. S., A. W. Neebe, and M. R. Rao (1974). "An Algorithm for the M-Median Plant Location Problem." *Transportation Science* **8**, 217–236.

Geoffrion, A. M. (1974). "Lagrangian Relaxation for Integer Programming." *Mathematical Programming Study* **2**, 82–114.

Grötschel, M. (1980). "On the Symmetric Travelling Salesman Problem: Solution of a 120-City Problem." *Mathematical Programming Study* **12**, 61–77.

Guignard, M. (1980). "Fractional Vertices, Cuts and Facets of the Simple Plant Location Problem." *Mathematical Programming Study* **12**, 150–162.

Guignard, M., and K. Spielberg (1977). "Algorithms for Exploiting the Structure of the Simple Plant Location Problem." *Annals of Discrete Mathematics* **1**, 247–271.

Hansen, P., and L. Kaufman (1972). "An Algorithm for Central Facilities Location under an Investment Constraint." In *Mathematical Programs for Activity Analysis*. (P. Van Moeseke, ed.). North-Holland, Publ., Amsterdam.

Held, M., P. Wolfe, and H. P. Crowder (1974). "Validation of Subgradient Optimization." *Mathematical Programming* **6**, 62–88.

Karp, R. M. (1972). "Reducibility among Combinatorial Problems." In *Complexity of Computer Computations* (R. E. Miller and J. W. Thatcher, eds.), pp. 85–104. Plenum, New York.

Khumwala, B. M. (1972). "An Efficient Branch and Bound Algorithm for the Warehouse Location Problem." *Management Science* **18**, 718–731.

Kolen, A. (1983). "Solving Covering Problems and the Uncapacitated Plant Location Problem on Trees." *European Journal of Operational Research* **12**, 266–278.

Krarup, J., and O. Bilde (1977). "Plant Location, Set Covering and Economic Lot Sizing: An *O(mn)* Algorithm for Structured Problems." In *Optimierung bei graphentheoretishen und ganzzahligen Probleme* (L. Collatz et al., eds.), pp. 155–180. Birkhaeuser, Basel, Switzerland.

Krarup, J., and P. M. Pruzan (1983). "The Simple Plant Location Problem: Survey and Synthesis." *European Journal of Operational Research* **12**, 36–81.

Kraus, A., C. Janssen, and A. McAdams (1970). "The Lock-Box Location Problem, a Class of Fixed Charge Transportation Problems." *Journal of Bank Research* **1**, 51–58.

Kuehn, A. A., and M. J. Hamburger (1963). "A Heuristic Program for Locating Warehouses." *Management Science* **9**, 643–666.

Magnanti, T. L., and R. T. Wong (1981). "Accelerated Benders Decomposition: Algorithmic Enhancement and Model Selection Criteria." *Operations Research* **29**, 464–484.

Marsten, R. E. (1972). *An Algorithm for Finding Almost All the Medians of a Network*, Discuss. Pap. 23. Center for Mathematical Studies in Econometrics and Management Science, Northwestern University, Evanston, Illinois.

Martin, C. K., and L. Schrage (1985). "Subset Coefficient Reduction Cuts for 0–1 Mixed Integer Programming." *Operations Research* **33**, 505–526.

Megiddo, N., E. Zemel, and S.L. Hakimi (1983). "Maximum Coverage Location Problem." *SIAM Journal on Algebraic and Discrete Methods* **4**, 253–261.

Mirzain, A. (1985). "Lagrangian Relaxation for the Star-Star Concentrator Location Problem: Approximation Algorithm and Bounds." *Networks* **15**, 1–20.

Morris, J. G. (1978). "On the Extent to Which Certain Fixed-Charge Depot Location Problems Can Be Solved by LP." *Journal of the Operational Research Society* **29**, 71–76.

Mukendi, C. (1975). "Sur l'implantation d'équipement dans un reseau: Le problème de *m*-centre." Thesis, University of Grenoble, France.

Mulvey, J. M., and H. L. Crowder (1979). "Cluster Analysis: An Application of Lagrangian Relaxation." *Management Science* **25**, 329–340.

Narula, S. C., U. I. Ogbu, and H. M. Samuelson (1977). "An Algorithm for the *p*-median Problem." *Operations Research* **25**, 709–713.

Nemhauser, G. L., and L. A. Wolsey (1978). "Best Algorithms for Approximating the Maximum of a Submodular Set Function." *Mathematics of Operations Research* **3**, 177–188.

Nemhauser, G. L., and L. A. Wolsey (1981). "Maximizing Submodular Set Functions: Formulations and Analysis of Algorithms." *Annals of Discrete Mathematics* **11**, 279–301.

Nemhauser, G. L., L. A. Wolsey, and M. L. Fisher (1978). "An Analysis of Approximations for Maximizing Submodular Set Functions. I." *Mathematical Programming* **14**, 265–294.

Padberg, M., and S. Hong (1980). "On the Symmetric Travelling Salesman Problem: A Study." *Mathematical Programming Study* **12**, 78–107.

Papadimitriou, C. H. (1981). "Worst-Case and Probabilistic Analysis of a Geometric Location Problem." *SIAM Journal on Computing* **10**, 542–557.

Polyak, B. T. (1969). "Minimization of Unsmooth Functionals." *USSR Computational Mathematics and Mathematical Physics* **9**, 509–521.

ReVelle, C. S., and R. S. Swain (1970). "Central Facilities Location." *Geographical Analysis* **2**, 30–42.

Schrage, L. (1975). "Implicit Representation of Variable Upper Bounds in Linear Programming." *Mathematical Programming Study* **4**, 118–132.

Simao, H. P., and J. M. Thizy (1986). *A Dual Simplex Algorithm for the Canonical Representation of the Uncapacitated Facility Location Problem*," Working Paper. Princeton University, Princeton, New Jersey.

Spielberg, K. (1969a). "Plant Location with Generalized Search Origin." *Management Science* **16**, 165–178.

Spielberg, K. (1969b). "Algorithms for the Simple Plant Location Problem with Some Side Conditions." *Operations Research* **17**, 85–111.

Trubin, V. A. (1969). "On a Method of Solution of Integer Linear Programming Problems of a Special Kind." *Soviet Mathematics Dokl.* (*English Translation*) **10**, 1544–1546.

Van Roy, T. J., and L. A. Wolsey (1986). "Valid Inequalities for Mixed 0-1 Programs." *Discrete Applied Mathematics* **14**, 199–213.

Wong, R., J. Ward, A. Oudjit, and P. Lemke (1984). "Linear Programming Models of the *K*-Median Location Problem on Special Structure." Presented at the Joint ORSA/TIMS National Meeting, Dallas, Texas.

4

Multiperiod Capacitated Location Models

Søren Kruse Jacobsen
The Institute of Mathematical Statistics and Operations Research
The Technical University of Denmark
Lyngby, Denmark

4.1. INTRODUCTION

The location models presented in Chapters 2 and 3 depict a single-period or static situation. The solutions to the models answer the question of *where* to locate facilities. As a byproduct the question of *what size* (capacity) is also answered. In a single-period model, capacity equals output and does not appear explicitly as a decision variable in the model.

The models presented in this chapter, commonly referred to as "dynamic location models," reflect a multiperiod situation where demand varies between time-periods; usually, demand is assumed to increase with time. In

173

addition to the two questions of *where* and *what size*, the solution to a multiperiod location model should also answer the question of *when* to establish a certain amount of productive capacity at a certain location. To illustrate the complications introduced by the *when* question, Section 4.2 is devoted to the problem of capacity expansion at a single location, that is, it concentrates on the questions of *when* and *what size*.

A fairly general multiperiod capacitated location (MCL) model is formulated in Section 4.3. The main extensions relative to the models in Chapters 2 and 3 are that data and decision variables become functions of time and that capacity must be treated explicitly and distinct from output as excess capacity may occur in certain periods at certain locations. Further, Section 4.3 presents some methods for solving an MCL model.

The term MCL does not refer to a specific well-defined model like the p-median and the UFL problems of Chapters 2 and 3 but rather to a class of models. Some of the models are reviewed in Section 4.4. The section also presents some methods of solution in addition to those described in Section 4.3. Thus, Section 4.4 gives a survey, not necessarily exhaustive, of the literature on MCL problems.

Section 4.5 is intended to provide the reader with some guidelines regarding the choice of solution method for a specific problem at hand. Computational experience with the methods described in Sections 4.3 and 4.4 is reported in that section. Finally, some concluding remarks and recommendations are given in Section 4.6.

The MCL problem is related to the challenging problems of sequencing and timing of interdependent projects in investment theory, where a "project" is represented by a location and a capacity to be added at that location. The number of projects is infinite if the choice of capacity expansions is not limited to a few standardized sizes. Thus, models for multiperiod locational decisions may be viewed as an interface between location theory and investment theory.

Historically, the study of MCL problems may be traced back to the mid-1960s. The book edited by Manne (1967) gives an excellent description of MCL problems motivated by decisions regarding the industrial development in India. Other roots to MCL models arise in problems where and when to establish dams and hydroelectric power stations; several such models were published in *Water Resources Research* in the early 1970s. Also, several "dynamic location models" have appeared in the operations research literature. With a few exceptions, motivation for the practical relevance is generally not given, but, nevertheless, good solution techniques for the models have been developed.

As mentioned earlier, the reader should bear in mind that, unlike the p-median or the uncapacitated facility location (UFL) models of Chapters 2 and 3, respectively, the so-called "dynamic location" models do not formulate a unique problem; many of the models have different underlying assumptions. Some models that have appeared in the literature should rather be termed "dynamic transhipment" or "dynamic inventory" models.

The theoretical sophistication of the state-of-the-art solution methods for MCL problems lags behind that of the single-period location models. Only small size MCL problems can be solved exactly; in most cases one must resort to heuristics, such as those described in Section 4.3. With the exception of the special model of Van Roy and Erlenkotter (1982), no computationally feasible exact method is available for medium or large scale problems.

4.2. CAPACITY EXPANSION AT A SINGLE LOCATION

As mentioned in the preceding section, the essential new feature of multiperiod capacitated location (MCL) models relative to the models presented in Chapters 2 and 3 is that their solutions also answer the question of *when* to establish capacity in addition to the usual questions on *where* and *what size*. To illustrate the complications introduced by the additional question of *when*, this section concentrates on the two questions of *what size* and *when*; the question of *where* is ignored. The problem to be examined is that of finding an optimal sequence of capacity expansions (in terms of size and timing) at a single location to meet given (time-varying) demands at a minimum discounted cost (present value).

To formulate a discrete time model of the capacity expansion problem, the following notation is needed.

$\tau(1), \tau(2), \ldots, \tau(T)$: a sequence of points in time when capacity expansion may take place; $\tau(t+1) > \tau(t)$. Quite often capacity expansion decisions are made every year, every quarter or the like; in that case $\tau(t) = t - 1$.

$\tau(T+1)$: the planning horizon.

z_t: the capacity expansion at time $\tau(t)$.

Z_t: the capacity (maximum output per unit time) available in time interval $[\tau(t), \tau(t+1))$, $t = 1, 2, 3, \ldots, T$. Observe that $Z_t = Z_{t-1} + z_t$.

Z_0: the initial capacity.

$F_t(z_t)$: the present value (at time $\tau(1)$) of the cost of a capacity expansion of size z_t at time $\tau(t)$. $F_t(z_t)$ is assumed to be increasing and concave in z_t representing economies of scale. Commonly used expressions for $F_t(z_t)$ are:

$$F_t(z_t) = f_t^0 \operatorname{sgn}(z_t) + f_t^1 z_t,$$

where f_t^0 and f_t^1 are given data or

$$F_t(z_t) = f_t z_t^{\psi_t}$$

where f_t and $0 < \psi_t < 1$ are given data. Note that to compute present values, a discount factor $(1 + r)^{-\tau(t)}$ is included in $F_t(z_t)$; r is the per unit time discount rate.

w_t: the demand per unit time during the time interval $[\tau(t), \tau(t + 1))$. Usually, w_t is nondecreasing with t, that is $w_{t+1} \geq w_t$.

Figure 4.1 illustrates for $T = 4$ how expansions are related to points on the time axis while demands and capacities are associated with time intervals. The problem of supplying the given demand in each time period at a minimal present value of capacity cost may now be formulated as follows:

$$
(S)\begin{cases}
\min \sum_{t=1}^{T} F_t(z_t) & & (4.2.1) \\
Z_t = Z_{t-1} + z_t, & t = 1, \ldots T, \quad Z_0 \text{ given} & (4.2.2) \\
Z_t \geq w_t, & t = 1, \ldots, T & (4.2.3) \\
z_t \geq 0, & t = 1, \ldots, T. & (4.2.4)
\end{cases}
$$

The model S may be solved by dynamic programming but the state variable Z_t assumes a continuum of values. It will be shown shortly, however, that the problem may be simplified substantially when the $F_t(z_t)$ are concave as assumed above.

Let $\hat{w}_t$ be defined by the recursion

$$
\hat{w}_t = \max\{w_t, \hat{w}_{t-1}\}, \qquad t = 1, 2, \ldots, T, \quad \hat{w}_0 = Z_0, \qquad (4.2.5)
$$

and let *model $\hat{S}$* be as S with w_t replaced by $\hat{w}_t$. Since capacity expansions must be positive and are the only costly elements, transformation (4.2.5) should not change the problem. This is confirmed by the following theorem.

Theorem 4.1. *Let $\hat{z}^*$ be an optimal solution to model $\hat{S}$ and let $\hat{Z}^*$ be the corresponding sequence of optimal states. Then $\hat{z}^*$ and $\hat{Z}^*$ are also optimal for model S.*

Proof. Since $\hat{w}_t \geq w_t$, $t = 1, \ldots, T$, $\hat{Z}^*$ is feasible for model S. Let OBJ $(\hat{Z}^*)$ be shorthand for the value of the objective (4.2.1). Assume there

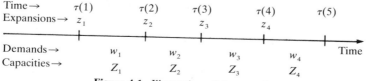

Figure 4.1. Illustration of the notation.

exists an optimal solution $\mathbf{Z}^0$ to S with a lower objective than OBJ $(\hat{\mathbf{Z}}^*)$. $\mathbf{Z}^0$ must be infeasible for $\hat{S}$, otherwise it would be optimal, contradicting the optimality of $\hat{\mathbf{Z}}^*$. Consider the first infeasibility, that is, the lowest t for which $Z_t^0 < \hat{w}_t$. By (4.2.5), $\hat{w}_t = w_t$ or $\hat{w}_t = \hat{w}_{t-1}$. As $Z_{t-1}^0 \le Z_t^0 < \hat{w}_t (z_t \ge 0)$, $\hat{w}_t = \hat{w}_{t-1}$ is impossible because t is the first infeasibility and hence $Z_{t-1}^0 \ge \hat{w}_{t-1}$. Consequently, $\hat{w}_t = w_t$ and Z_t^0 is also infeasible in S contradicting the assumed optimality. Thus, there cannot exist an optimal solution to S with a better objective than OBJ $(\hat{\mathbf{Z}}^*)$. $\square$

As a result of Theorem 4.1, the effort may be concentrated on solving model $\hat{S}$ which has nondecreasing demands because of (4.2.5) (i.e., $\hat{w}_{t-1} \le \hat{w}_t$). The "regeneration point" Theorem 4.2 below allows the continuum of Z_t values to be restricted to a finite number. A regeneration point is defined as follows.

Definition 4.1. A regeneration point is a point $\tau(t)$ in time such that $Z_{t-1} = \hat{w}_{t-1}$.

At a regeneration point (prior to a possible expansion z_t), the capacity equals demand and both may be forgotten; new expansions are built to serve new additional demand.

Theorem 4.2. (*Regeneration Point Theorem*). *Assume that all functions $F_t(\cdot)$, $t = 1, 2, \ldots, T$ in problem $\hat{S}$ are concave and increasing. Then there exists an optimal solution to $\hat{S}$ where $\hat{Z}_{t-1}^* = \hat{w}_{t-1}$ whenever $\hat{z}_t^* > 0$.*

Proof. A detailed proof is given by Manne (1967). However, an intuitive argument is as follows. Consider a feasible solution to $\hat{S}$ with two consecutive expansions $\hat{z}_s$ and $\hat{z}_t$ at instants $\tau(s) < \tau(t)$. The minimum size of $\hat{z}_s$ with $\hat{Z}_{s-1}$ kept fixed is

$$\hat{z}_s^{\min} = \max \{0, \hat{w}_{t-1} - \hat{Z}_{s-1}\},$$

while the maximum size of $\hat{z}_t$ with $\hat{Z}_t \ge \hat{w}_t$ kept fixed is

$$\hat{z}_t^{\max} = \hat{Z}_t - \max \{\hat{w}_{t-1}, \hat{Z}_{s-1}\}.$$

With $\hat{Z}_{s-1}$ and $\hat{Z}_t$ fixed, any $\hat{z}_s$ and $\hat{z}_t$ must satisfy

$$\hat{z}_s + \hat{z}_t = \hat{Z}_t - \hat{Z}_{s-1},$$

that is, if say $\hat{z}_s$ decreases then $\hat{z}_t$ must increase by the same amount. The cost of the two expansions is

$$F_s(\hat{z}_s) + F_t(\hat{z}_t) = F_s(p\hat{z}_t^{\max} + \hat{z}_s^{\min}) + F_t((1 - p)\hat{z}_t^{\max})$$

where

$$1 - p = \frac{\hat{z}_t}{\hat{z}_t^{\max}} \qquad \text{and} \qquad 0 \le p \le 1.$$

The concavity of F_s implies

$$F_s(p\hat{z}_t^{\max} + \hat{z}_s^{\min}) \ge (1 - p)F_s(\hat{z}_s^{\min}) + pF_s(\hat{z}_t^{\max} + \hat{z}_s^{\min}),$$

while the concavity of F_t implies

$$F_t((1 - p)\hat{z}_t^{\max}) \ge pF_t(0) + (1 - p)F_t(\hat{z}_t^{\max}).$$

Adding the two inequalities shows that

$$F_s(\hat{z}_s) + F_t(\hat{z}_t) \ge (1 - p)[F_s(\hat{z}_s^{\min}) + F_t(\hat{z}_t^{\max})] + p[F_s(\hat{z}_t^{\max} + \hat{z}_s^{\min}) + F_t(0)].$$

The right-hand side in the above inequality is an average of two terms and consequently greater than or equal to the smallest component; thus,

$$F_s(\hat{z}_s) + F_t(\hat{z}_t) \ge \min\,[F_s(\hat{z}_s^{\min}) + F_t(\hat{z}_t^{\max}), F_s(\hat{z}_t^{\max} + \hat{z}_s^{\min}) + F_t(0)].$$

Unless the two terms on the right-hand side are equal, the inequality is strict for $0 < p < 1$. Assuming that the two terms are different (this is the "intuitive" part), consider an optimal solution where $\hat{z}_s^* > 0$ and $\hat{z}_t^* > 0$. If $\hat{Z}_{s-1}^* > \hat{w}_{t-1}$ then

$$F_s(\hat{z}_s^*) + F_t(\hat{z}_t^*) = \min\,[F_s(0) + F_t(\hat{Z}_t^* - \hat{Z}_{s-1}^*), F_s(\hat{z}_t^{\max} + \hat{z}_s^{\min}) + F_t(0)],$$

which can only be true if either $\hat{z}_s^* = 0$ or $\hat{z}_t^* = 0$ when the minimands are different and F_s and F_t are increasing. Thus the assumption $\hat{Z}_{s-1}^* > \hat{w}_{t-1}$ produces a contradiction and consequently, $\hat{Z}_{s-1} \le \hat{w}_{t-1}$ in which case

$$F_s(\hat{z}_s^*) + F_t(\hat{z}_t^*) =$$

$$\min\,[F_s(\hat{w}_{t-1} - Z_{s-1}^*) + F_t(\hat{Z}_t^* - \hat{Z}_{s-1}^*), F_s(\hat{Z}_t^* - \hat{Z}_{s-1}^*) + F_t(0)].$$

By the same argument, $\hat{z}_s^* = 0$ produces a contradiction and consequently

$$\hat{z}_t^* = \hat{Z}_t^* - \hat{w}_{t-1} \qquad \text{and} \qquad \hat{z}_s^* = \hat{w}_{t-1} - \hat{Z}_{s-1}^*,$$

implying that

$$\hat{Z}_{t-1}^* = \hat{w}_{t-1} \qquad \square$$

The main implication of the regeneration point theorem is that the search for the optimal Z_t may be constrained to the set $\{\hat{w}_s, s = t, t+1, \ldots, T\}$ which in turn gives the values of z_t by (4.2.2). Manne (1967) notes that the problem of solving model $\hat{S}$ (and hence model S) simplifies to finding the shortest path through a network where the nodes correspond to the regeneration points, and the arc-length $d(t_1, t_2)$ corresponds to the cost of establishing the capacity $z_{t_1} = \hat{w}_{t_2-1} - \hat{w}_{t_1-1}$ at time $\tau(t_1)$ to serve demand up to the next regeneration point $\tau(t_2)$. Example 4.1 demonstrates the simplicity of the procedure.

Example 4.1. Consider a problem with a time-horizon of 4 years and assume that expansions may take place at the beginning of each year. The corresponding "time-graph" is shown in Figure 4.2, where each node corresponds to a regeneration point. Suppose the demands are $w_1 = 100$, $w_2 = 200$, $w_3 = 300$, $w_4 = 400$, and initial capacity is zero.

A path in the time-graph now implies an expansion plan. For example the path from node 1 via node 3 to node 5 corresponds to expansions of size 200 at nodes 1 and 3.

Let the cost of an expansion of size $z \geq 100$ at node t be

$$F_t(z) = (98.5079 + 0.7585\,(z - 100))(1.1)^{t+1}.$$

The arc-lengths $d(t_1, t_2)$ now become:

	$t_2 = 2$	$t_2 = 3$	$t_2 = 4$	$t_2 = 5$
$t_1 = 1$	98.5079	174.3579	250.2079	326.0579
$t_1 = 2$		89.5526	158.5072	227.4617
$t_1 = 3$			81.4115	144.0974
$t_1 = 4$				74.0104

The first row of elements ($t = 1$) is computed by $F_t(z)$ with $t = 1$ and $z = 100$, 200, 300, and 400, respectively. The next rows ($t_1 = 2, 3, 4$) are computed by shifting the previous row one position to the right and dividing by the discount factor 1.1. The computation is easy for two reasons. First, the

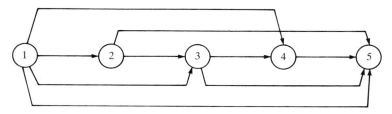

Figure 4.2. Time-graph for Example 4.1.

demand increases linearly with time allowing for the "one position to the right shift." Secondly, $F_t(z)$ only depends on t through the constant discount factor.

A path from node 1 to node 5 corresponds to an expansion plan satisfying the conditions of the regeneration point theorem and the length of the path is the cost of the expansion plan. Taking the path mentioned above from node 1 via node 3 to node 5, $d(1, 3) = 174.3579$ corresponds to $z_1 = 200$ which is exactly sufficient to satisfy the demands prior to the expansion at node 3, that is, $Z_2 = w_2 = 200$. Similarly, $d(3, 5) = 144.0974$ corresponds to $z_3 = Z_4 = w_4 = 400$, again satisfying the regeneration point theorem.

The minimum cost expansion plan is determined by finding the shortest path from node 1 to node 5. Any shortest path algorithm will produce the matrix of shortest path lengths shown below.

	$t_2 = 2$	$t_2 = 3$	$t_2 = 4$	$t_2 = 5$
$t_1 = 1$	98.5079	174.3579	250.2079	326.0579
$t_1 = 2$		188.0605	257.0151	325.9696
$t_1 = 3$			255.7694	318.4553
$t_1 = 4$				324.2183

The minimum cost of getting to node 5 (318.4553) is found in the column $t_2 = 5$ and row $t_1 = 3$, indicating that node 5 is reached from node 3. Similarly, the minimum cost to reach node 3 is found in the column $t_2 = 3$ and row $t_1 = 1$, indicating that the minimum cost path is from node 1 via node 3 to node 5. Once the optimal path is known, the size of the expansions may be determined by the regeneration point property. The optimal state variables are $Z_0^* = 0$, $Z_1^* = Z_2^* = w_2 = 200$, $Z_3^* = Z_4^* = w_4 = 400$, and, consequently, $z_1^* = Z_2^* - Z_0^* = 200$, $z_3^* = Z_4^* - Z_2^* = 200$. ○

The case where $F_t(\cdot)$ is concave is most relevant in practical applications. However, for the sake of completeness it should be mentioned that when $F_t(\cdot)$ is convex for all t and $F_s(z) > F_t(z)$ for all $s < t$ and all $z > 0$ then $\hat{Z}_t^* = \hat{w}_t$, that is, the established capacity should follow the demand as closely as possible, without decreasing with time. When $F_t(\cdot)$ is convex, the first equalities in the "proof" of Theorem 4.2 are reversed and the result follows (see also Exercise 4.1 at the end of the chapter).

The important result of this section is that an optimal expansion program can be derived from the shortest path through the time-graph which in turn is constructed by application of the regeneration point theorem. Unfortunately, the regeneration point theorem does not hold in the case of multiple locations. Nevertheless, the idea behind the time-graph will be used extensively in the sequel as it forms a good basis for explaining the heuristics to be presented in Sections 4.3 and 4.4. Further, experience seems to indicate that, in some practical applications, the transportation costs are relatively low compared to the costs of constructing and operating capacity; this implies that capacity should not be expanded until all existing capacity is exhausted and, thus, a type of regeneration point property exists even in the case of multiple locations.

4.3. THE MCL MODEL: FORMULATION AND HEURISTICS

In this section a discrete time multiperiod capacitated location (MCL) model is formulated and some heuristic solution procedures are presented. Brief descriptions of other model formulations and solution procedures are given in Section 4.4.

To formulate the model, the following notation is needed in addition to that already defined in Section 4.2. The index set $\{1, 2, \ldots, J\}$ denotes the set of locations indexed by j. The variables Z_{jt}, z_{jt} and the function $F_{jt}(\cdot)$ are the Z_t, z_t, and $F_t(\cdot)$ of Section 4.2 for location j. The index set $\{1, 2, \ldots, I\}$ denotes the set of clients indexed by i. The w_{it} is the demand per time unit in period t for clients i.

The imbedded transportation model uses the following symbols:

c_{jit}: the present value of the cost of producing one unit of flow at location j and shipping it to client i in period t.

y_{jit}: the flow from location j to client i in period t.

The MCL model now becomes:

$$\min \sum_{t=1}^{T} \sum_{j=1}^{J} \left[F_{jt}(z_{jt}) + \sum_{i=1}^{I} c_{jit} y_{jit} \right] \tag{4.3.1}$$

$$\sum_{j=1}^{J} y_{jit} = w_{it}, \qquad i = 1, \ldots, I; t = 1, \ldots, T \tag{4.3.2}$$

$$\sum_{i=1}^{I} y_{jit} \le Z_{jt}, \qquad j = 1, \ldots, J; t = 1, \ldots, T \tag{4.3.3}$$

$$Z_{jt} = Z_{j(t-1)} + z_{jt}, \qquad j = 1, \ldots, J; t = 1, \ldots, T \tag{4.3.4}$$

$$Z_{j0} \text{ given}$$

$$z_{jt} \ge 0, \qquad y_{jit} \ge 0. \tag{4.3.5}$$

The objective (4.3.1) is the minimization of the present value of total cost over the finite horizon $\tau(T + 1)$. The constraints (4.3.2) ensure that the demands are met, whereas (4.3.3) keep outputs below capacities. Constraint (4.3.4) is the system's "equation of motion" which describes the trajectory of the state-variable $\mathbf{Z}_t$ from the initial value $\mathbf{Z}_0$. The state-variables may be eliminated by substituting (4.3.4) into (4.3.3):

$$\sum_{i=1}^{I} y_{jit} < Z_{j0} + \sum_{s=1}^{t} z_{js} , \qquad j = 1, \ldots, J, t = 1, \ldots, T . \qquad (4.3.6)$$

The decision variables are z_{jt} and y_{jit}, with optimal values denoted by z_{jt}^* and y_{jit}^*. For given capacity expansions z_{jt}, it is straightforward to find the flows y_{jit} using a transportation algorithm.

It is assumed that the lifetime of all capacity exceeds the planning horizon or, equivalently, that worn-out capacity is automatically replaced. This implies that $F_{jt}(\cdot)$ includes maintenance and replacement costs. The possibility of combining replacement with relocation is not considered.

To solve the MCL model, one is required to find the minimum of the concave function (4.3.1) over the polyhedron described by the linear constraints (4.3.2), (4.3.5), and (4.3.6). From convex analysis it is known that the minimizing point is an extreme point of the polyhedron. Unfortunately, local minima may occur at several extreme points.

Now, consider the possibility of solving the MCL model by a gradient method. As the problem is nonconvex, there is a risk that termination occurs at a local minimum rather than at the desired global minimum. Another point is that the functions F_{jt} may not be differentiable everywhere; neither of the two examples given in Section 4.2 are differentiable at zero. Thus, for some F_{jt}, gradient methods may not be applicable, while dissatisfactory local minima may result in other cases. Consequently, it does not seem likely that a gradient method will perform very well on the MCL model, but no experience is available to support or dispel this view. In particular, the experience reported by Rao and Ruthenberg (1977) (see Section 4.5) suggests that a gradient method is essentially unable to improve a good heuristic solution.

Dynamic programming (DP) is another approach to solve the MCL model. The backward recursion for DP derived from formulation (4.3.1)–(4.3.5) becomes:

$$B_t(\mathbf{Z}) = \min_{\mathbf{z}} \left\{ \sum_j f_{jt}(z_j) + C_t(\mathbf{Z} + \mathbf{z}, \mathbf{w}_t) + B_{t+1}(\mathbf{Z} + \mathbf{z}) \right\}, \quad t = T, T-1, \ldots, 0$$
$$(4.3.7)$$

$$B_{T+1}(\cdot) = 0$$

where $C_t(\mathbf{a}, \mathbf{b})$ denotes the optimal objective function value of the following transportation model with source-capacities $\mathbf{a}$ and sink-demands $\mathbf{b}$:

$$C_t(\mathbf{a}, \mathbf{b}) = \min_{y} \sum_{i=1}^{I} \sum_{j=1}^{J} c_{ijt} y_{ij}$$

$$\sum_{j=1}^{J} y_{ij} \geq b_i , \qquad i = 1, \ldots, I$$

$$\sum_{i=1}^{I} y_{ij} \leq a_j , \qquad j = 1, \ldots, J \qquad (4.3.8)$$

$$y_{ij} \geq 0 , \qquad i = 1, \ldots, I, j = 1, \ldots, J .$$

In case of infeasibility, C_t in (4.3.8) is taken to be infinity. $B_t(\mathbf{Z})$ in (4.3.7) is the minimal cost of getting from state $\mathbf{Z}$ at time $\tau(t)^-$ to the end of the planning horizon $\tau(T+1)$ while satisfying demands. $B_0(\mathbf{Z}_0)$ is the optimal value of the objective (4.3.1).

The major single obstacle to the use of DP is the dimension of the state-vector. If the dimension is high, the number of different states to be evaluated at each stage t becomes very large and computationally prohibitive. This is often referred to as "the curse of dimensionality." Special considerations or approximations are needed to reduce the number of states evaluated. In (4.3.7) the dimension of the state-vector $\mathbf{Z}$ equals the number J of locations. The single location case discussed in Section 4.2 can be solved directly by DP since the regeneration point theorem reduces the set of states to be considered at stage t to $\{\hat{w}_s : s = t - 1, \ldots, T\}$. Unfortunately, the regeneration point theorem does not hold in the case of multiple locations. However, approximations that reduce the size of the state-space as though the theorem could be generalized create good heuristic procedures. In the rest of this section, three heuristics of this type are described.

4.3.1. One Shot Dynamic Programming (OSDP)

The first heuristic is the one shot dynamic programming (OSDP), originally developed by Jacobsen (1974); the reason for this name will become clearer after the procedure has been described. The OSDP procedure is based on the concept of the time-graph for the single location case (described in Section 4.2), and how it may be approximately extended to the multilocation case. Before we present OSDP we need some additional notation and algorithms for finding the shortest path in a time-graph.

Let $D(t)$ be the length of the shortest path found so far from node 1 to node t in the time-graph.

Let $P(t)$ be the node preceding node t on the path corresponding to $D(t)$.

Let $S(t)$ be the capacity available prior to an expansion at node t when the path corresponding to $D(t)$ is followed. In other words, $S(t)$ is the best value of Z_{t-1} found so far.

Algorithm 4.1 computes the shortest path through the time-graph.

Algorithm 4.1. To find the shortest path through a time-graph

INITIALIZATION	$D(1) := 0; D(t) := \infty, t = 2, \ldots, T + 1;$
	$S(1) := Z_0; P(1) := 0;$
START LOOP 1	for $t1 = 1, \ldots, T$ do:
START LOOP 2	for $t2 = t1 + 1, \ldots, T + 1$ do:
	$z^* := \hat{w}(t2 - 1) - S(t1)$

$$d(t1, t2) := F(t1, z^*)$$
if $D(t1) + d(t1, t2) < D(t2)$:
$$D(t2) := D(t1) + d(t1, t2),$$
$$S(t2) := S(t1) + z^*;$$
$$P(t2) := t1;$$

END LOOP 2
END LOOP 1

At the end of Algorithm 4.1, $D(T + 1)$ is the optimal value of the objective. The optimal expansions are found by backtracking through the time-graph as given in Algorithm 4.2. After a pass through Algorithm 4.1 and 4.2, $z(t)$, $t = 1, \ldots, T$ defines the optimal expansion schedule.

Algorithm 4.2. To find the optimal expansions by backtracking

$$t2 := T + 1; z(t) := 0, t = 1, \ldots, T;$$
LABEL 1 $\quad t1 := P(t2);$
$$z(t1) := S(t2) - S(t1)$$
if $t1 = 1$: stop
otherwise: $t2 := t1$; goto LABEL 1;

Considering the procedure of Algorithms 4.1 and 4.2 one may ask what *formal* changes are needed to apply them to the multilocation case. The issue is not whether the changes will produce an optimal or near optimal solution to the MCL model, but, rather, what changes can make the algorithms work logically on the MCL model. A proposition for these changes is as follows.

i. The scalars $S(t)$ should be replaced by J-dimensional vectors $S(t)$ with components $S(j, t)$. Similarly z^* in Algorithm 4.1 and $z(t)$ in Algorithm 4.2 should be replaced by J-dimensional vectors.

ii. The arc-length $d(t1, t2)$ in Algorithm 4.1 should be computed by the formula

$$d(t1, t2) = \sum_{j=1}^{J} F_j[t1, z^*(j)] + \sum_{t=t1}^{t2-1} C_t[S(t1) + z^*, w(t)]$$

where C_t is the previously defined optimal objective value in a transportation problem with known supplies and demands as arguments.

iii. The statement $z^* := \hat{w}(t2 - 1) - S(t1)$ in Algorithm 4.1 cannot be translated directly to vector form, as z^* and $S(t1)$ relate to a location and would thus become J-dimensional while $\hat{w}(t2 - 1)$ relates to a client and would become I-dimensional. Consequently, a more elaborate rule is needed to translate the statement into vector form. Such a rule is described below.

Thus, one may conclude that, except for the statement $z^* := \hat{w}(t2-1) - S(t1)$ in Algorithm 4.1, it is straightforward to generalize Algorithms 4.1 and 4.2 to the multilocation case. To complete the generalization, a rule that determines the vector $\mathbf{z}^*$ of capacity expansions at node $t1$ from $\mathbf{S}(t1) = \mathbf{Z}_{t-1}$ and $\mathbf{w}_t$, $t = t1, \ldots, t2-1$ is needed. As the overall purpose of Algorithm 4.1 is to find a shortest path, it seems reasonable to use a rule that minimizes $d(t1, t2)$ while maintaining feasibility in the MCL model. More specifically, $d(t1, t2)$ and $\mathbf{z}^*$ are found by solving the arc-length (AL) model (4.3.9) below.

$$d(t1, t2) = \min \sum_{j=1}^{J} \left[F_j(t1, z_j) + \sum_{t=t1}^{t2-1} \sum_{i=1}^{I} c_{jit} y_{jit} \right]$$

$$\sum_{j=1}^{I} y_{jit} \le S_j(t1) + z_j, \qquad t = t1, \ldots, t2-1, j = 1, \ldots, J,$$

$$\sum_{j=1}^{J} y_{jit} = w_{it} \qquad t = t1, \ldots, t2-1, i = 1, \ldots, I, \tag{4.3.9}$$

$$y_{jit} \ge 0; z_j \ge 0 \qquad \text{all } i, j \text{ and } t.$$

The AL model defined by (4.3.9) is in some sense a hybrid of the MCL model and a single-period facility model. The capacity must be established at the beginning of the time-period as in the single-period model, but the demand varies over the period.

Algorithm 4.3 below is a heuristic approach to solve the AL model. The heuristic is a combination of the greedy or ADD heuristic of Kuehn and Hamburger (1963) (see also Chapter 3) and the minimum entry or SMALC (ship most at least cost) heuristic of Kuhn and Baumol (1962). ADD determines the number of capacity expansions while the embedded transportation problems are solved approximately by SMALC. Before presenting Algorithm 4.3, a few more definitions and notation are needed.

Let $x(j) = 1$ if $z^*(j) > 0$ and $x(j) = 0$ if $z^*(j) = 0$.

Let $p_{\max}$ be an upper bound on the number of simultaneous expansions.

Let d^* be the best value of $d(t1, t2)$ found so far. Let d_p^* be the best value of $d(t1, t2)$ found so far with exactly p simultaneous expansions.

Let $z^{\max}$ be a (possibly infinite) upper bound on the size of a capacity expansion.

Algorithm 4.3. To solve AL model to determine $d(t1, t2)$ and $\mathbf{z}^*$.

INITIALIZATION $x(j) := 0$ for $j = 1, \ldots, J$;
                      $d^* := +\infty$;
START LOOP 3   for $p = 1, \ldots, p_{\max}$ do:
                      $d_p^* := +\infty$;

START LOOP 4   for $j = 1, \ldots, J$ do:

$\qquad\qquad\qquad\qquad$ if $x(j) \neq 0$ go to END LOOP 4;

$\qquad\qquad\qquad\qquad$ for $j1 = 1, \ldots, J$ do:

$\qquad\qquad\qquad\qquad$ if $j1 \neq j$ and $x(j1) = 0$: $z(j1) := 0$;

$\qquad\qquad\qquad\qquad$ if $j1 = j$ or $x(j1) = 1$: $z(j1) := z^{\max}$;

$\qquad\qquad\qquad\qquad$ $d := 0$

START LOOP 5   for $t = t1, \ldots, (t2 - 1)$ do:

$\qquad\qquad\qquad\qquad$ find $C_t(\mathbf{S}(t1) + \mathbf{z}, \mathbf{w}(t))$ and

$\qquad\qquad\qquad\qquad$ y_{jit}, $i = 1, \ldots, I$; $j = 1, \ldots, J$; by SMALC.

$\qquad\qquad\qquad\qquad$ $d := d + C_t$;

END LOOP 5

$$z(j1) := \max_{\substack{t1 < t \leq t2 - 1 \\ j}} \left\{ \sum_{j1=1}^{I} y_{j1it} \right\} - S_j(t1);$$

$$d := d + \sum_{j1=1}^{J} F_j(t1, z(j1))$$

$\qquad\qquad\qquad\qquad$ if $d < d_p^*$: $d_p^* := d$; $j^* := j$;

$\qquad\qquad\qquad\qquad$ if $d < d^*$: $d^* := d$; $\mathbf{z}^* := \mathbf{z}$;

END LOOP 4

$\qquad\qquad\qquad\qquad$ if $d_p^* > d^*$ go to LABEL 2

$\qquad\qquad\qquad\qquad$ $x(j^*) := 1$

END LOOP 3

LABEL 2 $d(t1, t2) := d^*$

In Algorithm 4.3 loop 3 controls the number p of capacity exansions at node $t1$. Loop 4 searches for the best location j^* for the pth expansion assuming that the previous $(p - 1)$ expansions are located as determined in earlier passes through loop 3. Loops 3 and 4 together constitute the ADD heuristic. Loop 5 solves the transportation problem for each time-period $[\tau(t), \tau(t + 1))$ on the arc $[t1, t2]$. Positive expansions are set to $z^{\max}$ before entering loop 5; after loop 5 the sizes of expansions are made as small as possible while maintaining the feasibility of the transportation solutions found in loop 5. Algorithm 4.3 terminates when the arc length d_p^* starts increasing as a function of p. This termination rule is based on the assumption that d_p^* is a convex function of p which is likely to be true in many applications but hard to prove in general.

By replacing the two statements $z^* := \ldots, ;$ $d(t1, t2) := \ldots$ in Algorithm 4.1 with Algorithm 4.3, and certain scalars by J-dimensional vectors as described earlier, we obtain a heuristic for solving the MCL model. The heuristic is the vector version of Algorithm 4.1 (using Algorithm 4.3 as a subroutine) followed by the vector version of Algorithm 4.2. We refer to the heuristic as OSDP (one shot dynamic programming) because only one value of the state vector $\mathbf{S}(t)$ is considered at each node t of the time graph. Strictly speaking OSDP is not a dynamic program (DP). A stage in DP corresponds to an arc $[t, t + 1]$ in the time-graph and the number of states at a stage equals the number of arcs in a vertical cut through the arc $[t, t + 1]$.

For example, in Figure 4.2 the number of states at stage $[1, 2]$ is 4 and at stage $[2, 3]$ the number of states is 5. In OSDP, the number of states is considerably reduced.

In the rest of this subsection we discuss some details that are important to a successful implementation of OSDP. A discussion of the quality of the solutions produced by OSDP is deferred to Section 4.5.

The computing time or time complexity of OSDP is mainly determined by the number of transportation problems solved in loop 5 of Algorithm 4.3. SMALC includes the sorting of the transportation costs c_{jit}, $i = 1, \ldots, I$, $j = 1, \ldots, J$ with complexity $O(IJ \log IJ)$, and a subsequent scanning of the sorted list for which the complexity is $O(IJ)$. Thus, the complexity of SMALC is $O(IJ \log IJ)$. The number of transportation problems for an arc $[t1, t2]$ is $t2 - t1$, that is, of order $O(T)$. Consequently, the complexity of loop 5 in Algorithm 4.3 is $O(TIJ \log (IJ))$. The complexity of loop 4 is $O(TIJ^2 \log (IJ))$ and the complexity of loop 3 is $O(p_{max}TIJ^2 \log IJ) < O(TIJ^3 \log (IJ))$ thus the complexity of Algorithm 4.3 is $O(TIJ^3 \log IJ)$.

The number of arcs scanned by loops 1 and 2 in Algorithm 4.1 is $O(T^2)$. Thus, the complexity of Algorithm 4.1 with Algorithm 4.3 as a subroutine becomes $O(T^3IJ^3 \log (IJ))$. Since the complexity of Algorithm 4.2 is $O(TJ)$, which is negligible, the complexity of OSDP thus becomes $O(T^3IJ^3 \log (IJ))$.

If the transportation costs c_{jit} has the form $c_{ji}R(t)$, the c_{ji} in SMALC need only be sorted once, and the complexity of OSDP reduces to $O(T^3IJ^3)$. Experiments have verified that when T is doubled, the computing time of OSDP increases by a factor of eight.

A closer look at Algorithms 4.1 and 4.3 reveals some other possibilities for reducing the computing time. First, the range of loop 2 in Algorithm 4.1 may be restricted such that $t1 + \theta_{min} < t2 \leq t1 + \theta_{max}$ where $1 \leq \theta_{min} \leq \theta_{max}$ are suitably chosen user-specified integer bounds. (When $t1 = 1$ the bounds should be $2 \leq t2 \leq \theta_{max} + 1$; when $t1 > T - \theta_{max}$ the bounds should be $t1 + 1 \leq t2 \leq T + 1$). The bounds should be chosen as tight as possible without being binding. Thus these bounds very much depend on the specific application at hand. The use of the pruning parameters θ_{min} and θ_{max} reduces the complexity of OSDP to $O(T^2(\theta_{max} - \theta_{min} + 1)IJ^3 \log (IJ))$. A further reduction results if range p_{max} of Algorithm 4.3 is made smaller. In some applications $p_{max} = 1$ is sufficient; this reduces the complexity to $O(T^2(\theta_{max} - \theta_{min} + 1)IJ^2 \log (IJ))$.

The number of AL models to be solved in OSDP is $O(T^2)$ (or $O(T(\theta_{max} - \theta_{min} + 1))$ if pruning is used) and, thus, a fairly efficient procedure for solving the AL model is required. Although any procedure that solves the AL model can be plugged into Algorithm 4.1 instead of the heuristic Algorithm 4.3, the trade-off between speed and quality must be considered for the choice of the solution method. First, it seems difficult to simplify Algorithm 4.3 further. On the other hand, it is questionable whether more complicated procedures can produce substantially better solutions to the AL model. Consider the possibility of replacing ADD and SMALC, respectively, by more sophisticated procedures. An obvious replacement for the greedy ADD heuristic is the interchange heuristic, but as the number of simultaneous capacity expansions is small and in many cases equal to one, this replacement is not likely to produce much improvement in return for the additional computing effort. SMALC could probably be replaced by an exact transportation algorithm like the simplex based PNET-I by Barr, Glover, and Klingman (1976). Utilizing fully the opportunities of an advanced starting basic solution in PNET-I, it should be possible to keep the computing time within reasonable limits. However, the benefits are likely to be small as SMALC usually produces good solutions and quite often obtains the optimum.

The final comments on OSDP all relate to capacity bounds. In loop 4 of Algorithm 4.3, the capacity expansion $z(j1)$ is set to some upper bound z^{max}. The capacity bounds and the discretization of time inherent in the time-graph are related. Several cases can be distinguished.

1. If the bound z_t^{max} is independent of the location j it is often a good idea to choose the function $\tau(t)$ such that the total demand increment over the time interval $[\tau(t-1), \tau(t)]$ equals z_t^{max}. If a finer time grid is used, the demand increment over corresponding intervals, for example $[\tau(t-2), \tau(t)]$ or $[\tau(t-3), \tau(t)]$, should be equal to z_t^{max}. The recommendation is based on two conditions. First and more important, the transportation cost should be small (although not necessarily negligible) relative to the capacity expansion costs so that a global regeneration property is likely to be present; that is, an expansion takes place only when total demand equals total capacity. Second, the function $\tau(t)$ must divide the time axis very finely so that only one expansion is made at each node of the time-graph.

2. If the upper bound z_{jt}^{max} depends both on time and location, it may be difficult to use OSDP. Assuming that the global regeneration point property is present, the difficulty is that $\tau(t2)$ will depend on the location chosen for the expansion at time $\tau(t1)$. It may be easier to adapt MACD, to be described below, to this situation. The alternative is to use OSDP with a very fine division of the time axis; however, as a consequence, T may become prohibitively large.

3. The upper bound z_{jt}^{max} may pertain to total capacity at location j, that is, $z_{jt}^{max} = z_j^{max} - S_j(t)$. In this case the only recourse for solution appears to be to choose $\tau(t)$ which defines a sufficiently fine division of the time axis so that the global regeneration property holds. The problem exception occurs when the bound z^{max} is independent of the location. Here, $\tau(t)$ should be chosen such that the total demand increment over the time interval $[\tau(t-1), \tau(t)]$ equals z^{max}/n for some integer $n > 1$; n should either be large (which is computationally expensive) or such that $z = kz^{max}/n$ are reasonable capacity expansion sizes for the integers $k \leq n$.

When the capacity bound z^{max} is finite, the function $\tau(t)$ defining the discretization of the time axis must be chosen *very carefully*. The ultimate resort is a very fine division of the time axis simulating continuous time. A poor choice of $\tau(t)$ is likely to be reflected in some small and uneconomical capacity expansions in the OSDP solution. Sometimes it may be useful to impose a global regeneration point property even when z^{max} is infinite. This is easy as long as $p_{max} = 1$ in Algorithm 4.3; then z^{max} is set to be the difference between the maximum total demand up to node $t2$ and the total capacity available prior to an expansion at node $t1$.

By and large, OSDP appears to be quite a flexible tool. No special assumption is made about the cost $F_{jt}(\cdot)$ of capacity expansions. Further, it is not difficult to distinguish between initial construction and expansion of existing capacity. The underlying transportation problem is assumed to be linear, but a method of solving a nonlinear transportation problem can easily be plugged into Algorithm 4.3, at the risk of a large increase in computational effort. The demands need not be linearly increasing, not even increasing. It should not be too difficult to generalize OSDP to the case of capacity with a finite lifetime; when setting the capacities for the transportation problem prior to loop 5 in Algorithm 4.3, account is simply made for obsolete or worn out capacity.

It should be noted, however, that OSDP has only been tested on the two problems reported in Section 4.5 and both problems are fairly simple. The above remarks concerning the wide applicability of OSDP still need support in terms of further empirical computational tests.

4.3.2. Minimum Annual Cost (MACD)

The second heuristic to be described is the minimum annual cost with discrete time (MACD). The continuous time version (MAC) is described in Section 4.4. The idea behind MACD is quite simple. Instead of solving the shortest path problem to optimality as in OSDP, an approximation is used. Assume that the node t_1 has been included on the path from node 1 to node $T + 1$ in the time-graph (initially $t_1 = 1$). Then the next node t_2^* (and hence the next arc (t_1, t_2^*)) to be included in the path is selected by the following rule:

$$a_2(t_1, t_2^*) = \min_{t_1 + 1 \le t_2 \le T + 1} \{a_2(t_1, t_2)\} \tag{4.3.10}$$

where $a_2(t_1, t_2)$ is the "annual cost" defined by

$$a_2(t_1, t_2) = \frac{d(t_1, t_2)}{\sum_{t=t_1}^{t_2-1} (1 + r)^{-\tau(t)}} \tag{4.3.11}$$

The annual cost is a constant cost distributed over the time periods covered by the arc $[t_1, t_2]$ such that the sum discounted back to time (t_1) equals $d(t_1, t_2)$. The idea behind $a_2(t_1, t_2)$ is to normalize $d(t_1, t_2)$ (which is an increasing function of t_2 when t_1 is given) such that arcs covering time intervals of different lengths may be compared.

The computer implementation of MACD is similar to that of OSDP. The main difference is that the next t_1 in the outmost loop is determined as the optimal t_2 from the previous pass through the next-to-outmost loop. This implies that the computing time for MACD is proportional to T^2 whereas it is proportional to T^3 in OSDP. As will be seen in Section 4.5, the price of the reduced computing effort is solutions of inferior quality.

4.3.3. Extended Minimum Annual Cost (MACDX)

The third heuristic is based on the following observation. In MACD the look-ahead is limited to one arc in the time-graph. With a look-ahead of $(K - 1) \geq 2$ arcs an extended MACD results with index a_K defined by

$$a_K(t_1, \ldots, t_K) = \frac{\displaystyle\sum_{k=1}^{K-1} d(t_k, t_{k+1})}{\displaystyle\sum_{t=1}^{t_K-1} (1 + r)^{-\tau(t)}} \qquad (4.3.12)$$

To find the next node t_2^* on the path from a given node t_1, a_K is minimized with respect to $t_2, t_3, \ldots, t_K$ by explicit enumeration. This increases the computational effort. However, as will be seen in Sections 4.4 and 4.5, Erlenkotter (1975a) has obtained very good results with $K = 5$ using IDP-MAC for the continuous time formulation of the MCL model; IDP-MAC is the continuous time counterpart of MACDX. MACDX has not been implemented and tested, but, the main reason for including its description here is that it serves as a good basis for describing IDP-MAC in the next section.

4.4. ALTERNATIVE MODELS AND METHODS: A SURVEY OF THE LITERATURE

Section 4.3 presented a discrete time formulation of the MCL problem and three DP-based heuristics to solve it. This section briefly discusses some alternative or closely related model formulations as well as some of the solution methods available in the literature. The reader is referred to the bibliographies by Erlenkotter (1975b) and by Domschke and Drexl (1985) and to the surveys by Erlenkotter (1981) and Luss (1982) for further information on multiperiod facility location problems.

4.4.1. The Multiperiod Uncapacitated Facility Location Model

Van Roy and Erlenkotter (1982) present the following multiperiod version of the UFL model from Chapter 3.

$$\min \sum_{t=1}^{T} \sum_{i=1}^{I} \sum_{s-1}^{T} \sum_{j=1}^{J} c_{ji}^{ts} y_{ji}^{ts} + \sum_{s=1}^{T} \sum_{j=1}^{J} f_{j}^{s} x_{j}^{s}$$

$$\sum_{j=1}^{J} \sum_{s=1}^{T} y_{ji}^{ts} = 1 , \qquad i = 1, \ldots, I , \quad t = 1, \ldots, T$$

$$y_{ji}^{ts} \le x_{j}^{s} , \qquad \text{all } (i, j, t, s) \tag{4.4.1}$$

$$y_{ji}^{ts} \ge 0 , \qquad x_{j}^{s} \in \{0, 1\} .$$

The data required for (4.4.1) is:

c_{ji}^{ts}: the cost of supplying client i in time period t from capacity established at location j at the beginning of time period s, with $c_{ji}^{ts} = +\infty$ for $t < s$.

f_{j}^{s}: the fixed cost of establishing capacity at location j at the beginning of time period s.

The decision variables in (4.4.1) are:

y_{ji}^{ts}: the fraction of client i's demand in time period t delivered from capacity established at the beginning of time period s at location number j.

x_{j}^{s}: binary variable indicating whether or not capacity is established at location j at the beginning of time period s.

In their original formulation, Van Roy and Erlenkotter (1982) allow for closing of old facilities as well as for opening of new facilities. For the purpose of conveying the essence of their formulation, only the latter possibility is included in (4.4.1).

Model (4.4.1) can be interpreted as a single-period model with "locations" $\{j, s\}$ and "clients" $\{i, t\}$ (see Exercise 4.12). Consequently, (4.4.1) can be solved by DUALOC (see Erlenkotter, 1978, also Chapter 3). However, by noting that

$$\sum_{s=1}^{T} x_{j}^{s} \le 1 , \qquad j = 1, \ldots, J \tag{4.4.2}$$

in an optimal solution ($f_{j}^{s} > 0$ is assumed) and by assuming that c_{ji}^{ts} is independent of s, Erlenkotter and Van Roy develop a substantially more efficient implementation which they refer to as DYNALOC.

DYNALOC is highly efficient in terms of computing time. However, formulation (4.4.1) is based on the assumption that the variable capacity cost is zero, that is

$$F_{js}(z_{js}) = f_j^s \cdot \mathrm{sgn}\,(z_{js}) \tag{4.4.3}$$

where $\mathrm{sgn}\,(z_{js})$ is the x_j^s in the objective of (4.4.1). This assumption somewhat restricts the applicability of the model.

4.4.2. Multiperiod Warehouse Location with External Capacity Bounds

Ballou (1968) and later Sweeney and Tatham (1976) solved the following discrete time warehouse location problem. In each period we have the usual capacitated warehouse location problem with capacity constraints (data) on both factories and warehouses. The single-period problems are tied together by fixed costs associated with moving capacities in or out of warehouse locations.

Ballou (1968) obtained an approximate solution by DP where the state space in each time period was restricted to the set of optimal single-period solutions.

Sweeney and Tatham (1976) also used DP but expanded the state space to include other reasonably good single-period solutions. By including all suboptimal single-period solutions which cost less than a given bound, the approach solves the problem to optimality. The sequence of suboptimal solutions to a single-period problem is computed by Benders Partitioning (see Chapters 3 and 5); when a solution $\mathbf{x}^*$ is found, the constraint

$$\sum_{j \in J1} x_j - \sum_{j \in J0} x_j \leq J1 - 1\,,$$

where $J1 = \{\,j: x_j^* = 1\,\}$ and $J0 = \{\,j: x_j^* = 0\,\}$, is added to the model; the constraint makes the solution $\mathbf{x}^*$ infeasible, and thus an inferior solution is found as the optimum in the next pass of the solution procedure.

In contrast to the MCL model of Section 4.3, the single-period models in the above problem are independent except for the fixed cost associated with moving capacities in or out of warehouse locations.

4.4.3. Continuous Time Formulation of the MCL Model (MAC and IDP-MAC)

Erlenkotter (1969, 1975a) gives a continuous time version of the MCL-model (4.3.1)–(4.3.5). All quantities indexed by t are replaced by functions of time, the summation over t in (4.3.1) is replaced by integration over time and the "equation of motion" in (4.3.4) becomes a differential equation.

The MAC heuristic described by Erlenkotter (1975a) is quite similar to MACD described in Section 4.3. MAC is based on the following assumptions.

i. Capacity expansions take place only at a single location each time and only at points in time when total capacity (before expansion) equals total demand.

ii. Total demand is an increasing function of time.

iii. The sizes of capacity expansion at each location j is limited to a finite set $\{z_{jm}, m = 1, 2, \ldots, M_j\}$.

Now, each of the size-location combinations are evaluated as follows. For each location, given the capacity prior to the expansion, the time τ_1 of expansion is found using assumptions (i) and (ii). Similarly, the time τ_2 of the next expansion is found since z_{jm} is known. Next, the cost $d_{jm}(\tau_1, \tau_2)$ incurred over the time interval $[\tau_1, \tau_2)$ is computed by solving a linear programming transportation problem with parametric right-hand side (demands) and adding the costs at time τ_1 of the expansion z_{jm}. The preferred expansion size and location is found by minimizing the MAC-index over all size and location combinations

$$a_2(\tau_1, \tau_2) = \frac{d_{jm}(\tau_1, \tau_2)}{\int_{\tau_1}^{\tau_2} e^{-r\tau} \, d\tau} , \qquad (4.4.4)$$

which is quite analogous to the discrete time expression (4.3.11). The MAC-heuristic may be seen as essentially a discrete time approximation since the time-axis is discretized implicitly by the three assumptions (i)–(iii) mentioned above.

Given the above description of the MAC-heuristic and the earlier developments for (4.3.12), it should be fairly straightforward to understand the continuous time analogy of the extended MAC index

$$a_K(\tau_1, \tau_2, \ldots, \tau_K) = \frac{\sum_{k=1}^{K-1} d(\tau_k, \tau_{k+1})}{\int_{\tau_1}^{\tau_K} e^{-r\tau} \, d\tau} \qquad (4.4.5)$$

For a specific sequence of size-location combinations $(z_{j_1 m_1}, z_{j_2 m_2}, \ldots, z_{j_{K-1} m_{K-1}})$, $\tau_2, \tau_3, \ldots, \tau_K$ can be computed (in that order) by the assumptions (i)–(iii). The costs $d(\tau_k, \tau_{k+1})$ are computed as in MAC. All size-location combinations are evaluated and the one minimizing a_K in (4.4.5) determines the preferred first decision, that is, the $z^*_{j_1 m_1}$ and τ_2^* which becomes the new τ_1 for the next pass of the procedure. The approach forms the core of the IDP-MAC-heuristic by Erlenkotter (1975a) (IDP stands for incomplete dynamic programming). To limit the computational effort, Erlenkotter evaluates only $M_j = 3$ different sizes at each location $j = 1, \ldots, J$ and $K - 1 = 4$ further expansions (of which only the expansion at time corresponding to $k = 1$ is implemented). As a refinement, quadratic interpolation between the three different values $z_{j_1 1}$, $z_{j_1 2}$, $z_{j_1 3}$ is used to find a better sized expansion at location j_1 at time τ_1.

Rao and Ruthenberg (1977) have suggested a gradient method to refine the continous time solution obtained by IDP-MAC. However, from the computational experience reported in Section 4.5 below, it appears that the trade-off between the improvement in the solution obtained and the computing effort is not quite favorable.

4.4.4. Interchange Heuristics for MCL Models

The two heuristics to be described in this subsection were originally designed to solve a special version of the MCL model (4.3.1)–(4.3.5) which is referred to as the fixed cost formulation. This terminology refers to the case where

$$F_{jt}(z_{jt}) = (f_{jt}^0 \cdot \text{sgn}(z_{jt})) + (f_{jt}^1 \cdot z_{jt})$$

which by replacing F_{jt} by $(f_{jt}^0 \cdot x_{jt}) + (f_{jt}^1 \cdot z_{jt})$ and adding the constraints

$$z_{jt} \leq z_{jt}^{\max} \cdot x_{jt}, \qquad j = 1, \ldots, J, \quad t = 1, \ldots, T$$

$$x_{jt} \in \{0, 1\}, \qquad j = 1, \ldots, J, \quad t = 1, \ldots, T$$

to the model (4.3.1)–(4.3.5) can be transformed to a MIP-formulation. Constant $z_{jt}^{\max}$ is a suitable upper bound on the size of a capacity expansion at location j at time $\tau(t)$.

Hung and Rikkers (1974) describe a fixed cost MCL model where the costs f_{jt}^0 and f_{jt}^1 may depend on whether an expansion is the initial construction at a point or an addition to an existing capacity. The accompanying heuristic is essentially a four-phase procedure that attempts to improve a known feasible solution. Briefly, the heuristic is as follows.

Phase 0. Obtain a feasible solution, for example, by MACD, OSDP or MACDX. Hung and Rikkers (1974) suggest an expansion at one location at the beginning of each time period with size based on an assumed global regeneration property. The location is selected according to minimum fixed cost.

Phase 1. Split the capacity established at one location in one period to several locations in an attempt to reduce transportation costs.

Phase 2. At each location, merge capacity expansions at different times to the earliest of the times considered to obtain economies of scale while maintaining feasibility. A suitable time-window specifies the expansions considered for merging.

Phase 3. Merge expansions at the same time but at different locations to one location in an attempt to obtain economies of scale.

Phase 4. Merge expansions at different times and different locations to one location and the earliest time considered.

Note the following. A loop repeats phases 2 and 3 as long as changes are observed. Not all of the possible changes indicated are considered; priority rules limit the number of changes examined (for details, see Hung, 1973). In all phases only changes that improve the objective are made. Erlenkotter (1981) reports that the procedure is sensitive to the numbering (labeling) of the locations.

Fong and Srinivasan (1981) have also developed an exchange heuristic for the fixed cost discrete time model. The basic phases are:

Phase 0. Obtain a feasible solution by MACD, OSDP or MACDX. Fong and Srinivasan offer two additional approaches. In the first, the fixed cost is ignored. In the second, the cheapest single expansion in each period is added where "cheapest" means that having the lowest transportation plus investment cost in the period considered.

Phase 1. Scan all pairs of locations (j_1, j_2). For each pair determine the optimal capacity exchange vector Δz such that (if possible) the expansion schedules $z_{j_1} - \Delta z$, $z_{j_2} + \Delta z$ are better than z_{j_1}, z_{j_2}. Determination of Δz requires the solution of a MIP model. This is done by branch-and-bound in which the fact that the dual of the LP relaxation is a parametric network flow model is utilized.

The final result is sensitive to the output from phase 0.

The computational experience reported in Section 4.5 indicates that the two interchange heuristics are fairly slow and may not improve much on the solution obtained by, for instance, IDP-MAC.

4.4.5. The SLOT Procedure

One of the earliest approaches to the MCL problem is the SLOT procedure by Manne (1967); SLOT is an acronym for Size Location and Time-phasing. Let indices (j, k) identify a specific expansion schedule for location j. Let z_{jkt}, $t = 1, \ldots, T$ be the corresponding capacity expansions and Z_{jkt}, $t = 1, \ldots, T$ the capacities available at location j in period t when schedule k is used. Let K_j be the number of different schedules considered for location j.

A total capacity expansion schedule is now uniquely determined by specifying a value of k, say $k(j)$ $(1 \le k(j) \le K_j)$, for each location j. A total expansion schedule can now be described by a vector of the form $(k(1), k(2), \ldots, k(j), \ldots, k(J))$ indicating that the expansions at location j are $z_{jk(j)t}$, $t = 1, \ldots, T$. Let

$$f_{jk} = \sum_{t=1}^{T} F_{jt}(z_{jkt}) \tag{4.4.6}$$

be the component of the expansion cost from location j if schedule k is used. Let x_{jk} be a binary variable indicating whether or not schedule k is used at location j. With the remaining notation as in Section 4.3, Manne's formulation of the MCL problem is:

$$\min \sum_{j=1}^{J} \sum_{k=1}^{K_j} f_{jk} x_{jk} + \sum_{t=1}^{T} \sum_{j=1}^{J} \sum_{i=1}^{I} c_{jit} \cdot y_{jit} \tag{4.4.7}$$

$$\sum_{i=1}^{I} y_{jit} \le \sum_{k=1}^{K_j} Z_{jkt} \cdot x_{jk} , \qquad j = 1, \ldots, J , \quad t = 1, \ldots, T \tag{4.4.8}$$

$$\sum_{j=1}^{J} y_{jit} = w_{it} , \qquad i = 1, \ldots, I , \quad t = 1, \ldots, T \tag{4.4.9}$$

$$\sum_{k=1}^{K_j} x_{jk} = 1 , \qquad j = 1, \ldots J \tag{4.4.10}$$

$$y_{jit} \ge 0 , \qquad x_{jk} \in \{0, 1\} . \tag{4.4.11}$$

The complication with the above MIP formulation is that the number K_j of expansion schedules for location j may be very large to make the model equivalent to the MCL model in Section 4.3. Thus, a rule (implying an approximation) for selection of a fairly small number of expansion schedules is needed. In SLOT, the problem is solved by a device motivated by the regeneration point theorem of Section 4.2. It is assumed that the demands w_i increase linearly with time, and, therefore, the optimal single location expansions occur with constant time intervals (cycle), provided that the cost-structure is

$$c_{jit} = c_{ji} \cdot e^{-r\tau(t)} , \qquad F_{jt}(z_{jt}) = F_j(z_{jt}) \cdot e^{-r\tau(t)} .$$

That is, costs are constant over time and discounted with a constant factor r. By extrapolation, the schedules considered in SLOT have a global "major cycle" corresponding to a global regeneration point (the planning horizon). Within the major cycle, "minor cycles" or local regeneration points are allowed; the minor cycles are divisors in the major cycle. If, for example, the major cycle is 24 years, the minor cycles are 1, 2, 3, 4, 6, 8, 12, 24 years. Each minor cycle may be "phased" or delayed. for instance, the 4-year cycle may be initiated with 0, 1, 2 or 3 years delay; the 12-year cycle can have delays of 0–11 years, and so on. The size of each expansion is determined by the minor cycles as the expansions should occur at local regeneration points. That is, the size of an expansion equals the increase of demand over the minor cycle, from the clients for which the location in question is closest.

The use of local and global regeneration points in SLOT for generating the expansion schedules may not be optimal (see Section 4.5). However, as pointed out by Manne (1967), the data for the model (4.4.7)–(4.4.11) can alternatively be obtained by column generation as done by Gilmore and Gomory (1961, 1963) in the cutting-stock problem. The generation of a column requires the solution of a one-dimensional DP model corresponding to an expansion schedule at a single location. However, this column generation approach has never been tested for SLOT.

4.5. COMPUTATIONAL EXPERIENCE AND COMPARISON OF HEURISTICS

The purpose of this section is to compare the various heuristic solution methods described in Sections 4.3 and 4.4. The comparison is in terms of objective values and computing times, and it is based on computational experience reported in the literature. This experience, of which parts are reproduced below, is admittedly a bit meager, but still, it does provide some idea of the capabilities of the methods.

First, a few remarks on generally applicable standard methods like dynamic programming (DP) or mixed integer programming (MIP). The standard DP approach will require a state-vector $(Z_{1t} \ldots Z_{Jt})$ specifying the capacity at each location j in each period t. The dimension of the state-vector is the number J of locations and if J exceeds 3 or 4, "the curse of dimensionality" prohibits the direct use of DP (cf. Erlenkotter, 1969, 1975a). Thomas (1977) suggests that the problem of dimensionality is overcome by an aggregation of locations, but this approach induces an approximation which may be at least as imprecise as that of the heuristics evaluated below.

If a MIP formulation (4.3.1)–(4.3.5) is used, a commercially available package like MPSX/MIP-370 (IBM), APEX IV (CDC) or a similar product may be applied. The number of rows is $T \cdot (I + J)$ which is not likely to be prohibitive. However, the number of binary variables is $T \cdot J$ which may be prohibitive. The main problem, however, is that the formulation (4.3.1)–(4.3.5) is not "tight." A "tight" formulation, as for the UFL model in Chapter 3, may be difficult to obtain but will also substantially increase the number of rows. A decade ago Hung and Rikkers (1974) used OPHELIE (a predecessor of APEX IV) on a problem with $(J, I, T) = (3, 4, 10)$ and could not prove optimality (in one run, no integer solution was obtained) within 5 min of CPU-time on a CDC 6600-computer. Although modern commercial codes like MPSX/MIP-370 offer a variety of user-specified strategies, it seems unlikely, for the near future, that a reasonably sized MCL model may be solved to optimality with a commercial standard code. Consequently, specially designed procedures such as those described in Sections 4.3 and 4.4, are needed to solve an MCL model.

Comparative evidence is available for the "caustic soda problem" and the "nitrogeneous fertilizers problem" described by Manne (1967). Both problems have $J = 15$, $I = 15$ while different planning horizons have been used in different studies. Two versions of the "nitrogenous fertilizers" problem have been studied, one with an upper bound of 250 and the other of 400 on the size of each capacity expansion. The sources of the evidence presented below are Erlenkotter (1975a, 1981) and Jacobsen (1977).

First some comments on the solutions produced by SLOT. Table 4.1 presents relative objective values and computing times for SLOT, MAC, OSDP and IDP-MAC on the "caustic soda problem." The SLOT solution is rather poor. The reason is probably that the major cycle (24 years) is too short. Table 4.2 shows that the capacity expansions tend to be smaller than those found with the other methods. With a longer major cycle, SLOT may become as complex as the general MIP formulation and, therefore, may

TABLE 4.1   **Relative Objective Values and Computing Times for the Caustic Soda Problem Solved by Various Heuristic Methods**

Method	Cost Index	CPU Time(s)	Computer
SLOT	108.02	n.a.	–
MACD	102.08	18	IBM 370/165
MAC	100.78	22	IBM 360/91
OSDP	100.68	49	IBM 370/165
MAC-Sarin	100.20	6	IBM 360/91
IDP-MAC	100.00	813	IBM 360/91

TABLE 4.2   **Expansion Schedules (Time, Size, Location) for the Caustic Soda Problem Obtained by Various Methods**

SLOT	MACD ($\Delta\tau = 1.0$)	OSDP ($\Delta\tau = 1.0$)	IDP-MAC
0, 101.4, 11	0, 175.8, 11	0, 117.2, 11	0.00, 114.42, 10
1, 88.8, 13	3, 175.8, 7	2, 175.8, 10	1.95, 153.86, 11
3, 81.7, 7	6, 175.8, 10	5, 117.2, 15	4.58, 110.23, 4
4, 100.8, 10	9, 175.8, 10	7, 117.2, 4	6.46, 133.35, 14
6, 101.4, 11	12, 175.8, 4	9, 175.8, 11	8.73, 118.72, 8
8, 62.4, 8	15, 175.8, 11	12, 175.8, 7	10.76, 157.53, 11
9, 81.6, 14	18, 175.8, 8	15, 117.1, 13	13.45, 111.98, 7

require a general purpose MIP-code. As it stands, SLOT does not appear to be a competitive approach; the solutions to the "nitrogeneous fertilizers problem" in Tables 4.3 and 4.5 further confirm this.

As could be expected from the construction of the heuristics, Tables 4.1, 4.3, and 4.5 show that the MAC, OSDP, and IDP-MAC solutions, in that order, have increasing quality but also require increasing computing effort. The question is which procedure to select for the solution of a specific problem.

The first recommendation is to use IDP-MAC if it is computationally feasible, that is, if the computing time can be afforded. From Tables 4.1, 4.3, and 4.5 it can be seen that some of the other procedures are substantially faster and produce solutions within less than 1% of that of IDP-MAC. However, from Tables 4.2 and 4.4 it is seen that the superiority of IDP-MAC stems from a different location-sequence for the *first* expansions which are the important ones from a decision-making point of view. Decisions concerning the near future must be made now and they are binding while longer term decisions may be revised in view of new information.

The second recommendation is to use OSDP if IDP-MAC is too expensive. It produces a better solution than MACD within the same computing

TABLE 4.3 Relative Objective Values and Computing Times for the Nitrogenous Fertilizers Problem Solved by Various Heuristic Methods (upper bound is 400 on the size of an expansion)

Method	Cost Index	CPU Time(s)	Computer
SLOT	111.39	n.a.	–
MACD	100.24	40	IBM 370/165
OSDP	100.17	74	IBM 370/165
MAC	100.09	11	IBM 360/91
IDP-MAC	100.00	546	IBM 360/91

TABLE 4.4 Expansion Schedules (Time, Size, Location) for the Nitrogenous Fertilizers Problem Obtained by Various Heuristic Methods (upper bound 400)

MACD ($\Delta\tau = 0.767$)	OSDP ($\Delta\tau = 0.767$)	MAC	IDP-MAC
0.00, 400, 6	0.00, 400, 6	0.00, 400, 6	0.00, 400, 11
1.53, 400, 11	1.53, 400, 11	1.53, 400, 11	1.53, 400, 2
3.07, 400, 2	3.07, 400, 2	3.07, 400, 2	3.07, 400, 6
4.60, 400, 15	4.60, 400, 15	4.60, 400, 15	4.60, 400, 15
6.13, 400, 4	6.13, 400, 4	6.13, 400, 4	6.13, 400, 4
7.67, 400, 9	7.67, 400, 9	7.67, 400, 9	7.67, 400, 9
9.20, 400, 12	9.20, 400, 12	9.20, 400, 12	9.20, 400, 12
10.73, 400, 8	10.73, 400, 8	10.73, 400, 6	10.73, 400, 6

time (see Table 4.6) for the soda problem and similar solutions for the fertilizers problem also with comparable computing effort (see Tables 4.3 and 4.5). Erlenkotter (1981) suggested that this may be due to the fact that the MAC (and MACD) expansions are too large although the sequence of locations may be the same as those obtained using OSDP.

The MAC procedure is recommended as a last resort, with several runs being made. The first run will give an indication of the size of expansions. In the subsequent runs, sizes lower than these should be tried. This may be done by restricting the choice of expansions to specific quantities as in the MAC-Sarin solution to the soda problem reported by Erlenkotter (1981) (see Table 4.1). In MACD, θ_{max} should be kept low; perhaps depending on the location considered for expansion, the lower the local demand increment the lower θ_{max} should be.

TABLE 4.5 Relative Objective Values and Computing Times for the Nitrogenous Fertilizers Problem Solved by Various Heuristic Methods (upper bound is 250 on the size of an expansion)

Method	Cost Index	CPU Time(s)	Computer
SLOT	111.65	n.a.	–
MACD	100.01	32	IBM 370/165
OSDP	100.01	33	IBM 370/165
MAC	100.01	10	IBM 360/91
IDP-MAC	100.00	619	IBM 360/91

TABLE 4.6 Expansion Plans, Both Produced within Approximately 50 s of CPU Time on an IBM 370/165*

OSDP			MACD		
Time	Location	Size	Time	Location	Size
0.0	11	117.2	0.00	11	146.50
2.0	7	146.5	2.50	7	146.50
4.5	15	117.2	5.00	15	146.50
6.5	10	146.5	7.50	10	146.50
9.0	4	117.2	10.00	4	146.50
11.0	11	175.8	12.50	11	161.15
14.0	13	117.2	15.25	13	131.85
16.0	8	146.5	17.50	8	161.15
18.5	9	117.2	20.25	11	161.15
20.5	11	117.2	23.00	2	117.20
22.5	2	146.5			

*In OSDP $\Delta\tau = 0.5$ years, OBJ = 854.96. In MACD $\Delta\tau = 0.25$ years, OBJ = 860.42. In both cases the horizon was 25 years and the problem was the caustic soda problem. The table illustrates the superiority of OSDP over MACD within a fixed computing budget.

Now, the question arises whether the improvement methods suggested by Fong and Srinivasan (1981), Hung and Rikkers (1974), and Rao and Ruthenberg (1977), respectively, can produce any substantial improvements compared to the construction methods discussed above.

Fong and Srinivasan (1981) solved a fixed cost, discrete time version of the nitrogeneous fertilizers problem with $T = 12$ and no upper bound on expansion size. The computing time was 12.9 min on an IBM 370/135 which is equivalent to approximately 53 s on an IBM 360/91. When the objective is evaluated using the fixed cost approximation, the Fong and Srinivasan approach gives a relative cost of 99.46 while IDP-MAC, constrained to discrete time expansions, produces a solution with relative cost 100. This comparison is not quite accurate because IDP-MAC "optimizes" with respect to the original smooth objective. Evaluated with respect to the original objective, the Fong and Srinivasan solution is 101.69, the IDP-MAC solution costrained to discrete time expansions is 101.30 and the original IDP-MAC solution from Table 4.3 is 100. The results cited are from Erlenkotter (1981).

Hung and Rikkers (1974) solved some problems with $J = 3$, $I = 4$, and $T = 10$. A heuristic solution was obtained within 3–4 s on a CDC 3600. In terms of objective function value, the heuristic was better than the best solution obtained with OPHELIE which terminated when the best integer solution was within an error tolerance of 6% over the lower bound. OPHELIE used 1–5 min on a CDC 6600. When the error tolerance was reduced to 1%, no integer solution was found within 5 min. Erlenkotter (1981) used the Hung and Rikkers (HR) procedure to improve on the discrete time constrained IDP-MAC solution (relative cost 100) for the nitrogenous fertilizers problem. The result was a relative cost of 99.76 while the original Hung and Rikkers procedure yielded 102.06. Here, all costs are evaluated with the fixed cost approximation. With the original cost data, the figures become: HR, 102.55; IDP-MAC/HR, 101.30; IDP-MAC (continuous time), 100. The improvement accomplished by HR on the IDP-MAC solution is minor: two expansions at time 7 and 8 years are merged to one expansion in year 7. For the caustic soda problem, the HR approach produced solutions which were 3% worse than the IDP-MAC solution.

The procedure by Rao and Ruthenberg (1977) used 6.9 min on a Univac 1108 to improve by 0.03% on the IDP-MAC solution for the nitrogeneous fertilizers problem.

The limited experience reported above shows that "improvement" or "interchange" methods do not substantially improve the solutions obtained using the "construction" methods mentioned earlier in this section. However, this may as well be an indication that the "construction" methods work quite well on the special problems considered here and not a general indication that "improvement" methods should be disregarded. For other data instances the results may be quite different and, in addition, it may turn out to be possible in the future to develop more efficient "improvement" methods.

For the other procedures discussed in Section 4.4 no comparative computational evidence is available. It may be noted, however, that Sweeney and Tatham (1976) solved a problem with $J = 5$, $I = 15$, and $T = 5$. For each time period it was necessary to find the 10–20 best static solutions, which consumed typically 1 min of CPU time on an IBM 370/168. Thus, the total computing time for the test problem (although not reported in the paper) must have been 5 min plus the time required to find the optimal sequence of static solutions by DP. The need for a fairly long planning horizon $\tau(T + 1)$ in order to render the first decisions independent of the rather arbitrary choice of $\tau(T + 1)$ has been discussed earlier in this section; this may render Sweeney and Tatham's approach computationally unattractive, especially as the number of static solutions to be considered increases with both J and T.

The DYNALOC procedure by Van Roy and Erlenkotter (1982) is extremely fast. A set of 48 problems with $J = 25$, $I = 50$, and $T = 10$ derived from the Kuehn and Hamburger's (1963) data was solved in less than 0.5 s (on the average) per problem on an IBM 3033. However, as mentioned in Section 4.4, the model is rather special as it does not account explicitly for the *size* of capacity expansions.

4.6. FURTHER DISCUSSION AND CONCLUSIONS

In this concluding section, the MCL model and the associated methods of solution are discussed in a broader context. More specifically the following three topics are addressed:

i. the state of the art regarding methods of solution, especially in comparison with that reported in Chapters 2 and 3.

ii. Some speculations on the future directions of research on the development of better heuristics and algorithms for the MCL model.

iii. A discussion of the validity of the MCL model.

A comparison between solution methods for single-period versus multiperiod location models provides a relative assessment of the quality of the procedures described in Sections 4.3 and 4.4 as well as some insights on the complications resulting from the introduction of multiple periods. First, a discussion of the *uncapacitated* case. As indicated in Chapters 2 and 3, medium sized $(200 \cdot 200)$ uncapacitated single period location models can be solved to optimality using Erlenkotter's (1978) DUALOC algorithm with the refined dual adjustment/ascent procedure by Van Roy and Erlenkotter (1982). Large-scale models can be solved to near optimality by greedy or interchange heuristics as described in Chapter 3. The multiperiod uncapacitated facility location model was introduced in Section 4.4 and it was shown that a simple change of variables reduces the model to a single-period model which can be solved by DUALOC or, more efficiently, by the specially adapted DYNALOC algorithm. By the same token, large-scale multiperiod models can be solved by one of the heuristics for the single-period model. Thus, equally good solution methods are available for uncapacitated single- and multiperiod models. The only difference is that multiperiod models tend to be larger in terms of the volume of input data.

With the *capacitated* case consideration for solution methods are quite different. In the multiperiod model, capacity bounds mean two things. First, output flow in any period should be below established capacity; second, established capacity at each location should be below some bound prescribed in the problem data. In the multiperiod model either one or both of the bounds may be active; in the MCL model of Section 4.3, output flow must be below established capacity while the Sweeney and Tatham (1976) model of Section 4.4 requires that established capacity is below an externally given bound. In the single-period model, capacity equals output flow and, consequently, only the bound on established capacity is active. This difference is reflected quite strongly in the methods of solution. Medium-sized single-period capacitated location models can be solved to optimality by a branch-and-bound algorithm, as, for instance, described by Christofides and Beasley (1983) who use a subgradient algorithm to compute the bounds on the objective function value. Large-scale single-period models can be solved by one of the greedy or interchange heuristics described by Jacobsen (1983). In contrast to the above, only small-scale multiperiod capacitated location models can be solved to optimality and the tool is either standard DP or MIP, which are general purpose algorithms.

Medium sized MCL models can be solved by one of the heuristics MAC (MACD), OSDP or IDP-MAC described in Sections 4.3 and 4.4. MAC, MACD, and IDP-MAC are pure greedy heuristics while OSDP may be said to have a slight interchange element (a choice between different paths through the time-graph) although still being essentially greedy. The improvement or interchange methods mentioned in Section 4.4 tend to be slow and they improve little on the solutions obtained by a greedy heuristic. This agrees to some extent with the experience on interchange heuristics for the single-period capacitated location model, except that the difference between computing efforts for the greedy and interchange heuristics is not as large as for the multiperiod case.

As for large-scale MCL-models, it is questionable whether even the greedy heuristics will perform reasonably in terms of computing time. The judgement depends to some extent on what is meant by large-scale. In the single-period case, most researchers will agree that a problem with $I = 100$ clients and $J = 100$ locations is medium-scale while a problem with $I = 1000$ clients and $J = 1000$ locations is large-scale. In the multiperiod case, the number of time-periods T is part of the definition of size in the discrete time formulation. If $I = 15$, $J = 15$, $T = 200$ is considered large-scale, MACD and OSDP can solve large-scale models, but nothing is known about the performance when I and J are large while T is a moderate number. In the continuous time formulations, such as MAC and IDP-MAC, T is replaced by the number of different expansion sizes examined, and here the maximum number tested is three while the maximum number of clients and locations reported is $I = 45$ and $J = 21$ (Erlenkotter, 1975a). Considering the computing times experienced with OSDP and IDP-MAC, it seems reasonable to conclude that only the pure greedy heuristics MACD and MAC can solve true large-scale MCL models.

Thus, one may conclude that the quality of the solution methods does not differ much between single- and multiperiod models in the uncapacitated case while there is quite a gap in the capacitated case. For the cases reported in Section 4.5, IDP-MAC tends to produce the best known solutions and one would tend to believe that perhaps these solutions are close to optimal. The belief is supported by the fact that nobody has been able to produce substantially improved solutions (the interchange heuristics contribute little, if any, improvement). But, theoretically all the heuristics could be quite far from the optimum, since we do not have an optimal solution or a good lower bound. In other words, the development of methods for solving the MCL model lags substantially behind the development of methods for similar single-period models where exact algorithms are available for medium-sized models.

The above observations lead naturally to a discussion of the future directions for the development of algorithms for the MCL model. One line of development might be a branch-and-bound based algorithm for the MIP version of the MCL model with lower bounds computed by a subgradient algorithm or by a dual ascent/adjustment procedure. The first hurdle to overcome is the development of a dual ascent/adjustment procedure for the single-period capacitated case. Another, and probably more far fetched, line of development is the possibility of using methods from the theory of optimal control to solve the MCL model. A serious difficulty in this context may be that the MCL model is a nonconvex optimization problem. Another difficulty is that it is not clear how the MCL problem should be appropriately formulated as a continuous time optimal control problem. The controls are the capacity expansions which are usually modeled as impulses or Dirac delta functions, and these are known to mathematicians as generalized functions that are not well behaved. A third line of development could be based on DP with the effort concentrated on the derivation of a state space which is computationally feasible but richer than the one used in OSDP. As mentioned in the introduction to this section, the above is speculations about future developments, but it could also serve as inspiration for future research.

Throughout this chapter it has been assumed that the MCL model under suitable circumstances may be a valid representation of reality and that the necessary data can be obtained. Neither is necessarily true.

First, a comment on the data acquisition problem. In cases where application of the MCL model is considered, the time interval between decision and implementation may be rather long, say 2–5 years. The computational experience in Section 4.5 indicates that a time-horizon of some 10–15 years is necessary to render the early decisions independent of the rather arbitrary time-horizon. Data for the future 10–15 years are likely to be highly uncertain and imprecise and constrained to projections of the present even if different scenarios are used to provide a sensitivity analysis. Trends may be forecast but jumps in prices or technology are difficult to foresee. The problem of obtaining even imprecise data for the MCL model may turn out to be, in specific applications, as least as hard as the problem of solving the model.

The second and final comment is on the validity of the MCL model itself. The question is whether the model (4.3.1)–(4.3.5) or similar models are valid representations of reality. The question should be considered very carefully in each individual prospective application of the MCL model as the consequences of using a wrong problem formulation (model) may be far worse than the deviations from optimum produced by a heuristic solution procedure. Although acceptance or rejection of the MCL model depends strongly on the case at hand, one general caution, however, is that the MCL model does not account for the uncertainties of the future. Part of the decision-maker's preferences may very well be a demand for flexibility or robustness that makes it possible to consider hedging and other decision actions to meet the uncertain future in an acceptable way.

In concluding this chapter, it may be worth noting that multiperiod locational decisions provide a rich area for future research both from a theoretical viewpoint of understanding the decision problems as well as for model formulation and development of algorithms to obtain good or optimal multiperiod locational decisions.

EXERCISES

The exercises for this fourth chapter are opportunities to study various extensions of the material presented in the chapter rather than numerical illustrations. There may not be easy and well-defined answers for some exercises. Some exercises may even turn out to be research projects if a full and well documented answer is desired.

4.1   In the single location multiperiod model of Section 4.2 it was assumed that the cost of a capacity expansion is concave. Discuss the structure of the optimal solution when the cost of each capacity expansion is convex in the size of the expansion.

4.2   Reformulate the single location multiperiod model (4.2.1)–(4.2.4) for the situation where capacity has a finite lifetime.

4.3   Assume that the demand is linearly increasing with time in the model
         (4.2.1)–(4.2.4). A long time-horizon is chosen in order to avoid the
         effects of finite horizon on the early expansion decisions. In order to
         save computing time the function $\tau(t)$ is chosen such that $\tau(t) - \tau(t -$
         $1)$ is a nondecreasing function of t as for instance: $\tau(1) = 0$; $\tau(2) = 1$;
         $\tau(3) = 2$; $\tau(4) = 3$; $\tau(5) = 5$; $\tau(6) = 8$; $\tau(7) = 13 \ldots$; $\tau(t) = \tau(t - 1) +$
         $\tau(t - 2)$, $t = 3, 4, \ldots$, (which are, by the way, the Fibonnaci
         numbers). Discuss the consequences of this choice of $\tau(t)$ both in
         terms of the capacity expansions and in terms of the costs. Compare
         with the choice $\tau(t) = (t - 1)$.

4.4   Reformulate the MCL model (4.3.1)–(4.3.5) to consider the finite
         lifetime of each capacity expansion.

4.5   Describe a greedy heuristic for the MCL model (4.3.1)–(4.3.5); that
         is, a heuristic which determines time, size, and location of each
         capacity expansion, one at a time.

4.6   Modify Algorithm 4.1 to implement MACD rather than OSDP.

4.7   Discuss how OSDP and MACD (Algorithms 4.1, 4.2, and 4.3) should
         be modified to take care of capacity expansions with a finite lifetime
         and the opportunity that results, which allows the relocation of
         capacity.

4.8   Discuss how MACD may be modified to take care of time and
         location dependent finite upper bounds $z_{jt}^{\max}$ on capacity expan-
         sions.

4.9   Discuss under what conditions the termination rule in Algorithm 4.3
         is optimal; that is, under what conditions on $F_{jt}(z)$ and w_{it} is d_p^* a
         convex function of p. It is known that $C_t(\mathbf{a}, \mathbf{b})$ is a convex function of
         $\mathbf{a}$.

4.10 Formulate a continuous time (optimal control) version of the MCL
         model (4.3.1)–(4.3.5). Comment: this is a research project and there
         may not be an easy answer. If the z_{jt} are transformed to $z_j(t)$ and
         considered as controls, the optimal controls will be Dirac delta
         functions (impulses) and trouble arises with the definition of the cost
         function $F_{jt}(z)$.

4.11 With reference to the description of MAC and the implicit discretiza-
         tion of time by the discrete set of allowed capacity expansions,
         compare MAC and MACD, and discuss advantages and drawbacks of
         the continuous time approach versus the discrete time approach.

4.12 The uncapacitated multiperiod facility location model by Van Roy
         and Erlenkotter was described in Section 4.4, and it was mentioned
         that the model is equivalent to a single-period model. Develop a
         greedy heuristic for this model by generalizing the greedy heuristic for
         the UFL model from Chapter 3.

4.13 In MAC and IDP-MAC (Section 4.4), the continuous time transportation model is solved by parametric programming of the right-hand side (PARA.RHS). This is straightforward when demands $w_i(t)$ increase linearly with time; the parameter in PARA.RHS is simply time. Discuss what happens when $w_i(t)$, $i = 1, \ldots, I$ are nonlinear increasing functions of time. Can PARA.RHS be used or must a discrete time formulation be used?

REFERENCES

Ballou, R. H. (1968). "Dynamic Warehouse Location Analysis." *Journal of Marketing Research* **5**, 271–276.

Barr, R. S., F. Glover and D. Klingman (1976). *Enhancements of Spanning Tree Labelling Procedures for Network Optimization*, Res. Rep. CCS 262. University of Texas, Austin.

Christofides, N., and J. E. Beasley (1983). "Extensions to a Lagrangian Relaxation Approach for the Capacitated Warehouse Location Problem." *European Journal of Operational Research* **12**(1), 19–28.

Domschke, W., and A. Drexl (1985). *Location and Layout Planning—An International Bibliography*. Springer-Verlag, Berlin and New York.

Erlenkotter, D. (1969). "Preinvestment Planning for Capacity Expansions: A Multi-Location Dynamic Model." Ph.D. Dissertation, Stanford University, Stanford, California.

Erlenkotter, D. (1975a). "Capacity Planning for Large Multilocation Systems: Approximate and Incomplete Dynamic Programming Approaches." *Management Science* **22**, 274–285.

Erlenkotter, D. (1975b). *Bibliography on Dynamic Location Models*, Discuss. Pap. No. 55. Management Science Study Center, Graduate School of Management, University of California, Los Angeles.

Erlenkotter, D. (1978). "A Dual-Based Procedure for Uncapacitated Facility Location." *Operations Research* **26**, 992–1009.

Erlenkotter, D. (1981). "A Comparative Study of Approaches to Dynamic Location Problems." *European Journal of Operational Research* **6**, 133–143.

Fong, C. O., and V. Srinivasan (1981). "The Multiregion Dynamic Capacity Expansion Problem. Parts I and II." *Operations Research* **29**, 787–816.

Gilmore, P. C., and R. E. Gomory (1961). "A Linear Programming Approach to the Cutting Stock Problem. Part I." *Operations Research* **9**, 849–859.

Gilmore, P. C., and R. E. Gomory (1963). "A Linear Programming Approach to the Cutting Stock Problem. Part II." *Operations Research* **11**, 863–888.

Hung, H. K. (1973). "A Heuristic Algorithm for the Multi-Period Facility Location Problem." Ph.D. Dissertation, University of Massachusetts, Amherst.

Hung, H. K., and R. F. Rikkers (1974). "A Heuristic Algorithm for the Multi-Period Facility Location Problem." Presented at the Joint ORSA/TIMS National Meeting, Boston, Massachusetts.

Jacobsen, S. K. (1974). *An Algorithm for Small-Scale Dynamic Plant-Location Problems*, Working Paper. IMSOR, Technical University of Denmark.

Jacobsen, S. K. (1977). *Heuristic Procedures for Dynamic Plant Location*, Working Paper. IMSOR, Technical University of Denmark.

Jacobsen, S. K. (1983). "Heuristics for the Capacitated Plant Location Model." *European Journal of Operational Research* **12**(3), 253–261.

Kuehn, A. A., and M. J. Hamburger (1963). "A Heuristic Program for Locating Warehouses." *Management Science* **9**(4), 643–666.

Kuhn, H. W., and M. J. Baumol (1962). "An Approximate Algorithm for the Fixed-Charges Transportation Problem." *Naval Research Logistics Quarterly* **9**(1), 1–15.

Luss, H. (1982). "Operations Research and Capacity Expansion Problems: A Survey."*Operations Research*, **30**(5), 907–947.

Manne, A. S., ed. (1967). *Investments for Capacity Expansion: Size, Location and Time-Phasing*. MIT Press, Cambridge, Massachusetts.

Rao, R. C., and D. P. Ruthenberg (1977). "Multilocation Plant Sizing and Timing." *Management Science* **23**, 1187–1198.

Sweeney, D. J., and R. L. Tatham (1976). "An Improved Long Run Model for Multiple Warehouse Location." *Management Science* **22**(7), 748–758.

Thomas, A. (1977). "Models for Optimal Capacity Expansion." Ph.D. Dissertation, Yale University, New Haven, Connecticut.

Van Roy, T. J., and D. Erlenkotter (1982). "A Dual-Based Procedure for Dynamic Facility Location". *Management Science* **28**(10), 1091–1105.

5

Decomposition Methods for Facility Location Problems

Thomas L. Magnanti
Sloan School of Management
Massachusetts Institute of Technology
Cambridge, Massachusetts

Richard T. Wong
Krannert Graduate School of Management
Purdue University
West Lafayette, Indiana

5.1.   INTRODUCTION

Discrete facility location problems pose many challenging optimization issues. In size alone, they can be difficult to solve: models of facility location applications often require thousands of variables and thousands of constraints. Moreover, the models are complicated: the basic yes-no decisions of whether or not to select candidate sites for facilities endow the models with a complex combinatorial structure. Even with as few as 30 candidate sites, there might be more than one billion potential combinations for the facility locations.

In treating large-scale problems with these complications, mathematical programming, like most disciplines, has relied heavily upon several key concepts. Throughout the years, the closely related notions of bounding techniques, duality, and decomposition have been central to many of the advances in mathematical programming. The optimization problems encountered in facility location have been no exception. Indeed, location problems have served as a fertile testing ground for many ideas from mathematical programming, and advances in location theory have stimulated more general developments in optimization.

In particular, since discrete facility location problems contain two types of inherently different decisions—where to locate facilities and how best to allocate demands to the resulting facilities—the problem class is an attractive candidate for decomposition. Once the discrete-choice facility location decisions have been made, the (continuous) allocation problem typically becomes much simpler to solve. Can we exploit this fact in designing algorithms? If not, decomposition may still be attractive. Even if location problems were not complicated by the discrete-choice site selection decisions and were to be formulated as simpler linear programs (e.g., by relaxing the integrality restrictions on the problem variables), they still would be very large and difficult to solve. Fortunately, however, the problems have a special structure that can be exploited by various decomposition techniques.

This chapter describes the use of decomposition as a solution procedure for solving facility location problems. It begins by introducing two basic decomposition strategies that are applicable to location problems. It then presents a more formal discussion of decomposition and examines methods for improving the performance of the decomposition algorithms, both in general and in the context of facility location models. This discussion emphasizes recent advances that have led to new insights about decomposition methods and that appear promising for future developments. It also stresses the relationships between bounding techniques, decomposition, and duality. Finally, the chapter discusses the importance of problem formulation and its effect upon the performance of decomposition methods. Most facility location problems can be stated as mixed integer programs in a variety of ways; choosing a "good" formulation from the available alternatives can have a pronounced effect upon the performance of an algorithm.

Most of the chapter, and particularly Sections 5.1, 5.2, 5.6, and 5.7, should be accessible to nonspecialists and requires only a general background in linear and integer programming. Sections 5.3–5.5 discuss more advanced material and contain some new results and interpretations that might also be of interest to specialists. A good knowledge of linear programming duality is useful for following the proofs in Sections 5.4 and 5.5.

5.1.1. Problem Formulations

Throughout our discussion, we assume that facilities are to be located at the nodes of a given network $G = (V, A)$ with node (vertex) set V and arc set A. We let $[i, j]$ denote the arc connecting nodes v_i and v_j.

We assume that if a facility is located at node $v_j \in V$, then the node has a demand (output) capacity of K_j units. If no facility is assigned to node $v_j \in V$, then the node cannot accommodate any demand.

For decision variables, we let

$$x_j = \begin{cases} 0, & \text{if a facility is not assigned to node } v_j \\ 1, & \text{if a facility is assigned to node } v_j, \end{cases}$$

and let

$$y_{ij} = \text{the flow on arc } [i, j] \in A.$$

Let $\mathbf{x} = (x_1, \ldots, x_n)$ denote the vector of location variables and $\mathbf{y} = (y_{ij})$ denote the vector of flow variables. For notational convenience, we will say that facility v_j is *open* if $x_j = 1$ and that it is *closed* if $x_j = 0$. In general, the set $\{v_1, v_2, \ldots, v_n\}$ of potential facility locations might be a subset of the nodes V. We let A_j denote the subset of arcs directed into the potential facility location v_j.

We assume that the location problem has been formulated as the following mixed integer program:

$$\text{minimize} \quad \mathbf{cx} + \mathbf{dy} \tag{5.1.1}$$

$$\text{subject to} \quad \mathbf{Ny} = \mathbf{w}, \tag{5.1.2}$$

$$\mathbf{y} \geq 0, \tag{5.1.3}$$

$$\sum_{[i,j] \in A_j} y_{ij} \leq K_j x_j, \quad j = 1, \ldots, n, \tag{5.1.4}$$

$$\mathbf{x} \in X, \tag{5.1.5}$$

$$(\mathbf{x}, \mathbf{y}) \in \text{SIDE}, \tag{5.1.6}$$

where $\mathbf{c} = (c_1, \ldots, c_n)$, $\mathbf{d} = (d_{ij})$, and $\mathbf{w} = (w_1, \ldots, w_n)$; in this formulation, d_{ij} denotes the per unit cost of routing flow on arc $[i, j]$, c_j denotes the cost for locating a facility at node v_j, $\mathbf{N}$ is a node-arc incidence matrix for the network G, and w_i denotes the net demand (weight) at node v_i. Therefore, (5.1.2) is the customary mass balance equation from network flows.

The inequalities (5.1.4) state that the total output* from node v_j cannot exceed the node's capacity K_j if a facility is assigned to that node (i.e., $x_j = 1$), and that the node can have no output if a facility is not assigned to it (i.e., $x_j = 0$). The set X contains any restrictions imposed upon the location decisions, including the binary restriction $x_j = 0$ or 1. For example, the set might include multiple choice constraints of the form $x_1 + x_2 + x_3 \le 2$ that state that at most two facilities can be assigned to nodes v_1, v_2, and v_3. It could also contain precedence constraints of the form $x_1 \le x_2$, stating that a facility can be assigned to node v_1 (i.e., $x_1 = 1$) only if a facility is assigned to node v_2.

Finally, the set SIDE contains any additional side restrictions imposed upon the allocation variables, or imposed jointly upon the location and allocation variables. For example, it might contain "bundle" constraints of the form $y_{ij} + y_{hk} + y_{rs} \le u$ that limit the total flow on three separate arcs $[i, j]$, $[h, k]$, and $[r, s]$ or of the form $y_{ij} + y_{hk} + y_{rs} = y_{pq}$ that relate the flow on several arcs. The last equation can be used to model multicommodity flow versions of the problem without the need for any additional notational complexity. In this case, we could view the arcs $[i, j]$, $[h, k]$, $[r, s]$, and $[p, q]$ as having been extracted from four separate copies of the same underlying network (i.e., $\mathbf{N}$ is block diagonal with four independent copies of the same node-arc incident matrix). The first three of these networks model different commodities and the fourth models total flow by all commodities. Similar types of specifications for the side constraints or for the topology of the underlying network would permit the formulation to model a wide variety of other potential problem characteristics, such as the distribution of goods through a multiechelon system of warehouses.

The following special case of this general model has received a great deal of attention in the facility location literature:

$$\text{minimize} \quad \mathbf{cx} + \mathbf{dy} \tag{5.1.7}$$

$$\text{subject to} \quad \sum_{j=1}^{n} y_{ij} = 1, \qquad i = 1, \ldots, m \tag{5.1.8}$$

$$y_{ij} \le x_j, \qquad i = 1, \ldots, m, \quad j = 1, \ldots, n \tag{5.1.9}$$

$$\sum_{j=1}^{n} x_j = p \tag{5.1.10}$$

$$y_{ij} \ge 0, \qquad i = 1, \ldots, m, \quad j = 1, \ldots, n \tag{5.1.11}$$

---

*The flow y_{ij} *into* node v_j represents the amount of service that node v_i is receiving *from* node v_j. Therefore, it seems natural to refer to this flow as an *output* (of service) from node v_j.

$$x_j = 0 \text{ or } 1, \quad \text{all } j = 1, \ldots, n. \tag{5.1.12}$$

In this model, y_{ij} denotes the fraction of customer demand at node v_i that receive service from a facility at node v_j. The "forcing" constraints (5.1.9), which we could have written as $\Sigma_i \, y_{ij} \le m x_j$ to conform with the earlier formulation (5.1.4), restricts the flow to only those nodes v_j that have been chosen as facility sites (i.e., have $x_j = 1$). Finally, constraint (5.1.10) restricts the number of facilities to a prescribed number p. In this formulation, the set of customer locations v_i could be distinct from the set of potential facility locations v_j. Or, both sets of locations might correspond to the same node set V of an underlying graph $G = (V, A)$. In the model (5.1.7)–(5.1.12), which is usually referred to as the *p-median problem*, d_{ij} denotes the cost of servicing demand from node v_i by a facility at node v_j (see Chapter 2). Throughout our discussion, when referring to the p-median problem, we will assume, as is customary, that each $c_j = 0$; that is, we do not consider the cost of establishing facilities, but merely limit their number.

Although much of our discussion in this chapter applies to the general formulation (5.1.1)–(5.1.6), or can be extended to apply to this model, for ease of presentation, we usually consider the more specialized model (5.1.7)–(5.1.12).

5.1.2. Chapter Outline

The remainder of the chapter is structured as follows. The next section introduces two forms of decomposition for facility location problems—Benders' (or resource directive) decomposition and Lagrangian relaxation (or price directive) decomposition. Section 5.3 describes these decomposition approaches in more detail and casts them in a more general and unifying framework of minimax optimization. The section also describes methods for improving the performance of these algorithms. Section 5.4 specializes one of these improvements to Benders' decomposition as applied to facility location problems. Section 5.5 discusses the important role of model formulation in applying decomposition to facility location problems. This section also focuses on Benders' decomposition (see Chapters 2 and 3 for related discussions of Lagrangian relaxation). Section 5.6 describes computational experience in applying Benders' decomposition to facility location and related transportation problems. Finally, Section 5.7 contains concluding remarks and cites references to the literature.

5.2. INTRODUCTION TO DECOMPOSITION

This section discusses two different decomposition strategies for obtaining lower bounds on the optimal objective function value of location problems. To introduce these concepts, we focus on the p-median location problem introduced in Chapter 2 and reformulated in Section 5.1. The next section derives these bounding techniques more generally for the entire class of location problems (5.1.1)–(5.1.6).

5.2.1. Resource Directive (Benders') Decomposition

Consider the five-node, two-median example of Figure 5.1. In Figure 5.1(a), the arc labels indicate the cost of traversing a particular link; assume that each node has a unit demand. The entries in the transportation cost matrix in Figure 5.1(b) specify costs d_{ij} of servicing the demand at node v_i from a facility located at node v_j. Suppose we have a current configuration with facilities located at nodes v_2 and v_5 (i.e., $x_2 = x_5 = 1$). The objective function cost for this configuration is $5 + 0 + 3 + 1 + 0 = 9$.

Relative to the current solution, let us evaluate the reduction in the objective function cost if facility 1 (i.e., the facility at node v_1) is opened and all other facilities retain their current, open versus closed, status. This new facility would reduce the cost of servicing the demands at node v_1 from $d_{12} = 5$ to $d_{11} = 0$. Therefore, the saving for opening facility 1 is 5 units. Similarly, by opening facility 3 we would reduce (relative to the current solution) node v_3 cost from $d_{34} + d_{45} = 3$ to $d_{33} = 0$ so the saving is 3 units. Opening facility 4 would reduce node v_3 cost from 3 to 2 and node v_4 cost from 1 to 0, for a total saving of $1 + 1 = 2$. Since facilities 2 and 5 are already open in the current solution, the saving for opening any of them is zero.

Note that when these savings are combined, the individual assessments might overestimate possible total savings since the computation might double count the cost reductions for any particular node. For example, our previous computations predict that opening both facilities 3 and 4 would reduce the node v_3 cost and give a total reduction of $3 + 1 = 4$ units even though the maximum possible reduction is clearly 3 units which is the cost of servicing node v_3 in the current solution.

With this savings information, we can bound the cost z of any feasible configuration $\mathbf{x}$ from below by

$$z \geq B_1(\mathbf{x}) = 9 - 5x_1 - 3x_3 - 2x_4 . \qquad (5.2.1)$$

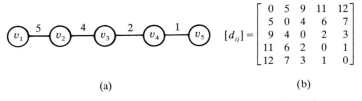

$$[d_{ij}] = \begin{bmatrix} 0 & 5 & 9 & 11 & 12 \\ 5 & 0 & 4 & 6 & 7 \\ 9 & 4 & 0 & 2 & 3 \\ 11 & 6 & 2 & 0 & 1 \\ 12 & 7 & 3 & 1 & 0 \end{bmatrix}$$

(a)   (b)

Figure 5.1. A two-median example: (a) the underlying transportation network; (b) the distance matrix.

Notice that specifying a *different* current configuration would change our savings computations and permit us to obtain a different lower bound function. For example, the configuration $x_1 = x_3 = 1$ would produce a lower bound inequality

$$z \geq B_2(\mathbf{x}) = 9 - 4x_2 - 4x_4 - 4x_5 \qquad (5.2.2)$$

on the objective function value z of any feasible solution, including the optimal solution of the problem.

Since each of these two bounding functions is always valid, by combining them we obtain an improved lower bound for the optimal two-median cost. Solving the following mixed integer program would determine the best location of the facilities that uses the combined lower bounding information:

$$
\begin{aligned}
\text{minimize} \quad & z \\
\text{subject to} \quad & z \geq B_1(\mathbf{x}) = 9 - 5x_1 \qquad - 3x_3 - 2x_4 \\
& z \geq B_2(\mathbf{x}) = 9 \qquad - 4x_2 \qquad - 4x_4 - 4x_5 \\
& x_1 + x_2 + x_3 + x_4 + x_5 = 2 \\
& x_j = 0 \text{ or } 1, \qquad j = 1, \ldots, 5 \qquad (5.2.3)
\end{aligned}
$$

which yields a lower bound of $z^* = 5$ obtained by setting $x_1^* = x_2^* = 1$ and $x_3^* = x_4^* = x_5^* = 0$ (or by setting $x_1^* = x_4^* = 1$, or $x_1^* = x_5^* = 1$, or $x_3^* = x_4^* = 1$, and all other $x_j^* = 0$ in each case).

This bounding procedure is the essential ingredient of Benders' decomposition. In this context, (5.2.3) is referred to as a Benders' *master problem* and (5.2.1) and (5.2.2) are called *Benders' cuts* or inequalities. When applied to mixed integer programs with integer variables $\mathbf{x}$ and continuous variables $\mathbf{y}$, Benders' decomposition repeatedly solves a master problem like (5.2.3) in the integer variables $\mathbf{x}$; at each step, the algorithm uses a "simple" savings computation to refine the lower bound information by adding a new Benders' cut to the master problem. Each solution $(z^*, \mathbf{x}^*)$ to the master problem yields a new lower bound z^* and a new configuration $\mathbf{x}^*$. For p-median problems, with the facility locations fixed at $\mathbf{x} = \mathbf{x}^*$, the resulting allocation problem becomes a trivial linear program (assign all demand at node v_i to the closest open facility, that is, minimize d_{ij} over all j with $x_j^* = 1$). The optimal solution $\mathbf{y}^*$ to this linear program generates a new feasible median solution $(\mathbf{x}^*, \mathbf{y}^*)$. The cost $\mathbf{dy}^*$ of this solution is an upper bound on the optimal objective function value of the p-median problem. As we will see in Section 5.4, the savings from any current configuration $\mathbf{x}^*$ can be viewed as dual variables for this linear program. Therefore, in general, the solution of a linear program (and its dual) would replace the simple savings computation.

The method terminates when the current lower bound z^* equals the cost of the best (least cost) configuration $\hat{x}$ found so far. This equality implies that the best upper bound equals the best lower bound and so $\hat{x}$ must be an optimal configuration.

Since Benders' decomposition generates a series of feasible solutions to the original median problem, it may be viewed as a primal method that utilizes dual information. We next discuss a *dual* method.

5.2.2. Price-Directive (Lagrangian) Decomposition

Lagrangian relaxation offers another type of decomposition technique that produces lower bounds. Consider a mixed integer programming formulation of the example of Figure 5.1:

$$\text{minimize} \quad \sum_{i=1}^{5} \sum_{j=1}^{5} d_{ij} y_{ij} \tag{5.2.4}$$

$$\text{subject to} \quad \sum_{j=1}^{5} y_{ij} = 1 , \quad i = 1, \ldots, 5 \tag{5.2.5}$$

$$y_{ij} \leq x_j , \quad i = 1, \ldots, 5 , \quad j = 1, \ldots, 5 \tag{5.2.6}$$

$$\sum_{j=1}^{5} x_j = 2 \tag{5.2.7}$$

$$y_{ij} \geq 0 , \quad x_j = 0 \text{ or } 1, \quad \begin{array}{l} i = 1, \ldots, 5 , \\ j = 1, \ldots, 5 . \end{array} \tag{5.2.8}$$

Larger versions of problem (5.2.4)–(5.2.8) are too complicated to solve directly, since with 100 nodes instead of 5 the problem would contain 10,000 variables y_{ij} and 10,000 constraints of the form (5.2.6).

As an algorithmic strategy for simplifying the problem, suppose that we remove the constraints (5.2.5), weighting them by Lagrange multipliers (dual variables) λ_i, and placing them in the objective function to obtain the *Lagrangian subproblem*:

$$L(\boldsymbol{\lambda}) = \min \sum_{i=1}^{5} \sum_{j=1}^{5} d_{ij} y_{ij} + \sum_{i=1}^{5} \lambda_i \left(1 - \sum_{j=1}^{5} y_{ij} \right) \tag{5.2.9}$$

subject to (5.2.6)–(5.2.8).

Each "penalty" term $\lambda_i (1 - \sum_{j=1}^{5} y_{ij})$ will be positive if λ_i has the appropriate sign and the ith constraint of (5.2.5) is violated. Therefore, by adjusting the penalty values λ_i, we can "discourage" the subproblem (5.2.9) from having an optimal solution that violates (5.2.5).

Note that since the penalty term is always zero for all λ_i whenever **y** satisfies (5.2.5), the optimal subproblem cost $L(\boldsymbol{\lambda})$ is always a valid lower bound for the optimal p-median cost.

The primary motivation for adopting this algorithmic strategy is that problem (5.2.9) is very easy to solve. Set $y_{ij} = 1$ only when $x_j = 1$ and the modified cost coefficient $(d_{ij} - \lambda_i)$ of y_{ij} is nonpositive. Thus, summed over all nodes v_i, the optimal benefit of setting $x_j = 1$ is

$$r_j = \sum_{i=1}^{5} \min (0, d_{ij} - \lambda_i)$$

and we can rewrite (5.2.9) as

$$L(\boldsymbol{\lambda}) = \min \sum_{j=1}^{5} r_j x_j + \sum_{i=1}^{5} \lambda_i \qquad (5.2.10)$$

subject to (5.2.7) and (5.2.8).

This problem is solved simply by finding the two smallest r_j values and setting the corresponding variables $x_j = 1$.

For example, let $\boldsymbol{\lambda} = (3, 3, 3, 3, 3)$. Then (5.2.10) becomes

$$L(\boldsymbol{\lambda}) = \min (-3x_1 - 3x_2 - 4x_3 - 6x_4 - 5x_5 + 15)$$

subject to (5.2.7) and (5.2.8).

The corresponding optimal solution for (5.2.9) has a Lagrangian objective value $L(\boldsymbol{\lambda}) = 15 - 6 - 5 = 4$; the solution has $x_4 = x_5 = 1$, $y_{34} = y_{44} = y_{45} = y_{54} = y_{55} = 1$, and all the other variables set to zero. Notice that this solution for the Lagrangian subproblem is not feasible for the p-median problem. Indeed, for any $i = 1, 2, \ldots, 5$, it does not satisfy the demand constraint (5.2.5).

For another dual variable vector $\boldsymbol{\lambda}^* = (5, 5, 3, 2, 3)$, (5.2.10) becomes

$$L(\boldsymbol{\lambda}^*) = \min (-5x_1 - 5x_2 - 4x_3 - 5x_4 - 4x_5 + 18)$$

subject to (5.2.7) and (5.2.8).

Its optimal objective function value $L(\boldsymbol{\lambda}^*) = 8$ is a tight lower bound since the optimal p-median cost is also 8.

This example illustrates the importance of using "good" values for the dual variables λ_i in order to obtain strong lower bounds from the Lagrangian subproblem. In fact, to find the sharpest possible Lagrangian lower bound, we need to solve the optimization problem

$$\max_{\boldsymbol{\lambda}} L(\boldsymbol{\lambda}).$$

This optimization problem in the variables $\boldsymbol{\lambda}$ has become known as a *Lagrangian dual* problem to the original facility location model. (See

Chapter 2 for further discussion of the use of the Lagrangian dual for the p-median problem, and Chapter 3 for applications to the uncapacitated facility location problem.)

5.3. DECOMPOSITION METHODS AND MINIMAX OPTIMIZATION

The previous section introduced two of the most widely used strategies for solving large-scale optimization problems. Lagrangian relaxation, or price directive decomposition, simplifies problems by relaxing a set of complicating constraints. Resource directed decomposition, which includes Benders' method as a special case, decomposes problems by projecting (temporarily holding constant) a set of strategic resource variables.

We noted how the techniques can be applied directly to location problems. In addition, they can be combined with other solution methods; for example, Lagrangian relaxation, rather than a linear programming relaxation, can be embedded within the framework of a branch-and-bound approach for solving location and other discrete optimization problems.

In this section, we study these two basic decomposition techniques by considering a broader, but somewhat more abstract, minimax setting that captures the essence of both the resource directive and Lagrangian relaxation approaches. That is, we consider the optimization problem

$$v = \min_{\mathbf{u} \in U} \max_{\mathbf{s} \in S} \{ f(\mathbf{s}) + \mathbf{u}g(\mathbf{s}) \} \qquad (5.3.1)$$

where U and S are given subsets of R^n and R^r, f is a real-valued function defined on S, and $g(\mathbf{s})$ is an n-dimensional vector for any $\mathbf{s} \in S$. Note that we are restricting the objective function $f(\mathbf{s}) + \mathbf{u}g(\mathbf{s})$ to be linear-affine in the outer minimizing variable $\mathbf{u}$ for each choice of the inner maximizing variable $\mathbf{s}$.

To relate this minimax setting to Benders' decomposition applied to the facility location problem (5.1.7)–(5.1.12), we can argue as follows. Let $X = \{\mathbf{x}: \Sigma_{j=1}^{n} x_j = p$ and $x_j = 0$ or 1 for $j = 1, \ldots, n\}$. An equivalent form of formulation (5.1.7)–(5.1.12) is

$$\min_{\mathbf{x} \in X} \min_{\mathbf{y} \geq 0} \{\mathbf{cx} + \mathbf{dy}: (5.1.8), (5.1.9), \text{ and } (5.1.11) \text{ are satisfied}\} . \qquad (5.3.2)$$

For any fixed value of the configuration vector $\mathbf{x}$, the inner minimization is a simple network flow linear program. Assume* the network flow problem is feasible and has an optimal solution for all $\mathbf{x} \in X$; then dualizing the inner mimimization problem over $\mathbf{y}$ gives the equivalent formulation

---

*These assumptions can be relaxed quite easily in our development, but the added complications would only cloud our main development.

$$\min_{\mathbf{x} \in X} \max_{(\boldsymbol{\lambda}, \boldsymbol{\pi}) \in \Lambda\Pi} \left\{ \sum_{i=1}^{m} \lambda_i - \sum_{j=1}^{n} \left(\sum_{i=1}^{m} \pi_{ij} \right) x_j + \mathbf{cx} \right\} \qquad (5.3.3)$$

where $\Lambda\Pi = \{(\boldsymbol{\lambda}, \boldsymbol{\pi}): \boldsymbol{\lambda} \in R^m, \boldsymbol{\pi} \in R^{mn}, \lambda_i - \pi_{ij} \le d_{ij}$ for all i, j and $\boldsymbol{\pi} \ge 0\}$. Observe that this problem is a special case of (5.3.1) with $(\boldsymbol{\lambda}, \boldsymbol{\pi})$ and $\mathbf{x}$ identified with $\mathbf{s}$ and $\mathbf{u}$, respectively. This reformulation is typical of the resource directive philosophy of solving the problem parametrically in terms of complicating variables like the configuration variables $\mathbf{x}$.

Dualizing (5.1.8) in the location model (5.1.7)–(5.1.12) gives a maximin form of the problem. The resulting Lagrangian dual problem is

$$\max_{\boldsymbol{\lambda}} \min_{(\mathbf{x}, \mathbf{y}) \in XY} \left\{ \mathbf{cx} + \mathbf{dy} + \sum_{i=1}^{m} \lambda_i \left(1 - \sum_{j=1}^{n} y_{ij} \right) \right\} \qquad (5.3.4)$$

or, equivalently,

$$\max_{\boldsymbol{\lambda}} \min_{(\mathbf{x}, \mathbf{y}) \in XY} \left\{ \mathbf{cx} + \sum_{i=1}^{m} \lambda_i + \sum_{i=1}^{m} \sum_{j=1}^{n} (d_{ij} - \lambda_i) y_{ij} \right\} \qquad (5.3.5)$$

where $XY = \{(\mathbf{x}, \mathbf{y}): \mathbf{x} \in X, \mathbf{y} \ge 0$ and (5.1.9)–(5.1.12) are satisfied$\}$ and $\boldsymbol{\lambda}$ and $(\mathbf{x}, \mathbf{y})$ correspond to $\mathbf{u}$ and $\mathbf{s}$ in (5.3.1).

Note that duality plays an important role in both the minimax formulation (5.3.3) and Lagrangian maximin formulation (5.3.5). Benders' decomposition uses duality to convert the inner minimization in (5.3.2) into a maximization problem and (5.3.5) is just a slightly altered restatement of the Lagrangian dual problem (5.3.4).

5.3.1. Solving Minimax Problems by Relaxation

For any $\mathbf{u} \in U$, let $v(\mathbf{u})$ denote the value of the maximization problem in (5.3.1); that is

$$v(\mathbf{u}) = \max_{\mathbf{s} \in S} \{ f(\mathbf{s}) + \mathbf{u}g(\mathbf{s}) \} . \qquad (5.3.6)$$

We refer to this problem, for a fixed value of $\mathbf{u}$, as a *subproblem*. Note that

$$v = \min_{\mathbf{u} \in U} v(\mathbf{u}) .$$

To introduce a "relaxation" strategy for solving this problem, let us rewrite (5.3.1) as follows:

$$\text{minimize} \quad z$$

$$\text{subject to} \quad z \ge f(\mathbf{s}) + \mathbf{u}g(\mathbf{s}) , \qquad \text{for all } \mathbf{s} \in S , \qquad (5.3.7)$$

$$\mathbf{u} \in U, z \in R .$$

Observe that this problem has a constraint for each point $s \in S$. Since S may be very large, and possibly even infinite, the problem (5.3.7) often has too many constraints to solve directly. Therefore, let us form the following relaxation of this problem:

$$\text{minimize} \quad z$$

$$\text{subject to} \quad z \geq f(\mathbf{s}^k) + \mathbf{u}g(\mathbf{s}^k), \qquad k = 1, 2, \ldots, K, \qquad (5.3.8)$$

$$\mathbf{u} \in U, z \in R.$$

which is obtained by restricting the inequalities on z to a finite subset $\{\mathbf{s}^1, \mathbf{s}^2, \ldots, \mathbf{s}^K\}$ of elements $\mathbf{s}^k$ from the set S. The solution $(\mathbf{u}^K, z^K)$ of this *master problem* (5.3.8) is optimal for (5.3.7) if it satisfies all of the constraints of that problem, that is, if $v(\mathbf{u}^K) \leq z^K$. If, on the other hand, $v(\mathbf{u}^K) > z^K$ and $\mathbf{s}^{K+1}$ solves* the subproblem (5.3.6) when $\mathbf{u} = \mathbf{u}^K$, then we add

$$z \geq f(\mathbf{s}^{K+1}) + \mathbf{u}g(\mathbf{s}^{K+1})$$

as a new constraint or, as it is usually referred to, a new "cut" to the master problem (5.3.8). The algorithm continues in this way, alternately solving the master problem and subproblem.

In Section 5.3.2, we give a numerical example that illustrates both the algorithm and the conversion of mixed integer programs into the minimax form (5.3.7).

Maximin problems like the Lagrangian dual problem (5.3.5) can be treated quite similarly. Restating the relaxation algorithm for these problems requires only minor, and rather obvious, modifications.

When applied to problem (5.3.3) this relaxation algorithm is known as Benders' decomposition and when applied to (5.3.5), it is known as generalized programming or Dantzig–Wolfe decomposition. For Benders' decomposition, the master problem is an integer program with one continuous variable z, and the subproblem (5.3.6) is a linear program whose solution $\mathbf{s}^*$ can be chosen as an extreme point of S. Since S has a finite number of extreme points, Benders' algorithm will terminate after a finite number of iterations. (In the worst possible case, eventually $\{\mathbf{s}^1, \mathbf{s}^2, \ldots, \mathbf{s}^K\}$ equals all extreme points of S and (5.3.8) becomes identical to (5.3.7)). For Dantzig–Wolfe decomposition applied to (5.3.5), the master problem is a linear program and, consequently, we can replace the set $S = XY$ by the set of its extreme points (since the inner minimization problem always solves at an extreme point). Consequently, the algorithm will again terminate in a

---

*As before, to simplify our discussion we assume that this problem always has at least one optimal solution.

finite number of iterations and the sequence of solutions $\{\boldsymbol{\lambda}^K\}_{K\geq 1}$ (i.e., the $\mathbf{u}$ variable for problem (5.3.1)) will converge to an optimum for (5.3.5) (see Section 5.7 for comments on more general convergence properties of the algorithm).

5.3.2. Accelerating the Relaxation Algorithm

A major computational bottleneck in applying Benders' decomposition is that the master problem, which must be solved repeatedly, is an integer program. Even when the master problem is a linear program as in the application of Dantzig–Wolfe decomposition, the relaxation algorithm has not generally performed well due to its poor convergence properties. There are several ways to improve the algorithm's performance:

1. make a good selection of initial cuts (i.e., initial values of the $\mathbf{s}^k$ for the master problem);
2. modify the master problem to alter the choice of $\mathbf{u}^K$ at each step, or to exploit the information available from master problems solved in previous iterations;
3. reduce the number of master problems to be solved by using alternative mechanisms to generate cuts (i.e., values of the $\mathbf{s}^k$);
4. formulate the problem "properly"; or
5. select good cuts, if there are choices, to add to the master problem at each step.

Let us briefly comment on each of these enhancements. Sections 5.5.6 and 5.5.7 cite computational studies that support many of the observations in this discussion.

1. Initial Cuts. Various computational studies have demonstrated that the initial selection of cuts can have a profound effect upon the performance of Benders' algorithm applied to facility location and other discrete optimization problems. The initial cuts can be generated from institutional knowledge about the problem setting being studied or from heuristic methods that provide "good" choices of $\mathbf{u}$ for the integer variables. Solving the subproblem (5.3.6) for these choices of $\mathbf{u}$ generates points $\mathbf{s}$ from S that define the initial cuts. Unfortunately, little theory is available to guide analysts in the choice of initial cuts.

2. Modifying the Master Problem. In the context of Dantzig–Wolfe decomposition, several researchers have investigated approaches for implementing the relaxation method more efficiently by altering the master problem. Scaling the constraints of the master problem to find the "geometrically centered" value of $\mathbf{u}^K$ at each step can be beneficial. Another approach is to restrict the solution to the master problem at each step to lie within a box centered about the previous solution. This procedure presents the solution from oscillating too wildly between iterations. When there are choices, selecting judiciously among multiple optima of the master problem can also result in better convergence.

We can also modify Benders' decomposition to exploit the inherent nesting of constraints in the sequence of master problems and thus avoid solving a complete integer program at each iteration. Let $\bar{z}_K$ be the value of the best solution from the points $\mathbf{u}^1, \mathbf{u}^2, \ldots, \mathbf{u}^K$ generated after K iterations, that is, $\bar{z}^K = \min \{v(\mathbf{u}^k): k = 1, 2, \ldots, K\}$. Instead of solving the usual master problem (5.3.8), consider the integer programming feasibility version of that problem.

Find $\mathbf{u} \in U$ satisfying

$$(\bar{z}^K - \varepsilon) \geq f(\mathbf{s}^k) + \mathbf{u}g(\mathbf{s}^k), \qquad \text{for } k = 1, 2, \ldots, K \qquad (5.3.9)$$

where ε is a prespecified target reduction in objective value. If this system has a feasible solution $\mathbf{u}^{K+1}$, then solve the subproblem (5.3.6) with $\mathbf{u} = \mathbf{u}^{K+1}$ to generate a new point $\mathbf{s}^{K+1}$ from S and add the associated cut to (5.3.9). Notice that the $(K + 1)$st system has a feasible region that is a proper subset of the Kth system (since $z^{K+1} \leq z^K$ and the $(K + 1)$st system has one more constraint). This property allows us to solve a sequence of these systems by incorporating information from previous iterations.

If $z = v$ and $\mathbf{u} = \mathbf{u}^*$ is optimal for (5.3.7), then $\mathbf{u}^*$ is feasible in (5.3.9) for any $\bar{z}^K \geq v + \varepsilon$. Therefore, if (5.3.9) is infeasible, then $\bar{z}^K < v + \varepsilon$ which implies that we have found a solution within ε-units of the optimal objective value. For this reason, this technique is referred to as the ε-*optimal method* for solving the Benders' master problem.

An implementation of the ε-optimal method has been very effective in solving facility location problems with a number of side constraints, that is, when the set U has a very complicated structure (see Section 5.6).

3. Avoiding the Master Problem (*Cross Decomposition*). An alternative to modifying the master problem is to reduce the number of master problems that must be solved. Although our discussion applies to any mixed integer program with continuous variables $\mathbf{y}$ and integer variables $\mathbf{x}$, for concreteness, consider the location model (5.1.7)–(5.1.12). Suppose we apply the relaxation algorithm to the Lagrangian dual problem (5.3.5) and obtain a master problem solution $\mathbf{u}^K = \boldsymbol{\lambda}^K$ and a solution $\mathbf{s}^K = (\mathbf{x}^K, \mathbf{y}^K)$ to the Lagrangian subproblem (5.3.6). Instead of solving another master problem (in this case a linear program) to generate $\boldsymbol{\lambda}^{K+1}$, we could fix the network configuration at $\mathbf{x} = \mathbf{x}^K$ and solve the inner maximization of the Benders' formulation (5.3.3) to obtain $(\boldsymbol{\lambda}^{K+1}, \boldsymbol{\pi}^{K+1})$. Solving the subproblem (5.3.6) with $\boldsymbol{\lambda} = \boldsymbol{\lambda}^{K+1}$, we obtain $(\mathbf{x}^{K+1}, \mathbf{y}^{K+1})$.

These computations can be carried out very efficiently. The inner maximization of (5.3.3) is the dual of a special transportation problem (i.e., the inner minimization problem in (5.3.2)) which can, as we saw in Section 5.2, be solved by inspection. This special linear program is the subproblem that arises when Benders' decomposition is applied to the location problem (5.1.7)–(5.1.12). Since this technique combines the advantages of an easily solved Lagrangian dual subproblem (5.3.6) and an easily solved Benders' subproblem, it is sometimes referred to as *cross decomposition*.

By exploiting two special structures of the facility location problem, cross decomposition can compute a new dual solution $\boldsymbol{\lambda}^{K+1}$ and a new cut corresponding to $(\mathbf{x}^{K+1}, \mathbf{y}^{K+1})$ much more quickly than the usual Dantzig–Wolfe decomposition algorithm, which needs to solve a linear programming master problem (5.3.8) to find a new dual solution $\mathbf{u}^{K+1} = \boldsymbol{\lambda}^{K+1}$. Cross decomposition iteratively continues this process of solving a Lagrangian subproblem and a Benders' subproblem. Periodically, the method solves a linear programming master problem corresponding to the Lagrangian dual (5.3.5) in order to guarantee convergence to a dual solution.

An implementation of cross decomposition has provided the most effective method available for solving certain capacitated plant location problems (see Section 5.6).

4. Improving Model Formulation. Current research in integer programming has emphasized the importance of problem formulation for improving the performance of decomposition approaches and other algorithms. Two different formulations of the same problem might have identical feasible solutions, but might have different computational characteristics. For example, they might have different linear programming or Lagrangian relaxations, one being preferred to the other when used in conjunction with algorithms like branch-and-bound or Benders' decomposition. Since the issue seems to be so essential for ensuring computational success, in Section 5.5 we discuss in some detail the role of model formulation in the context of Benders' decomposition applied to facility location problems.

5. Choosing Good Cuts. In many instances, the selection of good cuts at each iteration can significantly improve the performance of the relaxation algorithm as applied to minimax problems. For facility location models, the Benders' subproblem (5.3.6) often has multiple optimal solutions; equivalently, the dual problem is a transportation linear program which is renowned for its degeneracy.

In the remainder of this section, we introduce general methods and algorithms for choosing from the alternate optima to (5.3.6) at each iteration, a solution that defines a cut that is in some sense "best." Section 5.4 specializes this methodology to facility location models.

To illustrate the selection of good cuts to add to the master problem, consider the following example of a simple mixed integer program:

$$
\begin{aligned}
z = \text{minimize} \qquad & y_3 + u \\
\text{subject to} \qquad -y_1 + \quad & y_3 + 2u = 4 \\
& -y_2 + y_3 + 5u = 4 \\
y_1 \geq , \quad y_2 \geq 0, \quad & y_3 \geq 0 \\
u \geq 0 \qquad \text{and integer} .
\end{aligned}
$$

The equivalent formulation (5.3.7) written as the linear programming dual of this problem for any fixed value of u is

$$\text{maximize} \quad (4-2u)s_1 + (4-5u)s_2$$

$$s_1 \qquad\qquad\qquad \leq 0$$

$$-s_2 \qquad \leq 0$$

$$s_1 \qquad +s_2 \qquad \leq 1$$

The three extreme points of the dual feasible region S are $\mathbf{s}^1 = (0,0)$, $\mathbf{s}^2 = (1,0)$, and $\mathbf{s}^3 = (0,1)$. We can use these points in the equivalent formulation (5.3.8) to obtain the formulation:

$$\text{minimize} \quad z$$

$$\text{subject to} \quad z \geq u$$

$$z \geq 4 - u \qquad\qquad\qquad (5.3.10)$$

$$z \geq 4 - 4u$$

$$u \geq 0 \qquad \text{and integer}.$$

Notice that the inequalities in (5.3.10) are sufficient to represent all of the inequalities that can be generated from the dual feasible region S in (5.3.7) since $\mathbf{s}^1$, $\mathbf{s}^2$, and $\mathbf{s}^3$ are all of the extreme points of S. Hence, (5.3.10) is an equivalent representation of the original mixed integer program stated in terms of the variables $\mathbf{y}$ and u.

Suppose that we initiate the relaxation algorithm with the single cut $z \geq u$ in the master problem. The optimal solution is $z^1 = u^1 = 0$. At $u = u^1 = 0$, both the extreme points $\mathbf{s}^2$ and $\mathbf{s}^3$ (and every convex combination of them) solves the subproblem

$$\text{maximize} \quad (4-2u)s_1 + (4-5u)s_2 + u$$

$$\text{subject to} \quad (s_1, s_2) \in S.$$

Stated in another way, both the second and third constraints of (5.3.10) are most violated at $z = u = 0$. Thus, the corresponding extreme points $\mathbf{s}^2$ and $\mathbf{s}^3$ must solve this subproblem.

Adding the second constraint gives the optimal solution $z^2 = u^2 = 2$ to the original problem as the next solution to the master problem. Adding the third constraint gives the nonoptimal solution $z^2 = u^2 = 1$ and requires another iteration that adds the remaining constraint of (5.3.10).

In this instance, the second constraint of (5.3.10) dominates the third in the sense that

$$4 - u \geq 4 - 4u$$

whenever $u \geq 0$ with strict inequality if $u > 0$; that is, the second constraint provides a sharper lower bound on z.

To identify the dominant cut in this case, we check to see which of the second or third constraints of (5.3.10) has the largest right-hand side value for *any* $u^o > 0$. In terms of the subproblem, this criterion becomes: from among the alternate optimal solutions to the subproblem at $\hat{u} = 0$, choose a solution that maximizes the subproblem's objective function when $u = u^o > 0$.

Figure 5.2 illustrates this procedure and serves as motivation for our subsequent analysis. In the figure, we have plotted the three constraints from the dual version (5.3.10) of the subproblem. Note that as a funciton of u, the minimum objective function value $v(u)$ to the problem is the upper envelope of the three lines in the figure. At $\hat{u} = 0$, the lines $z = 4 - u$ and $z = 4 - 4u$ both pass through this lower envelope. Equivalently, the extreme points $\mathbf{s}^2 = (1, 0)$ and $\mathbf{s}^3 = (0, 1)$ of the dual feasible region S both solve the dual problem. Note, however, that as we increase u from $\hat{u} = 0$, the line $z = 4 - u$ lies above the line $z = 4 - 4u$. It, therefore, provides a better approximation to the dual objective function $v(u)$. To identify this preferred line, we can conceptually pivot about the solution point $(\hat{z}, \hat{u}) = (4, 0)$, choosing the line through this point that lies most to the "northeast." Note that to discover this line, we need to find which of the two lines through the pivot point $(\hat{z}, \hat{u})$ is higher for *any* value of $u > 0$.

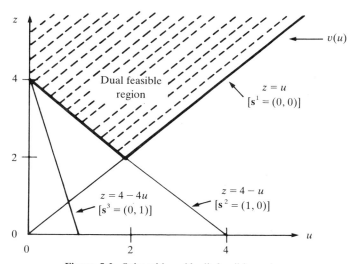

Figure 5.2. Subproblem (dual) feasible region.

Before extending this observation to arbitrary minimax problems, we formalize some definitions.

We say that the cut (or constraint)

$$z \geq f(\mathbf{s}^1) + \mathbf{u}g(\mathbf{s}^1)$$

in the minimax problem (5.3.7) *dominates* or is *stronger* than the cut

$$z \geq f(\mathbf{s}) + \mathbf{u}g(\mathbf{s})$$

if

$$f(\mathbf{s}^1) + \mathbf{u}g(\mathbf{s}^1) \geq f(\mathbf{s}) + \mathbf{u}g(\mathbf{s})$$

for all $\mathbf{u} \in U$ with a strict inequality for at least one point $\mathbf{u} \in U$. We call a cut *pareto-optimal* if no cut dominates it. Since a cut is determined by the vector $\mathbf{s} \in S$, we shall also say that $\mathbf{s}^1$ dominates (is stronger than) $\mathbf{s}$ if the associated cut is stronger, and we say that $\mathbf{s}$ is pareto-optimal if the corresponding cut is pareto-optimal.

In the previous example, we showed how to generate a pareto-optimal cut by solving an auxiliary problem defined by any point $u^o > 0$. Note that any such point is an interior point of the set $\{u: u \geq 0\}$. This set, in turn, is the convex hull of the set $U = \{u: u \geq 0 \text{ and integer}\}$.

The following theorem shows that this observation generalizes to any minimax problem of the form (5.3.7). Again, we consider the convex hull of U, denoted by U^c, but now we will be more delicate and consider the relative interior (or core)* of U^c, denoted ri (U^c), instead of its interior. The result will always be applicable since the relative interior of the convex set U^c is always nonempty. For notation, let us call any point u^o contained in the relative interior of U^c, a *core* point of U.

Theorem 5.1. *Let $\mathbf{u}^o$ be a core point of U, that is, $\mathbf{u}^o \in$ ri (U^o), and let $S(\mathbf{u})$ denote the set of optimal solutions to the optimization problem*

$$\max_{\mathbf{s} \in S} \{ f(\mathbf{s}) + \mathbf{u}g(\mathbf{s}) \} . \tag{5.3.11}$$

Also, let $\hat{\mathbf{u}}$ be any point in U and suppose that $\mathbf{s}^o$ solves the problem

$$\max_{\mathbf{s} \in S(\hat{\mathbf{u}})} \{ f(\mathbf{s}) + \mathbf{u}^o g(\mathbf{s}) \} . \tag{5.3.12}$$

Then $\mathbf{s}^o$ is pareto-optimal.

---

*The relative interior of a set is the interior relative to the smallest affine space that contains it. For example, the relative interior of a disk in 3-space (which has no interior) is the interior of the disk when viewed as a circle in 2-space.

Proof. Suppose to the contrary that $\mathbf{s}^o$ is not pareto-optimal; that is, there is a $\bar{\mathbf{s}} \in S$ that dominates $\mathbf{s}^o$. We first note that the inequalities

$$f(\bar{\mathbf{s}}) + \mathbf{u}g(\bar{\mathbf{s}}) \geq f(\mathbf{s}^o) + \mathbf{u}g(\mathbf{s}^o) \qquad \text{for all } \mathbf{u} \in U , \tag{5.3.13}$$

imply that

$$f(\bar{\mathbf{s}}) + \mathbf{u}g(\bar{\mathbf{s}}) \geq f(\mathbf{s}^o) + \mathbf{u}g(\mathbf{s}^o) \qquad \text{for all } \mathbf{u} \in U^c . \tag{5.3.14}$$

To establish the last inequality, recall that any point $\bar{\mathbf{u}} \in U^c$ can be expressed as a convex combination of a finite number of points in U, that is,

$$\bar{\mathbf{u}} = \sum_{\mathbf{u} \in U} \{\lambda_{\mathbf{u}} \mathbf{u} : \mathbf{u} \in U\} = 1$$

where $\lambda_{\mathbf{u}} \geq 0$ for all $\mathbf{u} \in U$, at most a finite number of the $\lambda_{\mathbf{u}}$ are positive, and $\sum_{\mathbf{u} \in U} \lambda_{\mathbf{u}} = 1$. Therefore, (5.3.14) with $\mathbf{u} = \bar{\mathbf{u}}$ can be obtained from (5.3.13) by multiplying the $\mathbf{u}$th inequality by $\lambda_{\mathbf{u}}$ and adding these weighted inequalities.

Also, note from the inequality (5.3.13) with $\mathbf{u} = \hat{\mathbf{u}}$ that $\bar{\mathbf{s}}$ must be an optimal solution to the optimization problem (5.3.11) when $\mathbf{u} = \hat{\mathbf{u}}$, that is, $\bar{\mathbf{s}} \in S(\hat{\mathbf{u}})$. But then, (5.3.12) and (5.3.13) imply that

$$f(\bar{\mathbf{s}}) + \mathbf{u}^o g(\bar{\mathbf{s}}) = f(\mathbf{s}^o) + \mathbf{u}^o g(\mathbf{s}^o) . \tag{5.3.15}$$

Since $\bar{\mathbf{s}}$ dominates $\mathbf{s}^o$

$$f(\bar{\mathbf{s}}) + \bar{\mathbf{u}}g(\bar{\mathbf{s}}) > f(\mathbf{s}^o) + \bar{\mathbf{u}}g(\mathbf{s}^o) \tag{5.3.16}$$

for at least one point $\bar{\mathbf{u}} \in U$. Also, since $\mathbf{u}^o \in \text{ri}\,(U^c)$ for some scalar $\theta > 1$

$$\mathbf{u} \equiv \theta \mathbf{u}^o + (1 - \theta)\bar{\mathbf{u}}$$

belongs to U^c. Multiplying (5.3.15) by θ, multiplying inequality (5.3.16) by $(1 - \theta)$, which is negative and reverses the inequality, and adding gives

$$f(\bar{\mathbf{s}}) + \mathbf{u}g(\bar{\mathbf{s}}) < f(\mathbf{s}^o) + \mathbf{u}g(\mathbf{s}^o) .$$

But this inequality contradicts (5.3.14), showing that our supposition that $\mathbf{s}^o$ is not pareto-optimal is untenable. $\square$

We should note that varying the core point $\mathbf{u}^o$ might conceivably generate different pareto-optimal cuts. Also, any implementation of Benders' algorithm has the option of generating pareto-optimal cuts at every iteration, or possibly, of generating these cuts only periodically. The trade-off will depend upon the computational burden of solving problem (5.3.12) as compared to the number of iterations that it saves.

In many instances, it is easy to specify a core point $\mathbf{u}^o$ for implementing the pareto-optimal cut algorithm. If, for example,

$$U = \{\mathbf{u} \in R^k : \mathbf{u} \geq 0 \text{ and integer}\}$$

then any point $\mathbf{u}^o > 0$ will suffice; if

$$U = \{\mathbf{u} \in R^k : u_j = 0 \text{ or } 1 \text{ for } j = 1, 2, \ldots, k\}$$

then any vector $\mathbf{u}^o$ with $0 > u_j^o > 1$ for $j = 1, 2, \ldots, k$ suffices; and if

$$U = \left\{\mathbf{u} \in R^k : \sum_{j=1}^{k} u_j \leq p, \mathbf{u} \geq 0 \text{ and integer}\right\}$$

as in the inequality version of the p-median problem (here $X = U$), then any $\mathbf{u}^o$ with $\mathbf{u}^o > 0$ and $\Sigma_{j=1}^n u_j^0 < p$ suffices. In particular, if $p > n/2$ then $\mathbf{u}^o = (1/2, 1/2, \ldots, 1/2)$ is a core point.

When Benders' decomposition is applied to the location model (5.1.7)–(5.1.12), problem (5.3.11) is a specially structured linear program that can be solved efficiently. The next section specifies details of this solution procedure.

5.4. ACCELERATING BENDERS' METHOD FOR FACILITY LOCATION

5.4.1. Introduction

Section 5.3 described both Benders' decomposition and Dantzig–Wolfe decomposition within a unifying framework of minimax optimization. This section, which is problem-specific and somewhat more detailed, considers Benders' decomposition as applied to facility location problems. The discussion will serve two purposes. First, it shows how decomposition can be streamlined to exploit the special structure of facility location problems. Second, it introduces several different types of Benders' cuts for facility location models that can be used to design new algorithms. In particular, they can be used as bounding procedures within branch-and-bound algorithms or can be used to design heuristic algorithms. For example, when interpreted properly, a number of successful heuristics for several classes of integer programming problems can be viewed as applying a (heuristic) version of Benders' decomposition that retains only the most recently generated Benders' cut(s) in the master problem. Therefore, the cuts themselves are of interest, independent of their use within decomposition.

Although solving the linear program (5.3.12) generates pareto-optimal cuts for Benders' method applied to general mixed integer programs, the special structure of facility location problems makes it possible to generate strong cuts more efficiently with specialized network algorithms. In this section, we discuss several different cut-generating procedures, ranging from those that produce cuts that dominate the standard Benders' cuts, to more elaborate algorithms that actually produce pareto-optimal cuts. In this discussion, we return to the notation used in Sections 5.1 and 5.2.

Suppose we fix $\mathbf{x} = \bar{\mathbf{x}} \in X$; then (5.1.7)–(5.1.12), and more generally (5.1.1)–(5.1.6), reduce to a pure linear programming subproblem in the variables y_{ij} which we will call the *associated linear program*:

$$v(\bar{\mathbf{x}}) = \text{minimum} \quad \sum_{i=1}^{m} \sum_{j=1}^{n} d_{ij} y_{ij} + \sum_{j=1}^{n} c_j \bar{x}_j$$

$$\text{subject to} \quad \sum_{j=1}^{n} y_{ij} = 1, \quad i = 1, \ldots, m \quad (5.4.1)$$

$$y_{ij} \leq \bar{x}_j$$

$$y_{ij} \geq 0, \quad i = 1, \ldots, m, \quad j = 1, \ldots, n.$$

For future reference, let us adopt the following notation:

$O = \{ j \mid \bar{x}_j = 1 \}$, the index set of *open* facilities, and

$C = \{ j \mid \bar{x}_j = 0 \}$, the index set of *closed* facilities

corresponding to the configuration $\mathbf{x} = \bar{\mathbf{x}}$.

The dual of the associated linear program is

$$v(\bar{\mathbf{x}}) = \text{maximum} \quad \sum_{i=1}^{m} \left[\lambda_i - \sum_{j=1}^{n} \bar{x}_j \pi_{ij} \right] + \sum_{j=1}^{n} c_j \bar{x}_j$$

$$\text{subject to} \quad \lambda_i - \pi_{ij} \leq d_{ij}, \quad i = 1, \ldots, m, \quad j = 1, \ldots, n \quad (5.4.2)$$

$$\pi_{ij} \geq 0, \quad i = 1, \ldots, m, \quad j = 1, \ldots, n.$$

Note that $\sum c_j \bar{x}_j$ in the objective function is a constant since the $\bar{x}_j$ are fixed. Any solution $\{\lambda_i, \pi_{ij}\}$ to this problem determines a cut of the form

$$z \geq \sum_{i=1}^{m} \left(\lambda_i - \sum_{j=1}^{n} \pi_{ij} x_j \right) + \sum_{j=1}^{n} c_j x_j. \quad (5.4.3)$$

Let us define

$$d_{ij(i)} = \min \{ d_{iq} : q \in O \}.$$

Therefore, facility $v_{j(i)}$ is a closest opened facility to node v_i. Then, with $x_j = \bar{x}_j$ for $j = 1, \ldots, n$, the associated linear program (5.4.1) has the following optimal solution:

$$y_{ij} = \begin{cases} 1, & \text{if } j = j(i) & i = 1, \ldots, m \\ 0, & \text{otherwise} & j = 1, \ldots, n . \end{cases}$$

Also, the dual program (5.4.2) has the following "natural" solution: For each $i = 1, 2, \ldots, m$,

$$\bar{\lambda}_i = d_{ij(i)}$$

$$\bar{\pi}_{ij} = 0 \qquad\qquad\qquad \text{if } j \in O, j = 1, \ldots, n \qquad (5.4.4)$$

$$\bar{\pi}_{ij} = \max (0, \bar{\lambda}_i - d_{ij}), \qquad \text{if } j \in C, j = 1, \ldots, n .$$

The optimal dual variables have a convenient interpretation: $\bar{\lambda}_i$ is the cost of servicing node v_i when $\mathbf{x} = \bar{\mathbf{x}}$; $\bar{\pi}_{ij}$ is the reduction in the cost of servicing node v_i when facility v_j is opened and $x_i = \bar{x}_i$ for all $i \neq j$. So from the dual subproblem solution, we can construct the following cut

$$z \geq \bar{\omega} - \sum_{j=1}^{n} \mu_j x_j + \sum_{j=1}^{n} c_j x_j \qquad (5.4.5)$$

whose coefficients ω and μ_j are defined by

$$\bar{\omega} = \sum_{i=1}^{m} \bar{\lambda}_i \qquad \text{and} \qquad \mu_j = \sum_{i=1}^{m} \bar{\pi}_{ij} .$$

Note that $\bar{\omega}$ is the total servicing costs when $\mathbf{x} = \bar{\mathbf{x}}$ and that μ_j is the total reduction in servicing costs if facility v_j is opened and all other facilities retain their current, open versus closed, status.

For reference purposes, we shall refer to the cut in (5.4.5) as a *usual cut*. We discussed this cut in our introduction to decomposition in Section 5.2.

For $\mathbf{x} = \bar{\mathbf{x}}$, the associated linear program can be viewed as a transportation problem with demand constraints (5.1.8) for each destination v_i and a set of unconstrained origins v_j (i.e., each has an unlimited supply). Typically, transportation problems have a degenerate optimal basis which implies that the dual problem (5.4.2) has multiple optimal solutions. Because of this property, it is usually possible to derive more than one Benders' cut. We next describe procedures for generating alternative cuts that will normally be superior to the usual cut (5.4.5).

An Improved Cut

In deriving the Benders' cut (5.4.5), we considered only the savings from opening a new facility, that is, changing some x_j from 0 to 1. We did not, however, consider the added servicing costs produced by closing a facility. If facility $v_{j(i)}$ is closed, then node v_i must be serviced from a *different* facility and the service cost for node v_i must be at least the cost $d_{ik(i)}$ of servicing node v_i from the best alternative node $v_{k(i)}$; that is,

$$d_{ik(i)} = \min \{d_{iq} : 1 \le q \le n \text{ and } q \ne j(i)\} .$$

Note that since $v_{j(i)}$ must be an open facility and $v_{k(i)}$ need not be open, $d_{ik(i)}$ might be less than $d_{ij(i)}$.

Let

$$\sigma_i = \max \{d_{ik(i)} - d_{ij(i)}, 0\} .$$

Whenever $\sigma_i > 0$, node v_i suffers an increase in service cost of at least σ_i if facility $v_{j(i)}$ is closed, that is, if $x_{j(i)}$ is changed from 1 to 0. Therefore,

$$\nu_j = \sum \{\sigma_i : 1 \le i \le n \text{ and } j = j(i)\} \tag{5.4.6}$$

is the minimum total service cost incurred from all customers by closing facility v_j. Therefore, we can write a new cut, which we will refer to as a *closing facility* cut, as follows:

$$z \ge \bar{\omega} + \sum_{j \in 0} (1 - x_j)\nu_j - \sum_{j \in C} \mu_j x_j + \sum_{j=1}^{m} c_j x_j . \tag{5.4.7}$$

Notice that whenever some $\nu_j \ne 0$ and $\hat{x}_j \ne 0$ for some $\hat{\mathbf{x}} \in X$, the closing facility cut will dominate the usual cut.

Example 5.1. To illustrate the concepts introduced in this subsection, we consider once again the two-median problem given in Figure 5.1. Let the current configuration $\bar{\mathbf{x}} = (1, 0, 1, 0, 0)$. Then from (5.4.4) we have the "natural" dual solution

$$\bar{\lambda}_1 = 0, \quad \bar{\lambda}_2 = 4, \quad \bar{\lambda}_3 = 0, \quad \bar{\lambda}_4 = 2, \quad \bar{\lambda}_5 = 3$$

and

$$\bar{\pi}_{ij} = \max (0, \bar{\lambda}_i - d_{ij}), \quad i = 1, 2, 3, 4, 5, \quad j = 1, 2, 3, 4, 5 .$$

Substituting into (5.4.5), we obtain the usual cut

$$z \ge 9 - 4x_2 - 4x_4 - 4x_5 \tag{5.4.8}$$

which we specified earlier as (5.2.2).

To compute the closing facility cut for the current configuration $\bar{\mathbf{x}}$, note that $d_{ik(i)} = 0$ for $i = 2, 4, 5$, $d_{1k(1)} = 5$, and $d_{3k(3)} = 2$. Therefore,

$$\nu_1 = \sigma_1 = 5$$

$$\nu_3 = \sigma_2 + \sigma_3 + \sigma_4 + \sigma_5 = 0 + 2 + 0 + 0 = 2$$

and substituting into (5.4.7) yields the closing facility cut

$$z \geq 9 + 5(1 - x_1) - 4x_2 + 2(1 - x_3) - 4x_4 - 4x_5 . \qquad (5.4.9)$$

Notice that in this example, since every node is a candidate for a facility, it is possible to open a facility at each closed node and consequently $d_{ik(i)} = 0$ for each closed node $v_i \in C$. In general, these costs could be positive. $\bigcirc$

5.4.2. Pareto-Optimal Cuts

In this section, we derive an efficient special purpose algorithm for solving the linear program for generating pareto-optimal cuts for the facility location model. The algorithm uses a parametric solution technique to solve each of the subproblems.

First, we note that for any choice of $\bar{x} \in X$, the linear program (5.4.2) decomposes into separate subproblems, one for each index $i = 1, 2, \ldots, m$. Also, the "natural solution" (5.4.4) to the linear programming dual problem (5.4.2) has the property that the optimal value of the ith subproblem is $v_i(\bar{x}) = \lambda_i$ and $(\lambda_i - \Sigma_{j=1}^{n} \bar{x}_j \pi_{ij}) \leq v_i(\bar{x})$ for any (λ, π) that is feasible for (5.4.2). Consequently,

$$\sum_{i=1}^{m} \left(\lambda_i - \sum_{j=1}^{n} \bar{x}_j \pi_{ij} \right) = v(\bar{x}) = \sum_{i=1}^{m} v_i(\bar{x}) - \sum_{j=1}^{n} c_j \bar{x}_j$$

if and only if $(\lambda_i - \Sigma_{j=1}^{n} \bar{x}_j \pi_{ij}) = v_i(\bar{x})$. This observation implies that we can also decompose (5.3.11) into a series of subproblems. For each i, solving the subproblem

$$\text{maximize} \qquad \lambda_i - \sum_{j=1}^{n} x_j^0 \pi_{ij}$$

$$\text{subject to} \qquad \lambda_i - \sum_{j=1}^{n} \bar{x}_j \pi_{ij} = \bar{\lambda}_i \qquad\qquad (5.4.10)$$

$$\lambda_i - \qquad \pi_{ij} \leq d_{ij}, \qquad j = 1, \ldots, m$$

$$\pi_{ij} \geq 0, \qquad j = 1, \ldots, m$$

provides a pareto-optimal vector with components λ_i and π_{ij} for $i = 1, \ldots, m$ and $j = 1, \ldots, n$. In this formulation, as before, $\bar{x}$ denotes the current value of the integer variables and x^o belongs to the core of X (which was S in Section 5.3); that is, $x^o \in \text{ri}(X^c)$.

Our first objective is to show that, for each i, the optimal value of the subproblem (5.4.10) is piecewise linear as a function of λ_i. Since the equality constraint of this problem reads

$$\lambda_i - \sum_{j \in 0} \pi_{ij} = \bar{\lambda}_i = d_{ij(i)},$$

and since $\lambda_i - \pi_{ij(i)} \leq d_{ij(i)}$ and $\pi_{ij} \geq 0$ for all j, we have $\pi_{ij} = 0$ for all $j \neq j(i)$, $j \in O$ and $\pi_{ij(i)} = \lambda_i - d_{ij(i)} = \lambda_i - \bar{\lambda}_i$. Also, if we substitute for λ_i in the objective function of (5.4.10) from the equality constraint, the objective becomes

$$\text{maximize } \bar{\lambda}_i + \sum_{j=1}^{n} (\bar{x}_j - x_j^0) \pi_{ij}.$$

For any index $j \in C$, $\bar{x}_j = 0$ and the coefficient $\varepsilon_j \equiv (\bar{x}_j - x_j^0)$ of π_{ij} is nonpositive. Thus, an optimal choice of π_{ij} in (5.4.10) is $\pi_{ij} = \max(0, \lambda_i - d_{ij})$.

Collecting these results, we see that the optimal value of problem (5.4.10) as a function of the variable λ_i is

$$\bar{\lambda}_i + \varepsilon_{j(i)}(\lambda_i - \bar{\lambda}_i) + \sum_{j \in C} \varepsilon_j \max(0, \lambda_i - d_{ij}). \tag{5.4.11}$$

To aid us in optimizing (5.4.10), we note that it is possible to impose upper (L_i) and lower ($\bar{\lambda}_i$) bounds on λ_i, $\bar{\lambda}_i \leq \lambda_i \leq L_i$; by definition, $L_i = \min\{d_{ij} : j \in O \text{ and } j \neq j(i)\}$. The lower bound is a simple consequence of the equality constraint of problem (5.4.10), because each $\bar{x}_j \geq 0$ and each $\pi_{ij} \geq 0$. The upper bound follows from our previous observation that $\pi_{ij} = 0$ whenever $j \neq j(i)$ and $j \in O$, and, therefore, for these j the constraint $\lambda_i - \pi_{ij} \leq d_{ij}$ becomes $\lambda_i \leq d_{ij}$.

Now, since the function (5.4.11) is piecewise linear and concave in λ_i, we can minimize it by considering its linear segments in the interval $\bar{\lambda}_i \leq \lambda_i \leq L_i$ in order from left to right until the slope of any segment becomes nonpositive. More formally, for a current configuration $\bar{x}$ and a core point x^o, we have the following procedure.

Pareto-Optimal Cut Generation Algorithm

0. For all $i = 1, \ldots, m$ and $j = 1, \ldots, n$, compute

$$\varepsilon_j = (\bar{x}_j - x_j^o)$$
$$d_{ij(i)} = \min\{d_{ij} : j \in O\}$$
$$L_i = \min\{d_{ij} : j \in O \text{ and } j \neq j(i)\}.$$

For every $i = 1, 2, \ldots, m$ perform the following steps.

1. Start with $\lambda_i = \bar{\lambda}_i$.
2. Let $T = \{j \in C: d_{ij} \leq \lambda_i\}$ and let $s = \varepsilon_{j(i)} + \sum \{\varepsilon_j: j \in T\}$; s is the slope of the function (5.4.11) to the right of λ_i.
3. If $s \leq 0$ then stop; λ_i is optimal. If $s > 0$ and $T = C$, then stop, $\lambda_i = L_i$ is optimal.
4. Let $d_{ik} = \min \{d_{ij}: j \in C \text{ and } j \notin T\}$. If $d_{ik} > L_i$, set $\lambda_i = L_i$ and stop. Otherwise, increase λ_i to d_{ik}, and go to step 2.

Once the optimal value of λ_i for each i is found using this algorithm, the remaining variables π_{ij} can be set using the rule $\pi_{ij} = \max(0, \lambda_i - d_{ij})$. Then, the cut obtained by substituting these values in (5.4.3) is pareto-optimal.

This algorithm is quite efficient. For each node v_i, at most n (the number of possible facilities) steps must be excuted, so the total number of steps required by this procedure is bounded by (number of demand nodes) × (number of possible facilities).

We might emphasize that this algorithm determines a pareto-optimal cut for any given point $\mathbf{x}^o$ in the core of X. Also, the algorithm applies to any of the possible modeling variations that we might capture in X, such as the contingency and configuration constraints mentioned in Section 5.1.

Example 5.2. Once again, consider the two-median example depicted in Figure 5.1. To apply the pareto-optimal cut generation algorithm, we must first choose a core point $\mathbf{x}^o \in \mathrm{ri}(\bar{X}^c)$ of the set

$$\bar{X} = \{\mathbf{x}: \sum_{i=1}^{5} x_i = 2 \text{ and } 0 \leq x_i \leq 1 \text{ for } 1 \leq i \leq 5\}.$$

One possible value for the core point is $\mathbf{x}^o = (1/2, 1/4, 1/2, 1/4, 1/2)$. The conditions of a core point are satisfied since

$$\sum_{i=1}^{5} x_i^o = \frac{1}{2} + \frac{1}{4} + \frac{1}{2} + \frac{1}{4} + \frac{1}{2} = 2$$

and $0 < x_i^o < 1$ for $1 \leq i \leq 5$.

As in Section 5.2, assume that the current configuration $\bar{\mathbf{x}}$ is $(1, 0, 1, 0, 0)$. From computations in Example 5.1, we know $\bar{\lambda} = (0, 4, 0, 2, 3)$.

Now we apply the steps of the pareto-optimal cut generation algorithm. For $i = 1$, we have $\bar{\lambda}_1 = 0 \leq \lambda_1 \leq L_1 = 9$. Step 1 initializes $\lambda_1 = 0$. Step 2 computes $T = \emptyset$ and $s = \varepsilon_1 = 1 - \frac{1}{2} = \frac{1}{2}$. Since $s > 0$, step 4 increases λ_1 to $d_{12} = 5$. Next we return to step 2 and find $T = \{2\}$ and $s = \varepsilon_1 + \varepsilon_2 = (1 - \frac{1}{2}) + (0 - \frac{1}{4}) = \frac{1}{4}$. Since $s > 0$, step 4 increases λ_1 to $d_{13} = 9$, and since $\lambda_1 = L_1 = 9$, we can stop with the optimal value $\lambda_1 = 9$.

Similar computations show that $\lambda_2 = 5$, $\lambda_3 = 3$, $\lambda_4 = 2$, and $\lambda_5 = 3$.

Using the values for $\boldsymbol{\lambda}$ permits us to compute the corresponding values for the π_{ij} from the relation

$$\pi_{ij} = \max\left(0, \lambda_i - d_{ij}\right).$$

Substituting these values of the λ_i and π_{ij} into (5.4.3) produces the following pareto-optimal Benders' cut for the two-median problem:

$$z \geq 22 - 9x_1 - 9x_2 - 4x_3 - 5x_4 - 4x_5. \quad \bigcirc \qquad (5.4.12)$$

5.4.3. Neighborhood Interpretation and a New Cut

As we noted in Section 5.4.1, the standard Benders' cut considers savings in servicing costs obtained by opening new facilities. The improved closing facility cut introduces additional servicing costs that must be incurred whenever an open facility is closed. In this section, we show that *any* Benders' cut generated from an optimal solution to the dual problem (5.4.2) has a similar interpretation. We also present a new type of cut for the p-median problem and discuss its interpretation.

An Interpretation

First, we introduce some new notation. The δ-*neighborhood*, denoted $N_i(\delta)$, of demand node v_i with respect to the dual variable $\lambda_i = \bar{\lambda}_i + \delta$, with value $\bar{\lambda}_i$ defined in (5.4.4), is the set of facility locations v_j satisfying $d_{ij} \leq \bar{\lambda}_i + \delta$. We define the interior of the δ-neighborhood as $N_i^o(\delta) \equiv \{v_j: d_{ij} < \bar{\lambda}_i + \delta\}$.

Recall from the last section that $\lambda_i \geq \bar{\lambda}_i$ in any optimal solution to the dual of subproblem (5.4.1); therefore, $\lambda_i = \bar{\lambda}_i + \delta_i$ for some $\delta_i \geq 0$ and varying δ_i (and hence the size of the δ-neighborhood) is equivalent to varying λ_i. The operation in the pareto-optimal cut generation algorithm of increasing λ_i until $s \leq 0$ has the following interpretation: increase the δ-neighborhood about node v_i until $\Sigma \{\varepsilon_j: v_j \in N_i(\delta_i)\} \leq 0$.

Figure 5.3 gives an example of a δ-neighborhood for the p-median example depicted in Figure 5.1. Assume distances in the figure are drawn to scale (they are not) and that the neighborhood is constructed around demand node v_5 with the current configuration $\bar{\mathbf{x}} = (1, 0, 0, 1, 0)$. As indicated in the figure, the current δ-neighborhood contains nodes v_5, v_4, v_3, and v_2. If $\varepsilon_5 + \varepsilon_4 + \varepsilon_3 + \varepsilon_2 = s > 0$, then the pareto-optimal cut algorithm would expand the neighborhood to the next nearest facility, which is node v_1.

The cut determined by the neighborhood pictured in Figure 5.3 has the following interpretation. As we noted in deriving (5.4.11) from (5.4.10), every optimal solution to (5.4.2) can be written as

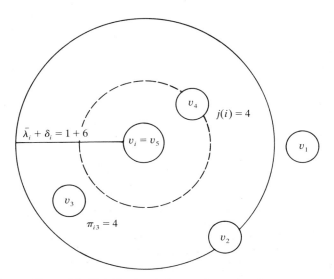

Figure 5.3. Neighborhood about a demand node $v_i = v_5$.

$$\lambda_i = \bar{\lambda}_i + \delta_i \qquad \text{for some } \delta_i \geq 0$$

$$\bar{\lambda}_i = d_{ij(i)} \equiv \min \{d_{ij}: j \in O\}$$

$$\pi_{ij} = \begin{cases} \lambda_i - \bar{\lambda}_i = \delta_i \,, & \text{if } j = j(i) \\ \lambda_i - d_{ij} \,, & \text{if } j \in C \cap N_i(\delta_i) \\ 0 \,, & \text{otherwise .} \end{cases}$$

For notational convenience, let us assume at this point that node v_5 is the only demand node. Substituting the dual variable values corresponding to Figure 5.3 into (5.4.3) yields (after some rearrangement) the cut

$$z \geq \bar{\lambda}_5 + \delta_5(1 - x_4) - (\bar{\lambda}_5 + \delta_5 - d_{53})x_3 - (\bar{\lambda}_5 + \delta_5 - d_{55})x_5$$

or

$$z \geq 1 + 6(1 - x_4) - 4x_3 - 7x_5 \,.$$

If we set $x_4 = 0$ to close facility 4, then node v_5 must be serviced from outside the neighborhood (or on its boundary) at a cost z of at least $\bar{\lambda}_5 + \delta_5 = 7$ unless a facility at node v_3 or node v_5 is opened. If facility 5 is opened, then the service cost for node v_5 becomes $d_{55} = 0$. The coefficient of x_5 compensates for this reduction in service cost when $x_5 = 1$. The coefficient for x_3 has a similar interpretation.

The general situation is much the same. Given any neighborhoods for the nodes, let $\bar{\omega} = \Sigma_{i=1}^m \bar{\lambda}_i$ be the current allocation cost, let

$$\nu_j = \sum \{\delta_i : 1 \le i \le n \text{ and } j = j(i)\} = \sum \{\pi_{ij} : 1 \le i \le j \text{ and } j = j(i)\},$$

and let

$$\mu_j = \sum_{i=1}^{n} \pi_{ij}.$$

Substituting these values in the form of the cut expressed in (5.4.3) gives

$$z \ge \bar{\omega} + \sum_{j \in O} \nu_j (1 - x_j) - \sum_{j \in C} \mu_j x_j + \sum_{j=1}^{n} c_j x_j. \qquad (5.4.13)$$

The coefficient ν_j accounts for the fact that the open facility ν_j might lie interior to several neighborhoods. Closing this facility increases allocation costs to the boundary of each of these neighborhoods unless some closed facility within any neighborhood is opened. The coefficient μ_j for $j \in C$ records the savings for opening facility ν_j considering all the neighborhoods that contain it.

Suppose, as before, that $d_{ik(i)}$ denotes the cost to the closest alternate facility $k(i) \ne j(i)$ to node ν_i. Setting $\lambda_i = \bar{\lambda}_i$, and $\delta_i = \max \{0, d_{ik(i)} - d_{ij(i)}\}$, reduces expression (5.4.13) to the closing facility cut introduced in Section 5.4.1.

Note that the cut (5.4.13) is only an *alternative* way of describing the Benders' cut (5.4.3) using the neighborhood interpretation. This alternative description not only provides a new interpretation, but will permit us to introduce a new type of Benders' cut that is easily described using the alternative form (5.4.13). We first use an example to illustrate the equivalence of the two cut descriptions (5.4.3) and (5.4.13).

Example 5.3. We continue Example 5.2 and discuss the two-median problem given in Figure 5.1 with $\bar{\mathbf{x}} = (1, 0, 1, 0, 0)$. Recall from the example that $\bar{\boldsymbol{\lambda}} = (0, 4, 0, 2, 3)$ and the final computed value for $\boldsymbol{\lambda}$ was $(9, 5, 3, 2, 3)$. We will translate this solution to our neighborhood interpretation and use it to show the equivalence to the two cut descriptions (5.4.3) and (5.4.13).

Using $\boldsymbol{\lambda}$ and the final value for $\boldsymbol{\lambda}$ permits us to compute $\delta_1 = \lambda_1 - \bar{\lambda}_1 = 9$, $\delta_2 = 5 - 4 = 1$, $\delta_3 = 3 - 0 = 3$, $\delta_4 = 2 - 2 = 0$, and $\delta_5 = 3 - 3 = 0$.

We can now determine the corresponding neighborhoods. For example, $N_1(9) = \{v_1, v_2, v_3\}$, $N_1^o(9) = \{v_1, v_3\}$, $N_2(1) = \{v_1, v_2\}$, and $N_2^o(1) = \{v_2\}$.

$$\bar{\omega} = \sum_i \bar{\lambda}_i = 0 + 4 + 0 + 2 + 3 = 9.$$

Also, since $\bar{x}_1$ and $\bar{x}_3$ are 1, we compute

$$\nu_1 = \delta_1 = 9$$

$$\nu_3 = \delta_2 + \delta_3 + \delta_4 + \delta_5 = 1 + 3 + 0 + 0 = 4.$$

In this case, $j(i) = 1$ for $i = 1$, and $j(i) = 3$ for $i = 2, 3, 4, 5$. Now $\bar{x}_2$, $\bar{x}_4$, and $\bar{x}_5$ are zero, so we compute

$$\mu_2 = \pi_{12} + \pi_{22} + \pi_{32} + \pi_{42} + \pi_{52} = 4 + 5 + 0 + 0 + 0 = 9$$

$$\mu_4 = \pi_{14} + \pi_{24} + \pi_{34} + \pi_{44} + \pi_{54} = 0 + 0 + 1 + 2 + 2 = 5$$

$$\mu_5 = \pi_{15} + \pi_{25} + \pi_{35} + \pi_{45} + \pi_{55} = 0 + 0 + 0 + 1 + 3 = 4 .$$

Substituting these values into (5.4.13), we obtain the cut

$$z \geq 9 + 9(1 - x_1) + 4(1 - x_3) - 9x_2 - 5x_4 - 4x_5$$

which is the same as (5.4.12), the cut computed from (5.4.3) in Example 5.2. ○

A New Cut for the p-Median Problem

When specialized, the cut-generating technique described in the last section provides a new type of Benders' cut for the p-median problem, one that dominates the closing facility cut. To simplify our development, we temporarily assume that all servicing costs d_{ij} are nonnegative and that $d_{ii} = 0$ for all i.

As we have seen, the closing facility cut introduces penalties for customers forced to travel to nodes other than the ones to which they are currently assigned. For the p-median problem, these penalties separate into two groups.

1. A demand node and a facility are located at the same node v_i: then the servicing cost for that demand node is $d_{ii} = 0$ and the penalty in servicing cost for this node is

$$d_{ik(i)} \equiv \min \{d_{ij}: j \neq i\}$$

   if the facility at node v_i is closed.

2. A demand node, but no facility, is located at node v_i: then the closing of any open facility need not incur any servicing penalty, since the demand node might conceivably be serviced by a facility at node v_i at cost $d_{ii} = 0$.

Stated in terms of the neighborhood interpretation, these observations imply that the δ_i-neighborhood about demand node v_i is of minimal size, $\delta_i = 0$, if $x_i = 0$ in the current solution x; if $x_i = 1$, then $d_{ij(i)} \equiv \min \{d_{ij}: j \in O\}$ and $\delta_i = d_{ij(i)}$ is the size of the neighborhood.

Since closing a facility at node v_j contributes to the penalty in the closing facility cut of the demand at only that node, the term $\nu_j \equiv \Sigma \{\delta_i: 1 \leq i \leq n$

and $j = j(i)$} equals $d_{jk(j)}$, the distance to node v_j's second nearest neighbor and the closing facility cut is written in the form of expression (5.4.13) as

$$z \geq \bar{\omega} + \sum_{j \in O} d_{jk(j)} (1 - x_j) - \sum_{j \in C} \mu_j x_j \qquad (5.4.14)$$

whose terms $\bar{\omega}$ and μ_j are defined as before in (5.4.5).

The algorithm presented in Section 5.4.1 shows how to expand the neighborhoods about every demand node from the values associated with the usual cut in order to obtain pareto-optimality. Although the new cut must be pareto-optimal, there is no guarantee that it *dominates* the usual cut or the closing facility cut.

To develop a cut that dominates the closing facility cut, we proceed as follows. *We maintain the neighborhood about nodes whose facilities are closed at their minimal size* $\delta_j = 0$, and we increase the neighborhoods about the other nodes all by the same amount $\bar{\delta}$; that is, we set $\delta_j = d_{jk(j)} + \bar{\delta}$ for every node v_j with $\bar{x}_j = 1$. This procedure avoids the formal slope checking mechanism of the algorithm for generating pareto-optimal cuts. Although other options are certainly possible, choosing to expand every neighborhood equally leads to a very simple implementation.

The choice of $\bar{\delta}$ for δ is governed by two restrictions. First, the resulting value of δ cannot be too large, since otherwise $\lambda_i = (\bar{\lambda}_i + \delta_i) = \bar{\lambda}_i + d_{ik(i)} + \delta$ for $i \in O$ will violate

$$\lambda_i \leq L_i = \min \{ d_{ij} : j \in O \text{ and } j \neq j(i) \} .$$

Recall that we identified this bound in Section 5.4.1 by considering the subproblem (5.4.10).

This bound on the λ_i is equivalent to the restriction that if $j \neq j(i)$ and $j \in O$, then $\lambda_i = (\bar{\lambda}_i + \delta_i) \leq d_{ij}$ or j *cannot* be in the interior of the neighborhood about node v_i. Since node $v_{j(i)}$ is in the interior of the neighborhood about node v_i whenever $\delta_i > 0$, this bound on λ_i is equivalent to the restriction that *the interior of every neighborhood may contain at most one open facility*. The second restriction is that *every closed facility lie interior to at most one neighborhood about an open facility*. Although this restriction is not imposed by the linear programs (5.4.10), later we will show by an example that the new cut need not dominate the closing facility cut if this condition is not fulfilled. *Our choice of δ is to make it as large as possible, consonant with these two restrictions.*

We will call the result of this procedure

$$v \geq \bar{\omega} + \sum_{j \in O} (d_{jk(j)} + \bar{\delta})(1 - x_j) - \sum_{j \in C} (\mu_j + \bar{\Delta}_j) x_j \qquad (5.4.15)$$

an expanding neighborhood cut (we will define $\bar{\Delta}_j$ shortly). Note that the coefficients of x_j for the closed facilities v_j must be altered from the values μ_j

in the closing facility cut (5.4.14). Since our restrictions on $\bar{\delta}$ ensure that every closed facility v_j lies interior to only one neighborhood $N_q(\delta)$, if any, about an open facility, as we increase δ only the term π_{qj} in the savings expression $\mu_j = \Sigma_{i=1}^{m} \pi_{ij}$ changes. Thus, we introduce a "compensation factor" $\bar{\Delta}_j$ to the savings expression that is equal to the difference between the values of $\pi_{qj} = \max(\lambda_q - d_{qj}, 0) = \max(d_{qk(q)} + \delta - d_{qj}, 0)$ at $\delta = 0$ and at $\delta = \bar{\delta}$ (see Section 5.4.1). Note that this observation implies that $\bar{\Delta}_j \leq \bar{\delta}$ for all $j \in C$.

In comparing cuts, we noted that the closing facility cut dominates the usual cut whenever at least one $\nu_j \neq 0$. The following result summarizes the relationship between closing facility and expanding neighborhood cuts.

Proposition 5.1. *For a given iteration of Benders' decomposition applied to the p-median problem, an expanding neighborhood cut will either dominate or be equivalent to a closing facility cut.*

Proof. Let $\mathbf{x} = \bar{\mathbf{x}}$ be any values for the configuration variables satisfying the p-median constraint $x_1 + x_2 + \cdots + x_n = p$. Let $R_E(\mathbf{x})$ and $R_C(\mathbf{x})$ denote the right-hand sides of the expanding neighborhood cut (5.4.15) and the closing facility cut (5.4.14). Then

$$R_E(x) - R_C(x) = \sum_{j \in O} \bar{\delta}(1 - x_j) - \sum_{j \in C} \bar{\Delta}_j x_j .$$

By the p-median constraint, if K of the facilities v_j for $j \in C$ are opened, then K of the facilities v_j for $j \in O$ must be closed. As we have noted just prior to the proposition, though, $\bar{\Delta}_j \leq \bar{\delta}$ for all $j \in C$. These two facts imply that $R_E(\mathbf{x}) - R_C(\mathbf{x}) \geq 0$, so the expanding neighborhood cut is always at least as strong as the closing facility cut. $\square$

Reviewing the definition of the expanding neighborhood cut and the proof of this proposition shows that our assumptions that service costs are nonnegative and that $d_{ii} = 0$ for all i are dispensable. These assumptions merely lead to more attractive interpretations and motivation.

Example 5.4. We continue discussing the two-median example of Figure 5.1 with the current configuration $\bar{\mathbf{x}} = (1, 0, 1, 0, 0)$. Recall from Example 5.1 that $\boldsymbol{\lambda} = (0, 4, 0, 2, 3)$, $d_{1k(1)} = 5$ and $d_{3k(3)} = 2$. Also, $\mu_2 = 4$, $\mu_4 = 4$, and $\mu_5 = 4$. Using the δ-neighborhood concept, we find that $\bar{\delta}$ equals 2 (for $\delta > 2$, node v_2 lies in the interior of the neighborhoods about node v_1 and node v_3), and we obtain the following expanding neighborhood cut

$$z \geq 9 + (5 + 2)(1 - x_1) - (4 + 2)x_2 + (2 + 2)(1 - x_3) - (4 + 2)x_4$$
$$- (4 + 1)x_5 . \qquad (5.4.16)$$

Note that the expanding neighborhood cut dominates the usual cut (5.4.8) and the closing facility cut (5.4.9).

If we ignored the restriction prohibiting node v_2 from being in the interior of the neighborhoods about both nodes v_1 and v_3, we could expand the neighborhoods until $\delta = 4$ and the cut would become

$$z \geq 9 + 9(1 - x_1) - 10x_2 + 6(1 - x_3) - 8x_4 - 7x_5 \,.$$

Observe that this cut does not dominate the closing facility cut (5.4.9) (take $x_1 = x_2 = 1$, $x_3 = x_4 = x_5 = 0$). The difficulty is that $\bar{\Delta}_2 = 6$ exceeds $\delta = 4$.

Finally, notice the expanding neighborhood cut (5.4.16) does not dominate the pareto-optimal cut (5.4.12) (take $x_4 = x_5 = 1$, $x_1 = x_2 = x_3 = 0$) nor does the pareto-optimal cut dominate it (take $x_1 = x_2 = 1$, $x_3 = x_4 = x_5 = 0$). ○

5.5. A MODEL SELECTION CRITERION FOR BENDERS' DECOMPOSITION

Selecting the "proper" model formulation is another important factor that affects the computational performance of Benders' decomposition applied to facility location and other mixed integer programming models. This section discusses a criterion for distinguishing between different, but "equivalent," formulations of the same mixed integer programming problem to identify which formulation is preferred in the context of Benders' decomposition.

Many network optimization problems have "natural" mixed integer programming formulations. For example, as we noted in Section 5.1, different variations of the facility location problem can be stated in several possible ways as mixed integer programs. In this section, we demonstrate why some formulations lead to such pronounced improvements over others in the performance of Benders' decomposition.

To illustrate the role of model selection, we consider an example of Benders' decomposition applied to the p-median facility location problem. In Section 5.1, (5.1.7)–(5.1.10) gives a formulation, say P, of the p-median problem when

$$X = \left\{ \mathbf{x} \colon \sum_{j=1}^{n} x_j = p \right\}.$$

Replacing (5.1.9), that is $y_{ij} \leq x_j$, with

$$\sum_{i=1}^{m} y_{ij} \leq mx_j, \qquad j = 1, \ldots, n, \tag{5.5.1}$$

gives an equivalent formulation, say Q. Note that (5.5.1) represents an aggregation of (5.1.9). Consequently, although P and Q are equivalent mathematical descriptions, if we relax the integrality constraints on the x_j, the feasible region for P is a proper subset of the feasible region for Q.

Let us examine the p-median problem represented in Figure 5.4. In this example, $m = n = 4$, $p = 2$, and all d_{ij} are 100 except for $d_{ii} = 0$.

The application of Benders' decomposition to this example with formulation Q yields the following set of Benders' cuts:

$$z \geq 200 - 400x_1 - 400x_2 + \quad 0x_3 + \quad 0x_4$$

$$z \geq 200 - 400x_1 + \quad 0x_2 - 400x_3 + \quad 0x_4$$

$$z \geq 200 - 400x_1 - \quad 0x_2 + \quad 0x_3 - 400x_4$$

$$z \geq 200 + \quad 0x_1 - 400x_2 - 400x_3 + \quad 0x_4$$

$$z \geq 200 + \quad 0x_1 - 400x_2 + \quad 0x_3 - 400x_4$$

$$z \geq 200 + \quad 0x_1 + \quad 0x_2 - 400x_3 - 400x_4$$

It turns out (see Exercise 5.8) that every single one of these cuts must be generated in order for Benders' algorithm to converge.

Recall from Section 5.4 that applying Benders' decomposition to our example with formulation P yields several different sets of cuts. The first set, consisting of the usual cuts, is identical to the previous set except that all coefficients of value -400 become -100. Thus, all six cuts are again necessary for convergence. In contrast, generating a set of closing facility cuts requires the single cut

$$z \geq 400 - 100x_1 - 100x_2 - 100x_3 - 100x_4$$

for convergence.

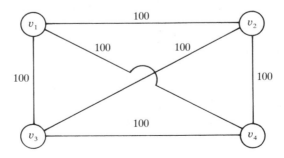

Figure 5.4. Example of a p-median problem with $n = 4$ and $p = 2$.

We can generalize this example in the following way: let $p = n/2$ and let $d_{ij} = 100$ for all $i \neq j$ and $d_{ii} = 0$ for all i. For this class of examples, the Q formulation requires an exponential number ($\binom{n}{n/2}$) of cuts for Benders' algorithm to converge. For these same problems, the P formulation in every case requires only one Benders' cut for convergence. This example certainly underscores the importance of intelligent model formulation for Benders' decomposition.

Now we present a formal framework for comparing model formulations for Benders' decomposition. Our results apply not only to facility location problems (5.1.1)–(5.1.6), but also to general mixed integer programming problems. Since it will facilitate our notation, we cast our development in its most general form. Later in this section, we discuss the application of this theory to specific facility location models.

Suppose we have two mixed integer programs P and Q that are represented as:

$$(P) \quad \min_{\mathbf{x} \in X} [v^P(\mathbf{x})] \text{ where } [v^P(\mathbf{x})] = \min_{\mathbf{y} \geq 0} \{\mathbf{cx} + \mathbf{dy} : H\mathbf{x} + G\mathbf{y} = \mathbf{h}\} \quad (5.5.2)$$

and

$$(Q) \quad \min_{\mathbf{x} \in X} [v^Q(\mathbf{x})] \text{ where } [v^Q(\mathbf{x})] = \min_{\mathbf{y} \geq 0} \{\mathbf{cx} + \mathbf{ty} : R\mathbf{x} + T\mathbf{y} = \mathbf{r}\} . \quad (5.5.3)$$

$\mathbf{x}$ and $\mathbf{y}$ are column vectors of problem variables; $\mathbf{h}$ and $\mathbf{r}$ are column vectors; $\mathbf{c}, \mathbf{d}$, and $\mathbf{t}$ are row vectors; H, G, R, and T are matrices with appropriate dimensions. The set X is a set of integer-valued vectors and captures the integer constraints of the problem. We assume that the set X is finite.

We will say that P and Q are *equivalent* mixed integer programming representations of the same problem if $v^P(\mathbf{x}) = v^Q(\mathbf{x})$ for all $\mathbf{x} \in X$. That is, the two models have the same integer variables, but may have different constraints and continuous variables; nevertheless, they always give the same objective function value for any feasible assignment of the integer variables. We will say that the two formulations are *identical* if $v^P(\mathbf{x}) = v^Q(\mathbf{x})$ for all $\mathbf{x}$ belonging to the convex hull of X.

Note that in the context of Benders' decomposition, $v^P(\mathbf{x})$ and $v^Q(\mathbf{x})$ represent the linear programming subproblems when Benders' decomposition is applied to P and Q. Consequently, the two models are equivalent if their respective Benders' subproblems always have the same optimal value.

We evaluate the two models (5.5.2) and (5.5.3) by comparing the cuts generated from the application of Benders' decomposition. Following the derivation of Benders' decomposition given in Section 5.3, we can rewrite P and Q, respectively, as*:

---

*As in earlier sections, we assume that the linear programming subproblems $v^P(\mathbf{x})$ and $v^Q(\mathbf{x})$ are feasible and have optimal solutions for all $\mathbf{x} \in X$. These restrictions can be relaxed, but with added complications that do not enrich the devlopment in an essential way.

$$(P) \qquad \min_{x \in X, z \in R} \{z: z \geq \pi(\mathbf{h} - H\mathbf{x}) + \mathbf{c}\mathbf{x} \text{ for all } \pi \in \Pi\}$$

where Π is the set of points in the polyhedron $\pi G \leq \mathbf{d}$; and

$$(Q) \qquad \min_{x \in X, z \in R} \{z: z \geq \gamma(\mathbf{r} - R\mathbf{x}) + \mathbf{c}\mathbf{x} \text{ for all } \gamma \in \Gamma\}$$

where Γ is the set of points in the polyhedron $\gamma T \leq \mathbf{t}$.

The inequalities $z \geq \pi(\mathbf{h} - H\mathbf{x}) + \mathbf{c}\mathbf{x}$ and $z \geq \gamma(\mathbf{r} - R\mathbf{x}) + \mathbf{c}\mathbf{x}$ will be referred to as the Benders' cuts for P and Q, respectively. We remark that our definition of Benders' cuts, in which a cut can be generated from *any* point in the subproblem dual feasible region, produces a larger set of possible cuts than the usual definition which restricts the cuts to those corresponding to the extreme points of the subproblem dual feasible region. The results of this section are not always valid for the usual definition of Benders' cuts (see Exercise 5.10). To compare equivalent model formulations, we adapt the concept of a pareto-optimal cut introduced in Section 5.3 by saying that a Benders' cut (or constraint) $z \geq \pi(\mathbf{h} - H\mathbf{x}) + \mathbf{c}\mathbf{x}$ for P *dominates* a Benders' cut $z \geq \gamma(\mathbf{r} - R\mathbf{x}) + \mathbf{c}\mathbf{x}$ for Q if $\pi(\mathbf{h} - H\mathbf{x}) + \mathbf{c}\mathbf{x} \geq \gamma(\mathbf{r} - R\mathbf{x}) + \mathbf{c}\mathbf{x}$ for all $\mathbf{x} \in X$ with a strict inequality for at least one point $\mathbf{x} \in X$.

A cut $z \geq \gamma(\mathbf{r} - R\mathbf{x}) + \mathbf{c}\mathbf{x}$ for Q will be called *unmatched* with respect to the formulation P if no cut for P is equal to it (in the sense that two cuts are equal if their right-hand sides are equal for all $\mathbf{x} \in X$) or dominates it.

A formulation Q is *cut richer* than P if they are equivalent formulations and the set of Benders' cuts for P is a "proper subset" of the Benders' cuts for Q (i.e., some cut in Q equals or dominates each cut in P and Q has a cut that is unmatched in P).

With these definitions, we can now prove several properties concerning model formulation and the strength of Benders' cuts.

Lemma 5.1. *Let P and Q be equivalent formulations of a mixed integer programming problem. Q has a Benders' cut that is unmatched with respect to P if, and only if, some $\mathbf{x}^o$ belonging to the convex hull X^c of X satisfies $v^Q(\mathbf{x}^o) > v^P(\mathbf{x}^o)$.*

Proof. To establish the necessity of the inequality condition, let $z \geq \gamma^*(\mathbf{r} - R\mathbf{x}) + \mathbf{c}\mathbf{x}$ be a Benders' cut that is unmatched with respect to P. That is, for every cut $z \geq \pi(\mathbf{h} - H\mathbf{x}) + \mathbf{c}\mathbf{x}$ in P, there is an $\mathbf{x} \in X$ with $\pi(\mathbf{h} - H\mathbf{x}) + \mathbf{c}\mathbf{x} < \gamma^*(\mathbf{r} - R\mathbf{x}) + \mathbf{c}\mathbf{x}$. Since we are assuming that the set X is finite, this inequality implies that

$$\max_{\pi G \leq \mathbf{d}} \left[\min_{\mathbf{x} \in X} \pi(\mathbf{h} - H\mathbf{x}) + \mathbf{c}\mathbf{x} - \gamma^*(\mathbf{r} - R\mathbf{x}) - \mathbf{c}\mathbf{x} \right] < 0.$$

Now observe that this inequality still holds if we replace the set X by X^c. Using linear programming duality theory, we can reverse the order of the max and min operations to obtain

$$\min_{\mathbf{x} \in X^c} \left[\max_{\pi G \leq \mathbf{d}} \boldsymbol{\pi}(\mathbf{h} - H\mathbf{x}) + \mathbf{cx} - \boldsymbol{\gamma}^*(\mathbf{r} - R\mathbf{x}) - \mathbf{cx} \right] < 0.$$

Linear programming duality theory, when applied to the inner maximization, allows us to rewrite this expression as

$$\min_{\mathbf{x} \in X^c, \mathbf{y} \geq 0} \{ \mathbf{cx} + \mathbf{dy} - [\boldsymbol{\gamma}^*(\mathbf{r} - R\mathbf{x}) + \mathbf{cx}] : H\mathbf{x} + G\mathbf{y} = \mathbf{h} \} < 0.$$

Now let $\mathbf{x}^o \in X^c$ be an optimal value for $\mathbf{x}$ in this problem. Then

$$\min_{\mathbf{y} \geq 0} \{ \mathbf{cx}^o + \mathbf{dy} : G\mathbf{y} = \mathbf{h} - H\mathbf{x}^o \} = v^P(\mathbf{x}^o) < \boldsymbol{\gamma}^*(\mathbf{r} - R\mathbf{x}^o) + \mathbf{cx}^o.$$

Another application of linear programming duality theory, in this case to Q, gives

$$v^P(\mathbf{x}^o) < \boldsymbol{\gamma}^*(\mathbf{r} - R\mathbf{x}^o) + \mathbf{cx}^o \leq \min_{\mathbf{y} \geq 0} \{ \mathbf{cx}^o + \mathbf{ty} : T\mathbf{y} = \mathbf{r} - R\mathbf{x}^o \}$$

or

$$v^P(\mathbf{x}^o) < v^Q(\mathbf{x}^o).$$

The sufficiency of this inequality condition has essentially the same proof with all the steps reversed. Explicit details are left as an exercise (see Exercise 5.9). □

This lemma leads to the following theorem concerning preferred formulations.

Theorem 5.2. *Let P and Q be equivalent formulations of a mixed integer programming problem. Q is cut richer than P if, and only if, $v^Q(\mathbf{x}) \geq v^P(\mathbf{x})$ for all $\mathbf{x} \in X^c$ with a strict inequality for at least one $\mathbf{x} \in X^c$.*

Proof. If $v^Q(\mathbf{x}) \geq v^P(\mathbf{x})$ for all $\mathbf{x} \in X^c$, Lemma 5.1 says that P does not have any Benders' cuts that are unmatched with respect to Q. But because there is a $\mathbf{x}^o \in X^c$ satisfying $v^Q(\mathbf{x}^o) > v^P(\mathbf{x}^o)$, Lemma 5.1 implies that Q has a cut that is unmatched in P. Thus, Q satisfies the definition of being cut richer than P.

If Q is cut richer than P, then P, by definition of cut richer, does not have any cuts that are unmatched with respect to Q. Lemma 5.1 then tells us that $v^Q(\mathbf{x}) \geq v^P(\mathbf{x})$ for all $\mathbf{x} \in X^c$. The definition of cut richer also states that Q has a cut that is unmatched with respect to P and using Lemma 5.1 we know that some $\mathbf{x}^o \in X^c$ satisfies $v^Q(\mathbf{x}^o) > v^P(\mathbf{x}^o)$. □

The implications of Theorem 5.2 may become more apparent when interpreted in another way. Let the *relaxed primal problem* for any formulation of a mixed integer program be defined by replacing X by its convex hull X^c. Theorem 5.2 states that the preferred formulation of a mixed integer program for generating strong Benders' cuts is the one with the smallest possible feasible region (or the "tightest" possible constraint set) for its relaxed primal problem. For any formulation P, a smaller feasible region for its relaxed primal problem will result in larger values of the function $v^P(\mathbf{x})$; this property is desirable because of Lemma 5.1 and Theorem 5.2.

As an example, consider the p-median problem of Figure 5.4. Formulations P and Q differ only in that P has constraints of the form $y_{ij} \leq x_j$ for all (i, j), whereas Q has constraints of the form

$$\sum_{i=1}^{4} y_{ij} \leq 4x_j \qquad \text{for all } j .$$

Since the latter set of constraints is an aggregation of the former set of constraints, the feasible region for the relaxed primal problem of P is no larger than that for Q. Thus, $v^P(\mathbf{x}) \geq v^Q(\mathbf{x})$ for all $\mathbf{x} \in X^c$. A straightforward computation shows that $v^P(\mathbf{x}^o) = 200 > v^Q(\mathbf{x}^o) = 0$ for $\mathbf{x}^o = (1/2, 1/2, 1/2, 1/2)$. Therefore, the formulation P is cut richer than Q for this example. The comparison of the cuts given at the beginning of this section dramatically illustrates the superiority of the Benders' cuts for formulation P.

As a general consequence of Theorem 5.2, for any mixed integer programming formulation, the convex hull of its feasible region will be a model formulation that is "optimal" for generating Benders' cuts since it has a relaxed primal problem whose feasible region is the smallest. In order to formalize this observation, for any formulation P of a mixed integer program as in (5.5.2), let $C(P)$ denote the mixed integer program whose feasible region is the convex hull of the feasible region for P.

Theorem 5.3. *Given any formulation P of a mixed integer program, $v^{C(P)}(\mathbf{x}) \geq v^Q(\mathbf{x})$ for all $\mathbf{x} \in X^c$ and for all equivalent formulations Q of this problem.*

Proof. Let $\mathbf{x}^* \in X^c$ be arbitrary and let $\mathbf{y}^*$ be an optimal solution to $C(P)$ when $\mathbf{x} = \mathbf{x}^*$; that is, $v^{C(P)}(\mathbf{x}^*) = \mathbf{cx}^* + \mathbf{dy}^*$. By the definition of convex hull, $(\mathbf{y}^*, \mathbf{x}^*)$ is a convex combination with weights λ_i of a finite number of points $(\mathbf{y}^i, \mathbf{x}^i)$ that are feasible in P. Linearity of the objective function $\mathbf{cx} + \mathbf{dy}$ implies that $\mathbf{cx}^* + \mathbf{dy}^* = \Sigma\, \lambda_i(\mathbf{cx}^i + \mathbf{dy}^i)$. Since $(\mathbf{y}^i, \mathbf{x}^i)$ is feasible in P, $v^P(\mathbf{x}^i) \leq \mathbf{cx}^i + \mathbf{dy}^i$. Therefore, $v^{C(P)}(\mathbf{x}^*) \geq \Sigma\, \lambda_i v^P(\mathbf{x}^i)$. But since P and Q are equivalent formulations, $v^{C(P)}(\mathbf{x}^*) \geq \Sigma\, \lambda_i v^Q(\mathbf{x}^i)$ and by convexity of $v^Q(\mathbf{x})$ the right-hand side of this last expression is no smaller than $v^Q(\mathbf{x}^*)$. Consequently, $v^{C(P)}(\mathbf{x}^*) \geq v^Q(\mathbf{x}^*)$ for all $\mathbf{x}^* \in X^c$. $\quad\square$

Combining this theorem with Theorem 5.2 establishes the following result.

Corollary 5.1. *Given any two equivalent formulations P and Q of a mixed integer program, the convex hull formulation C(P) of P is either cut richer than or identical to Q.*

Another distinguishing feature of the convex hull formulation of a problem is that when Benders' algorithm is applied to it, only one cut is necessary for it to converge. More formally, let us suppose that the constraints of the following problem define the convex hull of the mixed integer program P:

$$v^{C(P)} = \min_{\mathbf{x} \in X, \mathbf{y} \geq 0} \{\mathbf{cx} + \mathbf{dy} : H_1\mathbf{x} + G_1\mathbf{y} = \mathbf{h}_1\} .$$

Then we have the following result.

Theorem 5.4. *For any formulation of the mixed integer program (5.5.2), the convex hull formulation requires only one Benders' cut for convergence.*

Proof

$$v^{C(P)} = \min_{\mathbf{x} \in X} \min_{\mathbf{y} \geq 0} \{\mathbf{cx} + \mathbf{dy} : H_1\mathbf{x} + G_1\mathbf{y} = \mathbf{h}_1\} .$$

Since $C(P)$ is the convex hull formulation, we can substitute X^c for X without affecting the optimal solution value. Then, applying linear programming duality theory (and again assuming that $v^{C(P)}(\mathbf{x})$ is feasible for all $\mathbf{x} \in X$), we have

$$v^{C(P)} = \min_{\mathbf{x} \in X^c} \max_{\mathbf{u}G_1 \leq \mathbf{d}} \mathbf{u}(\mathbf{h}_1 - H_1\mathbf{x}) + \mathbf{cx} .$$

Another application of linear programming duality theory yields

$$v^{C(P)} = \min_{\mathbf{x} \in X^c} \{\mathbf{u}^*(\mathbf{h}_1 - H_1\mathbf{x}) + \mathbf{cx}\}$$

for some $\mathbf{u}^*$ satisfying $\mathbf{u}^*G_1 \leq d$. Since the last objective function is a linear function of $\mathbf{x}$, we can substitute X for its convex hull and write

$$v^{C(P)} = \min_{\mathbf{x} \in X, z \in R} \{z : z \geq \mathbf{u}^*(\mathbf{h}_1 - H_1\mathbf{x}) + \mathbf{cx}\} .$$

Let $\mathbf{x}^*$ be a solution of this problem. Then $v^{C(P)} = v^{C(P)}(\mathbf{x}^*)$. Therefore, the single Benders' cut generated by $\mathbf{u}^*$ is sufficient to solve the convex hull formulation $C(P)$. $\square$

For facility location problems, our results show that a formulation with a reduced feasible region for the relaxed primal problem is desirable. However, there are other issues that must be considered in selecting a model for use with Benders' decomposition.

First, constructing alternative models for mixed integer programming problems can be a difficult task. In principle, the convex hull formulation of a problem requires only a single Benders' cut for convergence. However, in general, it will be very difficult to determine this cut since finding the constraints to represent the convex hull of a set of points is a complex problem.

Recently, researchers have been successful in partially characterizing such constraints for the plant location problem (see Chapter 3). Section 5.7 cites a number of related studies.

5.6. COMPUTATIONAL RESULTS

The previous sections in this chapter discussed decomposition methods that apply to discrete location problems and other combinatorial optimization models. This section summarizes computational results for some of these techniques and discusses the strengths and weaknesses of decomposition methods. The discussion focuses mainly on Benders' decomposition and related techniques. Chapters 2 and 3 describe computations using Lagrangian or price directive decomposition methods. Since computational experience with a broad set of transportation problems is helpful in assessing the potential of decomposition methods for location applications, we also discuss some of these experiences.

Perhaps the earliest and most successful reported application of Benders' decomposition was a facility location study conducted about 15 years ago for Hunt-Wesson Foods, Inc. The model considered the flow of multiple commodities from factories to regional distribution centers (DCs) and then to final customers. It addressed several important interrelated decisions: the number, location, and sizing of the DCs, the assignment of each customer to a DC, and the routing of the goods from the factories to the customers. The overall problem can be viewed as a capacitated plant location model (see Chapter 4) with a number of complicating side constraints. Benders' decomposition, equipped with the ε-optimal method for solving the master problem (see Section 5.3.2), was used to solve this problem. The computational results were outstanding. For example, a problem with 30 potential DC sites and a total of 513 0–1 variables and about 140,000 continuous variables required five iterations of Benders' decomposition and 191 s on an IBM 360/91 to compute upper and lower bounds that were within 0.15% of each other. Other computational experiments verified the utility of tight model formulations as discussed in Section 5.5. For several problems, the use of an aggregated (looser) formulation increased the number of Benders' iterations by a factor of more than 10.

Benders' decomposition has also been used successfully in two other transportation applications: (i) constructing airline routes for long-haul passenger markets; and (ii) in railway planning for selecting the mix of engine types and scheduling the available engines to trains. The model for the first application chooses, for each given origin-destination city pair, a route plan consisting of intermediate stops and the number of passengers transported between pairs of cities on the route. The objective is to maximize revenue while honoring operational constraints such as the capacity of the aircraft. The mixed integer programming model for this problem contains a number of integer side constraints (constraints imposed upon the integer variables). The implementation of Benders' decomposition for this problem used the ε-optimal method for solving the master problem and an initial selection of cuts to accelerate convergence (see Section 5.3.2). For test problems with 40–160 0–1 variables (corresponding to routing problems over a 12- to 17-city network), the solution procedure required from 10 to 16 Benders' iterations and about 80 s per problem on a DEC-10 system. Comparative tests indicate that the initial selection of cuts substantially reduced the number of Benders' iterations.

In the railway planning application, several types of engines can be assigned to various trains in order to meet each train's power constraints. The movements of trains through space and time are modeled as a time-space network. Each node corresponds to a particular location at a particular time and each arc corresponds to a train whose departure and arrival time and location are determined by the two terminal nodes. The integer variables indicate the number of engines providing power to trains while the continuous flow variables represent the *total* number of engines assigned to a train. The total number of engines assigned to a train might exceed the number of engines providing power since it may be useful to send engines to a location where they are needed. The linear subproblem (assignment of engines to trains) can be solved as a minimum cost flow problem. The model also contains a number of integer side constraints that represent engine requirements for each particular train. For a problem with 432 0–1 variables, 986 continuous flow variables and 1972 integer side constraints, Benders' decomposition required nine iterations and 1500 s on a CYBER 74 computer to determine upper and lower bounds that differed by about 6.6%. For another version (with different costs) of the same model, the decomposition procedure was able to find upper and lower bounds within only 19.3% of each other after 20 iterations and 3168 s of computation time. This study concluded that the procedure was suitable for solving moderate-sized, but not large-scale problems.

In the context of facility location, computational experiments performed with p-median problems have tested the effectiveness of the usual, closing facility, and expanding neighborhood cuts that we discussed in Section 5.4.3. When applied to 10- and 33-node problems, the expanding neighborhood cut performed slightly better than the closing facility cut, but both cuts clearly outperformed the usual cut technique. Implementations using the first two types of cuts required at least two or three times fewer cuts than the usual cut implementation to achieve comparable levels of accuracy. These results indicate the relative utility of the improved Benders' cuts. However, the performance of all three cut types indicates that Benders' decomposition is not competitive for solving large-scale p-median problems (see Chapter 2). For example, a four-median problem on a 33-node network required ten Benders' iterations to compute bounds that were within 9% of each other. Also, for larger problems, all three cut types exhibited pronounced tailing effects, that is, the convergence of the bounds slowed considerably as the number of iterations increased.

The improved Benders' cut methodology has also been tested on a problem closely related to discrete location problems, namely, the uncapacitated fixed charge network design problem. (Splitting of nodes permits facility location problems to be converted into network design problems, and adding nodes to arcs permits network design problems to be converted to facility location models.) In the network design setting, multiple commodities must be routed over a network with linear flow costs and with a fixed charge cost on each arc. The solution procedure compared three types of Benders' cuts including a usual cut, a "strong" cut that dominates the usual cut, and a pareto-optimal cut computed with the methodology described in Section 5.3. For ten moderate-sized test problems with 35–45 0–1 variables and 1800–3600 continuous variables, the pareto-optimal cuts required from 8 to 30 Benders' iterations to solve a problem to optimality. The computation time on a VAX 11/780 ranged from 7 to 700 s. The strong cuts performed almost as well, but the usual cuts were much less effective and exhibited severe tailing effects. On average, the usual cut implementation required fifty times more computation time and four times as many iterations as the pareto-optimal cut implementation to solve a problem to optimality. For most of the test problems, the pareto-optimal cut implementation required fewer iterations than the strong cut implementation, though at the expense of larger computation time for generating each cut. Generating a pareto-optimal cut required the solution of the auxiliary problem (5.3.11) which, for the network design application, reduces to a series of minimum cost-flow problems. Generating a strong cut required additional work that was equivalent to solving only a shortest-path problem. The overall computational results seem to justify the additional complexity of using the pareto-optimal cuts.

These computational experiments also used a second set of 21 larger problems with 90 0–1 variables and 10,000–15,000 continuous variables. For these problems, with all three cut types, Benders' decomposition encountered severe convergence problems and required excessive numbers of iterations and computation times. However, a preprocessing technique based upon a dual ascent procedure (see Chapter 3) was able to significantly improve the computational performance for these problems. This procedure used dual information to eliminate variables and to provide an initial feasible solution as well as an initial Benders' cut. For 17 of the test problems, the preprocessing routine was usually able to eliminate 75–90% of the 0-1 variables. For these 17 problems, the pareto-optimal and strong cuts both performed significantly better than the usual cuts. The strong cuts were generally more effective than the pareto-optimal cuts except that neither implementation converged after 7000 s for five difficult problems. For these five problems, the pareto-optimal implementation produced slightly stronger lower bounds. In general, the pareto-optimal cuts strategy required more time to generate a cut than the strong-cut strategy. On the other hand, the pareto-optimal cuts seem to generate somewhat stronger cuts and the resulting improvements appear to be more pronounced for the more difficult problems.

Finally, in a recent study an implementation of cross decomposition (see Section 5.3.2) has been very successful in solving capacitated plant location problems. The implementation required only one full cross-decomposition iteration and did not require the solution of a Benders' master problem. It alternated between solving Benders' subproblems and Lagrangian subproblems while occasionally solving the master problem resulting from applying the relaxation algorithm to the Lagrangian dual problem (5.3.5). The method generated "strong" Benders' cuts that dominate the usual cuts derived from the transportation subproblems. Computational results indicate that the procedure is about ten times faster than other proposed techniques for the capacitated plant location problem. The cross-decomposition implementation has solved (computed upper and lower bounds within 0.12% of each other) a series of problems with 100 potential plant sites and 200 demand nodes in 6–400 s on an MV8000 computer.

The computation results discussed in this section indicate that Benders' decomposition and related techniques can be successful in solving discrete location problems and other combinatorial optimization models. The acceleration techniques discussed in this chapter appear to be quite effective. The cut selection techniques (for strong and pareto-optimal cuts) can further improve the performance of Benders' decomposition. Also, the selection of an appropriate mixed integer programming model is vital to the success of Benders' method. Other techniques such as the ε-optimal method for solving the master problem and making a good selection of initial cuts have also been quite useful in various applications.

However, these methods should be used with caution. For the multicommodity (Hunt-Wesson) location, airline route construction, and railway planning applications for which Benders' decomposition was fairly successful, the models were complicated by a large number of integer side constraints. The Benders' master problems inherited these side constraints and so in each application a specialized technique was used to exploit the unique structure of the master problem. We suspect that these tailored master problem algorithms contributed significantly to the successful use of Benders' decomposition. For the p-median problem, network design problem, and other generic optimization problems that are basically combinatorial, but do not have many complicating integer side constraints, Benders' decomposition by itself has been much less successful. The p-median problem, for example, has been solved more effectively with other decomposition techniques, most notably Lagrangian decomposition and dual ascent. Other problems have required that Benders' decomposition be combined with problem preprocessing or with Lagrangian relaxation and other decomposition schemes.

In summary, computational results support the effectiveness of decomposition methods for solving discrete location problems. Further, the Benders' cuts presented in this chapter can definitely enhance the performance of decomposition methods. However, for many problems it is also useful to exploit the problem structure of the integer side constraints or combine decomposition with other solution methods.

5.7. NOTES

Section 5.2
Over 20 years ago, Benders (1962) first introduced his resource directive decomposition scheme which he cast in a setting of general mixed integer programming. Later, Geoffrion (1972) generalized the approach to solve nonlinear programming problems. Balinski and Wolfe (1963), Balinski (1965), Geoffrion and Graves (1974), and Magnanti and Wong (1981) discuss the application of Benders' decomposition to facility location problems. In particular, Geoffrion and Graves have been able to solve complicated large-scale location problems that arise in distribution system design.

Lagrangian relaxation techniques have a long and illustrious history and have, over the last 200 years, become a staple of nonlinear programming. The use of this solution strategy for discrete optimization is much more recent, though, and dates to the seminal work of Held and Karp (1970, 1971) on the traveling salesman problem. Subsequently, the method has been applied to a vast range of combinatorial optimization problems (see Geoffrion, 1974; Shapiro, 1979; Fisher, 1981).

Numerous researchers have used Lagrangian techniques to analyze location models including Cornuejols, Fisher, and Nemhauser (1977a, b) and Cornuejols and Thizy (1982b) for uncapacitated facility location; Geoffrion and McBride (1978), and Christofides and Beasley (1983) for capacitated facility location; Narula, Ogbu, and Samuelson (1977), Christofides and Beasley (1982), Weaver and Church (1983), and Mirchandani, Oujdit, and Wong (1985) for the p-median problem and its variants; and Karkazis and Boffey (1981) for a multicommodity location problem.

Guignard and Spielberg (1979) and Van Roy and Erlenkotter (1982) proposed other dual-based methods. Bitran, Chandru, Sempolinski, and Shapiro (1981) proposed an inverse optimization approach using both Lagrangian and group theoretic techniques.

In an annotated bibilography, Wong (1985) discusses a number of other references in the facility location literature. See also the survey by Tansel, Francis, and Lowe (1983) and books by Francis and White (1974) and Handler and Mirchandani (1979).

Section 5.3
The minimax view of decomposition that we have adopted in this section is drawn from Magnanti (1976) and Magnanti and Wong (1981).

Because the general minimax problem (3.1) is typically nondifferentiable, a number of authors including Dem'yanov and Malozemov (1974), Lemarechal (1975), Mifflin (1977), and Wolfe (1975) have modified and extended differentiable optimization algorithms to solve these problems.

Dantzig (1963) and Magnanti, Shapiro, and Wagner (1976) discuss the convergence properties of Dantzig–Wolfe decomposition. The second of these references stresses the relationship between Dantzig–Wolfe decomposition and Lagrangian duality in the context of general mathematical programs (including discrete optimization problems).

Mevert (1979) and Richardson (1976) have studied the effect of the initial selection of cuts on the performance of Benders' algorithm.

Nemhauser and Widhelm (1971), O'Neill and Widhelm (1975), Marsten, Hogan, and Blankenship (1975), Marsten (19755), and Holloway (1973) have proposed alternatives for modifying the Dantzig–Wolfe decomposition master problem.

Van Roy (1983) introduced the cross-decomposition method. He has successfully applied the technique to solve large-scale capacitated plant location problems (see Van Roy, 1981, 1986).

Geoffrion and Graves (1974) have introduced the ε-optimality method when applying Benders' decomposition to distribution systems design, including facility location decisions.

Historically, the study of equivalent formulations for a discrete optimization model seems to have originated with the location problems (see Davis and Ray, 1969). Beale and Tomlin (1972), Williams (1974), Jeroslow and Lowe (1984, 1985), Eppen and Martin (1987), and Martin and Schrage (1985) have studied equivalent formulations for various discrete optimization models. Cornuejols et al. (1977a, b) studied equivalent formulations for an uncapacitated location model.

Section 2 of Magnanti and Wong (1981) discusses Theorem 5.1 and related material. Rockafellar (1970) discusses the relative interior of convex sets in great detail.

Section 5.4
The pareto-optimal cut generation algorithm is taken from Section 3 of Magnanti and Wong (1981). The algorithm is similar to dual ascent procedures for the plant location problem proposed by Bilde and Krarup (1977) and Erlenkotter (1978). Balinski (1965) originally introduced the idea of the closing facility cut. In an unpublished report, Magnanti and Wong (1977)

proposed the expanding neighborhood cut and gave computational results comparing the usual, closing, and expanding neighborhood cuts. Magnanti, Mireault and Wong (1986) discuss some computational results with the pareto-optimal Benders' cuts applied to a class of network design problems. Magnanti and Wong (1984) show that, when interpreted properly, several branch-and-bound and heuristic algorithms for network design problems use Benders' cuts for bounding the optimal objective function value. The cuts described in Section 5.4 could be used in similar ways.

Section 5.5
Our discussion of the Benders' decomposition model selection criteria is taken from Section 4 of Magnanti and Wong (1981).

In recent years, the mathematical programming research community has intensively studied facets of the convex hull of discrete optimization problems (see Pulleyblank, 1983; Nemhauser and Wolsey, 1988). Although facet inequalities have been used chiefly as cutting planes (see, e.g., Grötschel and Padberg, 1979a; Crowder and Padberg, 1980; Crowder, Johnson, and Padberg, 1983; Bárány, Van Roy, and Wolsey, 1984a, b; Johnson, Kostreva, and Suhl, 1985; and Grötschel, Junger, and Reinelt, 1984, 1985), they could also be used to derive alternative models for mixed integer programming problems. Several authors including Cornuejols et al. (1977a, b), Guignard (1980), Cornuejols and Thizy (1982a), Cho, Johnson, Padberg, and Rao (1983), Cho, Padberg, and Rao (1983), Van Roy and Wolsey (1985), Leung (1985), and Leung and Magnanti (1989) have studied valid inequalities and facets for plant location problems. Lemke (1986) and Lemke and Wong (1985) have studied facets for the p-median problem.

Section 5.6
The studies of the Hunt-Wesson Foods distribution system design, the airline route selection problem, and the railway engine scheduling application, using Benders' decomposition, were conducted, respectively, by Geoffrion and Graves (1974), Richardson (1976), and Florian, Guérin, and Bushel (1976).

Magnanti and Wong (1977) performed the computational results using several types of cuts for the p-median problem. Magnanti et al. (1986) discuss the acceleration of Benders' decomposition for fixed charge network design problems. Van Roy (1986) used cross decomposition to solve capacitated plant location problems.

ACKNOWLEDGMENTS

We are grateful to Pitu Mirchandani and to Rita Vachani for many constructive comments on an earlier version of this paper.

Thomas L. Magnanti was supported in part by grants 79-26225-ECS and

83-16224-ECS from the National Science Foundation's Program on Systems Theory and Operations Research.

Richard T. Wong was supported in part by grants 81-17876-ECS and 83-16224-ECS from the National Science Foundation's Program on Systems Theory and Operations Research and by the Office of Naval Research under University Research Initiative grant number N00014-86-k-0689.

EXERCISES

5.1 Consider the following capacitated facility location problem:

$$\text{minimize} \quad \mathbf{cx} + \mathbf{dy}$$

$$\text{subject to} \quad \sum_{j=1}^{n} y_{ij} = w_i \,, \qquad i = 1, \ldots, m$$

$$\sum_{i=1}^{m} y_{ij} \le K_j x_j \,, \qquad j = 1, \ldots, n$$

$$y_{ij} \ge 0 \,, \qquad i = 1, \ldots, m \,, \quad j = 1, \ldots, n$$

$$x_j = 0 \text{ or } 1 \,, \qquad j = 1, \ldots, n \,.$$

(a) Suppose that we apply Lagrangian relaxation to this problem by associating Lagrange multipliers $\alpha_j \ge 0$ with the constraints $\sum_{i=1}^{m} y_{ij} \le K_j x_j$ for $j = 1, \ldots, n$. Let $L(\boldsymbol{\alpha})$ denote the optimal value of the Lagrangian subproblem as a function of the Lagrange multipliers $\boldsymbol{\alpha} = (\alpha_1, \ldots, \alpha_n)$ and let $d = \max_{\sigma \ge 0} L(\boldsymbol{\alpha})$. Show that d equals the value v_{LP} of the linear programming relaxation of the original problem (obtained by replacing $x_j = 0$ or 1 by $0 \le x_j \le 1$ for all j).

(b) Suppose that we define another Lagrangian relaxation by associating Lagrange multipliers λ_i with the constraints $\sum_{j=1}^{m} x_{ij} = w_i$ for $i = 1, \ldots, m$. Let $\bar{L}(\boldsymbol{\lambda})$ denote the optimal value of the Lagrangian subproblem as a function of $\boldsymbol{\lambda} = (\lambda_1, \ldots, \lambda_m)$. Also let $\bar{d} = \max_{\lambda} \bar{L}(\boldsymbol{\lambda})$ and let d be defined as in part (a). Show that $\bar{d} \ge d$.

(c) Specify a numerical example to show that $\bar{d} > d$ is possible.

This exercise shows that some Lagrangian relaxations for solving location problems might provide sharper lower bounds than other Lagrangian relaxations.

5.2 Suppose that we add the valid inequalities

$$y_{ij} \le \min \{w_i, K_j\} x_j, \qquad i = 1, \ldots, m \,, \quad j = 1, \ldots, n$$

to the formulation in Exercise 5.1 and define the two Lagrangian relaxations specified in parts (a) and (b) of that exercise.

(a) How do the Lagrangian relaxations defined after the addition of the new valid inequalities compare with those defined before the addition of those inequalities?

(b) Show how to solve the new Lagrangian relaxations.

5.3   Outline the steps required to apply Benders' decomposition to the capacitated facility location problem formulated in Exercise 5.1. Show how to generate pareto-optimal cuts for this problem.

5.4   Suppose that we compare the formulation given in Exercise 5.1 with the formulation that adds the constraints specified in Exercise 5.2 Is one formulation necessarily cut richer than the other?

5.5   Consider a three-median problem defined on the network in Figure 5.5. The arc labels indicate the cost of traversing a particular link and the demands are assumed to be unity. Let the current configuration be $\bar{\mathbf{x}} = (0, 1, 0, 0, 1, 1)$.

(a) Compute the *usual cut* for the current configuration.

(b) Compute the *closing cut* for the current configuration.

(c) Compute a *pareto-optimal cut* for the current configuration using $(1/8, 5/8, 1/8, 4/8, 6/8, 7/8)$ as the core point.

(d) Compute the *expanding neighborhood cut* for the current configuration.

(e) For every cut generated, determine which of the other cuts dominates it.

5.6   Assume that the problem data of Exercise 5.5 corresponds to an uncapacitated facility location (UFL) problem. Let the current configuration be defined by $\bar{\mathbf{x}} = (1, 0, 1, 0, 0, 0)$ and assume that $c_1 = c_2 = c_3 = 5$ and $c_4 = c_5 = c_6 = 3$. Do parts (a)–(e) of Exercise 5.5 for this UFL problem.

5.7   Recall the two-median example described in Figure 5.1. Assume the current configuration is defined by $\bar{\mathbf{x}} = (1, 0, 1, 0, 0)$.

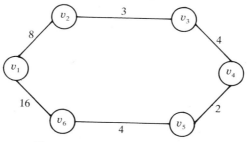

Figure 5.5. Three-median example.

(a) Formulate the linear subproblem that results from (5.1.7)–(5.1.12) when we fix $\mathbf{x} = \bar{\mathbf{x}}$. Formulate the dual subproblem (the dual of the linear subproblem).

(b) Compute the dual subproblem solution associated with the usual cut (5.4.5).

(c) Compute the dual subproblem associated with the closing facility cut (5.4.7).

(d) Compute the dual subproblem solution associated with the pareto-optimal cut generated by the core point (1/2, 1/4, 1/2, 1/4, 1/2).

(e) Show that the dual solutions computed in parts (b)–(d) are all optimal solutions for the dual subproblem.

(f) Formulate the optimization problem (5.3.12) specialized to the two-median example of Figure 5.1. Use $\mathbf{x}^o = (1/2, 1/4, 1/2, 1/4, 1/2)$.

(g) Show that the dual solutions computed in parts (b)–(d) are all feasible solutions for the optimization problem of part (f). Compute the objective function values for the three solutions.

Notice that the objective function value of the dual solution of part (d) is the largest of the three objective function values. This result is expected since the dual solution of part (d) is an optimal solution for the optimization problem of part (e).

5.8 Show that each of the cuts given in Section 5.5 are required for Benders' decomposition to converge for the two-median problem shown in Figure 5.4.

5.9 Prove the reverse implication of Lemma 5.1. That is, show that if some $\mathbf{x}^o$ belonging to the convex hull X^c of X satisfies $v^Q(\mathbf{x}^o) > v^P(\mathbf{x}^o)$, then Q has a Benders' cut that is unmatched with respect to P.

5.10 Consider the following pair of mixed integer programming formulations.

$$(P) \qquad \min_{x \in \bar{X} = \{0,1,2\}} v^P(x)$$

where

$$v^P(x) = \min y$$

$$\text{subject to} \qquad y \geq 0 + x$$

$$y \geq 2 + x$$

$$y \geq 0$$

and

$$(Q) \qquad\qquad \min_{x \in \bar{X}} v^Q(x)$$

where

$$v^Q(x) = \min (y_1 + \quad y_2)$$

$$\text{subject to} \qquad -y_1 \qquad\qquad + y_3 = \frac{1}{2} - x$$

$$y_2 \ - y_3 = \frac{3}{2} - x$$

$$y_1 \geq 0,\ y_2 \geq 0,\ y_3 \geq 0 .$$

(a) Show that the two integer programming formulations P and Q are *equivalent*.

(b) Show that the two integer programming formulations are not *identical*.

(c) Assume that *any* point in the subproblem's dual feasible region generates a Benders' cut. Show that Q *cannot* have a Benders' cut that is unmatched with respect to P. Also show that the formulation P is cut richer than the formulation Q.

(d) Now assume that *only* the extreme points of the subproblem's dual feasible region can generate a Benders' cut. Show that Q has a Benders' cut that is unmatched. Also, show that P is *not* cut richer than Q.

This exercise demonstrates that without the extended definition of a Benders' cut, given in part (c), some of the results in Section 5.5 might not be valid.

5.11 The network in Figure 5.6 describes a two-median problem: the arc labels indicate the cost of traversing a particular link and the demands are assumed to be unity. Let the current configuration be defined by $\bar{x} = (1, 0, 1, 0, 0)$.

(a) Compute the expanding neighborhood cut (5.4.15) for the current configuration.

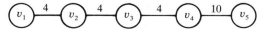

Figure 5.6. Two-median example.

(b) Show that the cut generated in part (a) is pareto-optimal. (Hint: compute the optimal dual objective function value $z_1(\mathbf{x})$ associated with the expanding neighborhood cut. Let

$$\bar{X} = \left\{ \mathbf{x}: \sum_{i=1}^{5} x_i = 2, 0 \le x_i \le 1, 1 \le i \le 5 \right\}.$$

Prove that for any cut corresponding to another optimal dual solution with objective function value $z_2(\mathbf{x})$, there is a $\hat{\mathbf{x}} \in \bar{X}$ satisfying $z_1(\hat{\mathbf{x}}) > z_2(\hat{\mathbf{x}})$.)

(c) Prove that the expanding neighborhood cut generated in part a *cannot* be generated as a solution to the optimization problem (5.3.11). That is, show that for any core point $\mathbf{x}^o \in \mathrm{ri}\,(\bar{X}^c)$, the dual solution corresponding to the expanding neighborhood cut is *not* a solution for (5.3.11).

This exercise demonstrates that some pareto-optimal cuts cannot be generated by solving (5.3.12). So although we are guaranteed that the solution to (5.3.12) generates a pareto-optimal cut, we cannot necessarily generate *all* pareto-optimal cuts with this technique.

REFERENCES

Balinski, M. L. (1965). "Integer Programming: Methods, Uses, Computation." *Management Science* **12**, 253–313.

Balinski, M. L., and P. Wolfe (1963). *On Benders Decomposition and a Plant Location Problem*, Working Paper ARO-27. Mathematica Inc., Princeton, New Jersey.

Bárány, I., T. J. Van Roy, and L. A. Wolsey (1984a). "Uncapacitated Lot-Sizing: The Convex Hull of Solutions." *Mathematical Programming Study* **22**, 32–43.

Bárány, I., T. J. Van Roy, and L. A. Wolsey (1984b). "Multi-Item Capacitated Lot Sizing Problems." *Management Science* **30**, 1255–1261.

Beale, E. M. L., and J. A. Tomlin (1972). "An Integer Programming Approach to a Class of Combinatorial Problems." *Mathematical Programming* **3**, 339–344.

Benders, J. F. (1962). "Partitioning Procedures for Solving Mixed Variables Programming Problems." *Numerische Mathematik* **4**, 238–252.

Bilde, O., and J. Krarup (1977). "Sharp Lower Bounds and Efficient Algorithms for the Simple Plant Location Problem." *Annals of Discrete Mathematics* **1**, 79–97.

Bitran, G., V. Chandru, D. Sempolinski, and J. Shapiro (1981). "Inverse Optimization: An Application to the Capacitated Plant Location Problem." *Management Science* **27**, 1120–1141.

Cho, D. C., E. L. Johnson, M. W. Padberg, and M. R. Rao (1983). "On the Uncapacitated Plant Location Problem. I. Valid Inequalities and Facets." *Mathematics of Operations Research* **8**, 579–589.

Cho, D. C., M. W. Padberg, and M. R. Rao (1983). "On the Uncapacitated Plant Location Problem. II. Facets and Lifting Theorems." *Mathematics of Operations Research* **8**, 590–612.

Christofides, N., and J. E. Beasley (1982). "A Tree Search Algorithm for the p-Median Problem." *European Journal of Operational Research* 10, 196–204.

Christofides, N., and J. E. Beasley (1983). "Extensions to a Lagrangian Relaxation Approach for the Capacitated Warehouse Location Problem." *European Journal of Operational Research* 12, 19–28.

Cornuejols, G., and J. M. Thizy (1982a). "Some Facets of the Simple Plant Location Polytope." *Mathematical Programming* 23, 50–74.

Cornuejols, G., and J. M. Thizy (1982b). "A Primal Approach to the Simple Plant Location Problem." *SIAM Journal on Algebraic Discrete Methods* 3, 504–510.

Cornuejols, G., M. L. Fisher, and G. L. Nemhauser (1977a). "On the Uncapacitated Location Problem." *Annals of Discrete Mathematics* 1, 163–177.

Cornuejols, G., M. L. Fisher, and G. L. Nemhauser (1977b). "Location of Bank Accounts to Optimize Float." *Management Science* 23, 789–810.

Crowder, H., and M. W. Padberg (1980). "Large Scale Symmetric Travelling Salesman Problems." *Management Science* 26, 495–509.

Crowder, H., E. L. Johnson, and M. W. Padberg (1983). "Solving Large-Scale Zero-One Linear Programming Problems." *Operations Research* 31, 803–834.

Dantzig, G. B. (1963). *Linear Programming and Extensions*. Princeton University Press, Princeton, New Jersey.

Davis, P. S., and T. L. Ray (1969). "A Branch-Bound Algorithm for Capacitated Facilities Location Problem." *Naval Research Logistics Quarterly* 16, 331–344.

Dem'yanov, V. F., and N. V. Malozemov (1974). *Introduction to Minimax* (translated from Russian by D. Louvish). Wiley, New York.

Eppen, G. D., and R. K. Martin (1987). "Solving Multi-Item Capacitated Lot Sizing Problems Using Variable Redefinition." *Operations Research* 35, 832–848.

Erlenkotter, D. (1978). "A Dual-Based Procedure for Uncapacitated Facility Location." *Operations Research* 26, 992–1009.

Fisher, M. (1981). "Lagrangian Relaxation Method for Solving Integer Programming Problems." *Management Science* 27, 1–18.

Florian, M., G. Guérin, and G. Bushel (1976). "The Engine Scheduling Problem in a Railway Network." *INFOR* 14, 121–138.

Francis, R., and J. White (1974). *Facility Layout and Location: An Analytic Approach*. Prentice-Hall, Englewood Cliffs, New Jersey.

Geoffrion, A. M. (1972). "Generalized Benders Decomposition." *Journal of Optimization Theory and Its Applications* 10, 237–260.

Geoffrion, A. M. (1974). "Lagrangian Relaxation and Its Uses in Integer Programming." *Mathematical Programming Study* 2, 82–114.

Geoffrion, A. M., and G. Graves (1974). "Multicommodity Distribution System Design by Benders' Decomposition." *Management Science* 5, 822–844.

Geoffrion, A. M., and R. McBride (1978). "Lagrangian Relaxation Applied to Facility Location Problems." *AIIE Transactions* 10, 40–47.

Grötschel, M., and M. W. Padberg (1979a). "On the Symmetric Travelling Salesman Problem. I. Inequalities." *Mathematical Programming* 16, 265–280.

Grötschel, M., and M. W. Padberg (1979b). "On the Symmetric Travelling Salesman Problem. II. Lifting Theorems and Facets." *Mathematical Programming* 16, 281–302.

Grötschel, M., M. Junger, and G. Reinelt (1984). "A Cutting Plane Algorithm for the Linear Ordering Problem." *Operations Research* 32, 1195–1220.

Grötschel, M., M. Junger, and G. Reinelt (1985). "Facets for the Linear Ordering Problem." *Mathematical Programming* 33, 43–60.

Guignard, M. (1980). "Fractional Vertices, Cuts and Facets of the Simple Plant Location Problem." *Mathematical Programming Study* **12**, 150–162.

Guignard, M., and K. Spielberg (1979). "A Direct Dual Method for the Mixed Plant Location Problem with Some Side Constraints." *Mathematical Programming* **17**, 198–228.

Handler, G. Y., and P. B. Mirchandani (1979). *Location on Networks: Theory and Algorithms.* MIT Press, Cambridge, Massachusetts.

Held, M., and R. M. Karp (1970). "The Travelling Salesman Problem and Minimum Spanning Trees." *Operations Research* **18**, 1138–1162.

Held, M., and R. M. Karp (1971). "The Travelling Salesman Problem and Minimum Spanning Trees. Part II." *Mathematical Programming* **1**, 6–25.

Holloway, C. (1973). "A Generalized Approach to Dantzig-Wolfe Decomposition for Concave Programs." *Operational Research* **21**, 210–220.

Jeroslow, R. G., and J. K. Lowe (1984). "Modelling with Integer Variables." *Mathematical Programming Study* **22**, 167–184.

Jeroslow, R. G., and J. K. Lowe (1985). "Experimental Results on the New Techniques for Integer Programming Formulations." *Journal of the Operational Research Society* **36**, 393–403.

Johnson, E. L., M. M. Kostreva, and U. H. Suhl (1985). "Solving 0–1 Integer Programming Problems Arising from Large Scale Planning Models." *Operations Research* **33**, 803–820.

Karkazis, J. and T. B. Boffey, (1981). "The Multi-Commodity Facilities Location Problem." *Journal of the Operational Research Society* **32**, 803–814.

Lemarechal, C. (1975). "An Extension of Davidson's Methods of Non-Differentiable problems." *Mathematical Programming Study* **3**, 95–103.

Lemke, P. (1986). *Some Properties of the K-Median Polytope.* Doctoral Dissertation, Rensselaer Polytechnic Institute, Troy, New York.

Lemke, P., and R. T. Wong (1985). "Valid Inequalities and Facets for the *K*-Median Location Problems." *TIMS/ORSA Bulletin* **19**, 170.

Leung, J. M. Y. (1985). *Polyhedral Structure of Capacitated Fixed Charge Problems and a Problem in Delivery Route Planning.* Ph.D. Thesis, Department of Electrical Engineering and Computer Science, Massachusetts Institute of Technology, Cambridge, Massachusetts.

Leung, J. M. Y., and T. L. Magnanti (1989). "Valid Inequalities and Facets of the Capacitated Plant Location Problem." *Mathematical Programming* **44**, 271–292.

Magnanti, T. L. (1976). "Optimization for Sparse Systems." In *Sparse Matrix Computations* (J. R. Bunch and J. F. Rose, eds.), pp. 147–176. Academic Press, New York.

Magnanti, T. L., and R. T. Wong (1977). "Network Design via Benders' Decomposition." Massachusetts Institute of Technology, Cambridge, Massachusetts (unpublished manuscript).

Magnanti, T. L., and R. T. Wong (1981). "Accelerating Benders' Decomposition: Algorithmic Enhancement and Model Selection Criteria." *Operations Research* **29**, 464–484.

Magnanti, T. L., and R. T. Wong (1984). "Network Design and Transportation Planning: Models and Algorithms." *Transportation Science* **18**, 1–55.

Magnanti, T. L., P. Mireault, and R. T. Wong (1986). "Tailoring Benders' Decomposition for Network Design." *Mathematical Programming Study* **26**, 112–154.

Magnanti, T. L., J. F. Shapiro, and M. H. Wagner (1976). "Generalized Linear Programming Solves the Dual." *Management Science* **22**, 1195–1203.

Marsten, R. E. (1975). "The Use of the BOXSTEP Method in Discrete Optimization." *Mathematical Programming Study* **3**, 127–144.

Marsten, R. E., W. W. Hogan, and J. W. Blankenship (1975). "The BOXSTEP Method for Large-Scale Optimization." *Operations Research* **23**, 389–405.

Martin, K., and L. Schrage (1985). "Subset Coefficient Reduction Cuts for 0/1 Mixed Integer Programming." *Operations Research* **33**, 505-526.

Mevert, P. (1977). "Fixed Charge Network Flow Problems: Applications and Methods of Solution." Presented at Large Scale and Hierarchical Systems Workshop, Brussels, Belgium, May.

Mifflin, R. (1977). "An Algorithm for Constrained Optimization with Semismooth Functions." *Mathematics of Operations Research* **2**, 191-207.

Mirchandani, P. B., A Oudjit, and R. T. Wong (1985). "Multidimensional Extensions and a Nested Dual Approach for the *M*-Median Problem." *European Journal of Operational Research* **21**, 121-137.

Narula, S. C., U. I. Ogbu, and H. M. Samuelsson (1977). "An Algorithm for the *P*-Median Problem." *Operations Research* **25**, 709-712.

Nauss, R. M. (1978). "An Improved Algorithm for the Capacitated Facility Location Problem." *Journal of the Operational Research Society* **29**, 1195-1201.

Nemhauser, G. L., and W. B. Widhelm (1971). "A Modified Linear Program for Columnar Methods in Mathematical Programming." *Operations Research* **19**, 1051-1060.

Nemhauser, G. L., and L. A. Wolsey (1988). *Integer and Combinatorial Optimization*, Wiley, New York.

O'Neill, R. P., and W. B. Widhelm (1975). "Computational Experience with Normed and Non-normed Column-Generation Procedures in Nonlinear Programming." *Operations Research* **23**, 372-382.

Pulleyblank, W. R. (1983). "Polyhedral Combinatorics." In *Mathematical Programming: The State-of-the-Art* (A. Bachem, M. Grötschel, and B. Korte, eds.), pp. 312-345. Springer-Verlag, Berlin and New York.

Richardson, R. (1976). "An Optimization Approach to Routing Aircraft." *Transportation Science* **10**, 52-71.

Rockafellar, R. T. (1970). *Convex Analysis*. Princeton Univ. Press, Princeton, New Jersey.

Shapiro, J. F. (1979). "A Survey of Lagrangian Techniques for Discrete Optimization." *Annals of Discrete Mathematics* **5**, 113-118.

Tansel, B. C., R. L. Francis, and T. J. Lowe (1983). "Location on Networks: A Survey. Parts I and II." *Management Science* **29**, 482-511.

Van Roy, T. J. (1981). "Cross Decomposition for Mixed Integer Programming with Applications to Facility Location." In *Operational Research* (J. P. Brans, ed.), pp. 579-587. North-Holland, Publ., Amsterdam.

Van Roy, T. J. (1983). "Cross Decomposition for Mixed Integer Programming." *Mathematical Programming* **25**, 46-63.

Van Roy, T. J. (1986). "A Cross Decomposition Algorithm for Capacitated Facility Location." *Operations Research* **34**, 145-163.

Van Roy, T. J., and D. Erlenkotter (1982). "A Dual-Based Procedure for Dynamic Facility Location." *Management Science* **28**, 1091-1105.

Van Roy, T. J., and L. A. Wolsey (1985). "Valid Inequalities and Separation for Uncapacitated Fixed Charge Networks." *Operations Research Letters* **4**, 105-112.

Weaver, J. R, and R. L. Church (1983). "Computational Procedures for Location Problems on Stochastic Networks." *Transportation Science* **17**, 168-180.

Williams, H. P. (1974). "Experiments in the Formulation of Integer Programming Problems." *Mathematical Programming Study* **2**, 180-197.

Wolfe, P. (1975). "A Method of Conjugate Subgradients for Minimizing Nondifferentiable Functions." *Mathematical Programming Study* **3**, 145-173.

Wong, R. T. (1985). "Location and Network Design." In *Combinatorial Optimization: Annotated Bibliographies* (M. O'hEigeartaigh, J. K. Lenstra, and A. H. G. Rinnooy Kan, eds.), pp. 127-147. Wiley (Interscience), New York.

6

Covering Problems

Antoon Kolen
Department of Quantitative Economics
University of Limburg
Maastricht, The Netherlands

Arie Tamir
Department of Statistics
Tel Aviv University
Ramat Aviv, Tel Aviv, Israel

6.1. INTRODUCTION

A class of location decision problems may be formulated as *covering problems*. We will study in this chapter some covering problems on *networks*. Here a set of clients, with given demands for services or commodities, are assumed to be located on the nodes or arcs of an underlying network. The problems require that facilities be established on the network to provide the necessary services or commodities for these clients. All facilities will be assumed to be of the same type and each of them to have sufficient capacity to serve all clients; that is, only the *uncapacitated* versions of the covering problems will be considered. Whenever a facility is "close enough," as defined by the problem statement, to serve a client we say that the client is *covered* by that facility. Generally, in the covering problems discussed here we determine the number and locations of the facilities so that the clients are covered with minimum cost, the cost function (or objective function) being defined by the problem statement.

In this introduction we give an informal description of the various location problems to be discussed in this chapter. Most of these problems are either covering problems or can be solved by a sequence of covering problems. Exact formulations are given in the succeeding sections where we present solution techniques.

In most of our models the clients are assumed to be located only at the nodes of the network. We refer to the case where clients are not restricted to be at the nodes as a *continuous location problem*. A point in the network where a facility may be established is referred to as a *potential site*.

We consider three types of costs involved with a given set of facility locations. The first is the *setup cost*, that is, the cost of establishing a facility at a given site. When the facilities may be located anywhere along the network we assume that all setup costs are equal. When the set of potential sites is finite, different setups will also be allowed. The second cost is the *transportation cost*, that is, the cost of transporting the service (or commodity) between a facility and a client. The transportation cost is assumed to be a nondecreasing function of the distance between the client and the serving facility. Since we have assumed that each facility has a sufficient capacity to serve all clients, each client will be served by its closest facility. Finally, we may have what we refer to as the *penalty cost*, a cost which is applied only if a client is not served by any facility. The penalty costs will, in general, depend on the particular clients not served.

The following constraints are also included in our models. The first is a *budget constraint* which models the upper bound on the total setup cost. If all setup costs are equal, then the budget constraint reduces to an upper bound on the number of facilities that may be established.

In addition we have *client constraints* and *facility constraints*. Through the client constraints, we model the requirement that each client be served by a facility which is located within a given distance (depending on the client) from that client. One can think of the set of points within a given distance from a client as the *region* of *attraction* for that client. Consider, for example, the problem of a new company which is interested in entering an existing market. We may assume that a client will switch to the new company only if the latter establishes a facility within his region of attraction.

The facility constraint refers to the case when a facility can only serve clients which are located within a given distance (depending on the facility) from it. Here we may assume that associated with clients who are located at large distances, are transportation costs that are too expensive for the serving company.

Common objective functions that arise are:

1. minimize the maximum transportation cost (the *center problem*);
2. minimize the sum of the transportation costs (the *median problem*);

3. minimize the sum of the transportation costs and the setup costs (the *uncapacitated facility location problem*);
4. minimize the sum of the setup costs and penalty costs (the *covering problem*);
5. minimize the penalty costs (the *coverage problem*).

In Section 6.2 we formulate both the client and facility constrained problems as $(0, 1)$ integer programming problems. We present a polynomial time algorithm to solve this problem whenever the integer programming problem satisfies certain properties. These properties are shown to be satisfied when the underlying network has a tree structure. We also show that the uncapacitated facility location (UFL) problem can be formulated as a client constrained covering problem. Hence, it can be solved in polynomial time in the case of a tree network by using the algorithm presented.

One aspect of location problems which is usually not addressed is the aspect of allocating the total locational cost among the clients. In Section 6.2 we discuss the problem of finding a cost allocation which is "acceptable" to all clients. After defining what is meant by "acceptable," we develop a relationship between the cost allocation problem and the dual of the covering problem. Acceptable allocations are shown to always exist for tree networks.

In the context of covering problems we also discuss the *multiple covering problem*. Here, each client must be served by a number (depending on the client) of facilities. There is also an upper bound (depending on the site) on the number of facilities we can establish at a given site. We show how the algorithm developed in Section 6.2 can be used to solve the multiple covering problem on tree networks when all setup costs are equal.

Section 6.3 is devoted to budget constrained center problems on trees. We show that for different setup costs this problem can be solved as a sequence of covering problems. In the case of equal setup costs, the budget constraint specifies the number of facilities, say p; in this case we obtain the classical p-center problem. Using the concept of a chordal graph we establish a duality result for a class of p-center problems.

An extension of the classical center problem is the *round-trip center problem*. In this problem we consider pairs of clients and a transportation company which has to transport services (or commodities) from one client to the other. A facility in this case is a depot where the vehicles of the company are to be located. The transportation cost is assumed to be a monotone nondecreasing function of the *round-trip distance*, that is, the distance a vehicle has to travel to deliver the service from one client to another, and then to return to its depot. Equivalently, the round trip distance is the sum of the distances between the depot and the two clients and the distance between the two clients. We prove that, unlike the center problem, the round-trip version is $\mathcal{NP}$-*hard* for different setup costs, even on tree networks.

When the facilities can be located anywhere along the tree, and the setup costs are equal, the round-trip p-center problem, and the p-center problem, can be solved in polynomial time. When we restrict the potential sites to the set of all nodes, again we can solve both problems in polynomial time. However, in the case when we restrict the sites to a strict subset of the nodes, the p-center problem can still be solved in polynomial time, while the round-trip p-center problem becomes $\mathcal{NP}$-hard.

In Section 6.4 we show that there is a strong relationship between the location problems and set covering problems on totally balanced matrices. We show that the solution technique for the covering problem developed in Section 6.2 is equally applicable to the case where the $(0, 1)$ matrix of the covering problem is totally balanced. We also discuss the budget constrained coverage problem with equal setup costs and the p-median problem, both on tree networks. These problems are special cases of integer programming problems on totally balanced matrices, and are also solvable in polynomial time.

6.2.   THE INTEGER PROGRAMMING APPROACH

As a general framework for the location problems we utilize the following integer covering program:

$$\text{minimize} \quad \sum_{j \in M_2} c_j x_j + \sum_{\omega \in M_1} p_\omega z_\omega$$

$$\text{subject to} \quad \sum_{j \in M_2} a_{\omega j} x_j + z_\omega \geq 1, \quad \forall \omega \in M_1, \quad (6.2.1)$$

$$x_j \in \{0, 1\}, \quad j \in M_2,$$

$$z_\omega \in \{0, 1\}, \quad \omega \in M_1,$$

where M_1, M_2 are finite index sets and $A = (a_{\omega j})$ is an $|M_1| \times |M_2|$ $(0, 1)$ matrix. Let $N = (V, E)$ be an undirected network with node set $V = \{v_1, v_2, \ldots, v_m\}$ and arc set E. Each arc $a \in E$ has a certain length $\alpha_a \geq 0$. If we consider each arc $a = [v_i, v_j]$ as a line segment of length α_a, then we can define a point on the arc by its distance on the segment from v_i. We define the *distance* $d(x, y)$ between two points x and y on N to be the length of a shortest path (denoted by $P[x, y]$) from x to y. The *distance* $D(y, X)$ between a point y on N and a closed set of points X on N is defined to be the distance $d(y, x)$ where x is a closest point to y in the set X. We also let $D(X, y)$ denote the distance $D(y, X)$. We assume that at each node there exists exactly one client. We refer to the client located at node v_i as *client i*, $i = 1, 2, \ldots, m$. If client i is not served by any facility, then a nonnegative penalty cost of p_i is incurred. We assume that the set of potential sites for the facilities is a subset of nodes of the network. Without loss of generality let this set be $V' = \{v_1, \ldots, v_n\}$, $n \leq m$. The nonnegative setup cost of establishing a facility at v_j is c_j, $j = 1, \ldots, n$. (We will refer to a facility established at site v_j as *facility* j, $j = 1, \ldots, n$.) The *covering problem* is to minimize the sum of setup costs and penalty costs, and it corresponds to the special case of the covering program (6.2.1) with $M_1 = \{1, \ldots, m\}$, $M_2 = \{1, \ldots, n\}$ and $a_{ij} = 1$ if and only if a facility at site v_j can serve client i. Thus, the covering problem is formulated as,

$$\text{minimize} \quad \sum_{j=1}^{n} c_j x_j + \sum_{i=1}^{m} p_i z_i$$

$$\text{subject to} \quad \sum_{j=1}^{n} a_{ij} x_j + z_i \geq 1, \quad i = 1, \ldots, m, \quad (6.2.2)$$

$$x_j \in \{0, 1\}, \quad j = 1, \ldots, n,$$

$$z_i \in \{0, 1\}, \quad i = 1, \ldots, m,$$

where $x_j = 1$ if and only if a facility is established at v_j and $z_i = 1$ if and only if client i is served by no facility.

The *client constrained covering problem* corresponds to the case where we have a region of attraction of radius r_i for client i and we set $a_{ij} = 1$ if and only if $d(v_i, v_j) \leq r_i$, $i = 1, \ldots, m$, $j = 1, \ldots, n$.

The *facility constrained covering problem* corresponds to the case where we have a radius s_j for facility j and we set $a_{ij} = 1$ if and only if $d(v_i, v_j) \leq s_j$, $i = 1, \ldots, m$, $j = 1, \ldots, n$.

The *uncapacitated facility location problem* (UFL) is to locate facilities at the nodes in order to minimize the sum of the setup and transportation costs. The transportation cost for client i is given by a nondecreasing function $f_i(d)$ of the distance d between client i and the facility serving it. We let $f_i(\infty)$ correspond to the case when client i is served by no facility. Due to the fact that facilities are uncapacitated and the transportation costs are nondecreasing, we will assume without loss of generality that each client is served by its closest facility. If S is the subset of nodes corresponding to established facilities, then the corresponding objective value of the UFL problem is given by

$$\sum_{j:\, v_j \in S} c_j + \sum_{i=1}^{m} f_i(D(v_i, S)) \quad (6.2.3)$$

where by convention $D(v_i, \varphi) = \infty$.

Let us return for a moment to the client constrained covering problem (that is, the case where $a_{ij} = 1$ if and only if $d(v_i, v_j) \leq r_i$), and minimize (6.2.2) for a given solution $x_j \in \{0, 1\}$, $j = 1, \ldots, n$. Define $S = \{v_j : x_j = 1\}$. Since $p_i \geq 0$ an optimal solution is given by $z_i = 1$ if

$$\sum_{j=1}^{n} a_{ij} x_j = 0 \quad (\text{or equivalently } D(v_i, S) > r_i),$$

and $z_i = 0$ if

$$\sum_{j=1}^{n} a_{ij}x_j \geq 1 \quad \text{(or equivalently } D(v_i, S) \leq r_i), \qquad i = 1, \ldots, m.$$

If we define the function $f_i(r)$, $i = 1, 2, \ldots, m$ by

$$f_i(r) = \begin{cases} 0, & \text{if } r \leq r_i, \\ p_i, & \text{if } r > r_i, \end{cases} \qquad (6.2.4)$$

then the optimal objective value of (6.2.2) corresponding to the set of established facilities S is given by (6.2.3).

We conclude that both the client constrained covering problem and the UFL problem can be formulated as

$$\underset{S \subseteq V'}{\text{minimize}} \left\{ \sum_{j: v_j \in S} c_j + \sum_{i=1}^{m} f_i(D(v_i, S)) \right\} \qquad (6.2.5)$$

where f_i, $i = 1, \ldots, m$ is a nondecreasing function.

We demonstrate next that the UFL problem can be formulated as a client constrained covering problem. Rewrite (6.2.5) as

$$\text{minimize} \qquad \left[\sum_{j=1}^{n} c_j x_j + \sum_{i=1}^{m} f_i \left(\min_{\{v_j : x_j = 1\}} \{d(v_i, v_j)\} \right) \right] \qquad (6.2.6)$$

$$\text{subject to} \qquad x_j \in \{0, 1\}, \qquad j = 1, \ldots, n$$

where $x_j = 1$ if and only if a facility is established at v_j.

By introducing $m \cdot n$ constraints and $m \cdot n$ new $(0, 1)$-variables we replace the nonlinear part in the objective function of (6.2.6) by a linear expression. The idea behind this transformation is the following. For each client (node) v_i, $i = 1, \ldots, m$, we denote by $r_{i1} \leq r_{i2} \leq \cdots \leq r_{in}$ the (sorted) sequence of distances from v_i to the n potential sites in V'. We also define $r_{i,n+1} = \infty$. If there is no established facility within distance r_{ik} from v_i, then the closest established facility is at a distance of at least $r_{i,k+1}$. In this case the transportation cost for client i is increased from $f_i(r_{ik})$ (the cost if the closest facility was at distance r_{ik}) to at least $f_i(r_{i,k+1})$. Therefore we can consider the difference $f_i(r_{i,k+1}) - f_i(r_{ik})$ as a nonnegative penalty for not establishing a facility within distance r_{ik} from v_i. Define the $(m \cdot n) \times n$ $(0, 1)$ matrix $A = (a_{ik,j})$ by

$$a_{ik,j} = 1 \text{ iff } d(v_i, v_j) \leq r_{ik}, \qquad i = 1, 2, \ldots, m$$

$$j, k = 1, 2, \ldots, n. \qquad (6.2.7)$$

We now introduce the $(0, 1)$ variables z_{ik}, where $z_{ik} = 1$ if and only if there is no facility established within distance r_{ik} from v_i, $i = 1, \ldots, m$, $k =$

$1, \ldots, n$. Let x_j, $j = 1, \ldots, n$ be some solution for (6.2.6). Then, we claim that the transportation cost for client i is given by

$$f_i\left(\min_{\{v_j \,:\, x_j = 1\}} \{d(v_i, v_j)\}\right) = \text{minimize} \sum_{k=1}^{n} (f_i(r_{i,k+1}) - f_i(r_{ik}))z_{ik} + f_i(r_{i1})$$

subject to

$$\sum_{j=1}^{n} a_{ik,j}x_j + z_{ik} \geq 1, \qquad k = 1, \ldots, n$$

$$z_{ik} \in \{0, 1\}, \qquad k = 1, \ldots, n. \qquad (6.2.8)$$

To show (6.2.8) observe that since the coefficient of z_{ik} in the objective function of (6.2.8) is nonnegative an optimal solution is obtained by making z_{ik} as small as possible, that is, by making

$$z_{ik} = \begin{cases} 0, & \text{if } \sum_{j=1}^{n} a_{ik,j}x_j \geq 1, \\ 1, & \text{if } \sum_{j=1}^{n} a_{ik,j}x_j = 0. \end{cases} \qquad (6.2.9)$$

If we let $t(i)$ be the smallest index such that $r_{it(i)} = \min_{\{v_j \,:\, x_j = 1\}} \{d(v_i, v_j)\}$ then the number of facilities established within distance r_{ik} from v_i is zero for $k < t(i)$, and at least one for $k \geq t(i)$. Since $\sum_{j=1}^{n} a_{ik,j}x_j$ counts the number of established facilities within distance r_{ik} from v_i we have

$$z_{ik} = \begin{cases} 0, & \text{if } k \geq t(i), \\ 1, & \text{if } k < t(i). \end{cases} \qquad (6.2.10)$$

Substituting this in the right-hand side of the objective in (6.2.8) validates our claim:

$$\sum_{k=1}^{t(i)-1} (f_i(r_{i,k+1}) - f_i(r_{ik})) + f_i(r_{i1}) = f_i(r_{it(i)})$$

$$= f_i\left(\min_{\{v_j \,:\, x_j = 1\}} \{d(v_i, v_j)\}\right). \qquad (6.2.11)$$

From (6.2.6) and (6.2.8) we obtain the following $(0, 1)$ integer programming formulation of the UFL problem

$$\text{minimize} \quad \sum_{j=1}^{n} c_j x_j + \sum_{i=1}^{m} \sum_{k=1}^{n} (f_i(r_{i,k+1}) - f_i(r_{ik}))z_{ik} + \sum_{i=1}^{m} f_i(r_{i1})$$

subject to $\displaystyle\sum_{j=1}^{n} a_{ik,j}x_j + z_{ik} \geq 1$, $i = 1, \ldots, m$, $k = 1, \ldots, n$

$$z_{ik} \in \{0, 1\}, \quad i = 1, \ldots, m, \quad k = 1, \ldots, n$$

$$x_j \in \{0, 1\}, \quad j = 1, \ldots, n. \tag{6.2.12}$$

Formulation (6.2.12) of the UFL problem is a client constrained covering problem (note that $a_{ik,j} = 1$ if and only if $d(v_i, v_j) \leq r_{ik}$).

Let us now consider the special case when the network is a tree. Let us denote a tree by $T = (V, E)$. A *subtree* is a closed connected subset of points of T (closedness is meant with respect to the metric induced by the distance function). A *neighborhood subtree* $N(x, r)$ is defined as the set of all points on the tree within a distance r (called the *radius*) from x (called the *center*), that is, $N(x, r) = \{y \in T: d(y, x) \leq r\}$. A neighborhood subtree of a tree is a generalization of an interval on a line segment. We will see that neighborhood subtrees possess some of the useful properties of intervals.

An *intersection matrix* of the set $\{S_1, \ldots, S_m\}$ versus $\{R_1, \ldots, R_n\}$, where S_i, $i = 1, \ldots, m$, and R_j, $j = 1, \ldots, n$ are subsets of a given set is defined to be the $m \times n$ (0, 1) matrix $A = (a_{ij})$ defined by $a_{ij} = 1$ if and only if $S_i \cap R_j$ is nonempty.

If in the client constrained covering problem we define a neighborhood subtree $S_i = \{y \in T: d(v_i, y) \leq r_i\}$, $i = 1, \ldots, m$ then the matrix $A = (a_{ij})$ of (6.2.2) is the intersection matrix of neighborhood subtrees versus nodes, that is, $a_{ij} = 1$ if and only if $v_j \in S_i$.

Similarly we can define $R_j = \{y \in T: d(y, v_j) \leq s_j\}$, $j = 1, \ldots, n$. In this case the matrix $A = (a_{ij})$ of (6.2.2) is the intersection matrix of nodes versus neighborhood subtrees, that is, $a_{ij} = 1$ if and only if $v_i \in R_j$.

We shall prove in Section 6.2.2 that for intersection matrices of nodes versus neighborhood subtrees of a tree there exists a permutation of the rows and a permutation of the columns (we give an efficient procedure to find these permutations), such that the transformed matrix does not contain a 2×2 submatrix of the form

$$\begin{bmatrix} 1 & 1 \\ 1 & 0 \end{bmatrix}. \tag{6.2.13}$$

A matrix that does not contain the above submatrix is said to be in *standard greedy form*. Since a matrix is in standard greedy form if and only if its transpose is in standard greedy form we can also transform the intersection matrix of neighborhood subtrees versus nodes into standard greedy form.

In Section 6.2.1 we give an $O(mn)$ algorithm to solve the covering problem on an $m \times n$ matrix in standard greedy form. We also define and solve the multiple covering problem for a matrix in this form.

In Section 6.2.2 we discuss how we can find the permutations which transform the intersection matrix of nodes versus neighborhood subtrees into standard greedy form.

In Section 6.2.3 we define a dual problem to the covering problem and relate it to the allocation of the total cost among the clients.

6.2.1. The Covering Algorithm for Standard Greedy Matrices

Consider the covering problem

$$\text{minimize} \quad \sum_{j=1}^{n} c_j x_j + \sum_{i=1}^{m} p_i z_i$$

$$\text{subject to} \quad \sum_{j=1}^{n} a_{ij} x_j + z_i \geq 1, \qquad i = 1, \ldots, m,$$

$$x_j \in \{0, 1\}, \qquad j = 1, \ldots, n,$$

$$z_i \in \{0, 1\}, \qquad i = 1, \ldots, m \qquad (6.2.14)$$

where $A = (a_{ij})$ is in standard greedy form. Without loss of generality we assume that $c_j > 0$, $j = 1, \ldots, n$ and $p_i > 0$, $i = 1, \ldots, m$; if $c_j = 0$, then we can take $x_j = 1$ and eliminate from (6.2.14) all rows i and variables z_i for which $a_{ij} = 1$; if $p_i = 0$, then we take $z_i = 1$ and eliminate row i from (6.2.14). Let us define the *LP-relaxation* of (6.2.14) as the problem obtained from (6.2.14) by replacing the integrality constraints by the nonnegativity constraints on the variables.

The algorithm we describe shortly starts by solving the dual of the LP-relaxation:

$$\text{maximize} \quad \sum_{i=1}^{m} y_i$$

$$\sum_{i=1}^{m} y_i a_{ij} \leq c_j, \qquad j = 1, \ldots, n,$$

$$0 \leq y_i \leq p_i, \qquad i = 1, \ldots, m. \qquad (6.2.15)$$

After a feasible solution y of (6.2.15) is obtained by our algorithm, it constructs a feasible $(0, 1)$-solution x, z of (6.2.14) which, together with y, satisfy the complementary slackness relations given by

$$y_i \left(\sum_{j=1}^{n} a_{ij} x_j + z_i - 1 \right) = 0, \qquad i = 1, \ldots, m, \qquad (6.2.16)$$

$$x_j \left(\sum_{i=1}^{m} y_i a_{ij} - c_j \right) = 0, \qquad j = 1, \ldots, n, \qquad (6.2.17)$$

$$z_i (y_i - p_i) = 0, \qquad i = 1, \ldots, m. \qquad (6.2.18)$$

It follows that x, z is an optimal solution of (6.2.14).

In the first phase, the algorithm starts by calculating $y_1, \ldots, y_m$ recursively by a greedy approach, that is, given $y_1, \ldots, y_{k-1}$ such that $\Sigma_{i=1}^{k-1} y_i a_{ij} \le c_j$, $j = 1, \ldots, n$ and $0 \le y_i \le p_i$, $i = 1, \ldots, k-1$ we give y_k the largest value such that $\Sigma_{i=1}^{k} y_i a_{ij} \le c_j$, $j = 1, \ldots, n$ and $0 \le y_k \le p_k$. So $y_1, \ldots, y_m$ is defined recursively by

$$y_k = \min \left\{ p_k, \min_{j \, : \, a_{kj} = 1} \left\{ c_j - \sum_{i=1}^{k-1} y_i a_{ij} \right\} \right\}, \qquad k = 1, \ldots, m .$$

(6.2.19)

If y_k is such that $\Sigma_{i=1}^{k-1} y_i a_{ij} < c_j$ and $\Sigma_{i=1}^{k} y_i a_{ij} = c_j$, then we say that constraint j is *saturated* by y_k. Constraint j is a *binding* constraint if $\Sigma_{i=1}^{m} y_i a_{ij} = c_j$. Index sets I and J play an important role in our algorithm, where I is defined to be the index set of the y-variables which saturate a constraint, and J is defined to be the index set of the binding constraints, that is, $I = \{i \,|\, y_i \text{ saturates a constraint}\}$ and $J = \{j \,|\, \text{constraint } j \text{ is binding}\}$.

In the second phase, the algorithm constructs a subset J^* of J. The $(0, 1)$ solution x, z of (6.2.14) is defined by

$$x_j = \begin{cases} 1, & \text{if } j \in J^*, \\ 0, & \text{otherwise}, \end{cases}$$

$$z_i = \begin{cases} 1, & \text{if } \sum_{j \in J^*} a_{ij} = 0, \\ 0, & \text{otherwise}. \end{cases}$$

The subset J^* of J is defined as follows (beginning with $J^* = \varphi$); add the largest index $k \in J$ to J^* and delete all indices $j \in J$ from J for which $a_{ij} = a_{ik} = 1$ for some $i \in I$; repeat until $J = \varphi$.

Clearly x, z, and y are feasible solutions. In order to prove that they are optimal solutions we show that the complementary slackness relations hold. Let us say that row i is *covered* by column j if $a_{ij} = 1$. The following properties, to be proven shortly, are required to show that x, y, and z are optimal.

Property 6.1. Each row $i \in I$ is covered by exactly one column $j \in J^*$.

Property 6.2. Each row $i \notin I$ with $y_i = 0$ is covered by at least one column $j \in J^*$.

Property 6.3. Each row $i \notin I$ with $y_i = p_i$ is covered by at most one column $j \in J^*$.

Theorem 6.1. *Let x, z and y be the solutions defined above. Then x, z and y are optimal solutions of (6.2.14) and (6.2.15), respectively.*

Proof. Since $J^* \subseteq J$ (6.2.17) is satisfied. From Property 6.1 and the definition of z it follows that $z_i = 0$ for $i \in I$. Equivalently it follows from

Property 6.2 that $z_i = 0$ for $i \not\in I$ and $y_i = 0$. From Property 6.3 and the definition of z it follows that $\Sigma_{j \in J^*} a_{ij} + z_i = 1$ for $i \not\in I$ and $y_i = p_i$. Hence the complementary slackness relations (6.2.16), (6.2.17), and (6.2.18) hold. □

Proof of Property 6.1. Let j be the largest constraint which is saturated by y_i. If $j \not\in J^*$, then j was deleted from J because there exists an index $k \in J^*$, $k > j$ and an index $p \in I$ such that $a_{pj} = a_{pk} = 1$. If $p = i$, then row i is covered by column k. If $p \neq i$, then since y_i saturates constraint j we must have $p < i$. (Note that $y_1, \ldots, y_m$ were defined recursively.) By the standard greedy form $a_{pj} = a_{pk} = a_{ij} = 1$ imply $a_{ik} = 1$. Therefore row i is covered by column $k \in J^*$. Thus each row $i \in I$ is covered at least once. Whenever we add $k \in J$ to J^* all indices $j \in J$ for which $a_{ij} = a_{ik} = 1$ for some $i \in I$, are deleted from J; hence each row $i \in I$ can be covered at most once. We conclude that row $i \in I$ is covered exactly once by a column from J^*. □

Proof of Property 6.2. Since $y_i = 0$ there exists a constraint j with $a_{ij} = 1$ which was saturated by y_p before y_i was calculated by the algorithm, that is, $p < i$. It follows from the proof of Property 6.1 that row p is covered by a column $k \in J^*$ which is at least as large as any $j \in J$ that is saturated by y_p. If $j = k$, then row i is covered by column k, else by the standard greedy form $a_{pj} = a_{pk} = a_{ij} = 1$ imply $a_{ik} = 1$, and again row i is covered by column k. We conclude that row $i \not\in I$ with $y_i = 0$ is covered at least once by a column from J^*. □

Proof of Property 6.3. Suppose that row i is covered by the two columns j, $k \in J^*$ with $j < k$. Let column j be saturated by y_p. Since $y_i > 0$ and $i \not\in I$ we have $p > i$. By the standard greedy form $a_{ij} = a_{ik} = a_{pj} = 1$ imply $a_{pk} = 1$. Hence row $p \in I$ is covered by columns j, $k \in J^*$, contradicting Property 6.1. We conclude that row $i \not\in I$, $y_i = p_i$ is covered at most once by a column from J^*. □

Let us give an example to demonstrate the algorithm.

Example 6.1. The matrix $A = (a_{ij})$ of (6.2.14) is given by

$$A = \begin{bmatrix} 0 & 0 & 0 & 0 & 1 & 0 \\ 0 & 1 & 1 & 0 & 0 & 1 \\ 0 & 1 & 1 & 0 & 0 & 1 \\ 0 & 1 & 1 & 0 & 0 & 1 \\ 1 & 1 & 1 & 0 & 0 & 1 \\ 0 & 0 & 0 & 1 & 0 & 1 \\ 0 & 0 & 0 & 1 & 1 & 1 \end{bmatrix}$$

We have $c_1 = 2$, $c_2 = 4$, $c_3 = 4$, $c_4 = 4$, $c_5 = 3$, $c_6 = 8$, $p_i = 2$, $i = 1, 2, \ldots, 7$. Using the algorithm we find $y_1 = 2$, $y_2 = 2$, $y_3 = 2$, $y_4 = 0$, $y_5 = 0$, $y_6 = 2$, $y_7 = 1$, $I = \{3, 7\}$ and $J = \{2, 3, 5\}$. Furthermore $x_3 = x_5 = 1$, all other x_j are zero, $z_6 = 1$, all other z_i are zero. The total cost is 9. This covering problem corresponds to the location problem of Example 6.2. $\bigcirc$

Notice that whenever y_i saturates more than one constraint we only need to keep the last one since all others will never be chosen by the algorithm. In the example, y_3 saturated constraints 2 and 3 so we only had to add 3 to J.

Let us now define the *multiple covering problem*. This can be formulated as

$$\text{minimize} \quad \sum_{j=1}^{n} c_j x_j$$

$$\text{subject to} \quad \sum_{j=1}^{n} a_{ij} x_j \geq b_i , \qquad i = 1, \ldots, m \qquad (6.2.20)$$

$$0 \leq x_j \leq u_j , \qquad x_j \text{ integer} , \qquad j = 1, \ldots, n ,$$

where b_i, $i = 1, \ldots, m$, u_j, $j = 1, \ldots, n$ are integers. Each client i has to be served by b_i facilities, $i = 1, \ldots, m$, and there may exist at most u_j facilities at location j, $j = 1, \ldots, n$. A feasible solution exists if and only if $\sum_{j=1}^{n} a_{ij} u_j \geq b_i$, $i = 1, \ldots, m$. Let us assume that this is the case and let us also assume that the matrix $A = (a_{ij})$ is in standard greedy form. When the setup costs c_j are not all equal we know of no procedure solving the problem in polynomial time, even on tree networks. In the case of equal setup costs we may assume that $c_j = 1$, $j = 1, \ldots, n$. Let us define $y_j = u_j - x_j$, $j = 1, \ldots, n$. The multiple covering problem in case of equal setup costs can be formulated as

$$\text{minimize} \quad \sum_{j=1}^{n} u_j - \sum_{j=1}^{n} y_j$$

$$\text{subject to} \quad \sum_{j=1}^{n} a_{ij} y_j \leq \sum_{j=1}^{n} a_{ij} u_j - b_i , \qquad i = 1, \ldots, m$$

$$(6.2.21)$$

$$0 \leq y_j \leq u_j , \ y_j \text{ integer} , \qquad j = 1, \ldots, n ,$$

or equivalently

$$\text{maximize} \quad \sum_{j=1}^{n} y_j$$

$$\text{subject to} \quad \sum_{j=1}^{n} a_{ij} y_j \leq \sum_{j=1}^{n} a_{ij} u_j - b_i , \qquad i = 1, \ldots, m ,$$

$$(6.2.22)$$

$$0 \leq y_j \leq u_j , \qquad y_j \text{ integer} , \qquad j = 1, \ldots, n .$$

Since A, and therefore also its transpose, is in standard greedy form, (6.2.22) is equivalent to (6.2.15). We have already proved that an optimal solution of (6.2.15) is given by (6.2.19). Furthermore, it follows that if c_j ($j = 1, \ldots, n$) and p_i ($i = 1, \ldots, m$) in (6.2.15) are integer, then the constructed solution is also integer. Assuming b_i ($i = 1, \ldots, m$) and u_j ($j = 1, \ldots, n$) are integer, the following algorithm will solve the multiple covering problem. Define the variables x_j in (6.2.20), for increasing index of j, to be as small as possible; that is, use the following recursive relation:

$$x_j = \max \left\{ 0, \max_{i : a_{ij} = 1} \left\{ b_i - \sum_{k=j+1}^{n} a_{ik} u_k - \sum_{k=1}^{j-1} a_{ik} x_k \right\} \right\}. \qquad (6.2.23)$$

Let us interpret (6.2.23). $\sum_{k=1}^{j-1} a_{ik} x_k$ is the number of times client i is "covered" (served) by facilities that have already been established. $\sum_{k=j+1}^{n} a_{ik} u_k$ is an upper bound on the number of times facilities, which might be setup at sites $\{v_{j+1}, \ldots, v_n\}$, can cover this client. Thus, if the sum of the two is less than b_i, then the difference should be accounted for by x_j. Note that if $a_{ij} = 1$, then $b_i - \sum_{k=j+1}^{n} a_{ik} u_k - \sum_{k=1}^{j-1} a_{ik} x_k \le u_j$ since $b_i \le \sum_{k=1}^{n} a_{ik} u_k$ by assumption.

6.2.2. Transformation to Standard Greedy Form

To be able to apply the algorithm given in the previous section to the covering problem (6.2.2) and the multiple covering problem (6.2.21) for both the client and facility constrained versions on trees, we need to show how to transform the intersection matrix of nodes versus neighborhood subtrees (of a tree) into standard greedy form. This transformation is based on the following theorem (see Kolen, 1983) which we shall prove later in this section.

Theorem 6.2. *Let $N(x_1, r_1)$ and $N(x_2, r_2)$ be two neighborhood subtrees containing an endpoint t_1 of a longest path in the tree. Then $N(x_1, r_1) \subseteq N(x_2, r_2)$ or $N(x_2, r_2) \subseteq N(x_1, r_1)$.*

Theorem 6.2 is no longer true if we replace the endpoint t_1 of a longest path by an arbitrary "tip node," that is, by a node which is adjacent to exactly one other node.

The result of Theorem 6.2 constitutes a generalization of the following property of intervals. If $[a, b]$ is some interval, and I_1 and I_2 are subintervals containing point a, then $I_1 \subseteq I_2$ or $I_2 \subseteq I_1$.

Before proving this theorem let us examine its implications. Consider the intersection matrix of m nodes versus n neighborhood subtrees of a tree T and suppose that we have ordered its rows such that the first row corresponds to a vertex, say t_1, which is an endpoint of a longest path in T. Then we know from Theorem 6.2 that all columns having a 1 in row 1 (that is all neighborhood subtrees containing t_1), can be totally ordered by inclusion, that is, for any two of them one is contained in the other. Since t_1 is a tip node of the tree we can remove it and the unique arc containing it from the tree T. Let T_1 be the resulting tree. It is easy to see that the intersection of a neighborhood subtree $N(x, r)$ of T with T_1 is a neighborhood subtree of T_1. Thus, there is a $y \in T_1$ and a radius s such that $N(y, s) = N(x, r) \cap T_1$ (see Exercise 6.1). Using this we can repeat the above argument. In general, let t_{i+1} be the node corresponding to row $i + 1$, were t_{i+1} is defined to be an endpoint of a longest path in T_i, and where T_i is the subtree obtained by deleting t_i and the unique arc of T_{i-1} containing t_i from T_{i-1}, $i = 1, \ldots, m - 1$. (T_0 is defined to be the original tree T.) Using Theorem 6.2 and Exercise 6.1 we have established that the intersection matrix of nodes (rows) versus neighborhood subtrees (columns) has the *nest ordering property for columns* whenever the rows of the intersection matrix are defined recursively above.

Property 6.4. An $m \times n$ $(0, 1)$ matrix has the *nest ordering property for columns* if for $i = 1, \ldots, m$ the following holds: all columns containing a 1 in row i can be totally ordered by inclusion when they are restricted to rows with index greater than or equal to i (see the matrix of Example 6.1 for an illustration).

To find the permutation of the m nodes (rows) corresponding to the nest ordering property for columns we use the following observation (see Exercise 6.2).

Property 6.5. Let v be a given node of a tree T. Then a node of T which is at a largest distance from v is an endpoint of a longest path in T (see the tree in Figure 6.3 for an example).

Thus the nodes $t_1, \ldots, t_m$, which are recursively defined above, and correspond to the permutation of the rows can be obtained as follows. Find the distances from some given node v to all m nodes of the tree (this takes $O(m)$ time). Sort these distances and suppose that $d(v, v_{i1}) \geq d(v, v_{i2}) \geq \cdots \geq d(v, v_{im})$. Then set $t_1 = v_{i1}$, $t_2 = v_{i2}, \ldots, t_m = v_{im}(= v)$. The effort involved in computing and sorting these distances is $O(m \log m)$. Therefore the permutation of the rows yielding a nest ordering property for columns is obtained in $O(m \log m)$ time.

Given this permutation of the rows, one more step is needed now to transform the matrix into the standard greedy form. For $(0, 1)$ vectors x and y, of the same dimension, we say that x is *lexical* larger than y if x and y are different and in the last coordinate in which they differ x has a 1 and y has a 0. (Note that this is not the same as lexicographically larger; in that case the first coordinate in which the vectors differ would be important.) We say that a set of vectors $x^1, \ldots, x^k$ is in *nondecreasing lexical order* if $x^i = x^{i+1}$ or x^{i+1} is lexical larger than x^i, $i = 1, \ldots, k - 1$.

Lemma 6.1. *If a* $(0, 1)$ *matrix has the nest ordering property for columns and the columns are ordered in a lexical nondecreasing order, then the matrix is in standard greedy form.*

Proof. Suppose we are given a 2×2 submatrix, as defined by the rows $i(1)$, $i(2)$ (with $i(1) < i(2)$) and columns $j(1)$, $j(2)$ (with $j(1) < j(2)$):

$$
\begin{array}{cc}
 & j(1) \quad j(2) \\
\begin{array}{c} i(1) \\ i(2) \\ i(3) \end{array} & \left[\begin{array}{cc} 1 & 1 \\ 1 & 0 \\ 0 & 1 \end{array}\right].
\end{array}
$$

Since columns $j(1)$ and $j(2)$ differ, $j(2)$ is lexical larger than $j(1)$. Therefore there exists a row $i(3)$ (with $i(3) > i(2)$) such that column $j(1)$ has a 0 and column $j(2)$ has a 1 in this row. But this contradicts the nest ordering property for the columns which implies that column $j(1)$ is contained in column $j(2)$ or vice versa, whenever we restrict these columns to rows with an index of at least $i(1)$. $\square$

Ordering n $(0, 1)$ vectors of dimension m in a lexical ordering can be done in $O(mn)$ time using a radix sort procedure (see Aho, Hopcroft, and Ullman 1974). We conclude that the transformation of the intersection matrix of the nodes of a tree (rows) versus n neighborhood subtrees (columns) into standard greedy form can be achieved in $O(nm + m \log m)$ time.

The following example illustrates the above concepts.

Example 6.2. Consider the tree shown in Figure 6.1. Let us root the tree at $v = v_3$ and calculate the distances to all other nodes and order them in nondecreasing order, say $d(t_1, v) \geq d(t_2, v) \geq \cdots \geq d(t_7, v)$ with $t_7 = v$. Then if we take t_i as the node corresponding to row i of the matrix, $i = 1, \ldots, 7$, this will give the desired permutation.

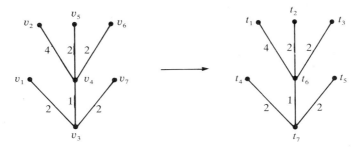

Figure 6.1. Tree of Example 6.2.

Let us consider the following neighborhood subtrees $N_5 = N(v_5, 4)$, $N_2 = N(v_2, 6)$, $N_1 = N(v_1, 3)$, $N_3 = N(v_3, 2)$, $N_7 = N(v_7, 1)$, $N_4 = N(v_4, 2)$, $N_6 = N(v_6, 4)$. A lexical nondecreasing ordering is given by the matrix.

$$
\begin{array}{c c}
 & \begin{array}{ccccccc} N_7 & N_4 & N_5 & N_6 & N_2 & N_1 & N_3 \end{array} \\
\begin{array}{c} t_1 \\ t_2 \\ t_3 \\ t_4 \\ t_5 \\ t_6 \\ t_7 \end{array} &
\left[\begin{array}{ccccccc}
0 & 0 & 0 & 0 & 1 & 0 & 0 \\
0 & 1 & 1 & 1 & 1 & 0 & 0 \\
0 & 1 & 1 & 1 & 1 & 0 & 0 \\
0 & 0 & 0 & 0 & 0 & 1 & 1 \\
1 & 0 & 0 & 0 & 0 & 0 & 1 \\
0 & 1 & 1 & 1 & 1 & 1 & 1 \\
0 & 1 & 1 & 1 & 1 & 1 & 1
\end{array}\right]
\end{array}
$$

(The transpose of the first six rows of the matrix was used in Example 6.1) ○

Let us return to Theorem 6.2.

Proof of Theorem 6.2.   Let $P[t_1, t_2]$ be a longest path in the tree T. $N(x_1, r_1)$ and $N(x_2, r_2)$ both contain t_1. Define T' to be the minimal subtree of T which contains $N(x_1, r_1) \cup N(x_2, r_2)$. Clearly, t_1 is in T'. Since t_1 is an endpoint of a longest path in T, it is also an endpoint of some longest path of every subtree of T containing t_1. Thus, let t_3 be some point in T' such that $P[t_1, t_3]$ is a longest path in T'. Due to the minimalilty of T' we have $t_3 \in N(x_1, r_1) \cup N(x_2, r_2)$. Suppose without loss of generality that $t_3 \in N(x_1, r_1)$. Then, $N(x_1, r_1)$ contains $P[t_1, t_3]$. Therefore $N(x_1, r_1) = T'$ (see Exercise 6.4), and $N(x_2, r_2) \subseteq T' = N(x_1, r_1)$. This completes the proof.   □

It was shown above that the intersection matrix of the m nodes of a tree (rows) versus n neighborhood subtrees (columns) can be transformed into standard greedy form in $O(nm + m \log m)$ time. Consider the case where the $m \times n$ matrix corresponds to the intersection of m neighborhood subtrees (rows) versus some subset of n (out of the m) nodes of the tree (columns) (each neighborhood is centered at some node of the tree). In this case the standard greedy form can be achieved in $O(nm)$ time only. To see that, consider the transpose of this matrix, which is $n \times m$ and transform it to standard greedy form.

First we permute the n rows (nodes) of this transposed matrix. The first row of the permuted matrix is obtained as follows. Iteratively remove all tips of the tree (with their adjacent arcs) which are not in the above subset of n nodes. The remaining tree has only tips belonging to this subset of n nodes. Then find a node which is an endpoint of a longest path of the remaining tree. This node will correspond to the first row. To find the second row, remove this node from the tree, and repeat the above process. Continuing this procedure for n iterations, we obtain the permutation of the rows.

From Property 6.5 it follows that each iteration can be performed in

$O(m)$ time. Therefore the permutation of the rows consumes $O(mn)$ time. The lexical ordering of the columns can also be done in $O(mn)$ time by radix sorting as discussed above. Thus, the standard greedy form is obtained in this case in total time of $O(mn)$.

Summarizing, we conclude that the results in Sections 6.2.1 and 6.2.2 imply the polynomial solvability of both the client and the facility constrained covering problems, as well as the UFL problem, on tree networks. For example, the methods in these sections solve the client constrained problem and the UFL problem on trees in $O(mn)$ and $O(mn^2)$ times, respectively. (Recall that the UFL has been formulated in (6.2.12) as a covering problem with an $(m \cdot n) \times n$ matrix in standard greedy form.)

Polynomial algorithms for these problems can also be constructed using dynamic programming principles. The dynamic programming approach utilizes the natural partial ordering of the nodes induced by rooting a tree at an arbitrary node (see Megiddo, Zemel, and Hakimi, 1983).

6.2.3. The Cost Allocation Problem

It has been shown earlier that both the covering problem and the UFL problem can be formulated as

$$\text{minimize} \quad \sum_{j=1}^{n} c_j x_j + \sum_{\omega \in M_1} p_\omega z_\omega$$

$$\text{subject to} \quad \sum_{j=1}^{n} a_{\omega j} x_j + z_\omega \geq 1 , \qquad \omega \in M_1 ,$$

$$x_j \in \{0, 1\} , \qquad j = 1, \ldots, n ,$$

$$z_\omega \in \{0, 1\} , \qquad \omega \in M_1 .$$

(6.2.24)

In both cases the variables $x_1, \ldots, x_n$ correspond, respectively, to the n potential facility sites. In the case of the covering problem with m clients M_1 is defined by $M_1 = \{1, \ldots, m\}$ and each index in M_1 is associated with a different client (see the definition of the covering problem). In the case of the UFL problem (see (6.2.12)), $|M_1| = m \cdot n$, and each index $\omega \in M_1$ corresponds to a pair (i, k) where i is a client and k is a facility site. In particular, each client i is associated with a subset of n indices in M_1. If we denote this subset by I_i, $i = 1, \ldots, m$, then $I_1, \ldots, I_m$ constitute a partition of M_1. Thus, in both the covering problem and the UFL problem we have a partition of the rows of the matrix $A = (a_{\omega j})$ into m subsets $I_1, \ldots, I_m$, where I_i, $i = 1, \ldots, m$, is associated with client i. For the covering problem $|I_i| = 1$, while for the UFL problem $|I_i| = n$, $i = 1, \ldots, m$.

We have shown how to solve the location models defined by (6.2.24) in the case where the matrix $A = (a_{\omega j})$ is in standard greedy form. However, we have not addressed two important issues related to these location models. First there exists the question of cooperation between the clients. Is there an incentive for them to cooperate? Suppose that each one of two subsets of clients operates on its own and establishes facilities serving its members only. Since we have assumed that there are no capacity constraints on the facilities, it is clear that if these two subsets of clients (coalitions) unite, their total cost will not increase. Therefore, viewing only the total cost of all clients, there exists an incentive for all of them to cooperate and act as a grand coalition.

The second question that arises is on the allocation of the total cost. Is there an "acceptable" allocation, an allocation such that no group of clients will have an incentive to not cooperate by splitting from the grand coalition and acting on its own? In game theory terminology such an allocation is called a *core allocation*. Namely, a core allocation of the total cost is such that no coalition can pay less than its part in this allocation if it establishes facilities that will serve its members only. The total cost incurred by a coalition of clients $I \subseteq \{1, \ldots, m\}$, if they want to act alone, is given by $v(I)$, where $v(I)$ is the optimum value of (6.2.25).

$$\text{minimize} \qquad \sum_{j=1}^{n} c_j x_j + \sum_{i \in I} \sum_{\omega \in I_i} p_\omega z_\omega$$

$$\text{subject to} \qquad \sum_{j=1}^{n} a_{\omega j} x_j + z_\omega \geq 1, \qquad \omega \in \bigcup \{I_i : i \in I\},$$

$$\tag{6.2.25}$$

$$x_j \in \{0, 1\}, \qquad j = 1, \ldots, n,$$

$$z_\omega \in \{0, 1\}, \qquad \omega \in \bigcup \{I_i : i \in I\}$$

where I_i is the set of constraints corresponding to client i, $i = 1, \ldots, m$.

Let us define the core of the covering problem by

$$\text{core}(\{1, \ldots, m\}) = \left\{ y \in R^m : \sum_{i=1}^{m} y_i = v(\{1, \ldots, m\}) \text{ and} \right.$$

$$\left. \sum_{i \in I} y_i \leq v(I) \text{ for all } I \subseteq \{1, \ldots, m\} \right\}. \tag{6.2.26}$$

If $y \in \text{core}(\{1, \ldots, m\})$, then it is called a core allocation and y_i denotes the part of the total cost paid by client i, $i = 1, \ldots, m$. It is clear that no coalition of clients would do better by breaking the cooperation between all clients if a core allocation is used to split the total cost. Thus a core allocation possesses a desirable stability property which seems to be necessary for an allocation to be acceptable by all the clients.

We next give an example of a covering problem for which the core is empty. The example is defined on a network which is a cycle. This motivates us to look at trees; we will show that for covering problems on trees the core is nonempty.

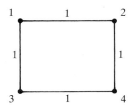

Figure 6.2. Network for Example 6.3.

Example 6.3. Consider the network shown in Figure 6.2. Each arc has length one. We consider the UFL problem with setup cost equal to 1.5 for all nodes and transportation costs which are equal to the respective distances from clients to their closest established facilities. It is easily verified that an optimal solution to the problem is given by establishing facilities at 1 and 2 and letting 3 and 4 be served by 1 and 2, respectively. The total cost is 5. If the UFL problem is restricted to any subset of three clients the optimum value is 3.5. Therefore every vector y in the core must satisfy:

$$y_1 + y_2 + y_3 + y_4 = 5$$
$$y_1 + \dot{y}_2 + y_3 \quad\quad \leq 3.5$$
$$y_1 + y_2 \quad\quad + y_4 \leq 3.5$$
$$y_1 \quad\quad + y_3 + y_4 \leq 3.5$$
$$y_2 + y_3 + y_4 \leq 3.5 \, .$$

Adding the four inequalities together yields $3(y_1 + y_2 + y_3 + y_4) \leq 14$. But the latter contradicts $3(y_1 + y_2 + y_3 + y_4) = 15$ which is the first equation. Therefore we conclude that the core is empty. ○

Having observed that cycles may yield an empty core, we turn to tree networks and prove that there the core is always nonempty. If u is the optimal solution of the dual of the LP-relaxation of (6.2.24), then we will show that $\hat{y}_i = \Sigma_{\omega \in I_i} u_\omega$, $i = 1, \ldots, m$, will generate a core allocation. Remember that I_i is the set of constraints corresponding to client i in (6.2.24).

Theorem 6.3. *If the problem (6.2.24) arises from a tree location problem, that is, the matrix $(a_{\omega j})$ is in standard greedy form, and u is an optimal solution to the dual of the LP-relaxation of (6.2.24), then $\hat{y} = (\hat{y}_1, \ldots, \hat{y}_m)$ defined by $\hat{y}_i = \Sigma_{\omega \in I_i} u_\omega$ is in the core defined by (6.2.26).*

Proof. It is shown in Section 6.2.1 that the optimal objective value of a covering problem, defined by a matrix in standard greedy form, is equal to the optimal value of its linear programming relaxation. Thus, duality yields

$$v(\{1, \ldots, m\}) = \sum_{\omega \in M_1} u_\omega = \sum_{i=1}^{m} \sum_{\omega \in I_i} u_\omega = \sum_{i=1}^{m} \hat{y}_i .$$

Therefore to prove that $\hat{y}$ is in the core it suffices to show that

$$\sum_{i \in I} \sum_{\omega \in I_i} u_\omega \leq v(I) \qquad \text{for all} \qquad I \subseteq \{1, \ldots, m\} .$$

Let $I \subseteq \{1, \ldots, m\}$ and consider the dual problem of the LP-relaxation of (6.2.25). Again by the results of Section 6.2.1 we know that the optimal solution to the dual of this problem is equal to $v(I)$. If we prove that u_ω, $\omega \in I_i$, $i \in I$ is a feasible solution to this dual problem, then the result follows from the weak duality property. Of course, we know that $0 \leq u_\omega \leq p_\omega$, $\omega \in M_1$, so that it suffices to prove that $\sum_{i \in I} \sum_{\omega \in I_i} u_\omega a_{\omega j} \leq c_j$ for $j = 1, \ldots, n$, but this is trivial since the left-hand side is less than or equal to $\sum_{\omega \in M_1} u_\omega a_{\omega j}$ for which we know that it is less than or equal to c_j, $j = 1, \ldots, n$. $\square$

We refer the reader to a paper by Tamir (1980) for a treatment on a more general cost-allocation game on trees.

6.3. CENTER PROBLEMS

In this section we discuss the budget constrained center and round-trip center problems on trees. We assume that clients are located only at the nodes of the tree. Each node is identified as a client. At the end of this section we also refer to other cases. We consider the case where facilities can be established only at the nodes as well as the infinite case where we may establish a facility anywhere along the tree.

The round-trip distance occurs, for example, in the context of a transportation problem in which a company has to execute a number of jobs. Job i consists of picking up goods at node a_i and delivering them at node b_i. The distance a vehicle located at a depot x has to travel in order to execute job i and return to its depot is given by the *round-trip distance* $d(x, a_i) + d(a_i, b_i) + d(b_i, x)$. If we let $D(P_i, x)$ denote the distance from x to the closest point on P_i, the shortest path connecting a_i and b_i, then the round-trip distance is given by $2[d(a_i, b_i) + D(P_i, x)]$ (see Figure 6.3). If X is a closed set of points on the network, then $D(P_i, X) := \min_{x \in X} \{D(P_i, x)\}$.

For ease of exposition we will assume, while defining the center problems, that the transportation cost between client i and the closest established facility x is $d(v_i, x)$. Similarly, the transportation cost between a pair of

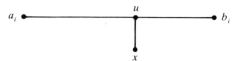

Figure 6.3. Illustrating that $D(P_i, x) = d(u, x)$, and round-trip distance $= 2[d(a_i, b_i) + D(P_i, x)]$.

clients a_i, b_i and x is $D(P_i, x)$. The case where these costs are nondecreasing functions of the distances can be treated similarly. Note that the round-trip distance $2[d(a_i, b_i) + D(P_i, x)]$ is a nondecreasing function of $D(P_i, x)$.

Let us start by considering the budget constrained center problem, where facilities can be established at the nodes only. The setup cost of establishing a facility at v_j is c_j, $j = 1, \ldots, m$. (Here we assume that all nodes are potential sites.) The *budget constrained center problem* is to minimize the maximum of the distances of the clients to their respective nearest facilities, subject to a budget constraint on the total setup cost. It is formulated as follows:

$$\text{minimize} \quad z \tag{6.3.1}$$

$$\text{subject to} \quad \min_{v_j \in S} \{d(v_i, v_j)\} \le z, \quad i = 1, \ldots, m, \tag{6.3.2}$$

$$\sum_{j:\, v_j \in S} c_j \le B, \quad S \subseteq V \tag{6.3.3}$$

where S denotes the set of established facilities. Notice that z can only take on values belonging to the set R, where

$$R = \{d(v_i, v_j): i, j = 1, \ldots, m\}. \tag{6.3.4}$$

It is easy to prove the following claim. The optimum value of (6.3.1) is the smallest value z, say z^*, in the set R for which the client constrained covering problem (6.2.2), with radius $r_i = z^*$, and penalty $p_i = \infty$, $i = 1, \ldots, m$, has a total setup cost which does not exceed B. Hence, we can solve this budget constrained center problem by solving a sequence of covering problems. Using a binary search over the above set R, the optimal solution will be found after solving $O(\log m)$ covering problems.

In the case when all setup costs are equal, the budget constraint simply specifies the number, say p, of facilities that may be established. In this case the problem is well recognized as *the p-center problem*. We will defer our discussion of this case, and treat it together with the respective case of the round-trip center problem. The general p-center problem is extensively discussed, in another perspective, in Chapter 7.

In contrast with the problem (6.3.1)–(6.3.3), the budget constrained round-trip center problem is $\mathcal{NP}$-hard when facilities, which are restricted to be located at the nodes, may differ in their setup costs. Recall that in this problem we are given q pairs of clients $\{a_i, b_i\}$, $i = 1, \ldots, q$, and the objective is to minimize the maximum of the distances of the pairs to their respective nearest facilities, subject to a budget constraint. Formally, the *budget constrained round-trip center problem* is:

$$\text{minimize} \quad z \tag{6.3.5}$$

$$\text{subject to} \quad \min_{v_j \in S} \{D(P_i, v_j)\} \le z, \quad i = 1, \ldots, q \tag{6.3.6}$$

$$\sum_{j: v_j \in S} c_j \le B, \quad S \subseteq V \tag{6.3.7}$$

where S denotes the set of established facilities (depots).

The $\mathcal{NP}$-hardness is proven by reducing the *node cover problem*, a known $\mathcal{NP}$-complete problem, to this problem. Given an undirected graph $G = (\bar{V}, \bar{E})$ with m nodes and a number $k \le m$, the node cover problem is to determine whether there exist a subset V' of $\bar{V}$ of at most k nodes, such that each arc contains at least one node in V'.

Consider the tree T in Figure 6.4. Suppose that $\bar{V} = \{u_1, \ldots, u_m\}$. Then $\{v_i, v_j\}$ is defined to be a pair of clients in T if and only if $[u_i, u_j]$ is an arc of G. The setup costs associated with the nodes of T are as follows: $c_i = 1$, $i = 1, \ldots, m$ and $c_{m+1} = m + 1$. Taking the budget constraint B to be k, it is then an easy task to verify that G has a node cover of cardinality k if and only if the solution to the budget constrained round-trip problem is equal to zero. We conclude that the budget constrained round-trip center problem on trees is $\mathcal{NP}$-hard, even for the case where all but one of the setup costs are equal. (Notice that the problem is in fact $\mathcal{NP}$-complete when posed as a recognition problem.) We will show later that if all setup costs are equal then this problem is polynomially solvable.

The above reduction leading to the $\mathcal{NP}$-hardness result is, in fact, valid for a larger class of objective functions. We may consider any nondecreasing objective function of the distances $D(P_1, X), \ldots, D(P_q, X)$, $X \subseteq V$, which is equal to zero if and only if $D(P_i, X) = 0$, $i = 1, \ldots, q$. For example, the median version of the problem, where we try to minimize $\Sigma_{i=1}^q D(P_i, X)$ over all feasible subsets X of cardinality p, is also $\mathcal{NP}$-hard when the set of potential location sites consists of all the nodes of the tree but one.

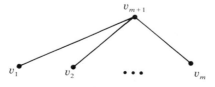

Figure 6.4. The tree of the reduction.

The difference in complexity between the budget constrained center problem and its round-trip counterpart is due to the fact that $T_i = \{y \in T: d(y, v_i) \le r\}$ is a neighborhood subtree, while, in general, this does not apply to $S_i = \{y \in T: D(P_i, y) \le r\}$. (Note that P_i is a path in the tree and not a node.)

Let us now introduce some theory to exhibit the polynomial solvability of the center and round-trip center problems, for the case where facilities are allowed to be located anywhere along the tree, with a constant setup cost.

We will assume that the tree is rooted at some arbitrary node, say v_m. For each node v_j define v_k to be a *child* of v_j if v_k is adjacent to v_j and v_j is on the shortest path from v_k to v_m. Note v_j is also called the *parent* of v_k. We also assume without loss of generality that the nodes are indexed in such a way that children have a smaller number than their parent. See Figure 6.5 for an illustration of a tree with 7 nodes rooted at v_7. The children of v_6 are v_1, v_2, and v_3.

Let $T_1, \ldots, T_n$ be subtrees of T. Without loss of generality we may assume that they are induced subgraphs, that is, each tip of a subtree belongs to the node set of T. (If this is not the case the tips are augmented to the node set.) With each subtree T_i we associate a node v_{ri}, called *the root of the subtree* T_i, which is the node with the largest index in T_i. This means that the root of T_i is on the shortest path connecting the root of T with any point in T_i. We then have the following observation.

Property 6.6. Given subtrees T_i and T_j with roots v_{ri} and v_{rj}, respectively, suppose that $ri \le rj$. Then

$$T_i \cap T_j \ne \varphi \qquad \text{iff} \qquad v_{ri} \in T_j.$$

From this we can obtain the Helly property for trees.

Property 6.7 (Helly Property). Given subtrees $T_1, \ldots, T_n$ such that $T_i \cap T_j$ is nonempty for $i \ne j$, then $\cap_{i=1}^n T_i$ is nonempty.

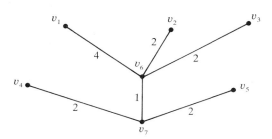

Figure 6.5. Illustration of node indexing.

Proof. Without loss of generality assume $r1 \leq r2 \cdots \leq rn$. Since $T_1 \cap T_i$ is nonempty for $i = 1, \ldots, n$, we have $v_{r_1} \in T_i$, $i = 1, \ldots, n$. □

Remark 6.1. It follows from the above proof that when $T_1, \ldots, T_n$ are induced subtrees whose intersection is nonempty, then this intersection contains a node.

The *intersection graph* corresponding to the subtrees $T_1, \ldots, T_n$ is the graph $G = (U, \bar{E})$, with $U = \{u_1, \ldots, u_n\}$ and $[u_i, u_j] \in \bar{E}$ if and only if $i \neq j$ and $T_i \cap T_j$ is nonempty.

A *chordal graph* is an undirected graph with the property that every simple cycle of length at least four contains a *chord*, that is, an arc connecting two nodes which are not adjacent in the cycle. The following theorem states that the intersection graph of subtrees of a tree is a chordal graph. The converse of this theorem is also true, so that every chordal graph is representable as the intersection graph of subtrees of some tree. This one-to-one correspondence between chordal graphs and intersection graphs of subtrees of a tree has been established by Walter (1972, 1978), Buneman (1974), and Gavril (1974). We will present a different and simpler proof for the chordality of the above intersection graph.

Theorem 6.4. *The intersection graph $G = (U, \bar{E})$ of the set of subtrees $T_1, \ldots, T_n$ of a given tree T is chordal.*

Proof. Without loss of generality we assume $r1 \leq r2 \leq, \ldots, \leq rn$. Consider a simple cycle of length at least four and suppose that u_i, the node of G corresponding to T_i, has the smallest index among all nodes of the cycle. Also, let $[u_i, u_j]$ and $[u_i, u_k]$, $k \neq j$, be two arcs in that cycle. Since we have $v_{ri} \in T_j \cap T_k$ (Property 6.6), $[v_j, v_k]$ is a chord of the cycle. □

Remark 6.2. Taking a closer look at the proof of Theorem 6.4 we see that we have actually proved the following. There exists an ordering of the indices of the nodes of the intersection graph, determined by the roots of the subtrees, such that all nodes u_j in G which are adjacent to u_i and have a larger index than u_i form a *clique* in G; that is, a set of nodes which are pairwise adjacent. An ordering with this property is called a *perfect elimination scheme* (see Example 6.4).

One can prove that there exists a perfect elimination scheme for a graph if and only if the graph is chordal (see Golumbic, 1980).

An *independent set* of a graph is a set of nodes such that no two of them are adjacent. A *clique cover* is a set of cliques with the property that each node of the graph is contained in at least one clique. Since each node of an independent set must be in a different clique of the cover we have a weak duality result. The cardinality of any independent set is less than or equal to the cardinality of any clique cover.

The existence of the above ordering for the intersection graph of subtrees of a tree enables us to prove a strong duality result for chordal graphs.

Theorem 6.5. *Let G be an intersection graph of the set of subtrees $T_1, \ldots, T_n$ of a given tree T. Then the maximum cardinality of an independent set in G is equal to the minimum cardinality of a clique cover.*

Proof. We shall construct an independent set and a clique cover of the same cardinality. Consider the perfect elimination scheme induced on the nodes of G by the roots of the subtrees $T_1, \ldots, T_n$. Suppose that u_i is a node of G which is smallest with respect to the ordering. Add this node to the current independent set. From Remark 6.2 we know that all nodes adjacent to u_i together with u_i form a clique in G. Add this clique to the current set of cliques. (Initially, both the independent set and the set of cliques are empty.) Remove the subgraph induced by u_i and its adjacent nodes from G. The remaining graph will still be an intersection graph of subtrees. We will repeat this procedure for the remaining graph, and this will produce the desired clique cover and independent set. $\square$

Example 6.4. Consider the tree shown in Figure 6.5. The subtrees will be given by their nodes, $T_1 = \{v_1\}$, $T_2 = \{v_1, v_2, v_6\}$, $T_3 = \{v_1, v_3, v_6\}$, $T_4 = \{v_4, v_7\}$, $T_5 = \{v_5, v_7\}$, and $T_6 = \{v_6, v_7\}$. We obtain $r1 = 1$, $r2 = 6$, $r3 = 6$, $r4 = 7$, $r5 = 7$, and $r6 = 7$. The intersection graph is given in Figure 6.6, where u_i corresponds to T_i.

It is easily observed that the ordering of the perfect elimination scheme corresponds to the indices of the nodes, u_i, $i = 1, \ldots, 7$. By the procedure described in the above proof $\{u_1, u_4\}$ is a maximum independent set, while $\{u_1, u_2, u_3\}$ and $\{u_4, u_5, u_6\}$ is a minimum clique cover. $\bigcirc$

Let us demonstrate how the duality result of Theorem 6.5 can be used to solve the p-center and round-trip p-center problems, when facilities can be established anywhere on the tree. It will be shown that both problems are solvable by a sequence of covering problems.

The covering problem for the p-center problem is

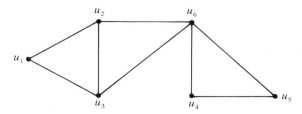

Figure 6.6. Intersection graph for Example 6.5.

$$\text{minimize} \qquad |X|$$

$$\text{subject to} \qquad D(v_i, X) \le r, \qquad i = 1, \ldots, m, \qquad (6.3.8)$$

$$X \subseteq T$$

where $D(v_i, X) = \min_{x \in X} \{d(v_i, X)\}$. (Since X is finite, $|X| \le m$, $D(v_i, X)$ is well defined.)

For the round-trip p-center problem we obtain the following covering problem

$$\text{minimize} \qquad |X|$$

$$\text{subject to} \qquad D(P_i, X) \le r, \qquad i = 1, \ldots, q, \qquad (6.3.9)$$

$$X \subseteq T$$

where $D(P_i, X) = \min_{x \in X} \{D(P_i, x)\}$.

Focussing first on (6.3.8), define the subtrees $T_i = \{y \in T : d(v_i, y) \le r\}$, $i = 1, \ldots, m$. It is easily verified that

$$T_i \cap T_j \qquad \text{is nonempty iff} \qquad d(v_i, v_j) \le 2r, \qquad i, j = 1, \ldots, m.$$
$$(6.3.10)$$

If $G = (U, \bar{E})$, $U = \{u_1, \ldots, u_m\}$ is the intersection graph of $T_1, \ldots, T_m$, then $[u_i, u_j] \in \bar{E}$ if and only if $i \ne j$ and $d(v_i, v_j) \le 2r$. If two clients v_i, v_j can be served by the same facility, then $T_i \cap T_j$ is nonempty. Therefore, clients which can be served by the same facility form a clique in G. Conversely, any two subtrees corresponding to nodes in the same clique are pairwise nondisjoint. According to the Helly property (Property 6.7), there exists a point of the tree which is contained in all subtrees corresponding to the same clique. This means that a facility located in such a point can serve all clients corresponding to this clique, that is, the distance of these clients to the facility is at most r. This proves that there is a one-to-one correspondence between the cliques of G and the subsets of the clients that can be served by the same facility. Therefore, finding the minimum number of facilities which can serve all clients within a radius r, is equivalent to finding a minimum clique cover in G.

By the duality result of Theorem 6.5 and (6.3.10), the minimum number of facilities is equal to the maximum number of clients for which the mutual distance is greater than $2r$. The latter problem is formulated as

$$\text{maximize} \qquad |I|$$

$$\text{subject to} \qquad d(v_i, v_j) > 2r, \qquad i, j \in I, \qquad i \ne j, \qquad (6.3.11)$$

$$I \subseteq \{1, 2, \ldots, m\}.$$

For the round-trip center problem we define $T_i = \{y \in T: D(P_i, y) \le r\}$, $i = 1, \ldots, q$. We leave it to the reader to show that

$$T_i \cap T_j \text{ is nonempty iff } \gamma_{ij} \le 4r \qquad (6.3.12)$$

where

$$\gamma_{ij} = d(a_i, a_j) + d(b_i, b_j) - d(a_i, b_i) - d(a_j, b_j), \qquad i, j = 1, \ldots, q.$$

Using exactly the same reasoning as for the center problem we can show that the optimal solution to (6.3.9) is equal to the solution of

maximize $\quad |I|$

subject to $\quad \gamma_{ij} > 4r, \quad i, j \in I, \quad i \ne j, \quad I \subseteq \{1, \ldots, q\}.$
$$(6.3.13)$$

The usefulness of these duality results is demonstrated by the next two theorems. They define sets (in fact of polynomial cardinality), that contain the optimal values for the p-center and round-trip p-center problems, respectively.

Theorem 6.6. *Suppose that $p < m$, then*

$$\max_{I \subseteq \{1, \ldots, m\}, |I| = p+1} \left\{ \min_{i, j \in I, i \ne j} \{d(v_i, v_j)/2\} \right\}$$

$$= \min_{X \subseteq T, |X| = p} \left\{ \max_{i=1, \ldots, m} \{D(v_i, X)\} \right\}. \qquad (6.3.14)$$

Proof. It is sufficient to show that for each $r \ge 0$, the right-hand side of (6.3.14) is less than or equal to r if and only if the left-hand side is less than or equal to r. The following equivalence is straightforward.

$$\min_{X \subseteq T, |X| = p} \left\{ \max_{i=1, \ldots, m} \{D(v_i, X)\} \right\} \le r$$

if and only if

$$\min \left\{ |X| : \left\{ \max_{i=1, \ldots, m} \{D(v_i, X)\} \right\} \le r, X \subseteq T \right\} \le p. \qquad (6.3.15)$$

Using the duality between (6.3.8) and (6.3.11), (6.3.15) is equivalent to

$$\max \{|I| : I \subseteq \{1, \ldots, m\}, d(v_i, v_j) > 2r, i, j \in I, i \ne j\} \le p,$$
$$(6.3.16)$$

which, in turn, is immediately observed to be equivalent to

$$\max_{I \subseteq \{1, \ldots, m\}, |I| = p+1} \left\{ \min_{i, j \in I, i \neq j} \{d(v_i, v_j)/2\} \right\} \leq r . \quad \square \qquad (6.3.17)$$

Performing the same analysis for the round-trip p-center problem we obtain the following theorem.

Theorem 6.7. *Suppose that $p < q$, then*

$$\max_{I \subseteq \{1, \ldots, q\}, |I| = p+1} \left\{ \min_{i, j \in I, i \neq j} \gamma_{ij}/4 \right\} = \min_{X \subseteq T, |X| = p} \left\{ \max_{i=1, \ldots, q} \{D(P_i, X)\} \right\} .$$

Theorem 6.6 implies that the optimal solution to the p-center problem is an element in the set

$$R = \{d(v_i, v_j)/2 : i, j = 1, \ldots, m\} . \qquad (6.3.18)$$

Similarly, Theorem 6.7 implies that the optimal solution to the round-trip p-center problem is an element in

$$R' = \{\gamma_{ij}/4 : i, j = 1, \ldots, q\} . \qquad (6.3.19)$$

This means that we can solve the two center problems as a sequence of covering problems. For example, the optimal solution to the p-center problem is the smallest element r in R for which the solution to the respective covering problem (6.3.8) is at most p. A similar observation applies to the round-trip p-center problem, when the respective covering problem is (6.3.9). Polynomial algorithms for the covering problems (6.3.8) and (6.3.9) are described by Kariv and Hakimi (1979a) and Kolen (1985), respectively. These algorithms work on the tree networks (see also Slater, 1976). One can also generate the respective intersection graphs and find minimum clique covers on these chordal graphs by the polynomial schemes of Gavril (1972) and Rose, Tarjan, and Lueker (1976).

An efficient implementation of the approach to solve the p-center problem on trees as a sequence of covering problems is presented by Megiddo, Tamir, Zemel, and Chandrasekaran (1981). It is based on an efficient search of the above set R (6.3.18), without explicitly generating it. To illustrate the idea of searching the above set R without explicitly generating its $|R| = O(m^2)$ elements, consider the special case where the tree is a path. In this case the nodes $\{v_1, \ldots, v_m\}$ may be identified as numbers on the real line. Suppose that $v_1 \leq v_2 \leq \cdots \leq v_m$. Then $R = \{\frac{1}{2}(v_j - v_i) : 1 \leq i \leq j \leq m\}$. Define

$$R_i = \{(v_j - v_i)/2 : j = i, i+1, \ldots, m\} , \qquad i = 1, \ldots, m .$$

Then R is the union of the sets R_i, $i = 1, \ldots, m$. The search in R for the optimal solution to the p-center problem consists of $O(\log m)$ steps. In each step we delete parts of the sets R_i, $i = 1, \ldots, m$, which are known not to contain the optimal value. Furthermore, the cardinality of R, the union of the sets R_i, $i = 1, \ldots, m$, will decrease by a factor of at least $1/4$ at each step.

Throughout the search each set R_i, $i = 1, \ldots, m$, will be represented as $R_i = \{(v_i - v_j)/2 : j = a(i), a(i) + 1, \ldots, b(i)\}$, where $i \le a(i) \le b(i) \le m$, and $a(i), b(i)$ are updated at each step. (Initially $a(i) = i$ and $b(i) = m$). So the elements of R_i are not calculated explicitly but represented by $a(i)$ and $b(i)$. The elimination of elements from R is performed as follows. We first compute the median element, s_i, of each set R_i, $i = 1, \ldots, m$. s_i is given by $(v_k - v_i)/2$, where $k = [\frac{1}{2}(b(i) - a(i) + 1)]$.

Having computed $\{s_1, \ldots, s_m\}$ we associate a weight, w_i, with s_i, $i = 1, \ldots, m$, where $w_i = b(i) - a(i) + 1$, is the number of elements in the current set R_i. Using the method of Aho et al. (1974), we then find in $O(m)$ time, the weighted median, say r, of the set $\{s_1, \ldots, s_m\}$. Next we solve the covering problem (6.3.8) for the value r, using the $O(m)$ procedure of Kariv and Hakimi (1979a). If the optimum of the covering problem is less than or equal to p, then the optimum value of the p-center problem is less than or equal to r. Therefore, if $s_i \ge r$, the elements in R_i which are at least as large as s_i can be deleted from R_i. Similarly, if the optimum to the covering problem is greater than p, the optimum value of the p-center problem is greater than r. Thus, if $s_i \le r$ the elements in R_i which are smaller than or equal to s_i can be discarded.

Since r is a weighted median of the sequence $\{s_1, \ldots, s_m\}$, it is easy to see that we will delete at each step at least $1/4$ of the elements in R, the union of the sets R_i, $i = 1, \ldots, m$. Note that the deletion of elements in a set R_i is done in constant time by increasing $a(i)$ or decreasing $b(i)$, depending on the case. Hence, the total time for one step of this procedure is $O(m)$. Since at each step the cardinality of R is decreased by a factor of at least $1/4$, after $O(\log m)$ steps, R will contain one element, the optimal value to the p-center problem. We conclude that the total complexity of this algorithm to solve the p-center problem on a tree which is a path is $O(m \log m)$.

The p-center problem on a tree with m nodes is solved by Megiddo et al. (1981) in $O(m \log^2 m)$ time. A further improvement of this implementation was achieved by Frederickson and Johnson (1983), who reduced the time bound to $O(m \log m)$. An $O(m)$ algorithm for the case $p = 1$ is given by Handler (1973). A more general case of the above p-center problem, where the transportation costs are arbitrary linear functions of the distance is solved by Megiddo and Tamir (1983) in $O(m \log^2 m \log \log m)$ time.

The set R' in (6.3.19) is the set of elements of the form $\frac{1}{2}D(P_i, P_j)$, $i, j = 1, \ldots, q$, where P_i and P_j are the shortest paths on T connecting the pair of clients a_i, b_i and a_j, b_j, respectively. When the clients are restricted to the nodes of T (as was assumed above), each distance $D(P_i, P_j)$ is also the distance between some two nodes of the tree. We conclude that R' in (6.3.19) is a subset of R in (6.3.18). Therefore, while looking for the optimal solution to the round-trip p-center problem, we can either search over R in (6.3.18) or R' in (6.3.19), depending on which is more convenient.

We remind the reader that duality results similar to Theorems 6.6 and 6.7 are easily obtained for more general transportation cost functions than the identity function we have chosen here for ease of exposition (see Tansel, Francis, Lowe, and Chen, 1982; Kolen, 1985).

A comment is in order with respect to the round trip p-center problem when facilities can be established only at the nodes of the tree. For this case we showed above that the problem becomes $\mathcal{NP}$-hard even if we exclude only one node from the set of potential sites (the set of nodes). However, we will use the above analysis, on chordal graphs to show that if *all* nodes of the tree are potential locations, then the round-trip p-center problem is polynomially solvable.

First note that in this case the optimal value of the objective is an element in R^2

$$R^2 = \{d(v_i, v_j): i, j = 1, \ldots, m\} . \tag{6.3.20}$$

Thus, the round-trip p-center problem is polynomially solvable if the following covering problem is polynomially solvable.

$$
\begin{aligned}
\text{minimize} \quad & |X| \\
\text{subject to} \quad & D(P_i, X) \le r , \qquad i = 1, \ldots, q , \tag{6.3.21} \\
& X \subseteq V .
\end{aligned}
$$

Define $S_i = \{y \in T: D(P_i, y) \le r\}$, $i = 1, \ldots, q$, and let S_i' be the subtree induced by the nodes of T that belong to S_i as well. We claim that (6.3.21) is equivalent to finding a minimum clique cover on the intersection graph corresponding to the induced subtrees $S_1', \ldots, S_q'$. In order to prove this claim by the above analysis (which was applied to the case where each point on a tree was a potential facility), it suffices to prove the following. If a subcollection $\{S_{i1}', \ldots, S_{it}'\}$ of $\{S_1', \ldots, S_q'\}$ has a nonempty intersection, then it contains a node. Since S_i', $i = 1, \ldots, q$, are induced subtrees the latter follows from Remark 6.1.

Therefore, we conclude that the round-trip p-center problem where facilities can be established at all nodes and only at nodes, at a constant setup cost, is polynomially solvable.

We conclude this section with a discussion on the continuous p-center problem, that is, where each point of the continuum of points on the tree is identified as a client. We consider two cases. The first one is where facilities can be established at the nodes only, while in the second case there are no restrictions on the potential location sites.

The first case is easily reducible to the case of a finite set of clients. It is shown by Chandrasekaran and Tamir (1982) that the solution to the problem is not affected if we assume that clients exist only at some finite set of points. Specifically, clients are located only at the nodes and at the midpoints of all shortest paths connecting nodes of the tree. Therefore, we can solve the budget constrained version of this problem by augmenting the above finite set of clients to the set of nodes of the tree and solving the resultant discrete p-center problem as before.

Efficient algorithms solving the second case, that is, when facilities can be established anywhere on the tree are given by Chandrasekaran and Daughety (1981), Chandrasekaran and Tamir (1980), Frederickson and Johnson (1983), and Megiddo and Tamir (1983). The most efficient algorithm known is that of Megiddo and Tamir that runs in $O(m \log^3 m)$ time.

A duality result for this continuous version of the p-center problem was obtained by Shier (1977), using a direct inductive proof. We will generalize his duality result by applying a theorem on infinite chordal graphs.

Consider the p-center problem where clients are located only at some subset of points $D \subseteq T$. D may be finite or infinite. Also suppose that facilities can be established anywhere on the tree. We will now define a generalized covering problem as follows.

Let each client $x \in D$ be associated with a positive radius r_x. Find a subset X of T of minimum cardinality, such that for each $x \in D$ there exists $y \in X$ with $d(x, y) \le r_x$.

For each x define $T_x = \{ y \in T : d(x, y) \le r_x \}$, and consider the intersection graph G of $\{T_x\}$, $x \in D$. G will have a node v_x for each neighborhood subtree T_x, and v_x and v_y will be adjacent if and only if $x \ne y$ and $T_x \cap T_y$ is nonempty, that is if and only if $d(x, y) \le r_x + r_y$. If D is infinite so is G. Like in the finite case it can be shown that G is an (infinite) chordal graph. The following theorem on infinite chordal graphs (see Hajnal and Súranyi, 1958; Wagon, 1978) is used to prove our duality result.

Theorem 6.8. *Let G be an infinite chordal graph. Let $\theta(G)$ denote the minimum cardinality of a clique cover, and let $\alpha(G)$ denote the maximum cardinality of an independent set. If either $\theta(G)$ or $\alpha(G)$ is finite, then both are finite and equal.*

To ensure the finiteness of $\alpha(G)$ or $\theta(G)$ for the chordal graph associated with our covering problem, we assume that the radii are uniformly bounded from below. There exists an $\varepsilon > 0$ such that $r_x \ge \varepsilon$ for all $x \in D$. It is easily observed that $\theta(G) \le m + \Delta/2\varepsilon$, where Δ is the sum of the arc lengths of the tree. Since the Helly property is still valid for this case (T_x is connected and closed, $x \in D$), $\theta(G)$ is the solution to the covering problem defined above.

Using Theorem 6.8 we obtain the following corollary for the case $r_x = r > 0$ for all $x \in D$.

Corollary 6.1. *Let D be a subset of T. Then for any $r > 0$,*

$$\min \{|X|: X \subseteq T, d(y, X) \le r \text{ for all } y \in D\}$$
$$= \max \{|Y|: Y \subseteq D, d(y_1, y_2) > 2r \text{ for all } y_1, y_2 \in Y, y_1 \ne y_2\} .$$

Corollary 6.1 generalizes the duality between (6.3.8) and (6.3.11) as well as the duality result obtained by Shier (1977) for the case $D = T$. When D is assumed to be closed we obtain the following duality result for the p-center problem.

Theorem 6.9. *Let D be a closed subset of T. Then for each positive p, $p < |D|$,*

$$\min_{X \subseteq T, |X| = p} \left\{ \max_{y \in D} \{d(y, X)\} \right\} = \max_{Y \subseteq D, |Y| = p+1} \left\{ \min_{x, z \in Y, x \ne z} \{d(x, z)/2\} \right\} .$$
$$(6.3.22)$$

Unlike the finite case, if D is infinite, Theorem 6.8 does not suggest a set R that includes r_p, the objective value of the p-center problem (the left-hand side of 6.3.22). This issue is resolved by Chandrasekaran and Tamir (1980) for the case where $D = T$, and by Tamir and Zemel (1982) for a more general case. For example, when $D = T$ it is shown by Chandrasekaran and Tamir (1980) that $r_p = d(x, y)/2k$, where x and y are some tip nodes of T and k is an integer less than or equal to p. Linear time algorithms solving the covering problem for $D = T$, and some generalizations are presented by Chandrasekaran and Tamir (1980) and Tamir and Zemel (1982), respectively.

6.4. TOTALLY BALANCED MATRICES

The covering problem on trees was introduced and solved in Section 6.2. Its formulation is given by (6.2.2).

The algorithm of Section 6.2 to solve the above integer program did not utilize the fact that the matrix A was obtained by row and column permutations from an intersection matrix of neighborhood subtrees versus nodes or vice versa. It relied only upon the information that the matrix $A = (a_{ij})$ was given in standard greedy form, and produced the optimal solution in $O(mn)$ time. This immediately raises the following questions. What is the class of matrices that can be permuted into standard greedy form? Is there an efficient procedure to recognize whether a $(0, 1)$ matrix is a member of this class?

To this end, define a $(0, 1)$ matrix to be *totally balanced* if it does not contain a square submatrix with row and column sums equal to 2 and no identical columns. Totally balanced matrices belong to the larger class of balanced matrices introduced by Berge (1972).

It is a simple observation that each matrix in standard greedy form is totally balanced (see Exercise 6.10). We will now prove the converse statement. Namely, each totally balanced matrix can be permutated into standard greedy form. This will characterize totally balanced matrices as the class of matrices which are permutable into standard greedy form. (Note that the property of total-balancedness is not affected by row or column permutations). The proof uses the concept of a lexical matrix which was introduced by Hoffman, Kolen, and Sakarovitch (1985).

We call a $(0, 1)$ matrix *lexical* if both the rows and columns are ordered in a lexical nondecreasing order. (See Section 6.2.2 for the definition of lexical nondecreasing order).

Let the matrices A_1, A_2 be given by

$$A_1 = \begin{bmatrix} 0 & 1 \\ 1 & 0 \end{bmatrix} \quad \text{and} \quad A_2 = \begin{bmatrix} 1 & 1 & 0 \\ 1 & 0 & 1 \\ 0 & 1 & 1 \end{bmatrix}.$$

Then matrix A_1 is totally balanced but not lexical; on the other hand, the matrix A_2 is lexical but not totally balanced. Thus the class of lexical matrices does not coincide with the class of totally balanced matrices.

An algorithm that transforms any $m \times n$ $(0, 1)$ matrix into a lexical matrix by permuting rows and by permuting columns of the matrix is presented by Hoffman et al. (1985). The algorithm consumes $O(nm^2)$ time (assuming that $m \le n$).

In the theorem below we show that a totally balanced matrix which is lexical is indeed in standard greedy form. In view of the above algorithm and the fact that total-balancedness is not affected by row and column permutations, the theorem implies that a totally balanced matrix is transformable by row and column permutations into standard greedy form.

Theorem 6.10. *Let $A = (a_{ij})$ be a totally balanced lexical matrix. Then A is in standard greedy form.*

Proof. Suppose that A is not in standard greedy form. Then there exist rows $i(1)$, $i(2)$, (with $i(1) < i(2)$) and columns $j(1)$, $j(2)$ (with $j(1) < j(2)$) such that $a_{i(1), j(1)} = a_{i(1), j(2)} = a_{i(2), j(1)} = 1$ and $a_{i(2), j(2)} = 0$. Let $i(3)$ be the last row in which columns $j(1)$, $j(2)$ differ, and let $j(3)$ be the last column in which rows $i(1)$ and $i(2)$ differ. Since A is lexical, $i(3) > i(2)$, $j(3) > j(2)$ and $a_{i(3), j(1)} = 0$, $a_{i(3), j(2)} = 1$, $a_{i(1), j(3)} = 0$, $a_{i(2), j(3)} = 1$. Furthermore since A is totally balanced, it does not contain a 3×3 submatrix with row and column sums equal to two. We can therefore conclude that $a_{i(3), j(3)} = 0$.

Consider now a square **submatrix** B of A of maximum order, say k, satisfying the following property: if $i(1) < i(2) < \cdots < i(k)$ and $j(1) < j(2) < \cdots < j(k)$ denote, respectively, the indices of the rows and columns of B, then

$$
\begin{array}{cccccc}
 & j(1) & j(2) & j(3) & \cdots & j(k) \\
i(1) & \begin{bmatrix} 1 \\ 1 \\ 0 \\ \vdots \\ \\ 0 \end{bmatrix} & \begin{matrix} 1 \\ 0 \\ 1 \\ \vdots \\ \\ \end{matrix} & \begin{matrix} 0 \\ 1 \\ 0 \\ \\ \\ 0 \end{matrix} & \begin{matrix} \cdots \\ \\ \\ \\ \\ 1 \end{matrix} & \begin{matrix} 0 \\ \\ \\ 0 \\ 1 \\ 0 \end{bmatrix} \end{matrix} \\
i(2) \\
i(3) \\
\vdots \\
\vdots \\
i(k)
\end{array}
$$

1. $i(p)$, $p = 3, \ldots, k$, is the last row in which columns $j(p-2)$ and $j(p-1)$ differ,
2. $j(p)$, $p = 3, \ldots, k$, is the last column in which rows $i(p-2)$ and $i(p-1)$ differ,
3. B has ones only in the lower and upper diagonal and the first element of the main diagonal and zero elsewhere.

(Note that $k \geq 3$ by the above argument.)

Using the fact that A is lexical define $i(k+1)$ $(>i(k))$ to be the last row in which columns $j(k-1)$ and $j(k)$ differ, and let $j(k+1)$ $(>j(k))$ be the last column in which rows $i(k-1)$ and $i(k)$ differ. We must have $a_{i(k+1)j(k-1)} = 0$, $a_{i(k+1)j(k)} = 1$, $a_{i(k-1)j(k+1)} = 0$, $a_{i(k)j(k+1)} = 1$. By the definition of $i(p)$ and $j(p)$ $(3 \leq p \leq k)$, we know that $a_{i(k+1)j(q)} = 0$ and $a_{i(q)j(k+1)} = 0$, $q = 1, 2, \ldots, k - 1$. Again, using the fact that A is totally balanced we know that A does not contain a $(k+1) \times (k+1)$ submatrix (with nonidentical columns) whose row and column sums are equal to two. Thus $a_{i(k+1)j(k+1)} = 0$, and the submatrix defined by the rows $i(1) < i(2) < \cdots < i(k+1)$ and columns $j(1) < j(2) < \cdots < j(k+1)$ contradicts the maximality of B. $\square$

As a consequence of the above theorem we conclude that an $m \times n$ matrix A is totally balanced if and only if the $O(nm^2)$ algorithm, which transforms any $m \times n$ $(0, 1)$ matrix into a lexical matrix, transforms A into standard greedy form. Testing whether a matrix is in standard greedy form can also be performed in $O(nm^2)$ time comparing each pair of rows. Testing for total-balancedness can therefore be done in $O(nm^2)$ time. Algorithms with lower complexity bounds have been developed recently by Lubiw (1987) and Paige and Tarjan (1987).

In the case of the covering problem on trees, the standard greedy form was obtained in $O(mn)$ and $O(mn + m \log m)$ times for the client constrained covering problem and the facility constrained covering problems, respectively (see Section 6.2.2). In particular the matrix A associated with this problem on a tree is also totally balanced. This matrix A is the intersection matrix of neighborhood subtrees versus nodes. The fact that such a matrix is totally balanced was first proved by Giles (1978). This result was generalized by Tamir (1983) who proved that the intersection matrix of neighborhood subtrees versus neighborhood subtrees is totally balanced. This latter result can also be proved using the lexical representation of a totally balanced matrix (see Hoffman et al., 1985). However, the converse that "every totally balanced matrix is the intersection matrix of neighborhood subtrees versus neighborhood subtrees of some tree," was proved to be false by Broin and Lowe (1986) who gave the following counterexample of such a matrix:

$$\begin{bmatrix} 1 & 0 & 0 & 0 & 1 & 0 \\ 0 & 0 & 1 & 0 & 1 & 0 \\ 0 & 1 & 0 & 0 & 0 & 1 \\ 0 & 0 & 0 & 1 & 0 & 1 \\ 1 & 1 & 0 & 0 & 1 & 1 \\ 0 & 0 & 1 & 1 & 1 & 1 \end{bmatrix}.$$

Recently, Tamir (1987) has presented other classes of totally balanced matrices defined by center location problems on trees.

In the remainder of this section we will discuss briefly some covering problems defined by totally balanced matrices.

The budget constrained *coverage problem* is to minimize the penalty costs given an upper bound on the setup costs. In case of equal setup costs the budget constraint reduces to an upperbound on the number of facilities say p. This problem can be formulated as

$$\text{minimize} \quad \sum_{i=1}^{m} p_i z_i$$

$$\text{subject to} \quad \sum_{j=1}^{m} a_{ij} x_j + z_i \geq 1, \qquad i = 1, \ldots, m,$$

$$\sum_{j=1}^{m} x_j \leq p \tag{6.4.1}$$

$$x_j \in \{0, 1\}, \qquad j = 1, \ldots, m,$$

$$z_i \in \{0, 1\}, \qquad i = 1, \ldots, m$$

where $a_{ij} = 1$ if client i can be served by a facility at v_j, $a_{ij} = 0$ otherwise.

The p-median problem on a tree turns out to be a special case of (6.4.1). The p-median problem is to locate p points $X = \{x_1, \ldots, x_p\}$ on the tree in order to minimize the sum of the transportation costs. In the case of linear transportation costs this problem can be formulated as

$$\text{minimize} \quad \sum_{i=1}^{m} w_i D(v_i, X)$$

$$\text{subject to} \quad X \subseteq T, \tag{6.4.2}$$

$$|X| = p$$

where w_i is a nonnegative weight corresponding to client i, $i = 1, \ldots, m$. It was proved by Hakimi (1965) that there exists an optimal solution with $X \subseteq V$. With this in mind we can easily verify that the p-median problem can be reformulated very similar to the UFL problem in Section 6.2.1 as a client constrained coverage problem. The reader is asked to construct such a formulation (see Exercise 6.13). Kariv and Hakimi (1979b) gave an $O(m^2 p^2)$ dynamic programming approach to solve the p-median problem on trees.

A second example is the maximum coverage problem considered by Megiddo et al. (1983). In this scenario they want to locate new facilities on the tree. In case a new facility is within distance r_i of client i this client will go to that new facility and this will generate a revenue of p_i, $i = 1, \ldots, m$. The *maximum coverage problem* is to establish at most p facilities on the tree so as to maximize the total revenue obtained from clients who will use the new facilities (equivalently, minimize the sum of revenues of clients who will not use the new facilities). It can be shown (as in the p-median problem), that facility locations may be restricted to a finite set of points on the tree. If the nodes are identified as clients, then the locations can be limited only to points on the tree that belong to the intersection of a maximal subset of neighborhood subtrees in the collection $N(v_i, r_i)$, $i = 1, \ldots, m$. It suffices to consider one point in the intersection of each maximal subset of neighborhood subtrees. From the discussion in Section 6.3, there is a one to one correspondence between maximal subsets of neighborhood subtrees (with nonempty intersection) and the maximal cliques of the intersection graph G of the subtrees $N(v_i, r_i)$, $i = 1, \ldots, m$. Therefore each maximal clique of G will contribute one potential facility location. Since G is a chordal graph with m nodes, it has at most m maximal cliques (see Exercise 6.8), and we can restrict our attention only to at most m potential locations corresponding to the maximal cliques.

Using the finiteness of the set of potential facility sites, the maximum coverage problem can be formulated as (6.4.1), and like the p-median problem it can be solved in $O(m^2 p^2)$ time.

Therefore we have two instances of problem (6.4.1) where A is a totally balanced matrix and which can be solved in polynomial time. The question immediately arises whether we can solve (6.4.1) polynomially for any totally balanced matrix A?

If A is totally balanced, then the matrix given by

$$\begin{bmatrix} A & I \\ e & 0 \end{bmatrix}$$

where I is the identity matrix and e is a row vector of all ones, is also totally balanced. In contrast to the LP-relaxation of (6.2.2) the LP-relaxation of (6.4.1) does not always give an integer optimal solution. This is shown by the following example. Let A be the 7×7 matrix given by

$$
\begin{bmatrix}
1 & 0 & 0 & 1 & 0 & 0 & 0 \\
0 & 1 & 0 & 0 & 1 & 0 & 0 \\
0 & 0 & 1 & 0 & 0 & 1 & 0 \\
1 & 0 & 0 & 1 & 0 & 0 & 1 \\
0 & 1 & 0 & 0 & 1 & 0 & 1 \\
0 & 0 & 1 & 0 & 0 & 1 & 1 \\
0 & 0 & 0 & 1 & 1 & 1 & 1
\end{bmatrix}.
$$

Take $p_i = 1$, $i = 1, \ldots, 6$, $p_7 = 0$, $p = 2$. An optimal solution of (6.4.1) is given by $x_1 = x_7 = 1$ and optimal value 2. If we take $x_1 = x_2 = x_3 = x_7 = \frac{1}{2}$ we get a solution of $3/2$. This example arises with the tree shown in Figure 6.7.

Broin and Lowe (1986) give an $O(mn^3 + p^2 n^3)$ dynamic programming algorithm to solve problem (6.4.1), when its matrix is of size $m \times n$ and $n \leq m$.

Consider the dominating set problem on a graph. Given a graph $G = (V, E)$ and an integer $k \leq |V|$ the *dominating set problem* is to determine whether there exists a subset of at most k nodes such that each node not in this subset is adjacent to at least one of these nodes. It is well known that this problem is $\mathcal{NP}$-complete even for chordal graphs (see Booth and Johnson, 1982).

Let us generalize the dominating set problem on a graph. Consider a graph $G = (V, E)$ with nodes v_i, $i = 1, \ldots, m$ and all arc lengths equal to one. With each node v_i we associate a nonnegative integer r_i and a cost c_i, $i = 1, \ldots, m$. The *generalized dominating set problem* is to minimize the total cost of a subset of nodes such that each node v_i, $i = 1, \ldots, m$ is within distance r_i from at least one of the nodes in this subset. This problem can be formulated as

$$
\text{minimize} \quad \sum_{j=1}^{m} c_j x_j
$$

$$
\text{subject to} \quad \sum_{j=1}^{m} a_{ij} x_j \geq 1, \quad i = 1, \ldots, m, \qquad (6.4.3)
$$

$$
x_j \in \{0, 1\}, \quad j = 1, \ldots, m
$$

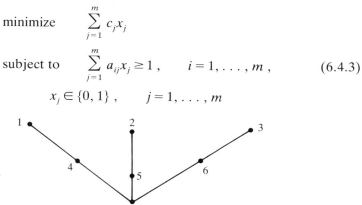

Figure 6.7. Arc lengths equal to one, $r_i = 1$, $i = 1, \ldots, 7$.

where $a_{ij} = 1$ if $d(v_i, v_j) \leq r_i$, $a_{ij} = 0$ otherwise. When $r_i = 1$ and $c_i = 1$, $i = 1, \ldots, m$ we get the dominating set problem.

There exists a subclass of chordal graphs for which the generalized dominating set problem can be solved in polynomial time. The *neighborhood matrix* of a graph $G = (V, E)$ with nodes $v_1, \ldots, v_m$ is the $m \times m$ $(0, 1)$ matrix defined by $a_{ii} = 1$, $i = 1, \ldots, m$ and $a_{ij} = 1$, $i \neq j$, if and only if $[v_i, v_j] \in E$. A graph is a *strongly chordal graph* if and only if its neighborhood matrix is totally balanced. For a given graph with nodes $v_1, \ldots, v_m$ and all arc lengths equal to 1, let us define the $m \times m$ $(0, 1)$ matrix A^k by $a_{ij}^k = 1$ if and only if $d(v_i, v_j) \leq k$. The neighborhood matrix is equal to A^1. It was proved by Lubiw (1982) that if A is totally balanced, then $[I|A^2| \cdots |A^k]$ ($[A|B]$ denotes the matrix where the first m columns are the columns of the matrix A and the last m columns are the columns of B) is totally balanced for every $k \geq 1$ (see Exercise 6.14). From this it follows that whenever we have a strongly chordal graph the matrix of (6.4.3) is totally balanced and hence we can solve (6.4.3) using the algorithm of Section 6.2.1 in $O(m^3)$ time by first transforming it into standard greedy form.

If we allow the arcs of the strongly chordal graph to have nonunit lengths, then problem (6.4.3) becomes $\mathcal{NP}$-hard even for the case where arcs have length equal to 1 or 2. The dominating set problem is reducible to this problem. Given a graph G with unit arc lengths, transform it into a complete graph (which is clearly strongly chordal) by augmenting all missing arcs and assigning each one of them a length of 2. The dominating set problem is then equivalent to the generalized dominating set problem (6.4.3) with $a_{ij} = 1$ if and only if $d(v_i, v_j) \leq 1$.

For further relationships between totally balanced matrices and strongly chordal graphs the reader is referred to Anstee and Farber (1984), Farber (1983, 1984), Chang (1982), Iijima and Shibata (1979), and Lubiw (1982).

ACKNOWLEDGMENT

This chapter was written with the support of the Erasmus University Rotterdam during the period Arie Tamir was a visiting professor at Erasmus University.

EXERCISES

6.1 Let $N(x, r)$ be a neighborhood subtree of a given tree T, and let t be a tip node of T. Define T_1 to be the subtree obtained from T by removing t and the unique arc adjacent to it. Prove that $N(x, r) \cap T_1$ is a neighborhood subtree of T_1.

6.2 Let v be a given node of a tree T. Prove that a node which is at a largest distance from v is an endpoint of a longest path in T.

6.3 Let t_1 and t_2 be the two endpoints of a longest (simple) path on a given tree T. Prove that the unique solution to the (unweighted) 1-center problem on T is obtained by setting the center at the middle point of the path $P[t_1, t_2]$.

6.4 Let t_1 and t_2 be the two endpoints of a longest (simple) path on a given tree T. Show that if a neighborhood subtree $N(x, r)$ contains t_1 and t_2, then $N(x, r) = T$.

Exercises 6.5, 6.6, and 6.7 deal with p-center problems on the real line. In all these problems assume that $v_1 < v_2 < \cdots < v_m$ are given real points on the line and $w_1, w_2, \ldots, w_m$ are nonnegative reals. The weighted p-center problem is given by

$$\text{minimize} \quad z$$

$$\text{subject to} \quad \min_{j=1,\ldots,p} \{w_i|v_i - x_j|\} \le z, \qquad i = 1, \ldots, m, \qquad (*)$$

$$x_1, x_2, \ldots, x_p \text{ reals}$$

6.5 Formulate the weighted 1-center problem on the line as a two-dimensional linear program with at most $2m$ constraints.

6.6 Consider the unweighted version of $(*)$, that is, $w_i = 1$, for $i = 1, \ldots, m$. Let z^* denote the optimal value of z in $(*)$. Design an algorithm of order $O(p \log m)$ to test whether or not z^* is greater than a given value r (this is equivalent to testing whether p-centers will suffice to cover each v_i, $i = 1, \ldots, m$ within a radius r).

6.7 Given a positive number r, define the $m \times m$ incidence matrix $A = (a_{ij})$ as follows

$$a_{ij} = \begin{cases} 1, & \text{if } w_i|v_i - v_j| \le r, \\ 0, & \text{otherwise.} \end{cases}$$

(a) Prove that A is totally balanced.

(b) Prove that every square nonsingular submatrix of A has a determinant ± 1, that is, A is totally unimodular.

6.8 Prove that a chordal graph on m nodes has at most m maximal cliques.

6.9 Construct an efficient algorithm that solves the budget constrained center problem on a cycle network G, that is, $G = (V, A)$ where

$$V = \{v_1, \ldots, v_m\}$$

and

$$A = \{[v_1, v_2], [v_2, v_3], \ldots, [v_{m-1}, v_m], [v_m, v_1]\}.$$

6.10 Show that a matrix in standard greedy form is totally balanced.

6.11 Let $V = \{v_1, \ldots, v_m\}$ be the node set of a tree T. Let $v_1, \ldots, v_k$ be the set of tip nodes. Let $P_i = P[v_1, v_i]$, $i = 1, \ldots, k$ denote the simple path connecting v_1 with v_i. Let $\{Q_1, \ldots, Q_n\}$ be a collection of paths on T such that each Q_j, $j = 1, \ldots, n$ is contained in some path of the collection $\{P_1, \ldots, P_k\}$. Define the $n \times m$ incidence matrix $A = (a_{ij})$ by

$$a_{ij} = \begin{cases} 1, & \text{if } v_j \in Q_i, \\ 0, & \text{otherwise}. \end{cases}$$

Prove that A is totally balanced. (Hint: Prove the nest ordering property and use Lemma 6.1 and Exercise 6.10.)

6.12 Let $T = (V, A)$, $V = \{v_1, \ldots, v_m\}$ be a tree. For each pair v_i and v_j of adjacent nodes on T replace the (undirected) arc $[v_i, v_j]$ by two directed arcs $[v_i, v_j]$ and $[v_j, v_i]$. Assign arbitrary nonnegative lengths to the directed arcs. The network resulting is called a *bitree*. For v_i, v_j let $d(v_i, v_j)$ denote the length of the shortest directed path from v_i to v_j. Given nonnegative reals $r_1, \ldots, r_m$, define the *outer neighborhood* $N(v_j, r_j) = \{v_i \in V : d(v_j, v_i) \leq r_j\}$, $j = 1, \ldots, m$. Prove that the $m \times m$ incidence matrix of outer neighborhood versus nodes is totally balanced.

6.13 Formulate the p-median problem as a client constrained coverage problem (see Section 6.4).

6.14 Let A be a neighborhood matrix of a graph. Suppose that A is totally balanced. Prove that the matrix $[I|A|A^2|\cdots|A^k]$ is totally balanced for all $k \geq 1$ (see Section 6.4 for the definition of A^i).

REFERENCES

Aho, A. V., J. E. Hopcroft, and J. D. Ullman (1974). *The Desing and Analysis of Computer Algorithms*. Addison-Wesley, Reading, Massachusetts.

Anstee, R. P., and M. Farber (1984). "Characterizations of Totally Balanced Matrices." *Journal of Algorithms* **5**, 215–230.

Berge, C. (1972). "Balanced Matrices." *Mathematical Programming* **2**, 19–31.

Booth, K. S., and J. H. Johnson (1982). "Dominating Sets in Chordal Graphs." *SIAM Journal on Computing* **11**, 191–199.

Broin, M. W., and T. J. Lowe (1986). "A Dynamic Programming Algorithm for Covering Problems with (Greedy) Totally-Balanced Constraint Matrices." *SIAM Journal on Algebraic and Discrete Methods* **7**, 348–357.

Buneman, P. (1974). "A Characterization of Rigid Circuit Graphs." *Discrete Mathematics* **9**, 205–212.

Chandrasekaran, R., and A. Daughety (1981). "Location on Tree Networks, p-Center and N-Dispersion Problems." *Mathematics of Operations Research* **6**, 50–57.

Chandrasekaran, R., and A. Tamir (1980). "An $O((n \log p)^2)$ Algorithm for the Continuous p-Center Problem on a Tree." *SIAM Journal on Algebraic and Discrete Methods* **1**, 370–375.

Chandrasekaran, R., and A. Tamir (1982). "Polynomially Bounded Algorithms for Locating *p*-Centers on a Tree." *Mathematical Programming* **22**, 304–315.

Chang, G.J. (1982). *K-Domination and Graph Covering Problems*. Ph.D. Dissertation, Cornell University, Ithaca, New York.

Farber, M. (1983). "Characterization of Strongly Chordal Graphs." *Discrete Mathematics* **43**, 173–189.

Farber, M. (1984). "Domination, Independent Domination and Duality in Strongly Chordal Graphs." *Discrete Applied Mathematics* **7**, 115–130.

Frederickson, G. N., and D. B. Johnson (1983). "Finding *k*-th Paths and *p*-Centers by Generating and Searching Good Data Structures." *Journal of Algorithms* **4**, 61–80.

Gavril, F. (1972). "Algorithms for Minimum Coloring, Maximum Clique, Minimum Covering by Cliques and Maximum Independent Set of a Chordal Graph." *SIAM Journal on Computing* **1**, 180–187.

Gavril, F. (1974). "The Intersection Graphs of Subtrees are Exactly the Chordal Graphs." *Journal of Combinatorial Theory, Series B* **16**, 47–56.

Giles, R. (1978). "A Balanced Hypergraph Defined by Subtrees of a Tree." *ARS Combinatorica* **6**, 179–183.

Golumbic, M. C. (1980). *Algorithmic Graph Theory and Perfect Graphs*. Academic Press, New York.

Hajnal, A., and J. Súranyi (1958). "Uber die Auflösung von Graphen in vollständige Teilgraphen." *Annales Universitatis Scientiarum Budapestinensis Eötvös Nominate, de Rolando Sectio Mathematica* **1**, 113–121.

Hakimi. S. L. (1965). "Optimum Distribution of Switching Centers in a Communication Network and Some Related Graph Theoretic Problems." *Operations Research* **13**, 462–475.

Handler, G. Y. (1973). "Minimax Location of a Facility in an Undirected Tree Graph." *Transportation Science* **7**, 287–293.

Hoffman, A. J., A. Kolen, and M. Sakarovitch (1985). "Totally Balanced and Greedy Matrices." *SIAM Journal on Algebraic and Discrete Methods* **6**, 721–730.

Iijima, K., and Y. Shibata (1979). *A Bipartite Representation of a Triangulated Graph and Its Chordality*, CS-79-1. Department of Computer Science, Gunma University, Japan.

Kariv, O., and S. L. Hakimi (1979a). "An Algorithmic Approach to Network Location Problems. Part 1. The *p*-Centers." *SIAM Journal on Applied Mathematics* **37**, 513–538.

Kariv, O., and S. L. Hakimi (1979b). "An Algorithmic Approach to Network Location Problems. Part 2. The *p*-Medians." *SIAM Journal on Applied Mathematics* **37**, 539–560.

Kolen, A. W. J. (1983). "Solving Covering Problems and the Uncapacitated Plant Location Problem on Trees." *European Journal of Operational Research* **12**, 266–278.

Kolen, A. W. J. (1985). "The Round-Trip *p*-Center and Covering Problem on a Tree." *Transportation Science* **19**, 222–234.

Lubiw, A. (1982). "*Γ*-Free Matrices." Master's Thesis, Faculty of Mathematics, University of Waterloo, Ontario, Canada.

Lubiw, A. (1987). "Doubly Lexical Ordering of Matrices." *SIAM Journal on Computing* **16**, 854–879.

Megiddo, N., and A. Tamir (1983). "New Results on *p*-Center Problems." *SIAM Journal on Computing* **12**, 751–758.

Megiddo, N., A. Tamir, E. Zemel, and R. Chandrasekaran (1981). "An $O(n \log^2 n)$ Algorithm for the *k*-th Longest Path in a Tree with Applications to Location Problems." *SIAM Journal on Computing* **10**, 328–337.

Megiddo, N., E. Zemel, and S. L. Hakimi (1983). "The Maximum Coverage Location Problem." *SIAM Journal on Algebraic and Discrete Methods* **4**, 253–261.

Paige, R., and R. E. Tarjan (1987). "Three Partition Refinement Algorithms." *SIAM Journal on Computing* **16**, 973–989.

Rose, D. J., R. E. Tarjan, and G. S. Lueker (1976). "Algorithmic Aspects of Vertex Elimination in Graphs." *SIAM Journal on Computing* **5**, 266–281.

Shier, D. R. (1977). "A Minimax Theorem for *p*-Center Problems on a Tree." *Transportation Science* **11**, 243–252.

Slater, P. S. (1976). "*R*-Domination in Graphs." *Journal of the Association for Computing Machinery* **23**, 446–450.

Tamir, A. (1980). *On the Core of Cost Allocation Games Defined on Location Problems*, Tech. Rep. Tel Aviv University, Tel Aviv, Israel.

Tamir, A. (1983). "A Class of Balanced Matrices Arising from Location Problems." *SIAM Journal on Algebraic and Discrete Methods* **4**, 363–370.

Tamir, A. (1987). "Totally Balanced and Totally Unimodular Matrices defined by Center Location Problems." *Discrete Applied Mathematics* **16**, 245–263.

Tamir, A., and E. Zemel (1982). "Locating Centers on Tree with Discontinuous Supply and Demand Regions." *Mathematics of Operations Research* **7**, 183–197.

Tansel, B. C., R. L. Francis, T. J. Lowe, and M. L. Chen (1982). "Duality and Distance Constraints for the Nonlinear *p*-Center Problem and Covering Problem on a Tree Network." *Operations Research* **30**, 725–744.

Wagon, S. (1978). "Infinite Triangulated Graphs." *Discrete Mathematics* **22**, 183–189.

Walter, J. R. (1972). *Representations of Rigid Cycle Graphs*. Ph.D. Dissertation, Wayne State University, Detroit, Michigan.

Walter, J. R. (1978). "Representations of Chordal Graphs as Subtrees of a Tree." *Journal of Graph Theory* **2**, 265–267.

7

p-Center Problems

Gabriel Y. Handler

Graduate School of Business Administration
Tel Aviv University
Ramat Aviv, Tel Aviv, Israel

7.1. INTRODUCTION

Let $N = (V, A)$ be an undirected network with a finite vertex set $V = \{v_1, v_2, \ldots, v_m\}$ and a finite set A of links. With every link $[i, j] \in A$ connecting v_i to v_j, associate a finite positive real number α_{ij} representing its length. A link may be considered as an infinite set of points. A point in link $[i, j]$ is specified by its distance from either of the end-points v_i, v_j. Let N also denote the set of all points in the graph including both the set of vertices and all points in all links. Define $d(x, y)$ as the length of a shortest path between $x, y \in N$. Let $X_p = \{x_1, x_2, \ldots, x_p\}$ denote a set of p points in N and let the quantity $D(y, X_p)$ be the generalization of $d(y, x)$ defined by

$$D(y, X_p) = \min_{x \in X_p} d(y, x) . \qquad (7.1.1)$$

Finally, let $H(X_p)$ be defined by

$$H(X_p) = \max_{y \in V} D(y, X_p) . \qquad (7.1.2)$$

We are now ready to formulate the "absolute *p*-center problem."

Definition 7.1.   For $p = 1, 2, \ldots$ a set of points $X_p^* \subseteq N$ is a set of *absolute p-centers* of N if for every $X_p \subseteq N$,

$$H(X_p^*) \le H(X_p)$$

where $H(X_p)$ is given by (7.1.2). Furthermore, the quantity $r_p = H(X_p^*)$ is known as the *absolute p-radius* of N.

A common application of the absolute *p*-center problem is the location of emergency service facilities on a transportation network, where x represents the location of such a facility and y represents the location of a demand point. For example, we may wish to locate p fire stations in a rural community in a manner that minimizes the maximum response time from the closest station to any farm house.

The absolute *p*-center problem defined above is but one example of a variety of minimax location problems on a network, some of which are introduced below. The common features of these "center" problems include the network representation and the minimax criterion. The network assumption often allows for more precise modeling in comparison with the use of rectilinear or Euclidean distance metrics. While the minimax criterion is particularly appropriate in emergency service scenarios, other objectives are frequently utilized, for example, the minisum criterion of "median" problems.

This chapter is devoted to a methodological discussion of computational procedures for center problems. As our point of departure we recall a statement by Hu (1971) to the effect that (by 1970) multifacility location problems on a network was one of the major areas of discrete optimization about which very little was known. Hu refers specifically to the center and median problems. It appears that much more is known today about network location, and our general aim here is to demonstrate that this is indeed the case with respect to center problems.

Specifically, our objectives are two-fold. First, employing the concepts of computational complexity, we shall briefly survey what is known about the complexity of center problems. In particular, we shall note that p-center problems are generally $\mathcal{NP}$-complete. Our second objective is to present exact procedures for finding p-centers of a graph. (In one case, that of the "continuous" problem treated in Section 7.4, the term exact is to be understood in an asymptotic sense. The algorithm presented there will sometimes provide an exact solution in a finite number of steps but at other times we may only be able to discover a δ-optimal solution with δ as small as we choose, except zero.) These procedures are often based on a relaxation framework that is effective for large-scale problems. Thus, we shall suggest that this class of problems is not particularly difficult or intractable in practice, despite its $\mathcal{NP}$ property, which indicates that these are "hard" problems in an asymptotic worst-case context.

As we indicated above, the absolute p-center problem introduced by Definition 7.1 is one of a variety of minimax location models. The following categories of model assumptions encompass much of this variety.

1. *Facility Location Sets.* Facilities may be situated on any points of N (vertices and interior points of the links) as in Definition 7.1, or they may be restricted to the set of vertices. In practice, facilities may well be restricted to a given finite set of possible locations.

2. *Demand Location Sets.* In Definition 7.1 demand is assumed to occur only at the vertices. A natural extension provides for demand generation at any point on the network. This would be appropriate, for example, in determining locations for emergency service stations along a highway network, since breakdowns and accidents can occur anywhere on the network.

3. *Inverse Center Problems.* Instead of looking for a set of locations which minimizes the maximum distance for a given number of facilities, it may be appropriate to answer the "inverse" question, namely: "what is the least number of facilities and their locations such that the maximum distance from a random incident to the closest facility is less than or equal to a specified value?" Referring to such problems as *inverse center* problems, we can formulate an inverse corresponding to each of the four multicenter problems introduced above. For example, the inverse associated with the absolute p-center problem of Definition 7.1 is to solve the optimization problem

$$h_\lambda = \min \{h : X_h \subseteq N, H(X_h) \le \lambda, h \ge 0 \text{ and integer}\} \qquad (7.1.3)$$

where h_λ is the minimum number of facilities needed for a maximum distance of λ and $H(\cdot)$ is given by (7.1.2). When the facility and demand location sets are restricted to vertices, then the corresponding inverse center problem is clearly a set covering problem (see Chapter 6). As we show in Section 7.4, other inverse center problems can also be solved as covering problems.

4. *Tree Networks*. An interesting special case of the center problems formulated above occurs when the network contains no cycles, that is, when the network is a tree, say T. This distinction presents a useful hierarchy in developing computational procedures for the general (cyclic) case. Furthermore, for those physical networks which do exhibit a tree-like structure, the special results for trees can be applied directly.

In order to facilitate identification of the center problems formulated above, we shall adopt the shorthand classification scheme shown in Table 7.1. The scheme is best explained by some examples. Consider the absolute p-center problem associated with Definition 7.1. This would be identified as $A/V/p/N$ since facilities may be established anywhere on the links, demand occurs only at the vertices, p facilities are to be located, and the network is a general (cyclic) graph. Now consider the inverse center problem defined by (7.1.3). That problem is identified as $A/V/\lambda^{-1}/N$, where the "-1" is used in "λ^{-1}" to distinguish λ from p when numbers replace symbols. As a final example, the 2-center problem on a tree network where facilities and demand can exist anywhere on the network would be denoted $A/A/2/T$.

The variety of center models may be further enriched by relaxing a host of implicit and explicit assumptions in the foregoing models. For example, facilities and demand points may be restricted to subsets of A or V; the network may be oriented (in which case we should differentiate between "out-centers" and "in-centers"); weights may be attached to demand points in multiplicative or additive fashion (so far we have implicitly assumed uniform weights, Exercise 7.4 refers to a weighted center problem); stochastic elements (representing variable travel time, for example) may be introduced; and so on. We shall restrict the discussion to the basic models introduced previously, though much of it extends directly to the generalized models indicated above. For some futher discussion of those and other extensions see Handler and Mirchandani (1979).

The literature on center problems is quite extensive, and, for a comprehensive survey on the state of the art until 1978, the reader is again referred to the previous reference. A more up to date survey is given by Tansel, Francis, and Lowe (1983). While the mathematical formulation and rudimentary analysis of location problems on a network can be traced back

TABLE 7.1   Classification Scheme for Center Problems*

Facility Location Set	Demand Location Set	Number of Centers Maximum Distance	Network
$\left\{ \begin{matrix} V \\ A \end{matrix} \right\}$	$\left\{ \begin{matrix} V \\ A \end{matrix} \right\}$	$\left\{ \begin{matrix} p \\ \lambda^{-1} \end{matrix} \right\}$	$\left\{ \begin{matrix} N \\ T \end{matrix} \right\}$

*V = vertex set; A = link set; p = number of centers; λ = maximum distance; N = general network; T = tree network.

at least to the nineteenth century, the source of the recent research efforts in this area is generally accredited to the seminal papers by Hakimi (1964, 1965).

In addition to the notation and definitions introduced previously, we shall make use of the following terminology. A minimum path spanning tree of a network N rooted at a point $x \in N$ is a spanning tree of N defined by the union of shortest paths from x to all nodes of N. It is denoted by MPT(x) and the matrix of shortest distances between all pairs of vertices in V is denoted by D. To evaluate the last two constructs, standard algorithms as reported by Dijkstra (1959) and Dreyfus (1969) can be used. We note here that for nonnegative link lengths, MPT(x) and D may be evaluated in $O(m^2)$ and $O(m^3)$ operations, respectively. The symbol VC is used to identify an optimal location in the "vertex center problem" $V/V/1/N$. The cardinality of any set S is denoted by $|S|$ and a bold symbol indicates a vector, for example $\mathbf{x}$.

We shall often use the following mathematical programming terminology. Consider the finite-dimensional optimization problem

$$z(C) = \inf_{\mathbf{x} \in C} f(\mathbf{x}) \tag{7.1.4}$$

where $f : E^k \to E$, $\mathbf{x} \in E^k$, $C \subseteq E^k$, and E^k denotes k-dimensional Euclidean space. A *relaxation* of (7.1.4) is any new problem with $C' \supset C$ replacing C in (7.1.4) while a *restriction* of (7.1.4) is defined by substituting $C'' \subset C$ for C in (7.1.4). If $z(C'') = z(C)$ we shall refer to C'' as a *dominant set* for C in (7.1.4).

Finally, we wish to distinguish between our usage of the terms "complexity" and "efficiency" in assessing the computational effort in solving optimization problems. In specifying the *complexity* of an algorithm (or of a problem) we have in mind the maximum number of operations needed to process the problem. This is a worst-case measure of computational effort. On the other hand, the *efficiency* of an algorithm has the less precise connotation of the computational effort involved in solving the problem in practice.

For expository purposes we initially confine our discussion to the class of absolute p-center problems $A/V/p/N$. This class may be considered generic to the other center models, which we shall consider subsequently. In Section 7.2 we summarize existing results concerning the complexity of absolute center problems, and in Section 7.3 we describe an exact procedure for solving these problems which is often effective for large networks. A final section is devoted to the remaining classes of center problems introduced above. Most of our discussion is devoted to solving problems on large-scale cyclic networks. While we very briefly indicate complexity results for tree networks, a fuller discussion of algorithmic results for trees is given in Chapters 6 and 8.

7.2. COMPLEXITY OF ABSOLUTE CENTER PROBLEMS

In this section we summarize existing results concerning the computational complexity of absolute center problems, denoted as $A/V/p/N$ in the classification scheme of the previous section. Categorizing this class of problems according to the number of facilities and the type of network, we obtain a broad spectrum of complexities ranging from $O(m)$ for the simplest problems to $\mathcal{NP}$-completeness for the most general ones.

The simplest problems occur when the network is a tree. In particular, the following algorithms, reproduced from Handler (1973, 1978), demonstrate that $O(m)$ algorithms are available for $p \leq 2$.

Algorithm 7.1 $(A/V/1/T)$

Step 1: Choose any point x on the tree and find a farthest point away, say e_1.

Step 2: Find a farthest point away from e_1, say e_2.

Step 3: The absolute center is at the midpoint of the path connecting e_1 to e_2.

The major computational effort involves finding the longest distance from each of two points (x and e_1). This requires sequentially labeling vertices by their distance from the given point x or e_1. Thus, computational complexity of the algorithm is of the order $O(m)$.

Algorithm 7.2 $(A/V/2/T)$

Step 1: Using Algorithm 7.1, find the absolute single center of T.

Step 2: Delete from T any arc that contains the absolute center and is on the path connecting e_1 to e_2; this forms two subtrees.

Step 3: An optimal pair of locations is given by the absolute single-centers of these two subtrees.

Since the procedure is composed of three applications of Algorithm 7.1, computational complexity of the algorithm is $O(m)$. Additional results and algorithms for p-centers on trees are given by Handler (1978), Handler and Mirchandani (1979), Hakimi, Schmeichel, and Pierce (1978), and Kariv and Hakimi (1979). With regard to the complexity of the p-center problem on trees for general values of p, Frederickson and Johnson (1983) have recently presented an $O(m \log m)$ algorithm for $A/V/p/T$.

Turning now to the general case of cyclic networks, Kariv and Hakimi (1979) have devised an $O(|A|m)$ algorithm for $A/V/1/N$ and an $O(|A|^p m^{2p-1}/(p-1)!)$ algorithm for $A/V/p/N$, where $p > 1$. Thus, for a *given* value of p, a polynomial-bounded algorithm exists for the most

TABLE 7.2   Complexity Results for Absolute Center Problems

Number of Centers, p	Type of Network	
	Tree	Cyclic
1	$O(m)$	$O(|A|m)$
2	$O(m)$	$O(|A|^p m^{2p-1}/(p-1)!)$
≥ 3	$O(m \log m)$	$\mathcal{NP}$-complete

general problem. However, when p is also taken as a varying input, such an algorithm is highly unlikely to exist. Kariv and Hakimi obtain this result by demonstrating that $A/V/p/N$ is $\mathcal{NP}$-complete.

In conclusion, existing results concerning the complexity of absolute center problems may be summarized as shown in Table 7.2. Of these results, the tree-based algorithms also provide practically effective procedures for finding absolute centers of a tree. The remaining results provide the best known upper bounds on the computational effort for the corresponding absolute center problems. However, the associated algorithms may be cumbersome from a practical standpoint, particularly for large problems. Furthermore, since the general problem is known to be $\mathcal{NP}$-complete, it may be expected that these are inherently "hard" problems. In the following section we present a relaxation strategy which appears promising for finding centers of large-scale networks in reasonable time. Indeed it would appear that, within the class of $\mathcal{NP}$-complete problems, center problems are quite tractable in practice.

7.3.   A RELAXATION ALGORITHM FOR ABSOLUTE CENTER PROBLEMS

In this section we describe an efficient methodology for locating p-centers in $A/V/p/N$ and determining the p-radius, r_p, defined by

$$r_p = \min_{X_p \subseteq N} H(X_p) . \tag{7.3.1}$$

All of the existing algorithms operate on the same principle, generating and solving a series of set-covering problems (CP). The major computational difficulty with these algorithms has to do with the size of the generated CP. The approach we describe here is a problem-oriented relaxation technique which is particularly appropriate for the large-scale CPs encountered in multicenter problems. Other approaches to finding r_p are given by Christofides and Viola (1971) and Kariv and Hakimi (1979). A general framework for m-center algorithms is presented by Halpern and Maimon (1982). Finally, the algorithms of Minieka (1970) and of Garfinkel, Neebe, and Rao (1977) are implicit in the procedure described below.

We describe first a rudimentary algorithm for $A/V/p/N$ which serves to introduce the CP framework and provides a point of departure for the subsequent developments. Consider first the following definition.

Definition 7.2. $\langle x, c, y \rangle$ denoting a *local center* at a point $c \in N$ with respect to a pair of vertices $x, y \in V$, is said to exist if the minimum distance from c to x equals the minimum distance from c to y and there is no direction from c in which the minimum distances to both x and y are decreasing. Formally, the conditions are:

  i. $d(x, c) = d(y, c)$,
  ii. $\{a \in A_c: \lim_{\theta \to 0} [(d(z, x_\theta^a) - d(z, c))/\theta] < 0,$ for $z = x, y\} = \emptyset$

where A_c is the set of links or partial links incident at c and x_θ^a is a point distant θ from c on link $a \in A_c$. Note that $\langle x, c, x \rangle$ exists if and only if $c = x$; in this case the local center $\langle x, x, x \rangle$ is referred to as the *null center* at x.

Let C denote the set of all points in N corresponding to local centers, that is

$$C = \{c \in N: \langle x, c, y \rangle \text{ exists for some } x, y \in V\} , \qquad (7.3.2)$$

Note that several local centers may coincide at a point $c \in N$, so that the cardinality of C is less than or equal to the number of local centers.

We now present a fundamental "mid-point property" for the case of single centers. We shall see that this simple observation for the case $p = 1$ will be crucial in subsequent developments for $p > 1$.

Theorem 7.1. *For the problem* $A/V'/1/N$, $V' \subseteq V$, *a global solution exists at a local center* $\langle x, c, y \rangle$, *where* $x, y \in V'$ *and* $d(c, x) = d(c, y) = \max \{d(x, z): z \in V'\}$.

Proof. Reasoning informally, this theorem follows because a location which does not fulfill the stated conditions can be shifted in the direction of a farthest vertex, thus reducing the maximum distance. □

7.3.1. Minieka's Approach

Noting that the cardinality of C is finite, Minieka (1970) developed a finite procedure for determining p-center locations. The following result enables the search for p-centers to be restricted from the infinite set of points in N to the finite set in C. We present a formal proof of this result, somewhat different from Minieka's analysis, to aid subsequent developments. Because the proof is based upon Theorem 7.1, we refer to the result as a corollary.

Corollary 7.1 (Minieka, 1970). *The finite set C defines a dominant set for the location of centers in* (7.3.1), *which can now be reformulated as*

$$r_p = \min_{X_p \subseteq C} H(X_p) \,. \tag{7.3.3}$$

Proof. The reasoning is similar to that for Theorem 7.1. A p-center $x \in C$ can be perturbed in the direction of any farthest vertex being "served" by it, without loss of optimality. The following formal proof will be useful farther on. Given a set of p-centers of N, any vertex of N can be associated arbitrarily with a p-center nearest to it, thus partitioning the vertex set into subsets $\{V_i\}_{i=1}^P$. Let Π denote the set of all such partitions of V. Then (7.3.1) may be reformulated as

$$r_p = \min_{\{V_i\}_{i=1}^P \in \Pi} \max_{i \in \{1, 2, \ldots, p\}} \min_{x \in N} \max_{y \in V_i} d(x, y) \,. \tag{7.3.4}$$

The final two operators in (7.3.4) define a 1-center problem as in Theorem 7.1, from which it follows that the set C is indeed a dominant location set for p-centers. $\square$

A solution strategy for (7.3.1) can now be devised by reformulating (7.3.3). Form the matrix $F = \{f_{ij}\}$, with m rows and $|C|$ columns, where f_{ij} denotes the shortest distance from v_i to the jth candidate center. Then (7.3.3) can be reformulated as

$$r_p = \min_{S_p \subseteq S} \max_{v_i \in V} \min_{j \in S_p} f_{ij} \tag{7.3.5}$$

where S_p is the index set of a set of p columns in F and $S = \{1, 2, \ldots, |C|\}$.

The following algorithm solves (7.3.5), and hence (7.3.1), in a finite number of operations.

Algorithm 7.3 $(A/V/p/N)$ (Minieka, 1970)

Step 0: Choose an arbitrary initial solution, S_p.
Step 1:

  i. Let $d = \max_{v_i \in V} \min_{j \in S_p} f_{ij}$
  ii. Update the matrix $B = \{b_{ij}\}$, where

$$b_{ij} = \begin{cases} 0, & \text{if } f_{ij} \geq d, \\ 1, & \text{otherwise} \end{cases} \quad \begin{array}{l} i = 1, 2, \ldots, m \\ j = 1, 2, \ldots, |C| \,. \end{array}$$

Step 2: Solve the CP

$$h = \min \mathbf{e}^T \mathbf{X} \tag{7.3.6}$$

$$BX \geq e \qquad (7.3.7)$$

$$x_j \in \{0, 1\}, \qquad j = 1, 2, \ldots, |C| \qquad (7.3.8)$$

where $e^T = (1, 1, \ldots, 1)$.

Step 3: If $h > p$, stop; $r_p = d$ is the value of an optimal solution. Otherwise, an improved solution has been obtained. S_p is now composed of the h indices in the optimal solution of the CP. Notice that h may be less than p. Go to Step 1.

7.3.2. Column Elimination

While the preceding algorithm locates *p*-centers in a finite number of steps, in practice the procedure is prohibitively time-consuming except for very small graphs. As m increases, $|C| = O(m^4)$ increases quite quickly. The result below has the effect of significantly reducing the number of columns in successive iterations of Step 2. Assume for the present that a candidate center $c \in C$ is generated uniquely by just one pair of vertices $x, y \in V$. Relaxing this assumption involves a notational complication which we address later. We define first an important quantity associated with any local center.

Definition 7.3. For any local center $\langle x, c, y \rangle$, let d_c denote its *radius*, defined as

$$d_c = d(x, c) = d(y, c). \qquad (7.3.9)$$

Corollary 7.2. *In Algorithm 7.3, if d is the value of the current solution for p-centers, then all candidate centers (columns) in the set $K = \{c \in C : d_c \geq d\}$ can be eliminated without loss of optimality.*

Proof. Let V_c be the set of vertices associated with the *p*-center at $\langle x, c, y \rangle$ for which $d_c \geq d$. We assert first that $r_p < d$ implies $x, y \in V_c$. This statement follows since otherwise, from (7.3.4), $r_p \geq d_c \geq d$. Furthermore, since

$$\min_{x \in N} \max_{y \in V_c} d(x, y) \leq \max_{y \in V_c} d(c, y) \qquad (7.3.10)$$

the *p*-center at c can be replaced by an optimal location in the problem defined in the left-hand side of (7.3.10) without loss of optimality. By Theorem 7.1, such an optimal location, c', exists at a local center $\langle x', c', y' \rangle$ where $x', y' \in V_c$. From the first statement, $c \neq c'$, so that the candidate center at c may be discarded. $\square$

The following result, again following directly from Theorem 7.1, renders the CP matrix considerably more sparse. Furthermore, together with Corollary 7.2, it eliminates the need for storing and working with the matrix F after the algorithm has been initiated.

Corollary 7.3. *In Algorithm 7.3, for any column j and row i, the initialization procedure $b_{ij} = 0$ if $f_{ij} > d_j$, where d_j is the radius of the candidate center associated with column j, can be made without loss of optimality.*

Proof. Consider the reformulation of (7.3.1) given by (7.3.4). From Theorem 7.1, there exists an optimal solution to any of the 1-center problems in (7.3.4) at a local center $c \in C$, where $d_c = \max\{d(c, y): y \in V_c\}$. For such an optimal solution, V_c does not contain vertices y such that $d(c, y) > d_c$. □

Corollaries 7.2 and 7.3 lead directly to the following improved version of Algorithm 7.3.

Algorithm 7.4 $(A/V/p/N)$

Step 0:

   i. Choose an arbitrary initial solution, S_p.
   ii. Let $d = \max_{v_i \in V} \min_{j \in S_p} f_{ij}$.
   iii. Set up matrix $B = \{b_{ij}\}$, where

$$b_{ij} = \begin{cases} 0, & \text{if } f_{ij} > d_j, \\ 1, & \text{otherwise}, \end{cases} \quad \begin{array}{l} i = 1, 2, \ldots, m \\ j = 1, 2, \ldots, |C|. \end{array}$$

Step 1: Eliminate from B all columns j such that $d_j \geq d$.
Step 2: Solve the CP (7.3.6)–(7.3.8).
Step 3: If $h > p$, stop; $r_p = d$ is the value of an optimal solution. Otherwise, an improved solution has been obtained. Update S_p; let $d = \max_{j \in S_p} d_j$ and return to Step 1.

In the revised algorithm, columns of B are eliminated, whereas previously elements of B were zeroed, leaving B, in general, with its original dimensions. The effect of this reduction in size becomes increasingly significant as p increases. Notice, however, that for small p we still encounter a great number of columns which, coupled with large m, renders the algorithm impractical for large problems. Before we proceed to tackle this issue we need to relax the restrictive assumption made earlier that only one local center may exist at a point in N.

Consider now the general case where k_c local centers $\{\langle x_i, c, y_i \rangle\}_{i=1}^{k_c}$ coincide at a point $c \in N$. Similar to C of (7.3.2), let C' denote the set of all local centers, that is

$$C' = \{\langle x_1, c, y_i \rangle : i = 1, 2, \ldots, k_c \text{ for all } c \in C\}. \tag{7.3.11}$$

To generalize the column elimination procedure to this case, assume that the set C in Corollaries 7.1 and 7.2 is replaced by C', so that a single point in N may be associated with several candidate centers.

The theory and algorithm apply as before. Notice, however, that the number of columns in the CP matrices may exceed the number of columns in Minieka's procedure. In particular, the initial B matrix now contains $|C'| \geq |C|$ columns. However, it is simple to show that all local centers at a point in N may be represented by at most one column in the CP matrix, and hence the CP matrix need never contain more than $|C|$ columns.

Suppose that after Step 1 of the algorithm the matrix B contains a set of k columns corresponding to k local centers at a point in N. Suppose the columns are indexed $j = 1, 2, \ldots, k$ so that $d_1 \geq d_j$, $j = 2, 3, \ldots, k$. Then, by construction, $b_{i1} \geq b_{ij}$, $i = 1, 2, \ldots, m$, $j = 2, 3, \ldots, k$, and the structure of (7.3.7) renders columns $j = 2, 3, \ldots, k$ redundant in the CP. Notice, however, that these columns must be stored for future use in case column one is eliminated at some later stage.

7.3.3. A Relaxation Strategy

The size of the CP matrices arising in Algorithm 7.3 is m rows by $|C'|$ columns. For networks with hundreds of vertices, the corresponding matrices are very large indeed. While in Algorithm 7.4 the number of columns is generally reduced, the CP matrices may still be large, particularly for small values of p. In both algorithms, solving the CPs in Step 2 is a major computational burden severely limiting the size of problems that can be optimally solved.

Comprehensive reviews of CPs appear in Garfinkel and Nemhauser (1972) and Christofides and Korman (1975). A more recent reference is Balas (1980). Further discussion of CPs is provided in Chapter 6. While significant algorithmic advances have been achieved, the state of the art does not permit efficient solution of truly large-scale general CPs. The following strategy for multicenter location constitutes a problem-oriented technique for solving the very large CPs arising in this context.

The "relaxation strategy" for $A/V/p/N$ is based upon two fundamental observations.

1. For any number of centers, p, there exists a set of critical vertices, a "relaxed" set, $R \subseteq V$, which determine the optimal location of centers. Moreover, $|R|$ will be relatively unaffected by m, and instead will be fairly closely related to p.

In relation to other mathematical programming problems, this observation and implied strategy is akin to a relaxation approach for minimax formulations where, again, the observation is that most of the constraints in the derived constrained problem will be nonbinding at an optimal solution.

2. Unlike general mathematical programming relaxation strategies, in this case both rows and columns are eliminated as a result of the manner in which columns (candidate centers) are generated by rows (vertices). Thus, a special feature here is that advantages which generally result from restrictions are also obtained, rendering the relaxation strategy particularly effective.

The following list of definitions together with previously defined quantities identifies notation used in the relaxation algorithm. We shall assume that a candidate center $c \in N$ is generated uniquely by one pair of vertices. As before, this restriction may be relaxed by replacing C of (7.3.2) with C' of (7.3.11).

$$C(x, y) = \{c \in C: \langle x, c, y \rangle \text{ exists for a given pair } x, y \in V\} .$$

$$C[(x, y): d] = \{c \in C(x, y): d_c < d\} .$$

$$C\{R: d\} = \bigcup_{x, y \in R} C[(x, y): d] \quad \text{where } R \subseteq V .$$

$\{h, \hat{X}_h, \hat{d}\}$ = optimal solution quantities for the CP where

h = value of objective function

$\hat{X}_h$ = identity of the h centers in the solution

$\hat{d} = \max_{c \in \hat{X}_h} \{d_c\} .$

Following is a statement of a procedure for determining p-centers, which combines Algorithms 7.3 and 7.4 in a relaxation framework. We shall state the algorithm in the context of solving $A/V/p/N$ for $p = 1, 2, \ldots, M$ for any given positive integer M. Minor adjustments for the case $p = k$, $k + 1, \ldots, M$, where $M \geq k > 1$, are made later. A flowchart of the algorithm appears in Figure 7.1.

Algorithm 7.5 $(A/V/p/N)$

Step 0: Initialization. Set $p = 1$ and select arbitrarily a vertex x. Let $R = \{X\}$, $d = \infty$, $C(R: d) = \langle x, x, x \rangle$, $\hat{d} = 0$, $\hat{X}_1 = x$. Proceed to Step 1.

Step 1: Improvement/Vertex-to-enter. If every vertex in $V-R$ is within a range of d from some $x \in \hat{X}_p$, then $\hat{X}_p$ is an improved solution; let $X_p = \hat{X}_p$ be the new current solution with $d = \hat{d}$ an upper bound on r_p; update $C\{R: d\}$ by eliminating candidate centers whose ranges exceed or equal d and go to Step 3. Otherwise, designate as vertex-to-enter a vertex v, which is farthest away from $\hat{X}_p$. If $\hat{d} < H(\hat{X}_p) < d$, then $\hat{X}_p$ is still an improved solution; set $d = H(\hat{X}_p)$ and let $X_p = \hat{X}_p$. In both cases proceed to Step 2.

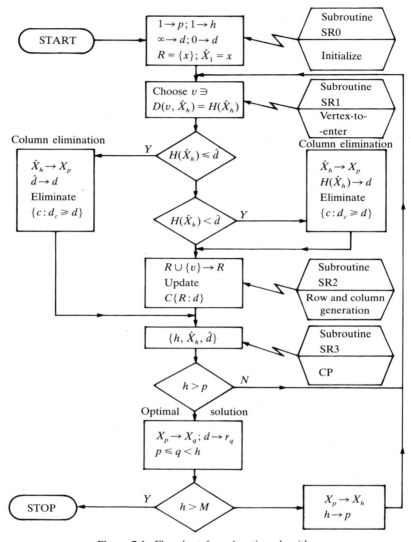

Figure 7.1. Flowchart for relaxation algorithm.

Step 2: Column generation. Add v to R and update $C\{R:d\}$ by adding candidate centers $C[(v, r):d]$ for all $r \in R$. Proceed to Step 3.

Step 3: Covering problem. Select from $C\{R:d\}$ an arbitrary set of p candidate centers, $\hat{X}_p$, "covering" all vertices in R and go to Step 1. If this is impossible, proceed to Step 4.

Step 4: Optimality. The current solution, X_p, constitutes a set of p-centers, with value $r_p = d$. If $p = M$, stop. Otherwise, let $p = p + 1$ and return to Step 3.

The basic computational building blocks, depicted as subroutines in the flowchart of Figure 7.1, need to be clarified.

A central issue in implementation of the algorithm concerns the computation of minimum path distances. For large-scale problems it is expedient to distinguish two modes of operation. In the first, minimum path distances are computed as needed. In the second, the matrix D is initially computed and stored for subsequent use as needed. The first option is generally preferable where M is small in relation to m. Otherwise, the second option is more efficient.

7.3.4. SR0: Initialization

The procedure in the flowchart is the simplest, though not necessarily the most efficient, for initiating the algorithm. The set R comprises initially any vertex x with upper bound $d = \infty > r_1$. It is often possible to speed up the process by deriving better (lower) initial values for d. For example, when D is initially computed, an optimal location (VC) in $V/V/1/N$, found by inspection, provides an upper bound on r_1, namely $d = H(VC) \geq r_1$. Furthermore, it is simple to show that a farthest apart pair of vertices p, q satisfying $d(p, q) \geq d(x, y)$ for all x, $y \in V$, provides a useful lower bound $\frac{1}{2} d(p, q) \leq r_1$. With this information it also seems appropriate to choose p or q as the initial element of R.

Consider now the case where $p = k(>1), \ldots, M$ centers are to be located. One possibility is to build up the solutions by first generating solutions for $p = 1, 2, \ldots, k - 1$. But a useful upper bound for r_k is easily obtained. Selecting arbitrarily a set of k vertices, X_k, an upper bound for r_k is given by $d = H(X_k) \geq r_k$, enabling the algorithm to commence directly with $p = k$.

7.3.5. SR1: Vertex-to-Enter

Assuming prior computation of D, it is straightforward to compute $H(X_h)$. Alternatively, in the absence of this matrix, it is necessary to compute MPT(x), for all $x \in X_h$. Note that since x is not necessarily a vertex, a slight modification is required in any standard MPT algorithm.

7.3.6. SR2: Row and Column Generation

The CP matrix needs to be updated by adding a row corresponding to the vertex chosen to enter and a set of columns corresponding to the new set of candidate centers generated by this vertex. Consider first the issue of column generation. $C\{R : d\}$ requires updating according to the expression

$$C\{R \cup \{v\} : d\} = C\{R : d\} \bigcup_{r \in R} C[(v, r) : d] \cup C(v, v) . \quad (7.3.12)$$

A procedure for generating all candidate centers generated by a given pair of vertices is described below. This procedure is performed for pairs $\{v, r\}$ for all $r \in R$. Note also the inclusion of the null center $C(v, v)$ in (7.3.12). For each candidate center c generated, we need to record its radius, d_c, and the subset $R_c \subseteq R$ covered by it, namely $R_c = \{r \in R: d(c, r) \le d_c\}$. For every new candidate center c, we add a new column to the CP matrix. An element of such a column equals 1 if the vertex corresponding to that row is a member of R_c; otherwise, the element equals 0.

To determine the row to be added to the CP matrix, we need to identify the subset $Q \subseteq C\{R : d\}$ covering vertex v, namely

$$Q = \{c \in C\{R : d\}: d(c, v) \le d_c\} \ .$$

Then an element of this row equals 1 if the candidate center associated with that column is a member of Q as well as when the column is among the newly generated columns. Otherwise, the element equals 0.

We turn now to the issue of generating $C[(x, y): d]$ for a given pair of vertices $\{x, y\}$, $x \ne y$. For a generating pair of vertices $\{x, y\}$ and a generic link $[i, j] \in A$, define the following terms:

$$C^{ij}(x, y) = \{c \in C(x, y): c \text{ is on } [i, j]\} \ ;$$

$$C^{ij}[(x, y) : d] = \{c \in C[(x, y) : d]: c \text{ is on } [i, j]\} \ ;$$

$$S^k(x, y) = \min \{d(k, x), d(k, y)\} \ , \qquad k \in \{i, j\} \ .$$

Definition 7.4. $\langle x, ij, y \rangle$, denoting a *flip-flop* condition on link $[i, j]$ with respect to a pair of vertices $\{x, y\}$, is said to exist if and only if

$$(S^i(x, y) - d(i, x))(S^j(x, y) - d(j, x)) + (S^i(x, y) - d(i, y))$$
$$\times (S^j(x, y) - d(j, y)) = 0 \ .$$

The following theorem leads to an efficient algorithm for generating candidate centers.

Theorem 7.2. $C^{ij}(x, y) \ne \emptyset$ *only if* $\langle x, ij, y \rangle$ *exists, in which case the following are mutually exclusive and exhaustive cases:*

1. $\langle x, c, y \rangle$ *exists at an interior point of* $[i, j]$, $|C^{ij}(x, y)| = 1$ *and the range and location of c are, respectively,*

$$d_c = \frac{1}{2} \left(\alpha_{ij} + S^i(x, y) + S^j(x, y) \right)$$

and

$$\alpha_{ic} = \frac{1}{2} \left(\alpha_{ij} + S^j(x, y) - S^i(x, y) \right).$$

2. $\langle x, c, y \rangle$ exists at v_k, $k = i$ or j, $|C^{ij}(x, y)| = 1$, and $d_c = S^k(x, y)$.
3. $\langle x, c_i, y \rangle$ and (x, c_j, y) exist at vertices v_i and v_j, respectively, $|C^{ij}(x, y)| = 2$, and $d_{c_k} = S^k(x, y)$ for $k = i$, j.
4. $C^{ij}(x, y) = \emptyset$.

Furthermore, when all links $[i, j] \in A$ are investigated, no candidate centers in $C(x, y)$ are lost by ignoring Case 3 for all links.

Proof. We shall refer to Figure 7.2. Consider first the general form of the function $f(\theta) = d(x, z(\theta))$, where $z(\theta)$ is a point on link $[i, j]$, θ units from v_i. It is readily established and illustrated in the example in Figure 7.2(a) that $f(0)$ is a concave, one- or two-piece linear function with magnitude of slope equal to unity.

We consider the relationship between $d(x, z(\theta))$ and $d(y, z(\theta))$ and distinguish three mutually exclusive and exhaustive cases:

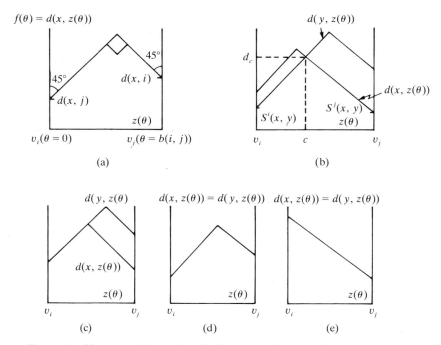

Figure 7.2. (a) Form of $d(x, z(\theta))$; (b) Case 1; (c) Case 2; (d) Case 3; (e) Case 3.

1. $d(x, k) \neq d(y, k)$, $k = i, j$. A necessary and sufficient condition for $\langle x, z(\theta), y \rangle$ to exist in the range $\theta \in (0, \alpha_{ij})$ is the existence of a flip-flop, $\langle x, ij, y \rangle$, as illustrated in Figure 7.2(b). Furthermore, such a local center, c, is unique. Finally, it is evident from the diagram that its range is given by $d_c = \frac{1}{2}(S^j(x, y) + S^i(x, y) + \alpha_{ij})$ and that the location of c is given by $\alpha_{ic} = \frac{1}{2}(\alpha_{ij} + S^j(x, y) - S^i(x, y))$.

2. $d(x, k) = d(y, k)$ for $k = i$ or $k = j$ but not both. Without loss of generality assume $k = i$ and consider the generic case depicted in Figure 7.2(c). Only the point $c = v_i$ can possibly satisfy $\langle x, c, y \rangle$ though information from adjacent links is required to confirm this. Note that $d_c = S^i(x, y)$.

3. $d(x, k) = d(y, k)$, $k = i, j$. Consider the generic case depicted in Figure 7.2(d). $d(x, z(\theta)) = d(y, z(\theta))$ for all $\theta \in [0, \alpha_{ij}]$ and only the points v_i and v_j are potential local centers, with radii $S^i(x, y)$, $S^j(x, y)$, respectively.

Note that $\langle x, ij, y \rangle$ exists whenever $d(x, k) = d(y, k)$ for $k = i$ or $k = j$ or both, as well as in the situation illustrated in Figure 7.2(b), thus establishing the four cases of the theorem.

We now wish to show that nothing is lost by ignoring local centers in Case 3 providing all links are investigated. Assuming Case 3 obtains, consider the two possibilities illustrated in Figure 7.2(d) and 7.2(e). Without loss of generality consider vertex v_i and let $\Delta(i)$ denote the set of vertices adjacent to v_i. All links incident to v_i are in Cases 2 or 3. In Figure 7.2(d), existence of $\langle x, i, y \rangle$ implies there exists a vertex $v_k \in \Delta(i)$ such that link (i, k) is in Case 2. The contrary implies $x = y(= v_i)$ which, by assumption, is impossible. In Figure 7.2(e), $\langle x, i, y \rangle$ does not exist. In conclusion, to generate $C(x, y)$ it suffices to inspect all links $[i, j] \in A$ in Cases 1 and 2 alone. □

Theorem 7.2 leads directly to an efficient algorithm for generating $C[(x, y) : d] = \cup_{(i,j) \in A} C^{ij}[(x, y) : d]$ as described in the flowchart in Figure 7.3.

7.3.7. SR3: Set-Covering Problem

In this subroutine, the CP defined in (7.3.6)–(7.3.8) is solved, with matrix B updated in SR2. We have already indicated that the relaxation strategy in its entirety can be viewed as a problem-oriented technique for solving the large-scale CPs arising in minimax facility location problems. Operationally, we have transformed a succession of large-scale CPs into a succession of small CPs, each of which requires relatively minor computational effort for its solution.

The size of a generic CP matrix in Algorithm 7.5 is $|R|$ rows by $|C\{R : d\}|$ columns, compared with m by $|C|$ and m by $|C\{V : d\}|$ in Algorithms 7.3 and 7.4, respectively. Since $|R|$ is generally related to p (independently of m), it is evident tht for small p the CP is indeed manageable and often

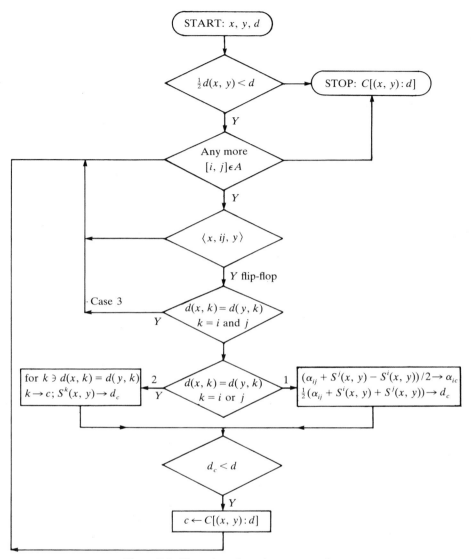

Figure 7.3. Flow chart for column generation.

amenable to hand solution. This is particularly true as a consequence of the sequential nature of the algorithm, enabling the CP to be solved as the following feasibility problem: find a binary vector $\mathbf{x}$ satisfying $B\mathbf{x} \geq \mathbf{e}$ and $\mathbf{e}^T\mathbf{x} = p$, or determine that no such vector exists. For further discussion of CP algorithms, the reader is referred to the survey by Christofides and Korman (1975), the text by Garfinkel and Nemhauser (1972), and a more recent approach due to Balas (1980).

The examples below illustrate the relaxation algorithm for location of *p*-centers. In the first example we consider a tree network and in the second a general cyclic network.

Example 7.1. $(A/V/p/T, p = 1, 2, \ldots, 7)$. The tree network with 60 vertices is shown in Figure 7.4. The example illustrates how a nontrivial tree-based problem can be solved manually. We shall let x_{pq} denote the mid-point of the path connecting p to q and, for compactness, we shall refer

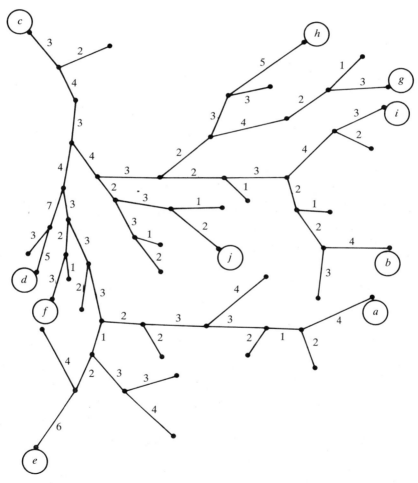

Figure 7.4. Network for Example 7.1. Numbers represent link lengths, encircled vertex labels $a, b, \ldots, j$ represent successive additions to R.

to x_{pq} as pq in labeling columns of CP matrices. The null center at a vertex x and its associated column is denoted as x.

$p = 1$. Use Algorithm 7.1 for $A/V/1/T$ to obtain $X_1^* = x_{ab}$ and $r_1 = 23$.

$p = 2$. Use Algorithm 7.2 for $A/V/2/T$ to obtain $X_2^* = \{x_{bc}, x_{ad}\}$ and $r_2 = 17$.

$p = 3$. Initiate the relaxation algorithm arbitrarily, with the following upper bound solution derived by breaking up the maximal radius in X_2^*:

$$X_3 = \{x_{bc}, x_{ae}, x_{df}\}, \qquad d = 15, \qquad R = \{a, b, c, d, e, f\}.$$

Update $C(R:d)$ to obtain the following CP matrix and radii:

	ae	af	cd	cf	df	ef	a	b	c	d	e	f
a	1	1							1			
b								1				
c			1	1					1			
d			1		1					1		
e	1	1				1					1	
f		1	1	1	1	1						1

$$d_c \; [\; 11 \quad 12 \quad 13 \quad 11 \quad 10 \quad 10 \quad 0 \quad 0 \quad 0 \quad 0 \quad 0 \quad 0 \;]$$

Obtain, by inspection, $h = 3$, $\hat{X}_3 = \{x_{af}, x_{cd}, b\}$, and $\hat{d} = 13$. Now $H(\hat{X}_3) = D(g, \hat{X}_3) = d(g, x_{cd}) = 21 \geq 15 = d$. Adding g to R and updating $C\{R:d\}$, obtain the following enlarged CP matrix and radii:

	ae	af	cd	cf	df	ef	gb	gc	a	b	c	d	e	f	g
a	1	1									1				
b							1			1					
c			1	1				1			1				
d			1		1							1			
e	1	1				1							1		
f		1	1	1	1	1								1	
g							1	1							1

$$d_c \; [\; 11 \quad 12 \quad 13 \quad 11 \quad 10 \quad 10 \quad 12 \quad 14 \quad 0 \quad 0 \quad 0 \quad 0 \quad 0 \quad 0 \quad 0 \;]$$

Obtain, by inspection, $h = 3$, $\hat{X}_3 = \{x_{af}, x_{cd}, x_{gb}\}$, and $\hat{d} = 13$. Since $H(\hat{X}_3) = 13$, we have an improved global solution with $d = 13$. Attempting to improve upon this, eliminate columns with $d_c \geq 13$, thus obtaining the following CP matrix and radii:

	ae	af	cf	df	ef	gb	a	b	c	d	e	f	g
a	1	1					1						
b						1		1					
c			1						1				
d				1						1			
e	1	1			1						1		
f		1	1	1	1							1	
g						1							1

d_c [11 12 11 10 10 12 0 0 0 0 0 0 0]

We find $h = 4$, $\hat{X}_4 = \{x_{af}, x_{cf}, x_{df}, x_{gb}\}$, and $\hat{d} = 12$. Hence, the current solution is optimal for $p = 3$, namely,

$$X_3^* = \{x_{af}, x_{cd}, x_{gb}\} \qquad \text{and} \qquad r_3 = 13 .$$

$p = 4$. Since $H(\hat{X}_4) = 12$, we have an improved solution $X_4 = \hat{X}_4$ with $d = 12$. Eliminating columns with $d_c \geq 12$, the following CP matrix and radii are obtained:

	ae	cf	df	ef	a	b	c	d	e	f	g
a	1				1						
b						1					
c		1					1				
d			1					1			
e	1			1					1		
f		1	1	1						1	
g											1

d_c [11 11 10 10 0 0 0 0 0 0 0]

We find $h = 5$, $\hat{X}_5 = \{x_{ae}, x_{cf}, x_{df}, b, g\}$, and $\hat{d} = 11$. Hence, the current solution is optimal for $p = 4$, namely,

$$X_4^* = \{x_{af}, x_{cf}, x_{df}, x_{gb}\} \qquad \text{and} \qquad r_4 = 12 .$$

$p = 5$. $H(\hat{X}_5) = D(h, \hat{X}_5) = 12 = d$. Adding h to R and updating $C\{R : d\}$, we obtain the following enlarged CP matrix and radii:

$$
\begin{array}{c}
\quad ae,\quad cf,\quad df,\quad ef,\quad hy,\quad hb,\quad a,\quad b,\quad c,\quad d,\quad e,\quad f,\quad g,\quad h \\[4pt]
\begin{array}{c}
a\\b\\c\\d\\e\\f\\g\\h
\end{array}
\left[
\begin{array}{cccccccccccccc}
1 & & & & & & 1 & & & & & & & \\
 & & & & & 1 & & 1 & & & & & & \\
 & 1 & & & & & & & 1 & & & & & \\
 & & 1 & & & & & & & 1 & & & & \\
1 & & & 1 & & & & & & & 1 & & & \\
 & 1 & 1 & 1 & & & & & & & & 1 & & \\
 & & & & 1 & & & & & & & & 1 & \\
 & & & & 1 & 1 & & & & & & & & 1
\end{array}
\right]
\end{array}
$$

$$d_c \quad [\; 11 \quad 11 \quad 10 \quad 10 \quad 8\tfrac{1}{2} \quad 11\tfrac{1}{2} \quad 0 \quad 0 \quad 0 \quad 0 \quad 0 \quad 0 \quad 0 \quad 0 \;]$$

We find $h = 5$, $\hat{X}_5 = \{x_{ae}, x_{cf}, x_{df}, x_{hg}, x_{hb}\}$, and $\hat{d} = 11\tfrac{1}{2}$. Since $H(\hat{X}_5) = 11\tfrac{1}{2}$, $X_5 = \hat{X}_5$ is an improved global solution for $p = 5$ with $d = 11\tfrac{1}{2}$. Eliminating columns with $d_c \geq 11\tfrac{1}{2}$ and solving the revised CP, we obtain $h = 5$, $\hat{d} = 11$, and $H(\hat{X}_5) = D(i, \hat{X}_5) \geq d$. Adding vertex i to R and updating $C\{R:d\}$, we obtain a new CP of size (9×7) (excluding null variables) yielding $h = 5$, $\hat{d} = 11$, and $H(\hat{X}_5) = D(j, \hat{X}_5) \geq d$. Adding vertex j to R and updating $C\{R:d\}$, we obtain an enlarged CP of size (10×10) yielding $h = 5$, $\hat{d} = 11$, and $H(\hat{X}_5) = 11$, so that $X_5 = \hat{X}_5$ is an improved solution with $d = 11$. Eliminating columns with $d_c \geq 11$ and solving again the CP of size (10×7) yields $h = 6$ and $d = 10\tfrac{1}{2}$ so that X_5 is an optimal solution with $r_5 = 11$.

$p = 6$. Since $H(\hat{X}_6) = 10\tfrac{1}{2}$, $X_6 = \hat{X}_6$ is an improved global solution for $p = 6$ with $d = 10\tfrac{1}{2}$. Eliminating columns with $d_c \geq 10\tfrac{1}{2}$ results in a CP of size (10×5), which yields $h = 7$ and $\hat{d} = 10$, so that X_6 is optimal and $r_6 = 10\tfrac{1}{2}$.

$p = 7$. $H(\hat{X}_7) = 20$ so that $X_7 = \hat{X}_7$ is an improved global solution for $p = 7$ with $d = 10$. Eliminating columns with $d_c \geq 10$, we obtain a CP of size (10×2) yielding $h = 8$, $\hat{d} = 8\tfrac{1}{2}$, so that X_7 is optimal and $r_7 = 10$.   ○

Example 7.2. $(A/V/p/N, p = 1, 2, 3, 4)$. The network, with 53 vertices and 81 links, is shown in Figure 7.5. For the cyclic network problem the task of updating $C\{R:d\}$ is tedious for a manual mode while the CPs are often amenable to manual solution by inspection. In this example an interactive approach was adopted with successive updates of $C\{R:d\}$ by computer and manual solutions of CPs by inspection. Details are reproduced only for $p = 1$ and $p = 2$. Computational data for this problem appear in Table 7.3.

$p = 1$. Computing first the matrix D, we locate a vertex center, yielding an upper bound solution $H(16) = 37$. Hence, $r_1 \leq 37$. A most distant pair of vertices is $\{40, 53\}$. Initiate the algorithm by setting $d = 37$, $R = \{40\}$, $\hat{X}_1 = 40$, and $\hat{d} = 0$. Then $H(40) = d(40, 53) = 71$. Let $R = \{40, 53\}$ and generate $c[(40, 53):37]$ to obtain the following CP matrix and radii:

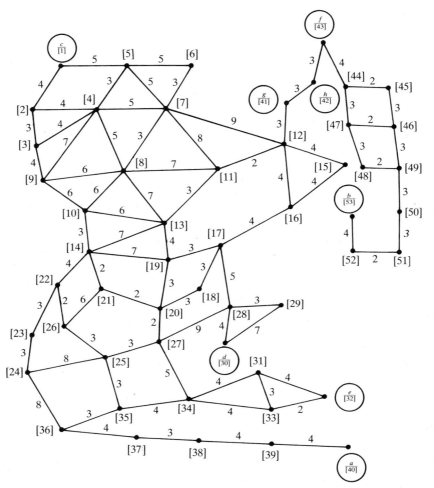

Figure 7.5. Network for Example 7.2. Numbers on links represent link lengths, numbers in brackets identify vertices, and encircled vertex labels $a, b, \ldots, h$ represent successive additions to R.

$$
\begin{array}{cccc}
x^{11,13}_{40,53} & x^{12,16}_{40,53} & 40 & 53
\end{array}
$$

$$
\begin{array}{c}
40 \\
53
\end{array}
\left[
\begin{array}{cccc}
1 & 1 & 1 & \\
1 & 1 & & 1
\end{array}
\right]
$$

$$
d_c \quad \left[\; 35\tfrac{1}{2} \quad 36\tfrac{1}{2} \quad 0 \quad 0 \; \right]
$$

Here, $x^{i,j}_{p,q}$ denotes the candidate center on link $[i, j]$ generated by the pair of vertices p, q. The columns associated with a null center at p is labeled p. The set of columns associated with the null centers is termed the null set.

Choosing $\hat{X}_1 = x_{40,53}^{11,13}$, $\hat{d} = 35\frac{1}{2}$, we find $H(\hat{X}_1) = 35\frac{1}{2}$ so that $X_1 = \hat{X}_1$ and $d = 35\frac{1}{2}$. Eliminating columns with $d_c \geq 35\frac{1}{2}$ reduces the CP matrix to the null set, from which one column is insufficient to cover the elements in R. Hence, a 1-center is given by $X_1^* = x_{40,53}^{11,13}$ and $r_1 = 35\frac{1}{2}$.

$p = 2$. The solution to the reduced CP yields $h = 2$, $\hat{X}_2 = \{40, 53\}$, and $\hat{d} = 0$. Since $H(\hat{X}_2) = D(1, \hat{X}_2) > 0$, vertex v_1 is added to R. Updating $C\{R : d\}$ yields the new CP matrix and radii:

$$
\begin{array}{cccccccccc}
 & x_{40,1}^{22,26} & x_{40,1}^{20,27} & x_{40,1}^{21,26} & x_{53,1}^{42,43} & x_{40,1}^{22,23} & x_{40,1}^{27,28} & 40 & 53 & 1 \\
40 & \left[\begin{array}{c} 1 \end{array}\right. & 1 & 1 & & 1 & 1 & 1 & & & \left.\begin{array}{c}\end{array}\right] \\
53 & & & & 1 & & & & 1 & \\
1 & \left[\begin{array}{c} 1 \end{array}\right. & 1 & 1 & 1 & 1 & 1 & & & 1 \left.\begin{array}{c}\end{array}\right] \\
d_c & [\;\; 25 & 25 & 26 & 26 & 27 & 32\frac{1}{2} & 0 & 0 & 0\;]
\end{array}
$$

Solving the CP yields $h = 2$, $\hat{X}_2 = \{x_{40,1}^{20,27}, 53\}$, $\hat{d} = 25$. Since $H(\hat{X}_2) = 25$, we have an improved global solution $X_2 = \hat{X}_2$, $d = 25$. Eliminating all columns with $d_c \geq 25$ reduces the CP matrix to the null set. Since three columns are now required to cover all elements of R, a set of 2-centers is given by $X_2^* = \{x_{40,1}^{20,27}, 53\}$ and $r_2 = 25$.

$p = 3$. Proceeding as before, an initial solution is given by the null set and a most distant vertex, v_{30}, is added to R. After five iterations an optimal solution for $p = 3$ is achieved with $R = \{40, 53, 1, 30, 32\}$ and $r_3 = 18$.

$p = 4$. Five iterations are needed to achieve optimality with $R = \{40, 53, 1, 30, 32, 43, 41, 42\}$ and $r_4 = 12\frac{1}{2}$. ◯

To validate the relaxation algorithm we state and prove the following theorem.

Theorem 7.3. *Algorithm 7.5 locates a set of p-centers in $A/V/p/N$ in a finite number of steps.*

Proof. **1.** *Optimality.* A simple relaxation argument suffices. The algorithm finds an optimal solution, X_p^*, to $A/R/p/N$ for some $R \subseteq V$ according to Algorithm 7.4. Furthermore,

$$
\min_{X_p \subseteq N} \max_{y \in R} D(y, X_p) = \max_{y \in V} D(y, X_p^*) \tag{7.3.13}
$$

according to the algorithm. Now consider $A/R/p/N$ reformulated as

$$
\min \{d : X_p \subseteq N, d \geq D(y, X_p) \text{ for all } y \in R\}, \tag{7.3.14}
$$

indicating that $A/R/p/N$ is a relaxation of $A/V/p/N$. Expressions (7.3.13) and (7.3.14) establish that X_p^* is also optimal for $A/V/p/N$.

2. *Finite Convergence.* An iteration of the algorithm consists of a CP and subsequent row/column generation, clearly a finite operation. At each iteration one and only of the following occurs:

(a) One row is added with possible column additions and eliminations.

(b) At least one column is eliminated and none added.

Since m is finite, a necessary condition for an infinite number of iterations is that (b) is repeated infinitely for a given R. Since $|C\{R:d\}|$ is finite this is impossible and finite convergence is guaranteed. □

7.3.8. Computational Efficiency and Experience

The critical factor determining computational efficiency is the cardinality of R at the optimal solution for a given p. In the worst case, Algorithm 7.5 will perform roughly as Algorithm 7.4. For example, consider $A/V/1/N$ where N is a single loop and vertices are distributed at equal intervals. Then $|R| \approx m$ at the optimal solution (see the example in Figure 7.6 and Table 7.6). However, apart from such pathological cases yielding rather unattractive computational upper bounds, the algorithm can be expected to perform efficiently. Preliminary computational experience suggests $|R| \leq 6 \cdot p$ is a good approximation. This indicates a significant relative advantage over Algorithm 7.4 when p is small. Since the latter algorithm is particularly efficient for large p, it turns out that the proposed algorithm, by combining both features, is well suited for all values of p.

We now wish to focus attention on the number of candidate centers $|C\{R:d\}|$ which, apart from the direct dependence on $|R|$, is based upon the generic quantities $|C[(x, y):d]|$. From Theorem 7.2 we can assert that $|C[(x, y):d]| \leq |A|$. However, the following observations indicate why this bound is usually a gross overestimate of the true number. Note first that in the previous inequality, A may be replaced by the set of links derived by amalgamating adjacent links at vertices with degree 2. This observation is particularly important for $A/A/p/N$ (Section 7.4). Consider next the following theorem.

Theorem 7.4.   *The existence of $\langle x, c, y \rangle$ implies that $\langle x, z, y \rangle$ does not exist at any point $z \neq c$ on a minimal distance path from c to x or to y.*

Proof.   Suppose, for example, that $z \neq c$ is a point on a minimum path from c to y, and assume $\langle x, c, y \rangle$ exists. Then by the latter assumption

$$d(c, x) < d(c, z) + d(z, x) = d(c, y) - d(z, y) + d(z, x)$$

so that $d(z, y) < d(z, x)$, which implies that $\langle x, z, y \rangle$ cannot exist. □

The preceeding comments apply to $|C(x, y)|$. The effect of d in reducing $|C[(x, y):d]|$ is all-important. For small p, the induced "spread" of vertices in R sharpens this effect. For example, note that $d(x, y) \geq 2d$ implies $|c[(x, y): d]| = 0$. For large p, small values of d again contribute to its effectiveness in reducing the cardinality of the set of candidate centers.

While $|C\{R : d\}|$ represents the number of distinct candidate centers at any iteration, the number of distinct columns in the corresponding CP matrix may generally be smaller. This follows since several candidate centers can give rise to an identical column in the CP matrix. In solving the CP, it is clearly desirable to ignore duplicate columns. To illustrate the point, consider Example 7.2. In the matrix for $p = 2$, five candidate centers produce an identical column so that the effective number of columns is two instead of six (exclusive of null columns).

Finally, note the special case of trees where $|C(x, y)| = 1$. Since now both CP and matrix generating efforts are minimal, it appears that tree-based problems can be solved manually for quite large networks.

We now present some computational results for the relaxation algorithm. Table 7.3 summarizes computational data for Example 7.2.

The advantages accruing from the relaxation scheme can be readily seen in this example. The number of vertices in R, identical to the number of rows in the CPs, is about twice the number of centers, p, in place of the full set of vertices, here 53. This represents a saving in orders of magnitude with repect to the resultant CPs and matrix generation. Indeed, it is doubtful whether Algorithm 7.3 can reasonably handle this problem, given the enormous number of generated columns. Employing Algorithm 7.5, the

TABLE 7.3 Computational Data for Example 7.2 for Network with 53 Vertices and 81 Links*

	Computation of D matrix	cpu (seconds) 0.24
Number of Centers, p	CP (rows × columns)	
1	(2×2)	0.03
2	(3×6)	0.04
3	$(4 \times 10); (4 \times 9); (4 \times 2); (5 \times 2); (5 \times 4)$	0.09
4	$(6 \times 16); (6 \times 7); (7 \times 18); (8 \times 26); (8 \times 16)$	0.22

*1. The program was written in FORTRAN IV, compiled under level G1, and run on an IBM-370–165.

2. Times are incremental. (To solve for a given number of centers, M, would not neccessitate solving for all previous $p < M$.)

3. A large fixed cost was incurred in this example by first computing D. This is very inefficient for small values of p. Thus, for $p = 1$, total time would be approximately 0.05 s instead of 0.27 as indicated.

4. CPs were solved manually by inspection.

5. The number of columns in the CPs does not include the $|R|$ columns associated with the null centers at the vertices.

TABLE 7.4   Size of CPs for Example 7.1 for Tree with 60 Vertices

Number of Centers, p	CP (Rows × Columns)
1, 2	Direct techniques (Section 7.2)
3	$(6 \times 6); (7 \times 8); (7 \times 6)$
4	(7×4)
5	$(8 \times 6); (8 \times 5); (9 \times 7); (10 \times 10); (10 \times 7)$
6	(10×5)
7	(10×2)

major computational effort is due to minimum path computations for matrix generation, while the CPs are small enough to allow solution by hand.

In the case of tree networks, since minimum path computations are particularly simple, the whole problem is often amenable to manual solution. Example 7.1, summarized in Table 7.4, illustrates this for a tree with 60 vertices. Notice that, in contrast, Algorithm 7.3 involves generating and solving a sequence of CPs of size (60×1770) or, in general for trees $(m \times \frac{1}{2}m(m-1))$, excluding m null columns.

The effectiveness of the relaxation procedure is best demonstrated with large-scale networks, which are altogether beyond the computational bounds of rudimentary procedures such as Algorithm 7.3. Table 7.5 summarizes computational data for several problems with the number of vertices

TABLE 7.5   Computational Data for Some Random Networks*

Number of Centers, p	Number of Vertices, m Number of Links, $|A|$	200 305	300 442	400 591	800 1216
1	cpu(s)	2.62	14.67	10.37	69.45
	CP_f(rows × columns)	3×2	5×14	3×2	6×27
	CPs	5	10	5	11
2	cpu(s)	4.31	16.14	50.53	211.07
	CP_f(rows × columns)	5×3	7×17	8×31	12×82
	CPs	5	8	12	18
3	cpu(s)	2.8	5.7	54.71	
	CP_f(rows × columns)	6×4	7×12	11×58	
	CPs	2	3	8	
4	cpu(s)	6.75		83.54	
	CP_f(rows × columns)	8×6		15×112	
	CPs	4		8	

*1. The program was written in FORTRAN IV, compiled under level 4.1 and run on a CDC-6600 in an interactive mode.

2. cpu times are incremental.

3. CP_f indicates the size of the final CP matrix excluding null centers and duplicate columns.

4. CPs indicates the number of CPs solved for the current value of p. These were solved manually by inspection.

ranging from 200 to 800. The examples were constructed by generating random transit-like networks, with the probability of link length decreasing as a function of link length. To avoid the large fixed cost of computing D, minimum path distances were computed as needed.

7.4. EXTENSIONS TO OTHER CENTER PROBLEMS

So far we have focused our discussion of complexity and efficiency in minimax network location on the class of absolute center problems denoted as $A/V/p/N$ in the classification scheme of Section 7.1. We now consider the remaining varieties of center problems introduced in that section.

Recalling the results concerning the complexity of absolute center problems from Section 7.2, we note first that here too for the simplest cases of single centers of a tree, $O(m)$ procedures are available. Specifically, Algorithm 7.1 solves $A/A/1/T$ and a variant thereof solves $V/V/1/T$ and $V/A/1/T$ (Handler, 1973). For $A/A/2/T$ a procedure similar to Algorithm 7.2 also involves $O(m)$ operations (Handler, 1978). $V/V/p/T$ and $V/A/p/T$, $p \geq 2$, are solvable in $O(m \log m)$ time (Frederickson and Johnson, 1983). The best complexity bounds known to date for $A/A/p/T$ are $O((m \log p)^2)$ (Chandrasekaran and Tamir, 1980) and $O(m \log^3 m)$ (Megiddo and Tamir, 1983).

Turning now to cyclic networks, the single center problems $V/V/1/N$ and $V/A/1/N$ are essentially solved once the shortest distance matrix is available, so that these can be processed in $O(m^3)$ time. Frank's (1967) procedure for $A/A/1/N$ appears also to be bounded by a low order polynomial in p. Finally, the general multicenter problems $A/A/p/N$, $V/V/p/N$, $V/A/p/N$, and all the inverse center problems appear to be at least as "hard" as $A/V/p/N$, namely, at least as complex as $\mathcal{NP}$-complete. Specifically, $V/A/p/N$ is $\mathcal{NP}$-complete since the vertex cover problem is a special case and $V/V/p/N$ is $\mathcal{NP}$-complete since the dominating set problem reduces to it (Garey and Johnson, 1979). The continuous problem $A/A/p/N$ is $\mathcal{NP}$-hard (Megiddo and Tamir, 1983; for a discussion of the distinction between $\mathcal{NP}$-completeness and $\mathcal{NP}$-hardness, see Garey and Johnson, 1979). As before, however, these results do not imply that these problems are necessarily difficult to solve in practice. The relaxation strategy of the previous section can be modified to provide effective algorithms for these problems, which we consider in turn.

7.4.1. $A/A/p/N$

The continuous p-center problem is perhaps the most challenging of the variety of minimax network location problems. Physically, it represents what is often the most realistic situation while $A/V/p/N$ is some discretized approximation of it. One way of approaching this problem is indeed to discretize the set of demand generating points as finely as is desired and then solve as $A/V/p/N$. Without the relaxation technique, such a scheme becomes unwieldy as the approximation is tightened because of the critical effect of a large number of vertices in other techniques. Before we continue with $A/A/p/N$ we note again that efficient algorithms for $A/A/p/T$ are available (Chandrasekaran and Tamir, 1980; Megiddo and Tamir, 1983). Finally, we note that an exact finite procedure for $A/A/p/N$ has been given by Tamir (1983). While Tamir's result is very important from a theoretical standpoint the algorithm is not necessarily recommended by its author for practical problems. In an exercise at the end of this chapter we suggest the possibility of embedding this algorithm in a relaxation framework.

Consider now the relaxation approach described in the previous section. All along we have been solving relaxed problems, $A/R/p/N$, $R \subseteq V$, as surrogates for $A/V/p/N$. The only conceptual change here is that V is now the infinite set of points in N. The basic strategy remains unaltered.

In Algorithm 7.3, $H(X_p)$ is now changed to $H'(X_p)$ defined as

$$H'(X_p) = \max_{y \in N} D(y, X_p) \tag{7.4.1}$$

and vertex-to-enter is changed to *point-to-enter* (pte).

Although $A/A/p/N$ utilizes to the fullest extent the capabilities of the relaxation method and provides the most striking context of its application, the algorithm nevertheless remains deficient in its convergence properties when applied to $A/A/p/N$. We have seen that for $A/V/p/N$ the algorithm converges finitely to an optimal solution. If the algorithm converges finitely for $A/A/p/N$, then the solution is optimal. However, the algorithm may not be finite for $A/A/p/N$.

The following example illustrates this. Consider the network in Figure 7.6 composed of a single cycle, and solve the problem $A/A/1/N$. Then application of the algorithm beginning at some arbitrary point, a, will lead to an infinitely convergent series of intermediate solutions. The labels $a, b, c, \ldots$ in Figure 7.6 represent successive additions to R as determined by (7.4.1). Successive iterations of the algorithm yield intermediate results as shown in Table 7.6.

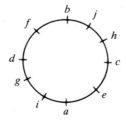

Figure 7.6. A single cycle network to illustrate $A/A/1/N$.

TABLE 7.6 Intermediate Results for $A/A/1/N$ in the Single Cycle Network Example

R	$\hat{X}_1$	$2\hat{d}$	$2H'(\hat{X}_1)$
a	a	0	1
a,b	d	$1/2$	1
a,b,c	c	$1/2$	1
a,b,c,d	f	$3/4$	1
a,b,c,d,e	e	$3/4$	1
a,b,c,d,e,f	h	$3/4$	1
a,b,c,d,e,f,g	g	$3/4$	1
a,b,c,d,e,f,g,h	j	$7/8$	1
etc.			

In this example, of course, any point on the cycle is a bona fide single center. However, the algorithm has difficulty in recognizing optimality. It will only do so in a limiting sense.

When the algorithm fails to terminate finitely, it is possible that the limiting solution will not be optimal. To illustrate this consider the problem of locating continuous 2-centers on a graph composed of a single link of length 1, as in Figure 7.7. Denote points on the line by their distance from the left end-point. Solving first for $p = 1$, we find the optimal solution at $\frac{1}{2}$. The quantities at the end of this stage are: $R = \{0, 1\}$, $d = \frac{1}{2}$, $C\{R : d\} = \{0, 1\}$, $X_1^* = \frac{1}{2}$. Solving now for $p = 2$, we initiate the search with the quantities $\hat{X}_2 = \{0, 1\}$, $d = 0$, $H'(\hat{X}_2) = \frac{1}{2}$, pte $= \frac{1}{2}$, $R = \{0, \frac{1}{2}, 1\}$, $C\{R : \frac{1}{2}\} = \{0, \frac{1}{4}, \frac{1}{2}, \frac{3}{4}, 1\}$, which yields the CP matrix and radii:

$$
\begin{array}{c}
0 \\
\frac{1}{2} \\
1
\end{array}
\left[
\begin{array}{ccccc}
1 & 1 & & & \\
 & 1 & 1 & 1 & \\
 & & & 1 & 1
\end{array}
\right]
$$

$$
d_c \quad [\, 0 \quad \tfrac{1}{4} \quad 0 \quad \tfrac{1}{4} \quad 0 \,]
$$

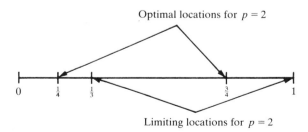

Optimal locations for $p = 2$

Limiting locations for $p = 2$

Figure 7.7. A single link network to illustrate that Algorithm 7.5 will *not* converge to optimal solution.

The CP contains three possible solutions, of which we choose $\hat{X}_2 = \{\frac{1}{4}, 1\}$, $\hat{d} = \frac{1}{4}$, $H'(\hat{X}_2) = \frac{3}{8}$, pte $= \frac{5}{8}$, $R = \{0, \frac{1}{2}, \frac{5}{8}, 1\}$, $C\{R : \frac{1}{2}\} = \{0, \frac{1}{4}, \frac{5}{16}, \frac{1}{2}, \frac{9}{16}, \frac{5}{8}, \frac{3}{4}, \frac{13}{16}, 1\}$ which yields the CP matrix and radii:

$$
\begin{array}{c}
0 \\
\frac{1}{2} \\
\frac{5}{8} \\
1
\end{array}
\left[
\begin{array}{ccccccccc}
1 & 1 & 1 & & & & & & \\
 & 1 & 1 & 1 & 1 & & 1 & & \\
 & & 1 & & 1 & 1 & 1 & 1 & \\
 & & & & & & 1 & 1 & 1
\end{array}
\right]
$$

$$
d_c \quad [\, 0 \quad \tfrac{1}{4} \quad \tfrac{5}{16} \quad 0 \quad \tfrac{1}{16} \quad 0 \quad \tfrac{1}{4} \quad \tfrac{3}{16} \quad 0 \,]
$$

Choosing $\hat{X}_2 = \{\frac{5}{16}, 1\}$ we find $\hat{d} = \frac{5}{16}$, $H'(\hat{X}_2) = \frac{11}{32}$, pte $= \frac{21}{32}$. Continuing in this manner, we can obtain an infinite series of solutions as indicated in Table 7.7, where

$$
a_k = \sum_{i=0}^{K-1} \frac{4^i}{4^K} = \frac{1}{3} - \frac{1}{3 \cdot 4^k}, \qquad k \geq 1.
$$

We thus find $\lim_{k \to \infty} a_k = \frac{1}{3}$. The limiting solution $\hat{X}_2 = \{\frac{1}{3}, 1\}$ yields $\hat{d} = \frac{1}{3}$, $H'(\hat{X}_2) = \frac{2}{3}$, pte $= \frac{2}{3}$ while the optimal solution is $X_2^* = (\frac{1}{4}, \frac{3}{4})$.

We have seen an example where the relaxation algorithm applied to $A/A/p/N$ converges infinitely to a suboptimal solution. In conclusion, the relaxation algorithm solves $A/A/p/N$ if it converges finitely. Otherwise, we need to develop a different strategy to solve $A/A/p/N$.

We now present a modified version of Algorithm 7.5 which guarantees convergence to an optimal solution for $A/A/p/N$. This strategy has been developed by Handler and Rozman (1985). The modification is to solve the relaxed problem $A/R/p/N$ optimally for every R. In terms of Algorithm 7.5 this implies a modification of Step 3 to read:

Step 3': Covering problem. Select from $C\{R : d\}$ a set of p candidates centers X_p "covering" all points in R *with minimal d* and go to Step 1. If this is impossible, proceed to Step 4.

TABLE 7.7   Intermediate Results for $A/A/2/N$ in the Single Link Network Example

K	$\hat{X}_2$	$\hat{d}$	pte
0	$\{0, 1\}$	0	$\frac{1}{2}$
1	$\{\frac{1}{4}, 1\}$	$\frac{1}{4}$	$\frac{5}{8}$
2	$\{\frac{5}{16}, 1\}$	$\frac{5}{16}$	$\frac{21}{32}$
3	$\{\frac{21}{64}, 1\}$	$\frac{21}{64}$	$\frac{85}{128}$
$\vdots$	$\vdots$	$\vdots$	$\vdots$
k	$\{a_k, 1\}$	a_k	$2a_{k+1}$

Implementation of the new Step 3' involves, in general, a series of old Step 3s. We begin by identifying, if possible, an arbitrary set $\hat{X}_p$ covering the points in R. We then delete from $C\{R:d\}$ all columns with $d_c \geq d$. We continue in this manner till it is impossible to cover R, so that the last set X_p represents an optimal solution to $A/R/p/N$. With this solution, we proceed to Step 1. It is important to observe, however, that the algorithm continues with the original set of candidate centers $C\{R:d\}$. Finally, we note that Algorithm 7.5 is also modified to compute $H'(X_p)$ and pte as indicated above. The procedure for this is given in Algorithm 7.6 below.

The modified algorithm may be viewed as a generalization of the original algorithm since it can solve not only $A/A/p/N$ but $A/V/p/N$ as well. The latter fact is obvious since in the modified algorithm, Step 3' is merely refined to reduce the degree of freedom in the original Step 3. We now proceed to prove the assertion that the modified algorithm solves $A/A/p/N$.

Let r_p be the p-radius in $A/A/p/N$ and let r_p^K be the p-radius in $A/R/p/N$ where the cardinality of R is K. By r_p^{K+1}, we refer to the p-radius in $A/R'/p/N$ were $R' = R \cup \{y\}$, $y \in N$. We state without proof the fact that the modified relaxation algorithm yields r_p^K at every iteration of Step 3'. The proof of this is similar to the proof of Algorithm 7.5 as given in Theorem 7.3. To prove that $\lim_{K \to \infty} r_p^K = r_p$, we need several lemmas. The first lemma is obvious and is stated without proof.

Lemma 7.1. $r_p^K \leq r_p^{K+1}$ for each K.

Lemma 7.2. The sequence of bounds $\{d^K\}_1^\infty$ in successive iterations of the modified algorithm is a nonincreasing sequence.

Proof. From the algorithm

$$d^{K+1} = \begin{cases} H^{K'}(\hat{X}_n), & \text{if } H^{K'}(\hat{X}_n) < d^K \\ d^K, & \text{otherwise} \end{cases}, \quad k = 0, 1, 2, \ldots$$

$$d^0 = \infty. \quad \square$$

Lemma 7.3. The subsequence of bounds $\{d^K\}_1^\infty$ is bounded from above $d^K \leq d^1 < \infty$, $K = 2, 3, \ldots$

Proof. Initially $d^0 = \infty$ and $d = 0$, so that a pte is introduced to R and $d^1 = H^{1'}(X_p) < \infty$. $\quad \square$

Lemma 7.4. The sequence $\{r_n^K\}_{K=0}^\infty$ is bounded from above.

Proof. From the algorithm $r_n^K \leq d^K$ for each K. Then using Lemmas 7.2 and 7.3, we have $r_n^K \leq d^1 < \infty$. $\quad \square$

Lemma 7.5 follows from Lemmas 7.1 and 7.4.

Lemma 7.5. $\{r_n^K\}_{K=0}^{\infty}$ *is a convergent sequence.*

Lemma 7.6. *At every iteration of the modified algorithm*

$$r_p^K \le r_p \le H^{K\prime}(\hat{X}_p) .$$

Proof. Both inequalities of the expression, $r_p^K \le r_p$ and $r_p \le H^{K\prime}(\hat{X}_p)$, obviously hold. $\square$

Lemma 7.7. $\lim_{K \to \infty} (H^{K\prime}(\hat{X}_p) - r_p^K) = 0$.

Proof. Suppose on the contrary that

$$\lim_{K \to \infty} (H^{K\prime}(X_p) - r_p^K) = \delta > 0 ,$$

and consider the situation arising at each iteration of the algorithm. In Step 3′, a new pte is added to R. Two cases are possible:

1. pte $\in V$;
2. pte $\notin V$.

Clearly, Case 1 can occur only a finite number of times so that for K sufficiently large all pte are of Case 2. We shall now demonstrate by contradiction that Case 2 also can only occur a finite number of times. Assume it can occur an infinite number of times. Consider a generic Case 2 as illustrated in Figure 7.8. The shaded portions represent segments covered by $\hat{X}_p$ within radius r_p^K. The arrows point away from the centers. The point farthest away, pte, is located at the mid-point of line segment AB of at least 2δ in length which represents points outside the radius r_p^K. Since pte is now incorporated into R, it will be covered in all future iterations. The center which covers pte will lie either (a) outside the 2δ interval, or (b) inside it. We now wish to determine the amount of the 2δ interval covered, together with pte, in all future iterations. Denote this quantity by I.

For Case (a): $I \ge \delta$.

For Case (b): $I \ge \min \{\delta, r_p^K\}$.

According to our original supposition, every iteration of the algorithm will

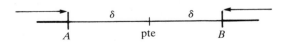

Figure 7.8. Line segment AB to illustrate case 2 for proof of Lemma 7.7.

yield (in Case 2) at least one uncovered interval of size greater than or equal to 2δ. And for each of these intervals a portion $I \geq \min \{\delta, r_p^K\}$ will be covered in future iterations. Summing these, we obtain an infinite network. This contradiction implies that Case 2 can only occur a finite number of times. $\square$

We are now ready to state and prove Theorem 7.5.

Theorem 7.5. *The modified relaxation algorithm converges to an optimal solution in $A/A/p/N$.*

Proof. When convergence is finite, proof of optimality is essentially the same as for $A/V/p/N$ as given in Section 7.3. For infinite convergence, we find from Lemmas 7.5, 7.6, and 7.7

$$\lim_{K \to \infty} H^{K\prime}(\hat{X}_p) = \lim_{K \to \infty} r_p^K = r_p . \quad \square$$

Before proceeding with an example we have yet to resolve one computational issue. The quantity $H'(X_p)$, defined in (7.4.1), is somewhat more difficult to compute than its counterpart $H(X_p)$. We present here a practical procedure for calculating $H'(X_p)$ and pte. The algorithm is presented without proof, the proof being straightforward.

Algorithm 7.6 $(H'(X_p)$ and pte)

Step 1: Compute

$$d_i = d(v_i, X_p) , \qquad i = 1, \ldots, p$$

$$l = H(X_p) = \max \{d_i \mid i = 1, \ldots, m\} .$$

Step 2: Compute

$$I(K, L) = \max_{[i,j] \in A'} \{I(i, j) = \alpha_{ij} + d_i + d_j - 2l\}$$

where A' is the set of arcs not containing $x \in X_p$, in the interior portion of the arcs.

Step 3: Compute

$$H'(X_p) = \begin{cases} l , & \text{if } A' = \emptyset , & \text{no pte} \\ l , & \text{if } I(K, L) \leq 0 , & \text{no pte} \\ l + (I(K, L)/2) , & \text{otherwise} , & \text{pte is } H'(X_p) - d_K \\ & & \text{from } v_K \text{ along } [K, L] . \end{cases}$$

Example 7.3 $(A/A/p/N, p = 1, 2)$. Consider the network in Figure 7.9.

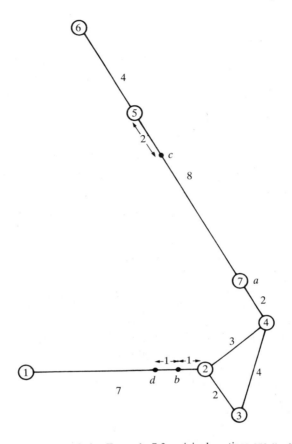

Figure 7.9. Network for Example 7.3, original vertices are v_1–v_6.

The original vertex set of the network consists of six vertices. Candidate centers will be labeled alphabetically and the corresponding columns will also be denoted by a pair i–j indicating the generating pair of vertices.

$p = 1$. Setting initially $R = \{1\}$, we have $\hat{X}_1 = \{1\}$, $\hat{d} = 0$, $H(\hat{X}_1) = 24$ $H'(\hat{X}_1) = 24$, pte $= \{6\}$, and $d = 24$. Then for $R = \{1, 6\}$ we obtain the CP matrix and radii

$$
\begin{array}{c}
1\text{--}6 \\
\begin{array}{cc}
a & 1 \quad 6
\end{array} \\
\begin{array}{c} 1 \\ 2 \end{array}
\left[\begin{array}{ccc}
1 & 1 & \\
1 & & 1
\end{array} \right]
\end{array}
$$

$$
d_c \; [\, 12 \quad 0 \quad 0 \,]
$$

We now obtain $\hat{X}_1 = \{a\}$, $\hat{d} = 12$, $H(\hat{X}_1) = 12$, $H'(\hat{X}_1) = 12$, and $d = 12$.

Having obtained a feasible solution to the global problem, we may now eliminate column a from the CP matrix. The resulting CP matrix is the 2×2 identity matrix and since two columns are needed to solve the CP we have found a solution for $p = 1$, namely $X_1^* = \{a\}$, $r_1 = 12$ (note that this is also a solution to $A/V/1/N$). Proceeding from this identity matrix we continue with the 2-center problem.

$p = 2$. We have $\hat{X}_2 = \{1, 6\}$, $\hat{d} = 0$, $H(\hat{X}_2) = 10$, $H'(\hat{X}_2) = 12$, pte $= \{7\}$, and $d = 12$. Note that the point 7 has now been added to the original vertex set. For $R = \{1, 6, 7\}$, we have the CP matrix and radii:

$$
\begin{array}{c}
\begin{array}{cc} 1\text{-}7 & 6\text{-}7 \\ b & c \quad 1 \quad 6 \quad 7 \end{array} \\
\begin{array}{c} 1 \\ 6 \\ 7 \end{array}
\left[
\begin{array}{ccccc}
1 & & 1 & & \\
 & 1 & & 1 & \\
1 & 1 & & & 1
\end{array}
\right]
\end{array}
$$

$$ d_c \ [\,6 \quad\quad 6 \quad\; 0 \quad 0 \quad 0\,] $$

Solving the CP we find $\hat{X}_2 = \{b, c\}$, $\hat{d} = 6$, $H(\hat{X}_2) = 6$, $H'(\hat{X}_2) = 6$, and $d = 6$. A feasible solution to the original problem is at hand and we may eliminate columns b and c from the CP matrix. The resulting CP matrix is the 3×3 identity matrix which requires three columns for a cover. Thus, we have a solution for $p = 2$, namely $X_2^* = \{b, c\}$ and $r_2 = 6$. (Note that a solution to $A/V/2/N$ is $X_2^* = \{d, 6\}$, $r_2 = 5$.) $\bigcirc$

7.4.2. $V/V/p/N$

A method for determining optimal locations in $V/V/p/N$ due to Toregas, Swan, ReVelle, and Bergman (1971) corresponds to Minieka's scheme for $A/V/p/N$ (Algorithm 7.3) with the dominant set of candidate centers C replaced by the set V. The mid-point property embodied in Corollary 7.1 no longer holds, though centers are now, by definition, restricted to a finite set of points. Indeed, with respect to the rudimentary framework of Algorithm 7.3 for solving $A/V/p/N$, $V/V/p/N$ is by far the easier of the two problems since, in general, $|C| > \binom{m}{2} + m \gg m$. In fact, we shall see that this observation, though intuitively appealing, is quite misleading.

The relaxation approach can be applied here with some modification. Note first that the column elimination scheme utilized in Algorithm 7.4 is no longer applicable since that scheme is inextricably tied up with the mid-point property. Consequently, columns cannot be eliminated, and the full set of m candidate centers must be carried explicitly throughout. Otherwise, the relaxation scheme applies as before and, clearly, finite convergence is guaranteed in this case.

Though the improvement over the rudimentary procedure is not as dramatic as for $A/V/p/N$ and $A/A/p/N$, substantial savings can be expected because of the importance of the number of rows to the solution of CPs. Furthermore, even in the single center case where no CP need be solved, substantial savings are obtained. To illustrate this point consider the example given by Toregas et al. (1971). Table 7.8 reproduces the D matrix for 30 locations in New York State. Consider now the problem of locating a solution VC to $V/V/1/N$. The classical approach is initially to compute D and inspect the matrix for an optimal solution. Employing instead the relaxation technique and beginning arbitrarily with $R = \{1\}$ results in the series of solutions to $V/R/1/N$ shown in Table 7.9, derived by inspection of the relevant columns and rows in Table 7.8. Thus, $VC = 27$ and $l(VC) = 254$ is a solution to $V/V/1/N$. Notice that to arrive at the solution we only require computation of MPT(x), for $x \in \{1, 11, 7, 4, 3, 21, 27\}$, in place of the full D matrix.

Although, as we have seen, $V/V/p/N$ can be profitably solved with the relaxation algorithm, the advantages due to this approach are not quite as dramatic as for $A/V/p/N$ and $A/A/p/N$. This serves to emphasize the special features of the relaxation scheme when applied to these problems. With respect to $V/V/p/N$, the relaxation technique can be viewed as a classical application of relaxation concepts to a minimax problem with corresponding elimination of constraints. But for $A/V/p/N$ and $A/A/p/N$ the technique is ideally suited because the linkage between rows and columns results in *both* row and column eliminations. Thus, problem relaxation here carries the advantages of both relaxation and restriction.

Finally, note the relative computational difficulty for these problems. $V/V/p/N$ can often be the more difficult problem to solve, contrary, perhaps, to intuition.

7.4.3. $V/A/p/N$

Once again, the relaxation approach is well suited to this problem. The procedures outlined for $V/V/p/N$ and $A/A/p/N$ can be readily combined to form a solution strategy for $V/A/p/N$. An important distinction from $A/A/p/N$ is contained in the following theorem.

Theorem 7.6. *The relaxation algorithm, appropriately modified to solve $V/A/p/N$, converges to an optimal solution in a finite number of steps.*

Proof.   An iteration of the algorithm results in one of the following two cases:

1. a new artificial vertex is added to R;
2. at least one nonzero element of the CP matrix is changed to zero.

To prove finite convergence it suffices to show that R has finite maximal

TABLE 7.8 The Minimum Distance Matrix for 30 Locations in New York State (Distances Are in Miles)

	1	2	3	4	5	6	7	8	9	10	11	12	13	14	15	16	17	18	19	20	21	22	23	24	25	26	27	28	29	30
1	0	244	140	128	281	196	181	51	248	167	338	54	203	146	295	211	295	78	169	38	167	112	71	220	157	16	135	7	90	165
2	244	0	158	359	37	111	66	268	60	112	101	278	272	328	51	222	77	200	106	281	332	263	294	33	284	233	109	248	161	164
3	140	158	0	202	194	56	92	170	117	46	215	137	256	170	209	206	160	62	114	177	279	105	136	136	239	129	78	144	92	148
4	128	359	202	0	395	258	294	179	319	248	416	90	331	61	410	339	361	176	290	200	295	106	70	337	285	143	254	293	211	293
5	281	37	194	395	0	145	102	305	275	148	69	317	309	366	19	259	74	236	143	318	369	299	330	70	321	272	254	285	211	201
6	196	111	56	258	145	0	60	229	61	34	159	189	269	226	162	219	104	118	112	233	315	161	192	100	274	185	146	200	198	161
7	181	66	92	294	102	60	0	208	67	47	157	225	262	262	117	175	114	134	59	218	279	197	228	46	237	170	49	185	101	117
8	51	268	170	179	305	229	208	0	275	195	366	105	319	226	162	175	322	108	186	81	315	106	228	242	237	170	159	48	107	175
9	248	60	117	319	275	61	67	275	0	87	111	152	66	287	319	180	56	175	126	285	346	222	253	60	304	41	116	252	128	184
10	167	112	46	248	148	34	47	195	87	0	185	179	235	216	88	185	130	93	79	204	281	151	182	90	240	156	57	171	171	127
11	338	101	215	416	69	159	157	366	111	185	0	348	373	381	329	323	55	273	207	375	433	316	351	385	211	327	206	342	258	265
12	54	278	137	90	317	189	225	105	152	179	348	0	257	95	323	250	293	86	205	65	221	58	20	254	46	69	169	61	126	204
13	203	272	256	331	309	269	262	319	66	235	373	257	0	349	323	66	93	179	157	332	383	314	345	239	303	161	178	200	219	108
14	146	328	170	61	366	226	262	226	287	216	381	95	349	0	379	343	326	179	284	144	60	69	84	306	46	193	248	151	219	297
15	295	51	209	410	19	162	117	162	319	88	329	323	323	379	0	273	289	251	157	332	313	69	75	84	335	161	160	299	212	215
16	211	222	206	339	259	219	175	175	180	185	323	250	66	343	273	0	289	86	205	65	126	69	345	189	92	128	206	342	129	58
17	295	77	160	361	74	104	114	322	56	130	55	293	93	326	289	289	0	218	207	332	261	293	270	106	351	92	163	61	215	231
18	78	200	62	176	236	118	134	108	175	93	273	86	179	179	251	86	218	0	130	118	124	124	106	178	194	156	94	200	64	146
19	169	106	114	290	143	112	59	186	126	79	207	205	157	284	157	205	207	130	0	206	219	123	225	73	180	79	36	171	79	60
20	38	281	177	200	318	233	218	81	285	204	375	65	332	144	332	65	332	118	206	0	191	123	76	257	187	52	172	37	127	202
21	167	332	279	295	369	315	279	315	346	281	433	221	383	60	313	126	261	124	219	191	0	279	238	299	52	157	230	162	187	168
22	112	263	105	106	299	161	197	106	222	151	316	58	314	69	69	69	293	124	123	123	279	0	60	241	269	127	183	119	164	247
23	71	294	136	70	330	192	228	228	253	182	351	20	345	84	75	345	270	106	225	76	238	60	0	272	228	86	189	76	146	224
24	220	33	136	337	70	100	46	242	60	90	385	254	239	306	84	189	106	178	73	257	299	241	272	0	251	209	85	224	135	131
25	157	284	239	285	321	274	237	237	304	240	211	46	303	46	335	92	351	194	180	187	52	269	228	251	0	147	188	154	135	120
26	16	233	129	143	272	185	170	170	41	156	327	69	161	193	161	128	92	156	79	52	157	127	86	209	147	0	124	15	77	152
27	135	109	78	254	254	146	49	159	116	57	206	169	178	248	160	206	163	94	36	172	230	183	189	85	188	124	0	139	52	70
28	7	248	144	293	285	200	185	48	252	171	342	61	200	151	299	342	61	200	171	37	162	119	76	224	154	15	139	0	92	167
29	90	161	92	211	211	198	101	107	128	171	258	126	219	219	212	129	215	64	79	127	187	164	146	135	135	77	52	92	0	83
30	165	164	148	293	201	161	117	175	184	127	265	204	108	297	215	58	231	146	60	202	168	247	224	131	120	152	70	167	83	0

TABLE 7.9   Intermediate Solutions for $V/V/1/N$ Using the Relaxation Technique in the New York State Example

R	VC	$\hat{d}$	$H(VC) = d(VC, v)$
1	1	0	$338 = d(1, 11)$
1, 11	7	181	$294 = d(7, 4)$
1, 11, 4	3	215	$279 = d(3, 21)$
1, 11, 4, 21	27	254	254

cardinality. According to the algorithm, $R \subseteq Q$ where

$$Q = \{q \in N: D(q, X_p) = H'(X_p) \text{ for some } X_p \subseteq V\} \ .$$

Since m, the cardinality of V, is finite so is $|Q|$ and therefore convergence is guaranteed. $\square$

7.4.4.   Inverse Center Problems

Consider first $A/V/\lambda^{-1}/N$ and let h_λ denote the minimal number of centers needed to insure a maximum distance not exceeding λ from any vertex to a nearest center. The relationship between h_λ and the solution, r_p, to $A/V/p/N$ is illustrated in Figure 7.10.

Solving $A/V/\lambda^{-1}/N$ requires minor and generally simplifying modifications to any procedure that solves $A/V/p/N$. Thus, Algorithms 7.3 or 7.4 can be used on a "one-shot" basis, solving just one CP. As before, however, the relaxation technique is more efficient. Setting $d = \lambda$ from the outset and ignoring intermediate updates of X_p where $h > p$, Algorithm 7.5 will yield $h_\lambda = h$ when $H(\hat{X}_h) = \lambda$ for the first time.

Extensions to the cases $A/A/\lambda^{-1}/N$, $V/V/\lambda^{-1}/N$, and $V/A/\lambda^{-1}/N$ are straightforward.

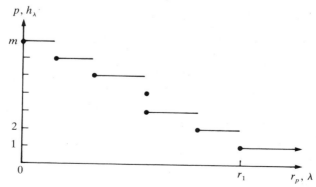

Figure 7.10. Relationship between $A/V/p/N$ and $A/V/\lambda^{-1}/N$; ● represents solution to $A/V/p/N$; — represents solution to $A/V/\lambda^{-1}/N$.

ACKNOWLEDGMENTS

Some of the figures used in this chapter first appeared in Handler and Mirchandani (1979). MIT Press has kindly allowed their use here. The cooperation of Dr. Yishai Feldman in generating the computational data of Table 7.5 is gratefully acknowledged.

EXERCISES

7.1 Continue the solution of $A/V/p/T$ in Example 7.1 for $p = 8, 9, 10$.

7.2 Solve $A/A/2/N$ for the network in Figure 7.7 using Algorithm 7.5 with Step 3' and Algorithm 7.6.

7.3 Describe a network N such that in solving $A/V/p/N$ we find $r_1 = r_p$, $p = 2, \ldots, (m - 1)$.

7.4 Consider the weighted absolute p-center problem obtained by reformulating (7.1.2) as

$$H(X_p) = \max_{y \in V} D(y, X_p) w(y)$$

where $w(y)$ is a positive weight associated with vertex y.

   (a) Describe some practical scenarios that may require such a weighted formulation. (Note that at first glance the weights appear to be irrelevant in a minimax emergency service model.)

   (b) Describe the changes to be made in the relaxation algorithm for $A/V/p/N$ in order to solve the weighted version.

7.5 Consider the absolute p-center problem based on a directed network. Distinguish between "in-centers" (e.g., air-raid shelters) and "out-centers" (e.g., ambulance stations).

   (a) Prove that the search for candidate centers may be restricted to the vertices of the network.

   (b) Construct a relaxation algorithm for this problem. (Hint: The algorithm is similar to the algorithm described for one of the p-center problems.)

7.6 (Research Problem) Apply relaxation ideas to p-center problems in the plane, based on Euclidean and rectilinear distance measures. Compare these to the network based problem.

7.7 (Research Problem) Devise a practical finite algorithm for $A/A/p/N$ by applying relaxation ideas to the algorithm presented by Tamir (1983).

REFERENCES

Balas, E. (1980). "Cutting Planes from Conditional Bounds: A New Approach to Set Covering." *Mathematical Programming* **12**, 19–36.

Chandrasekaran, R., and A. Tamir (1980). "An $O((n \lg p)^2)$ Algorithm for the Continuous *p*-Center Problem on a Tree." *SIAM Journal on Algebraic Discrete Methods* **1**, 370–375.

Christofides, N., and S. Korman (1975). "A Computational Survey of Methods for the Set Covering Problem." *Management Science* **21**, 591–599.

Christofides, N., and R. Viola (1971). "The Optimum Location of Multi-Centers on a Graph." *Operational Research Quarterly* **22**, 145–154.

Dijkstra, E. W. (1959). "A Note on Two Problems in Connexion with Graphs." *Numerische Mathematik* **1**, 269–271.

Dreyfus, S. E. (1969). "An Appraisal of Some Shortest-Path Algorithms." *Operations Research* **17**, 395–412.

Frank, H. (1967). "A Note on a Graph Theoretic Game of Hakimi's." *Operations Research* **15**, 567–570.

Frederickson, G. N., and D. B. Johnson (1983). "Finding *k*-th Paths and *p*-Centers by Generating and Searching Good Data Structures." *Journal of Algorithms* **4**, 61–80.

Garey, M. R., and D. S. Johnson (1979). *Computers and Intractability—A Guide to the Theory of $\mathcal{NP}$-Completeness*. Freeman, San Francisco, California.

Garfinkel, R. S., and G. L. Nemhauser (1972). *Integer Programming*. Wiley, New York.

Garfinkel, R. S., A. W. Neebe, and M. R. Rao (1977). "The *m*-Center Problem: Minimax Facility Location." *Management Science* **23**, 1133–1142.

Hakimi, S. L. (1964). "Optimum Locations of Switching Centers and the Absolute Centers and Medians of a Graph." *Operations Research* **12**, 450–459.

Hakimi, S. L. (1965). "Optimum Distribution of Switching Centers in a Communication Network and Some Related Graph Theoretic Problems." *Operations Research* **13**, 462–475.

Hakimi, S. L., E. F. Schmeichel, and J. G. Pierce (1978). "On *p*-Centers in Networks." *Transportation Science* **12**, 1–15.

Halpern, J., and O. Maimon (1982). "Algorithms for the *m*-Center Problems: A Survey." *European Journal of Operational Research* **10**, 90–99.

Handler, G. Y. (1973). "Minimax Location of a Facility in an Undirected Tree Graph." *Transportation Science* **7**, 287–293.

Handler, G. Y. (1978). "Finding Two-Centers of a Tree: The Continuous Case." *Transportation Science* **12**, 93–106.

Handler, G. Y., and P. B. Mirchandani (1979). *Location in Networks: Theory and Algorithms*. MIT Press, Cambridge, Massachusetts.

Handler, G. Y., and M. Rozman (1985). "The Continuous *m*-Center Problem on a Network." *Networks* **15**, 191–204.

Hu, T. C. (1971). "Some Problems in Discrete Optimization." *Mathematical Programming* **1**, 102–112.

Kariv, O., and S. L. Hakimi (1979). "An Algorithmic Approach to Network Location Problems. Part 1. The *P*-Centers." *SIAM Journal on Applied Mathematics* **37**, 539–560.

Megiddo, N., and A. Tamir (1983). "New Results on *p*-Center Problems." *SIAM Journal on Computing* **12**, 751–758.

Minieka, E. (1970). "The *m*-Center Problem." *SIAM Review* **12**, 138–139.

Tamir, A. (1983). *A Finite Algorithm for the Continuous Center Location Problem on a Graph.* Tel Aviv University, Tel Aviv, Israel.

Tansel, B. C., R. L. Francis, and T. J. Lowe (1983). "Location on Networks: A Survey." *Management Science* **29**, 482–511.

Toregas, C., R. Swan, C. ReVelle, and L. Bergman (1971). "The Location of Emergency Service Facilities." *Operations Research* **19**, 1366–1373.

8

Duality: Covering and Constraining p-Center Problems on Trees

B. C. Tansel
Department of Industrial Engineering
Bilkent University
Bilkent, Ankara, Turkey

Richard L. Francis
Department of Industrial and Systems Engineering
University of Florida
Gainesville, Florida

T. J. Lowe
College of Business Administration
University of Iowa
Iowa City, Iowa

8.1. INTRODUCTION

In this chapter we study the problem of determining the locations of a number of identical "service" centers on a network in the presence of constraints on the center locations. Throughout this chapter we use the word "center" as a synonym for "facility." The centers provide a service to demand points located at the nodes of the network. Given the locations of service centers, each demand point obtains service from the closest (in terms of distance or travel time) service center. Each demand point has a service "loss" (or disutility) function which is continuous and strictly increasing and whose argument is the distance (or travel time) between the demand point and the closest center. An example of such a loss function is given by Halpern (1979) in the context of percentage loss of property as a function of response time, by fire-fighting equipment, to the site of a fire. The object is to locate the centers on the network such that the maximum of the losses is minimized.

We are concerned with the case of locating a total of p such service centers, where p is a parameter in the problem. The constraints on center locations specify a nonnegative upper bound on the distance (or travel time) between each demand point and its nearest center. Thus, each constraint in effect specifies a maximum tolerable loss (as measured by the loss function) that can be incurred by a demand point. Similarly, since each loss function is strictly increasing, by knowing the maximum tolerable loss for a given demand point, it is easy to convert this value to a distance constraint. We call this problem the *monotonic, distance-constrained, p-center problem*. For convenience, we will refer to this problem as (P-C).

We restrict our analysis to the case where the underlying network is a tree network. A tree network is a network where there is only one (shortest) path among the arcs of the network between any two points on the network.

Our work is related to that in Chapter 7 in that we solve a p-center problem on a tree network by solving a sequence of covering problems. However, because our network is a tree we can dispense with the use of mathematical programming, and work directly with the tree network. By so doing we can offer efficient computational approaches, and include both distance constraints and nonlinear loss functions which are absent in Chapter 7. In addition, we concentrate on the use of duality, and place considerable emphasis on giving a physical interpretation to the dual of our p-center problem.

An example of a facility location problem on a transport network with tree structure is the regional planning problem studied by Patel (1979). Patel describes the use of operations research techniques in planning road networks and social service centers to provide health, educational, and other services, for the Dharampur area in India. Given that there was a fixed regional planning budget for roads and service centers, a "minimum cost" (tree) road network was specified so that a larger portion of the budget would be available for the establishment of the service centers. Tree-like road networks are often encountered in sparsely occupied regions. Also they appear when introducing "cycles" is very expensive; in the United States, approximately one half of the states have the property that the portion of the Interstate Highway System enclosed within the state's borders exhibits a tree network structure. Simple distribution systems with a single distribution center at the "hub" can often be modeled as star-like trees. Related examples are the "hub and spoke" route structures of two major US airlines with Atlanta as the hub in one case and Chicago as the hub in the other case.

Another example of travel on a tree-like transport network is by boat on a river system and its tributaries. It is usually the case that the underlying links of the river system form a tree network.

We now give a brief overview of the remainder of the chapter. In Section 8.2, we formally define (P-C) and a problem which is dual to (P-C), which we denote as (DP-C). In addition, we state a cover problem $(C(r))$ and a problem which is dual to $(C(r))$, which we denote as $(DC(r))$. The covering problem $(C(r))$ is to locate the minimum number of centers such that the loss function value of each demand point does not exceed the parameter r. The solution to (P-C) is intimately related to the solution of $(C(r))$. Further, the two dual problems (DP-C) and $(DC(r))$ are not only interesting problems in their own right, but also provide input for the solution of the primal problems. At the end of Section 8.2 we provide a brief survey of relevant literature and give a numerical example.

In Section 8.3, we give interpretations of the four problems mentioned above in an "attacker-defender" context.

In Section 8.4, we study the covering problem and present an algorithm, COVER, for solving it. The covering algorithm provides the basis of our solution procedure to (P-C) and (DP-C) and yields a constructive approach for proving strong duality results, that is, the objective values at optimality of the dual and primal problem are equal. We also present an algorithm, DUALOPT, which provides a constructive proof of a strong duality theorem, while solving the dual problem (DP-C). In addition, in Section 8.4 we give an algorithm, PRIMOPT, which solves (P-C). We present necessary analysis in Section 8.5. In Section 8.6, we provide supplementary results for evaluating certain inverse functions used in DUALOPT.

8.2. PROBLEM STATEMENTS AND RELATED LITERATURE

Given a finite undirected tree network with positive arc lengths, denote by T an imbedding of the network, defined by Dearing and Francis (1974). An example of an imbedded network is a road network. For any two points $x, y \in T$, let $d(x, y)$ denote the shortest-path distance between x and y; $d(x, y)$ has the following metric properties: $d(x, y) \geq 0$; $d(x, y) = 0$ if and only if $x = y$; $d(x, y) = d(y, x)$; $d(x, y) \leq d(x, z) + d(z, y)$ for every $x, y, z \in T$.

As a convenience, we summarize the notation and definitions to follow in the glossary given in Table 8.1. Let $V = \{v_1, \ldots, v_m\}$ denote the set of

TABLE 8.1   Glossary

T	imbedding of given tree network
$V = \{v_1, \ldots, v_m\}$	distinct node locations of "demand points" or "forces"
$M = \{1, 2, \ldots, m\}$	index set of node locations
$X = \{x_1, \ldots, x_p\}$	a p-center, $1 \le p \le m$, with $X \subset T$
$D(X, v_i) = \min \{(x, v_i): x \in X\}$	distance between v_i and its nearest center
$\delta_i = \max \{d(x, v_i): x \in T\},\ i \in M$	distance between v_i and farthest point in T
$\{u_i: i \in M\}$	given positive numbers, "upper bounds," $u_i \le \delta_i,\ i \in M$
f_i	strictly increasing and continuous "loss" function with domain $[0, \delta_i]$, $i \in M$ (indexing convention: for $i < j$, $f_i(u_i) \le f_j(u_j)$)
K	a "dual threat," any nonempty subset of M
$f(X : K) = \max \{f_i(D(X, v_i)): i \in K\}$	maximum loss for X given K
$S_p(K) = \{X: X \subset T,\ |X| = p,\ D(X, v_i) \le u_i,\ i \in K\}$	set of feasible p-centers, given K
$r_p(K) = \min \{f(X : K): X \in S_p(K)\}$	minimax loss given K
$f(X) = f(X : M),\ S_p = S_p(M),\ r_p = r_p(M)$	
$\beta_{ij} = r_1(\{i, j\}),\ 1 \le i < j \le m$ (with $\beta_{ij} \equiv \infty$ if $S_1(\{i, j\}) = \emptyset$)	
$\alpha(K) = \max \{f_i(0): i \in K\},$ $\alpha = \max \{f_i(0): i = 1, \ldots, m\}$	
$\beta(K) = \min \{\beta_{ij}: i, j \in K,\ i < j\},$ $\beta = \max \{\beta_{ij}: 1 \le i < j \le m\}$	
$g(K) = \max \{\alpha(K), \beta(K)\}$	
C_q	collection of all subsets of N with cardinality at least q, $2 \le q \le m$

distinct node locations of "demand points" or "forces." Let $M = \{1, 2, \ldots, m\}$ denote the index set of node locations. For $1 \le p \le m$, let $X = \{x_1, \ldots, x_p\}$ denote a p-center, with $X \subset T$. For each $v_i \in V$ and p-center X, define $D(X, v_i) = \min \{d(x, v_i): x \in X\}$, the distance between v_i and its nearest center. For $i \in M$, define $\delta_i = \max \{d(x, v_i): x \in T\}$, the distance between v_i and any farthest point in T. We are given a set of positive numbers $\{u_i: i \in M\}$, "upper bounds," with $u_i \le \delta_i,\ i \in M$. (The distance constraints require that the closest center be within u_i of v_i, $i = 1, \ldots, m$.) Associated with each demand point v_i is a given, strictly increasing and continuous (monotonic) "loss" function f_i with domain $[0, \delta_i]$, $i \in M$. (As an indexing convention, for $i < j$ we assume, without loss of generality, that $f_i(u_i) \le f_j(u_j)$.) Each loss function f_i is a function of the distance, $D(X, v_i)$, between v_i and a closest center from among the p-centers in $X = \{x_1, \ldots, x_p\}$. We will find it convenient to pose problems on subsets of the demand points, and so with K denoting any given nonempty subset of M, $S_p(K)$ is a set of p-centers which satisfy the distance constraints for K; that is, $S_p(K) = \{X: X \subset T,\ |X| = p,\ D(X, v_i) \le u_i,\ i \in K\}$. Likewise, we define $f(X : K) = \max \{f_i(D(X, v_i)): i \in K\}$ so that given a p-center X,

$f(X:K)$ measures the maximum loss over K. (To motivate the dual problems, we shall also refer to K as a *threat*.) Likewise, $r_p(K) = \min\{f(X:K): X \in S_p(K)\}$ is the minimax loss given K. For convenience, when $K = M$, we let $f(X) = f(X:M)$, $S_p = S_p(M)$, and $r_p = r_p(M)$. The *p-center problem* is to find a p-center X^* for which $f(X^*) = r_p$, with $X^* \in S_p$.

A restatement of the p-center problem appears in the upper left-hand corner of Table 8.2. In the upper right-hand corner of Table 8.2 we state the *covering problem*, C(r) (as we will show soon, C(r) is intimately related to the p-center problem). In the *covering problem*, a maximum loss value, say r, is fixed. The problem is to find the fewest number of centers such that the loss function value of each demand point v_i does not exceed r and that the distance constraints are satisfied. The problems in the lower portion of Table 8.2 are dual problems which we will describe shortly. We give an extensive interpretation of the dual problems in Section 8.3.

To describe the dual problems of Table 8.2, we define $\beta_{ij} = r_1(\{i, j\})$ for $1 \le i \le j \le m$. Note that β_{ij} is the minimax loss for the 1-center problem with only two demand points, v_i and v_j. If $S_1(\{i, j\}) = \emptyset$, that is, if it is the case that no point x in T is feasible in the sense of satisfying the distance constraints $d(x, v_i) \le u_i$ and $d(x, v_j) \le u_j$, we let $\beta_{ij} \equiv \infty$. For any dual threat K, we define $\alpha(K) = \max\{f_i(0): i \in K\}$, $\beta(K) = \min\{\beta_{ij}: i, j \in K, i < j\}$, and $g(K) = \max\{\alpha(K), \beta(K)\}$. We let $\alpha = \max\{f_i(0): i = 1, \ldots, m\}$, $\beta = \max\{\beta_{ij}: 1 \le i < j \le m\}$, and denote by C_q the collection of all subsets of M with cardinality at least q, $2 \le q \le m$.

Table 8.2 states the two pairs of primal and dual problems of interest. The dual of the p-center problem (P-C) is the problem we call the *dual threat problem*, denoted by (DP-C). Likewise the covering problem, C(r), has as its dual DC(r), which we call the *dual divergence problem*. For fixed p, the object of (DP-C) is to find a subset $K^* \subset M$, $K^* \in C_{p+1}$ (i.e., $|K^*| \ge p + 1$) such that $g(K^*) \ge g(K)$ for all $K \subset C_{p+1}$, where g evaluated on any subset K of M is the larger of $\alpha(K)$, the maximum $f_i(0)$ over K, and $\beta(K)$, the minimum β_{ij} over distinct i, j in K. The object of (DC(r)) is to find a subset $U^* \subset M$, $g(U^*) > r$ such that $|U^*| \ge |U|$ for all $U \subset M$ where $g(U) > r$. Thus in each pair of dual problems, the primal problem is a minimization problem and the dual problem is a maximization problem.

TABLE 8.2 Summary of Primal-Dual Problems

Problems	Loss Measures	Cardinality Measures
Primal	(P-C): p-center problem $r_p = \min\{f(X): X \in S_p\}$	(C(r)): covering problem $s(r) = \min\{|X|: f(X) \le r\}$, $D(X, v_i) \le u_i, i \in M\}$ $(\alpha \le r < r_1)$
Dual	(DP-C): dual threat problem $\bar{r}_p = \max\{g(K): K \in C_{p+1}\}$	(DC(r)): dual divergence problem $\bar{s}(r) = \max\{|U|: g(U) > r, U \subset M\}$ $(\alpha \le r < r_1)$

Subsequently, for each pair of problems we prove a weak duality theorem (WDT), which asserts that any primal objective function value is at least as large as any dual objective function value. We also prove a strong duality theorem (SDT) for each pair, which asserts that optimal objective function values are equal. We remark that only the strong duality theorems require the assumption that the given network is a tree. In effect, network cycles may create a "duality gap."

We now discuss related literature. With three exceptions, Dearing (1977), Francis (1977), and Tansel, Francis, Lowe, and Chen (1982), each function f_i is given in this literature by $f_i(y) = w_i y$, where w_i is a positive "weight." When w_i is taken to be 1 for each i, we refer to the corresponding problem as the _unweighted problem_.

Apparently, the first center type problem on a general network was formulated by Hakimi (1964), who considered a 1-center problem and suggested a solution procedure based on evaluating all local minima on every arc. The p-center problem ($p \geq 2$) on a network was formulated by Hakimi (1965). Minieka (1970) suggested solving the _p_-center problem on a general network by solving a finite series of set covering problems.

Handler (1978) provided an $O(m)$ algorithm for the unweighted 2-center problem. His procedure is based upon the 1-center procedure given by Handler (1973). Hakimi, Schmeichel, and Pierce (1978) presented a procedure for solving the unweighted _p_-center problem; Kariv and Hakimi (1979) gave a computationally more efficient procedure for the weighted problem.

Interesting work on various versions of the unweighted and weighted _p_-center problem can be found in Chandrasekaran and Daughety (1981) and Chandrasekaran and Tamir (1980, 1982). These authors present polynomially bounded algorithms for solving not only the weighted _p_-center problem, but also the problem where the centers are restricted to a subset of the tree. In addition, the authors efficiently solve the "continuous" _p_-center problem (each point of the entire network must be covered).

Kolen (1980) studied a _p_-center version of the round-trip problem given by Chan and Francis (1976), extending directly the methodology presented by Tansel et al. (1982) (in the absence of distance constraints).

The _p_-center problem on a general network was shown to be $\mathcal{NP}$-hard by Hsu and Nemhauser (1979) and Kariv and Hakimi (1979). Due in part to the computational complexity of location problems on general networks, a great deal of attention has been given to the special case of a tree network with $p = 1$. For a discussion, see Dearing (1977), Dearing and Francis (1974), Dearing, Francis, and Lowe (1976), Francis (1977), Goldman (1972), Handler (1973), and Lin (1975).

Duality relationships for location problems on trees are given by Meir and Moon (1975) and Cockayne, Hedetniemi, and Slater (1979). The strong duality results given in this chapter can be established by using the known graph theory results of Cockayne et al. or Gavril (1972). Shier (1977) discovered a duality relationship between the continuous unweighted _p_-

center problem and $p + 1$ point "dispersement" problem, and provided a procedure for solving the 2 and 3 point dispersement problems. Chandrasekaran and Tamir (1982) studied the duality relationship between the linear p-center problem (either centers or demands are restricted to finite subsets of the tree) and a $p + 1$ point dispersement problem. For an extensive discussion of the p-center problem on networks (as well as other network location problems) see Tansel, Francis, and Lowe (1983a,b). In addition, see Chapter 7.

Example 8.1. We now give an example of a monotonic p-center problem. Consider the tree network and loss function data given in Figure 8.1. The tree has six nodes and the loss function for node v_i, $i = 1, \ldots, 6$ is given by $f_i(y) = w_i(y + h_i)^2$ for $y \in [0, u_i]$. Note that there are explicit distance constraint upper bounds for nodes v_1 and v_2 ($i_1 = 15$ and $u_2 = 20$), but that $u_i = \delta_i$ for $i = 3, 4, 5,$ and 6. Clearly the loss functions are strictly increasing in this example.

Figure 8.2 illustrates the β_{ij} values for this example along with the computation of $f_i(0)$, $i = 1, \ldots, 6$. In Section 8.6 of this chapter, we provide a means for computing the β_{ij} in general. The numbers in Figure 8.2 can be verified using the computational procedures of Section 8.6. Here, it suffices to point out that β_{ij} is the minimax loss of a 1-center problem involving only two nodes, v_i and v_j, and thus β_{ij} is the minimum value of the function $\max \{ f_i d(x, v_i)), f_j(d(x, v_j)) \}$ over all x feasible for the constraints $d(x, v_i) \le u_i$ and $d(x, v_j) \le u_j$. Of course, if no such feasible x exists, then β_{ij} is set equal to infinity. On this latter point, note that $\beta_{12} = \infty$; the reason is that the upper bounds $u_1 = 15$ and $u_2 = 20$ do not permit any feasible location for a single center to service nodes v_1 and v_2 (i.e., $S_1(\{1, 2\}) = \emptyset$ since the distance between v_1 and v_2 is 50).

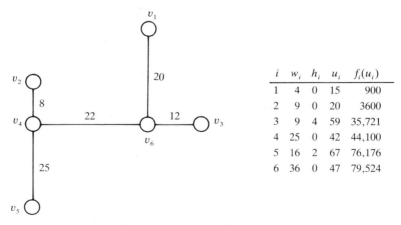

i	w_i	h_i	u_i	$f_i(u_i)$
1	4	0	15	900
2	9	0	20	3600
3	9	4	59	35,721
4	25	0	42	44,100
5	16	2	67	76,176
6	36	0	47	79,524

Figure 8.1. Data for Example 8.1.

	2	3	4	5	6
1	∞	3249	18,225	46,656	900
2		5184	225	3600	3600
3			455,625	11,664	784
4				3600	3600
5					13,829.76

i	$f_i(0)$
1	0
2	0
3	144
4	0
5	64
6	0

Figure 8.2. The β_{ij} and $f_i(0)$ for Example 8.1.

Figure 8.3 is a graphical representation (dual graph) of the data in Figure 8.2. The nodes in the dual graph correspond to the nodes of the tree where demands are located. The number on each arc $[i, j]$ is β_{ij}. The number in the square next to node v_i gives $f_i(0)$ for each i. We present the dual graph since it provides a pictorial representation of the dual problem data. Figure 8.3 illustrates the data in Figure 8.2.

We now discuss the dual threat problem (D-C) for this example. The example is small enough for (DP-C) to be solved by inspection. We shall later present an algorithm in Section 8.4 to solve (DP-C) for any p. First we note that the largest $f_i(0)$ (i.e., $f_3(0) = 144$) is strictly less than the smallest β_{ij} (i.e., $\beta_{24} = 225$). Thus, for this example $\alpha(K) < \beta(K)$ for any dual threat K and so $\alpha(K)$ can be ignored in computing $g(K)$. With $p = 1$ it is clear that the optimal threat is $\{1, 2\}$ since $\beta_{12} = \infty$. In fact, $\{1, 2\}$ is the unique optimal solution to (DP-C) for $p = 1$ since all other β_{ij} values are finite. Thus we have $\bar{r}_1 = \infty$.

For $p = 2$, each of the threats $\{1, 2, 5\}$, $\{1, 4, 5\}$, $\{2, 5, 6\}$, $\{2, 3, 5\}$, $\{3, 4, 5\}$, and $\{4, 5, 6\}$ is optimal. For each of these threats it can be verified that the associated $g(K)$ value is 3600. For example, for $\{1, 2, 5\}$ we have $\beta_{25} = 3600$ and $\beta_{ij} > 3600$ for any other i, j pair over 1, 2, and 5. Also note that any subset of M, other than those listed above, with cardinality at least three must contain at least one of the subsets $\{1, 3\}$, $\{1, 6\}$, $\{2, 4\}$, or $\{3, 6\}$. But each of $\beta_{1,3}$, $\beta_{1,6}$, $\beta_{2,4}$, and $\beta_{3,6}$ is strictly less than 3600 so that any member of C_3 which contains $\{1, 3\}$, $\{1, 6\}$, $\{2, 4\}$, or $\{3, 6\}$ will have a $g(K)$ value smaller than 3600. Hence $\bar{r}_2 = 3600$.

For $p = 3$, the optimal threats are $\{1, 2, 3, 5\}$ and $\{1, 3, 4, 5\}$ where each of these threats has a $g(K)$ value of 3249. The optimality of these threats is due to the fact that any other member of C_4 contains at least one of the subsets $\{1, 6\}$, $\{2, 4\}$, or $\{3, 6\}$. Thus $\bar{r}_3 = 3249$. Continuing in a similar manner, for $p = 4$, the optimal threats are $\{1, 2, 3, 5, 6\}$ and $\{1, 3, 4, 5, 6\}$ with a $g(K)$ value of 784 implying $\bar{r}_4 = 784$. Finally, for $p = 5$, the $g(K)$ value of $\{1, 2, 3, 4, 5, 6\}$ is 225 implying that $\bar{r}_5 = 225$.

Later in this chapter we prove a strong duality theorem relating problems (P-C) and (DP-C) in that for fixed p, $r_p = \bar{r}_p$. Thus, the optimal solution values for problem (P-C) with $p = 1, 2, 3, 4$, and 5 are ∞, 3600, 3249, 784, and 225, respectively. ○

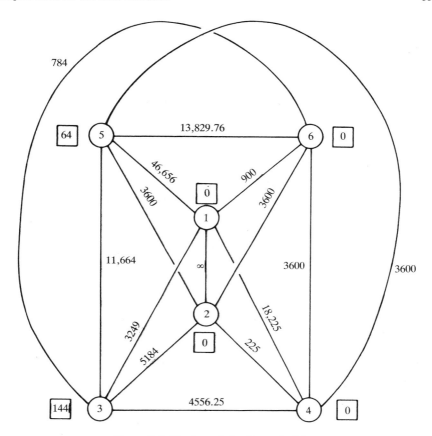

Figure 8.3. Dual graph for Example 8.1.

8.3. INTERPRETATIONS FOR THE DUAL PROBLEMS

Duality is generally most useful in obtaining necessary and sufficient conditions for optimality. Usually it is not particularly easy to give dual problems physical interpretations (if you doubt this we suggest you try to do so before reading what follows). Giving physical interpretations for the dual problems is thus something of an accomplishment in itself. Perhaps more important, however, is the fact that doing so requires us to think very carefully about interpretations of the primal problems, and about the assumptions the primal models are based on.

Imagine two conservative adversaries, an aggressor A, and a defender, D. A and D could represent opposing armed forces. Alternatively, A could represent a group of criminals and D could represent a law enforcement agency, or A could represent "Mother Nature," while D could represent a government agency responsible for emergency planning. D has "defense" forces placed at node locations $v_1, \ldots, v_m$. D knows A will "attack" a single node, but will know the node attacked only when the attack occurs.

D has p response forces which must be positioned at locations defined by a p-center X. Interpret tree distances as travel times, so that $D(X, v_i)$ is the minimum time to respond to v_i from a center in X. Assume A knows D's "loss" functions $\{ f_i: i \in M \}$ where $f_i(D(X, v_i))$ is D's loss if A attacks v_i and D responds to the attack in a time of $D(X, v_i)$. For convenience, we refer to the loss A inflicts on D as A's *gain*.

A knows D has p response forces, but does not know how D will position the response forces. Thus, A acts conservatively, and uses a worst-case analysis in making a decision. If A decides to attack v_i without threatening any other nodes, A reasons that D will correctly guess that v_i will be attacked and will position a response force at v_i. Hence, A assumes a gain of $f_i(0)$ if A decides to attack v_i immediately without a prior threatening strategy. In order to gain more, A decides to threaten, that is pretend to attack, s nodes, with $s > 1$, so that even if D knows which s nodes A threatens, D does not know which node A will attack until the attack occurs. Thus, D is forced to respond to the threat by positioning response forces optimally with respect to these s nodes. (Given that v_i is one of the nodes threatened, we can interpret u_i in the constraint $D(X, v_i) \le u_i$ as the maximum tolerable response time (as determined by D) involving v_i and the nearest response force. We also assume A knows $u_1, \ldots, u_m$.) Hence, if A threatens $K \subset M$, with $|K| = s$, then A assumes D will choose a p-center which solves

$$\min \{ (f(X : K): X \in S_p(K) \} \ .$$

In what follows, for $K \subset M$, define $V(K) = \{ v_i: i \in K \}$.

With $s \le p$, A assumes D knows K and will position a response force at every node in $V(K)$, so that A can gain at most $\alpha(K)$. The best A can do in this case is to choose a K which contains some index t for which $f_t(0) = \alpha \ge f_i(0)$, $v_i \in V$. Hence, if $s \le p$, A can gain *at most* $f_t(0) = \alpha$. On the other hand, if A chooses a subset K of M, with $|K| = s > p$, then D is unable to position a response force at every node in $V(K)$, even if D knows K, *so* A will gain *at least* $\alpha(K)$. Hence, A observes that by choosing some K', with $|K'| = s > p$ which contains an index t for which $\alpha = f_t(0)$, then A gains at least $\alpha = \alpha(K')$. However, A recognizes that there may be some other K, with $|K| = s$ and $s > p$, which may or may not contain t, but which yields a gain of more than α. For this reason A considers only those subsets of M with cardinality greater than p. A realizes by choosing some K, with $|K| = s > p$, that there is at least one pair of nodes in $V(K)$ which D can cover by only a single response force. If v_i and v_j are one such pair in $V(K)$ which are covered by only a single response force, say at x', where $d(x', v_k) \le u_k$, $k = i, j$, then clearly A obtains a gain of at least β_{ij} where

$$\beta_{ij} = \min \{ f(x : \{i, j\}): x \in S_1(\{i, j\}) \}$$
$$\leq \max \{ f_i(d(x', v_i)), f_j(d(x', v_j)) \} \, .$$

Since A does not know which pairs of nodes D will cover by single response forces, A acts conservatively once A chooses K, and assumes that D will cover a pair v_a, $v_b \in V(K)$ for which $\beta_{ab} = \min \{ \beta_{ij}: i, j \in K \}$. Thus, by choosing a K with $s > p$, A is guaranteed a gain of at least $\beta_{ab} = \beta(K)$. Hence A's minimum gain due to threatening K is $g(K) = \max \{ \alpha(K), \beta(K) \}$, so A chooses a $K^* \in C_s$ with $s > p$ which maximizes $g(K)$ over all $K \in C_s$, thus, solving (DP-C).

The question arises as to why A should choose $p + 1$ nodes to threaten, and no more. By virtue of a WDT, if X^* is an optimum p-center then $f(X^*) \geq g(K)$ for all $K \in C_{p+1}$. Thus, $r_p = f(X^*)$ is an upper bound on A's gain due to threatening K. But a SDT asserts that there is a threat of cardinality $p + 1$, say K^*, which attains this upper bound. Hence, A need threaten no more than $p + 1$ nodes to maximize A's gain, since A can gain no more by threatening more than $p + 1$ nodes. Similarly, we conclude D may as well minimize $f(X)$ instead of $f(X : K)$, and thus D solves (P-C).

There is also the possibility that A will make a "false threat," that is, attack a node not among the threatened nodes. If D knows that the threat is false and continues to act conservatively, D will simply choose a p-center X^* to minimize f. But since there exists a threat K^* of cardinality $p + 1$ such that $g(K^*) = f(X^*)$, the greatest loss D can incur, given X^*, is the same as if D believes A's optimal threat to be real, and acts accordingly. Hence, A cannot gain more by making a false threat.

Consider now the "divergence" problem (DC(r)) which is dual to the covering problem, (C(r)). We chose the term "divergence" to represent the physical interpretation, discussed below, in which the attacker A chooses a "divergent" set of nodes to threaten. Further, the term permits making a distinction between the two different dual problems.

It will be seen shortly that the problem (DC(r)) is to find a maximum number of existing facilities no two of which can be jointly covered by a single center within a radius of r. Equivalently, among all threats whose gain is more than r, the problem is to find a threat of maximum cardinality. Recall $\beta = \max \{ \beta_{ij}: 1 \leq i < j \leq m \}$. The dual problem is feasible for $r < \beta = r_1$ while if $r \geq \beta = r_1$ we show subsequently that there exists no subset U of M for which $g(U) > r$. On the other hand, the primal cover problem is feasible for $r \geq \alpha$. Hence, we shall restrict r in (DC(r)) to $\alpha \leq r < \beta = r_1$ in order to ensure feasibility to both problems. Let us now interpret (C(r)) and (DC(r)). The defender D specifies an upper bound r on the loss incurred due to an attack of any node, and chooses response force positions X as necessary so that the loss will not exceed r, while satisfying the distance constraints $D(X, v_i) \leq u_i$ for $i \in M$. Each response force is an "expense" for D. Hence, D's problem is to choose the fewest possible response forces.

The attacker A knows that D will not tolerate a loss exceeding r. Hence A recognizes that, no matter how many nodes are threatened, D will have a sufficiently large number of forces to respond and that the loss A inflicts on D will always be at most r. For this reason, A decides to force D into using as many response forces as possible. Hence, should A choose to threaten a subset U of M with $g(U) > r$, A knows that no two nodes with indices in U can be jointly covered by a single response force by D within the specified upper bound r. Thus, D, not tolerating a loss exceeding r, will have to allocate one response force for every node whose index is in U. In total, any feasible X which D chooses will satisfy $|X| \geq |U|$, which is what the WDT for $(C(r))$ and $(DC(r))$ asserts. By virtue of the corresponding SDT, if U' is A's optimal choice, then D can choose exactly $|U'|$ response forces positioned at, say X', with $|X'| = |U'|$ and still respond to an attack of any node without incurring a loss exceeding r.

If A threatens more than $\bar{s}(r) = |U'|$ nodes, say a subset U of M, then $|U| > \bar{s}(r)$ implies $g(U) \leq r$ (dual infeasibility). Thus, D would not be forced into allocating a single response for every member of U. Thus, if each threat is an "expense" for A, then A need threaten at most $\bar{s}(r)$ nodes. D, on the other hand, adopts an optimal strategy against A's best threat by minimizing the number of response forces with respect to M.

8.4. ALGORITHMS

In this section we present algorithms for solving all four problems (the correctness of the algorithms is established in the next section). Our primary interest in the algorithms is that they provide constructive approaches for proving results about the primal and dual problems. For this reason we purposely keep the algorithms simple, and use an analog string model to provide insight. The development of both the string model and the covering algorithm is motived by an earlier string algorithm given in Francis, Lowe, and Ratliff (1978). We remark that two efficient $O(m)$ algorithms of Chandrasekaran and Tamir (1982) and Kariv and Hakimi (1979) exist for solving the unconstrained covering problem, but they do not lend themselves readily to our needs.

Remark 8.1.   Define

$$e_i(r) \equiv f_i^{-1} \left(\min \{r, f_i(u_i)\} \right), \qquad i \in M, \qquad f_i(0) \leq r. \qquad (8.4.1)$$

It can be readily shown that an equivalent form of the covering problem $(C(r))$ is

$$\begin{aligned} \text{minimize} \quad & |X| \\ \text{subject to} \quad & D(X, v_i) \leq e_i(r), \qquad i \in M. \end{aligned} \qquad (8.4.2)$$

Further, the function e_i, $i \in M$, has domain $[f_i(0), \infty]$, and range $[0, u_i]$, and is given by

$$e_i(r) = \begin{cases} f_i^{-1}(r), & f_i(0) \le r \le f_i(u_i), \\ u_i, & f_i(u_i) \le r. \end{cases} \tag{8.4.3}$$

We will refer to our covering algorithm as COVER. In order to state COVER a few definitions are convenient. We may imagine that the tree network is represented appropriately by inscribing straight-line segments on a planar surface such that each segment represents an arc. We *fasten* a string of length $e_i(r)$ to each node v_i, $i \in M$, of the inscribed tree, where, by convention, we allow strings of zero length. Every fastened string has one end permanently affixed to the planar surface. In addition, during the use of the algorithm we *engage* previously fastened strings at various points on the tree. When a string is engaged, some point of the string is permanently affixed to the tree such that there is no slack in the portion of the string so far engaged. When strings are *removed*, we imagine that they are physically deleted from the string model.

During each iteration of the procedure, we partition the original tree into two subsets; one green, the other brown. The green subset is always a tree, denoted as GT (for green tree), while the brown subset consists of one or more subtrees of the original tree T, each of which is "rooted" at a node of the green tree. By convention, a root node t will be in both GT and the associated brown subtree, denoted as $BT(t)$.

The object of the algorithm is to place the fewest possible number of centers on the tree so that each node v_i has at least one center within the upper bound (string length) $e_i(r)$. The algorithm accomplishes this by pulling the "loose" end-points of the strings tight along the arcs of the tree towards the interior of the current green tree. The strings are pulled tight in a systematic manner working with one arc of the green tree at a time. Whenever it is the case that some string can no longer be pulled tight, because its end-point has been reached, then a center is placed on the green tree at the point where the end-point of that string is to be affixed. When a center is placed on the tree, all strings which can reach that center are assigned to that center, and then removed from the model. The procedure continues until either all strings are removed, or the green tree degenerates into a single point. In the latter case, a center is placed on the green tree and all remaining strings are assigned to this last center.

During the procedure, a record is kept of certain "critical" nodes, which we call the "distinguished" nodes, to be defined subsequently. These critical nodes provide a solution to the associated dual problem as we will show in the next section when we prove the optimality of the procedure and establish our strong duality results.

The algorithm COVER uses a number of subroutines which we now define. In what follows, when t is a chosen tip of GT, and GT is nontrivial, we will let $a(t)$ denote the adjacent vertex to t in GT. Each set SS_i is originally the set of strings fastened at v_i for all i in M; the sets SS_i are updated in the course of the algorithm; x_k is the location of the kth center as determined by the algorithm.

Initialize. Let $GT = T$. Let $k = 0$. For each tip vertex v_i of T let $BT(v_i)$ be the set initially consisting of only the vertex v_i. For each i in M fasten a string of length $e_i(r)$ at v_i. Let $X_0 = \emptyset$.

Revise GT. When some string in SS_t does not reach $a(t)$ we remove from GT the subarc $[t, x_k]$; in case all strings in SS_t do reach $a(t)$ we remove from GT the arc $[t, a(t)]$.

Revise BT(t). When some string in SS_t does not reach $a(t)$ we attach to $BT(t)$ the arc $[t, x_k]$; in case all strings in SS_t do reach $a(t)$ we attach to $BT(t)$ the arc $[t, a(t)]$.

Revise $SS_{a(t)}$. Engage at $a(t)$ all the tightly pulled strings reaching $a(t)$ from t, and include all these strings in $SS_{a(t)}$.

Construct U_k. Choose a shortest string engaged or fastened at t. (In case GT consists of the vertex t alone, *any* string engaged or fastened at t can be chosen.) Find the (unique) vertex, say $v_{(k)}$, at which the chosen string is fastened. Include (k) in U_{k-1} to obtain U_k.

Construct x_k. Choose a shortest string engaged or fastened at t. Find the farthest point, say y, from t on $[t, a(t)]$ to which the chosen string can reach. Locate x_k at y.

Covering Algorithm

```
01   BEGIN
02      initialize;
03      SS₀ := set of all strings;
04      SSᵢ := set of all strings at vᵢ for all i;
05      U₀ := ∅

06      choose a tip t of GT;

07      WHILE GT ≠ [t] and SS₀ ≠ ∅ DO
08        BEGIN
09          find a(t); (the vertex in GT adjacent to t)

10          IF SSₜ ≠ ∅ THEN

11           . BEGIN
12              pull strings at t towards a(t);

13              IF some string in SSₜ does not reach a(t) THEN
14                BEGIN
15                  k := k + 1;
16                  construct Uₖ;
17                  construct xₖ;
```

18   revise SS_0; (remove each string in GT reaching x_k)
20   END
21   ELSE
22   BEGIN
23   engage strings from t at $a(t)$;
24   revise $SS_{a(t)}$;
25   END;
26   END;

27   revise GT;
28   revise $BT(t)$;

29   choose a tip t of GT;

30   END;

31 IF $SS_0 \neq \emptyset$ THEN

32   BEGIN
33          $k := k + 1$;
34   construct U_k;
35          $x_k := t$;
36   END;

37 $X := [x_1, \ldots, x_k]$; (solves $(C(r))$
38 $U := U_k$; (solves $(DC(r))$
39 END.

We shall later use COVER as part of two other algorithms, which solve (P-C) and (DP-C); in such cases the solution to $(DC(r))$ in Step 38 of COVER, is, of course, omitted.

Note that each time COVER places a center x_k in Step 17, it identifies an associated node $v_{(k)}$, in Step 16, through its index (k), which we shall call the *primary node associated with* x_k. When centers $x_1, \ldots, x_k$ have been placed in Step 17, we call $U_k = \{(1), \ldots, (k)\}$ the *primary set of indices associated with* $\{x_1, \ldots, x_k\}$. Supposing the algorithm places s centers in total, the set U, defined in Step 38 of the algorithm, consists of indices $(1), \ldots, (s)$, the first $s - 1$ of which correspond to primary nodes (when $s \geq 2$). The last index corresponds to a primary node only if x_s is placed in Step 17. Letting $X = \{x_1, \ldots, x_s\}$, we call U the *distinguished set associated with* X, and call $v_{(i)}((i))$, the *distinguished node (index) associated with* x_i, $i = 1, \ldots, s$. Note that the distinguished nodes $v_{(1)}, \ldots, v_{(s)}$ are distinct, for as soon as a distinguished node is identified, its string is removed, and thus the node is not available for any subsequent identification. Likewise, the centers $x_1, \ldots, x_s$ are distinct, for if $x_i = x_j$ with $i < j$, then all strings assigned to x_j would have been assigned earlier to x_i, and so x_j would not have been located. Hence, it follows that $|U| = |X| = s$, and $U \neq \emptyset$. since $|X| \geq 1$.

The worst-case bound on COVER is $O(m^2)$ and is determined by Step 18. This step is performed each time a new center is placed. Each repetition requires at most m comparisons to identify the strings which can reach the last center. With at most m repetitions of this step, the result is an $O(m^2)$ algorithm.

We now describe a modified version of COVER whose worst-case bound is $O(m)$. First, remove Step 18. When a new center is placed, no string in the current green tree will be checked.

For each tip vertex t of the green tree, define a parameter $\delta(t)$ as follows: if there is at least one center already located in $BT(t)$, then $\delta(t)$ is the distance from t to a nearest center in $BT(t)$. Otherwise, $\delta(t) = \infty$.

The modified version of COVER proceeds as follows. Let t be the tip vertex selected. Let $s(t)$ be the length of a shortest string fastened or engaged at t. If $s(t) > \delta(t)$, then the shortest string and hence all strings at t can reach a nearest center in $BT(t)$. Assign them to such a center, remove them, color $[t, a(t)]$ brown, and continue with a new tip. In the remaining case, $s(t) < \delta(t)$, and so there is at least one string at t which cannot be assigned to any existing center in $BT(t)$. In this case, the algorithm proceeds just as in the old version. In the event there are no strings at t or $\delta(t) = \infty$, we simply proceed as in the old version.

It is clear that one comparison $(s(t) : \delta(t))$ is done for each tip t selected by the algorithm. The algorithm selects at most $2m$ tips, which are either vertices or center locations. Thus, the modified version of the algorithm is $O(m)$.

We note that Kariv and Hakimi (1979) provided another $O(m)$ algorithm for a linear version of the covering problem. Here, we shall use the $O(m^2)$ version of COVER as a theoretical tool to prove several results.

As the following remark indicates, we can use COVER to check whether or not (P-C) has any feasible solution.

Remark 8.2. Use COVER to compute

$$s = \min \{|X| : D(X, v_i) \le u_i, \, i \in M, \, X \subset T\} . \qquad (8.4.4)$$

(In initialization, fasten a string of length u_i instead of length $e_i(r)$ at v_i, $i \in M$.) We have $S_p \ne \emptyset$ if and only if $s \le p$.

Now we consider solving (P-C). First let us define the set R as follows:

$$R = \{\beta_{ij} : 1 \le i < j \le m\} \cup \{f_i(0) : i \in M\} . \qquad (8.4.5)$$

It is easy to establish that the following algorithm PRIMOPT, solves (P-C), given that $r_n \in R$, a fact we shall prove later in Section 8.5.

PRIMOPT
BEGIN
   IF $S_p \neq \emptyset$ THEN (check for $S_p \neq \emptyset$ using Remark 8.2 or Theorem 8.4)
     BEGIN
        compute $b(p)$; (smallest b in R for which $s(b) \leq n$)
        $X :=$ solution to $(C(b(p)))$;
        $r_n := b(p)$;
        $X' :=$ extension of X; (append any $p - b(p)$ locations to X to obtain
                    X')
        (X' solves (P-C))
     END
   ELSE
     write ("No feasible solution exists.")
END.

We remark that PRIMOPT is similar to the procedures of Chandrasekaran and Tamir (1982) and Kariv and Hakimi (1979) for solving the p-center problem on a tree network, and that bisection search (over R) discussed therein can be used to compute $b(p)$ efficiently.

Given the minimum objective function value for (P-C), say $r_p \equiv$ min $\{ f(X): X \in S_p \}$, we can state an algorithm, DUALOPT, to solve (DP-C).

DUALOPT
BEGIN
   compute r_p; (use PRIMOPT)
   IF $r_p = f_s(0)$ (in this case $r_p = \alpha$)
     THEN
        construct K^*; (choose any feasible K^* in V with s in K^*)
   ELSE
     BEGIN
        compute r_p'; (largest entry in R less than r_p)
        choose r; (r is any number satisfying $r_p' < r < r_p$)
        solve $C(r)$; (use COVER; let U solve $DC(r)$)
        construct K^*; (choose any $p + 1$ elements of U as K^*)
     END
   write ("K^* solves (DP-C)."); (note $r_p = g(K^*)$)
END.

In summary, we can solve all four problems of Table 8.1 using COVER. One application of COVER solves $(C(r))$ and $(DC(r))$ directly. We can solve (P-C) by solving a sequence of covering problems. Once we solve (P-C) one additional application of COVER permits us to solve (DP-C).

Example 8.1 (*continued*).   We now demonstrate the use of DUALOPT (and COVER) by determining an optimal solution to (DP-C) with $p = 3$ for the example problem given in Figure 8.1. From our analysis at the end of Section 8.2, $r_3 = 3249$. Since $r_3 > \alpha = 144$, we compute (from Table 8.2) $r_3' = \max \{ \beta_{ij} : \beta_{ij} \in R, \beta_{ij} < r_3 \} = 900$. We next apply COVER using a value of r where $900 < r < 3249$. Figure 8.4 shows the results of using COVER with $r = 1296$. In the figure we show the loose ends of the strings as wavy lines. The number adjacent to each string is the length of the loose end. Brown subtrees are shown as crosshatched arcs of the original tree. Figure 8.4(a) shows the strings fastened to nodes prior to the application of COVER. Note that the length of the string fastened at v_i is the minimum of $f_i^{-1}(1296)$ and u_i. For $i = 1$, $f_i^{-1}(1296) = 18$. However, $u_1 = 15$ and so the string fastened at v_1 is of length 15. For $i = 2, \dots, 6$, the length of corresponding string is $f_i^{-1}(1296)$ since in each case this value is less than u_i. Each separate drawing, (b)–(g), is for a subsequent iteration (choice of a tip of GT) of COVER. At each iteration, we indicate the tip of GT chosen. For example, in Figure 8.4(b), the tip v_2 is chosen, (i.e., $t = v_2$). Then $a(v_2) = v_4$ and since the string fastened at v_2 reaches v_4, its remaining length, when engaged at v_4, is $12 - 8 = 4$. We then color the arc between v_2 and v_4 brown. In Figure 8.4(c), we choose the tip $t = v_5$ and find $a(v_5) = v_4$. Since the string fastened at v_5 cannot reach v_4, we construct x_1 on the arc $[v_5, v_4]$ at a distance of 7 from v_5. Also, we place 5 (corresponding to v_5) in index set U_1.

At the final iteration, we note that U is the set $\{5, 2, 3, 1\}$ which, from our previous analysis, is known to be an optimal solution to (DP-C) when $p = 3$.   ○

8.5. ANALYSIS

We now develop some properties of COVER, as well as properties of $C(r)$ and $DC(r)$.

It is convenient to state the following lemma, due to Horn (1972), with alternate proofs given by Chan and Francis (1976) and Francis et al. (1978).

Lemma 8.1.   *Given any $v_1, \dots, v_m$ in T and nonnegative upper bounds $b_1, \dots, b_m$, there exists some x in T satisfying $d(x, v_i) \leq b_i$, $i \in M$, if and only if $d(v_i, v_j) \leq b_i + b_j$, $1 \leq i < j < m$.*

Using our string analogy, if we imagine a string of length b_i at each v_i, the foregoing lemma establishes the fact that all m strings will overlap at some point x in T if and only if each pair of strings overlap when pulled tight along the arcs of T towards one another.

Suppose now the conditions of Lemma 8.1 fail to hold for at least one

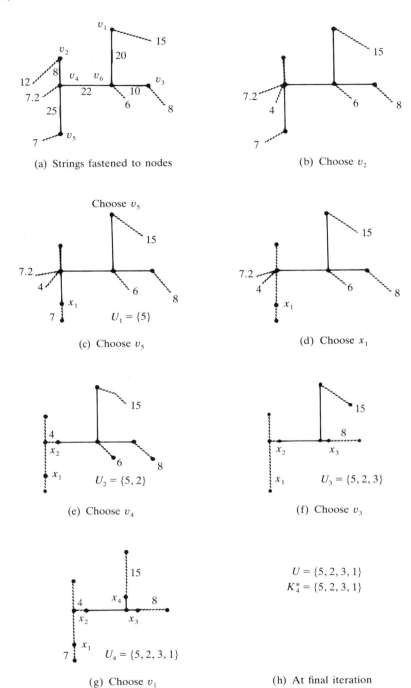

(a) Strings fastened to nodes

(b) Choose v_2

(c) Choose v_5

(d) Choose x_1

(e) Choose v_4

(f) Choose v_3

(g) Choose v_1

(h) At final iteration

Figure 8.4. DUALOPT for $p = 3$ for Example 8.1.

pair of nodes v_s and v_q. That is, we have $d(v_s, v_q) > b_s + b_q$. If we pull the strings at these nodes tight towards one another along the path connecting v_s and v_q, the end-points of these strings will not meet and a portion of the path will remain uncovered by either string. Hence, any x which covers v_s will then fail to cover v_q, and vice versa. The existence of such a pair implies then that we need at least two distinct centers, one for v_s, one for v_q, and possibly other ones to cover the remaining nodes.

Moving one step further, suppose that there are several such pairs whose strings do not reach one another. The question arises: what is the least number of centers needed so that each node has a closest center within the specified upper bound? The answer is not so obvious. However, it is quite easy to find a lower bound on the least number of centers required. Suppose we isolate a subset K of V with the property that if v_i and v_j are any two distinct nodes in K, then the strings at v_i and v_j do not overlap anywhere on T. Clearly then, any center which covers a given node in K will fail to cover any of the remaining nodes in K. Then, the least number of centers to cover all nodes in V is at least as large as the number of nodes in K. Furthermore, the larger the number of nodes in K, the tighter the lower bound will be. In particular, if K^* is a largest subset of V with no two strings in K^* overlapping, then the least number of centers will be bounded below by $|K^*|$. This is essentially what our weak duality theorem asserts, the one difference being that the string lengths are defined by $e_i(r)$ in the problems $C(r)$ and $DC(r)$. Subsequently, we shall show that for the case of a tree network the lower bound on the least number of centers is always attainable, thereby giving our strong duality result for $C(r)$ and $DC(r)$.

The foregoing discussion provides the framework for our subsequent analysis. We shall now proceed to establish some properties of COVER. Given the parameter r and the string lengths $e_i(r)$, $i \in M$, COVER attempts to solve $C(r)$ and $DC(r)$ simultaneously. The set of centers found by COVER is clearly feasible to $C(r)$ since no string is removed by the algorithm unless it reaches some center which has already been placed. Furthermore, each time the algorithm places a center, it identifies a primary node associated with that center. If we assume, without loss of generality, that the nodes are labeled so that v_j is the primary node associated with center x_j, then the length of the string at v_j is the same as the length of the unique path connecting v_j to x_j, as this string has been pulled tight and engaged at various points along the path until eventually its end-point has determined the location of x_j. These claims are summarized in parts (a) and (b) of Lemma 8.2 which follows. The primary nodes together with the last node placed in Step 35 (if any) form the *distinguished set* of nodes. The distinguished set U is a subset of M with the property that if v_i and v_j are any two distinct distinguished nodes, then their strings cannot overlap. This last claim is established in part (c) of Lemma 8.2. Part (d) of the same lemma is a direct consequence of part (c) and the definition of $\beta(U)$.

Lemma 8.2

  a. COVER *finds a feasible solution* X *to the covering problem with* $|X| \le m$.

  b. *For any nonempty primary set* U_k, *with nodes numbered so that* $U_k = \{1, \ldots, k\}$, *we have*

$$v_j \in BT(x_j), \qquad j \in U_k, \tag{8.5.1}$$

$$d(x_j, v_j) = e_j(r), \qquad j \in U_k. \tag{8.5.2}$$

  c. *Let* $X = \{x_1, \ldots, x_s\}$ *be the feasible solution constructed by* COVER, *with nodes numbered so that* $U = \{1, \ldots, s\}$ *is the distinguished set associated with* X. *Assume* $s > 1$. *Then*

$$d(v_i, v_j) > e_i(r) + e_j(r), \qquad for \ 1 \le i < j \le s. \tag{8.5.3}$$

  d. *Whenever* $s = s(r) > 1$ *and* $\alpha \le r$, *any distinguished set* U *associated with* X *satisfies* $\beta(U) > r$.

Proof. Parts (a) and (b) are straightforward; we shall only prove parts (c) and (d) below.

  c. We know the first $s - 1$ members of U are primary indices. Hence, part (b) implies

$$v_i \in BT(x_i), \qquad 1 \le i \le s - 1, \tag{8.5.4}$$

$$d(v_i, x_i) = e_i(r), \qquad 1 \le i \le s - 1. \tag{8.5.5}$$

For $i < j$, x_i is placed prior to x_j. Since v_j is assigned to x_j and not assigned earlier to x_i, v_j was not a node in the brown subtree rooted at x_i, and the string at v_j did not reach x_i. Hence

$$v_j \in T - BT(x_i), \qquad 1 \le i < j \le s, \tag{8.5.6}$$

$$d(x_i, v_j) > e_j(r), \qquad 1 \le i < j \le s. \tag{8.5.7}$$

Expressions (8.5.4) and (8.5.6) imply x_i is on the unique path connecting v_i and v_j and so $d(v_i, v_j) = d(v_i, x_i) + d(x_i, v_j)$ for $1 \le i < j \le s$. But (8.5.5) and (8.5.7) imply that $d(v_i, v_j) > e_i(r) + e_j(r)$. Thus (8.5.3) follows.

  d. Let a, b be indices in U for which $\beta(U) = \beta_{ab} = \min \{\beta_{ij}: i, j \in U, i < j\}$. If $\beta_{ab} = \infty$ clearly $\beta(U) > r$. Assume β_{ab} is finite. Then, the constraints $d(x, v_i) \leq u_i$, $i = a, b$, admit a solution. By definition, β_{ab} is the minimum objective value of the problem min $\{\lambda: f_i(d(x, v_i)) \leq \lambda, d(x, v_i) \leq u_i, i = a, b\}$. Utilizing Remark 8.1, β_{ab} is the smallest λ for which there exists $x \in T$ with $d(x, v_i) \leq e_i(\lambda)$, $i = a, b$. Lemma 8.1 thus implies β_{ab} is the smallest λ for which $d(v_a, v_b) \leq e_a(\lambda) + e_b(\lambda)$. Hence, $d(v_a, v_b) \leq e_a(\beta_{ab}) + e_b(\beta_{ab})$, while from part (c), $e_a(r) + e_b(r) < d(v_a, v_b)$. Defining $e_{ab}(\theta) = e_a(\theta) + e_b(\theta)$, for θ in the domain of e_a and e_b, the last two inequalities imply $e_{ab}(r) < e_{ab}(\beta_{ab})$. Due to monotonicity of e_a and e_b, the function e_{ab} is also monotone and so $r < \beta_{ab} = \beta(U)$. $\square$

Later we shall use the results of Lemma 8.2 to prove our strong duality result for $C(r)$ and $DC(r)$. We now turn our attention to problems $C(r)$ and $DC(r)$, with the purpose of establishing the weak duality theorem. First we give an interpretation of $C(r)$ and $DC(r)$ in terms of the string lengths $e_i(r)$, $i \in M$. Then the weak duality theorem will naturally follow. We remark that the discussion which follows is independent of the results of Theorem 8.2.

Let us first focus on $C(r)$. Given the value of the parameter r, $C(r)$ seeks the least number of centers X so that each node v_i, $i \in M$, has a closest center within the upper bound u_i, and that the loss $f_i(D(X, v_i))$ at node v_i does not exceed r. If $r < f_k(0)$ for some node index k, then even if we did locate a center at v_k, the loss at v_k would be $f_k(0)$ and would exceed r. Hence $C(r)$ does not admit a feasible solution unless $r \geq \alpha$, the maximum of $f_k(0)$, $k \in M$. Given that $r \geq \alpha$, the loss at v_i will not exceed r if and only if $D(X, v_i) \leq f_i^{-1}(r)$. Hence, in effect, each node v_i has two upper bounds, namely u_i and $f_i^{-1}(r)$ and the smaller of the two will be the effective upper bound on v_i. From our definition of $e_i(r)$, $C(r)$ becomes the problem of finding the least number of centers so that each node v_i has a closest center within a distance of $e_i(r)$.

What is then the dual problem $DC(r)$? Assuming $r \geq \alpha$, by definition, $DC(r)$ seeks a largest subset U of M for which $g(U) > r$. $g(U)$ is either $\alpha(U)$ or $\beta(U)$, whichever is larger. But whenever $g(U) = \alpha(U)$, U will not be feasible to $DC(r)$ since feasibility of U would imply $\alpha(U) > r$ while the assumption $r \geq \alpha$ would imply $r \geq \alpha \geq \alpha(U)$ which is impossible. So, any feasible U to $DC(r)$ will satisfy $g(U) = \beta(U) > r \geq \alpha(U)$. But $\beta(U) > r$ is equivalent to $\beta_{ij} > r$ for each pair $i, j \in U$, $i < j$. Now, β_{ij} is the objective value of the 1-center solution when the nodes of interest are v_i and v_j. If β_{ij} is infinite then it is not possible to cover v_i and v_j by a single center within the upper bound u_i and u_j. On the other hand, if β_{ij} is finite then any single center x, for which $d(x, v_i) \leq u_i$ and $d(x, v_j) \leq u_j$, will yield a loss given by max $\{f_i(d(x, v_i)), f_j(d(x, v_j))\}$ and this loss will be at least as large as β_{ij}. Since $\beta_{ij} > r$, any single center which provides service to both v_i and v_j would yield a loss exceeding r. Thus, whenever a subset K of M contains some two indices i and j with the property that v_i and v_j can be jointly covered by a center x within the string lengths $e_i(r)$ and $e_j(r)$, then K is not feasible to DC(r). Hence, DC(r) becomes the problem of finding a largest subset U of M such that for any two nodes v_i and v_j with $i, j \in U$, $i < j$, it is not possible to cover v_i and v_j by a single center within the upper bounds $e_i(r)$ and $e_j(r)$. With these interpretations of the problems C(r) and DC(r), we can now establish the following theorem.

Theorem 8.1 (Weak Duality Theorem). *Assume $\alpha \leq r < \beta$. For any feasible solution X to C(r) and any feasible solution U to DC(r), we have $|U| \leq |X|$.*

Proof. Let V_U be the node set induced by U. Since r is finite and $r \geq \alpha$, the string lengths $e_i(r)$, $i \in M$, are well defined. The feasibility of U to DC(r) implies any point x which covers a node v_i in V_U within the string length $e_i(r)$ fails to cover any of the remaining nodes in V_U within their string lengths. Hence, any feasible X to C(r) requires at least $|U|$ centers, one for each node in V_U, and possibly additional ones for nodes in $V - V_U$. Thus $|U| \leq |X|$. □

We are now in a position to prove the optimality of COVER and the strong duality theorem.

Theorem 8.2. *Let $X = \{x_1, \ldots, x_s\}$ be the set of centers placed by COVER and let the nodes be numbered so that $U = \{1, \ldots, s\}$ is the distinguished set associated with X.*

a. *If $s = 1$, X solves C(r), there exists no feasible solution to DC(r) and $\beta \leq r$.*
b. *If $s \geq 2$, X solves C(r), U solves DC(r), and $r < \beta$.*

Proof. Lemma 8.2a implies X is a feasible solution to C(r).
a. If $s = 1$, then $X = \{x\}$ clearly solves C(r). Hence $d(x, v_i) \leq e_i(r)$, $i \in M$, and thus Remark 8.1 implies $f_i(d(x, v_i)) \leq r$, $d(x, v_i) \leq u_i$, $i \in M$. Then for every pair $i, j \in M$, $i < j$, $\beta_{ij} \leq \max \{f_i(d(x, v_i)), f_j(d(x, v_j))\} \leq r$ as β_{ij} is the minimax loss for nodes v_i and v_j. Thus $\beta \leq r$ and there exists no feasible solution to DC(r).
b. From Lemma 8.2c $d(v_i, v_j) > e_i(r) + e_j(r)$, $1 \leq i < j \leq s$. Hence Lemma 8.2d gives $\beta(U) > r$. Since $g(U) \geq \beta(U) > r$, U is feasible to DC(r) and since $\beta \geq \beta(U) > r$, we have $\beta > r$. The feasibility of X to C(r) and the feasibility of U to DC(r) imply $s(r) \leq |X|$ and $\bar{s}(r) \geq |U|$ while Theorem 8.1 implies $|X| \geq s(r) \geq \bar{s}(r) \geq |U|$. Because $|X| = |U|$, each inequality holds as an equality and thus X is optimal to C(r) while U is optimal to DC(r). □

As an immediate corollary of Theorem 8.2 we obtain the following.

Theorem 8.3 (Strong Duality Theorem). *Assume $\alpha \leq r < \beta$. We have $\bar{s}(r) = s(r) \geq 2$, and* COVER *solves both* C(r) *and* DC(r).

This completes the analysis of COVER and C(r) and DC(r). We now focus our attention on problems (P-C) and (DP-C), as well as the algorithms PRIMOPT and DUALOPT.

First, let us consider the conditions under which (P-C) admits a feasible solution. There exists a feasible solution to (P-C) if and only if there exists a point set X such that $|X| = p$ and $D(X, v_i) \leq u_i$, $i \in M$. Let us reverse the question and ask the following: when is it *not* possible to satisfy the constraints $D(X, v_i) \leq u_i$, $i \in M$, and $|X| = p$? We shall again look at subsets of V to answer this question. Suppose we isolate a subset K of V with the property that K has at least $p + 1$ nodes and that no two nodes v_i and v_j in K can obtain service from the same center, say x, without violating at least one of the constraints $d(x, v_i) \leq u_i$ and $d(x, v_j) \leq u_j$. Then each node in K requires a distinct center and additional ones may be needed for nodes in $V - K$. Since $|K| \geq p + 1$, it is not possible to cover all nodes in V within their upper bounds using only p centers. Thus, if there exists a feasible solution X to (P-C) then no subset K of V of cardinality at least $p + 1$ satisfies $d(v_i, v_j) > u_i + u_j$, $i, j \in K$, $i < j$. Stated differently, if $S_p \neq \emptyset$ then for every $K \in C_{p+1}$ there exist distinct s and q in K for which $d(v_s, v_q) \leq u_s + u_q$. This last condition is a *necessary* condition for $S_p \neq \emptyset$. The question arises now: is the same condition also sufficient for S_p to be nonempty? The answer is in the affirmative. To see this, assume that whenever $K \in C_{p+1}$, $d(v_s, v_q) \leq u_s + u_q$ for some two distinct indices s and q in K. Apply the algorithm COVER with the string lengths u_i, $i \in M$. Let U be the distinguished set found by COVER. Then part (c) of Lemma 8.2 implies $d(v_i, v_j) > u_i + u_j$ for $i, j \in U$, $i < j$. Clearly then U is not in C_{p+1} and thus $|U| \leq p$. If X is the solution found by COVER, then $|X| = |U| \leq p$ and thus X is feasible to (P-C). Thus, we have the following theorem.

Theorem 8.4. *We have $S_p \neq \emptyset$ if and only if for every $K \in C_{p+1}$ there exist distinct s and q for which*

$$d(v_s, v_q) \leq u_s + u_q \tag{8.5.8}$$

if and only if

$$g(K) < \infty \qquad \text{for every } K \in C_{p+1}. \tag{8.5.9}$$

We remark that the equivalence of (8.5.8) and (8.5.9) is an immediate consequence of (8.5.8) and the definition of $g(K)$.

Lemma 8.3. *Assume $S_p \neq \emptyset$. For any $X \in S_p$ and any $K \in C_{p+1}$, we have $\beta(K) \leq f(X)$.*

Proof. Since $|X| < |K|$, some center, say at $x \in X$, must be closest to two distinct nodes, say, v_p and v_q, with $p, q \in K$, $p < q$. Thus, for $i = p, q$, $d(x, v_i) = D(X, v_i) \le u_i$ so that $S_1(\{p, q\}) \ne \emptyset$ and β_{pq} is finite, and $f_i(d(x, v_i)) = f_i(D(X, v_i)) \le f(X)$. It follows now, from the definition of β_{pq} and $\beta_{pq} < \infty$ that

$$\beta(K) \le \beta_{pq} \le \max\{f_p(d(x, v_p)), f_q(d(x, v_q))\} \le f(X).$$

(Note also that $d(v_p, v_q) \le d(v_p, x) + d(x, v_q) \le u_p + u_q$.) □

We can establish now a weak duality theorem for (P-C) and (DP-C).

Theorem 8.5 (Weak Duality Theorem). *Assume $S_p \ne \emptyset$. For any $X \in S_p$ and $K \in C_{p+1}$ we have*

$$g(K) \le f(X). \qquad (8.5.10)$$

Proof. Lemma 8.3 gives $\beta(K) \le f(X)$. Also, $\alpha(K) \le \alpha \le f(X)$ as $f_j(0) \le f_j(D(X, v_j))$ for each $j \in M$. It follows that $\max\{\alpha(K), \beta(K)\} \equiv g(K) \le f(X)$. □

We remark that Theorem 8.5 does not depend on the structure of the network under consideration. As long as S_p is nonempty, for any $X \in S_p$ and $K \in C_{p+1}$, the monotonicity of the functions f_j, $j \in M$, and the definition of $\alpha(K)$ imply $\alpha(K) \le f(X)$. Furthermore, in establishing $\beta(K) \le f(X)$ in Lemma 8.3, we have only used the definition of $\beta(K)$ and β_{ij} together with the fact that the maximum loss at any v_i and v_j is certainly no more than the maximum loss at $v_1, \ldots, v_m$. Thus, Theorem 8.5 holds for general networks as well as tree networks.

We shall now establish a strong duality theorem for (P-C) and (DP-C). Our proof is constructive in that we use the algorithm DUALOPT which, given an optimal solution to the primal, constructs an optimal solution to the dual problem. We then show that the objective values of the pair of problems are equal. As a byproduct, the proof also establishes that $r_p \in R$ (R is defined by (8.4.5)).

First, we establish that DUALOPT constructs an optimal solution to (DP-C).

Theorem 8.6. *Given r_p, $1 \le p \le m - 1$, K^* constructed by DUALOPT solves (DP-C) and satisfies*

$$\bar{r}_p = g(K^*) = \max\{g(K): K \in C_{p+1}\} = r_p = \min\{f(X): X \in S_p\}. \qquad (8.5.11)$$

Proof. Let $X^* \in S_p$ be an optimum p-center solution to the primal problem so that $|X^*| = p$ and $f(X^*) = r_p$. Since $r_p \geq \alpha$, we consider the cases $r_p = \alpha$ and $r_p > \alpha$. Let us apply DUALOPT for each case.

For $r_p = \alpha$, K^* is chosen by DUALOPT so that $|K^*| = p + 1$ and K^* contains an index s for which $\alpha = f_s(0) = \alpha(K^*)$. Since X^* is a feasible p-center and $K^* \in C_{p+1}$, Theorem 8.5 gives $g(K^*) \leq f(X^*)$. But then, $\alpha = \alpha(K^*) \leq g(K^*) \leq f(X^*) = r_p = \alpha$, so that each inequality holds as an equality and (8.5.11) follows.

Consider now the case $r_p > \alpha$. In this case, the algorithm DUALOPT identifies the largest member r_p' of R from among those which are less than r_p. Clearly r_p' is well defined since $\alpha \in R$ and $\alpha < r_p$. Then the algorithm chooses some r for which $r_p' < r < r_p$, applies COVER to solve $C(r)$ and obtains an optimum solution X to $C(r)$ together with the distinguished set U. Since $r < r_p$, and since X is feasible to $C(r)$, X must consist of at least $p + 1$ centers. Clearly then $|U| \geq p + 1$ as $|X| = |U|$. Let K^* be that subset of U identified by DUALOPT with $|K^*| = p + 1$.

Since $K^* \in C_{p+1}$, Theorem 8.5 gives $r_p = f(X^*) \geq g(K^*)$ while the definition of $g(K^*)$ implies $g(K^*) \geq \beta(K^*)$. But $\beta(K^*)$ is no smaller than $\beta(U)$ since K^* is a subset of U. Hence, we have

$$r_p = f(X^*) \geq g(K^*) \geq \beta(K^*) \geq \beta(U) . \tag{8.5.12}$$

If we can show $\beta(U) \geq r_p$, then each inequality in (8.5.12) must hold as an equality and the proof will be complete.

We now show $\beta(U) \geq r_p$. From Lemma 8.2d we have $\beta(U) > r$ and so the definition of $\beta(U)$ implies

$$\beta_{ij} > r , \qquad i, j \in U , \qquad i < j . \tag{8.5.13}$$

But r is chosen so that $r_p' < r < r_p$ and thus no member β_{ij} of R falls in the open interval (r, r_p). Thus, whenever $\beta_{ij} > r$ then it is not possible to have $r < \beta_{ij} < r_p$. It follows that $\beta_{ij} > r$ implies $\beta_{ij} \geq r_p$. But then (8.5.13) gives

$$\beta_{ij} \geq r_p , \qquad i, j \in U , \qquad i < j ,$$

and thus $\beta(U) = \min \{\beta_{ij} : i, j \in U, i < j\} \geq r_p$, and the proof of (8.5.11) is complete.

The assertion that K^* solves the dual problem is immediate from $f(X^*) = g(K^*)$ and Theorem 8.5. $\square$

We note that Theorem 8.6 provides a proof of the strong duality theorem (SDT) for (P-C) and (DP-C) since, in the statement of the SDT, we take $X^* \in S_p$ to be any optimum p-center solution to the primal problem and K^* as constructed by DUALOPT. We also note that the duality theory provides necessary and sufficient conditions for a p-center to be optimal.

Theorem 8.7 (Strong Duality Theorem). *For any* p, $1 \leq p \leq m - 1$, *with* $S_p \neq \emptyset$, *there exists a* p-*center*, $X^* \in S_p$, *and a dual threat* $K^* \in C_{p+1}$ *such that* $|K^*| = p + 1$ *and* $g(K^*) = f(X^*)$. (*It is evident from the weak duality theorem that* X^* *solves* (P-C) *and that* K^* *solves* (DP-C).)

Another immediate consequence of Theorem 8.6 is that $r_p \in R$, a fact we exploited in algorithm PRIMOPT.

For the special case $p = 1$, r_1 will be finite if and only if $d(v_i, v_j) \leq u_i + u_j$ for $i, j \in M$, $i < j$. Assuming that this is the case, each β_{ij} is then finite. Clearly, $r_1 \geq \alpha$ and $r_1 \geq \beta_{ij}$ for each $i, j \in M$, $i < j$, as β_{ij} is the minimum objective value of the relaxation of the 1-center problem (hereafter denoted as (1-C)) defined only for nodes v_i and v_j. Hence, $r_1 \geq \max(\alpha, \beta)$. The fact that $r_1 \in R$ implies then $r_1 = \max(\alpha, \beta)$. Furthermore, clearly $\beta_{ij} \geq \max\{f_i(0), f_j(0)\}$, for each pair $i, j \in M$, $i < j$, and thus $\beta \geq \alpha$. We conclude then that $r_1 = \beta \geq \alpha$ whenever r_1 is finite.

In Section 8.6, we provide supplementary results which permit the computation of the β_{ij}. Hence, (1-C) can be solved directly by computing β. Once β is computed, two "critical" nodes v_a and v_b are identified for which $\beta = \beta_{ab}$. The 1-center solution x which solves the relaxed problem for nodes v_a and v_b will also solve (1-C).

8.6. COMPUTATION OF THE β_{ij}

Because $r_p \in R$ and the algorithms PRIMOPT and DUALOPT use as input the β_{ij}, we provide several supplementary results in this section which permit the computation of the β_{ij}.

For convenience, let us define $M^2 = \{(i, j): i, j \in M, i < j\}$. For $(i, j) \in M^2$, the definition of β_{ij} implies β_{ij} is the smallest r for which there exists a solution x in T with constraints $d(x, v_k) \leq u_k$, $f_k(d(x, v_k)) \leq r$, $k = i, j$. Lemma 8.1 implies β_{ij} is finite if and only if $d(v_i, v_j) \leq u_i + u_j$. We shall assume β_{ij} is finite. Let us define $a_{ij} = \max\{f_i(0), f_j(0)\}$. Clearly β_{ij} can be no smaller than a_{ij} and hence we can restrict our attention to values of r for which $r \geq a_{ij}$. But $r \geq a_{ij}$ implies r is in the range of f_i and f_j and thus $f_i^{-1}(r)$ and $f_j^{-1}(r)$ are well defined. Clearly then, β_{ij} is the smallest r for which there exists x in T with

$$d(x, v_k) \leq e_k(r) = f_k^{-1}(\min\{r, f_k(u_k)\}), \qquad k = i, j. \qquad (8.6.1)$$

Lemma 8.1 implies then that β_{ij} is the smallest r for which

$$d(v_i, v_j) \leq e_{ij}(r) \equiv e_i(r) + e_j(r), \qquad (8.6.2)$$

and

$$a_{ij} \leq r. \qquad (8.6.3)$$

It is useful at this point to analyze the function $e_{ij}(r)$ defined by (8.6.2): the analysis is related to, and extends that of Dearing (1977) and Francis (1977) for the unconstrained problem.

For $(i, j) \in M^2$, as the domain of e_{ij} is the intersection of the domains of e_i and e_j, we conclude that the domain of e_{ij} is $[a_{ij}, \infty)$, provided, of course, $S_1(\{i, j\}) \neq \emptyset$.

Let us first concentrate on $e_i(r)$ for $r \in [f_i(0), \infty)$. By definition, e_i is the inverse function f_i^{-1} evaluated at either r or $f_i(u_i)$, whichever is smaller.

For the case $r \in [f_i(0), f_i(u_i)]$, clearly $e_i(r) = f_i^{-1}(r)$, while $r \in [f_i(u_i), \infty)$ implies $e_i(r) = f_i^{-1}(f_i(u_i)) = u_i$, a constant. In Figure 8.5(a) we give an

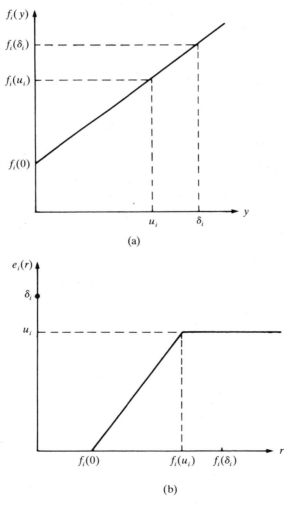

Figure 8.5. Example of (a) loss function f_i and (b) function e_i.

example loss function f_i with domain $[0, \delta_i]$ and range $[f_i(0), f_i(\delta_i)]$. In the same figure, since $0 < u_i < \delta_i$, we have $f_i(0) < f_i(u_i) < f_i(\delta_i)$, as depicted on the vertical axis. The function $e_i(r)$ is shown in Figure 8.5(b). For r in the subinterval $[f_i(0), f_i(u_i)]$, $e_i(r)$ is the monotone function $f_i^{-1}(r)$, while for $r \in [f_i(u_i), f_i(\delta_i)]$, $e_i(r)$ is the constant u_i. Clearly e_j will be similar, consisting, in general, of a monotone portion on $[f_j(0), f_j(u_j)]$ and of a flat portion on $[f_j(u_j), \infty)$.

It is direct then to conclude that e_{ij}, the pointwise sum of e_i and e_j, is monotone on any interval where at least one of e_i, e_j is monotone, and that e_{ij} is the constant $u_i + u_j$ whenever both e_i and e_j are constant on a given interval. Figures 8.6(a) and 8.7(a) illustrate the construction of $e_{ij}(r)$ shown with bold lines. In Figure 8.6(a), the lower limit a_{ij} of the domain of $e_{ij}(r)$ is defined by $f_j(0)$. As r varies on the horizontal axis from $f_j(0)$ toward $f_i(u_i)$, both e_i and e_j are monotone and are defined by f_i^{-1} and f_j^{-1}, respectively. Their pointwise sum on this subinterval is $e_{ij}(r) = f_i^{-1}(r) + f_j^{-1}(r)$, the first "steep" portion of the bold line. As r continues to vary from $f_i(u_i)$ toward $f_j(u_j)$, e_i is the constant u_i while e_j remains monotone on this subinterval. Hence, $e_{ij}(r)$ is the function $u_i + f_j^{-1}(r)$ on this subinterval and is the second monotone piece as shown in the same figure. For $r \geq f_j(u_j)$, e_i and e_j are constant and thus $e_{ij}(r) = u_i + u_j$, the flat portion of the function.

We remark that $f_i(u_i) \leq f_j(u_j)$ for $i < j$ due to our earlier indexing convention. For this reason $f_j(u_j)$ is further to the right of $f_i(u_i)$ in Figure 8.6(a). It is conceivable that $f_i(u_i)$ may be smaller than $f_j(0)$. In this case, since $f_j(0) \leq f_i(u_i) < f_j(0)$, the lower limit a_{ij} of the domain of $e_{ij}(r)$ will be defined by $f_j(0)$. This case is illustrated in Figure 8.7(a). With reference to Figure 8.7(a), it is the case that e_i is monotone only on $[f_i(0), f_i(u_i)]$, a subinterval disjoint from $[a_{ij}, \infty]$. For this reason, $e_{ij}(r)$ is defined by $u_i + f_j^{-1}(r)$ as r varies on $[a_{ij}, f_j(u_j)]$ and is the monotonic bold portion in Figure 8.7(a). For $r \geq f_j(u_j)$, $e_{ij}(r)$ becomes the constant $u_i + u_j$, the flat bold piece in Figure 8.7(a).

We summarize the foregoing observations in the following lemma.

Lemma 8.4. *Let* $(i, j) \in M^2$, $S_1(\{i, j\}) \neq \emptyset$, *and* $a_{ij} \leq r$.

a. *If* $f_j(0) \leq f_i(u_i)$ *then*

$$
e_{ij}(r) = \begin{cases} f_i^{-1}(r) + f_j^{-1}(r), & a_{ij} \leq r \leq f_i(u_i), \\ u_i + f_j^{-1}(r), & f_i(u_i) \leq r \leq f_j(u_j), \\ u_i + u_j, & f_j(u_j) \leq r. \end{cases}
$$

b. *If* $f_i(u_i) < f_j(0)$ *then*

$$
e_{ij}(r) = \begin{cases} u_i + f_j^{-1}(r), & a_{ij} = f_j(0) \leq r \leq f_j(u_j), \\ u_i + u_j, & f_j(u_j) \leq r. \end{cases}
$$

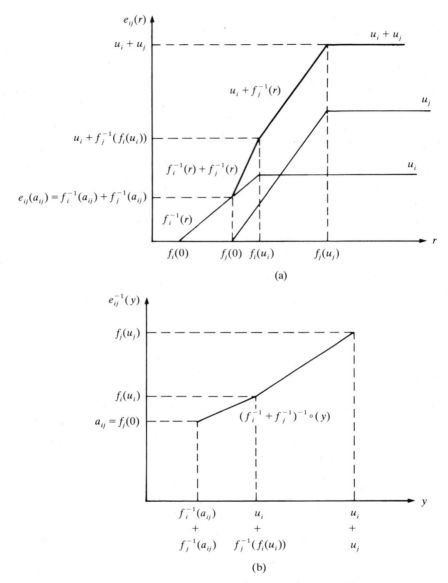

Figure 8.6. Example of functions (a) $e_{ij}(r)$ and (b) $e_{ij}^{-1}(y)$ for the case $a_{ij} \le f_j(0) \le f_i(u_i)$.

We observe that $e_{ij}(r)$ is a continuous function and is monotone on the interval $[a_{ij}, f_j(u_j)]$; thus its restriction to this interval has an inverse, which we denote by $e_{ij}^{-1}(\cdot)$.

The construction of $e_{ij}^{-1}(\cdot)$ for the case of $f_j(0) \le f_i(u_i)$ and for the case of $f_i(u_i) < f_j(0)$ is illustrated, respectively, in Figures 8.6(b) and 8.7(b). The domain of $e_{ij}^{-1}(\cdot)$ is the same as the range of $e_{ij}(r)$, where $e_{ij}(r)$ is restricted

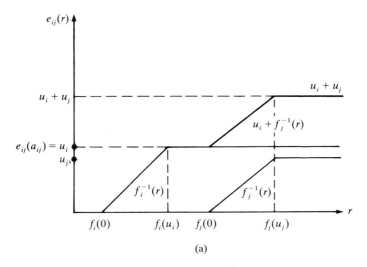

(a)

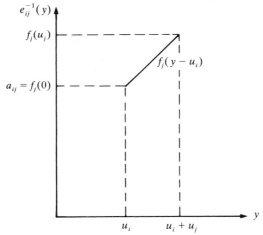

Figure 8.7. Example of (a) function $e_{ij}(r)$ and (b) $e_{ij}^{-1}(y)$ for the case $f_i(u_i) < a_{ij} = f_j(0)$.

to the interval $[a_{ij}, f_j(u_j)]$. (In the figures and elsewhere in the chapter, given a function f, $f \circ (y)$ means f evaluated at y.)

It is direct to verify that the construction of $e_{ij}^{-1}(\cdot)$ is as follows.

Lemma 8.5. *Let $(i, j) \in M^2$ and $S_1(\{i, j\}) \neq \emptyset$.*

a. *If $f_j(0) \leq f_i(u_i)$, then*

$$e_{ij}^{-1}(y) = \begin{cases} (f_i^{-1} + f_j^{-1})^{-1} \circ (y), & \text{if } e_{ij}(a_{ij}) = (f_i^{-1} + f_j^{-1}) \circ (a_{ij}) \leq y \\ & \leq u_i + f_j^{-1}(f_i(u_i)), \\ f_j(y - u_i), & \text{if } u_i + f_j^{-1}(f_i(u_i)) \leq y \leq u_i + u_j. \end{cases}$$

b. If $f_i(u_i) < f_j(0)$, then

$$e_{ij}^{-1}(y) = f_j(y - u_i), \qquad u_i \le y \le u_i + u_j.$$

Lemmas 8.4 and 8.5 provide us with the necessary machinery to compute e_{ij} and e_{ij}^{-1}. The question arises now how one uses this machinery to compute β_{ij}. Recall that in relation to expression 8.6.2, we had concluded that β_{ij} is the smallest r for which

$$d(v_i, v_j) \le e_{ij}(r), \tag{8.6.4}$$

$$a_{ij} \le r. \tag{8.6.5}$$

Clearly then $\beta_{ij} \ge a_{ij}$. Two cases may arise: either $r = a_{ij}$ satisfies (8.6.4) or else it does not. In the former case, clearly $\beta_{ij} = a_{ij}$. In the latter case, $r = a_{ij}$ is too small and thus must be made just large enough to satisfy (8.6.4). We shall see now just how large r must be. The fact that $d(v_i, v_j) > e_{ij}(a_{ij})$ implies $d(v_i, v_j)$ is in the range of $e_{ij}(\cdot)$ and therefore is in the domain of $e_{ij}^{-1}(\cdot)$. Then $r \in [a_{ij}, \infty)$ satisfies (8.6.4) if and only if the same r satisfies $e_{ij}^{-1}(d(v_i, v_j)) \le r$. Clearly then the smallest r for which (8.6.4) and (8.6.5) hold is $e_{ij}^{-1}(d(v_i, v_j))$. In conclusion, we have the following lemma.

Lemma 8.6. Let $(i, j) \in M^2$, $S_1(\{i, j\}) \ne \emptyset$. Then

$$\beta_{ij} = \begin{cases} a_{ij}, & \text{if } d(v_i, v_j) \le e_{ij}(a_{ij}), \\ e_{ij}^{-1}(d(v_i, v_j)), & \text{if } d(v_i, v_j) > e_{ij}(a_{ij}). \end{cases}$$

We remark, if β_{ij} is to be determined by the closed form expression $\beta_{ij} = (f_i^{-1} + f_j^{-1})^{-1} \circ (d(v_i, v_j))$ and if the expression is difficult to evaluate, then numerical methods for finding roots may be used to compute β_{ij} to the necessary degree of accuracy, since β_{ij} is the unique root of the strictly increasing and continuous function $f_i^{-1}(y) + f_j^{-1}(y) - d(v_i, v_j)$.

8.7. SUMMARY AND CONCLUSIONS

In this chapter, we have studied the p-center and covering problems on a tree network, where each of the demand points on the network has a nonlinear loss function, which is nondecreasing in distance to the nearest center. We have shown the existence of problems which are dual to these primal problems and have demonstrated that strong duality holds.

We have provided an algorithm COVER to solve the covering problem and its dual. In addition, we have presented an algorithm, PRIMOPT, which solves the p-center problem. Likewise, algorithm DUALOPT solves the dual of the p-center problem.

The reader will gain further understanding of the material in this chapter by solving the exercises given below.

EXERCISES

8.1 For the tree network in Figure 8.8, determine the least number of centers to locate so that each node has at least one center within a distance of 6 units.

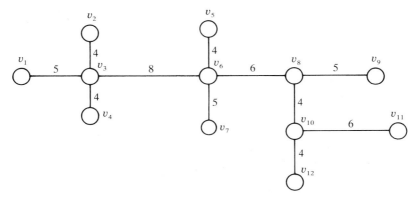

Figure 8.8

8.2 For $p = 1, 2, \ldots, 6$, solve the p-center problem and its dual for the data in Figure 8.9.

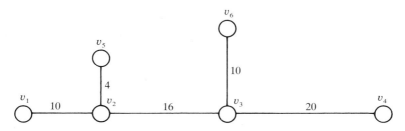

Figure 8.9. $f_i(y) = y$ for $y \in [0, \delta_i]$, $i = 1, \ldots, 6$

$$u_i = \delta_i, \ i = 1, \ldots, 6$$

8.3 During a military conflict, the blue forces positioned themselves at base locations $v_6, \ldots, v_{13}$ as shown in Figure 8.10. The access from the main road to the bases is via the pathways shown in broken lines.

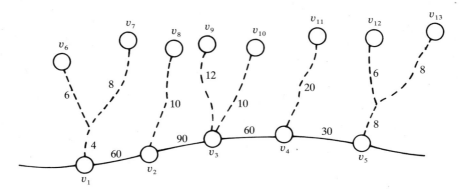

Figure 8.10

It is desired to locate two supply centers in order to minimize the longest time it takes to deliver supplies from the centers to the bases. Because this is a rugged terrain, military trucks can operate on the main road, but not on the pathways. For this reason, the supply centers have to be located along the main road. Travel along the pathways will be by carts. The distances (in miles) between bases and access points $v_1, \ldots, v_5$, as well as the distances between access points are indicated by the numbers next to arcs. The trucks can travel at an average speed of 30 mph along the main road while the carts can travel at an average speed of 2 mph along the pathways. The supplies will be delivered from supply centers to access points by trucks, and will then be loaded on carts which wait at the access points. The time it takes to load and unload is negligible. If you were the Commander, where would you advise the supply centers be located?

8.4 Two fire stations are located at points x_1 and x_2 as shown in Figure 8.11. It is desired to locate two additional fire stations at points x_3 and x_4 on the tree network so as to minimize the maximum response time to a potential fire at any node. The travel times along the arcs are as indicated in the figure. Each node will receive service from the nearest fire station, which may be x_1, x_2, x_3, or x_4. Determine the optimal locations for x_3 and x_4.

8.5 For the data in Exercise 8.4, a new analysis revealed that fire damage increases in proportion to the square of the response time and that the factor of proportionality varies from node to node. Let w_i be the factor of proportionality for node v_i so that $w_i y^2$ is the fire damage at node v_i if the response time from the nearest fire station to node v_i is y. Where would you locate the two new fire stations in this case if you wanted to minimize the maximum fire damage, given that $w_1 = w_2 =$

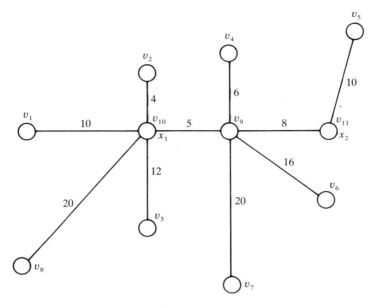

Figure 8.11

$w_4 = 4$, $w_3 = w_5 = w_9 = w_{10} = w_{11} = 2$, and $w_6 = w_7 = w_8 = 1$? If you were able to relocate the stations at x_1 and x_2, what would be the optimal locations for x_1, x_2, x_3, and x_4?

8.6 For a p-center problem on a tree network, the loss functions are of the form $f_i(y) = w_i(y + h_i)^2$ for $y \in [0, \delta_i]$, where w_i, h_i are given constants with $w_i > 0$ for each i.

(a) Specify the domain and range of $f_i^{-1}(\cdot)$ and give an expression for computing $f_i^{-1}(r)$ for r in the domain of $f_i^{-1}(\cdot)$.

(b) Define $f_{ij}(r) = f_i^{-1}(r) + f_j^{-1}(r)$. Specify the domain and range of $f_{ij}(\cdot)$ and give an expression for computing $f_{ij}(r)$.

(c) Let $f_{ij}^{-1}(\cdot)$ be the inverse of $f_{ij}(\cdot)$. Specify the domain and range of $f_{ij}^{-1}(\cdot)$ and give an expression for computing $f_{ij}^{-1}(y)$.

(d) Suppose the upper bounds u_i are such that $u_i = \delta_i$ for each i. Give a closed form expression to compute β_{ij}.

8.7 Given loss functions of the form $f_i(y) = w_i(y + h_i)^2$, for the data in Figure 8.12.

(a) Compute $f_i(0)$ for $i = 1, \ldots, 6$.

(b) Compute β_{ij} for $1 \le i < j \le 6$.

(c) Solve the problems $C(r)$ and $DC(r)$ where r is the sixth largest β_{ij}.

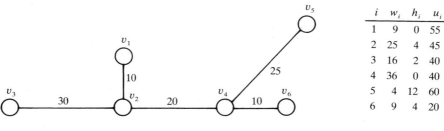

i	w_i	h_i	u_i
1	9	0	55
2	25	4	45
3	16	2	40
4	36	0	40
5	4	12	60
6	9	4	20

Figure 8.12

(d) Solve the *p*-center problem and its dual for $p = 1, \ldots, 6$ and verify the strong duality theorem.

8.8 Is it possible to have $r_p = r_{p-1}$ for the problem on a tree network? If not, explain why. If yes, construct an example tree consisting of six nodes so that $r_1 = r_2 = r_3 = r_4 > r_5 > r_6 = 0$.

8.9 In Section 8.4 we defined $e_j(r) = f_j^{-1}(\min \{r, f_j(u_j)\})$ for $j \in M$, $f_j(0) \leq r$. Show that an equivalent definition of $e_j(r)$ is $e_j(r) = \min \{u_j, f_j^{-1}(r)\}$ for $j \in M$, $f_j(0) \geq r$.

8.10 Give a rigorous justification for Remark 8.1; that is, prove that problems (P10.1) and (P10.2) below are equivalent.

$$\min \{|X|: f(X) \leq r, D(X, v_i) \leq u_i, i \in M\} \qquad \text{(P10.1)}$$

$$\min \{|X|: D(X, v_i) \leq e_i(r), i \in M\} \qquad \text{(P10.2)}$$

8.11 Give a rigorous justification for the fact that, whenever β is finite, $r_1 = \beta$. What can you say about r_1 and (1-C) when $\beta = \infty$?

8.12 Prove that for $\alpha \leq r < \beta$, the dual problem (DC(r)) is equivalent to

$$\text{maximize} \qquad |U|$$

$$\text{subject to} \qquad \beta(U) > r$$

where U is any subset of M with cardinality at least two.

8.13 Suppose $\alpha = \beta$. What can be said about (C(r)) and (DC(r)) in this case? What can be said about (P-C) and (DP-C)?

8.14 Show that if $\alpha = \beta$, the optimal 1-center is unique and is that node v_a for which $f_a(0) = \alpha$.

8.15 Suppose that $\alpha = \beta$ and there are two distinct nodes v_a and v_b such that $f_a(0) = f_b(0) = \alpha$. From Exercise 8.14, the optimal 1-center is unique and must be located at v_a and v_b, which is absurd. How do we resolve this apparent paradox?

8.16 In our interpretation of the problems (P-C) and (DP-C), we assumed that the attacker will attack a single node (even though he threatens

$p + 1$ or more nodes). If you were the defender, what kind of strategy would you have adopted (in placing the centers) if you had sufficient information to believe that

(a) the attacker will attack 2 nodes,

(b) the attacker will attack $p + 1$ nodes,

(c) the attacker will attack simultaneously a single node and the nearest center to that node.

8.17 Let $L_1, \ldots, L_m$ be intervals on the real line. From a stack of colors, it is desired to assign a color to each interval so that all intervals of the same color have a common point and that the minimum number of colors is used. Solve this problem using the results of this chapter. Prove, also, that the minimum number of colors to use is the same as the largest number of intervals, no two of which intersect. Can you extend your conclusions to the case where each L_i is a subtree of a tree T?

REFERENCES

Chan, A. W., and R. L. Francis (1976). "A Round-Trip Location Problem on a Tree Graph." *Transportation Science* **10**, 35–51.

Chandrasekaran, R., and A. Daughety (1981). "Location on Tree Networks: p-Center and n-Dispersion Problems." *Mathematics of Operations Research* **6**, 50–57.

Chandrasekaran, R., and A. Tamir (1980), "An $O(n \log p)^2$ Algorithm for the Continuous p-Center Problem on a Tree." *SIAM Journal on Algebraic Discrete Methods* **1**, 370–375.

Chandrasekaran, R., and A. Tamir (1982). "Polynomially Bounded Algorithms for Locating p-Centers on a Tree." *Mathematical Programming* **22**, 304–315.

Cockayne, E. J., S. T. Hedetniemi, and P. J. Slater (1979). "Matchings and Transversals in Hypergraphs, Domination and Independence in Trees." *Journal of Combinatorial Theory*, *Series B* **26**, 78–80.

Dearing, P. M. (1977). "Minimax Location Problems with Nonlinear Costs." *Journal of Research of the National Bureau of Standards* **82**, 65–72.

Dearing, P. M., and R. L. Francis (1974). "A Minimax Location Problem on a Network." *Transportation Science* **8**, 333–343.

Dearing, P. M., R. L. Francis, and T. J. Lowe (1976). "Convex Location Problems on Tree Networks." *Operations Research* **24**, 628–642.

Francis, R. L. (1977). "A Note on a Nonlinear Minimax Location Problem in a Tree Network." *Journal of Research of the National Bureau of Standards* **82**, 73–80.

Francis, R. L., T. J. Lowe, and H. D. Ratliff (1978). "Distance Constraints for Tree Network Multifacility Location Problems." *Operations Research* **26**, 570–596.

Gavril, F. (1972). "Algorithm for Minimum Coloring, Maximum Clique, Minimum Covering by Cliques and Maximum Independent Set of a Chordal Graph." *SIAM Journal on Computing* **1**, 180–187.

Goldman, A. J. (1972). "Minimax Location of a Facility in a Network." *Transportation Science* **6**, 407–418.

Hakimi, S. L. (1964). "Optimal Locations of Switching Centers and the Absolute Centers and Medians of a Graph." *Operations Research* **12**, 450–459.

Hakimi, S. L. (1965). "Optimal Distribution of Switching Centers in a Communications Network and Some Related Graph-Theoretic Problems." *Operations Research* **13**, 462–475.

Hakimi, S. L., E. F. Schmeichel, and J. G. Pierce (1978). "On p-Centers in Networks." *Transportation Science* **12**, 1–15.

Halpern, J. (1979). "Fire Loss Reduction: Fire Detectors vs. Fire Stations." *Management Science* **25**, 1082–1092.

Handler, G. Y. (1973). "Minimax Location of a Facility in an Undirected Tree Graph." *Transportation Science* **7**, 287–293.

Handler, G. Y. (1978). "Finding Two-Centers of a Tree: The Continuous Case." *Transportation Science* **12**, 93–106.

Horn, W. A. (1972). "Three Results for Trees, Using Mathematical Induction." *Journal of Research of the National Bureau of Standards, Section B* **76B** (1 and 2), 39–45.

Hsu, W., and G. L. Nemhauser (1979). "Easy and Hard Bottleneck Location Problems." *Discrete Applied Mathematics* **1**, 209–215.

Kariv, O., and S. L. Hakimi (1979). "An Algorithmic Approach to Network Location Problems. Part 1. The *P*-Centers." *SIAM Jopurnal of Applied Mathematics* **37**, 513–538.

Kolen, A. (1980). *Duality and the Nonlinear Round-Trip 1-Center Problem and Covering Problems on a Tree*, Working Paper BW 123. Stichting Mathematisch Centrum, Kruislaan 413, 1098, SJ Amsterdam, The Netherlands.

Lin, C. C. (1975). "On Vertex Addends in Minimax Location Problems." *Transportation Science* **9**, 165–168.

Meir, A., and J. W. Moon (1975). "Relations between Packing and Covering Numbers of a Tree." *Pacific Journal of Mathematics* **61**, 225–233.

Minieka, E. (1970). "The *M*-Center Problem." *SIAM review* **12**, 138–139.

Patel, N. R. (1979). "Locating Rural Social Service Centers in India." *Management Science* **25**, 22–30.

Shier, D. P. (1977). "A Min-Max Theorem for Network Location Problems on a Tree." *Transportation Science* **11**, 243–252.

Tansel, B. C., R. L. Francis, T. J. Lowe, and M. L. Chen (1982). "Duality and Distance Constraints for the Nonlinear *p*-Center Problem and Covering Problem on a Tree Network." *Operations Research* **30**, 725–744.

Tansel, B. C., R. L. Francis, and T. J. Lowe (1983a). "Location on Networks: A Survey. Part I. The *p*-Center and *p*-Median Problems." *Management Science* **29**, 482–497.

Tansel, B. C., R. L. Francis, and T. J. Lowe (1983b). "Location on Networks: A Survey. Part II. Exploiting Tree Network Structure." *Management Science* **29**, 498–511.

9

Locations with Spatial Interactions: The Quadratic Assignment Problem

Rainer E. Burkard

Institute for Mathematics
Technical University Graz
Graz, Austria

9.1. INTRODUCTION AND EXAMPLES

In many locational problems the cost associated with placing a facility at a certain site depends not only on the distances from other facilities and the demands, but also on the *interaction* with other facilities. Koopmans and Beckmann (1957) were the first to formulate a mathematical model for locating facilities for this scenario. The model, now known as the quadratic assignment problem (QAP) is: given a set $N \equiv \{1, 2, \ldots, n\}$ and real numbers c_{ik}, a_{ik}, b_{ik} for $i, k = 1, 2, \ldots, n$, find a permutation φ of the set N which minimizes

$$z = \sum_{i=1}^{n} c_{i\varphi(i)} + \sum_{i=1}^{n} \sum_{k=1}^{n} a_{ik} b_{\varphi(i),\varphi(k)} .$$

Later we will extend this problem to the general QAP as introduced by Lawler (1963): given real numbers d_{ijkl} $(i, j, k, l \in N)$, find a permutation $\varphi : N \to N$ which minimizes

$$z = \sum_{i=1}^{n} \sum_{k=1}^{n} d_{i,\varphi(i), k, \varphi(k)} . \qquad (9.1.1)$$

As a first illustrative example we describe a campus planning model due to Dickey and Hopkins (1972). On a campus, new buildings are to be erected. They are to be placed in order to minimize the total walking distances for students and staff. Suppose we have n available sites and n buildings to locate. Each building has a special function, for example, it may serve as a lecture hall, an office building, a campus shop or a dormitory. Let a_{ik} be the walking distance between the two sites i and k where the new buildings can be erected. Let the quantities b_{jl} denote the number of people per week who travel between buildings j and l. The problem is to assign buildings to sites so that the walking distance is minimized. Each assignment can mathematically be described as a permutation φ of the underlying index set $N = \{1, 2, \ldots, n\}$. The product $a_{ik} b_{\varphi(i),\varphi(k)}$ describes the weekly walking distance of people who travel between buildings $j = \varphi(i)$ and $l = \varphi(k)$, if building j is erected on site i and building l is erected on site k. Therefore the problem of minimizing the total walking distance becomes

$$\underset{\varphi}{\text{minimize}}\ z = \sum_{i=1}^{n} \sum_{k=1}^{n} a_{ik} b_{\varphi(i),\varphi(k)} .$$

Consider the small numerical example where we wish to locate four buildings A, B, C, and D on the four sites a, b, c, and d. The distances (in meters) between the four sites (see Figure 9.1) are given by the distance matrix

$$\{a_{ik}\} = \begin{bmatrix} 0 & 340 & 320 & 400 \\ 340 & 0 & 360 & 200 \\ 320 & 360 & 0 & 180 \\ 400 & 200 & 180 & 0 \end{bmatrix} \begin{matrix} a \\ b \\ c \\ d \end{matrix} .$$
$$\quad\ \ a \quad\ \ b \quad\ \ c \quad\ \ d$$

Building A serves as a lecture hall, building B hosts offices, campus shops are in building C and building D is a dormitory. The "connections" between these buildings are described by the "connection matrix" $\{b_{jl}\}$, where b_{jl} is a measure for the number of persons and the frequency with which they walk from building j to building l.

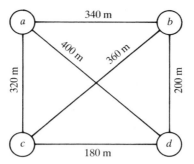

Figure 9.1. Routes between the sites a, b, c, and d.

$$\{b_{jl}\} = \begin{bmatrix} 0 & 80 & 40 & 30 \\ 80 & 0 & 30 & 20 \\ 40 & 30 & 0 & 10 \\ 30 & 20 & 10 & 0 \end{bmatrix} \begin{matrix} A \\ B \\ C \\ D \end{matrix} \, .$$
$$\qquad\qquad A \quad B \quad C \quad D$$

If we assume that building A is erected on site a, building B on site b, building C on site c and building D on site d, we then obtain the following objective function value

$$z = \sum_{i=1}^{n} \sum_{k=1}^{n} a_{ik} b_{ik} = 2[340 \times 80 + 320 \times 40 + 400 \times 30$$

$$+ \, 360 \times 30 + 200 \times 20 + 180 \times 10] = 137{,}200 \, .$$

This solution corresponds to the permutation $\varphi(i) = i$ for $i = 1, 2, 3, 4$. If we assume that A is erected at site d, B at b, C at c, and D at a, we then have the permutation $\varphi(1) = 4$, $\varphi(2) = 2$, $\varphi(3) = 3$, $\varphi(4) = 1$ and the objective function value is now

$$z = \sum_{i=1}^{n} \sum_{k=1}^{n} a_{ik} b_{\varphi(i),\varphi(k)} = 2[340 \times 20 + 320 \times 10 + 400 \times 30$$

$$+ \, 360 \times 30 + 200 \times 80 + 180 \times 40] = 112{,}000 \, .$$

The quadratic assignment problem asks for the best assignment of the buildings to the available sites to minimize the objective function value.

An important area of application of QAPs is the "wiring" problem. Suppose that n modules have to be placed on a board and be connected by "wires." The modules should be placed such that the total wire length is minimal. This leads to the same mathematical model as before (see Steinberg, 1961). Let us denote the distance between positions i and k on the board by a_{ik}. Let b_{jl} be the number of connections between module j and module l. We are looking for a permutation φ of the set $N = \{1, 2, \ldots, n\}$ which assigns a position on the board to every module. If j is placed on position i and l is placed on position k the product $a_{ik}b_{\varphi(i),\varphi(k)}$ is the wire length between modules $j = \varphi(i)$ and $l = \varphi(k)$. Therefore the total wire length is

$$\sum_{i=1}^{n} \sum_{k=1}^{n} a_{ik}b_{\varphi(i),\varphi(k)} \, ,$$

and our problem becomes

$$\text{minimize } z = \sum_{i=1}^{n} \sum_{k=1}^{n} a_{ik}b_{\varphi(i),\varphi(k)} \, .$$

A similar QAP formulation is applicable for design of control panels and typewriter keyboards (see Burkard and Offermann, 1977; Pollatschek, Gershoni, and Radday, 1976). Suppose the keys of a typewriter are to be arranged on the keyboard such that the time needed to write a text in a certain language is minimal. The set $N = \{1, 2, \ldots, n\}$ is the set of symbols to be arranged on the keyboard. We denote the mean frequency of a pair of letters in the considered language by a_{ik}. In the study by Burkard and Offermann (1977) these quantities were determined by evaluating German, English, and French texts with 100,000 letters and punctuation marks. The entry b_{jl} of the matrix $\{b_{jl}\}$ is the number of times key l is pressed after pressing key j. (These numbers were obtained from an ergonometric study.) In the keyboard design problem, we have to assign symbols to the keys, that is, we have to find a permutation φ of the set N. If k is assigned to key $l = \varphi(k)$ and symbol i is assigned to key $j = \varphi(i)$ the product $a_{ik}b_{\varphi(i),\varphi(k)}$ is the time needed to write symbol k after symbol i. In order to minimize the average time for writing a text we have to solve the QAP. Based on the data of Burkard and Offermann, the resulting QAP, solved by heuristic methods, designed keyboards that would require 10% less time for writing a text, than on the international standard keyboard.

There have been many other proposed applications of QAPs, for example,

- in building layout problems, Elshafei (1977) and J. Krarup (personal communication, 1976) have used QAPs for hospital planning,
- in sports, Heffley (1977) models the ranking of a team in a relay race as a QAP,
- in machine scheduling, minimizing average job completion time can be regarded as a QAP,
- in information retrieval, an optimal ordering of interrelated data on a magnetic tape leads to a QAP,

- in chemistry, QAPs have been used for analyzing chemical reactions for organic compounds (Ugi et al., 1979),
- in archaeology, Krarup and Pruzan (1978) model the ranking of archaeological data as a QAP,
- in balancing turbine runners, see Schlegel (1987) as well as Laporte and Mercure (1988).

In the next section we describe some integer programming formulations for QAPs which are useful for solution methods and the design of heuristics. In Section 9.3 we point out some efficiently solvable special cases and comment on the computational complexity of QAPs. Bounds on partial solutions are useful in many exact solution methods. Therefore, in Section 9.4, several methods for deriving good lower bounds are discussed. Exact algorithms for solving QAPs are given in Section 9.5. It is rather time consuming to solve QAPs optimally, even with large computers. Therefore, a need for good heuristics exists and several strategies for the design of efficient heuristics are described in Section 9.6. Computational experiences with some available computer codes are reported in Section 9.7. The asymptotic behavior of QAPs is discussed in Section 9.8. We shall show that the relative difference between the worst and the optimal value of the objective function becomes arbitrarily small with a probability that tends to 1 as the size of the problems tends to infinity. An extensive reference list concludes the chapter.

9.2. INTEGER PROGRAMMING FORMULATIONS OF QAPs

In the last section we defined the QAP as the following combinatorial optimization problem: Given a set $N \equiv \{1, 2, \ldots, n\}$ and real numbers d_{ijkl} $(i, j, k, l \in N)$ find a permutation $\varphi : N \to N$ such that

$$\sum_{i=1}^{n} \sum_{k=1}^{n} d_{i,\varphi(i),k,\varphi(k)} \tag{9.2.1}$$

becomes minimal.

In the examples of Section 9.1 the coefficients d_{ijkl} have the special form

$$d_{ijkl} = a_{ik} b_{jl} . \tag{9.2.2}$$

QAPs with cost coefficients of the form (9.2.2) are sometimes called Koopmans–Beckmann problems, since they appeared as such in their original work (Koopmans and Beckmann, 1957). These problems are by far the most common in practice. Therefore, we shall mainly deal with QAPs in Koopmans–Beckmann form instead of QAPs with general cost coefficients.

However, all results of this chapter also hold, in an analogous way, for "general" QAPs as introduced by Lawler (1963).

The name "quadratic assignment problem" stems from the following linear description of these problems: a permutation $\varphi : N \to N$ corresponds in a unique way to a permutation matrix $X = \{x_{ij}\}$ with

$$\sum_{i=1}^{n} x_{ij} = 1 \qquad \text{for } j = 1, 2, \ldots, n,$$

$$\sum_{j=1}^{n} x_{ij} = 1 \qquad \text{for } i = 1, 2, \ldots, n,$$

$$x_{ij} \in \{0, 1\} \qquad \text{for } i, j = 1, 2, \ldots, n.$$

For example, the permutation φ defined by $\varphi(1) = 4$, $\varphi(2) = 2$, $\varphi(3) = 3$, $\varphi(4) = 1$ corresponds to the permutation matrix

$$X \equiv \{x_{ij}\} = \begin{bmatrix} 0 & 0 & 0 & 1 \\ 0 & 1 & 0 & 0 \\ 0 & 0 & 1 & 0 \\ 1 & 0 & 0 & 0 \end{bmatrix}.$$

That is $x_{i,\varphi(i)} = 1$ for $i = 1, 2, \ldots, n$ and all other elements of X are zero. Thus, a permutation matrix has in every row and column exactly one nonzero entry, namely 1; all other entries are zero.

Utilizing the concept of permutation matrices, QAPs can be reformulated in the following manner

$$\text{minimize} \qquad z = \sum_{i=1}^{n} \sum_{j=1}^{n} \sum_{k=1}^{n} \sum_{l=1}^{n} d_{ijkl} x_{ij} x_{kl}$$

$$\text{such that} \qquad \sum_{i=1}^{n} x_{ij} = 1 \qquad \text{for all } j = 1, 2, \ldots, n,$$

$$\sum_{j=1}^{n} x_{ij} = 1 \qquad \text{for all } i = 1, 2, \ldots, n, \qquad (9.2.3)$$

$$x_{ij} \in \{0, 1\} \qquad \text{for all } i, j = 1, 2, \ldots, n.$$

This is an integer programming formulation of a QAP with a quadratic objective function; hence the term "quadratic assignment problem."

If there happens to be a fixed cost c_{ij} for assigning item j to site i, then the objective function of the problem includes a linear term. That is, we now minimize

$$z = \sum_{i=1}^{n} \sum_{j=1}^{n} \sum_{k=1}^{n} \sum_{l=1}^{n} d_{ijkl} x_{ij} x_{kl} + \sum_{i=1}^{n} \sum_{j=1}^{n} c_{ij} x_{ij}.$$

However, we can redefine

$$d_{ijij} \leftarrow d_{ijij} + c_{ij} \qquad \text{for } i, j = 1, 2, \ldots, n \qquad (9.2.4)$$

and again obtain a purely quadratic objective function with cost coefficients d_{ijkl}. Since linear problems are easier to solve than those with a quadratic objective function, there have been many attempts to get rid of the quadratic terms in the objective function. Lawler (1963), for example, proposed to replace the products $x_{ij}x_{kl}$ by n^4 new binary variables y_{ijkl}:

$$y_{ijkl} \equiv x_{ij}x_{kl} ,$$

and showed that the QAP is equivalent to a linear integer program with $O(n^4)$ variables and constraints.

Theorem 9.1. *The QAP is equivalent to the integer linear program of the form*

$$minimize \qquad z = \sum_{i=1}^{n} \sum_{j=1}^{n} \sum_{k=1}^{n} \sum_{l=1}^{n} d_{ijkl} y_{ijkl}$$

$$subject\ to \qquad \sum_{i=1}^{n} \sum_{j=1}^{n} \sum_{k=1}^{n} \sum_{l=1}^{n} y_{ijkl} = n^2 ,$$

$$x_{ij} + x_{kl} - 2y_{ijkl} \geq 0 \qquad for\ i, j, k, l = 1, 2, \ldots, n ,$$

$$\sum_{i=1}^{n} x_{ij} = 1 \qquad for\ j = 1, 2, \ldots, n , \qquad (9.2.5)$$

$$\sum_{j=1}^{n} x_{ij} = 1 \qquad for\ i = 1, 2, \ldots, n ,$$

$$x_{ij} \in \{0, 1\} \qquad for\ i, j = 1, 2, \ldots, n ,$$

$$y_{ijkl} \in \{0, 1\} \qquad for\ i, j, k, l = 1, 2, \ldots, n .$$

Proof. Let x_{ij} describe a feasible solution of (9.2.3) and define $y_{ijkl} \equiv x_{ij}x_{kl}$. Then all constraints of (9.2.5) are fulfilled and the problems (9.2.3) and (9.2.5) yield, for the corresponding solutions, the same objective function value.

Conversely, let x_{ij}, y_{ijkl} be a feasible solution of (9.2.5). From $x_{ij} + x_{kl} - 2y_{ijkl} \geq 0$, $x_{ij} \in \{0, 1\}$, $y_{ijkl} \in \{0, 1\}$ it follows that

$$y_{ijkl} = 1 \Rightarrow x_{ij} = x_{kl} = 1 .$$

If we assume $x_{ij} = x_{kl} = 1$, but $y_{ijkl} = 0$, we obtain a contradiction to the constraint

$$\sum_{i=1}^{n} \sum_{j=1}^{n} \sum_{k=1}^{n} \sum_{l=1}^{n} y_{ijkl} = n^2 \ .$$

Therefore

$$y_{ijkl} = 1 \Leftrightarrow x_{ij} = x_{kl} = 1 \ ,$$

which can be written as $y_{ijkl} = x_{ij}x_{kl}$. Thus the objective function of (9.2.5) yields the same value as that of (9.2.3). $\square$

For computational purposes the linearization of the QAP due to Theorem 9.1 is rather inconvenient because of the large additional amount of variables and constraints. Thus, efforts have been made to find linearizations with fewer variables and constraints. The smaller the number of additional variables and constraints the easier the linearized problem can be solved by standard computer software. Bazaraa and Sherali (1980) proved the equivalence of the QAP with a mixed integer linear program having n^2 binary variables, $n^2(n-1)^2/2$ real variables, and $2n^2$ linear constraints. The smallest linearization (with respect to the number of variables and constraints), however, is due to Kaufman and Broeckx (1978).

In order to simplify the developments below we introduce the following convenient notation for summation:

$$\sum_{i=1}^{n} \sum_{j=1}^{n} a_{ij}b_{ij} \equiv A \cdot B (= B \cdot A) \ ,$$

where $(n \times n)$ matrices A and B are defined by $\{a_{ij}\}$ and $\{b_{ij}\}$, respectively. The array of the n^4 general cost coefficients d_{ijkl}, $i, j, k, l \in N$ can now be written in the form

$$\{D_{ij}\} \ , \quad i, j = 1, 2, \ldots, n \ ,$$

where every D_{ij} corresponds to an $(n \times n)$ matrix

$$D_{ij} \equiv \{d_{ijkl}\} \ , \quad k, l = 1, 2, \ldots, n \ .$$

Using this notation the objective function of (9.2.1) can be written as

$$z = \sum_{i=1}^{n} \sum_{j=1}^{n} \sum_{k=1}^{n} \sum_{l=1}^{n} d_{ijkl}x_{ij}x_{kl} = \sum_{i=1}^{n} \sum_{j=1}^{n} (D_{ij} \cdot X)x_{ij} \ ,$$

where $X \equiv \{x_{ij}\}$.

We derive now the mixed integer linear program formulation of Kaufman and Broeckx (1978) who define n^2 new real variables w_{ij} by

$$w_{ij} = x_{ij}(D_{ij} \cdot X) = x_{ij}\left(\sum_{k=1}^{n} \sum_{l=1}^{n} d_{ijkl}x_{kl}\right) .$$

Let $W \equiv \{w_{ij}\}$. The objective function can now be rewritten as

$$\text{minimize } z = \sum_{i=1}^{n} \sum_{j=1}^{n} (D_{ij} \cdot X) x_{ij} = \sum_{i=1}^{n} \sum_{j=1}^{n} w_{ij} \,.$$

The following theorem shows the equivalence of the QAP to a mixed integer program with n^2 real and n^2 integer variables and $O(n^2)$ constraints.

Theorem 9.2. *A QAP with nonnegative cost coefficients d_{ijkl} is equivalent to the mixed integer linear program*

$$\textit{minimize} \quad z = \sum_{i=1}^{n} \sum_{j=1}^{n} w_{ij}$$

$$\textit{subject to} \quad \sum_{i=1}^{n} x_{ij} = 1 \qquad \qquad \textit{for } j = 1, 2, \ldots, n \,,$$

$$\sum_{j=1}^{n} x_{ij} = 1 \qquad \qquad \textit{for } i = 1, 2, \ldots, n \,, \tag{9.2.6}$$

$$c_{ij} x_{ij} + (D_{ij} \cdot X) - w_{ij} \le c_{ij} \qquad \textit{for } i, j = 1, 2, \ldots, n \,,$$

$$x_{ij} \in \{0, 1\}, \, w_{ij} \ge 0 \qquad \textit{for } i, j = 1, 2, \ldots, n \,,$$

where $c_{ij} \equiv \sum_{k=1}^{n} \sum_{l=1}^{n} d_{ijkl}$.

Note that we can assume $d_{ijkl} \ge 0$ without loss of generality, since adding a constant to all cost coefficients does not change the optimal solution.

Proof. If x_{ij}, $i, j = 1, 2, \ldots, n$, is a feasible solution of the QAP, then we obtain a feasible solution of (9.2.6) with the same objective function value by defining

$$w_{ij} \equiv x_{ij}(D_{ij} \cdot X) \,.$$

Now let us assume x_{ij} and w_{ij} form an optimal solution of (9.2.6). We have to prove

$$w_{ij} = x_{ij}(D_{ij} \cdot X) \,, \tag{9.2.7}$$

thus showing that the elements x_{ij} form an optimal solution of the QAP. If $x_{ij} = 0$, then $w_{ij} = 0$, since we minimize the sum of the numbers w_{ij} and w_{ij} is feasible. Therefore (9.2.7) holds. If $x_{ij} = 1$, then constraint

$$c_{ij} x_{ij} + (D_{ij} \cdot X) - w_{ij} \le c_{ij}$$

implies

$$w_{ij} \geq (D_{ij} \cdot X) .$$

Again the argument that we minimize the sum of the w_{ij}, yields

$$w_{ij} = (D_{ij} \cdot X) ,$$

thus showing (9.2.7). □

A similar linearization of QAPs, originally proposed by Balas and Mazzola (1980), and used in a recent code of Burkard and Bönniger (1983) is as follows. Let S be the set of $(n \times n)$ permutation matrices and let c_{ij} be an upper bound for $\{D_{ij} \cdot X: X \in S\}$. We define for every $Y \in S$ the elements $a_{kl}(Y)$ of a matrix $A(Y)$ by

$$a_{kl}(Y) \equiv c_{kl}y_{kl} + \sum_{i=1}^{n} \sum_{j=1}^{n} d_{ijkl}y_{ij} , \qquad (9.2.8a)$$

and a real number $b(Y)$ by

$$b(Y) \equiv C \cdot Y . \qquad (9.2.8b)$$

Then we have the following result.

Theorem 9.3. *Every optimal solution X^* of a QAP with nonnegative cost coefficients d_{ijkl} corresponds uniquely to an optimal solution (z^*, X^*) of the integer program*

$$\begin{aligned} &\text{minimize} \quad z \\ &\text{subject to} \quad z \geq A(Y) \cdot X - b(Y) \qquad \text{for all } Y \in S . \end{aligned} \qquad (9.2.9)$$

Proof. For any $Y \in S$ we obtain by definition (9.2.8)

$$A(Y) \cdot X - b(Y)$$

$$= \sum_{k=1}^{n} \sum_{l=1}^{n} \left(c_{kl}y_{kl} + \sum_{i=1}^{n} \sum_{j=1}^{n} d_{ijkl}y_{ij} \right) x_{kl} - C \cdot Y$$

$$= \sum_{i=1}^{n} \sum_{j=1}^{n} \left(\sum_{k=1}^{n} \sum_{l=1}^{n} d_{ijkl}x_{kl} \right) y_{ij}$$

$$+ \sum_{k=1}^{n} \sum_{l=1}^{n} c_{kl}x_{kl}y_{kl} - \sum_{k=1}^{n} \sum_{l=1}^{n} c_{kl}y_{kl}$$

$$= \sum_{i=1}^{n} \sum_{j=1}^{n} (D_{ij} \cdot X + c_{ij}(x_{ij} - 1))y_{ij} = W(X) \cdot Y$$

where $W(X) \equiv \{w_{ij}(X)\}$, and

$$w_{ij}(X) \equiv D_{ij} \cdot X + c_{ij}(x_{ij} - 1).$$

Therefore we obtain

$$\min \{z : z \geq W(X) \cdot Y\} = \min_{X \in S} \left(\max_{Y \in S} W(X) \cdot Y \right).$$

For fixed $X \equiv \bar{X}$ an optimal solution of

$$\max_{Y \in S} W(\bar{X}) \cdot Y$$

is given by $Y \equiv \bar{X}$, since

$$\bar{x}_{ij} = 1 \Rightarrow w_{ij}(\bar{X}) = D_{ij} \cdot \bar{X} + c_{ij}(\bar{x}_{ij} - 1) = D_{ij} \cdot \bar{X} \geq 0,$$
$$\bar{x}_{ij} = 0 \Rightarrow w_{ij}(\bar{X}) = D_{ij} \cdot \bar{X} - c_{ij} \leq 0.$$

Note that this Y is feasible, since $\bar{X} \in S$. Furthermore

$$W(\bar{X}) \cdot Y = W(\bar{X}) \cdot \bar{X}$$
$$= \sum_{i=1}^{n} \sum_{j=1}^{n} \sum_{k=1}^{n} \sum_{l=1}^{n} d_{ijkl} \bar{x}_{ij} \bar{x}_{kl} + \sum_{i=1}^{n} \sum_{j=1}^{n} c_{ij}(\bar{x}_{ij} - 1) \bar{x}_{ij}.$$

Since $\bar{x}_{ij} \in \{0, 1\}$ implies $(\bar{x}_{ij} - 1)\bar{x}_{ij} = 0$ for all i and j, we obtain

$$W(\bar{X}) \cdot \bar{X} = \sum_{i=1}^{n} \sum_{j=1}^{n} \sum_{k=1}^{n} \sum_{l=1}^{n} d_{ijkl} \bar{x}_{ij} \bar{x}_{kl}.$$

Therefore

$$\min_{X \in S} \left(\max_{Y \in S} W(X) \cdot Y \right) = \min \sum_{i=1}^{n} \sum_{j=1}^{n} \sum_{k=1}^{n} \sum_{l=1}^{n} d_{ijkl} x_{ij} x_{kl}. \quad \square$$

For other linearizations and equivalent integer programming formulations of QAPs, see Frieze and Yadegar (1983) and Love and Wong (1976).

9.3. SPECIAL CASES AND COMPUTATIONAL COMPLEXITY

Many well-known combinatorial optimization problems can be formulated as a QAP, such as *linear assignment problems* (LAP), *traveling salesman problems* (TSP), and the so-called *triangulation problem*. If a linear assignment problem with cost matrix $C = \{c_{ij}\}$ is given, we define

$$d_{ijkl} \leftarrow \begin{cases} c_{ij}, & \text{for } (i, j) = (k, l), \\ 0, & \text{otherwise}. \end{cases}$$

Then the objective function of the given LAP is equivalent to the QAP objective

$$\min \sum_{i=1}^{n} \sum_{j=1}^{n} \sum_{k=1}^{n} \sum_{l=1}^{n} d_{ijkl} x_{ij} x_{kl}.$$

We can now show how the traveling salesman problem (TSP) may be formulated as a QAP. Let $N \equiv \{1, 2, \ldots, n\}$. A permutation $\varphi : N \rightarrow N$ is called *cyclic*, if for all $k = 1, 2, \ldots, n - 1$,

$$\varphi^{k}(1) \neq 1,$$

where $\varphi^{k}(1)$ is defined recursively by

$$\varphi^{k}(1) = \varphi(\varphi^{k-1}(1)) \qquad \text{for } k = 2, \ldots, n - 1.$$

For example the permutation φ defined by

$$\varphi(1) = 2, \qquad \varphi(2) = 3, \qquad \varphi(3) = 4, \qquad \varphi(4) = 1$$

is a cyclic permutation. However, the permutation ψ defined by

$$\psi(1) = 2, \qquad \psi(2) = 1, \qquad \psi(3) = 4, \qquad \psi(4) = 3$$

is not cyclic, since $\psi^{2}(1) = 1$ and the exponent $2 = k < n - 1 = 3$.

Cyclic permutations correspond in a unique way to hamiltonian circuits in complete graphs. If the vertices of the graph correspond to the cities which the salesperson has to visit, $\varphi(i) = j$ expresses that the salesperson travels from city i to city j. If we compose an arbitrary permutation φ of N with a fixed cyclic permutation τ of N by

$$\varphi \rightarrow \varphi \circ \tau \circ \varphi^{-1} \equiv \tau',$$

where φ^{-1} is the inverse permutation of φ, we again obtain a cyclic permutation τ', and *all* cyclic permutations of N can be generated in this way with any fixed cyclic permutation τ.

For example, let $N \equiv \{1, 2, 3, 4\}$ and consider the cyclic permutation

$$\tau = \begin{bmatrix} 1 & 2 & 3 & 4 \\ 2 & 3 & 4 & 1 \end{bmatrix}.$$

If we take any other permutation φ, say

$$\varphi = \begin{bmatrix} 1 & 2 & 3 & 4 \\ 2 & 1 & 4 & 3 \end{bmatrix},$$

then we obtain by $\varphi \circ \tau \circ \varphi^{-1}$ another cyclic permutation τ'. In our example φ equals φ^{-1} and therefore

$$\tau' = \varphi \circ \tau \circ \varphi^{-1} = \begin{bmatrix} 1 & 2 & 3 & 4 \\ 4 & 1 & 2 & 3 \end{bmatrix}$$

which yields the cycle 1-4-3-2-1.

Let the cyclic permutation τ correspond to the matrix $B = \{b_{jl}\}$, that is $b_{j,\tau(j)} = 1$ and all other elements $b_{jl} = 0$. Then the matrix corresponding to $\varphi \circ \tau \circ \varphi^{-1}$ is obtained by permuting simultaneously the rows and columns of B according to φ. Therefore $\varphi \circ \tau \circ \varphi^{-1}$ corresponds to $\bar{B} = \{b_{\varphi(j),\varphi(l)}\}$. Thus the TSP can be written in the form

$$\min_{\varphi} \sum_{i=1}^{n} \sum_{k=1}^{n} a_{ik} b_{\varphi(i),\varphi(k)} ,$$

where $\{a_{ik}\}$ is the distance matrix between n cities and $\{b_{jq}\}$ is a fixed cyclic permutation matrix, for example

$$B = \{b_{jq}\} = \begin{bmatrix} 0 & 1 & 0 & 0 & \cdots & 0 & 0 & 0 \\ 0 & 0 & 1 & 0 & \cdots & 0 & 0 & 0 \\ 0 & 0 & 0 & 1 & \cdots & 0 & 0 & 0 \\ \vdots & \vdots & \vdots & \vdots & \ddots & \vdots & \vdots & \vdots \\ & & & & & 0 & 1 & 0 \\ 0 & 0 & 0 & 0 & \cdots & 0 & 0 & 1 \\ 1 & 0 & 0 & 0 & \cdots & 0 & 0 & 0 \end{bmatrix} .$$

This shows that TSPs are special quadratic assignment problems.

In the case of triangulation problems an $(n \times n)$ matrix $A = \{a_{ij}\}$ is given. The rows and the columns of this matrix have to be permuted simultaneously such that ths sum of the elements in the permuted matrix above the main diagonal is minimized. For modeling this problem we introduce a matrix $B = \{b_{jq}\}$ of the form

$$B = \{b_{jq}\} = \begin{bmatrix} 0 & 1 & 1 & 1 & \cdots & 1 & 1 \\ 0 & 0 & 1 & 1 & \cdots & 1 & 1 \\ 0 & 0 & 0 & 1 & \cdots & 1 & 1 \\ \vdots & \vdots & \vdots & \vdots & \ddots & \vdots & \vdots \\ 0 & 0 & 0 & 0 & \cdots & 0 & 1 \\ 0 & 0 & 0 & 0 & \cdots & 0 & 0 \end{bmatrix} .$$

Now the triangulation problem can be formulated as a special QAP

$$\min_{\varphi} \sum_{i=1}^{n} \sum_{k=1}^{n} a_{ik} b_{\varphi(i),\varphi(k)} .$$

Triangulation problems play an important role in connection with input-output matrices in economic models.

We turn now to the complexity of QAPs. The main result is that QAPs are $\mathcal{NP}$-*hard*. This follows from the fact that the TSP is a special QAP and, on the other hand, any QAP can be solved by enumerating all of its $n!$ feasible solutions. Sahni and Gonzalez (1976) showed that QAPs belong even to the hard core of this complexity class. Namely, they proved that even the following approximation problem is $\mathcal{NP}$-complete: let an arbitrarily small $\varepsilon > 0$ be given; for all problem instances find a permutation $\bar{\varphi}$ with objective function value $z(\bar{\varphi})$ such that the relative difference between the optimal objective function value z^* and $z(\bar{\varphi})$ is less than ε, that is

$$\left| \frac{z^* - z(\bar{\varphi})}{z^*} \right| < \varepsilon \, .$$

Up to now $\mathcal{NP}$-hard problems can be solved only by enumeration methods. The enumeration methods known today do not solve QAPs with arbitrary data and problem size of $n > 20$ in a reasonable time. Thus there is a special need for good heuristics, which we shall describe in Section 9.6, since nearly all QAPs arising in practice have larger problem sizes.

On the other hand one can ask: Are there specially structured cases which can be solved by a polynomial algorithm? In this regard, Christofides and Gerrard (1976) investigate the conditions under which a Koopmans–Beckmann problem may be solved by a polynomial algorithm. They show that a Koopmans–Beckmann problem can be solved in $O(n^2)$ steps if the matrices A and B are each a weighted adjacency matrix of a tree. If only one of these matrices is such a "tree-matrix," the problem remains $\mathcal{NP}$-hard; but it can be solved by a special dynamic programming approach (Christofides and Benavent, 1982) for problem sizes of up to $n \approx 30$.

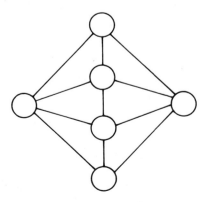

Figure 9.2. A "double-star" graph.

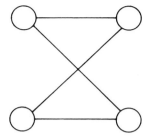

Figure 9.3. The bipartite graph $K_{2,2}$.

Another solvable case, described by Christofides and Gerrard (1976), occurs when A is the weighted adjacency matrix of a double star (see Figure 9.2). In this case the QAP can be solved by a series of linear assignment problems. Rendl (1986) proved that Koopmans–Beckmann problem can be solved in $O(n^3)$ steps if both matrices are weighted adjacency matrices of series-parallel graphs containing no bipartite graph $K_{2,2}$ (see Figure 9.3). If the series-parallel graph contains a $K_{2,2}$ the corresponding QAP remains $\mathcal{NP}$-hard.

9.4. BOUNDS FOR QAP

Let a QAP of the form

$$z = \min_{\varphi} \sum_{i=1}^{n} \sum_{k=1}^{n} d_{i,\varphi(i),k,\varphi(k)} + \sum_{i=1}^{n} c_{i,\varphi(i)}$$

·be given. We want now to derive a good lower bound for z. As in (9.2.4) we can redefine

$$c_{ij} \leftarrow c_{ij} + d_{ijij} \qquad \text{for } i, j = 1, 2, \ldots, n .$$

The coefficients d_{ijil} with $j \neq l$ and d_{ijkl} with $i \neq k$ can never occur in the objective function, since φ is a one-to-one mapping. Therefore we can assume

$$d_{ijkl} = 0 \qquad \text{for } i = k, j \neq l \text{ or } i \neq k, j = l . \tag{9.4.1}$$

Now let f_{ij} be a lower bound for the value of the LAP

$$\min_{\varphi} \sum_{k=1}^{n} d_{ijk,\varphi(k)} \tag{9.4.2}$$

with fixed indices i and j such that $\varphi(i) = j$. The values f_{ij} can be determined by solving LAPs with an $(n-1) \times (n-1)$ cost matrix.

Because of (9.4.1) and (9.4.2)

$$\sum_{i=1}^{n} f_{i,\varphi(i)} \leq \sum_{i=1}^{n} \sum_{k=1}^{n} d_{i,\varphi(i),k,\varphi(k)}$$

holds for any permutation φ. Therefore, the objective function value z is bounded from below by

$$\underline{z} \equiv \min_{\varphi} \sum_{i=1}^{n} (f_{i,\varphi(i)} + c_{i,\varphi(i)}) . \tag{9.4.3}$$

For general QAPs, this lower bound can be computed by solving n^2 LAPs of problem size $(n-1)$ in order to determine the values f_{ij} and one LAP of size n defined by (9.4.3).

The quality of the bound can be improved if we try to shift as much information as possible from the quadratic term of the objective function to the linear term. This procedure, known as *reduction*, was originally proposed by Conrad (1971) and further studied by Burkard (1973), Roucairol (1979), Edwards (1980), Frieze and Yadegar (1983), and recently by Finke, Burkard, and Rendl (1987).

Let us confine ourselves to Koopmans–Beckmann problems with cost coefficients $d_{ijkl} = a_{ik}b_{jl}$. We decompose the given coefficients a_{ik}, b_{jl} in the following way:

$$a_{ik} = \bar{a}_{ik} + f_k , \qquad 1 \leq i, k \leq n, \quad i \neq k ,$$
$$b_{jl} = \bar{b}_{jl} + h_l , \qquad 1 \leq j, l \leq n, \quad j \neq l . \tag{9.4.4}$$

Frieze and Yadegar (1983) showed that the more general decomposition

$$a_{ik} = \bar{a}_{ik} + e_i + f_k , \qquad 1 \leq i, k \leq n, \quad i \neq k ,$$
$$b_{jl} = \bar{b}_{jl} + g_j + h_l , \qquad 1 \leq j, l \leq n, \quad j \neq l$$

does not lead to better bounds. From (9.4.4) we have

$$\bar{a}_{ik}\bar{h}_{jl} = (a_{ik} - f_k)(b_{jl} - h_l) = a_{ik}b_{jl} - h_l a_{ik} - f_k b_{jl} + f_k h_l .$$

Therefore

$$\sum_{i=1}^{n} \sum_{k=1}^{n} a_{ik}b_{\varphi(i),\varphi(k)} + \sum_{k=1}^{n} c_{k,\varphi(k)}$$
$$= \sum_{i=1}^{n} \sum_{k=1}^{n} \bar{a}_{ik}\bar{b}_{\varphi(i),\varphi(k)} + \sum_{k=1}^{n} \bar{c}_{k,\varphi(k)} ,$$

with

$$\bar{c}_{kl} \equiv c_{kl} + f_k \sum_{j=1}^{n} b_{jl} + h_l \sum_{i=1}^{n} a_{ik} - (n-1)f_k h_l .\qquad (9.4.5)$$

In the literature, different rules have been suggested on how to choose f_k and h_l. The choice we adopt here is

$$f_k = \min \{a_{ik}: 1 \le i \le n, i \ne k\} ,$$
$$h_l = \min \{b_{jl}: 1 \le j \le n, j \ne l\} .\qquad (9.4.6)$$

Then

$$\bar{a}_{ik} = a_{ik} - f_k \ge 0 , \qquad 1 \le i, k \le n, \quad i \ne k ,$$
$$\bar{b}_{jl} = b_{jl} - h_l \ge 0 , \qquad 1 \le j, l \le n, \quad j \ne l .$$

Example 9.1. Let

$$A = \begin{bmatrix} 2 & 3 & 4 & 0 \\ 3 & 0 & 5 & 7 \\ 8 & 2 & 1 & 7 \\ 0 & 0 & 4 & 2 \end{bmatrix} , \qquad B = \begin{bmatrix} 1 & 8 & 3 & 1 \\ 0 & 4 & 2 & 7 \\ 0 & 0 & 3 & 7 \\ 2 & 1 & 0 & 7 \end{bmatrix} , \qquad C = 0 .$$

When we split the problem into linear and quadratic parts by redefining $c_{kl} \leftarrow c_{kl} + a_{kk}b_{ll}$, we obtain

$$A = \begin{bmatrix} 0 & 3 & 4 & 0 \\ 3 & 0 & 5 & 7 \\ 8 & 2 & 0 & 7 \\ 0 & 0 & 4 & 0 \end{bmatrix} , \qquad B = \begin{bmatrix} 0 & 8 & 3 & 1 \\ 0 & 0 & 2 & 7 \\ 0 & 0 & 0 & 7 \\ 2 & 1 & 0 & 0 \end{bmatrix} , \qquad C = \begin{bmatrix} 2 & 8 & 6 & 14 \\ 0 & 0 & 0 & 0 \\ 1 & 4 & 3 & 7 \\ 2 & 8 & 6 & 14 \end{bmatrix} .$$

Now we reduce the matrices A and B and obtain

$$f_1 = f_2 = f_4 = 0 , \quad f_3 = 4 , \qquad h_1 = h_2 = h_3 = 0 , \quad h_4 = 1 ,$$

$$\bar{A} = \begin{bmatrix} 0 & 3 & 0 & 0 \\ 3 & 0 & 1 & 7 \\ 8 & 2 & 0 & 7 \\ 0 & 0 & 0 & 0 \end{bmatrix} , \qquad \bar{B} = \begin{bmatrix} 0 & 8 & 3 & 0 \\ 0 & 0 & 2 & 6 \\ 0 & 0 & 0 & 6 \\ 2 & 1 & 0 & 0 \end{bmatrix} .$$

The linear part becomes

$$\bar{C} = \begin{bmatrix} 2 & 8 & 6 & 14+11 \\ 0 & 0 & 0 & 0+5 \\ 1+8 & 4+36 & 3+20 & 7+60+13-12 \\ 2 & 8 & 6 & 14+14 \end{bmatrix} = \begin{bmatrix} 2 & 8 & 6 & 25 \\ 0 & 0 & 0 & 5 \\ 9 & 40 & 23 & 68 \\ 2 & 8 & 6 & 28 \end{bmatrix} . \qquad \bigcirc$$

The original problem with matrices A, B, and C is equivalent to a QAP with matrices $\bar{A}$, $\bar{B}$, and $\bar{C}$. Gilmore (1962) showed that the solution of the subproblems (9.4.2) can be considerably simplified in the case of Koopmans–Beckmann problems. In this case, (9.4.2) is of the following form

$$\min_{\varphi} \sum_{k=1}^{n} a_{ik} b_{j,\varphi(k)} \qquad \text{for } i, j \text{ fixed and } \varphi(i) = j . \qquad (9.4.7)$$

The problems (9.4.7) are therefore of the following kind: given two vectors $(a_1, \ldots, a_r)$, $(b_1, \ldots, b_r)$, find a permutation φ of the indices such that $\sum_{i=1}^{n} a_i b_{\varphi(i)}$ is minimal. The theorem below (see Hardy, Littlewood, and Polya, 1952, Theorem 368) solves these problems.

Theorem 9.4.   *The solution of*

$$\min \sum_{i=1}^{n} a_i b_{\varphi(i)} \qquad (9.4.8)$$

is obtained by reordering the elements of a and b such that the elements of a are in increasing order and the elements of b in decreasing order. The scalar product of these two rearranged vectors gives the minimal value of (9.4.8).

Example 9.2.   Let $a \equiv (0, -1, 5, 4)$ and $b \equiv (3, -1, 2, 7)$. Rearrangements of a and b are

$$\tilde{a} = (-1, 0, 4, 5) , \qquad \tilde{b} = (7, 3, 2, -1) .$$

Then

$$\langle \tilde{a}, \tilde{b} \rangle = (-1) \times 7 + 0 \times 3 + 4 \times 2 + 5 \times (-1) = -4 ,$$

which is minimal.   ○

Proof of Theorem 9.4.   Without loss of generality we can assume that $a_1 \leq a_2 \leq \cdots \leq a_r$.

Assume an optimal solution of (9.4.8) is obtained by a permutation φ such that for a pair (i, j) of indices with $i < j$ the relation

$$b_{\varphi(i)} < b_{\varphi(j)} \qquad (9.4.9)$$

holds. Now define the new permutation $\bar{\varphi}$ by

$$\bar{\varphi}(i) \equiv \varphi(j) , \qquad \bar{\varphi}(j) \equiv \varphi(i) , \qquad \bar{\varphi}(k) \equiv \varphi(k) , \qquad \text{for } k \neq i, j .$$

Then

$$\sum_{\substack{k=1}}^{n} a_k b_{\bar\varphi(k)} = \sum_{\substack{k=1\\k\neq i,j}}^{n} a_k b_{\bar\varphi(k)} + a_i b_{\bar\varphi(i)} + a_j b_{\bar\varphi(j)}$$

$$= \sum_{\substack{k=1\\k\neq i,j}}^{n} a_k b_{\varphi(k)} + a_i b_{\varphi(j)} + a_j b_{\varphi(i)}$$

$$< \sum_{\substack{k=1\\k\neq i,j}}^{n} a_k b_{\varphi(k)} + a_{ib\varphi(i)} + a_i b_{\varphi(j)} \, ,$$

since $a_i \leq a_j$ and $b_{\varphi(i)} < b_{\varphi(j)}$ imply $a_j(b_{\varphi(j)} - b_{\varphi(i)}) > a_i(b_{\varphi(j)} - b_{\varphi(i)})$ and therefore $a_i b_{\varphi(j)} + a_j b_{\varphi(i)} < a_i b_{\varphi(i)} + a_j b_{\varphi(j)}$. Thus we have a contradiction to the optimality of the permutation φ, and therefore (9.4.9) cannot occur in an optimal solution. $\square$

To solve (9.4.7) we arrange in increasing order, for fixed index i, the elements a_{ik}, $k \neq i$, and, for fixed index j, the elements b_{jl}, $l \neq j$, in decreasing order. The scalar product of these rearranged vectors gives the minimal value for (9.4.7).

Example 9.3. In Example 9.1, the third row of $\bar{A}$ is $(8, 2, 0, 7)$ and the first row of $\bar{B}$ is $(0, 8, 3, 0)$. Deleting the elements a_{33} and b_{11}, and rearranging the remaining elements we obtain

$$\tilde a = (2, 7, 8) , \qquad \tilde b = (8, 3, 0) .$$

Thus

$$f_{31} = \langle \tilde a, \tilde b \rangle = 16 + 21 + 0 = 37 . \quad \bigcirc$$

In order to generate the matrix $\{f_{ij}\}$ for problem (9.4.3) we have to simply calculate n^2 such minimal scalar products instead of solving n^2 LAPs.

Example 9.4. To determine a lower bound for the problem instance of Example 9.1, we compute the matrix $F = \{f_{ij}\}$ from the matrices $\bar{A}$ and $\bar{B}$ of Example 9.1. The rearranged row vectors are

$$\tilde a_1 = (0, 0, 3) , \qquad \tilde b_1 = (8, 3, 0) ,$$
$$\tilde a_2 = (1, 3, 7) , \qquad \tilde b_2 = (6, 2, 0) ,$$
$$\tilde a_3 = (2, 7, 8) , \qquad \tilde b_3 = (6, 0, 0) ,$$
$$\tilde a_4 = (0, 0, 0) , \qquad \tilde b_4 = (2, 1, 0) .$$

Therefore $F = \{f_{ij}\} = \{\langle \tilde{a}_i, \tilde{b}_j \rangle\}$ is

$$\begin{bmatrix} 0 & 0 & 0 & 0 \\ 17 & 12 & 6 & 5 \\ 37 & 26 & 12 & 11 \\ 0 & 0 & 0 & 0 \end{bmatrix}.$$

Thus $\{f_{ij} + c_{ij}\}$ becomes

$$\tilde{C} = \begin{bmatrix} 2 & 8 & 6 & 25 \\ 17 & 12 & 6 & 10 \\ 46 & 66 & 35 & 79 \\ 2 & 8 & 6 & 28 \end{bmatrix}.$$

The solution of a LAP with cost matrix $\tilde{C}$ now yields the lower bound $\underline{z}$ on z: $\underline{z} = 55$. $\bigcirc$

We summarize the above procedure in the following algorithm.

Algorithm 9.1. For the lower bound computation for a QAP of the form

$$\min_{\varphi} \sum_{k=1}^{n} c_{k,\varphi(k)} + \sum_{i=1}^{n} \sum_{k=1}^{n} a_{ik} b_{\varphi(i),\varphi(k)}.$$

Given data are $A = \{a_{ik}\}$, $B = \{b_{jl}\}$, $C = \{c_{kl}\}$, for $i, j, k, l = 1, 2, \ldots, n$. Let index sets $I = J = \{1, 2, \ldots, n\}$, and let $t \equiv n - 1$.

Step 1: Redefine for $k \in I$, $j \in J$

$$c_{kl} \leftarrow c_{kl} + a_{kk} b_{ll}, \qquad a_{kk} = b_{ll} = 0.$$

(These elements are not considered any more and, thus, may be deleted.)
Step 2: Reduction of A: determine for $k \in I$

$$I_k \equiv I \backslash \{k\}, \qquad f_k \equiv \min\{a_{ik}: i \in I_k\}, \qquad a_k \equiv \sum_{i \in I_k} a_{ik}.$$

Replace for all $i \in I_k$

$$a_{ik} \leftarrow a_{ik} - f_k.$$

Step 3: Reduction of B: determine for all $l \in J$

$$J_l \equiv J \backslash \{l\}, \qquad h_l \equiv \min\{b_{jl}: j \in J_l\}, \qquad b_l \equiv \sum_{j \in J_l} b_{jl}.$$

Replace for all $j \in J_l$

$$b_{jl} \leftarrow b_{jl} - h_l.$$

Step 4: Define for all $k \in I$, $l \in J$

$$c_{kl} \leftarrow c_{kl} + f_k b_l + a_k h_l - f_k h_l t \, .$$

Step 5: Gilmore–Lawler bounds: arrange for all (fixed) $i \in I$ the numbers $\{a_{ik} : k \neq i\}$ in increasing order, $a^{(i)} = (a_{ik_1}, \ldots, a_{ik_r})$. Arrange for all (fixed) $j \in J$ the numbers $\{b_{jl} : l \neq j\}$ in decreasing order, $b^{(j)} = (b_{jl_1}, \ldots, b_{jl_r})$. Compute for all $i \in I$, $j \in J$ the scalar product

$$f_{ij} = \langle a^{(i)}, b^{(j)} \rangle \, .$$

Step 6: Redefine for all $k \in I$, $l \in J$

$$c_{kl} \leftarrow c_{kl} + f_{kl} \, .$$

Step 7: Solve the linear assignment problem with cost matrix C. The optimal objective function value z is a lower bound for the objective function value of the QAP.

In branch-and-bound algorithms and some heuristics we often have to compute bounds under the additional assumption that some of the indices are already fixed. Let $M \subseteq N = \{1, 2, \ldots, n\}$ and let $\varphi(i)$ be fixed for $i \in M$. We denote the mapping $\varphi(i)$, $i \in M$, by (M, φ) and call it a *partial permutation*. Later on we shall use the notation $\varphi(M)$ for $\{j : j = \varphi(i), i \in M\}$. Thus the partial permutation (M, φ) is a one-to-one mapping of M to $\varphi(M)$, whereas $\varphi(M)$ is the set of indices which are already fixed by this partial permutation. Now, given a partial permutation (M, φ), then what is an upper bound for

$$z(\varphi) = \sum_{i=1}^{n} \sum_{k=1}^{n} a_{ik} b_{\varphi(i), \varphi(k)} \, ,$$

under the constraint $\varphi(i)$ fixed for $i \in M$? Fortunately such an upper bound is easily available by extending the partial permutation to a permutation of the set N and by evaluating the corresponding objective function value $z(\varphi)$.

Example 9.5. Let

$$A = \begin{bmatrix} 2 & 3 & 4 & 0 \\ 3 & 0 & 5 & 7 \\ 8 & 2 & 1 & 7 \\ 0 & 0 & 4 & 2 \end{bmatrix}, \qquad B = \begin{bmatrix} 1 & 8 & 3 & 1 \\ 0 & 4 & 2 & 7 \\ 0 & 0 & 3 & 7 \\ 2 & 1 & 0 & 7 \end{bmatrix},$$

and $M = \{1, 2\}$ with $\varphi(1) = 2$, $\varphi(2) = 3$. We extend the partial permutation in an arbitrary way, for example, by $\varphi(3) = 1$, $\varphi(4) = 4$. Now we rearrange

B by permuting first the rows and then the columns of B according to φ^{-1}

$$\bar{B} = \{\bar{b}_{ik}\} = \{b_{\varphi(i),\varphi(k)}\} = \begin{bmatrix} 4 & 2 & 0 & 7 \\ 0 & 3 & 0 & 7 \\ 8 & 3 & 1 & 1 \\ 1 & 0 & 2 & 7 \end{bmatrix}.$$

As in Section 9.2 the term $\sum_{i=1}^{n} \sum_{k=1}^{n} a_{ik} b_{\varphi(i),\varphi(k)} = \sum_{i=1}^{n} \sum_{k=1}^{n} a_{ik} \bar{b}_{ik}$ can be written as $A \cdot \bar{B}$, namely

$$A \cdot \bar{B} = \begin{bmatrix} 2 & 3 & 4 & 0 \\ 3 & 0 & 5 & 7 \\ 8 & 2 & 1 & 7 \\ 0 & 0 & 4 & 2 \end{bmatrix} \begin{bmatrix} 4 & 2 & 0 & 7 \\ 0 & 3 & 0 & 7 \\ 8 & 3 & 1 & 1 \\ 1 & 0 & 2 & 7 \end{bmatrix}$$

$$= 8 + 6 + 49 + 64 + 6 + 1 + 7 + 8 + 14 = 163 \, ,$$

and this corresponds to an upper bound.   ○

The problem to obtain good lower bounds for z is more difficult. We can rewrite the objective function using the fact that the indices $\varphi(i)$, $i \in M$, are already fixed. For any permutation φ of N with $\varphi(i) = \bar{\varphi}(i)$ for $i \in M$ we obtain

$$z(\varphi) = \sum_{i \in M} \sum_{k \in M} a_{ik} b_{\bar{\varphi}(i),\bar{\varphi}(k)}$$

$$+ \sum_{i \in M} \sum_{k \notin M} [a_{ik} b_{\bar{\varphi}(i),\varphi(k)} + a_{ki} b_{\varphi(k)\bar{\varphi}(i)}]$$

$$+ \sum_{i \notin M} \sum_{k \notin M} a_{ik} b_{\varphi(i),\varphi(k)} \, . \tag{9.4.10}$$

The first sum in (9.4.10) is a constant, since $\bar{\varphi}$ is fixed. For the second and third sum in (9.4.10) a lower bound can be derived by solving a linear assignment problem with cost coefficients c_{ik}, for $i \notin M$, $k \notin \bar{\varphi}(M)$. The coefficients c_{ik}, $i \notin M$, $k \notin \bar{\varphi}(M)$, are chosen as lower bounds for the contribution of the single assignment $i \rightsquigarrow k$, namely $\varphi(i) = k$, to the objective function value $z(\varphi)$. These lower bounds consist of a part induced by the partial permutation $(M, \bar{\varphi})$, a reduction part, and the "Gilmore–Lawler"-bound applied to the reduced elements.

Note that

$$a_{ii} b_{kk} + \sum_{l \in M} [a_{li} b_{\bar{\varphi}(l),k} + a_{il} b_{k,\bar{\varphi}(l)}]$$

is that contribution to c_{ik} which is implied by the partial permutation $(M, \bar{\varphi})$. Furthermore, the third term in the sum (9.4.10) can be viewed as objective function of a QAP with problem size $n - |M|$. Therefore, we can use the ideas given at the beginning of this section to obtain a lower bound for this term. In particular, a reduction can be applied and the Gilmore–Lawler bounds can be computed. Summarizing, we obtain the following algorithm.

Algorithm 9.2. For the lower bound computation for a QAP of the form

$$\min_{\varphi} \sum_{i=1}^{n} c_{i,\varphi(i)} + \sum_{i=1}^{n} \sum_{k=1}^{n} a_{ik} b_{\varphi(i),\varphi(k)} ,$$

where the indices $\varphi(i)$, $i \in M$, are fixed. Given data are

$$M \subseteq \{1, 2, \ldots, n\}, \varphi(i), i \in M ,$$
$$I \equiv \{1, 2, \ldots, n\} \setminus M ,$$
$$J \equiv \{1, 2, \ldots, n\} \setminus \{\varphi(i): i \in M\} ,$$
$$A = \{a_{ik}\}_{i \in I, k \in I}, \ B = \{b_{jl}\}_{j \in J, l \in J}, \ C = \{c_{kl}\}_{k \in I, l \in J} .$$

Let

$$\underline{z} \equiv \sum_{i \in M} \sum_{k \in M} a_{ik} b_{\varphi(i),\varphi(k)} , \qquad t \equiv |I| - 1 .$$

Step 1: Replace, for $k \in I$, $l \in J$

$$c_{kl} \leftarrow c_{kl} + a_{kk} b_{ll} + \sum_{r \in M} [a_{kr} b_{l,\varphi(r)} + a_{rk} b_{\varphi(r),l}] , \quad a_{kk} \leftarrow b_{ll} \leftarrow 0 .$$

(These elements are not needed further.)

Step 2: Perform Steps 2–6 of Algorithm 9.1.

Step 3: Solve a linear assignment problem with cost matrix C. Let its optimal objective function value be z_L. Then $\underline{z} \leftarrow \underline{z} + z_L$ is a lower bound.

Example 9.6. We have $M = \{1, 2\}$ with $\varphi(1) = 2$, $\varphi(2) = 3$ and therefore $I = \{3, 4\}$, $J = \{1, 4\}$,

$$A = \begin{bmatrix} 2 & 3 & 4 & 0 \\ 3 & 0 & 5 & 7 \\ 8 & 2 & 1 & 7 \\ 0 & 0 & 4 & 2 \end{bmatrix}, \qquad B = \begin{bmatrix} 1 & 8 & 3 & 1 \\ 0 & 4 & 2 & 7 \\ 0 & 0 & 3 & 7 \\ 2 & 1 & 0 & 7 \end{bmatrix}, \qquad C = 0 .$$

Thus

$$\underline{z} = \sum_{i=1}^{2} \sum_{k=1}^{2} a_{ik} b_{\varphi(i),\varphi(k)} = a_{11} b_{22} + a_{12} b_{23} + a_{21} b_{32} + a_{22} b_{33}$$

$$= 8 + 6 + 0 + 0 = 14 .$$

This partial permutation implies now the following contribution to c_{ik} ($i = 3, 4$; $k = 1, 4$):

$$c_{31} = 1 \times 1 + (4 \times 0 + 5 \times 0 + 8 \times 8 + 2 \times 3) = 71 ,$$

$$c_{34} = 1 \times 7 + (4 \times 7 + 5 \times 7 + 8 \times 1 + 2 \times 0) = 78 ,$$

$$c_{41} = 2 \times 1 + (0 \times 0 + 7 \times 0 + 0 \times 8 + 0 \times 3) = 2 ,$$

$$c_{44} = 2 \times 7 + (0 \times 7 + 7 \times 7 + 0 \times 1 + 0 \times 0) = 63 .$$

Now we redefine a (2×2) matrix C by

$$C = \begin{bmatrix} c_{31} & c_{34} \\ c_{41} & c_{44} \end{bmatrix} = \begin{bmatrix} 71 & 78 \\ 2 & 63 \end{bmatrix} .$$

Reduction of A yields

for $k = 3$: $I_k = \{4\}$, $f_3 = 4 = a_3$, $a_{43} = 0$;

for $k = 4$: $I_k = \{3\}$, $f_4 = 7 = a_4$, $a_{34} = 0$.

Reduction of B yields

for $l = 1$: $j_l = \{4\}$, $h_1 = 2 = b_1$, $b_{41} = 0$;

for $l = 4$: $J_l = \{1\}$, $h_4 = 1 = b_4$, $b_{14} = 0$.

Redefining C using Step 1 of Algorithm 9.2

$$c_{31} = 71 + 8 + 8 - 8 = 79 \quad \text{(since } t = 1\text{) ,}$$

$$c_{34} = 78 + 4 \qquad\quad = 82 ,$$

$$c_{41} = 2 + 14 \qquad\quad = 16 ,$$

$$c_{44} = 63 + 7 \qquad\quad = 70 .$$

Moreover $f_{ij} = 0$ for $i \in I$, $j \in J$. Therefore we have to solve a LAP with

$$C = \begin{bmatrix} 79 & 82 \\ 16 & 70 \end{bmatrix} .$$

Its optimal value is $z_L = 82 + 16 = 98$. Therefore $\underline{z} \leftarrow \underline{z} + z_L = 14 + 98 = 112$ is a lower bound. Note that for $|M| = n - 2$, Algorithm 9.2 yields the exact values of a feasible permutation. Thus, there is a permutation, namely $\varphi(1) = 2$, $\varphi(2) = 3$, $\varphi(3) = 4$, $\varphi(4) = 1$ with value $z = \underline{z} = 112$.

The other completion of the partial permutation yields the upper bound

$$z = 14 + 79 + 70 = 163$$

as the direct computation in Example 9.5 showed.   ○

We shall discuss in the next section how these bounds can be used in branch-and-bound algorithms.

Finke et al. (1987) propose a different approach for the computation of lower bounds in the case of Koopmans–Beckmann problems with *symmetric* matrices A and B.

Let $\lambda_1, \ldots, \lambda_n$ be the eigenvalues of the symmetric matrix A and let $\mu_1, \ldots, \mu_n$ be the eigenvalues of the symmetric matrix B. Since A and B are symmetric, the eigenvalues are real and we can assume the ordering

$$\lambda_1 \le \lambda_2 \le \cdots \le \lambda_n \quad \text{and} \quad \mu_1 \ge \mu_2 \ge \cdots \ge \mu_n \,.$$

Now the following theorem holds.

Theorem 9.5. *For all permutations φ*

$$\sum_{i=1}^{n} \lambda_i \mu_i \le \sum_{i=1}^{n} \sum_{k=1}^{n} a_{ik} b_{\varphi(i),\varphi(k)} \le \sum_{i=1}^{n} \lambda_i \mu_{n-i} \,.$$

The proof is given by Finke et al. This theorem shows that the objective function value of a QAP with symmetric matrices A and B ranges between

$$\sum_{i=1}^{n} \lambda_i \mu_i \quad \text{and} \quad \sum_{i=1}^{n} \lambda_i \mu_{n-1} \,. \tag{9.4.11}$$

In order to make the range in (9.4.11) smaller, a reduction may be applied to the matrices A and B which still preserves their symmetry. One way to decrease the difference between upper and lower bounds in (9.4.11) is to minimize the *spreads* $s(A)$ and $s(B)$ of the matrices A and B. The spread of a symmetric matrix is defined as the difference between its largest and smallest eigenvalues

$$s(A) = \min_{i,j} |\lambda_i - \lambda_j| \,, \qquad s(B) = \min_{i,j} |\mu_i - \mu_j| \,.$$

Unfortunately, there is no simple formula to compute the spread. However, we can minimize the following approximation of the spread due to Mirsky (1956)

$$s(T) \le \left[2 \sum_{i=1}^{n} \sum_{j=1}^{n} t_{ij}^2 - \left(\frac{2}{n} \right) \left(\sum_{i=1}^{n} t_{ii} \right)^2 \right]^{1/2} \equiv m(T) \,,$$

where T is any symmetric $(n \times n)$ matrix. Minimizing $m(T)$ leads to a system of linear equations, from which the coefficients of the reduction can be computed explicitly. The reduction of $T = \{t_{ik}\}$ to $\bar{T} = \{\bar{t}_{ik}\}$ has the form

$$t_{ik} = \bar{t}_{ik} + e_i + e_k + r_{ik} \,, \tag{9.4.12}$$

where the coefficients e_i, e_k, and r_{ik} are computed by

$$z = \frac{1}{2(n-1)} \left(\sum_{i=1}^{n} \sum_{k=1}^{n} t_{ik} - \sum_{i=1}^{n} t_{ii} \right),$$

$$e_i = \frac{1}{n-2} \left(\sum_{j=1}^{n} t_{ij} - t_{ii} - z \right), \qquad (9.4.13)$$

$$r_{ik} = \begin{cases} t_{ii} - 2e_i, & \text{for } i = k, \\ 0, & \text{otherwise}. \end{cases}$$

Obviously, the reduced matrix $\bar{T}$ has zeros in the diagonal and is again symmetric. Moreover, every row and column sum of $\bar{T}$ equals 0. Using these properties, a simple formula for a lower bound can be derived as follows. Reduce the matrix $A = \{a_{ik}\}$ to $\bar{A} = \{\bar{a}_{ik}\}$ by

$$a_{ik} = \bar{a}_{ik} + e_i + e_k + r_{ik},$$

and the matrix $B = \{b_{jl}\}$ to $\bar{B} = \{\bar{b}_{jl}\}$ by

$$b_{jl} = \bar{b}_{jl} + f_j + f_l + s_{jl}.$$

Then a straightforward calculation yields, for any permutation,

$$\sum_{i=1}^{n} \sum_{k=1}^{n} \bar{a}_{ik} \bar{b}_{\varphi(i),\varphi(k)}$$

$$= \sum_{i=1}^{n} \sum_{k=1}^{n} a_{ik} b_{\varphi(i),\varphi(k)} - \sum_{i=1}^{n} \sum_{k=1}^{n} (e_i + e_k + r_{ik}) b_{\varphi(i),\varphi(k)}$$

$$- \sum_{i=1}^{n} \sum_{k=1}^{n} \bar{a}_{ik} (f_{\varphi(i)} + f_{\varphi(k)} + s_{\varphi(i),\varphi(k)}).$$

But $\bar{a}_{ik} = 0$ for $i = k$ and all row and column sums of the symmetric matrix $\bar{A}$ are zero. Therefore

$$\sum_{i=1}^{n} \sum_{k=1}^{n} \bar{a}_{ik} (f_{\varphi(i)} + f_{\varphi(k)} + s_{\varphi(i),\varphi(k)}) = 0.$$

Moreover, by the symmetry of B we obtain

$$\sum_{i=1}^{n} \sum_{k=1}^{n} (e_i + e_j + r_{ik}) b_{\varphi(i),\varphi(k)} = \sum_{i=1}^{n} a_{ii} b_{\varphi(i),\varphi(i)} + 2 \sum_{i=1}^{n} e_i \left(\sum_{\substack{k=1 \\ k \neq i}}^{n} b_{\varphi(i),\varphi(k)} \right).$$

Let us now define a matrix $C = \{c_{ij}\}$ by

$$c_{ij} \equiv a_{ii} b_{jj} + 2e_i \sum_{\substack{k=1 \\ k \neq j}}^{n} b_{jk}$$

and let $\bar{\lambda}_1, \ldots, \bar{\lambda}_n$ and $\bar{\mu}_1, \ldots, \bar{\mu}_n$ be the ordered eigenvalues of the reduced matrices $\bar{A}$ and $\bar{B}$, respectively. Then

$$\sum_{i=1}^{n} \bar{\lambda}_i \bar{\mu}_i + \min_{\varphi} \sum_{i=1}^{n} c_{i\varphi(i)}$$

is a lower bound for the QAP. Computational experiments have shown that, in general, this bound is sharper than the Gilmore–Lawler bound for larger sized problems.

Example 9.7 (Rendl, 1985).   Let two matrices of a Koopmans–Beckmann problem be given as follows

$$A = \begin{bmatrix} 0 & 1 & 1 & 3 \\ 1 & 0 & 4 & 4 \\ 1 & 4 & 0 & 5 \\ 3 & 4 & 5 & 0 \end{bmatrix}, \qquad B = \begin{bmatrix} 0 & 1 & 3 & 1 \\ 1 & 0 & 4 & 2 \\ 3 & 4 & 0 & 2 \\ 1 & 2 & 2 & 0 \end{bmatrix}.$$

The reduction of A yields the values

$$z = 6, \qquad e_1 = -\frac{1}{2}, \qquad e_2 = \frac{3}{2}, \qquad e_3 = 2, \qquad e_4 = 3,$$

$$r_{11} = 1, \qquad r_{22} = -3, \qquad r_{33} = -4, \qquad r_{44} = -6,$$

and

$$\bar{A} = \frac{1}{2} \begin{bmatrix} 0 & 0 & -1 & +1 \\ 0 & 0 & +1 & -1 \\ -1 & +1 & 0 & 0 \\ +1 & -1 & 0 & 0 \end{bmatrix}$$

with eigenvalues $\bar{\lambda}_1 = -1$, $\bar{\lambda}_2 = \bar{\lambda}_3 = 0$, $\bar{\lambda}_4 = 1$.

   The reduction of B yields the values

$$z = \frac{13}{3}, \qquad f_1 = \frac{1}{3}, \qquad f_2 = \frac{4}{3}, \qquad f_3 = \frac{7}{3}, \qquad f_4 = \frac{1}{3},$$

$$s_{11} = -\frac{2}{3}, \qquad s_{22} = -\frac{8}{3}, \qquad s_{33} = -\frac{14}{3}, \qquad s_{44} = -\frac{2}{3},$$

and

$$\bar{B} = \frac{1}{3} \begin{bmatrix} 0 & -2 & 1 & 1 \\ -2 & 0 & 1 & 1 \\ 1 & 1 & 0 & -2 \\ 1 & 1 & -2 & 0 \end{bmatrix}$$

with eigenvalues

$$\bar{\mu}_1 = \bar{\mu}_2 = \frac{2}{3}, \qquad \bar{\mu}_3 = 0, \qquad \bar{\mu}_4 = -\frac{4}{3}.$$

Since the diagonal elements of A are zero we can solve the LAP $\min \Sigma_{i=1}^{n} c_{i\varphi(i)}$ by a minimal scalar product of the vectors

$$e \equiv (-1, 3, 4, 6) \qquad \text{and} \qquad b \equiv (9, 7, 5, 5).$$

Thus

$$\underline{z} = \langle \bar{\lambda}, \bar{\mu} \rangle + \langle e, b \rangle = -2 + 62 = 60.$$

Therefore, the minimal value of this Koopmans–Beckmann problem is at least 60. For this example the Gilmore–Lawler bound yields the value 59. The optimal value is known to be 60. $\bigcirc$

Equations (9.4.13) provide a reduction that yields smaller spreads for the matrices A and B. The idea behind it is to minimize the range of values in Theorem 9.5. Recently, a different reduction scheme has been proposed by Rendl and Wolkowicz (1988) where the lower bound of the reduced QAP is maximized. This reduction is determined iteratively and relies on techniques for nonsmooth optimization and matrix analysis. Hadley, Rendl, and Wolkowicz (1989) provide a refinement of Theorem 9.5 by using the matrix formulation (9.2.3) of the QAP and exploiting the special structure of orthogonal matrices having constant row and column sums.

9.5.   EXACT ALGORITHMS FOR SOLVING QAPs

Since QAPs are $\mathcal{NP}$-hard, only implicit enumeration methods are known for solving them optimally. Essentially, there are three different types of algorithms that have been used for implicit enumeration, namely

1. branch-and-bound type algorithms,
2. cutting plane methods,
3. dynamic programming.

Cutting plane methods for QAPs were introduced by Bazaraa and Sherali (1980), but the computational experience has not been satisfactory. However, such methods are useful for finding good suboptimal solutions (see also Burkard and Bönniger, 1983, for a cutting plane method as a heuristic).

Branch-and-bound methods are most widely used for solving QAPs exactly. Three different types of approaches are reported in the literature:

1. single assignment algorithms,
2. pair assignment algorithms,
3. relative positioning algorithm.

In pair assignment algorithms, a fixed pair (i, k) is assigned to a pair (j, l) and the corresponding increase of the objective function (or a lower bound thereof) is computed. Pair assignment algorithms were developed by Land (1963), Gavett and Plyter (1966), and Nugent, Vollmann, and Ruml (1968), among others. Pierce and Crowston (1971) designed a method based on the exclusion of such pair assignments. Several computational studies have revealed that pair assignment and pair exclusion algorithms are computationally not very efficient and cannot compete with single assignment algorithms.

In the relative positioning algorithm of Mirchandani and Obata (1979) the levels in the branch-and-bound tree do not correspond to assignments of facilities to sites. The partial placements at each level are in terms of distances between facilities, that is, their relative positions. The authors claim favorable behavior of this algorithm for problems with sparse connection matrices.

The first single assignment algorithm goes back to Gilmore (1962) and was extended to general QAPs by Lawler (1963). In single assignment algorithms just one facility is assigned to a location and the contribution to the objective function caused by such an assignment (or rather a lower bound for that contribution) is computed. For this computation, Algorithm 9.2 can be used.

We describe now a single assignment algorithm in more detail. With a partial permutation (M, φ) we associate a lower bound $\underline{z}(M, \varphi)$ which, for example, can be computed by Algorithm 9.2. If now the partial permutation (M, φ) is extended by an additional assignment $i \rightsquigarrow \varphi(i)$ for $i \notin M$, $\varphi(i) \notin \varphi(M)$, a new lower bound $\underline{z}(\bar{M}, \varphi)$ can be computed from the matrix C without much effort. To do this, we delete in C the row corresponding to i and the column corresponding to $\varphi(i)$. The remaining coefficients c_{ij} represent minimal amounts which need to be added to $\underline{z}(M, \varphi)$ if an assignment $i \rightsquigarrow j$ were to be made. Thus, important information can be obtained without updating the elements c_{ij} by Algorithm 9.2 (see the following example).

To describe the branch-and-bound scheme for the single assignment algorithm, let $\bar{z}$ denote an upper bound for the optimal objective function value of the QAP. We start with the partial permutation corresponding to $M = \emptyset$. If for a given partial permutation (M, φ) the relation $z(M, \varphi) < \bar{z}$ holds, then we choose a pair of indices $i \notin M$, $j \notin \varphi(M)$ and replace M by

$$M \leftarrow M \cup \{i\}, \qquad \varphi(i) = j.$$

Then a new bound is derived, either by considering the last updated matrix C or by applying Algorithm 9.2 to the new M. If $|M| = n - 2$, the remaining two completions of M are compared with $\bar{z}$. If one of them leads to a value less than $\bar{z}$, this newly found solution is stored as a possible candidate for the optimal solution and $\bar{z}$ is improved.

If $\underline{z}(M, \varphi) \geq \bar{z}$, one returns to the last found partial permutation (M, φ) with $\underline{z}(M, \varphi) < \bar{z}$. The assignment $i \rightsquigarrow j$, chosen at the transition of (M, φ) to its successor, is now blocked, for example by defining $c_{ij} \equiv \infty$. If the blocked element is the first blocked one in the matrix C, then a new assignment is chosen either for i or for $\varphi(k) = j$. If, however, row i (column j) of C already contains more blocked elements, the new assignment has to be chosen in the same row (column) of C. This rule prevents the same problem being considered several times in the branching tree. The optimality of the stored solution is verified as soon as the empty set is reached again. See Figure 9.5 for an example of a branching tree.

A favorable selection of the pair (i, j) for a new branching can be made by the following *rule of alternative costs*. Let c_{ij}, $i \not\in M$, $j \not\in \varphi(M)$ be a lower bound for the increase of the objective function value if i is assigned to j. (Such a matrix is constructed in Algorithm 9.2. In Step 4 of this algorithm a LAP with the cost matrix $\{c_{ij}\}$ is solved. In its optimal tableau for every i and every j there is an entry $c_{ij} = 0$.) We can assume that there is a one-to-one mapping φ^* of the rows to the columns of C with $c_{i,\varphi^*(i)} = 0$. (Otherwise the lower bound for the current solution could be increased.) Now we compute for every $(i, \varphi^*(i))$

$$u_i = \min \{c_{ij} \mid j \not\in \varphi(M), j \neq \varphi^*(i)\},$$

$$v_{\varphi^*(i)} = \min \{c_{k\varphi^*(i)} \mid k \not\in M, k \neq i\}.$$

The value $u_i + v_{\varphi^*(i)}$ yields a lower bound for the increase of the bound z_L, if the assignment $i \rightsquigarrow \varphi^*(i)$ would *not* be used (*alternative costs*). In order to exclude as many problems as possible at an early stage in the branching tree, one of those pairs $(i, \varphi^*(i))$ should be chosen for the next assignment which has maximal alternative costs. Two such branches are added, one corresponds to $i \rightsquigarrow \varphi^*(i)$, the other to $i \not\rightsquigarrow \varphi^*(i)$; in the second case the lower bound is at least

$$z_L + u_i + v_{\varphi}^*(i).$$

We illustrate the above branch-and-bound procedure by a numerical example.

Example 9.8. We will continue with Example 9.4. For $M = \emptyset$ we had to solve a LAP with cost matrix

$$C = \begin{bmatrix} 2 & 8 & 6 & 25 \\ 17 & 12 & 6 & 10 \\ 46 & 66 & 35 & 79 \\ 2 & 8 & 6 & 28 \end{bmatrix}.$$

reducing first the rows of C (according to the so-called Hungarian method) we obtain $z_L = 45$ and

$$C_1 = \begin{bmatrix} 0 & 6 & 4 & 23 \\ 11 & 6 & 0 & 4 \\ 11 & 31 & 0 & 44 \\ 0 & 6 & 4 & 26 \end{bmatrix}.$$

A column reduction leads to $z_L = 55$ and

$$C_2 = \begin{bmatrix} 0^* & 0 & 4 & 19 \\ 11 & 0 & 0 & 0^* \\ 11 & 25 & 0^* & 40 \\ 0 & 0^* & 4 & 22 \end{bmatrix}.$$

Fortunately, this reduction yields an optimal assignment for the first LAP with $z_L = 55$. The corresponding permutation is $\varphi(1) = 1$, $\varphi(2) = 4$, $\varphi(3) = 3$, and $\varphi(4) = 2$. For the given QAP the objective function value for this assignment is $z = 63$, which can now be used as an upper bound. According to the rule of alternative costs, we now choose the single assignment $\varphi(2) = 4$ for the next branching.

Thus we have the branching shown in Figure 9.4. Since $\varphi(2) \neq 4$ would result in an increase of the objective function value of at least 19 which exceeds $z = 63$, we can delete this branch. Now we delete in C_2 the second row and the fourth column and obtain

$\diagdown \, j$ $i \, \diagdown$	1	2	3
1	0	0	4
C_3: 3	11	25	0
4	0	0	4

By solving a LAP with C_3, the lower bound z_L cannot be improved, but the rule of alternative costs permits us to fix another assignment. If we branch on $\varphi(3) = 3$ and $\varphi(3) \neq 3$, then $\varphi(3) \neq 3$ leads to an increase of the lower bound of at least $11 + 4 = 15$. Thus $z_L = 55 + 15 > 63$; in this case also we can delete this branch.

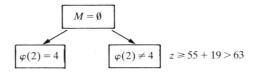

Figure 9.4. Branching from assignment $\varphi(2) = 4$.

Now $M = \{2, 3\}$ with $\varphi(2) = 4$, $\varphi(3) = 3$ and only two completions of M are left, namely $\varphi(1) = 1$, $\varphi(4) = 2$ or $\varphi(1) = 2$, $\varphi(4) = 1$. We can now compute the objective function value of the completion $\varphi(1) = 2$, $\varphi(4) = 1$ (the other was already determined to be 63)

$$\begin{bmatrix} 2 & 3 & 4 & 0 \\ 3 & 0 & 5 & 7 \\ 8 & 2 & 1 & 7 \\ 0 & 0 & 4 & 2 \end{bmatrix} \begin{bmatrix} 4 & 7 & 2 & 0 \\ 1 & 7 & 0 & 2 \\ 0 & 7 & 3 & 0 \\ 8 & 1 & 3 & 1 \end{bmatrix} = 37 + 17 + 17 + 14 = 85 .$$

This is worse than the result of 63 known so far. Therefore $\varphi(1) = 1$, $\varphi(2) = 4$, $\varphi(3) = 3$, $\varphi(4) = 1$ solves the given QAP optimally and yields an objective function value of $z = 63$. Figure 9.5 shows the branch-and-bound tree for this example.

For a computer implementation it would be better to proceed first to a good solution and then to scan the remaining branches. For this example the algorithm could proceed as follows. Starting from node 1 (see Figure 9.5) with $M = \emptyset$ and an upper bound $\bar{z} = 63$ the algorithm proceeds via node 2 and node 3 to the comparison of the remaining two possibilities (node 4 and node 5). Then it searches for a solution with better objective function value, but can find it neither at node 6 nor at node 7. Thus, $M = \emptyset$ is reached again and all feasible solutions are fathomed. Therefore $z = 63$ is optimal. ○

A *parallel* branch-and-bound algorithm has recently been described Roucairol (1987).

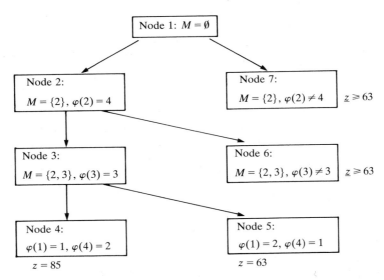

Figure 9.5. Branch-and-bound tree for Example 9.8.

9.6. HEURISTICS FOR QAPs

Since even with very large computers it is rather time consuming to solve QAPs optimally for large problem sizes, say of $n \geq 20$, there is a special need for good heuristics for QAPs. Some desirable features required of heuristics for combinatorial optimization problems are:

- Heuristics should yield a near optimal solution.
- Often, not one but several good feasible solutions are required by the decision-maker to make a choice.
- It is preferable that the methods are easy to implement, and the storage requirements are small enough so that they may be implemented on small computers.
- Heuristics should have a short running time compared with exact (implicit enumeration) methods.

It is nearly impossible to design a heuristic for QAP that has all of the above features. However, different approaches give different desirable features. Known heuristics for QAPs can be classified into four categories:

1. Limited enumeration methods,
2. construction methods,
3. improvement methods,
4. simulation approaches.

9.6.1. Limited Enumeration Methods

In branch-and-bound methods, it is often noticed that an optimal or good suboptimal solution is found at an early stage in the branching tree, but it takes a very long time to improve this solution or prove its optimality. For example, the optimal solution the example of Nugent et al. (1968) example with $n = 15$ was found after 23.48 CPU-seconds on a CDC CYBER 76, yet, more than an hour of CPU-time was further needed to prove the optimality of this solution. There are several ways to take advantage of this behavior:

1. *Time Limits.* We can stop the enumeration process after a prespecified time limit (depending on the problem size) has been reached. Or, we can stop the enumeration if no improvement is made within a given time interval.

2. *Method of Decreasing Requirements.* We can modify the upper bound to decrease our requirement for optimality. For example, whenever improvement is not found after a given time interval, the upper bound is decreased by a certain specified percentage. This process makes deeper cuts in the decision tree. Although the optimal solution may be cut off by this

TABLE 9.1 Objective Function Values and CPU-Times (in Seconds) Found by Modified Branch-and-Bound Methods for Selected Test Problems of Nugent et Al. (1968) and Steinberg (1961)

Example	Best Known Objective Function Value	By Time Limits		By Decreasing Requirements	
		Value	CPU-Time	Value	CPU-Time
Nugent ($n = 15$)	1150 (optimal)	1150	382	1150	37
Nugent ($n = 20$)	2570	2658	251	2658	90
Nugent ($n = 30$)	6124	6302	260	6302	392
Steinberg R.D. ($n = 36$)	4774	5791	352	5791	1122

approach, the enumeration process is speeded up. Moreover, one can estimate that the optimal value differs from the suboptimal one by not more than the specified percentage.

Table 9.1 shows some results obtained with the modified branch-and-bound methods. The corresponding CPU-times lie between 35 s and 7 min on a CDC CYBER 76.

Methods using bounds based on statistical considerations also belong to this class of heuristics. Graves and Whinston (1970) showed that expected value and variance of the objective function value can easily be computed for completion of partial permutations. Such considerations were used by West (1983) in his efficient and powerful computer program for solving QAPs suboptimally.

Good experience has also been obtained from performing cutting-plane methods suboptimally. Bazaraa and Sherali (1980) and Burkard and Bönniger (1983) describe such approaches. Burkard and Bönniger use the QAP linearization of Theorem 9.3 and propose the following procedure to obtain a suboptimal solution of formulation (9.2.9) for the QAP.

Algorithm 9.3. Suboptimal cutting plane method for solving QAPs. Given data are $N = \{1, 2, \ldots, n\}$, $A = \{a_{ik}\}$, $i, k \in N$, $B = \{b_{jl}\}$, $j, l \in N$. Set parameters R and S.

Step 1: Compute for $i, j \in N$ upper bounds

$$c_{ij} = n\left(\max_{1 \le k \le n} a_{ik}\right)\left(\max_{1 \le l \le n} b_{jl}\right)$$

and define

$$h_{ij}^0 \equiv 0 .$$

Step 2: Generate randomly an $(n \times n)$ permutation matrix $\{y_{kl}\}$, compute

$$\bar{z} = \sum_{i=1}^{n} \sum_{j=1}^{n} \sum_{k=1}^{n} \sum_{l=1}^{n} a_{ik} b_{jl} y_{kl}$$

and goto Step 3.

Step 3: Define $X^1 \equiv Y$, $s \equiv 1$ and goto Step 4.

Step 4: Compute for $k, l \in M$

$$f_{kl} \equiv \sum_{i=1}^{n} \sum_{j=1}^{n} a_{ik} b_{jl} x_{ij}^s + c_{kl} x_{kl}^s ,$$

$$g \equiv \sum_{i=1}^{n} \sum_{j=1}^{n} c_{ij} x_{ij}^s .$$

Step 5: Solve the LAP

$$z = \min_{X} \sum_{k=1}^{n} \sum_{l=1}^{n} f_{kl} x_{kl} ,$$

where $\{x_{kl}\}$ is an $(n \times n)$ permutation matrix.

Step 6: Compute

$$d \equiv \max(1, |z - g|) ,$$

$$h_{ij}^s \equiv h_{ij}^{s-1} + \frac{1}{d} f_{ij} , \qquad \text{for } i, j \in N .$$

Step 7: Solve the LAP

$$z^{s+1} \equiv \min \sum_{i=1}^{n} \sum_{j=1}^{n} h_{ij}^s x_{ij} ,$$

where $\{x_{ij}\}$ is an $(n \times n)$ permutation matrix. Let X^{s+1} be the solution of this problem and z^{s+1} be the corresponding objective function value.

Step 8: If $z^{s+1} < \bar{z}$, replace $\bar{z} \leftarrow z^{s+1}$.

Step 9: If $s < S$, replace s by $s + 1$ and goto Step 4; else goto Step 10.

Step 10: Store $\bar{z}$ and the corresponding solution. If $r < R$, goto Step 2; else stop.

This algorithm yields r suboptimal solutions and objective function values $\bar{z}$. Computational tests have shown that a good choice of the parameters R and S is

$$R = 3n \qquad \text{and} \qquad S \equiv \begin{cases} 10, & \text{if } n < 20 \\ 15, & \text{if } 20 < n < 40 . \end{cases}$$

For more details and a FORTRAN program of this method see Burkard and Bönniger (1983). Their computational experience revealed that the algorithm has a stable behavior. Starting with arbitrary chosen permutations, in almost all cases a suboptimal solution was found for which the objective function value deviated from the best known value by less than 1%.

In conclusion, we may state that modified enumeration methods yield solutions of quite good quality. The codes, however, are often involved and have rather large storage requirements.

9.6.2. Construction Methods

As the name suggests, these methods construct a suboptimal solution step by step, for example, by enlarging a partial permutation according to given criteria, until a permutation of the whole index set is obtained. A typical construction method, the basic idea of which was first introduced by Gilmore (1962), is an iterated use of Algorithm 9.2.

Algorithm 9.4.   Refined Gilmore heuristic for solving

$$\min_{\varphi} \sum_{i=1}^{n} c_{i,\varphi(i)} + \sum_{i=1}^{n} \sum_{k=1}^{n} a_{ik} b_{\varphi(i),\varphi(k)} \, .$$

Given data are $N = \{1, 2, \ldots, n\}$,

$$A = \{a_{ik}\}, \qquad i \in N, \, k \in N,$$
$$B = \{b_{jl}\}, \qquad j \in N, \, l \in N,$$
$$C = \{c_{ij}\}, \qquad i \in N, \, j \in N.$$

Step 1: Initialize $M = \emptyset$.

Step 2: Perform Algorithm 9.2, in particular solve the LAP of Step 3 in Algorithm 9.2. Let its optimal solution be

$$\varphi(i) \qquad \text{for } i \in M \, .$$

Step 3: Determine the index i^*, for which

$$c_{i^*,\varphi(i^*)} = \max \{c_{i,\varphi(i)} \, | \, i \in M\} \, .$$

(Here the c_{ij} are the original, nonreduced cost coefficients of Step 6 in Algorithm 9.1.) Update $M \leftarrow M \cup \{i^*\}$ and let $\varphi^*(i^*) = \varphi(i^*)$. If $M = N$, stop; φ^* is the constructed solution. Otherwise goto Step 2.

Aside from the different rule for fixing indices in the partial permutation this algorithm describes exactly the first phase (until a feasible solution is reached) of the branch-and-bound algorithm of Section 9.5. We replace the rule of alternative cost since it was particularly appropriate in the branch-and-bound framework but not necessarily in this context.

There is another construction method that yields quite good results: the "increasing degree of freedom" method of Müller-Merbach (1970). We start with $M = \emptyset$ and arrange the indices $1, 2, \ldots, n$ in a fixed order: $r_1, r_2, \ldots, r_n$. Proceeding from a partial permutation (M, φ) with $M = \{r_1, \ldots, r_{k-1}\}$, we expand M to $\bar{M} = M \cup \{r_k\}$. Now we consider the following $k(n - k + 1)$ different cases:

> At first we assign the index r_k to an index $j \notin \varphi(M)$ and compute the corresponding increase $\Delta z(j)$ of the objective function value. There are $(n - k + 1)$ different values $\Delta z(j)$. Then we assign the index r_k to $j \in \varphi(M)$. Since, however, $j \in \varphi(M)$ is already occupied by an assignment, say $r_i \rightsquigarrow j$, we reassign r_i now to an index k not contained in $\varphi(M)$ and compute again the corresponding increase $\Delta z(j, k)$, $j \in \varphi(M)$, $k \notin \varphi(M)$, of the objective function value. There are $(k - 1)(n - k + 1)$ different values $\Delta z(j, k)$. We compare in total $k(n - k + 1)$ different values for the increase of the objective function value and choose among them that assignment which leads to a minimal value.

The result of the method of increasing degree of freedom depends on the initially chosen arrangement of the indices $1, 2, \ldots, n$. Therefore, this method can be applied several times with different initial arrangements, which usually leads to a better overall result. As a rule of thumb $n/3$ performances of the algorithm are recommended.

Example 9.9. Let

$$A = \begin{bmatrix} 2 & 3 & 4 & 0 \\ 3 & 0 & 5 & 7 \\ 8 & 2 & 1 & 7 \\ 0 & 0 & 4 & 2 \end{bmatrix}, \qquad B = \begin{bmatrix} 1 & 8 & 3 & 1 \\ 0 & 4 & 2 & 7 \\ 0 & 0 & 3 & 7 \\ 2 & 1 & 0 & 7 \end{bmatrix}.$$

Let us fix the indices in the order they appear, that is, $r_k = k$ for $k = 1, 2, \ldots, n$. In the first step we have co compare four values, namely

$$a_{11} b_{jj} \qquad \text{for } j = 1, 2, 3, 4 .$$

The minimum is attained for $j = 1$. Therefore we obtain $M = \{1\}$ with $\varphi(1) = 1$. Now we have to compare the three values

$$a_{11} b_{11} + a_{12} b_{1j} + a_{21} b_{j1} + a_{22} b_{jj} \qquad \text{for } j = 2, 3, 4 .$$

The minimum is attained for $j = 3$ and $j = 4$ and has the value 11. Since the sums

$$a_{11}b_{jj} + a_{12}b_{j1} + a_{21}b_{1j} + a_{22}b_{11} \qquad \text{for } j = 2, 3, 4$$

all have a value greater than 11, we obtain $M = \{1, 2\}$ with $\varphi(1) = 1, \varphi(2) = 3$.

In the third step we have to evaluate six sums, namely

$$(a_{11}b_{11} + a_{22}b_{33} + a_{12}b_{13} + a_{21}b_{31}) + (a_{13}b_{1j} + a_{23}b_{3j} + a_{31}b_{j1}$$
$$+ a_{32}b_{j3} + a_{33}b_{jj}) \qquad \text{for } j = 2, 4 \,,$$

and

$$(a_{11}b_{jj} + a_{22}b_{33} + a_{12}b_{j3} + a_{21}b_{3j}) + (a_{13}b_{j1} + a_{23}b_{31} + a_{31}b_{1j}$$
$$+ a_{32}b_{13} + a_{33}b_{11}) \qquad \text{for } j = 2, 4 \,,$$

and

$$(a_{11}b_{11} + a_{22}b_{jj} + a_{12}b_{1j} + a_{21}b_{j1}) + (a_{13}b_{13} + a_{23}b_{j3} + a_{31}b_{31}$$
$$+ a_{32}b_{3j} + a_{33}b_{22}) \qquad \text{for } j = 2, 4 \,.$$

The minimal value is 48 and is attained by the last sum; therefore we let $M = \{1, 2, 3\}$ with $\varphi(1) = 1$, $\varphi(2) = 4$, and $\varphi(3) = 3$.

In the last step we have to evaluate four permutations, namely

$$\begin{array}{llll}
\varphi(1) = 1 \,, & \varphi(2) = 4 \,, & \varphi(3) = 3 \,, & \varphi(4) = 2 \,, \\
\varphi(1) = 2 \,, & \varphi(2) = 4 \,, & \varphi(3) = 3 \,, & \varphi(4) = 1 \,, \\
\varphi(1) = 1 \,, & \varphi(2) = 2 \,, & \varphi(3) = 3 \,, & \varphi(4) = 4 \,, \\
\varphi(1) = 1 \,, & \varphi(2) = 4 \,, & \varphi(3) = 2 \,, & \varphi(4) = 3 \,.
\end{array}$$

The first permutation gives the minimal value $z = 63$. This is optimal as we know from Example 9.8.   ○

Usually, construction methods are easy to implement, have short running times and can be run on a small computer. However, the quality of their solutions, in particular for larger sized problems, may not be very good.

9.6.3. Improvement Methods

Improvement methods start with a feasible solution (permutation) and try to improve it by interchanges of assignments. Widely used such methods are pair exchange algorithms where all $\binom{n}{2}$ possible pairwise exchanges are evaluated in a systematic way.

A pair exchange is performed in the following manner. We start with a permutation φ, select two indices i and k and define a new permutation $\bar{\varphi}$ by

$$\bar{\varphi}(i) \equiv \varphi(k), \qquad \bar{\varphi}(k) \equiv \varphi(i),$$
$$\bar{\varphi}(l) \equiv \varphi(l), \qquad \text{for } l = 1, 2, \ldots, n, \quad l \neq i, k.$$

Connected with this exchange, $i \rightsquigarrow \varphi(k)$ and $k \rightsquigarrow \varphi(i)$, is the following change of the objective function value

$$
\begin{aligned}
d \equiv \sum_{\substack{l=1 \\ l \neq i,k}}^{n} & [(a_{il} - a_{kl})(b_{\varphi(i),\varphi(l)} - b_{\varphi(k),\varphi(l)}) \\
& + (a_{li} - a_{lk})(b_{\varphi(l),\varphi(i)} - b_{\varphi(l),\varphi(k)})] \\
& + (a_{ii} - a_{kk})(b_{\varphi(i),\varphi(i)} - b_{\varphi(k),\varphi(k)}) \\
& + (a_{ik} - a_{ki})(b_{\varphi(i),\varphi(k)} - b_{\varphi(k),\varphi(i)}).
\end{aligned}
\tag{9.6.1}
$$

If $d > 0$, then $\bar{\varphi}$ yields a lower objective function value than φ. There are several strategies for performing pair-exchanges:

1. *Method of First Improvement.* Pairwise exchanges are examined in fixed order until an improvement of the objective is found; the exchange is made and the process restarts from the beginning.
2. *Method of Best Improvement.* All possible pairwise exchanges are examined; the one which leads to the largest improvement is implemented and the process restarts.
3. *Heider's Method* (Heider, 1972). Pairwise exchanges are examined in a fixed order and an exchange is made as soon as it yields an improvement. Several exchanges can be made during a single iteration.

All of the above methods stop if no improvement is found during a complete cycle of $\binom{n}{2}$ trials.

Analogous to a pairwise exchange, an improvement in the objective function value may be obtained by a cyclic exchange of three indices. Since for these cyclic "triple exchanges" the running times grow considerably from $\binom{n}{2}$ to $\binom{n}{3}$, it is usually not very useful to replace pair by triple exchange algorithms, in particular because triple exchange algorithms do not yield much better results. Triple exchange algorithms can be used, however, to supplement pair exchange algorithms. In particular, the "mixed exchange algorithm" of Mirchandani and Obata (1979), where, along with all pairwise exchanges, some three-way and four-way exchanges are evaluated without many additional computations (the complexity still being $O(n^2)$), appears to considerably improve the performance of straight pair exchange algorithms

Note that improvement methods can easily be combined with construction methods.

9.6.4.   Simulation Approaches

A recently developed heuristic that fulfills many of the requirements for a good heuristic is based on a *simulation approach*. Kirkpatrick, Gellat, and Vecchi (1983) applied a thermodynamical simulation procedure to traveling salesman and placement problems. Burkard and Rendl (1984) have applied this "simulated annealing" method to QAPs and computational tests show a very favorable behavior of the method. The main idea is to perform pairwise exchanges but a new solution is accepted (that is, the exchange is carried out) not only if it yields a lower objective function value, but also, with a positive probability, if it deteriorates this value. Thus, in this process it is possible to leave local optima. The acceptance probability depends on the difference between the previously accepted and the current objective function value and on a formal parameter which decreases during the procedure. By choosing the parameters differently, one can either have a fast method, comparable to construction methods, or a close to exact method comparable, for example, to Algorithm 9.3. In any case, this simulation procedure is very simple to implement and requires only a small memory. Thus, it is also well suited for small computers.

Algorithm 9.5. Simulation procedure for QAPs. Given data are $A = \{a_{ik}\}$, $i, k \in \{1, 2, \ldots, n\}$, $B = \{b_{jl}\}$, $j, l \in \{1, 2, \ldots, n\}$. Formal parameters controlling computation time and efficiency of the algorithm are: $t > 0$; $r \in N$; $a \in (0, 1)$; $b > 0$.

Step 1: Set t to an appropriately high value.
Step 2: Select an arbitrary feasible solution for the QAP, that is, a permutation of the set $\{1, 2, \ldots, n\}$. Let the corresponding objective function value be $z(\varphi)$.
Step 3: Set the logical variable "change" to "true."
Step 4: If the variable "change" has value "false," then stop.
Step 5: Set "change" to "false."
Step 6: Repeat the following steps 1–9 r times.

1. Perform an arbitrary pairwise exchange in the permutation yielding the permutation $\bar{\varphi}$.
2. Evaluate the corresponding change, d, of the objective function value according to (9.4.14).
3. If $d < 0$ then goto 7.
4. Let $P(d) \equiv \exp(-d/t)$.
5. Generate a random number x, uniformly distributed in $(0, 1)$.
6. If $x \geq P(d)$ then goto 9.
7. Accept the new permutation

$$\varphi \leftarrow \bar{\varphi}, \qquad z(\varphi) \leftarrow z(\varphi) + d.$$

TABLE 9.2   Performance of the Simulation Procedure on Nugent et Al.'s (1968) Test Problems of Size n

n	Best Known Value	Simulation 1		Simulation 2	
		Value	CPU	Value	CPU
12	578 (optimal)	612	0.9	578	4
15	1150 (optimal)	1182	1.9	1150	9
20	2570	2620	7.7	2570	70
30	6124	6236	25.6	6150	130

In Simulation 1 the parameters were chosen such that it terminates soon. In Simulation 2 the parameters were chosen in order to obtain a high quality solution. All times are in CPU-seconds on a UNIVAC 1100/81 of the Research Center, Graz.

8. If $d \neq 0$ then set "change" to "true."

9. End of repeat.

Step 7: Reduce t by the factor a and increase r by the factor b,

$$t \leftarrow ta , \quad r \leftarrow rb .$$

Step 8: Goto Step 4.

When the algorithm stops, the suboptimal solution is φ with objective function value $z(\varphi)$. By setting $r = O(n)$, $a = 0.5$, b close to but greater than 1, one obtains a very fast procedure. The higher the variable r and closer the parameter a is to 1, the more time consuming is the procedure. On the other hand, the quality of the solution improves. In addition, the procedure may be restarted several times with different starting solutions in Step 2 to give a series of good supoptimal solutions. Some computational tests on Nugent et al.'s (1968) test problems are reported in Table 9.2.

9.7. SOME AVAILABLE COMPUTER CODES AND COMPUTATIONAL EXPERIENCES

Several authors have developed computer codes for QAPs and have reported their computational experiences (see, for example, Bazaraa and Sherali, 1980, Burkard and Stratmann, 1978; Mirchandani and Obata, 1979). We have tried in this chapter to take the essence thereof and described only those methods that have led to good results according to computational tests. Computational results with a promising parallel branch-and-bound algorithm have been reported recently by Roucairol (1987).

There are only few sources for complete computer programs. In the book of Burkard and Derigs (1980), a branch-and-bound code for Koopmans–Beckmann problems is listed in FORTRAN. The program requires a storage capacity of $n^3 + 5.5n^2 + 17.5n$. The CPU-times utilized by the code

TABLE 9.3 Running Times of a Branch-and-Bound Code	
n	Time (s)
5	0.005
6	0.021
7	0.059
8	0.263
12	46.771
15	2947.320

TABLE 9.4 Running Times of the Heuristic Code QAPH3	
n	Time (s)
20	5
30	26
36	58

for the test examples of Nugent et al. on a CDC CYBER 76 are given in Table 9.3. In the same book, two other heuristic codes are described. One is a fast heuristic called QAPH1, which is an implementation of the method of increasing degree of freedom. The other heuristic, QAPH2, is outperformed by a FORTRAN routine, QAPH3, for Algorithm 9.3 given by Burkard and Bönniger (1983). QAPH3 needs a storage capacity of $6n^2 + 4n$ and its running times per restart are given in Table 9.4. The authors recommend 10 restarts for problems of size $n < 20$ and 15 restarts for larger problems.

An efficient heuristic that makes use of expectation values for partial permutations has been published by West (1983). The complete code is available from the ACM Algorithms Distribution Service.

Complete computer program listings have been presented in several theses. We mention here only Obata (1979). Obata presents detailed computational comparisons with various codes and test examples. In his thesis, program listings for various heuristics and an exact branch-and-bound code are given.

A computer code for the simulation approach has not yet been published. It can be written, however, without difficulty following the lines given in Section 9.6.4.

9.8.   THE ASYMPTOTIC BEHAVIOR OF QAPs

A surprising feature of QAPs is that the relative difference between the worst and the optimal solution becomes arbitrarily small with a probability tending to 1 as the problem size tends to infinity. This behavior was first shown for QAPs in the plane, that is, for problems where the elements a_{ik} correspond to Euclidean distances in the plane (see Burkard and Fincke, 1983). This behavior is also true for quadratic assignment problems with a bottleneck objective (see Exercise 9.2; Burkard and Fincke, 1982) and for general QAPs (see Burkard and Fincke, 1985). Frenk, Van Houweninge, and Rinnooy Kan (1985) as well as Rhee (1988) have improved the order of convergence and shown that convergence holds almost everywhere.

Let us outline here the theorem and the proof for the general case. We consider a family (P_n), $n \in N$, of QAPs, with problem size n. Then the problem has $n!$ feasible solutions and in the objective function

$$\sum_{i=1}^{n} \sum_{k=1}^{n} d_{i,\varphi(i),k,\varphi(k)}$$

there are at most n^2 nonzero coefficients.

Theorem 9.6. *For $i, j, k, l = 1, 2, \ldots, n$, $n \in N$, let d_{ijkl} be identically distributed random variables in $[0, 1]$ with expected value $E \equiv E(d_{ijkl})$ and variance $\sigma^2 \equiv \sigma^2(d_{ijkl}) > 0$. For every fixed permutation φ of $\{1, 2, \ldots, n\}$ let $d_{i,\varphi(i),k,\varphi(k)}$ be independently distributed. For a given $\varepsilon > 0$ let ε_0 fulfill $0 < \varepsilon_0 \leq \sigma^2$ and $0 < (E + \varepsilon_0)/(E - \varepsilon_0) \leq 1 + \varepsilon$. Then*

$$P\left\{ \frac{\max\limits_{\varphi} \sum\limits_{i=1}^{n} \sum\limits_{k=1}^{n} d_{i,\varphi(i),k,\varphi(k)}}{\min\limits_{\varphi} \sum\limits_{i=1}^{n} \sum\limits_{k=1}^{n} d_{i,\varphi(i),k,\varphi(k)}} < 1 + \varepsilon \right\} \geq 1 - 2(n!) \exp\left(-\lambda_0 n^2\right) \xrightarrow[n \to \infty]{} 1$$

with

$$\lambda_0 = 2\left(\frac{\varepsilon_0 \sigma}{\varepsilon_0 + 2\sigma^2} \right)^2.$$

In the proof of Theorem 9.6, the following Lemma of Renyi (1970) is used.

Lemma 9.1. *Let $X_1, \ldots, X_n$ be independent random variables with $|X_k - E(X_k)| < K$ for $k = 1, 2, \ldots, n$. Denote $D \equiv \sum_{k=1}^{n} \sigma^2(X_k)$ and let μ be a positive real number with $\mu < D/k$. Then*

$$P\left\{ \left| \sum_{k=1}^{n} (X_k - E(X_k)) \right| \geq \mu D \right\} \leq 2 \exp\left(-\frac{\mu^2}{2(1 + \mu K/2D)^2} \right).$$

Proof of Theorem 9.6 (a Sketch). We consider first the following chain of inequalities

$$P\left\{ \exists \varphi : \left| \sum_{i=1}^{n} \sum_{k=1}^{n} (d_{i,\varphi(i),k,\varphi(k)} - E) \right| \geq \varepsilon_0 n^2 \right\}$$

$$\leq \sum_{\varphi} P\left\{ \left| \sum_{i=1}^{n} \sum_{k=1}^{n} (d_{i,\varphi(i),k,\varphi(k)} - E) \right| \geq \varepsilon_0 n^2 \right\}$$

$$\leq (n!) P\left\{ \left| \sum_{i=1}^{n} \sum_{k=1}^{n} (d_{i,\varphi(i),k,\varphi(k)} - E) \right| \geq \frac{\varepsilon_0 n}{\sigma} \, n\sigma \right\} \equiv A.$$

Now we apply Lemma 9.1 with

$$D = \left[\sum_{i=1}^{n} \sum_{k=1}^{n} \sigma^2(d_{i,\varphi(i),k,\varphi(k)}) \right]^{1/2} = n\sigma \, , \qquad K = 1 \, ,$$

and by defining

$$\mu \equiv \frac{\varepsilon_0 n}{\sigma} \, .$$

Thus we obtain

$$A \leq (n!)2 \exp\left(-\left(\frac{\varepsilon_0 n}{\sigma} \right)^2 \frac{1}{2[1 + (\varepsilon_0 n/\sigma)(1/2n\sigma)]^2} \right)$$

$$= 2(n!) \exp\left(-n^2 \lambda_0 \right) \qquad \text{by definition of } \lambda_0 \, .$$

Since $\lim_{n \to \infty}(n!) \exp\left(-\lambda_0 n^2 \right) = 0$, the right-hand side tends to zero as n approaches infinity. Therefore, we have shown

$$P\left\{ \exists \varphi : \left| \sum_{i=1}^{n} \sum_{k=1}^{n} (d_{i,\varphi(i),k,\varphi(k)} - E \right| \geq \varepsilon_0 n^2 \right\} \leq 2(n!) \exp\left(-\lambda_0 n^2 \right) \to 0 \, .$$

But this is equivalent to

$$P\left\{ \forall \varphi : \left| \sum_{i=1}^{n} \sum_{k=1}^{n} (d_{i,\varphi(i),k,\varphi(k)} - E) \right| < \varepsilon_0 n^2 \right\} \geq 1 - 2(n!) \exp\left(-\lambda_0 n^2 \right) \to 1 \, .$$

Thus we obtain

$$\frac{\max\limits_{\varphi} \sum\limits_{i=1}^{n} \sum\limits_{k=1}^{n} d_{i,\varphi(i),k,\varphi(k)}}{\min\limits_{\varphi} \sum\limits_{i=1}^{n} \sum\limits_{k=1}^{n} d_{i,\varphi(i),k,\varphi(k)}} < \frac{\varepsilon_0 n^2 + E n^2}{-\varepsilon_0 n^2 + E n^2} \leq 1 + \varepsilon \, ,$$

with probability tending to 1 as n approaches infinity. $\square$

As a corollary we obtain a similar result for QAPs of Koopmans–Beckmann type, since for independent and identically distributed random variables a_{ik}, b_{jl}, $i, j, k, l = 1, 2, \ldots, n$, the products $a_{ik} b_{\varphi(i)\varphi(k)}$ are independently distributed for a fixed permutation φ, as required by Theorem 9.6.4.

Theorem 9.6 even holds for combinatorial optimization problems which are more general than QAPs, but not for linear assignment problems and traveling salesman problems. For a further discussion of this issue see Burkard and Fincke (1985), where it is shown that the number of feasible solutions and the number of coefficients in the objective function govern the asymptotic behavior of such problems. Whenever the number of coefficients in the objective function increases faster than the logarithm of the number of feasible solutions, a behavior described by Theorem 9.6 can be expected.

Recently, Bonomi and Lutton (1986) relate the asymptotic behavior of QAPs to the statistical mechanic approach which underlies the simulated annealing algorithm of Section 9.6.4.

Whereas the results above suggest that any algorithm almost always finds a good solution, Dyer, Frieze, and McDiarmid (1986) show that the expected duality gap between a QAP and a linear relaxation thereof is enormous. The following theorem is due to them.

Theorem 9.7.   *Consider any branch-and-bound algorithm for solving QAP (9.2.1) which branches by setting variables x_{ij} to 0 and 1 and bounds by using the LP relaxation of (9.2.5). Then the number of branch nodes explored is at least*

$$n^{(1-O(1))n/4}$$

with a probability $1 - O(1)$ as n tends to infinity.

This means that any branch-and-bound algorithm which uses the common LP bounds has to explore exponentially many nodes in the branching tree with a probability which tends to 1.

APPENDIX.   NUGENT ET AL.'S TEST EXAMPLES

The matrices A and B are symmetric, the linear part (main diagonal) is zero. The data can therefore be given in a square array in the following manner: the numbers *above* the main diagonal are the elements of A, the numbers *below* the main diagonal are the elements of B.

Size n = 5

$$(B \backslash A) = \begin{bmatrix} 0. & 1 & 1 & 2 & 3 \\ 5 & 0. & 2 & 1 & 2 \\ 2 & 3 & 0. & 1 & 2 \\ 4 & 0 & 0 & 0. & 1 \\ 1 & 2 & 0 & 5 & 0 \end{bmatrix}.$$

Optimal objective function value $z = 50$. Optimal solutions (in cyclic representation) are

$$(1,4,2) \ (3,5)$$

$$(1,4,2,5,3).$$

Size n = 6

$$(B\ A) = \begin{bmatrix} 0. & 1 & 2 & 1 & 2 & 3 \\ 5 & 0. & 1 & 2 & 1 & 2 \\ 2 & 3 & 0. & 3 & 2 & 1 \\ 4 & 0 & 0 & 0. & 1 & 2 \\ 1 & 2 & 0 & 5 & 0. & 1 \\ 0 & 2 & 0 & 2 & 10 & 0. \end{bmatrix}.$$

Optimal objective function value $z = 86$. Optimal solutions (in cyclic representation) are:

$$(1)\ (2)\ (3)\ (4)\ (5)\ (6)$$
$$(1,3)\ (2)\ (4,6)\ (5)$$
$$(1,4)\ (2,5)\ (3,6)\ .$$

Size n = 7

$$(B\backslash A) = \begin{bmatrix} 0. & 1 & 2 & 3 & 2 & 3 & 4 \\ 5 & 0. & 1 & 2 & 1 & 2 & 3 \\ 2 & 3 & 0. & 1 & 2 & 1 & 2 \\ 4 & 0 & 1 & 0. & 3 & 2 & 1 \\ 1 & 2 & 0 & 5 & 0. & 1 & 2 \\ 0 & 2 & 2 & 2 & 10 & 0. & 1 \\ 0 & 2 & 5 & 2 & 0 & 5 & 0. \end{bmatrix}.$$

Optimal objective functions value $z = 148$. An optimal solution (in cyclic representation) is:

$$(1,2)\ (3,4,5)\ (6,7)\ .$$

Size n = 8

$$(B\backslash A) = \begin{bmatrix} 0. & 1 & 2 & 3 & 1 & 2 & 3 & 4 \\ 5 & 0. & 1 & 2 & 2 & 1 & 2 & 3 \\ 2 & 3 & 0. & 1 & 3 & 2 & 1 & 2 \\ 4 & 0 & 0 & 0. & 4 & 3 & 2 & 1 \\ 1 & 2 & 0 & 5 & 0. & 1 & 2 & 3 \\ 0 & 2 & 0 & 2 & 10 & 0. & 1 & 2 \\ 0 & 2 & 0 & 2 & 0 & 5 & 0. & 1 \\ 6 & 0 & 5 & 10 & 0 & 1 & 10 & 0. \end{bmatrix}.$$

Optimal objective functions value $z = 214$. An optimal solution (in cyclic representation) is:

$$1,2)\ (3,4,5)\ (6,8)\ (7)\ .$$

EXERCISES

9.1 Consider the following situation. At a wedding breakfast n persons are invited. The guests are seated around a round table, where each can easily communicate with his right and left neighbors and it is still possible for him to speak with their neighbors to the right and left, respectively. The hosts know (or guess) a coefficient a_{ik} which measures the pleasure that person i gets from communicating with person k. They want to place the guests such that their total pleasure is as high as possible.

Model the problem as a QAP. In what way does the shape of the table influence the model? How does the problem change for a square or a long rectangular table?

9.2 In hospital layout planning, the following problem, known as "quadratic bottleneck assignment problem" (cf. Burkard, 1974) arises. Certain uses are to be attached to the rooms. Let $A = \{a_{ik}\}$ be the distance matrix between the rooms. The matrix $B = \{b_{jl}\}$ describes if a doctor or nurse being in a room with use j may be called to a room with use l; that is, B plays the rôle of a "connection matrix." Now the problem is to assign the uses to the rooms such that the longest distance that a doctor or nurse has to walk in an emergency is minimal. Model this situation with a bottleneck objective function. Prove a result analogous to Theorem 9.3 for this quadratic bottleneck assignment problem.

9.3 Show in Example 9.1 that an additional rowwise reduction of the matrices A and B does not improve the lower bound $\underline{z}$.

9.4 Describe simplifications, if any, that can be made in the lower bound computations for symmetric matrices A and B.

9.5 Given the matrices

$$A = \begin{bmatrix} 7 & 3 & 2 & 4 \\ 5 & 4 & 3 & 1 \\ 6 & 2 & 0 & 6 \\ 8 & 1 & 5 & 3 \end{bmatrix}, \quad B = \begin{bmatrix} 2 & 1 & 4 & 3 \\ 1 & 4 & 2 & 1 \\ 4 & 2 & 2 & 3 \\ 3 & 1 & 3 & 5 \end{bmatrix},$$

solve the corresponding QAP optimally. (The optimal objective function value is $z = 132$.)

9.6 Generalize the lower bound computations to QAPs of the form (9.1.1) and optimally solve the general QAP given by

$$
D = \begin{bmatrix}
3 & \cdot & \cdot & \cdot & \infty & 4 & 8 & 9 & \infty & 2 & 7 & 3 & \infty & 8 & 3 & 4 \\
 & 7 & \cdot & \cdot & 1 & \infty & 3 & 4 & 2 & \infty & 3 & 7 & 2 & \infty & 8 & 4 \\
 & & 3 & \cdot & 2 & 1 & \infty & 9 & 1 & 2 & \infty & 7 & 3 & 2 & \infty & 1 \\
 & & & 4 & 7 & 8 & 9 & \infty & 2 & 1 & 3 & \infty & 1 & 4 & 3 & \infty \\
 & & & & 8 & \cdot & \cdot & \cdot & \infty & 2 & 3 & 1 & \infty & 4 & 2 & 1 \\
 & & & & & 7 & \cdot & \cdot & 3 & \infty & 1 & 8 & 9 & \infty & 2 & 4 \\
 & & & & & & 2 & \cdot & 2 & 2 & \infty & 1 & 2 & 3 & \infty & 1 \\
 & & & & & & & 6 & 7 & 8 & 9 & \infty & 1 & 2 & 3 & \infty \\
 & & & & & & & & 7 & \cdot & \cdot & \cdot & \infty & 8 & 3 & 4 \\
 & & & & & & & & & 6 & \cdot & \cdot & 7 & \infty & 2 & 1 \\
 & & & & & & & & & & 5 & \cdot & 1 & 5 & \infty & 1 \\
 & & & & & & & & & & & 4 & 3 & 2 & 1 & \infty \\
 & & & & & & & & & & & & 1 & \cdot & \cdot & \cdot \\
 & & & & & & & & & & & & & 6 & \cdot & \cdot \\
 & & & & & & & & & & & & & & 4 & \cdot \\
 & & & & & & & & & & & & & & & 1 \\
\end{bmatrix}
$$

(The optimal objective function value is $z = 27$.)

9.7 Describe the lower bound computations for the quadratic bottleneck assignment problem and solve the quadratic bottleneck assignment problem with the data of Example 9.5. (The optimal objective function value is $z = 20$.)

9.8 Find an efficient recursive way to perform the "increasing degree of freedom" heuristic.

9.9 Write computer programs for

(a) The refined Gilmore heuristic,

(b) the "increasing degree of freedom" heuristic and test your programs on Nugent et al.'s problems of sizes $n = 5, 6, 7,$ and 8.

9.10 Write a computer program for the pair exchange algorithm (Heider's version) and try to improve the solutions found in Exercise 9.9.

9.11 Write a computer program for the simulation procedure and test this program using different choices for the parameters. Compare your results with those of Exercises 9.9 and 9.10.

REFERENCES

Balas, E., and J. B. Mazzola (1980). "Quadratic 0-1 Programming by a New Linearization." Presented at the Joint ORSA/TIMS National Meeting, Washington, D.C.

Bazaraa, M. S., and M. D. Sherali (1980). "Benders' Partitioning Scheme Applied to a New Formulation of the Quadratic Assignment Problem." *Naval Research Logistics Quarterly* **27**, 29–41.

Bonomi, E., and J. L. Lutton (1986). "The Asymptotic Behaviour of Quadratic Sum Assignment Problems: A Statistical Mechanics Approach." *European Journal of Operational Research* **26**, 295–300.

Burkard, R. E. (1973). "Die Störungsmethode zur Lösung quadratischer Zuordnungsprobleme." *Operations Research Verfahren* **16**, 84–108.

Burkard, R. E. (1974). "Quadratische Bottleneckprobleme." *Operations Research Verfahren* **18**, 26–41.

Burkard, R. E., and T. Bönniger (1983). "A Heuristic for Quadratic Boolean Programs with Applications to Quadratic Assignment Problems." *European Journal of Operational Research* **13**, 374–386.

Burkard, R. E., and U. Derigs (1980). *Assignment and Matching Problems: Solution Methods with FORTRAN-Programs*. Springer-Verlag, Berlin and New York.

Burkard, R. E., and U. Fincke (1982). "On Random Quadratic Bottleneck Assignment Problems." *Mathematical Programming* **23**, 227–232.

Burkard, R. E., and U. Fincke (1983). "The Asymptotic Probabilistic Behaviour of Quadratic Sum Assignment Problems." *Zeitschrift für Operations Research* **27**, 73–81.

Burkard, R. E., and U. Fincke (1985). "Probabilistic Asymptotic Properties of Some Combinatorial Optimization Problems." *Discrete Applied Mathematics* **12**, 21–29.

Burkard, R. E., and J. Offermann (1977). "Entwurf von Schreibmaschinentastaturen mittels quadratischer Zuordnungsprobleme." *Zeitschrift für Operations Research* **21**, B121–B132.

Burkard, R. E., and F. Rendl (1984). "A Thermodynamically Motivated Simulation Procedure for Combinatorial Optimization Problems." *European Journal of Operational Research* **17**, 169–174.

Burkard, R. E., and K.-H. Stratmann (1978). "Numerical Investigations on Quadratic Assignment Problems." *Naval Research Logistics Quarterly* **25**, 129–148.

Christofides, N., and E. Benavent (1982). *An Exact Algorithm for the Tree-QAP,"* Res. Rep., Department of Management Science, Imperial College, London.

Christofides, N., and M. Gerrard (1976). *Special Cases of the Quadratic Assignment Problem*, Manage. Sci. Res. Rep. No. 391. Carnegie Mellon University, Pittsburgh, Pennsylvania.

Christofides, N., and M. Gerrard (1981). "A Graph Theoretic Analysis of Bounds for the Quadratic Assignment Problem." In *Studies on Graphs and Discrete Programming* (P. Hansen, ed.). North-Holland Publ., Amsterdam.

Conrad, K. (1971). *Das quadratische Zuweisungsproblem und zwei seiner Spezialfalle*. Mohr-Siebeck, Tübingen.

Dickey, J. W., and J. W. Hopkins (1972). "Campus Building Arrangement Using TOPAZ." *Transportation Research* **6**, 59–68.

Dyer, M. E., A. M. Frieze, and C. J. H. McDiarmid (1986). "On Linear Programs with Random Costs." *Mathematical Programming* **35**, 3–16.

Edwards, C. S. (1980). "A Branch and Bound Algorithm for the Koopmans-Beckmann Quadratic Assignment Problem." *Mathematical Programming Study* **13**, 35–52.

Elshafei, A. N. (1977). "Hospital Lay-Out as a Quadratic Assignment Problem." *Operational Research Quarterly* **28**, 167–179.

Finke, G., R. E. Burkard, and F. Rendl (1987). "Quadratic Assignment Problems." *Annals of Discrete Mathematics* **31**, 61–82.

Frenk, J. C. B., M. van Houweninge, and A. H. G. Rinnooy Kan (1985). "Asymptotic Properties of Assignment Problems." *Mathematics of Operations Research* **10**, 100–116.

Frieze, A. M., and J. Yadegar (1983). "On the Quadratic Assignment Problem." *Discrete Applied Mathematics* **5**, 89–98.

Gavett, J. W., and N. V. Plyter (1966). "The Optimal Assignment of Facilities to Locations by Branch and Bound." *Operations Research* **14**, 210–232.

Gilmore, P. C. (1962). "Optimal and Suboptimal Algorithms for the Quadratic Assignment Problem." *SIAM Journal on Applied Mathematics* **10**, 305–313.

Graves, G. W., and A. B. Whinston (1970). "An Algorithm for the Quadratic Assignment Problem." *Management Science* **17**, 453–471.

Hadley, S. W., F. Rendl, and H. Wolkowicz (1989). *A New Lower Bound via Elimination for the Quadratic Assignment Problem*, Rep. 136. Mathematical Institute, Technical University Graz, Austria.

Hardy, G. H., and J. E. Littlewood, and G. Polya (1952). *Inequalities*. Cambridge Univ. Press, London and New York.

Heffley, D. R. (1977). "Assuming Runners to a Relay Team." In *Optimal Strategies in Sports* (S. P. Ladany and R. E. Machol, eds.), North-Holland Publ., Amsterdam, pp. 169–171.

Heider, C. H. (1972). *A Computationally Simplified Pair Exchange Algorithm for the Quadratic Assignment Problem*, Pap. No. 101. Center for Naval Analyses, Arlington, Virginia.

Kaufman, L., and F. Broeckx (1978). "An Algorithm for the Quadratic Assignment Problem Using Benders' Decomposition." *European Journal of Operational Research* **2**, 204–211.

Kirkpatrick, S., C. D. Gelatti, Jr., and M. P. Vecchi (1983). "Optimization by Simulated Annealing." *Science* **220**, 671–680.

Koopmans, T. C., and M. J. Beckmann (1957). "Assignment Problems and the Location of Economic Activities." *Econometrica* **25**, 53–76.

Krarup, J., and P. M. Pruzan (1978). "Computer-Aided Layout Design." *Mathematical Programming Study* **9**, 75–94.

Land, A. M. (1963). "A Problem of Assignment with Interrelated Costs." *Operational Research Quarterly* **14**, 185–198.

Laporte, G. and H. Mercure (1988). "Balancing Hydraulic Turbine Runners: A Quadratic Assignment Problem." *European Journal of Operations Research* **35**, 378–382.

Lawler, E. L., (1963). "The Quadratic Assignment Problem." *Management Science* **9**, 586–599.

Love, R. F., and J. Y. Wong (1976). "Solving Quadratic Assignment Problems with Rectangular Distances and Integer Programming." *Naval research Logistics Quarterly* **23**, 623–627.

Mirchandani, P. B., and T. Obata (1979). *Locational Decisions with Interactions Between Facilities: The Quadratic Assignment Problem—A Review*, Working Paper PS-79-1. Rensselaer Polytechnic Institute, Troy, New York.

Mirsky, L. (1956). "The Spread of a Matrix." *Mathematika* **3**, 127–130.

Müller-Merbach, H. (1970). *Optimale Reihenfolgen*, pp. 158–171. Springer-Verlag, Berlin and New York.

Nugent, C. E., T. E. Vollmann, and J. Ruml (1968). "An Experimental Comparison of Techniques for the Assignment of Facilities to Locations." *Operations Research* **16**, 150–173.

Obata, T. (1979). *The Quadratic Assignment Problem: Evaluation of Exact and Heuristic Algorithms*, Tech. Rep. TRS-7901. Rensselaer Polytechnic Institute, Troy, New York.

Pierce, J. F., and W. B. Crowston (1971). "Tree Search Algorithms for Quadratic Assignment Problems." *Naval Research Logistics Quarterly* **18**, 1–36.

Pollatschek, M. A., H. Gershoni, and Y. T. Radday (1976). "Optimization of the Typewriter Keyboard by Computer Simulation." *Angewandte Informatik* **10**, 438–439.

Rendl, F. (1985). "Ranking Scalar Products to Improve Bounds for the Quadratic Assignment Problem." *European Journal of Operational Research* **20**, 363–372.

Rendl, F. (1986). "Quadratic Assignment Problems on Seriell-Parallel Digraphs." *Zeitschrift für Operations Research* **30**, A161–A173.

Rendl, F., and H. Wolkowicz (1988). *Applications of Parametric Programming and Eigenvalue Maximization to the Quadratic Assignment Problem*, Rep. 113. Mathematical Institute, Technical University Graz, Austria. To appear in *Mathematical Programming*.

Renyi, A. (1970). *Probability Theory*. North-Holland Publ., Amsterdam.

Rhee, W. T. (1988). "A Note on Asymptotic Properties of the Quadratic Assignment Problem." *Operations Research Letters* **7**, 197–200.

Roucairol, C. (1979). "A Reduction Method for Quadratic Assignment Problems." *Operations Research Verfahren* **32**, 183–187.

Roucairol, C. (1987). "A Parallel Branch and Bound Algorithm for the Quadratic Assignment Problem. *Discrete Applied Mathematics* **18**, 211–225.

Sahni, S., and T. Gonzalez (1976). "*P*-Complete Approximation Problems." *Journal of the Association for Computing Machinery* **23**, 555–565.

Schlegel, D. (1987). *Die Unwucht-optimale Verteilung von Turbinenschaufeln als quadratisches Zuordnungsproblem*. Ph.D. Thesis, ETH Zürich, Switzerland.

Steinberg, L. (1961). "The Backboard Wiring Problem: A Placement Algorithm." *SIAM Review* **3**, 37–50.

Ugi, I., J. Bauer, J. Brandt, J. Friedrich, J. Gasteiger, C. Jochum, and W. Schubert (1979). "Neue Anwendungsgebiete für Computer in der Chemie." *Angewandte Chemie* **91**, 99–111.

West, D. H. (1983). "Algorithm 608: Approximate Solution of the Quadratic Assignment Problem." *ACM Transactions on Mathematical Software* **9**, 461–466.

10

Locations with Spatial Interactions: Competitive Locations and Games

S. Louis Hakimi
Department of Electrical Engineering and Computer Science
University of California
Davis, California

10.1. INTRODUCTION

A great deal of the literature about the modeling and the analysis of location problems involves locating facilities (which belong to a single organization) to provide a service (or goods) to the customers (or consumers) who are located at the given sites in a "satisfactory manner." The "satisfactory manner" or, at the very best, the optimum manner to the supplier of the service, ordinarily means the way in which the total cost (usually the transportation cost) of providing the service to the consumers is the minimum possible. The p-median problem is an idealized model for locating p facilities to serve the consumers so that the transportation cost (to the supplier or provider) is minimum. This cost may be ultimately passed on to the customers, but, nevertheless, the supplier may wish to keep this cost as small as possible.

On the other hand, each customer, if he is expected to provide his own transportation to a facility (possibly indirectly), may be interested in minimizing his transportation cost (or equivalently improving the quality of service provided by the supplier). Furthermore, some consumer groups often are able to express their interests in a sufficiently forceful manner to have an impact on the supplier's decision as to where to locate his facilities. For public service facilities such as fire stations, schools, hospitals, or parks the above notions translate into the desire to be within close proximity of a facility. The p-center problem is an idealized model for locating p facilities to serve the consumers so that the distance between a farthest consumer and its closest facility is minimized.

Although any analysis of this nature must be carried out for use by a *single* organization (the supplier), in much of reported locational analyses the possibility of the existence of other organizations, which also wish to provide the same service (or goods) to the customers, is ignored. Thus it is often assumed that the customer has *no choice* among suppliers and he must use one of the facilities provided by a single supplier; that is, there is *no competition* for providing the service to the customers. Although there certainly are many applications in the public or the private sector where the above assumption does hold, there are possibly even more applications in which it does not.

There is one other implicit assumption that is normally made. This assumption is that the level of demand of each customer (or the used portion of the purchasing power of each customer) is not a function of how far or close the customer is to a facility, that is, the level is fixed. This assumption tends to hold if the service provided by the supplier is an essential service (such as hospitals, police stations, or supermarkets), but it certainly will not hold if the service provided by the supplier is not an essential service (such as restaurants, ice cream parlors, or liquor stores). We shall refer to these two service (or demand) types as *essential* and *nonessential*.

In this chapter we will assume that a customer's preference, among the facilities available to him, is based purely on a function of the relative distances to these facilities rather than the quality of service provided by the competing suppliers. In usual analyses, one assumes a *binary* preference (all or none) model where a consumer selects a facility based on which supplier provides the closest facility to him; he uses that facility to satisfy his entire demand. In some situations, it is more valid to assume that a consumer's purchasing power is divided up among the facilities according to a function of relative distances to the various facilities. We shall refer to these two cases as the binary and the proportional customer preferences.

Finally, as it is required in many applications, we will model location problems on both networks and the plane.

The above discussion leads to eight classes of competitive location problems. These eight classes arise from the following combinations of choices: whether the demands are essential or nonessential, whether the customers' preferences are binary or proportional, and finally whether the problem is defined on a network or on the plane. We shall have much to say in this chapter about these eight classes of problems. In particular, in the next section we present an outline of the known results in competitive location theory, on a network and on the plane, with essential demands and binary consumers preferences. In Section 10.3, we review the p-median problem in the context of a noncompetitive location problem for nonessential demands. In Section 10.4, we study competitive location problems when the demands are nonessential and/or consumers' preferences are proportional. In Section 10.5, we discuss certain game theoretic problems and concepts which arise from the study of location problems in a competitive environment. Some concluding remarks are given in Section 10.6.

The reader who is interested in an overview of this subject may well skip over the proofs of many of the theorems that follow. However, a deeper understanding is attained by careful examinations of the proofs.

10.2. LOCATION THEORY IN A COMPETITIVE ENVIRONMENT: ESSENTIAL DEMANDS AND BINARY PREFERENCES

10.2.1. Locations on Networks

We will begin by formulating some problems on locating facilities on a network. In the next subsection we discuss the same problems for the plane. A network $N(V, A)$ is a weighted graph with node set $V = \{v_1, v_2, \ldots, v_n\}$ and arc set A where with each node $v \in V$, we associate a weight $w(v)$ (≥ 0) and with each arc $a \in A$, we associate a length $l(a)$ (>0). It is assumed that $w(v)$ represents the demand (or the purchasing power) at vertex $v \in V$ for the service provided by the facilities to be located. Also $l(a)$ represents the transportation cost (per unit service) along the arc a. Suppose, now, there already exist p facilities located at the given points $X_p = \{x_1, x_2, \ldots, x_p\}$ on the network $N(V, A)$. We wish to locate r new facilities at points (to be computed) $Y_r = \{y_1, y_2, \ldots, y_r\}$ on $N(V, A)$ which are to compete with the existing facilities at X_p for providing service to the customers (who are all at the nodes). In this section we assume that the demands are essential and that the consumers' preferences are binary. Furthermore, we explicitly assume that a customer will change his habit and use the closest new (contemplated) facility if and only if it is closer to him than the closest old facility (that is, the ties are broken in favor of the old facilities). Before we discuss the implications of the above assumption, let us introduce some additional notation. For a set of points Z on $N(V, A)$, let $D(v, Z) = \min\{d(v, z) \mid z \in Z\}$ where $d(v, z)$ is the length of a shortest path in $N(V, A)$ from v to z. Now given $N(V, A)$ and the locations of the p existing facilities X_p, we wish to find Y_r such that the sum of the weights of the vertices in $V(Y_r \mid X_p)$ is maximized, where $V(Y_r \mid X_p) = \{v \in V \mid D(v, Y_r) < D(v, X_p)\}$. We define $W(Y_r \mid X_p) = \Sigma\{w(v) \mid v \in V(Y_r \mid X_p)\}$. Note that $W(Y_r \mid X_p)$ represents the "market share" controlled by the r new facilities at the points Y_r.

We have assumed that if for a customer at v, $D(v, Y_r) = D(v, X_p)$, then this customer will use the closest old facility. This is a questionable assumption and it may be more reasonable to assume that if $D(v, Y_r) = D(v, X_p)$, then either the purchasing power of the customer at v is shared equally by the competing suppliers, or the customer uses a new facility. To see why we have made the above assumption, consider the special case when $p = r = 1$. Furthermore, let us choose $Y_1 = X_1$, then in the former case the new and old facilities get equal shares of the market and in the latter case the new facility controls the entire market. Our assumption was designed to avoid such trivial solutions. Given $N(V, A)$ and X_p, let Y_r^* be such that $W(Y_r^* \mid X_p) \geq W(Y_r \mid X_p)$ for all possible choices of Y_r on $N(V, A)$. We call Y_r^* an $(r \mid X_p)$-medianoid of $N(V, A)$. It is easy to show that even $(1 \mid X_1)$-medianoid is not necessarily at a vertex of $N(V, A)$ (see Exercise 10.1).

At this point it is instructive to demonstrate that the problem of computing an $(r \mid X_1)$-medianoid is $\mathcal{NP}$-hard (Hakimi, 1983) which implies that it is unlikely that a polynomial-time algorithm for its computation can ever be found (Garey and Johnson, 1979).

Theorem 10.1. *The problem of finding an $(r \mid X_1)$-medianoid of a network is $\mathcal{NP}$-hard.*

Proof. We prove this theorem by reducing the dominating set (DS) problem (Garey and Johnson, 1979, p. 190) to the $(r \mid X_1)$-medianoid problem. We begin by stating the DS problem.

DS Problem. Given graph $G(V, A)$ with node set V and arc set A and an integer $r < |V|$, is there a subset $V' \subset V$ such that $|V'| \leq r$ and $D_G(v, V') \leq 1$ for all $v \in V$, where $D_G(v, V')$ is defined for a graph as was $D(v, Z)$ for a network with the assumption that the length of all arcs in the graph is equal to one.

Given an instance of the DS problem, we construct a network N_1 with node set $V \cup \{x_1\}$ and arc set $A \cup \{(x_1, v) \mid v \in V\}$. In N_1, we let the node weights all equal one and if arc $a = (x_1, v)$, then $l(a) = 2$, otherwise $l(a) = 1.5$.

We prove the theorem by showing that there exists a set of r points Y_r on N_1 such that $W(Y_r | x_1) \geq |V|$, if and only if the DS problem has a solution. If DS has a solution, then there exists $V' \subset V$ with $|V'| = r$ such that $D_G(v, V') \leq 1$ for all $v \in V$. Let $Y_r = V'$. Then it is easy to see that $W(Y_r | x_1) = |V|$; this is because $D(v, Y_r) \leq 1.5 < d(v, x_1) = 2$ for all $v \in V$.

On the other hand, suppose Y_r on N_1 is such that $W(Y_r | x_1) \geq |V|$. Then for each $v \in V$, $D(v, Y_r) < d(v, x_1) = 2$. If Y_r consisted of only nodes, then Y_r would obviously yield a solution to the DS problem in G. Suppose, therefore, that Y_r contains some nonnode point, say y_1, on arc $a = (u, v)$. It is a simple matter to show that y_1 can be replaced by one of the end nodes of a and the resulting Y_r' would still satisfy $W(Y_1' | x_1) \geq |V|$. This process can be continued until Y_r contains no nonnode points. Then the existence of a solution to DS is implied. $\square$

It may be noted from the above proof that even if the $(r | X_1)$-medianoid were defined to be restricted to the nodes only, the problem would remain $\mathcal{NP}$-hard.

Let $N(V, A)$ be a network and assume X_p on N represent the locations of the present facilities on N. For each $v \in V$, let $B(v, X_p) = \{$points z on $N \,|\, d(v, z) < D(v, X_p)\}$. Then it is easy to see that the customer located at v will use one of the new facilities located at a point in Y_r if and only if $Y_r \cap B(v, X_p) \neq \emptyset$. For $V' \subset V$, let $B(V', X_p) = \cap \{B(v, X_p) \,|\, v \in V'\}$. Observe that if $B(V', X_p) \neq \emptyset$ and if a new facility is located at a point in $B(V', X_p)$, then this facility will be used by all customers at the nodes in V'; we will say that this facility *covers* V'. This idea can be used to find an $(r | X_p)$-medianoid in $O(|V|^r \cdot |A|^r / r!)$ time (Megiddo, Zemel, and Hakimi, 1983). This implies that for each fixed r this algorithm has polynomial time complexity, but if r is an arbitrary "input variable," then it is not polynomial time. This does not violate our $\mathcal{NP}$-hardness proof because in that proof r was assumed to be part of the input specifications.

Megiddo et al. (1983) use the above concept to devise an algorithm for finding an $(r | X_p)$-medianoid of a tree network in $O(n^2 r)$ time. Due to the complexity of this algorithm we will not describe it here and refer the interested reader to the original paper.

Now suppose that we are contemplating on locating p facilities on a network $N(V, A)$ where at present no other competing facilities exist. However, we wish to avoid the possibility of a major loss of customers should another organization in the future enter into our market by introducing, say r, new facilities on the network. More precisely, let X_p be a potential set of p locations on N. Let $Y_r^*(X_p)$ be the optimum r sites on N for locating r new facilities which compete with the existing facilities located at X_p. We note that $Y_r^*(X_p)$ is an $(r | X_p)$-medianoid of N given X_p. Here, however, our goal is to find X_p such that $W(Y_r^*(X_p) | X_p)$ is minimized. Let

X_p^* be such that $W(Y_r^*(X_p^*) \,|\, X_p^*) \leq W(Y_r^*(X_p) \,|\, X_p)$ for all X_p on N. We will call X_p^* an $(r \,|\, p)$-centroid of N. We note that X_p^* is a minimax location problem (somewhat similar to the p-center problem) and we may write $\min_{X_p} \max_{Y_r} W(Y_r(X_p) \,|\, X_p) = W(Y_r^*(X_p^*) \,|\, X_p^*)$.

Given the network and integers r and p, the problem of finding an $(r \,|\, p)$-centeroid, X_p^*, seems exceedingly difficult. It is known that, for example, a $(1 \,|\, 1)$-centroid of a network may not be a node of that network (Wendell and McKelvey, 1981; Hakimi, 1983), but it is easy to see that an $(r \,|\, 1)$-centroid is always at a node for $r \geq 2$. Slater (1975) and Wendell and McKelvey (1981) through different considerations showed that a $(1 \,|\, 1)$-centroid of a tree network is at a node; and, in fact, it is a 1-median of that tree network. This result can be obtained as follows.

Let $T(V, A)$ be a tree network. For each $v \in V$, let $T - v$ denote the network obtained from T by removing node v and the arcs incident at v from T. We observe that $T - v$ will contain exactly $d(v)$ components (connected parts) where $d(v)$ is the degree of node v in $T(V, A)$. If T_i is a component of $T - v$, let $W(T_i)$ denote the sum of the weights of the nodes of T_i. Let $H(v) = \max \{W(T_i) \,|\, T_i$ is a component of $T - v\}$. If v^* is such that $H(v^*) \leq H(v)$ for all $v \in V$, then v^* is called a centroid of T (Goldman, 1971; Kariv and Hakimi, 1979). It is known (as Jordan's Theorem) that a centroid of a tree is either a unique node or one of a pair of adjacent nodes in T (see, e.g., Harary, 1969)]. If X_1 is located at node v, it is easy to see that a choice for $Y_1^*(X_1)$ (or the $(1 \,|\, X_1)$medianoid) is then at the node adjacent to v in a heaviest component of $T - v$. Furthermore, it can be seen that $W(Y_1^*(X_1) \,|\, X_1) = H(v)$. This implies that an optimum choice for X_1 is at v^*, which is a centroid of T; and if there are two choices for a centroid of T, then any point along the arc joining the two choices for a centroid could serve as a $(1 \,|\, 1)$-centroid of T. It is known that a centroid of a tree network can be found in $O(n)$ time and that a centroid of a tree network is the same as its 1-median (Goldman, 1971; Kariv and Hakimi, 1979).

We now present two related $\mathcal{NP}$-hardness results that demonstrate the difficulty of the problem of finding an $(r \,|\, p)$-centroid of a network.

Theorem 10.2. *The problem of finding a $(1 \,|\, p)$-centroid of a network is $\mathcal{NP}$-hard.*

Proof. We prove this theorem by reducing the vertex cover (VC) problem (Garey and Johnson, 1979, p. 190) to the $(1 \,|\, p)$-centroid problem.

VC Problem. Given graph $G(V, A)$ and an integer $p < |V|$, is there a subset $V' \subset V$ with $|V'| \leq p$ such that each arc $a \in A$ has at least one end node in V'?

Given an instance of the VC problem, we construct a network $N_1(V_1, A_1)$ from G by replacing each arc $a_i = [u, v]$ in G by the "structure" shown in Figure 10.1. This structure is called a "diamond" joining u and v in N_1. The

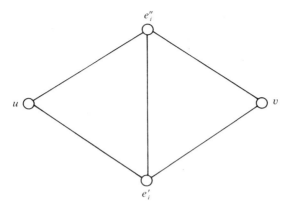

Figure 10.1. The "diamond structure" used in the proof of Theorem 10.2.

lengths of all arcs and the weights of all nodes in N_1 are equal to one. It may be worth noting that $|A_1| = 5|A|$ and $|V_1| = |V| + 2|A|$. We prove our theorem by showing that there exists a set of p points X_p on N_1 such that $W(Y_1(X_p) | X_p) \leq 3$ for every point $Y_1(X_p)$ on N_1, if and only if VC has a solution.

Suppose V' is a solution to the VC problem in G of cardinality p. Let $X_p = V'$ on N_1. Then for any diamond joining u and v in N_1, either u or v belong to $V' = X_p$. Then it is easy to see that $W(Y_1(X_p) | X_p) \leq 3$ for every point $Y_1(X_p)$ on G.

Now let us suppose that a set of p points X_p on N_1 is such that $W(Y_1(X_p) | X_p) \leq 3$ for every choice of point $Y_1(X_p)$ on N_1. If on each diamond of N_1 there exists at least one point of X_p, then one can move these points to ($\leq$) p nodes $V' \subset V$ such that each diamond has a node in V'. Then V' would provide a solution to the VC problem in G. Thus let us assume there is a diamond in N_1 joining, say, u and v on which no point of X_p lies. Suppose $\min \{D(u, X_p), D(v, X_p)\} > 1$; then it is easy to see that $W(e'_i | X_p) \geq 4$, where e'_i is an interior node of the diamond joining u and v. Thus, we may assume that $0 < \min \{D(u, X_p), D(v, X_p)\} \leq 1$, and without loss of generality, let $\min \{D(u, X_p), D(v, X_p)\} = D(u, X_p)$. Now consider another diamond in N_1 joining u and v' with $v' \neq v$. If on this diamond there lies exactly one point of X_p, then we select $Y_1(X_p)$ to lie on the arc of this diamond incident at u on which no point of X_p lies such that $0 < D(u, Y_1(X_p)) < D(u, X_p)$. It can now be seen that $W(Y_1(X_p) | X_p) \geq 4$. This implies that there must be at least two points of X_p on the diamond joining u and v'. In general, we can show that, if there are no points of X_p on some diamond in N_1 then there are at least two points of X_p on an "adjacent" diamond of N_1 (in fact on every adjacent diamond of N_1). Therefore, there certainly are enough points to "cover" all diamonds in N_1. The existence of a solution to VC in G is immediately implied. $\quad\square$

One can also prove (in fact the proof is simpler) that if $(1 \mid p)$-centroid was defined to be restricted to the nodes, the problem would remain $\mathcal{NP}$-hard.

We now wish to prove that even the problem of finding an "approximate" solution to the $(1 \mid p)$-centroid problem is $\mathcal{NP}$-hard (Garey and Johnson, 1979). We say X_p^a is an approximate $(1 \mid p)$-centroid if $W(Y_1^*(X_p^a) \mid X_p^a) \leq \alpha W(Y_1^*(X_p^*) \mid X_p^*)$ for a fixed positive integer α where X_p^* is a $(1 \mid p)$-centroid and α is not a function of the size of the network.

Theorem 10.3.   *The problem of finding an approximate $(1 \mid p)$-centroid of a network is $\mathcal{NP}$-hard.*

Proof.   We again prove this by reducing the VC problem to the approximate $(1 \mid p)$-centroid problem. The details follow the previous proof fairly closely.

Given an instance of the VC problem, we construct a network $N_1(V_1, A_1)$ from G by replacing each arc $a_i = [u, v]$ in G by the structure (diamond) shown in Figure 10.2, where the nodes $e_i^1, e_i^2, \ldots, e_i^{3\alpha-1}$ form a clique (i.e., are pairwise adjacent) and u and v are also adjacent to each of these nodes. The lengths of all arcs and weights of all nodes in N_1 are equal to one. We first show that there exists a set of p points X_p on N_1 such that $W(Y_1(X_p) \mid X_p) \leq 3\alpha$ for every point $Y_1(X_p)$, if and only if VC has a solution.

Suppose V' is a solution to the VC problem in G of cardinality p. Let $X_p = V'$ in N_1. Then for any diamond joining u and v in N_1, either u or v belong to X_p. Then it is easy to see that $W(Y_1(X_p) \mid X_p) \leq 3 \leq 3\alpha$.

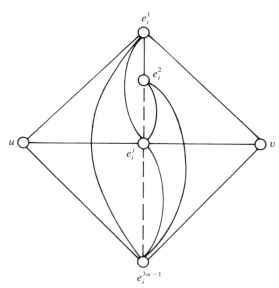

Figure 10.2. The "diamond structure" used in the proof of Theorem 10.3.

Now, suppose X_p on N_1 is such that $W(Y_1(X_p) \mid X_p) \leq 3\alpha$ for every choice of the point $Y_1(X_p)$ in N_1. As before, if on each diamond there is a point of X_p, then one can certainly obtain a node cover V' of G with $|V'| \leq p$. Suppose there is a diamond in N_1 joining u and v on which no point of X_p lies. If $\min\{D(u, X_p), D(v, X_p)\} > 1$, then it is easy to see that $W(e_i^j \mid X_p) \geq 3\alpha + 1$. Thus, we may assume that

$$0 < \min\{D(u, X_p), D(v, X_p)\} \leq 1,$$

and, without loss of generality, that $\min\{D(u, X_p), D(v, X_p)\} = D(u, X_p)$. Consider another diamond in N_1 joining, say, u and v' with $v' \neq v$. If on this diamond there lies exactly one point of X_p, then we select $Y_1(X_p)$ to lie on an arc of this diamond incident at u on which no point of X_p lies such that $0 < D(u, Y_1(X_p)) < D(u, X_p)$. It can now be seen that $W(Y_1(X_p) \mid X_p) \geq 3\alpha + 1$. This implies that there must be at least two points of X_p on the diamond $u - v'$. The existence of VC in G follows immediately as in the proof of Theorem 10.2.

Furthermore, we can also similarly prove that there exists X_p on N_1 such that $(W(Y_1(X_p) \mid X_p) \leq 3$ for every point $Y_1(X_p)$ on G, if and only if VC has a solution. We can then conclude that $W(Y_1(X_p) \mid X_p) \leq \alpha w(Y_1^*(X_p^*)(X_p^*)(\leq 3\alpha)$ if and only if VC has a solution. This completes the proof of Theorem 10.3. $\square$

We remark, without further details, that Hansen and Labbé (1984) have developed a polynomial time algorithm for finding a $(1 \mid 1)$-centroid of a network. Whether or not there exists a polynomial time algorithm for finding an $(r \mid p)$-centroid of a tree network is an interesting and open problem.

10.2.2. Locations on the Plane

In this subsection, we demonstrate that certain competitive location problems can be effectively solved on the plane and possibly in a Euclidean space of higher dimension. In view of the possible implications of these results on spatial voting theory (Simpson, 1969; Greenberg, 1979; Wendell and McKelvey, 1981), we will present them here. As the results are not prerequisites for understanding the future sections, the reader may skip over this subsection.

Let us now assume that we are given the set of demand points $V = \{v_1, v_2, \ldots, v_n\}$ on the plane which we denote by R^2 with $w(v_i)$ representing the demand (or the purchasing power) at point $v_i \in V$ for the service to be provided by the facilities. Suppose as usual X_p denote the locations of the first (i.e., the existing) set of p facilities and Y_r is the location of the second (i.e., the competing) set of r facilities. As before, we assume that the demands are essential and that the customers' preferences are binary. For any set Z of points on the plane, we define $D(v, Z) = \min\{d(v, z) \mid z \in Z\}$

where $d(v, z)$ is the Euclidean distance between points v and z. Define as before $V(Y_r | X_p) = \{v \in V \mid D(v, Y_r) < D(v, X_p)\}$ and $W(Y_r | X_p) = \Sigma \{w(v) \mid v \in V(Y_r | X_p)\}$. Given V and X_p on the plane and integer r we call Y_r^* an $(r | X_p)$-medianoid if $W(Y_r^* | X_p) \geq W(Y_r | X_p)$ for all sets of r points Y_r on the plane. Finally given V on the plane and positive integers r and p, we call X_p^* an $(r | p)$-centroid if $W(Y_r^*(X_p^*) | X_p^*) \leq W(Y_r^*(X_p) | X_p)$ for all sets of p points X_p on the plane where $Y_r^*(X_p)$ is an $(r | X_p)$-medianoid given V, X_p, and r. The results presented here are based on a paper by Drezner (1982). We begin by presenting a solution to the $(1 | X_1)$-medianoid problem.

Suppose Y_1 is a candidate site (point) for a facility on the plane to compete with the existing facility at point X_1. Consider the open half-plane containing Y_1 which is generated by the perpendicular bisector of the (straight) line segment joining points X_1 and Y_1. Note that all (and only those) customers located in this open half-plane will use the facility at Y_1. Suppose we now move the point Y_1 closer to X_1 but along the original line segment from X_1 to Y_1. We observe that in this process the facility at Y_1 will not lose customers, until $Y_1 = X_1$ at which time the facility at Y_1 will lose all customers to the facility at X_1. This implies that an optimum choice for Y_1 would be infinitesimally close to X_1 but at a particular angle from X_1. The choice of this angle determines the number of customers that will use the new facility at Y_1; or more precisely the market share controlled by the facility at Y_1. Let v be a point on the plane and let $A(X_1, v)$ be the angle (say in degrees) of the line passing through X_1 and v with respect to the positive x-axis. Let $H(X_1, v) = \{z \in R^2 \mid A(X_1, v) \leq A(X_1, z) < A(X_1, v) + 180°\}$. Note that $H(X_1, v)$ is a "semi" open half-plane defined by the line from X_1 through v. We define the point $Y_1(v)$ to be infinitesimally close to X_1 such that $A(X_1, Y_1(v))$ is less than but infinitesimally close to $A(X_1, v) + 90°$. It can now be seen that $W(Y_1(v) | X_1) = \Sigma \{w(v_i) \mid v_i \in V$ and $v_i \in H(X_1, v)\}$. The following theorem presents the basic idea behind the procedure for computing $(1 | X_1)$-medianoid.

Theorem 10.4

$$\max_{Y_1 \in R^2} W(Y_1 | X_1) = \max_{v \in R^2} W(Y_1(v) | X_1) = \max_{v_i \in V} W(Y_1(v_i) | X_1).$$

Proof. The fact that $\max_{Y_1 \in R^2} W(Y_1 | X_1) = \max_{v \in R^2} W(Y_1(v) | X_1)$ is established by the fact that we already know that a $(1 | X_1)$-medianoid Y_1 must be infinitesimally close to X_1 and the only matter is to decide the angle of the line from X_1 to Y_1. As V is a finite subset of R^2, it is clear that $\max_{v \in R^2} W(Y_1(v) | X_1) \geq \max_{v_i \in V} W(Y_1(v_i) | X_1)$. Suppose for some point $v' \in R^2$ we have $W(Y_1(v') | X_1) > \max_{v_i \in V} W(Y_1(v_i) | X_1)$. This implies that the semi-infinite line from X_1 through v' does not pass through any points in V. Now suppose we rotate the semi-infinite line from X_1 through v' in the counterclockwise direction about the point X_1 until it touches a point, say v_j in V. Then it is easy to see that

$$\sum \{w(v_i) \mid v_i \in H(X_1, v_j)\} \geq \sum \{w(v_i) \mid v_i \in H(X_1, v')\}.$$

This immediately implies that $W(Y_1(v') \mid X_1) \leq W(Y_1(v_j) \mid X_1)$, which contradicts the previous inequality and hence the theorem is proved. $\square$

This theorem suggests the following simple algorithm for finding a $(1 \mid X_1)$-medianoid which is determined by $v' \in V$ such that $W(Y_1(v') \mid X_1) = \max_{v \in V} W(Y_1(v) \mid X_1)$. First we sort the angles $A(X_1, v)$ for $v \in V$ in a nondecreasing order starting with the smallest angle no less than zero. Suppose then we have the sorted list $0 \leq A(X_1, v_1') \leq A(X_1, v_2') \leq \cdots \leq A(X_1, v_n') < 360°$. Note that to compute $W(Y_1(v_1') \mid X_1)$ requires $O(n)$ operations. However, in general, if we have already computed $W(Y_1(v_i') \mid X_1)$, then we can compute $W(Y_1(v_{i+1}') \mid X_1)$ efficiently as follows: if $A(X_1, v_i') = A(X_1, v_{i+1}')$, then $W(Y_1(v_{i+1}') \mid X_1) = W(Y_1(v_i') \mid X_1)$; if $A(X_1, v_i') < A(X_1, v_{i+1}')$, then $W(Y_1(v_{i+1}') \mid X_1) = W(Y_1(v_i' \mid X_1) - \sum \{w(v) \mid v \in V \text{ and } A(X_1, v) = A(X_1, v_i')\} + \sum \{w(v) \mid v \in V \text{ and } A(X_1, v_i') + 180° \leq A(X_1, v) < A(X_1, v_{i+1}') + 180°\}$.

The sorting step in the above algorithm takes $O(n \log n)$ operations and the computation of $W(Y_1(v_{i+1}') \mid X_1)$ from $W(Y_1(v_i') \mid X_1)$ takes at most $O(\log n)$ operations. (It is possible by a slight modification of this algorithm to find $W(Y_1(v_i') \mid X_1)$ for $i = 1, 2, \ldots, n$ in linear time. But this would require a slightly more complex notation and would not effect the overall complexity.) Thus this algorithm finds a $(1 \mid X_1)$-medianoid in $O(n \log n)$ operations.

As an example for finding a $(1 \mid X_1)$-medianoid, let us consider the case shown in Figure 10.3 where the demand points and their purchasing power and the location of the first facility at X_1 are as indicated. We note that $W(Y_1(v_i) \mid X_1) = \sum \{w(v) \mid v \in V \text{ and } A(X_1, v_i) \leq A(X_1, v) < A(X_1, v_i) + 180°\}$. Consequently, $W(Y_1(v_1) \mid X_1) = 4$, $W(Y_1(v_2) \mid X_1) = 5$, $W(Y_1(v_3) \mid X_1) = 4$, $W(Y_1(v_4) \mid X_1) = W(Y_1(v_5) \mid X_1) = 5$, and $W(Y_1(v_6) \mid X_1) = 7$. This means that $(1 \mid X_1)$medianoid is at $Y_1(v_6)$ where $Y_1(v_6)$ is a point close to X_1 with $-\delta < A(X_1, Y_1(v_6)) < 0$, where the size of δ is determined by the angle shown in Figure 10.3.

This algorithm can be modified to yield a range of values for the infinitesimals for the distance of Y_1 from X_1 as well as the angle of Y_1. However, one may envision applications in which one is not allowed to locate a new facility closer than d from X_1. Drezner (1982) also presents an approach to this variation of the $(1 \mid X_1)$-medianoid problem which we shall briefly review here. To begin with, it is clear from our previous discussion that one may limit the choice of the candidates for Y_1 to the points on (the circumference of) a circle of radius d centered at X_1. Let Y_1 be such a point. Then the perpendicular bisector of the line segment from X_1 to Y_1 is the boundary line for the customers using the facilities at X_1 and at Y_1 with

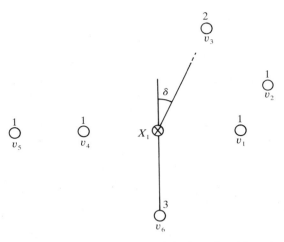

Figure 10.3. An example for computing $(1|X_1)$-medianoid on the plane.

customers on the bisector itself using the facility at X_1. This bisector is in fact a tangent to the cirlce C_1 of radius $d/2$ centered at X_1. Thus, instead of examining lines passing through X_1 and demand points $v \in V$, we really need to examine lines which are tangent to the circle C_1 and pass through demand points $v \in V$, in particular those $v \in V$ which are outside of circle C_1. This also leads to an $O(n \log n)$ algorithm for the restricted $(1|X_1)$-medianoid problem. The details of the algorithm are quite similar to the previous case (see Drezner, 1982).

We now turn our attention to solving the $(1|1)$-centroid problem on the plane. To begin with, suppose, for some given positive number w_0, we wish to find the location $X_1(w_0)$ of the first facility (if possible) such that for all $Y_1 \in R^2$, $W(Y_1|X_1(x_0)) < w_0$. The following theorem, due to Drezner (1982), characterizes the locations of all such points, $X_1(w_0)$.

Theorem 10.5. $W(Y_1|X_1(w_0)) < w_0$ *for all* $Y_1 \in R^2$ *if and only if* $X_1(w_0)$ *belongs to* $\cap H$ *where* $\cap H$ *is the intersection of all closed half-planes, H, for which* $\Sigma \{w(v)|v \in H\} \geq w_0$.

Proof. Suppose $X_1(w_0) \in \cap H$ and $W(Y_1|X_1(w_0)) \geq w_0$ for some $Y_1 \in R^2$. Then the open half-plane H_0', which contain Y_1 and is defined by perpendicular bisector of the line segment from Y_1 to $X_1(w_0)$ must also have the property that $\Sigma \{w(v)|v \in H_0'\} \geq w_0$. Then the closed half-plane defined by H_0' and its boundary satisfies the above property but does not contain $X_1(w_0)$. This is a contradiction to the hypothesis that $X_1(w_0) \in \cap H$. Now suppose $w(Y_1|X_1(w_0)) < w_0$ for all $Y_1 \in R^2$ and $X_1(w_0) \not\in \cap H$. Then there exists a closed half-plane H_c which does not contain $X_1(w_0)$ such that $\Sigma \{w(v)|v \in H_c\} \geq w_0$. Suppose we select Y_1 to be the mirror image of

$X_1(w_0)$ with respect to the line which defines H_c. Let Y_1' be infinitesimally closer to $X_1(w_0)$ than Y_1 and along the line segment from Y_1 to $X_1(w_0)$. Then it is easy to see that $w(Y_1' | X_1(w_0)) \geq w_0$. This is a contradiction and thus it completes the proof. $\square$

Thus to find a point $X_1(w_0)$ such that $W(Y_1 | X_1(w_0)) < w_0$ for all $Y_1 \in R^2$, we need to find a point in the intersection of all closed half-planes H for which $\Sigma \{ w(v) | v \in H \} \geq w_0$. We shall call such a plane a closed half-plane with purchasing power $\geq w_0$. We claim that we need concern ourselves with only those closed half-planes with purchasing power $\geq w_0$ which are generated by lines passing through at least two demand points. To prove this claim consider a closed half-plane generated by line L and assume that the closed half-plane "below" L has the purchasing power $\geq w_0$. If there is no demand point on L, then we may move L "down" but parallel to its original position until it touches a demand point. Call this new line L_1. We note that the closed half-plane below L_1 still has the purchasing power $\geq w_0$. If there is exactly one demand point, say v_1, on L_1, then we rotate about v_1 the line L_1 once in the clockwise (respectively, once in the counterclockwise) direction until it touches another demand point v_2 (respectively, v_3). Let the resulting lines be L_1' and L_1''. Again it is clear that the closed half-planes below L_1' and L_2'' both have the desired property. As the intersection of these two closed half-planes is a subset of the closed half-plane below L, our claim is proved.

For each pair of demand points, v_i and v_j, we have two closed half-planes generated by the lines (say) L_{ij} passing through v_i and v_j. If neither closed half-planes has the purchasing power $\geq w_0$, then we may ignore the line L_{ij}. If one (or respectively, both) closed half-planes have the purchasing power $\geq w_0$, then $X_1(w_0)$ lies in that half-plane (or respectively on L_{ij}). There are $n(n-1)/2$ such lines. Finding a feasible point, if there exists one, is reduced to finding $X_1(w_0) \in R^2$ which satisfies a set of, at most, $n(n-1)/2$ inequalities. This problem is essentially a linear program in R^2 which is solvable in time proportional to n^2 (Megiddo, 1983, 1984) as the number of inequalities is in the order of n^2. To determine the inequalities, it takes $n^2 \log n$. This is because we first have to compute the purchasing power of each closed half-plane. This requires $O(n^2 \log n)$ time (see Exercise 10.10). Then for each line L which may be written as $ax + by = c$, based on the purchasing powers of the resulting two half-planes we must decide whether the point $X_1(w_0)$ with coordinates (x_1, y_1) lies above, on, or below this line by writing $ax_1 + by_1 \geq c$, $ax_1 + by_1 = c$ or $ax_1 + by_1 \leq c$. If neither closed half-planes generated by L has the purchasing power $\geq w_0$, then no inequality corresponding to this line need be written. Thus, given w_0, one can find a feasible point $X_1(w_0)$ (if there exists one) or determine that no such feasible point exists, in time proportional to $n^2 \log n$. However, to solve the $(1|1)$-centroid problem on the plane, we need to find the smallest value w_0^* for which a feasible site $X_1(w_0^*)$ exists such that $W(Y_1 | X_1(w_0^*)) < w_0^*$ for all

$Y_1 \in R^2$. As there are at most $n(n-1)$ values for the purchasing powers, each associated with a closed half-plane, to find a $(1|1)$-centroid we may restrict the value of w_0^* to these values only. We observe that the value of $W(Y_1^*(X_1^*)|X_1^*)$ is not the smallest value w_0^* for which $X_1(w_0^*)$ exists; see the example below. In fact, it can be seen that $W(Y_1^*(X_1^*)|X_1^*)$ is equal to the largest half-plane purchasing power $< w_0^*$. This can be found in constant time. In any case, the purchasing powers associated with half-planes can be sorted and a binary search on these values will produce the smallest feasible value for w_0^*; the resulting feasible point $X_1(w_0^*)$ is the $(1|1)$-centroid. This leads to an $O(n^2 \log^2 n)$ algorithm for finding a $(1|1)$-centroid on the plane.

The following example demonstrates the steps involved in the algorithm for finding a $(1|1)$-centroid on the plane.

Example 10.1. Suppose the demand points and their purchasing powers are as indicated in the Figure 10.4(a). There are six lines which pass through distinct pairs of these points. These lines generate closed half-planes with purchasing powers 2, 3, 4, 5, and 6. To find a $(1|1)$-centroid we must find the smallest value $w^* \in \{2, 3, 4, 5, 6\}$ for which a feasible site $X_1(w^*)$ exists such that $W(Y_1|X_1(w^*)) < w^*$ for all $Y_1 \in R^2$. As the first candidate for w^* we pick the middle value, that is, $w^* = 4$. We observe that as both closed half-planes generated by the line L_{23} have purchasing power of 4, $X_1(4)$ must be restricted to this line. The same statement holds true for lines L_{24} and L_{13}, thus $X_1(4)$ must be restricted to the intersection of L_{13}, L_{23}, and L_{24}. Since this intersection is empty, $w^* = 4$ is not feasible. The next candiate for w^* is 5. The intersection of all closed half-planes with purchasing power ≥ 5 is shown as the shaded area in Figure 10.4(b). Any point in or

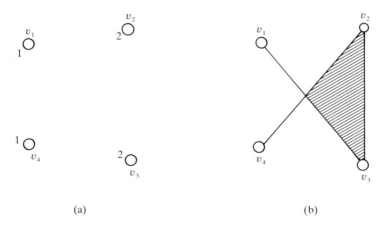

(a)   (b)

Figure 10.4. (a) An example for computing a $(1|1)$-centroid on the plane; (b) shaded area indicates all possible choices for a $(1|1)$-centroid.

on the boundary of the shaded area can be used as the candidate for $X_1(5)$. Since $w^* = 5$ is the smallest value for which $X_1(w^*)$ exists, any point in the shaded area is a candidate for a $(1|1)$-centroid. We finally note that $W(Y_1^* | X_1(5)) = 4$, that is, the market share controlled by the first player is equal to $6 - 4 = 2$ assuming he selects a best choice site. ○

We now briefly turn out attention to the more general problems of computing an $(r | X_p)$-medianoid and an $(r | p)$-centroid on the plane. The $(r | p)$-centroid problem when $p > 1$ seems very difficult and we have nothing further to say about it. But with $p = 1$, it is easy to solve the $(r | 1)$-centroid problem for $r \geq 2$; the solution is always at the node with maximum purchasing power. The proof of this assertion is simple and is left as an exercise for the reader (see Exercise 10.11). Now, with regard to the $(r | X_p)$-medianoid problem, a solution approach for $r > 1$ is not available, but for $r = 1$, Drezner (1981) presents an approach which we briefly outline below.

As before, let $B(v, X_p) = \{z \in R^2 \mid d(v, z) < D(v, X_p)\}$ and for $V' \subset V$, let $B(V', X_p) = \cap \{B(v, X_p) \mid v \in V'\}$. If $B(V', X_p) \neq \emptyset$, then all customers at the nodes V' will use a new facility located at $Y_1 \in B(V', X_p)$. Note that $B(v, X_p)$ represent all points inside a circle of radius $D(v, X_p)$ centered at v. Now let us consider the circles centered at $v_1, v_2, \ldots, v_n$ of radii, $D(v_1, X_p), D(v_2, X_p), \ldots, D(v_n, X_p)$, respectively. Any two of these circles intersect in at most two points. Thus in each circle there are at most $2(n - 1)$ intersection points. As we move, say in clockwise direction, on a circle we can mark each intersection point such that it reveals to us which circle we are entering or leaving. This would lead to finding an interval on each circle with the "maximum market share" should a facility be located there. To find this interval, one first needs to sort the angles of the intersections points about each circle with respect to its center. For each circle this requires $O(n \log n)$. As we must do this for all circles, this leads to an $O(n^2 \log n)$ algorithm. The reader should note that the actual location of Y_1 must be "infinitesimally" inside all relevant circles. However, a very important fact that makes this algorithm work is that if any two of the above circles intersect at any (interior) point of the two circles then they do also intersect at a circumference point; that is, no circle is entirely inside another circle. Thus, the study of the circumference intersection points provides all information about the intersections of these circles.

We feel that some of the results of this subsection can be generalized to higher dimension Euclidean spaces and such results may have applications to voting theory. Possibly more important applications of these results are, say, to find approximate solutions to $(1|1)$-centroid or $(1|X_1)$-medianoid of a network where the network itself is a road map of a state or a country. This is because, in such a network, the nodes and arcs may be assumed to be entities on the plane.

10.3. THE p-MEDIAN PROBLEM: A NONCOMPETITIVE LOCATION THEORY FOR NONESSENTIAL DEMANDS

Let $N(V, A)$ be a network. Suppose X_p represents p sites for locating facilities on $N(V, A)$ with all facilities belonging to a *single* organization. Assume, without loss of generality that $p < n$ because when $p = n$ the solution will be trivial and if $p > n$ the problem has no mathematical significance. Let $f_v(D(v, X_p))$ be the portion of the purchasing power, $w(v)$, of the customer(s) at v which will be spent at a closest facility (i.e., of distance $D(v, X_p)$) given that the p facilities are located at X_p. We assume that for $v \in V, f_v(D(v, X_p)) \leq w(v)$ and furthermore we assume that $f_v(D(v, x_p))$, which maps nonnegative real numbers into positive numbers, is a nonincreasing convex function of the distance, $D(v, X_p)$. Let $F(X_p) = \Sigma \{ f_v(D(v, X_p)) | v \in V \}$. The following may be considered the fundamental theorem of location theory for nonessential demands.

Theorem 10.6. *Suppose $f_v(x)$ is a nonincreasing convex function of real variable x with $f_v(0) > 0$ for all $v \in V$. Then there exists a subset $V_p \subset V$ with $|V_p| = p$ such that $F(V_p) \geq F(X_p)$ for all sets of p points X_p on $N(V, A)$.*

Remark 10.1. It should be noted that this is really a special case of the "generalized p-median theorem" (see Chapter 2). To see this consider

$$F'(X_p) \overset{\triangle}{=} \sum_{v \in V} [w(v) - f_v(D(v, X_p))]$$

$$= \sum w(v) - \sum f_v(D(v, X_p)) = \sum w(v) - F(X_p)$$

and note that if X_p^* minimizes $F'(X_p)$, then X_p^* maximizes $F(X_p)$. Observe that for each v, $w(v) - f_v(D(v, X_p))$ is a nondecreasing concave function of $D(v, X_p)$. It is known that there exists $V_p \subset V$ such that $F'(V_p) \leq F'(X_p)$ for all X_p on G (Hakimi and Maheshwari, 1972; Wendell and Huster, 1973). This, of course, immediately implies the desired result (see also Chapter 2).

The reader should convince himself that the hypothesis of this theorem cannot be easily weakened for the theorem to still hold (see Exercise 10.12).

10.4. TOWARD MORE PRACTICAL MODELS FOR LOCATIONS IN A COMPETITIVE ENVIRONMENT

We develop in this section competitive location models where consumer preference behavior is *not binary* when two organizations compete for customers. To illustrate, suppose we have two supermarket chains A and B. Suppose that chain A has p stores located at p points X_p and the chain B has

r stores located at r points Y_r. Consider a particular customer located at $v \in V$ who makes special trips to a supermarket. Suppose this customer's preference behavior is not binary; that is, on a given day, he may select either chain A or chain B and the percentages of times that he picks A or B are inversely proportional to some functions of the distances $D(v, X_p)$ and $D(v, Y_r)$. However, once he picks chain A (or otherwise chain B), he will use the closest facility in chain A (or otherwise chain B). We will refer to this model of customer's behavior as a partially binary preference; the associated location models, for essential and nonessential demands, are discussed in Sections 10.4.1 and 10.4.2, respectively.

Now consider a different model for customer preference behavior in which a customer decides he must go to a supermarket but does not select which chain he will patronize that day; instead he selects stores $1, 2, \ldots, (p + r)$ with probabilities that are inversely proportional to functions of his distances to these stores. We will analyze location models with this customer behavioral assumption, which we will call proportional preferences, in Sections 10.4.3 and 10.4.4

Before we introduce the models and their analyses, we will state without proof a simple convexity lemma that is needed in the analyses.

Lemma 10.1. *Let f be a function of a nonnegative real variable. If $f(x)$ is a nondecreasing and concave function of x, then $F(x) = a/(b + f(x))$ is a nonincreasing and convex function of x provided real constants a and b are such that $a > 0$ and $b + f(0) > 0$.*

10.4.1. Partially Binary Customers' Preferences and Essential Demands

Consider a network $N(V, A)$. Let X_p be the locations of existing p facilities which are serving the customers at the nodes V. Let Y_r be a candidate for the locations of r new facilities which are to compete with the existing facilities. We assume that the demands are essential and the customers' preferences are partially binary. More precisely, let $w_x(v)$ and $w_y(v)$ represent, respectively, the portions of the customer(s) purchasing power at node $v \in V$ which are spent at a facility in the first set and a facility in the second set. Then the following two relations define the model considered in this subsection:

$$w_x(v) + w_y(v) = w(v), \qquad \text{for } v \in V,$$

and

$$\frac{w_y(v)}{w_x(v)} = \frac{f_v(D(v, X_p))}{f_v(D(v, Y_r))},$$

where f_v is a function mapping nonnegative real numbers into positive real numbers. From the above two relations we have

$$w_y(v) = w(v) \, \frac{f_v(D(v, X_p))}{f_v(D(v, X_p)) + f_v(D(v, Y_r))} \, .$$

Then, we can define in this model

$$W(Y_r \mid X_p) = \sum_{v \in V} w_y(v) = \sum_{v \in V} \frac{w(v) f_v(D(v, X_p))}{f_v(D(v, X_p)) + f_v(D(v, Y_r))} \, .$$

We can now proceed to define an $(r \mid X_p)$-medianoid in this model to be Y_r^* such that $W(Y_r^* \mid X_p) \geq W(Y_r \mid X_p)$ for all Y_r on $N(V, A)$, that is, Y_r^* maximizes $W(Y_r \mid X_p)$. Similarly X_p^* is an $(r \mid p)$-centroid if

$$W(Y_r^*(X_p^*) \mid X_p^*) \leq W(Y_r^*(X_p) \mid X_p)$$

for all X_p on $N(V, A)$ where $Y_r^*(X_p)$ is an $(r \mid X_p)$-medianoid.

Theorem 10.7. *Let f_v be a nondecreasing and concave function of a nonnegative real variable and $f_v(0) > 0$ for all $v \in V$. Then there exists a $V_r \subset V$ with $|V_r| = r$ which is an $(r \mid X_p)$-medianoid of $N(V, A)$.*

Proof. We first define

$$F_v(D(v, Y_r)) = \frac{w(v) f_v(D(v, X_p))}{f_v(D(v, X_p)) + f_v(D(v, Y_r))} \, .$$

Let $D(v, Y_r) = z$ and observe that $f_v(D(v, X_p))$ is a constant. Then by Lemma 10.1, we have that $F_v(z)$ is a nonincreasing and convex function of the real variable z. We note that $W(Y_r \mid X_p) = \Sigma \{F_v(D(v, Y_r)) \mid v \in V\}$ and therefore the theorem immediately follows from Theorem 10.6. $\square$

Let us briefly consider the medianoid model for competitive locations on the plane. All definitions carry over as before with, of course, all distances now denoting Euclidean distances. However, unlike Theorem 10.7 for $(r \mid X_p)$-medianoids on a network, node optimality does not apply to these locations. To see this, consider the following example.

Example 10.2. Suppose we have three demand points, $\{v_1, v_2, v_3\}$ which are at the corners of an equilateral triangle whose sides are of length one and with $w(v) = 1$ for $v \in \{v_1, v_2, v_3\}$. Consider the case of $(1 \mid X_1)$-medianoid problem and assume X_1 is located at v_1. Assume that $f_v(\cdot) = f(\cdot)$ for $v \in V$. Note that regardless of what the function $f(\cdot)$ is, $W(Y_1 \mid X_1) = 1.5$ for $Y_1 \in \{v_1, v_2, v_3\}$. Suppose now that $f_v(z) = 1 + z$, X_1 is at v_1 and choose Y_1 to be at the center of the triangle. Then

$$W(Y_1 \mid X_1) = \sum_{v \in V} \frac{w(v)(1 + d(v, X_1))}{1 + d(v, X_1) + 1 + d(v, Y_1)}$$

$$= \frac{1 + 0}{1 + 0 + (1 + \sqrt{3}/3)} + \frac{1 + 1}{1 + 1 + (1 + \sqrt{3}/3)}$$

$$+ \frac{1 + 1}{1 + 1 + (1 + \sqrt{3}/3)} = 1.506 .$$

This implies that Y_1^* is not at any of the demand points for this particular case even though $f(z)$ is an increasing and concave function of z. ○

Now let us consider the $(r \mid p)$-centroid problem for this consumer behavioral model. Note that the $(r \mid p)$-centroid X_p^* is a set of points that minimizes $W(Y_r^*(X_p) \mid X_p)$ over all possible choices of X_p, where $Y_r^*(X_p)$ is an $(r \mid X_p)$-medianoid of $N(V, A)$. But minimizing

$$W(Y_r^*(X_p) \mid X_p) = \sum_{v \in V} \frac{w(v) f_v(D(v, X_p))}{f_v(D(v, X_p)) + f_v(D(v, Y_r^*(X_p)))}$$

is equivalent to maximizing

$$\sum_{v \in V} (v) - W(Y_r^*(X_p) \mid X_p) = \sum_{v \in V} \frac{w(v) f_v(D(v, Y_r^*(X_p)))}{f_v(D(v, X_p)) + f_v(D(v, Y_r^*(X_p)))} .$$

It seems difficult to prove any convexity properties of these functions as X_p varies. Nevertheless, it is possible that an $(r \mid p)$-centroid in this model is at a set of p vertices.

10.4.2. Partially Binary Customers' Preferences and Nonessential Demands

In this section, we present a possible extension of the results of the previous subsection to the case where the demands are nonessential. As before we assume that we have a network $N(V, A)$ where the customers are located at the nodes and X_p and Y_r are the possible facility locations for the first and the second competitors. Let $w(v)$ be the demand at node $v \in V$. Let $w_x(v)$ and $w_y(v)$ be the portions of this demand which use a facility at X_p and a facility at Y_r, respectively. Let f_v be a function which maps nonnegative, real numbers into positive real numbers. In contrast to the case of essential demands, here we cannot write $w_x(v) + w_y(v) = w(v)$; however, we wish to make sure that $w_y(v)$ (or $w_x(v)$) "decreases" as $D(v, Y_r)$ (or $D(v, X_p)$) increases. Suppose that $w_x(v)$ is the portion of $w(v)$ which uses a facility at X_p, then $w(v) - w_x(v)$ is the portion that is available to use a facility at Y_r. Thus, we may write

$$w_y(v) = \frac{w(v) - w_x(v)}{f_v(D(v, Y_r))} ,$$

and similarly

$$w_x(v) = \frac{w(v) - w_y(v)}{f_v(D(v, X_p))} .$$

From the above two equations, we obtain

$$w_x(v) = \frac{w(v)(f_v(D(v, Y_r)) - 1)}{[f_v(D(v, X_p))f_v(D(v, Y_r))] - 1} ,$$

$$w_y(v) = \frac{w(v)(f_v(D(v, X_p)) - 1)}{[f_v(D(v, X_p)) \cdot f_v(D(v, Y_r))] - 1} .$$

These values of $w_x(v)$ and $w_y(v)$ make sense only if $f_v(0) \geq 1$ and $f_v(z)$ is a nondecreasing function of z for all $v \in V$. For simplicity, we will assume that $f_v(0) > 1$ for all $v \in V$.

Thus, we may write

$$W(Y_r | X_p) = \sum_{v \in V} w_y(v) = \sum_{v \in V} \frac{w(v)(f_v(D(v, X_p)) - 1)}{[f_v(D(v, X_p))f_v(D(v, Y_r))] - 1} .$$

Given $N(V, A)$ and X_p, then Y_r^* is called a $(r | X_p)$-medianoid if $W(Y_r^* | X_p) \geq W(Y_r | X_p)$ for all possible choices of Y_r on $N(V, A)$. At this time we define, analogously,

$$W(X_p | Y_r) = \sum_{v \in V} w_x(v) = \sum_{v \in V} \frac{w(v)(f_v(D(v, Y_r)) - 1)}{[f_v(D(v, X_p))f_v(D(v, Y_r))] - 1} .$$

It should be noted here that $W(X_p | Y_r) + W(Y_r | X_p) \leq \Sigma \{w(v) | v \in V\}$ and the chronological order in which the organizations enter into the market is irrelevant.

Theorem 10.8. *Let f_v be a nondecreasing and concave function of a nonnegative real variable and $f_v(0) > 1$ for all $v \in V$. Then there exists a $V_r \subset V$ with $|V_r| = r$ which is an $(r | X_p)$-medianoid of $N(V, A)$.*

Proof. We claim that

$$F_v(D(v, Y_r)) = \frac{w(v)[f_v(D(v, X_p)) - 1]}{[f_v(D(v, X_p))f_v(D(v, Y_r))] - 1}$$

is a nonincreasing convex function of the variable $D(v, Y_r) (\geq 0)$. To prove this we let $D(v, Y_r) = z$ and $D(v, X_p) = b$. Then, we have

$$F_v(z) = \frac{w(v)[f_v(b) - 1]}{f_v(b)f_v(z) - 1} .$$

The claim then follows immediately from Lemma 10.1. As $W(Y_r | X_p) = \{F_v(D(v, Y_r)) | v \in V\}$ the validity of this theorem is implied by Theorem 10.7. $\square$

Finally, with regard to defining an $(r | p)$-centroid when the demands are nonessential, one has two reasonable choices:

1. As before, we may define X_p^* to be an $(r | p)$-centroid if $W(Y_r^*(X_p^*) | X_p^*) \le W(Y_r^*(X_p) | X_p)$ for all possible choices of X_p on $N(V, A)$. This means X_p^* is a set of sites which the first competitor selects to minimize the market share of the second competitor knowing that the second competitor will select r sites which maximizes his market share given X_p^*.

2. We may define X_p^* to be an $(r | p)$-centroid if X_p^* is the set of sites which maximizes the first competitor's share of the market knowing that the second competitor will select r sites which maximizes his market share.

The reader should note that if the demands are essential, then these two definitions of $(r | p)$-centroid are equivalent.

10.4.3. Proportional Customers' Preferences and Essential Demands

In the models developed in the previous two subsections, we, in a sense, ignored the competitive interaction among the facilities belonging to the same organization. Although there may be applications in which such interactions are irrelevant, we provide a model in which such interactions are taken into account. It will be seen that the results are consistent with our previous results and are in fact extensions of them.

To simplify the notation, we assume that a candidate for all facility locations is given by $X_{p+r} = \{x_1, x_2, \ldots, x_{p+r}\}$ of which the first p belong to the first competitor and the remaining r belong to the second competitor. The customers' preference behavior is assumed to be independent of which organization the facility belongs to. More precisely, let $w_{x_i}(v)$ be the portion of customers at $v \in V$ which use the facility at $x_i \in X_{p+r}$. As before, we may write $w_{x_i}(v) / w_{x_j}(v) = f_v(d(v, x_j)) / f_v(d(v, x_i))$. For simplicity, we will denote $f_v(d(v, x_i))$ by $f_v(x_i)$ for all $v \in V$ and $x_i \in X_{p+r}$. Then the purchasing behavior of the customers at node $v \in V$ can be defined by the following equations:

$$w_{x_1}(v) + w_{x_2}(v) + \cdots + w_{x_{p+r}}(v) = w(v), \qquad v \in V,$$

$$w_{x_i}(v) f_v(x_i) = w_{x_j}(v) f_v(x_j), \qquad x_i \text{ and } x_j \in X_{p+r} \text{ and } v \in V.$$

Using the above equations, we obtain

$$w_{x_i}(v) = \frac{w(v) / f_v(x_i)}{\sum\limits_{j=1}^{p+r} 1 / f_v(x_j)}, \qquad x_i \in X_{p+r} \text{ and } v \in V.$$

This means that a certain percentage of customers' purchasing power at v is spent at the facility at x_i, the percentage being inversely proportional to the cost of getting to the facility at x_i.

Now an $(r \mid X_p)$-medianoid for this scenario is the set of points $\{x^*_{p+1}, x^*_{p+2}, \ldots, x^*_{p+r}\}$ which maximizes

$$\sum_{v \in V} \sum_{i=p+1}^{p+r} w_{x_i}(v) \overset{\triangle}{=} F(x_{p+1}, x_{p+2}, \ldots, x_{p+r})$$

when $\{x_1, x_2, \ldots, x_p\}$ are fixed and given. Similarly an $(r \mid p)$-centroid is the set of points $\{x^*_1, x^*_2, \ldots, x^*_p\}$ which minimizes the

$$\max F(x_{p+1}, x_{p+2}, \ldots, x_{p+r}),$$

where the maximum is taken over all possible choices of x_{p+1}, $x_{p+2}, \ldots, x_{p+r}$.

We now state and prove a theorem similar to the theorems of the previous two sections.

Theorem 10.9. *Let $N(V, A)$ be a network and assume $p + r \leq |V|$. Assume for each $v \in V$, f_v is a nondecreasing and concave function mapping nonnegative real numbers into positive numbers. Then there exists a set $V_r \subset V$ with $|V_r| = r$ and which is a $(r \mid X_p)$-medianoid of $N(V, A)$ given $X_p = \{x_1, x_2, \ldots, x_p\}$ on $N(V, A)$.*

Proof. Suppose otherwise and let $\{x^*_{p+1}, x^*_{p+2}, \ldots, x^*_{p+r}\}$ be an $(r \mid X_p)$-medianoid with the least number of nonnode points and assume without loss of generality that $x^*_{p+1} \in \{x^*_{p+1}, \ldots, x^*_{p+r}\} = X^*_r$ is such a point on arc $[u, v] \in A$. We would like to show that we may move x^*_{p+1} to either u or v while keeping the locations of all other facilities fixed without decreasing $F(x^*_{p+1}, x^*_{p+2}, \ldots, x^*_{p+r})$ or equivalently move x^*_{p+1} to either node u or node v without increasing $F(x_1, x_2, \ldots, x_p)$ where

$$F(x_1, x_2, \ldots, x_p) \overset{\triangle}{=} \sum_{v \in V} \sum_{i=1}^{p} w_{x_i}(v)$$

$$= \sum_{v \in V} \sum_{i=1}^{p} \frac{w(v)/f_v(x_i)}{\displaystyle\sum_{i=1}^{p} [1/f_v(x_i)] + \sum_{i=p+1}^{p+r} [1/f_v(x^*_i)]}.$$

Keeping the positions of all locations except x^*_{p+1} fixed, we may write

$$F(x_1, x_2, \ldots, x_p) = \sum_{v \in V} \sum_{i=1}^{p} \frac{w(v)/f_v(x_i)}{[1/f_v(x_{p+1}^*)] + G_v(X_{p+r}^-)},$$

where

$$G_v(X_{p+r}^-) = \sum_{i=1}^{p} \frac{1}{f_v(x_i)} + \sum_{i=p+2}^{p+r} \frac{1}{f_v(x_i^*)}.$$

Suppose now that the position of the facility currently at x_{p+1}^* on $[u, v] \in A$ is given by the variable z which represents the distance of this facility from u along the arc $[u, v]$. Thus $0 \le z \le l(u, v)$ and assume the current position of x_{p+1}^* is denoted by the particular value z_0. As the positions of all other facilities are fixed, we may write $F(x_1, x_2, \ldots, x_p) = F_1(z)$ and we would like to show that $F_1(z)$ achieves its minimum value at either $z = 0$ or $z = l(u, v)$. Let $Y(u, x_{p+1}^*)$ (respectively $Y(v, x_{p+1}^*)$) be the set of nodes (demand points) $v' \in V$ for which the shortest route from v' to the current position of x_{p+1}^* at z_0 passes through u (respectively, v) and assume that "ties" are broken in favor of u. Then, let us define

$$F_1'(z) = \sum_{v' \in Y(u, x_{p+1}^*)} \sum_{i=1}^{P} \frac{w(v')/f_{v'}(x_i)}{[1/f_{v'}(d(v', u) + z)] + G_v(X_{p+1}^-)}$$

$$+ \sum_{v' \in Y(v, x_{p+1}^*)} \sum_{i=1}^{P} \frac{w(v')/f_{v'}(x_i)}{\{1/[f_{v'}(d(v', v) + l(u, v) - z)]\} + G_v(X_{p+1}^-)}.$$

Because $F_1(z)$ is defined with shortest path routings, and $F_1'(z)$ is not, we have $F_1(z) \le F_1'(z)$ for $0 \le z \le l(u, v)$. As $f_{v'}$ is a nondecreasing concave function of z, one can show, using a variation of Lemma 10.1 that each function in the first summation in the above equation is also a nondecreasing concave function of z. Consequently the first term is a nondecreasing concave function of z. Similarly, the second term is a nonincreasing concave function of z. This implies that $F_1'(z)$ is a concave function of z, $0 \le z \le l(u, v)$. This, in turn, implies that $\min_z F_1'(z) = \min \{F_1'(0), F_1'(l(u, v))\}$. Let $z' \in \{0, l(u, v)\}$ be such that $\min_z F_1'(z) = F_1'(z')$. Then $F_1'(z_0) \ge F_1'(z')$. Therefore, we have $F_1(z_0) = F_1'(z_0) \ge F_1'(z') \ge F_1(z') \ge F_1(z_0)$, and thus, $F_1(z') = F_1(z_0)$. This implies that the facility which was located at X_{p+1}^* can be either moved to u or to v without increasing $F(x_1, x_2, \ldots, x_p)$, which in turn proves the theorem. $\square$

10.4.4. Proportional Customers' Preferences and Nonessential Demands

In this subsection, we would like to repeat the analysis of the previous section assuming that demands are nonessential. The analysis is somewhat similar except that, in this case, $w_{x_1}(v) + w_{x_2}(v) + \cdots + w_{x_{p+r}}(v) \le w(v)$

where, as before, w_{x_i} denotes the portion of a customer's purchasing power at $v \in V$ which is spent at the facility located at x_i. Assume $f_v(d(v, x_j))$ are given functions for all $v \in V$ and $x_j \in X_{p+r}$. Analogous to the model of Section 10.4.3, we use the following relation to model the interaction among the facilities and the behavior of the customers at node $v \in V$:

$$w_{x_i}(v) = \frac{w(v) - \sum_{j=1, j \neq i}^{p+r} w_{x_j}(v)}{f_v(d(v, x_i))} = \frac{w(v) - \sum_{j=1}^{p+r} w_{x_j}(v) + w_{x_i}(v)}{f_v(d(v, x_i))} .$$

To make our notation simpler we will denote $w_{x_i}(v)$ by $w_i(v)$ and $f_v(d(v, x_i))$ by $f_v(x_i)$ and let $m = p + r$. Then the above equation may be rewritten as

$$w_1(v) + w_2(v) + \cdots + w_{i-1}(v) + w_i(v)f_v(x_i) + w_{i+1}(v)$$
$$+ \cdots + w_m(v) = w(v) ,$$

$v \in V, i = 1, 2, \ldots, m$. This leads to the following system of linear algebraic equations for each $v \in V$.

$$
\begin{bmatrix}
f_v(x_1) & 1 & 1 & \cdots & 1 & \cdots & 1 \\
1 & f_v(x_2) & 1 & \cdots & 1 & \cdots & 1 \\
\cdot & & \cdot & & \cdot & & \cdot \\
\cdot & & \cdot & & \cdot & & \cdot \\
1 & 1 & 1 & \cdots & f_v(x_i) & \cdots & 1 \\
\cdot & & \cdot & & \cdot & & \cdot \\
\cdot & & \cdot & & \cdot & & \cdot \\
1 & 1 & 1 & \cdots & 1 & \cdots & f_v(x_m)
\end{bmatrix}
\begin{bmatrix}
w_1(v) \\
w_2(v) \\
\cdot \\
\cdot \\
w_i(v) \\
\cdot \\
\cdot \\
w_m(v)
\end{bmatrix}
=
\begin{bmatrix}
w(v) \\
w(v) \\
\cdot \\
\cdot \\
w(v) \\
\cdot \\
\cdot \\
w(v)
\end{bmatrix} .
$$

If we subtract the first equation from the second through mth, we obtain,

$$
\begin{bmatrix}
f_v(x_1) & 1 & 1 & \cdots & 1 & \cdots & 1 \\
1 - f_v(x_1) & f_v(x_2) - 1 & 0 & \cdots & 0 & \cdots & 0 \\
\cdot & & \cdot & & \cdot & & \cdot \\
\cdot & & \cdot & & \cdot & & \cdot \\
1 - f_v(x_1) & 0 & 0 & \cdots & f_v(x_i) - 1 & \cdots & 0 \\
\cdot & & \cdot & & \cdot & & \cdot \\
\cdot & & \cdot & & \cdot & & \cdot \\
1 - f_v(x_1) & 0 & 0 & \cdots & 0 & \cdots & f_v(x_m) - 1
\end{bmatrix}
\begin{bmatrix}
w_1(v) \\
w_2(v) \\
\cdot \\
\cdot \\
w_i(v) \\
\cdot \\
\cdot \\
w_m(v)
\end{bmatrix}
=
\begin{bmatrix}
w(v) \\
0 \\
\cdot \\
\cdot \\
0 \\
\cdot \\
\cdot \\
0
\end{bmatrix} ,
$$

or

$$
\begin{bmatrix}
f_v(x_1) & 1 & 1 & \cdots & 1 & \cdots & 1 \\
\dfrac{1-f_v(x_1)}{f_v(x_2)-1} & 1 & 0 & \cdots & 0 & \cdots & 0 \\
\cdot & \cdot & \cdot & & \cdot & & \cdot \\
\cdot & \cdot & \cdot & & \cdot & & \cdot \\
\cdot & \cdot & \cdot & & \cdot & & \cdot \\
\dfrac{1-f_v(x_1)}{f_v(x_i)-1} & 0 & 0 & \cdots & 1 & \cdots & 0 \\
\cdot & \cdot & \cdot & & \cdot & & \cdot \\
\cdot & \cdot & \cdot & & \cdot & & \cdot \\
\cdot & \cdot & \cdot & & \cdot & & \cdot \\
\dfrac{1-f_v(x_1)}{f_v(x_m)-1} & 0 & 0 & \cdots & 0 & \cdots & 1
\end{bmatrix}
\begin{bmatrix}
w_1(v) \\
w_2(v) \\
\cdot \\
\cdot \\
\cdot \\
w_i(v) \\
\cdot \\
\cdot \\
\cdot \\
w_m(v)
\end{bmatrix}
=
\begin{bmatrix}
w(v) \\
0 \\
\cdot \\
\cdot \\
\cdot \\
0 \\
\cdot \\
\cdot \\
\cdot \\
0
\end{bmatrix}
.
$$

If we now subtract equations 2 through m from the first equation in the above system of equations, we obtain

$$
\left(f_v(x_1) + \sum_{j=2}^{m} \frac{f_v(x_1)-1}{f_v(x_j)-1} \right) w_1(v) = w(v) .
$$

Consequently,

$$
w_1(v) = \frac{w(v)}{f_v(x_1) - 1 + \displaystyle\sum_{j=1}^{m} (f_v(x_1)-1)/(f_v(x_j)-1)}
$$

$$
= \frac{w(v)/(f_v(x_1)-1)}{1 + \displaystyle\sum_{j=1}^{m} 1/(f_v(x_j)-1)} .
$$

It is easy to see that, in general

$$
w_i(v) \overset{\triangle}{=} w_{x_i}(v) = \frac{w(v)/(f_v(x_i)-1)}{1 + \displaystyle\sum_{j=1}^{m} 1/(f_v(x_j)-1)}
$$

$$
\text{for } i = 1, 2, \ldots, p+r \quad \text{and} \quad v \in V .
$$

As before an $(r \mid X_p)$-medianoid is the set of points $\{x_{p+1}^*, \ldots, x_{p+r}^*\}$ which, given $N(V, A)$ and $\{x_1, \ldots, x_p\}$, maximizes

$$\sum_{v \in V} \sum_{i=p+1}^{p+r} w_{x_i}(v) \overset{\triangle}{=} F(x_{p+1}, x_{p+2}, \ldots, x_{p+r}) \, .$$

Similarly, one definition of an $(r \mid p)$-centroid is the set of points $\{x_1^*, \ldots, x_p^*\}$ which minimizes the

$$\max \{ F(x_{p+1}, x_{p+2}, \ldots, x_{p+r}) \mid \{x_{p+1}, \ldots, x_{p+r}\} \} \, .$$

As in Section 10.4.2, another definition of an $(r \mid p)$-centroid is the set of points $\{x_1^*, x_2^*, \ldots, x_p^*\}$ which maximizes $\Sigma_{v \in V} (w_{x_1}(v) + w_{x_2}(v) + \cdots + w_{x_p}(v))$ given $\{x_{p+1}, x_{p+2}, \ldots, x_{p+r}\}$ maximizes $F(x_{p+1}, x_{p+2}, \ldots, x_{p+r})$.

It seems difficult to find conditions on the network $N(V, A)$ or the functions f_v such that there exists an $(r \mid X_p)$-medianoid which consists entirely of r nodes for this case where we have nonessential demands with proportional preferences. However, for a slightly different objective, where the goal of the second competitor is to minimize the first competitor's sales, we do have the node optimality result. Consider for a moment the case where we had *essential* demands and proportional preferences. If the goal of the second competitor, who chooses the locations of the facilities at x_{p+1}, $x_{p+2}, \ldots, x_{p+r}$, is not to maximize his "sales" but rather to minimize his competitor's sales, he automatically maximizes his own sales. Thus the node optimality result holds for both objectives. In the case of nonessential demands with proportional preferences, node optimality holds only for the second objective. We state this result as a theorem.

Theorem 10.10.   *Let $N(V, A)$ be a network and assume $p + r \leq |V|$. Let, for each $v \in V$, f_v be a nondecreasing and concave function that maps nonnegative real numbers into positive real numbers, and $f(0) > 1$. Then there exists a set $V_r \subset V$ with $|V_r| = r$ such that $\{x_{p+1}, x_{p+2}, \ldots, x_{p+r}\} = V_r$ minimizes $\Sigma_{v \in V} w_{x_1}(v) + w_{x_2}(v) + \cdots - w_{x_p}(v))$.*

As the proof is similar to the proof of Theorem 10.9 it is not presented here, but is left as an exercise for the reader.

The above result is interesting, but not very useful. We have shown that the second competitor can select the r sites for his facilities at r nodes which minimizes the first competitor's share of the market. We have changed the original objective of the second competitor to prove the node optimality result. However, since the service is nonessential, the resulting choice may not maximize the second competitor's own share of the market. Also, the result is meaningless if there is only one competitor ($p = 0$) and all facilities belong to one organization.

However, in the case of linear $f_v(\cdot)$, if the second competitor's objective is to maximize his own market share, we can still prove node optimality for the $(r \mid X_p)$-medianoid problem with nonessential demands.

Theorem 10.11. *Let $N(V, A)$ be a network and assume $p + r \le |V|$. Let, for each $v \in V$, $f_v(x) = a_v x + b_v$ with $a_v \ge 0$ and $b_v > 1$. Then there exists a set $V_r \subset V$ with $|V_r| = r$ such that $\{x_{p+1}, x_{p+2}, \ldots, x_{p+r}\} = V_r$ is an $(r \mid X_p)$-medianoid of $N(V, A)$ given $X_p = \{x_1, x_2, \ldots, x_p\}$.*

Proof. Suppose otherwise, and as before, assume that $\{x^*_{p+1}, \ldots, x^*_{p+r}\}$ is an $(r \mid X_p)$-medianoid with the least number of nonnode points and that x^*_{p+1} on arc $[u, v] \in A$ be one such point. we will show that x^*_{p+1} can be moved to either u or v without decreasing $F(x^*_{p+1}, x^*_{p+2}, \ldots, x^*_{p+r})$ where

$$F(x^*_{p+1}, \ldots, x^*_{p+r}) = \sum_{v' \in V} \frac{w(v') \sum_{j=p+1}^{p+r} 1/[f_v(x^*_j) - 1]}{1 + \sum_{j=1}^{p} \{1/[f_v(x_j) - 1]\} + \sum_{j=p+1}^{p+r} \{1/[f_v(x^*_j) - 1]\}}.$$

The position of x^*_{p+1} on $[u, v]$ is denoted by the variable z which is distance from u with its current position being z_0. Let $Y(u, x^*_{p+1})$ and $Y(v, x^*_{p+1})$ be defined as before. We define

$$F_1(z) = \sum_{v' \in Y(u, x^*_{p+1})} w(v') \frac{\{1/[f_{v'}(d(v', u) + z) - 1]\} + G'_{v'}}{\{1/[f_{v'}(d(v', u) + z) - 1] + G'_{v'} + G''_{v'}}$$

$$+ \sum_{v' \in Y(v, x^*_{p+1})} w(v') \frac{\{1/[f_{v'}(d(v', v) + l(u, v) - z) - 1]\} + G'_v}{\{1/[f_{v'}(d(v', v) + l(u, v) - z) - 1]\} + G'_{v'} + G''_{v'}}$$

where

$$G'_{v'} = \sum_{j=p+2}^{p+r} \frac{1}{f_{v'}(x^*_j) - 1} \quad \text{and} \quad G''_{v'} = 1 + \sum_{j=1}^{p} \frac{1}{f_{v'}(x_j) - 1}.$$

Since $f_v(x) = a_v x + b_v$, it can be seen that each term in the first summation will have the form $(A + Bz)/(C + Dz)$ with A, B, C, and $D > 0$ and $BC < DA$. This implies that each term in the first summation is nonincreasing and convex function of z. Each term in the second summation will have the form $(A - Bz)/(C - Dz)$ with A, B, C, and $D > 0$ and with $BC < DA$ and $C/D > l(u, v)$. These conditions imply that each term in the second summation is nondecreasing and convex (for $z \le l(u, v)$). We conclude that $F_1(z)$ is convex and $\max \{F_1 \mid 0 \le z \le l(u, v)\} = \max \{F_1(0), F_1(l(u, v))\} \overset{\triangle}{=} F_1(z')$. Because $F(x^*_{p+1}, x^*_{p+2}, \ldots, x^*_{p+r}) = F(z)$ is defined with shortest path routings and $F_1(z)$ is not, we have $F(z) \ge F_1(z)$. From the above discussion, we conclude that

$$F(z_0) = F_1(z_0) \le F_1(z') \le F(z') \le F(z_0),$$

which implies that $F_1(z') = F(z_0)$. This means that x^*_{p+1} can be moved to either u or v without decreasing the value of $F(x^*_{p+1}, \ldots, x^*_{p+r})$. This completes the proof of Theorem 10.11. $\square$

In contrast with Theorem 10.10, in Theorem 10.11 the second competitor chooses his r locations which maximize his share of the market. It can be noted that if we set $p = 0$ in the above theorem, we have a node-optimality result for nonessential demands and proportional preferences. In this case, the total sales by the single organization when its facilities are located at $X_p = \{x_1, x_2, \ldots, x_p\}$ may be written as follows

$$F(X_p) = \sum_{v \in V} \frac{w(v) \sum_{i=1}^{p} 1/[f_v(x_i) - 1]}{1 + \sum_{i=1}^{p} 1/[f_v(x_i) - 1]}.$$

Below we state, without proof, the associated node-optimality result.

Theorem 10.12. *Let $N(V, A)$ be a network and assume $p \leq |V|$. Let for each vertex $v \in V$, $f_v(x) = a_v x + b_v$ with $a_v \geq 0$ and $b_v > 1$. Then there exists a set $V_p \subset V$ with $|V_p| = p$ such that $F(V_p) \geq F(X_p)$ for all X_p on $N(V, A)$.*

Finally, as a remark, to contrast with the models for binary preferences in Section 10.2, we have the case when customers preferences are *binary* and the demands are *nonessential*. In this case there may not exist a node which is a $(1 \,|\, X_1)$-medianoid (see Exercise 10.1).

10.5. COMPETITIVE LOCATIONS AND GAMES

One may think of the problems in this chapter, in particular the $(r \,|\, p)$-centroid problem, as games. In each of these games there are two competitors (players). In the various versions of the problems, with the exception of that of Theorem 10.10, both players have the same objective, that is, to control as large a share of the market as possible. With this in mind, consider the following game. We begin with a network $N(V, A)$ and two positive integers p and r. The first player selects p points X_p (on $N(V, A)$) for his facilities, the second player having knowledge of X_p selects r points Y_r. At this stage the "pay off" to the second player is $W(Y_r \,|\, X_p)$ and the "pay off" to the first player is $W(X_p \,|\, Y_r)$. (The reader should note that we are implicitly redefining $W(X_p \,|\, Y_r)$ for the case of essential demands and binary preferences to be $\sum \{w(v) \,|\, v \in V\} - W(Y_r \,|\, X_p)$; in all other cases this is consistent with our earlier definitions.) As the problem is presently stated each player has exactly one move and he has to make the best move possible. This is especially true in situations where the facilities are expensive to construct, and once the facilities are constructed no further moves can be contemplated. The first player knows that once he selects his p sites, the second player will then select the best possible r sites for his facilities. Thus the first player picks his p sites at an $(r \mid p)$-centroid X_p^* while the second player responds by picking Y_r^* at an $(r \mid X_p^*)$-medianoid and the game is over.

One may pose two possible scenarios for this game to continue beyond the first move by each player.

1. The facilities are mobile but for each player it takes a certain amount of time to respond to the other player's choice of sites (move), assuming that the players do have the computational power to make the best move at each step.

2. The first player does not have the computational power to find an $(r \mid p)$-centroid while each player does have the capability of finding $(r \mid X_p)$-medianoid (or $(p \mid Y_r)$-medianoid) of the network. For both cases, the question arises on where the two players will end up.

Before we attempt to analyze the above scenarios, we describe the game by defining each player's ith move. The first player's ith move, for $i > 1$, is the optimum selection of p points denoted by $X_p(i)$ given the $(i - 1)$th move of the second player which was the selection of r points $Y_r(i - 1)$. The second player's $(i - 1)$th move for $i > 1$ is the optimum selection of r points $Y_r(i - 1)$ given the $(i - 1)$th move of the first player which was the selection of $X_p(i - 1)$. The first move of the first player is an arbitrary set of p points $X_p(1)$. More precisely (for $i > 1$) $X_p(i)$ is a $(p \mid Y_r(i - 1))$-medianoid of $N(V, A)$ and $Y_r(i - 1)$ is an $(r \mid X_p(i - 1))$-medianoid of $N(V, A)$ and $X_p(1)$ is an arbitrary set of p points. Unless explicitly stated otherwise, we assume that the demands are essential and preferences are binary.

We will now consider two examples to illustrate some game-theoretic concepts. Consider first the network of Figure 10.5(a) and assume $p = r = 1$ and $w(v_j) = 1$ for $j = 1, 2, 3$ and the arc lengths are 1.

In Figure 10.5(b) both players' first moves are indicated where $Y_1(1)$ is the mid-point on the edge (v_2, v_3) which is a $(1 \mid X_1(1))$-medianoid. At this stage, it is the first player's turn to move. His move and the second player's response to it are shown in Figure 10.5(c). Finally, Figure 10.5(d) indicates the third move of the first player and the second player's response to that. At this stage it is clear that the game will continue indefinitely. Whichever player quits first is the loser and will control exactly 1/3 of the market leaving the rest to the other player. This example illustrates a situation where the game does not reach an "equilibrium," that is, where each player finds that he must continue to move or accept his share of the market to be one third of the total. Note that in the above example the first move by the first player, that is the choice of $X_1(1)$, is a $(1 \mid 1)$-centroid of the network.

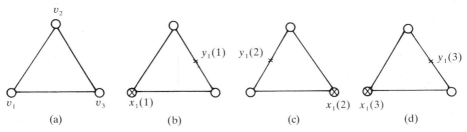

Figure 10.5. Moves by the players not leading to an equilibrium state.

Let us now consider the network of Figure 10.6(a) and assume $w(v_j) = 1$ for $j = 1, 2, \ldots, 9$ and $p = r = 2$ and the arc lengths are 1.

The first player's move $X_2(1) = \{x_1(1), x_2(1)\}$ and the second player's response $Y_2(1) = \{y_1(1), y_2(1)\}$ are shown in Figure 10.6(b). The first player's second move $X_2(2) = \{x_1(2), x_2(2)\}$ and the second player's second move $Y_2(2) = \{y_1(2), y_2(2)\}$ are shown in Figure 10.6(c). The players' third moves $X_2(3) = \{x_1(3), x_2(3)\}$ and $Y_2(3) = \{y_1(3), y_2(3)\}$ are shown in Figure 10.6(d). Now it is the first player's turn. He knows, of course, $Y_2(3)$ and finds that his present location is at a $(2 \mid Y_2(3))$-medianoid. Thus he will not move from his present position which implies that the second player also will not move and the game is over. Thus this game terminates in an "equilibrium state." We note that $X_2(3)$ is in fact a $(2 \mid 2)$-centroid of this tree network.

At this time, it is instructive to define an equilibrium state. Suppose after i moves by both players we have the position pair $(X_p(i), Y_r(i))$. We call $(X_p(i), Y_r(i))$ the state of the game after i steps. We remind the reader that the game's first move, $X_p(1)$, is by the first player and its last move $Y_r(i)$ is

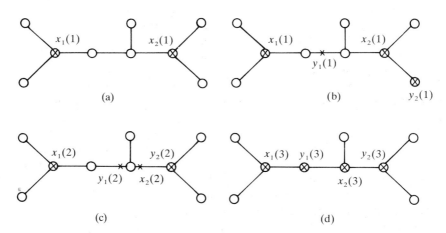

Figure 10.6. Moves by the players leading to an equilibrium state. $X_2(3)$ is a $(2 \mid 2)$-centroid.

made by the second player and, in fact, $Y_r(i)$ is an $(r \mid X_p(i))$-medianoid of the network $N(V, A)$. The state $(X_p(i), Y_r(i))$ is called an equilibrium state, if $X_p(i)$ is a $(p \mid Y_r(i))$-medianoid of $N(V, A)$. It should be noted that when $X_p(i)$ is a $(p \mid Y_r(i))$-medianoid, the next "move" $X_p(i+1)$ by the first player can be picked to be equal to $X_p(i)$ and consequently $Y_p(i+1)$ can be picked to be equal to $Y_p(i)$. Hence, it is possible that the game will remain in its present state indefinitely. Two simple observations can be made about this equilibrium state.

1. Suppose $X_p(i)$ is an $(r \mid p)$-centroid. Then the question arises: is $(X_p(i), Y_r(i))$ an equilibrium state? The answer is "no," as the example of Figure 10.5(a) indicates. Suppose we restrict the network $N(V, A)$ to be a tree network. The answer is still "no." To see this consider the network of Figure 10.7(a). Assume that $w(v) = 1$ for all $v \in V$ and all arc lengths are equal to 1. A $(2 \mid 1)$-centroid for this network is at $X_1(1)$ as indicated in Figure 10.7(b), where a choice for $Y_2(1) = \{y_1(1), y_2(1)\}$ is also indicated. In Figure 10.7(c), the choice for $X_1(2)$ of the first player and the response $Y_2(2) = \{y_1(2), y_2(2)\}$ of the second player are shown. It is clear that this game will never reach an equilibrium even though the first player's first move was a $(2 \mid 1)$-centroid of the tree network. Let us now study the same question, when the network is a tree but $p = r = 2$.

Consider the network of Figure 10.8(a) with all node weights and arc lengths equal to 1 and suppose the first player has selected $X_2(1) = \{x_1(1), x_2(1)\}$ and subsequently the second player has picked $Y_2(1) =$

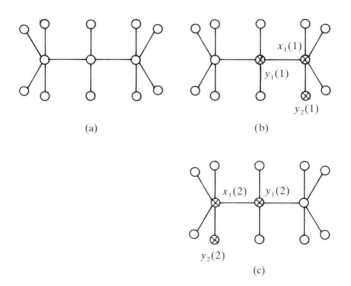

(a)   (b)

(c)

Figure 10.7. A game which does not reach equilibrium even though $X_1(1)$ is a $(2 \mid 1)$-centroid.

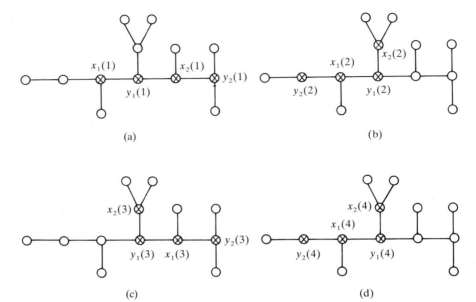

Figure 10.8. A game which does not reach an equilibrium even though $X_2(1)$ is a $(2|2)$-centroid.

$\{y_1(1), y_2(1)\}$ as indicated in Figure 10.8(a). At this time the first player picks $X_2(2) = \{x_1(2), x_2(2)\}$ and then the second player picks $Y_2(2) = \{y_1(2), y_2(2)\}$ as shown in Figure 10.8(b). The players then move to $X_2(3) = \{x_1(3), x_2(3)\}$ and $Y_2(3) = \{y_1(3), y_2(3)\}$ as shown in Figure 10.8(c). Finally, $X_2(4) = \{x_1(4), x_2(4)\}$ and $Y_2(4) = \{y_1(4), y_2(4)\}$ are shown in Figure 10.8(d). As $X_2(4) = X_2(2)$ and $Y_2(4) = Y_2(2)$, the game does not reach an equilibrium. We point out that $X_2(1)$ above is in fact a $(2|2)$-centroid of the above tree.

However, it is known that if $p = r = 1$, the game will reach an equilibrium (Slater, 1975; Wendell and McKelvey, 1981) when the network is a tree (see also Exercise 10.14).

2. Suppose $(X_p(i), Y_r(i))$ is an equilibrium state of the above game. Is it necessary that either $X_p(i)$ be an $(r \mid p)$-centroid or $Y_r(i)$ be a $(p \mid r)$-centroid? The answer is "no," even if the network is a tree and $p = r = 2$. To see this consider the example of Figure 10.9(a) with all node weights and arc lengths being equal to 1. The first move of the first player $X_2(1) = \{x_1(1), x_2(1)\}$ and the response of the second player $Y_2(1) = \{y_1(1), y_2(1)\}$ are indicated in Figure 10.9(b). We know that $(X_2(1), Y_2(1))$ is an equilibrium state. The $(2|2)$-centroid $X_2 = \{x_1, x_2\}$ is shown in Figure 10.9(c), which is neither equal to $X_2(1)$ nor equal to $Y_2(1)$. However, if $p = r = 1$ and the network is a tree, then the answer to the above question is "yes" (see Exercise 10.14).

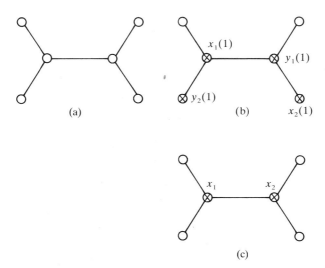

Figure 10.9. A game which reaches an equilibrium but not at the $(2|2)$-centroid shown in (c).

From the preceding discussion, one can conclude that there are a number of interesting questions that remain to be investigated about the above game and its equilibrium. The general question is: given positive integers p and r, can we determine the class of networks for which the game reaches an equilibrium for certain starting choices of $X_p(1)$ of the first player? This problem seems difficult. However, we remind the reader that if either the second player can respond immediately or the facilities are not mobile, then the best choice for the first player is X_p^* which is an $(r|p)$-centroid of $N(V, A)$, and of course the second player will subsequently pick Y_r^* to be at an $(r|X_p^*)$-medianoid of $N(V, A)$. No further move by either player can lead to an advantage.

Proving the existence of an equilibrium state, or its nonexistence, when the game is played on a network with nonessential demands, or when the game is played on a plane, is a fertile ground for further study. We will end this chapter with a brief presentation of a class of locational games formulated and analyzed by Penn, Kariv, and Halpern (1982).

In these games, there is exactly one move by each of the two players; that is, the first player makes a choice X_p for the sites for his facilities and then the second player responds by choosing the sites Y_r for his facilities and the game is over. The two player's may or may not have the same goals (objective functions). There are four reasonable objective functions for each player and these are

α, the player wishes to maximize his share of the market;

β, the player wishes to minimize his competitor's share of the market;

γ, the player wishes to maximize the difference between his share and his competitor's share of the market;

σ, the player wishes to insure that he will not lose the game; that is, his share of the market is no less than his competitor's share of the market.

If the first player acts according to objective function $u \in \{\alpha, \beta, \gamma, \delta\}$ and the second player acts according to objective function $v \in \{\alpha, \beta, \gamma, \delta\}$ then, the game will be called an $R(u, v)$-game. This leads to 16 seemingly distinct games. By a solution (X_p, Y_r) to the game $R(u, v)$, we mean that the first player has optimally selected X_p according to objective function u and the knowledge that his rival's move Y_r will be an optimum choice according to the objective function v and the knowledge of the sites X_p.

Two simple observations can be made about this class of games.

1. If the sum of the market shares of the two players is equal to $\Sigma \{w(v) | v \in V\}$, then the objectives α, β and γ are identical. In particular, in the locational games previously considered, if the demands are essential, then α, β and γ are identical, but if the demands are nonessential then α, β and γ may not be identical.
2. There is always a solution (X_p, Y_r) to any $R(u, v)$ game if $u, v \in \{\alpha, \beta, \gamma\}$. However, if either $u = \delta$ or $v = \delta$, then the game $R(x, y)$ may not have a solution.

Penn et al. (1982) make some additional assumptions to make the problem manageable and yet interesting. These assumptions are:

1. the network $N(V, A)$ is a tree network;
2. $p = r = 1$;
3. the demands are nonessential, in particular the portion of the purchasing power at node v which uses the facility located at x is given by the function $f_v(d(v, x)) = a_v - b_v d(v, x)$ and a_v and b_v are given for each $v \in V$ and are such that $a_v - b_v d(v, x) \geq 0$ for all x on $N(V, A)$ (as a special case, Penn et al. assume that $b_v = 1$ and $a_v = a$ for all $v \in V$);
4. the customers' preferences are binary, in particular the customer at v always uses the facility closer to him with the ties broken in the favor of the first player's facility;
5. the locations of X_1 and Y_1 are restricted to the nodes.

If the solution to the game is (X_1, Y_1), then the players' market shares are given as follows:

$$W(X_1 | Y_1) = \Sigma \{f_v(d(v, X_1)) | v \in V \text{ and } d(v, X_1) \leq d(v, Y_1)\}$$

for the first player, and

$$\bar{W}(X_1 \mid Y_1) = \sum \{ f_v(d(v, Y_1)) \mid v \in V \text{ and } d(v, X_1) > d(v, Y_1) \}$$

for the second player.

We shall now state without proofs, two theorems which are representatives of the type of results that Penn et al. (1982) were able to establish. These results apply to tree networks with $w(v) = 1$.

Theorem 10.13. *If v_m is a 1-median of a tree (i.e., $v_m \in V$ is such that $\sum \{d(v, v_m) \mid v \in V\} \leq \sum \{d(v, v') \mid v \in V\}$ for all $v' \in V$) and (X_1, Y_1) is a solution for the game $R(u, v)$ with u and $v \in \{\alpha, \beta, \gamma\}$, then v_m, X_1 and Y_1 lie on a path in the tree.*

Note that the 1-median as defined in the statement of Theorem 10.13 and the 1-median for nonessential demands as defined in Section 10.3 ($v_m \in V$ is such that $\sum \{f_v(d(v, v_m)) \mid v \in V\} \geq \sum \{f_v d(v, v') \mid v \in V\}$ for all $v' \in V$) coincide. This is because $f_v(d(v, v_m)) = a - d(v, v_m)$.

Let v_k be a node of degree d_k in the tree $T(V, A)$. If we delete v_k from T, we will obtain d_k components (subtrees). Let these subtrees be denoted by $T_{k1}, T_{k2}, \ldots, T_{kd_k}$ such that $|T_{k1}| \geq |T_{k2}| \geq \cdots \geq |T_{kd_k}|$ where $|T_{ki}|$ is the number of nodes in T_{ki}.

Theorem 10.14. *Let v_m be a 1-median of $T(V, A)$. If $|T_{m1}| \leq 1/3|V|$, then:*

a. *for the games $R(u, v)$ with $u \in \{\alpha, \beta, \delta\}$, $v \in \{\alpha, \beta\}$ and for the games $R(\alpha, \beta)$, $R(\beta, \alpha)$, and $R(\delta, \beta)$, $X_1 = v_m$,*
b. *there exists no solution for the games $R(u, \delta)$ with $u \in \{\alpha, \gamma, \delta\}$.*

10.6. CONCLUSIONS

The material in this chapter must be viewed as an introduction to the subject of competitive location theory. As the subject matter is quite new and the literature appears to be rather limited, this chapter was written from the personal perspective of the author. The choices of the models, their formulations, and the hypotheses in many of the theorems are to some extent ad-hoc even though considerable thinking went into them. It is fully expected that some of these results will be generalized, modified, or their proofs will be simplified in the future. The subject of competitive location theory seems to be a particularly interesting research area; there is greater flexibility here than in traditional location theory in the selection of problems or models for further study. The problems are also quite challenging but, admittedly, their solutions are not as elegant as for, say, the p-center and p-median problems.

In the next chapter the same general subject is studied from a different perspective by Hansen, Thisse, and Wendell. The emphasis there is on a selection of a single point on a network with essential demands and binary preferences: Such a point, referred to as a Simpson (1969) point in the chapter, may be a $(1|1)$-centroid. The authors also introduce a new and interesting concept called a Condorcet point which is a point X_1 such that $W(Y_1|X_1) \leq 1/2 \Sigma \{w(v)|v \in V\}$ for all Y_1 on $N(V, A)$. A Condorcet point may not always exist. However, for those networks for which it does exist the first competitor's market share is guaranteed to be no less than 50% (assuming that the second competitor competes with a single facility). In this connection, Greenberg (1979) has shown that the first competitor on the plane can choose his locations such that he can control at least $1/3$ of the entire market if a second competitor enters into his market with a single facility.

The subject of competitive location theory is likely to be an active field of future research. It is hoped that the material in this chapter will stimulate greater interest on the subject.

For a somewhat expanded treatment of the material presented in Sections 10.3 and 10.4, the reader is referred to Hakimi (1986).

ACKNOWLEDGMENTS

I would like to express my thanks to the anonymous referees whose suggestions and comments improved the presentation of the chapter and simplified the proofs of Theorems 10.7 and 10.8. Martine Labbé's comments and suggestions are also gratefully acknowledged. The work reported in this chapter was supported by the National Science Foundation through Grant ECS-8121741.

EXERCISES

10.1 Consider a network $N(V, A)$ consisting of three nodes and three arcs each joining a distinct pair of nodes. Assume that all nodes have weight one and all arcs have length one. Assume essential demands and binary preferences.

(a) Show that for certain choices of X_1, $(1|X_1)$-medianoid is not at a node.

(b) Show that any point in $N(V, A)$ is a $(1|1)$-centroid of N.

(c) Suppose demands are nonessential but still binary. Suppose $f_v(x) = w(v)/(1 + d(v, x))$, $v \in V$ and X_1 is at a node. Show that no vertex is a $(1|X_1)$-medianoid.

10.2 Consider a network $N(V, A)$ and let X_p be the location of p existing facilities on N. Show that $B(v, X_p)$ intersects at most two points belonging to any arc in N. Using this idea prove that one can find an $(r \mid X_p)$-medianoid of N in $O(|V|^r |A|^r / r!)$ time.

10.3 Consider the network N shown in Figure 10.10. Assume we have essential demands and binary preferences. Show that the mid-point of the arc (v_1, v_1') is the $(1 \mid 1)$-centroid of N. Does this imply that a $(1 \mid 1)$-centroid of a network is not necessarily at a 1-median?

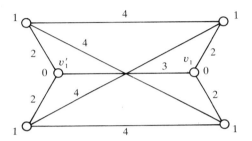

Figure 10.10. The network for Exercise 10.3.

10.4 Show that if $r \geq 2$, then an $(r \mid 1)$-centroid of a network is always at a node even if demands are nonessential so long as we have binary preferences. Assume demand at vertex v for service provided at point x is $w(v) / 1 + d(v, x)$.

10.5 Find the set of all points each of which is a $(1 \mid 1)$-centroid of the tree network of Figure 10.11. Assume that demands are essential with binary preferences.

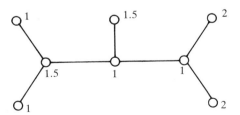

Figure 10.11. The network for Exercise 10.5.

10.6 Find a tree network for which a $(1 \mid 3)$-centroid is not at three of its nodes.

10.7 Find $(1|X_1)$-medianoid for the network of Figure 10.12. Assume that demands are essential with binary preferences. The lengths of the arcs and weights of the demand points are indicated in the figure.

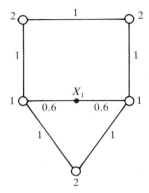

Figure 10.12. The network for Exercise 10.7.

10.8 Suppose we have the following demand points on the plane: $(2, 0)$, $(1, 1)$, $(-2, 1)$, and $(-1, -2)$. Assume X_1 is at $(0, 0)$ and all demands are essential and equal to 1 and the preferences are binary. Using the algorithm described in this chapter,

(a) find a $(1|X_1)$-medianoid,

(b) find the set of all $(1|X_1)$-medianoid, and

(c) find the $(1|X_1)$-medianoid, given that the Euclidean distance between X_1 and $Y_1 > \sqrt{2}$.

10.9 Suppose we have the following demand points on the plane: $v_1 = (0, 0)$, $v_2 = (1, 1)$, $v_3 = (-1, 1)$, and $v_4 = (0, -1)$, with purchasing powers $w(v_1) = 1/8$, $w(v_2) = 1/2$, $w(v_3) = 1/4$, and $w(v_4) = 1$, respectively. Find the $(1|1)$-centroid assuming that the demands are essential and consumer preferences are binary.

10.10 Suppose we have n points $V = \{v_1, v_2, \ldots, v_n\}$ on the plane with v_i having a purchasing power $w(v_i)$. Give an $O(n^2 \log n)$ algorithm for computing the purchasing powers of all closed half-planes defined by two points in V. Hint: Start with planes $v_1 - v_i$, $i = 2, 3, \ldots, n$.

10.11 Prove that a $(2|1)$-centroid in the plane is always located at a demand point with the maximum purchasing power.

10.12 Show that if in Theorem 10.6, $f_v(x)$ was not a nonincreasing concave function of x, then the theorem would not hold. What if $f_v(x)$ was a nondecreasing function of x? Is there any application for such a result?

10.13 Give a detailed proof of Theorem 10.10. Why is it that this proof cannot be completed if the second competitor merely attempts to maximize his sales?

10.14 Suppose we have a tree network $N(V, A)$. Suppose that $w(v) = 1$ for $v \in V$ and $l(e) = 1$ for all $e \in A$ and $p = r = 1$.

(a) Show that the game described in Section 10.5 always terminates in an equilibrium state regardless of the choice of the initial move.

(b) Show that at the equilibrium state $(X_1(i), Y_1(i))$ either $X_1(i)$ or $Y_1(i)$ is at a $(1 \mid 1)$-centroid of the tree.

10.15 Repeat Exercise 10.14 given $w(v) \geq 0$ for all $v \in V$, and $l(e) > 0$ for all $e \in A$.

REFERENCES

Drezner, Z. (1981). "On a Modified 1-Center Model." *Management Science* **17**, 848–851.

Drezner, Z. (1982). "Competitive Location Strategies for Two Facilities." *Regional Science and Urban Economics* **12**, 485–493.

Garey, M. R., and D. S. Johnson (1979). *Computers and Intractability: A Guide to the Theory of $\mathcal{NP}$-Completeness*. Freeman, San Francisco, California.

Goldman, A. J. (1971). "Optimal Center Location in Simple Networks." *Transportation Science* **5**, 212–221.

Greenberg, J. (1979). "Consistent Majority Rules over Compact Sets of Alternatives." *Econometrica* **47**, 627–636.

Hakimi, S. L. (1983). "On Locating New Facilities in a Competitive Environment." *European Journal of Operational Research* **12**, 29–35.

Hakimi, S. L. (1986). "p-Median Theorems for Competitive Locations." In *Location Decisions: Methodology and Applications, Annals of Operations Research* (J. P. Osleeb and S. J. Ratick, eds.), Vol. 6, pp. 77–98.

Hakimi, S. L., and S. N. Maheshwari (1972). "Optimum Locations of Centers in Networks." *Operations Research* **12**, 967–973.

Hansen, P., and M. Labbé (1984). "Algorithms for Condorcet and Simpson Points on a Network." Faculté Universitaire Catholique de Mons (unpublished).

Harary, F. (1969). *Graph Theory*. Addison-Wesley, Reading, Massachusetts.

Kariv, O., and S. L. Hakimi (1979). "An Algorithmic Approach to Network Location Problems. II. The p-Medians." *SIAM Journal on Applied Mathematics* **37**(3), 539–560.

Megiddo, N. (1983). "Linear-time Algorithm for Linear Programming in R^3 and Related Problems." *SIAM Journal on Computing* **12**(4), 759–776.

Megiddo, N. (1984). "Linear Programming in Linear-Time When the Dimension Is Fixed." *Journal of the Association for Computing Machinery* **31**, 114–127.

Megiddo, N., E. Zemel, and S. L. Hakimi (1983). "The Maximum Coverage Location Problem." *SIAM Journal on Algebraic and Discrete Methods* **4**(2), 253–261.

Penn, M., O. Kariv, and J. Halpern (1982). "Competitive Locations in Trees." Department of Industrial and Management Engineering, Technicon, Haifa, Israel (unpublished).

Simpson, P. (1969). "On Defining Areas of Voter Choice." *Quarterly Journal of Economics* **83**, 478–487.

Slater, P. J. (1975). "Maximin Facility Location." *Journal of Research of the National Bureau of Standards, Series B*, **79B**, 107–115.

Wendell, R. E., and A. P. Hurter (1973). "Optimal Locations in Networks." *Transportation Science* **7**, 18–33.

Wendell, R. E., and R. D. McKelvey (1981). "New Perspectives in Competitive Location Theory." *European Journal of Operational Research* **6**, 174–182.

11

Equilibrium Analysis for Voting and Competitive Location Problems

Pierre Hansen
RUTCOR
Rutgers University
New Brunswick, New Jersey

Jacques-François Thisse
Center for Operations Research and Econometrics
Université Catholique de Louvain
Louvain-la-Neuve, Belgium

Richard E. Wendell
The Joseph M. Katz Graduate School of Business
University of Pittsburgh
Pittsburgh, Pennsylvania

11.1. INTRODUCTION

Most locational models address situations where facilities are under the control of a single decision-maker. On the other hand, as in Chapter 10, a new class of problems, which we refer to as *competitive location problems*, arise when we consider locating a facility with respect to other competing facilities (e.g., department stores) under the control of independent decision-makers (e.g., entrepreneurs). These are modeled and studied within the framework of noncooperative game theory. Here a natural solution is a locational configuration of the facilities such that no facility would attract (e.g., be closer to) more clients at an alternate location.

Also in contrast to the main body of facility location theory, consider the problem of locating facilities as the result of a collective action in which clients pursue their own interest within the mutual dependency imposed by a voting rule. Thus, in this situation the focus shifts to the confrontation of individual preferences. Given the assumption that clients prefer to have the facilities located as close as possible to them, there exists no way in general to meet simultaneously the ideals of all clients. To illustrate, think of the problem of locating a school in a given community, where the choice of a particular site will affect the well-being of all community members. Consequently, the locational pattern must necessarily be a compromise. Here a new family of problems, called *voting location problems*, emerges. A natural solution to such problems is a location where no other location is preferred by (i.e., is closer to) a majority of clients.

In both classes of problems, a major difficulty arises in that the existence of "solutions" is not guaranteed. In other words, for a competitive location problem, any configuration of competing facilities may be such that there is an incentive for at least one facility to be moved; for a spatial voting problem, no locational pattern may always secure a majority of votes when compared to any other one. This indicates a need for alternate solution concepts. In this regard, two lines of research can be investigated: one restricts the set of locations to be compared in order to obtain "local" solution concepts; the other relaxes the equilibrium conditions to obtain "weaker" solution concepts. Both approaches are discussed here. More precisely, we discuss the existence of, and the relationships among, different possible solution concepts in competitive location and spatial voting problems.

Throughout this chapter the following are assumed: (i) in competitive location models, *two* facilities compete for a given market; and (ii) in voting location models, clients vote in order to locate *one* facility. Such simplifying assumptions may at first surprise the reader familiar with more general formulations in spatial economics. Indeed, a considerable amount of research has been devoted to spatial competition and spatial voting theory by economists (some references are noted in Section 11.2). However, simple and particular representations of space—for example, a uniform distribution of clients along a line or a circle—are usually considered there. Network formulations have only recently been studied. As a result, only a few papers have been published and only a limited number of results are yet available on network formulations.

We also compare competitive and voting solutions with solutions resulting from centralized location planning, for example, the locational configurations which minimize average distance from the clients. In doing so, we can illustrate and compare the impact of different institutional mechanisms—competition, voting, and planning—on the resulting locational patterns.

The chapter is organized as follows. The model is introduced and solution concepts are discussed in Section 11.2. The main results dealing with existence and comparison of solution concepts are stated and discussed in Section 11.3. Algorithmic considerations are taken up in Section 11.4. Finally, Section 11.5 summarizes our conclusions and discusses some possible extensions.

11.2. THE MODEL AND SOLUTION CONCEPTS

The model used here is a classical one in location theory and can be viewed as consisting of two "sides," a transportation side and a demand side. To describe the model we first consider the transportation side. Let $N = (V, A)$ be a simple (no loops or multiple links), finite, undirected, and connected *network* with $V = (v_1, \ldots, v_n)$ as its set of *vertices* and with A as its set of *arcs*. The length of each arc $[v_i, v_j] \in A$ is given by a positive number α_{ij}. Each point $x \in N$ is on some arc $[v_i, v_j] \in A$ but x may or may not be a vertex. For any two points $x, y \in [v_i, v_j]$ the set of points between and including x and y is called a *subarc* $[x, y]$. When x and y are distinct, the length of the subarc $[x, y]$ is also given by a positive number. The set of paths joining $x \in N$ and $y \in N$ is denoted by $P(x, y)$. Note that if for all arbitrary and distinct points x and y in N the set $P(x, y)$ consists of a unique path, the network is a *tree*. The set of shortest paths joining x and y will be denoted by $P^*(x, y)$. The length of a path belonging to $P^*(x, y)$ is called the *shortest distance* between x and y; it is denoted $d(x, y)$. Clearly, d satisfies the symmetry and triangle inequality properties. We say that x is *between* v_i and v_j in V if $d(v_i, x) + d(x, v_j) = d(v_i, v_j)$; let $B(v_i, v_j)$ be the set of points in N between v_i and v_j. Finally, for any $x \in N$ and for any $\varepsilon > 0$ we define an ε-*neighborhood* of x as the set $N(x; \varepsilon) = \{y \in N : d(x, y) \le \varepsilon\}$.

The demand side of our model is as follows. There is a finite set U of clients; for any subset S of U, $|S|$ stands for the number of elements in S. A *client* $u \in U$ is described by his *vertex location* $v(u) \in N$ and by a monotonic utility function that reflects the desire of the client to have the facility located as close as possible to him so that, when a client chooses between two facilities, he will patronize the nearest one. It is possible that $v(u) = v(u')$ for $u \neq u'$ in which case clients u and u' are both located at the same vertex. For any two locations, $x, y \in N$ we simplify notation by characterizing the number of clients who are closer to x than y via $|x < y| = |\{u \in U : d(v(u), x) < d(v(u), y)\}|$; we also denote the number of clients equidistant from x and y by $|x \sim y| = |\{u \in U : d(v(u), x) = d(v(u), y)\}|$.

We now turn to the solution concepts associated with the voting, competitive, and planning processes, respectively. As mentioned in the introduction, the possible nonexistence of "natural" solutions for the voting and competitive processes forces us to introduce alternate (less demanding) solution concepts, the existence of which can be established under general conditions. This explains the large number of definitions given below.

11.2.1. The Voting Process

Assuming that one facility is to be located for servicing a given set of clients, the voting location problem consists of finding a location which is supported by a majority of the clients. This was recently considered by Hansen and Thisse (1981). The solution to this problem is thus a location such that no other location is closer to a larger set of clients. In voting theory this is called a plurality solution, formally defined as follows.

Definition 11.1. A point $p \in N$ is called a *plurality solution* if $|x < p| \le |p < x|$ for every $x \in N$.

To emphasize the fact that the above definition is true for all $x \in N$, we also refer to a plurality solution as a *global plurality solution* and we let P_g denote the set of such points.

Unfortunately, as illustrated by the example in Figure 11.1, plurality solutions do not necessarily exist. First, observe that any point interior to an arc is defeated by the nearest vertex. Consequently, only the vertices are candidate plurality solutions. But then, any of them is defeated by the mid-point of the opposite arc.

Another popular voting concept is a Condorcet solution. This concept is defined below for network location problems (Hansen and Thisse, 1981).

Definition 11.2. A point $p \in N$ is called a *Condorcet solution* if $|x < p| \le |U|/2$ for every $x \in N$.

Observe that a Condorcet solution is a location for which no more than

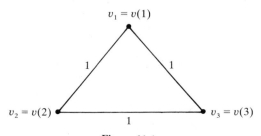

Figure 11.1

one half of the clients would prefer any other point on the network. Again, to emphasize the global nature of this concept, we sometimes refer to a Condorcet solution as a *global Condorcet solution* and we let C_g denote the set of such points. Note that $P_g \subset C_g$. In fact, Figure 11.2 illustrates a case where $P_g = \{v_5\}$ and $C_g = \{v_1, v_5\}$. Unfortunately, just as for plurality solutions, Figure 11.1 also indicates that Condorcet solutions do not necessarily exist.

One way to get around the problem of nonexistence is to consider a voting concept less demanding as far as $|x < p|$ is concerned. Here we follow a proposal in voting theory made by Simpson (1969).

Definition 11.3. A point $p \in N$ is called a *Simpson solution* if

$$\max \{|y < p|: y \in N\} \le \max \{|y < x|: y \in N\}$$

for every $x \in N$; the *score* of p is the number $\max \{|y < p|: y \in N\}$.

Thus, a Simpson solution is least objectionable in that no other solution has less clients wanting to move to another point. Note that the score of a Simpson solution is a measure of how objectionable it is. If the score is smaller than or equal to $|U|/2$ then a Simpson solution is a Condorcet point. Otherwise, the difference between $|U|/2$ and the score measures how close a Simpson solution comes to being a Condorcet solution.

Let S denote the set of Simpson solutions. Since $|U|$ is finite, it is easy to verify that in general $S \ne \emptyset$. In Figure 11.1 observe that $S = N$ with a corresponding score of 2 out of 3. In Figure 11.2, $S = \{v_5\}$ with a corresponding score of 2 out of 6 so that $\{v_5\}$ is a Condorcet point; note that $\{v_4\}$ is a Condorcet point but not a Simpson solution.

Whereas the concept of a Simpson solution relaxes the equilibrium conditions in order to obtain existence, we now consider an alternate approach to existence by restricting the locations to be compared. Specifically, we characterize local plurality and local Condorcet solutions as follows.

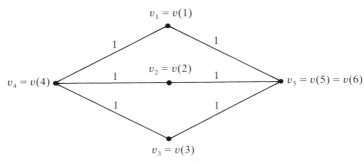

Figure 11.2

Definition 11.4. A point $p \in N$ is called a *local Condorcet solution* if there exists $\varepsilon > 0$ such that $|x < p| \leq |U|/2$ for all $x \in N(p; \varepsilon)$; further p is said to be a *local plurality solution* if $|x < p| \leq |p < x|$ for all $x \in N(p; \varepsilon)$.

We denote the set of local plurality solutions as P_l and the set of local Condorcet solutions as C_l. As with P_g and C_g, note that $P_l \subset C_l$. In Figure 11.1, we have $P_l = C_l = \{v_1, v_2, v_3\}$ and in Figure 11.2 we have $P_l = P_g$ and $C_l = C_g$.

For a further discussion of these (and other) concepts the reader is referred to Demange (1983). An intuitive introduction to voting theory in a geographical setting is given by Rushton, McLafferty, and Ghosh (1981).

11.2.2. The Competitive Process

Assuming that two facilities compete to attract clients from a given area, the competitive location problem is to find a pair of locations such that no facility can increase its number of clients by moving to another point on the network, given the location of its competitor. This problem was first formulated by Hotelling (1929) in the case of a uniform distribution of clients along a linear segment. More recently, it was considered within a network context by Wendell and McKelvey (1981). For a survey of previous work, see Graitson (1982). Following Wendell and McKelvey, we assume that each client has to obtain one unit of a given commodity from a facility. (This assumption is not restrictive, in that a client purchasing n units of the commodity can be viewed as n clients buying one unit each.) Observe that the concept of a plurality solution is also a natural solution concept in our two firm competitive location problem. In fact, assuming that clients equidistant between two facilities split their purchases equally between the two facilities, local and global plurality solutions are, respectively, local and global Nash solutions, which are defined as follows.

Definition 11.5. A pair $a_1, a_2 \in N$ is a *local Nash solution* if $\varepsilon > 0$ exists such that for all $x \in N(a_1; \varepsilon)$ and for all $y \in N(a_2; \varepsilon)$

$$|a_1 < a_2| + \frac{1}{2}|a_1 \sim a_2| \geq |x < a_2| + \frac{1}{2}|x \sim a_2|,$$

and

$$|a_2 < a_1| + \frac{1}{2}|a_2 \sim a_1| \geq |y < a_1| + \frac{1}{2}|y \sim a_1|;$$

the number $|a_i > a_j| + \frac{1}{2}|a_i \sim a_j|$ is called the *payoff* of facility i. When $\varepsilon \geq \max\{d(x, y): x, y \in N)\}$, (a_1, a_2) is called a *global Nash solution*.

In other words, a local Nash solution is a pair of locations (not necessarily identical) such that facility i, with $i = 1, 2$, has no incentive to move from a_i

to any location in $N(a_i; \varepsilon)$, given the location of facility j at a_j, $j \neq i$. To illustrate the relationship between plurality solutions and Nash solutions first we consider a point $p \in P_l$. Now, observe that by letting $a_1 = p$ and $a_2 = p$ we have a local Nash solution. Furthermore, consider a local Nash solution (a_1, a_2). Given that each facility can secure half of the total demand by having the same location as its competitor, the payoffs of the two facilities must be equal. Therefore, (a_1, a_1) and (a_2, a_2) are also local Nash solutions and it follows that a_1 and a_2 are local plurality solutions.

By introducing the element of time we can consider yet another solution, the Stackelberg solution, to the competitive problem (akin to the Simpson solution in the voting problem).

Definition 11.6. A pair $s_1, s_2 \in N$ is called a *Stackelberg solution* if

$$\min \left\{ |s_1 < x| + \frac{1}{2} |s_1 \sim x| : x \in N \right\} \geq \min \left\{ |y < x| + \frac{1}{2} |y \sim x| : x \in N \right\}$$

and

$$|s_2 < s_1| + \frac{1}{2} |s_2 \sim s_1| \geq |z < s_1| + \frac{1}{2} |z \sim s_1|$$

for every $y, z \in N$.

In other words, a Stackelberg solution is a pair of locations such that the second facility, called the follower, chooses its location given the decision of its competitor and such that the first facility, called the leader, selects its location anticipating the reaction of its competitor. This equilibrium concept, which is well known in game theory, has been placed within the framework of location theory by Prescott and Visscher (1977) and has been used in network location theory by Hakimi (1983) (see also Chapter 10). In the example of Figure 11.1, a Stackelberg solution is given either by a vertex and a point interior to the opposite arc or by a point interior to an arc and an adjacent vertex. In general, the set of Stackelberg solutions is nonempty. Interestingly, the asymmetry between the two facilities is reflected by the fact that the payoff of the leader is always smaller than or equal to the payoff of the follower. When both payoffs are equal, the corresponding Stackelberg solution is a global Nash solution. For a further discussion of the Stackelberg solution, see Chapter 10.

The relationships between Stackelberg and Simpson solutions are as follows. Let (s_1, s_2) be a Stackelberg solution. If $|s_1 \sim s_2| = 0$, then the location of the leader s_1 is a Simpson solution (the $(1|1)$-centroid of Chapter 10). Conversely, if p is a Simpson solution, then p is the location of the leader in a Stackelberg solution (p, s) when $|p \sim s| = 0$.

11.2.3. The Planning Process

Again assuming that each client purchases one unit of a commodity, a natural solution concept in centralized planning is a location where the total distance covered by all clients to the facility is minimized. Such a model was introduced in location theory by Weber (1927) and was first used within the framework of network location by Hua et al. (1962) and Hakimi (1964). To give a formal definition, we simplify notation by denoting the total distance as $F(x) = \Sigma\{d(v(u), x): u \in U\}$ for each $x \in N$.

Definition 11.7. A point $p \in N$ is said to be a *local Weber solution* if there exists $\varepsilon > 0$ *such that* $F(p) \leq F(x)$ for every $x \in N(p; \varepsilon)$. When $\varepsilon \geq \max\{d(x, y): x, y \in N\}$, p is called a *global Weber solution*.

The sets of local Weber solutions and global Weber solutions are denoted W_l and W_g, respectively; of course $W_g \subseteq W_l$. In the network context, the global Weber solution is also referred to as the 1-median of the network. See Chapter 2 and Tansel, Francis, and Lowe (1983a, b) for a further discussion of this and related problems.

11.3. LOCALIZATION THEOREMS

As seen in the previous section, the existence of global plurality and Condorcet solutions is not guaranteed. However, when the network is a tree, such solutions exist.

Theorem 11.1 (Hansen, Thisse, and Wendell, 1986). *If N is a tree, then* $W_g = P_g = C_g = W_l = P_l = C_l$.

Proof. Recall that $P_l \subseteq C_l$, $P_l \subseteq P_g$, $C_l \subseteq C_g$, and $P_g \subseteq C_g$. Also, since N is a tree it follows from Tansel et al. (1983b) that $W_l = W_g$. Thus, we need only to show that $W_l \subseteq P_l$ and $C_g \subseteq W_g$.

If $p \in W_l$ then by definition there exists some $\varepsilon > 0$ where $F(p) \leq F(x)$ for all $x \in N(p; \varepsilon)$. Let ε be sufficiently small so that $x \in N(p; \varepsilon)$ and $x \neq p$ imply there is no $u \in U$ where $x = v(u)$. Also, for each $x \in N(p; \varepsilon)$ and $x \neq p$ let

$$U_x = \{u \in U: d(x, v(u)) < d(p, v(u))\}$$

and

$$U_p = \{u \in U: d(p, v(u)) < d(x, v(u))\}.$$

By the choice of ε it follows that $U_x \cup U_p = U$. Observe that

$$F(p) = \sum\{d(v(u), p): u \in U_p\} + \sum\{d(v(u), x): u \in U_x\}$$
$$+ \sum\{d(x, p): u \in U_x\}$$

and that

$$F(x) = \sum \{d(v(u), p): u \in U_p\} + \sum \{d(p, x): u \in U_p\}$$
$$+ \sum \{d(v(u), x): u \in U_x\}.$$

Thus, $F(p) - F(x) \leq 0$ implies that $|U_x| \leq |U_p|$ and, therefore, x being arbitrary implies that $p \in P_l$.

Showing that $C_g \subseteq W_g$ also follows from basic arguments and is given as an exercise at the end of the chapter. $\square$

The result has some interesting implications. First, since $W_g \neq \emptyset$ the identity in the above theorem tells us that a global plurality (and Condorcet) solution always exists when the network admits no cycles. Second, it provides us with a simple condition under which the planning, voting, and competitive processes lead to the same outcome. This equivalence is interesting from the social perspective since it reconciles both planning and voting procedures in making locational decisions: the optimal solution is supported by a majority of clients and the location chosen through a vote of the clients is optimal. Also, it shows that competition between two facilities yields a locational pattern which does not make clients better off than in the case of a single facility minimizing total distance. In both cases, indeed, clients bear identical travel costs. Third, sets P_g and C_g are easy to obtain; it is indeed sufficient to determine W_g by using the algorithm of Goldman (1971), which has a linear complexity.

When N is not a tree, this equivalence property may not hold. One example is when P_g is empty as in Figure 11.1. Also, recall that in the example of Figure 11.2 we have $P_g \neq C_g$. Figure 11.3 gives an example where $P_g \neq \emptyset$ and $P_g \neq W_g$ in that $P_g = \{v_6\}$ but $W_g = \{v_5\}$. A characterization of those networks for which sets W_g and C_g are identical is now given.

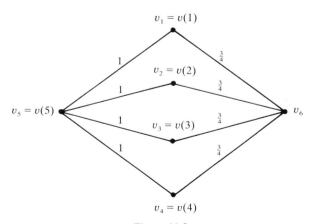

Figure 11.3

Assume that redundant arcs of N, that is, arcs $[v_i, v_j] \in A$ with $\alpha_{ij} > d(v_i, v_j)$, have been removed.

Theorem 11.2 (Bandelt, 1985). $W_g = C_g$ *if and only if the network N is such that the following two conditions hold*:

> **1.** *for any three vertices v_i, v_j, and v_k of V, there exists one and only one vertex v_p (with, possibly, $v_p \in \{v_i, v_j, v_k\}$) which is simultaneously between v_i and v_j, v_j and v_k, and v_i and v_k;*
> **2.** *for any vertex $v \in V$ and any set $\bar{V}$ of vertices, $\cap \{B(v, \bar{v}): \bar{v} \in \bar{V}\} = \{v\}$ implies that $B(v, \bar{v}_1) \cap B(v, \bar{v}_2) = \{v\}$ for some $\bar{v}_1 \in \bar{V}$ and $\bar{v}_2 \in \bar{V}$.*

An example satisfying the above conditions is provided by the rectangular network depicted in Figure 11.4 (see also Wendell and Thorson, 1974).

Furthermore, Bandelt has shown that any global Weber solution contained in V also belongs to C_g if and only if condition 2 holds while, in condition 1, it is required that the intersection of $B(v_i, v_j)$, $B(v_j, v_k)$, and $B(v_i, v_k)$ is nonempty.

A partial equivalence may also be obtained in the following case.

Theorem 11.3 (Labbé, 1985).   *If any two cycles of N intersect at most at one vertex, then either $C_g = W_g$ or $C_g = \emptyset$.*

See Figure 11.5 for an example in which $C_g = W_g = \{v_6\}$. There is also a local equivalence in a general network as given below.

Theorem 11.4 (Hansen et al., 1986).   *In a general network N, $W_l = P_l = C_l$.*

The following comments are in order. First, local plurality solutions always exist in the network case. This is in contrast to nonexistence in

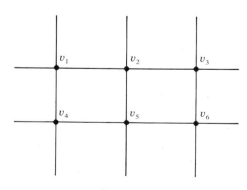

Figure 11.4

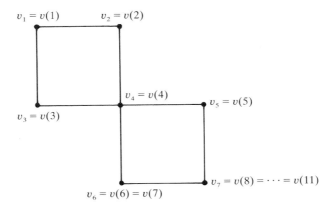

Figure 11.5

multidimensional continuous models (Kramer and Klevorick, 1974). Second, the local equivalence shows that a location which minimizes total distance can always be locally sustained by a majority vote. Also, the fact that no majority agrees to depart from the existing situation implies that the status quo is locally optimal, if not globally, from the planning standpoint. Third, using the property of having local Weber solutions at vertices, we have the following corollary.

*Corollary 11.1** (Wendell and McKelvey, 1981). *In a general network N, $V \cap P_l$ is nonempty; furthermore, if $|U|$ is odd then $P_l \subset V$.*

Note that this result is not true for global solutions since P_g may be empty and, even when $P_g \neq \emptyset$, $V \cap P_g$ may be empty. This later possibility was indicated by Wendell and McKelvey and is illustrated here by the example in Figure 6 from Hakimi (1983). In this example observe that v_1 is defeated by the mid-point of the arc $[v_2, v_5]$. By symmetry, the same holds for v_3, v_4, and v_6. Now suppose that v_2 (or v_5) is chosen as a candidate. Then v_2 (or v_5) is defeated by v_1 (or v_4). Finally, it is easy to check that the mid-point of the arc $[v_2, v_5]$ is a global plurality solution.

On the other hand, since $P_l = C_l$ and $C_g \subset C_l$, the latter part of Corollary 11.1 is true for global Condorcet solutions (and, hence, for global plurality solutions).

Corollary 11.2 (Hansen and Thisse, 1981). *If $|V|$ is odd, then $C_g \subset V$.*

With respect to global plurality solutions and global Weber solutions, there is at least a partial equivalence in a general network as given below.

Let σ be a permutation defined on U. Given $x \in N$, we say that x has the *betweeness property* for σ if $x \in B(v(u), v(\sigma(u)))$ for all $u \in U$.

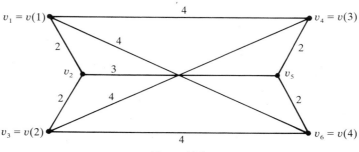

Figure 11.6

Theorem 11.5 (Hansen et al., 1986). *Let σ be a permutation on U. If $x \in N$ and if x has the betweeness property for σ, then $x \in W_g \cap P_g$.*

Note that vertex v_5 in Figure 11.2 satisfies the betweeness property under the permutation $\sigma: v_1 \rightarrow v_6$, $v_6 \rightarrow v_1$, $v_2 \rightarrow v_3$, $v_3 \rightarrow v_2$, $v_4 \rightarrow v_5$, $v_5 \rightarrow v_4$. Interestingly, points in the set P_g of Figure 11.6 do not satisfy the betweeness property. Thus, this property, which expresses a kind of symmetry of the network around a point, is only sufficient for the existence of a global plurality solution. This can be contrasted with corresponding conditions which are also necessary in the continuous approach; see Theorem 3.1 of Wendell and McKelvey (1981). The question of what conditions are necessary to guarantee the existence of a global plurality solution in a network remains open.

To determine which points (if any) satisfy the betweeness property, the following corollary shows that it is sufficient to consider the vertices of the network.

Corollary 11.3 (Hansen et al., 1986). *If $x \in N$ satisfies the betweeness property for some permutation σ, then either $x \in V$ or there exists an arc $[v_i, v_j]$ containing x such that $[v_i, v_j] \subset P_g \cap W_g$.*

Theorem 11.5 reduces to a simple condition when x is a cut-vertex of the network. Recall that $x \in V$ is a *cut-vertex* when the deletion of x and of the arcs adjacent to x from N yields disjoint connected subnetworks.

Corollary 11.4 (Hansen et al., 1986). *Assume that $x \in V$ is a cut-vertex and let $N_1, N_2, \ldots, N_t$ be the subnetworks obtained from the deletion of x. If $|\{u \in U: v(u) \in N_k\}| \leq |U|/2$ for each $k = 1, \ldots, t$, then $x \in P_g \cap W_g$.*

The sufficient condition on the distribution of clients given in Corollary 11.4 can be made necessary provided an additional restriction is imposed on x. We say that $a \in A$ is a *cut-arc* if deleting arc a yields two disjoint subnetworks; $x \in V$ is called a *strong cut-vertex* when all arcs adjacent to x are cut-arcs.

Corollary 11.5 (Hansen et al., 1986). *Assume that $x \in V$ is a strong cut-vertex and let $N_1, N_2, \ldots, N_t$ be the subnetworks obtained from the deletion of x. Then $x \in P_g \cap W_g$ if and only if $|\{u \in U : v(u) \in N_k\}| \leq |U|/2$ for each $k = 1, \ldots, t$.*

The above condition on the distribution of clients assumes that they are spread out around a vertex. On the other hand, we now observe that a concentration of a majority of clients at one vertex is also sufficient to obtain the equivalence of the different solutions. While the result is a simple consequence of Theorem 11.5, we also give a short independent proof.

Corollary 11.6 (Witzgall, 1965). *If $|\{u : v(u) = v_i\}| \geq |U|/2$, then $v_i \in W_g \cap P_g$. Furthermore, if the inequality is strict , then $\{v_i\} = W_g = P_g$.*

Proof. Since it is obvious that $v_i \in P_g$, we show that $v_i \in W_g$. For $x \in N$ we have

$$F(v_i) = \Sigma\{d(v(u), v_i) : u \in U\}$$
$$= \Sigma\{d(v(u), v_i) : v(u) \neq v_i, \, u \in U\}$$
$$\leq \Sigma\{d(v(u), x) + d(x, v_i) : v(u) \neq v_i, \, u \in U\}$$
$$= \Sigma\{d(v(u), x) : v(u) \neq v_i, \, u \in U\}$$
$$+ \Sigma\{d(v(u), x) - d(v(u), x) : v(u) = v_i, \, u \in U\}$$
$$+ \Sigma\{d(x, v_i) : v(u) \neq v_i, \, u \in U\}$$
$$= F(x) - d(v_i, x)[|\{u : v(u) = v_i, \, u \in U\}| - |\{u : v(u) \neq v_i, \, u \in U\}|]$$
$$\leq F(x) ,$$

where the first inequality follows from the triangle inequality and the second follows from the hypothesis. When the inequality in the hypothesis is strict, the result is straightforward. □

Even when a global Condorcet solution exists, we may observe a divergence with the global Weber solution. The next theorem gives the maximum value of the bias.

Theorem 11.6 (Labbé, 1985). *Let x and y be global Condorcet and Weber solutions, respectively. Then*

$$\frac{F(x)}{F(y)} \leq \frac{2|U| - \left(\left\lceil \dfrac{|U|}{2} \right\rceil + 1\right)}{\left\lceil \dfrac{|U|}{2} \right\rceil + 1} .$$

Thus, in a general network, an important loss in accessibility may result from selecting the facility location by means of a vote of the clients; similarly the competition between two facilities may yield a substantial inefficiency from the social point of view. This is reinforced by the fact that the above bound is the *best possible*. Consider the network represented in Figure 11.7. It is easy to verify that $v(\lceil |U|/2\rceil + 2)$ is the unique global Weber solution while $v(\lceil |U|/2\rceil + 3)$ is the unique global plurality solution. Consequently, for $y = v(\lceil |U|/2\rceil + 2)$ and $x = v(\lceil |U|/2\rceil + 3)$, we have $F(y) = \lceil |U|/2\rceil + 1$ and $F(x) = 2|U| - (\lceil |U|/2\rceil + 1) - \varepsilon|U|$ so that

$$\frac{F(x)}{F(y)} = \frac{2|U| - \left(\left\lceil \dfrac{|U|}{2}\right\rceil + 1\right)}{\left\lceil \dfrac{|U|}{2}\right\rceil + 1} - \frac{\varepsilon|U|}{\left\lceil \dfrac{|U|}{2}\right\rceil + 1}.$$

As ε can be made arbitrarily small, the bound can be made arbitrarily close to the first term.

In particular, this theorem yields the following simple inequality. For this result we also give a short proof independent of Theorem 11.6.

Corollary 11.7 (Hansen and Thisse, 1981). *Let x and y be global Condorcet and Weber solutions, respectively. Then $F(x)/F(y) \le 3$.*

Proof.   Let $\bar{U} = \{u:\ d(v(u), x) \le d(v(u), y)\}$ and let $\bar{u}$ be defined by $d(v(\bar{u}), y) \equiv \min \{d(v(u), y):\ u \in U\}$. By the triangle inequality we have $d(v(u), x) \le d(v(u), y) + d(y, v(\bar{u})) + d(v(\bar{u}), x)$ for all $u \in U - \bar{U}$. Hence,

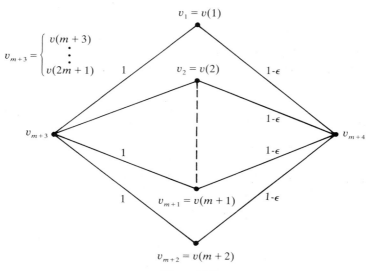

Figure 11.7

it follows that

$$
\begin{aligned}
\frac{F(x)}{F(y)} &= \left[\sum \{ d(v(u), x): u \in \bar{U} \} + \sum \{ d(v(u), y): u \in U - \bar{U} \} \right. \\
&\quad \left. + \sum \{ d(y, v(\bar{u})) + d(v(\bar{u}), x): u \in U - \bar{U} \} \right] \\
&\quad \times \left[\sum \{ d(v(u), y): u \in \bar{U} \} + \sum \{ d(v(u), y): u \in U - \bar{U} \} \right]^{-1} \\
&\leq \left[\sum \{ d(v(u), x): u \in \bar{U} \} + \sum \{ d(y, v(\bar{u})) + d(v(\bar{u}), x): u \in U - \bar{U} \} \right] \\
&\quad \times \left[\sum \{ d(v(u), y): u \in \bar{U} \} \right]^{-1} \\
&\leq 1 + 2 \left[d(v(\bar{u}), y) | U - \bar{U} | \Big/ \sum \{ d(v(u), y): u \in \bar{U} \} \right] \\
&\leq 1 + 2 [| U - \bar{U} | / | \bar{U} |] \leq 3,
\end{aligned}
$$

where the first two inequalities follow from elementary arithmetic and the fact that $F(y) \leq F(x)$, where the next two inequalities follow from the definitions of $\bar{U}$ and $v(\bar{u})$, and where the last inequality follows from the fact that $| \bar{U} | \geq | U - \bar{U} |$. $\quad \square$

Conversely, locating the facility at the global Weber solution may dissatisfy a large number of clients, the example in Figure 11.8, due to Bandelt and Labbé (1986), shows that up to $|U| - 1$ clients may prefer another location. In the example, observe that one client is located at v_1 and m clients are located at each of the other vertices (v_2 and v_3). Clearly, $W_g = \{ v_1 \}$ for $\varepsilon < 1/m$, but $2m = |U| - 1$ clients prefer the middle point on the arc $[v_2, v_3]$ to v_1.

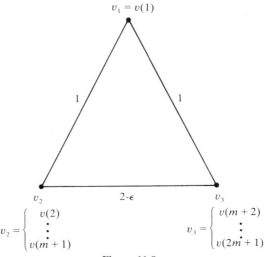

Figure 11.8

11.4. ALGORITHMS

Finding the (possibly empty) set of Condorcet points of a network, or the set of S of Simpson points can be done in polynomial time (Hansen and Labbé, 1988). We consider here the easiest case, that is, the determination of C_g when $|U|$ is odd. We know from Corollary 11.2 that $C_g \subset V$. The principle of the algorithm is to first set $C_g = V$ and then to remove vertices defeated by other vertices, or by points on arcs. The former case is straightforward. For the latter case, consider a vertex v_j and an arc $[v_k, v_l]$; the set of clients U will be partitioned into five sets according to whether the subset of $[v_k, v_l]$ closer to $v(u)$ than v_j is empty, a subarc containing v_k, a subarc containing v_l, two disjoint subarcs or the whole arc $[v_k, v_l]$ (see Figure 11.9):

$$U_1 = \{u \in U: d(v(u), v_j) \le \min \{d(v(u), v_k), d(v(u), v_l)\} \,,$$

$$U_2 = \{u \in U: d(v(u), v_k) < d(v(u), v_j) \le d(v(u), v_l)\} \,,$$

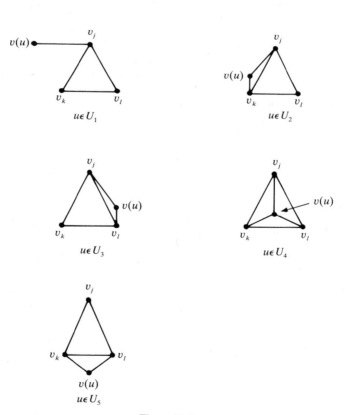

Figure 11.9

$$U_3 = \{u \in U: d(v(u), v_l) < d(v(u), v_j) \le d(v(u), v_k)\},$$

$$U_4 = \{u \in U: \min \{d(v(u), v_k), d(v(u), v_l)\} < d(v(u), v_j) <$$
$$[d(v(u), v_k) + d(v(u), v_l) + \alpha_{kl}]/2\},$$

$$U_5 = U/\{U_1 \cup U_2 \cup U_3 \cup U_4\}.$$

In order to specify the above-mentioned subarcs we map continuously $[v_k, v_l]$ into the unit segment $[0, 1]$ through a parameter θ. Then compute for all $u \in U \cup U_4$ the number

$$\vec{t}_u = [d(v(u), v_j) - d(v(u), v_k)]/\alpha_{kl},$$

and for all $u \in U_3 \cup U_4$ the number

$$\vec{t}_u = 1 - [d(v(u), v_j) - d(v(u), v_l)]/\alpha_{kl},$$

that is, the values of θ for which the subarc containing v_k ends and for which the subarc containing v_l begins, respectively. We then check systematically to see if some point of $[v_k, v_l]$ belongs to at least $\lceil U/2 \rceil$ such subarcs.

The rules of the algorithm are as follows:

a. *Pairwise Comparison of Vertices.* Set $C_g = V$. For each $v_j \in V$ and each $v_k \in V$ in turn compute $|v_k < v_j|$. If $|v_k < v_j| \ge \lceil U/2 \rceil$ remove v_j from C_g. Stop if $C_g = \emptyset$, the network having no Condorcet point.

b. *Comparison of Vertices and Arcs.* For each $v_j \in C_g$ and each arc $[v_k, v_l]$ in turn (with $k < l$ to avoid duplication) partition the set of clients U into the sets $U_1, U_2, \ldots, U_5$. If $|U_1| \ge \lceil U/2 \rceil$ proceed to the next arc. Otherwise sort the $\vec{t}_u$ and the $\overleftarrow{t}_u$ together by order of increasing values. Set $k = |U_2| + |U_4| + |U_5|$ and explore in sequence the sorted list, adding 1 to k each time a $\vec{t}_u$ is found and subtracting 1 from k each time a $\overleftarrow{t}_u$ is found. If during this procedure one obtains $k \ge \lceil U/2 \rceil$ remove v_j from C_g and proceed to the next vertex of C_g (unless C_g is empty). if k remains smaller than $\lceil U/2 \rceil$ proceed to the next arc. Once all vertices and edges have been considered, C_g is equal to the set of Condorcet points of N.

This algorithm requires $O(qa|U| \log |U|)$ operations in the worst case (where a is the number of arcs).

Finding C_g when $|U|$ is even is more difficult: indeed $C_g \subset V$ need not hold anymore, and, as shown by the example of Figure 11.6, one may have $C_g \neq \emptyset$ and $C_g \cap V = \emptyset$. So, even to find a single Condorcet point it is necessary to consider candidate points on arcs. To show that all points of some subarc of an arc $[v_k, v_l]$ are farther away for a majority of clients than one or several points of an arc $[v_r, v_s]$, we first partition both of these arcs into subarcs along which all distance functions are monotonic (i.e., subarcs limited by vertices or *bottleneck points*; see Church and Garfinkel, 1978). We call such subarcs *segments*. Then we detect dominance of subarcs of a segment of $[v_k, v_l]$ by subarcs of a segment of $[v_k, v_l]$ using a two-parameter procedure which generalizes the one-parameter method of the previous algorithm. This yields an algorithm to determine C_g with an $O(|U|^3 a^2 \log |U| a)$ worst-case complexity.

To find S, as the score p (i.e., the maximum number of clients preferring a location not in S) is unknown a priori, a dichotomous search on its value is made. Adapting the algorithm defined for finding C_g with $|U|$ even, and using in the dominance tests the tentative values for p generated during the search, gives an $O(|U|^4 a^2 \log |U| a \log |U|)$ algorithm to determine S.

The sufficient, but not necessary, condition of Theorem 11.5, for a given $x \in N$ to be a Condorcet point can be easily checked algorithmically (Hansen et al., 1986). Recall that a permutation σ must be found on U such that x is between u and its image $\sigma(u)$ for all $u \in U$. We proceed as follows:

a. Construct a bipartite graph $G = (V', V'', A')$: the $|U|$ vertices of V' and the $|U|$ vertices of V'' are, respectively, denoted by $v'(u)$ and $v''(u)$ and associated with the locations $v(u)$ of the clients. The arc set A' is such that both $(v'(u), v'(\sigma(u)))$, and $(v'(\sigma(u)), v''(u))$ belong to A if and only if $x \in B(v(u), v(\sigma(u)))$.

b. Determine a maximum matching of G, that is, a set of pairwise non-adjacent arcs of largest possible cardinality. If this matching is perfect (i.e., contains $|U|$ arcs), it defines a permutation $\sigma : U \rightarrow U$ satisfying the requirements of Theorem 11.5. Otherwise no such permutation exists.

Step (a) takes $O(|U|^2)$ operations provided the shortest distances between pairs of locations and between these locations and x are known. Step (b) takes $O(|U|^{5/2})$ operations (Hopcroft and Karp, 1973).

Finally, let us note that a polynomial algorithm has been recently proposed to check if the necessary and sufficient conditions of Theorem 11.2 hold, regardless of the number and locations of the clients (Bandelt, 1985).

11.5. CONCLUSIONS AND EXTENSIONS

Both competitive location theory and spatial voting theory incorporate strategic features in that the final outcomes of the so-considered processes are influenced by the choices made by independent decision-makers. Here we have considered some basic models of these problems which, in turn, open the door to a vast domain of possible extensions. It is not possible, within the format of this section, to give a complete overview of these extensions. We will, however, briefly discuss some recent work and make some suggestions for future research.

Within the framework considered here, a variety of issues remain to be addressed. One such issue concerns the properties of the Simpson solution. In this regard, it would be interesting to characterize the class of networks for which at least one global Weber solution is a Simpson solution, that is, a solution of maximum consensus, and to determine the maximum divergence between the two solutions for the remaining cases (Bandelt and Labbé, 1986). Another issue is how other concepts from voting theory (Vohra, 1987) and game theory (Granot, 1987; Holzman, 1986) could be applied to the above problems. Also, issues relating to the existence of a Condorcet solution and to its comparison with the Weber solution could also be studied empirically by using distance data drawn from real transportation networks. In this way, an attempt could be made to estimate the average divergence (instead of the maximal one) between the two solutions.

In terms of extending the framework, one possibility was recently considered by de Palma, Ginsburgh, Labbé, and Thisse (1989). Specifically, this extension considers the possibility that different facilities may have different inherent characteristics so that a client might not simply go to the nearest facility. As suggested by modern discrete choice theory (Manski, 1977), the utility of a client u with respect to a facility located at $x \in N$ may be represented as $a(u) - d(v(u), x) + \varepsilon$ where ε is a continuous random variable with a zero mean representing unobservable variations in taste. Then, provided that the standard deviation of ε is large enough, the set W_g can be shown to coincide with the set of global Nash solutions. Other extensions include (i) considerations of several facilities to be located in the voting process (Cremer, de Kerchove, and Thisse, 1985) or in the competitive process (Hakimi, 1983, ReVelle, 1987), and (ii) the possibility for the facilities to deliver their product to the clients and to choose location-specific prices (Lederer and Thisse, 1987).

In conclusion, we believe that location problems on a network offer novel and interesting applications of game and voting theory, many of which are yet to be explored. This should yield new insights into such location problems. Furthermore, in as much as one can sometimes obtain solution results on networks that do not yield elsewhere (e.g., local plurality solutions exist on a network in contrast to nonexistence in multidimensional continuous models), we also believe that the study of network location problems can open new perspectives in game and voting theory.

EXERCISES

11.1 For the situation indicated in Figure 11.10, show that $v_4 \in P_g \cap W_g$.

11.2 (Wendell and McKelvey, 1981) Consider the situation in Figure 11.11

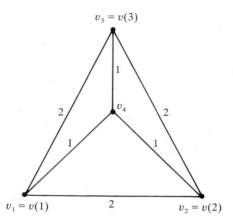

Figure 11.10

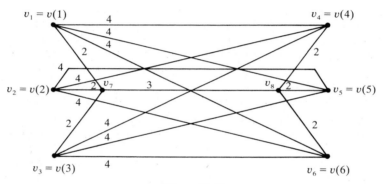

Figure 11.11

(i) Identify C_g and P_g.

(ii) Identify W_g. Does $W_g = P_g$?

(iii) Identify P_l.

11.3 If N is a tree, prove that $C_g \subset W_g$.

11.4 Verify that $S \neq \emptyset$.

11.5 Prove or disprove: $C_g \neq \emptyset$ implies that $P_g \neq \emptyset$.

11.6 (Wendell and McKelvey, 1981) Define a set of strong global plurality points P'_g as follows:

$$P'_g \equiv \{p: |x < p| < |p < x| \text{ for all } x \neq p \text{ in } N\}.$$

(i) Show that $P'_g \subset P_g$.

(ii) Give an example where $P'_g = P_g$ and an example where $P'_g \neq P_g$.

(iii) Give a definition of an analogous concept for local plurality points. Discuss its properties.

11.7 Assume that three facilities compete in order to attract the largest possible number of clients from a given population and that clients patronize the nearest facility. A Nash solution is a triplet of locations such that no facility can increase its volume of sales by a unilateral move. Give an example where no Nash solution exists when N is a tree.

11.8 (Sloss, 1978) Consider a characterization of client preferences where each client is indifferent between two facilities whose distances from his location differ no more than α kilometers (where α is some specified positive number).

(i) Generalize the definition of P_l and P_g for this case.

(ii) If $\alpha > 0$ show that $P_l = N$.

(iii) Show that for α sufficiently large $P_g = N$.

(iv) Discuss the relationship between the size of α and the existence of global plurality points.

11.9 (Hansen and Thisse, 1981) A point $r \in N$ is said to be a *Rawls solution* if and only if $G(r) \equiv \max \{d(v(u), r): \ u \in U\} \leq \max \{d(v(u), x): u \in U\} \equiv G(x)$ for every $x \in N$. Contrast the interpretations of the Rawls with the Weber solution. Compare the Rawls and plurality solution and, letting p denote a plurality solution, prove that

(i) $G(p)/G(r) \leq 2$ when N is a tree,

(ii) $G(p)/G(r) \leq 3$ for a general network.

Show by an example that each upper bound is the best possible.

11.10 (Labbé, 1982) A facility at $x \in N$ is said to be *obnoxious* if the utility of a client at $v(u)$ is given by $a(u) + d(v(u), x)$. Give a definition of a plurality solution for such a facility and prove that

(i) when N is a tree, there exists a plurality solution in the set of tips,

(ii) if a plurality solution exists and if $|U|$ is odd, then any plurality solution belongs to the set of tips and bottleneck points of a general network.

Show by an example that, on a tree, the plurality solution does not maximize the sum of the distances to the clients and give a counterexample of the existence of a plurality solution in the case of a general network.

11.11 (Fujita, 1981) Consider two facilities $i = 1, 2$. Facility i is linked to vertex $v_i \in V$ through a weight $w_i \geq 0$ and to facility j through weight $w_{ij} > 0$. The objective of facility i is to minimize the sum of the weighted distances to the vertices and to facility j, that is, $\Sigma\{w_i d(v, x_i) + w_{ij} d(x_i, x_j): v \in V\}$. The *competitive Weber problem* consists of locating facilities 1 and 2 in a way that no facility has an incentive to move given the location of the other, that is, at a Nash solution. Show that a Nash solution exists when N is a tree and give a counterexample of the existence of a Nash solution in the case of a general network.

REFERENCES

Bandelt, H.-J. (1985). "Networks with Condorcet Solutions." *European Journal of Operational Research* **20**, 314–326.

Bandelt, H.-J., and M. Labbé (1986). "How Bad Can a Voting Solution Be?" *Social Choice and Welfare* **3**, 125–145.

Church, R. L., and R. S. Garfinkel (1978). "Locating an Obnoxious Facility on a Network." *Transportation Science* **8**, 107–118.

Cremer, H., A.-M. de Kerchove, and J.-F. Thisse (1985). "An Economic Theory of Public Facilities in Space." *Mathematical Social Sciences* **9**, 249–262.

Demange, G. (1983). "Spatial Models of Collective Choice." In *Locational Analysis of Public Facilities*, (J.-F. Thisse and H. G. Zoller, eds.), pp. 153–182. North Holland Publ., Amsterdam.

de Palma, A., V. Ginsburgh, M. Labbé, and J.-F. Thisse (1989). "Competitive Location with Random Utilities." Forthcoming in *Transportation Science*. (Mimeo. Department of Economics, Université Libre de Bruxelles.)

Fujita, M. (1981). "Location of Firms with Input Transactions." *Environment and Planning A* **13**, 1401–1414.

Goldman, A. J. (1971). "Optimal Center Location in Simple Networks." *Transportation Science* **5** 212–221.

Graitson, D. (1982). "Spatial Competition à la Hotelling: A Selective Survey." *Journal of Industrial Economics* **31**, 13–25.

Granot, D. (1987). "The Role of Cost Allocation in Locational Models." *Operations Research* **35**, 234–248.

Hakimi, S. L. (1964). "Optimum Location of Switching Centers and the Absolute Centers and Medians of a Graph." *Operations Research* **12**, 450–459.

Hakimi, S. L. (1983). "On Locating New Facilities in a Competitive Environment." *European Journal of Operational Research* **12**, 29–35.

Hansen, P., and M. Labbé (1988). "Algorithms for Voting and Competitive Location on a Network." *Transportation Science* **22**, 278–288.

Hansen, P., and J.-F. Thisse (1981). "Outcomes of Voting and Planning: Condorcet, Weber and Rawls Locations." *Journal of Public Economics* **16**, 1–15.

Hansen, P., J. F. Thisse, and R. W. Wendell (1986). "Equivalence of Solutions to Network Location Problems." *Mathematics of Operations Research* **11**, 672–678.

Holzman, R. (1986). "An Axiomatic Approach to Location on Networks." Forthcoming in *Mathematics of Operations Research*. (Mimeo. RUTCOR, Rutgers University, New Brunswick, New Jersey.)

Hopcroft, J. E., and R. M. Karp (1973). "An $n^{5/2}$ Algorithm for Maximum Matchings in Bipartite Graphs." *SIAM Journal on Computing* **2**, 225–231.

Hotelling, H. (1929). "Stability in Competition." *Economic Journal* **39**, 41–57.

Hua, L.-K. and others (1962). "Applications of Mathematical Methods to Wheat Harvesting." *Chinese Mathematics* **2**, 77–91.

Kramer, G. H., and A. K. Klevorick (1974). "Existence of a 'Local' Cooperative Equilibrium in a Class of Voting Games." *Review of Economic Studies* **41**, 539–547.

Labbé M. (1982). "Equilibre de Condorcet pour le problème de localisation d'une installation polluante." *Cahiers du Centre d'Etudes de Recherche Operationnelle* **24**, 305–312.

Labbé M. (1985). "Outcomes of Voting and Planning in Single Facility Location Problems." *European Journal of Operational Research* **20**, 299–313.

Lederer, P. J., and J.-F. Thisse (1987)."Competitive Location on Networks under Discriminatory Pricing." Forthcoming in *Operations Research Letters*. (INSEAD Discuss. Pap. No. 8735.)

Manski, C. F. (1977). "The Structure of Random Utility Models." *Theory and Decisions* **8**, 229–254.

Prescott, E. C., and M. Visscher (1977). "Sequential Location among Firms with Foresight." *Bell Journal of Economics* **8**, 378–393.

ReVelle C. (1987). "The Maximum Capture or 'Sphere of Influence' Location Problem: Hotelling Revisited on a Network." *Journal of Regional Science* **26**, 343–358.

Rushton, G., S. McLafferty, and A. Ghosh (1981). "Equilibrium Locations for Public Services: Individual Preferences and Social Choice." *Geographical Analysis* **13**, 196–202.

Simpson, P. (1969). "On Defining Areas of Voter Choice: Professor Tullock on Stable Voting." *Quarterly Journal of Economics* **83**, 478–487.

Sloss, J. L. (1978) "Stable Outcomes in Majority Voting Games." *Public Choice* **15**, 19–48.

Tansel, B. C., R. L. Francis, and T. J. Lowe (1983a). "Location on Networks: A Survey. Part I. The p-Center and p-Median Problems." *Management Science* **29**, 482–497.

Tansel, B. C., R. L. Francis, and T. J. Lowe (1983b). "Location on Networks: A Survey. Part II. Exploiting Tree Network Structure." *Management Science* **29**, 498–511.

Vohra, R. V. (1987). "Distance Weighted Voting and a Single Facility Location Problem." Forthcoming in *European Journal of Operational Research*. (Mimeo. Faculty of Management Sciences, Ohio State University, Columbus.)

Weber, A. (1927). *Ueber den Standort der Industrien*. Tübingen (*The Theory of the Location of Industries*. Chicago University Press, Chicago, Illinois).

Wendell, R. E., and R. D. McKelvey (1981). "New Perspectives in Competitive Location Theory." *European Journal of Operational Research* **6**, 174-182.

Wendell, R. E., and S. J. Thorson (1974). "Some Generalizations of Social Decisions under Majority Rules." *Econometrica* **42**, 893–912.

Witzgall, C. (1965). *Optimal Location of a Central Facility: Mathematical Models and Concepts*, Rep. No. 8388. U.S. National Bureau of Standards, Washington, D.C.

12

Location of Mobile Units in a Stochastic Environment

Oded Berman
College of Management
University of Massachusetts
Boston, Massachusetts

Samuel S. Chiu
Engineering-Economic Systems Department
Stanford University
Stanford, California

Richard C. Larson
Operations Research Center
Massachusetts Institute of Technology
Cambridge, Massachusetts

Amedeo R. Odoni
Operations Research Center
Massachusetts Institute of Technology
Cambridge, Massachusetts

Rajan Batta
Department of Industrial Engineering
State University of New York at Buffalo
Buffalo, New York

12.1. INTRODUCTION

A locational decision is a spatial allocation of resources. The decision goal is usually to optimize some objective or set of objectives, subject to various types of constraints. The spatially deployed resources, often called "facilities," function within a complex operating system that includes a local transportation network and spatially dispersed system users. Much of the work in mathematical location theory has dealt with systems operating over large regions, such as warehousing systems, in which network travel costs or times can reasonably be modeled as known constants and in which facility capacity to respond to customers is never severely taxed.

More recently, particularly in dense urban areas, it has been found that the environment in which locational decisions are made is beset with uncertainties. First, there are uncertainties related to the users or customers of the system whose facilities are being located. Customers provide at least three types of uncertainty: namely, with respect to customer location, time of arrival (or time of service request), and amount (duration) of service required. If customers are further categorized, say by urgency of the service request, then additional uncertainty arises.

In the face of all these uncertainties, the types of service systems that operate within an urban environment are, however, finite capacity systems (i.e., they can only provide a limited amount of service at any given time). Under current severe budget constraints, urban public sector services often find this capacity to be decreasing. The result is the possibility that queueing-like congestion will occur. In fact, queueing delays for such systems may be an order of magnitude greater than the corresponding travel times in some scenarios. However, standard locational models often focus on travel times and neglect congestion delays. There is clearly a need to develop locational theories incorporating as a fundamental system performance measure "system response time," comprising both travel time and queueing delay.

But there is also another source of uncertainty: the transit time on any given network arc can vary because of random traffic surges or breakdowns, or because of periodic influences such as morning and evening rush hours. A locational decision-maker might be tempted to replace time of day periodic variations with 24-hour time averages and/or to ignore randomness by utilizing average values for arc travel times. Such an approach can yield locational decisions far from optimal.

The urban systems that share many, if not all, of the stochastic elements outlined above are found both in the public and private sectors. They usually house one or more mobile service units at one or more fixed facility locations. However, sometimes the planned location of a unit, not constrained to any single fixed facility, can be varied by time of day or by system state. In the public sector, examples include ambulance services, emergency street repair and other public property repair services, fire departments, and certain functions of police departments (e.g., detectives, special situation teams). In the private sector, examples include emergency repair services for utilities (e.g., gas, electricity, water) and for various products (e.g., windows, locks, typewriters, computers), taxicab fleets and private transportation companies.

All of our concerns can be illustrated by the ambulance example. Until recently, it was not uncommon for ambulance queueing delays in New York City to be 45 minutes or more, nearly an order of magnitude greater than travel times. Some ambulance services station their units at fixed garages, often located at hospitals, while others (such as those in Boston, Massachusetts) utilize satellite locations (on the street) which can be moved by time of day or system state. In fact, due to severe rush-hour traffic congestion of two underharbor tunnels (arcs in the transportation network) Boston routinely repositions an ambulance on the outer harbor side of the tunnel during rush hours (ordinarily it is stationed on the other, "downtown," side).

Such complex ambulance location decisions and similar decisions for other services call for the development of locational decision models and algorithms that begin to incorporate the uncertainties discussed above. In this chapter, we examine separately those uncertainties due to queueing-like congestion, and those due to travel time fluctuations.

In the first and more extensive part of this chapter (Section 12.2), we focus on various locational models that incorporate queueing behavior (and alternative queueing strategies) in a natural way. The most striking aspect of our results is the marked sensitivity of system performance to server locations, even for the case of a single-server system. It is clear that, for locational decisions in which queueing time represents a significant component of system response time, it is essential that queueing delay be explicitly considered in the optimization process.

In the second part of the chapter (Section 12.3) we examine travel time uncertainties, including both random components and time-of-day variability in travel times. Earlier work in this area (see, for example, Mirchandani and Odoni, 1979, and Chapter 2, this book) has demonstrated that a deterministic approximation to the stochastic network situation, where the approximation consists of replacing the travel time random variables with their expected values, can yield results far from optimum. Thus, a locational decision-maker should explicitly consider the distribution of travel times throughout the network when examining the consequences of alternative decisions. Now we carry these ideas further by developing more realistic representations of the dynamic behavior of stochastic transportation networks and by analyzing the placement of mobile servers on such networks.

12.2. FACILITY LOCATION WITH QUEUEING-TYPE CONGESTION

12.2.1. Introduction

To queue or not to queue—often we do not have a choice. Queueing related delays can affect almost any spatially distributed service system. The time between a customer's initial desire for service and the initiation of that service comprises a travel time (to transport either the customer to the server's location or the server to the customer's location) plus any time waiting in line, that is, a queueing delay. When the customer travels to the service facility, the queueing delay usually occurs after the travel time (e.g., waiting in line to place an order for hamburgers). When the server travels to the customer, the queueing delay occurs before the travel time, reflecting the fact that the server to be assigned is busy elsewhere with another customer.

As we will see in this chapter, the explicit incorporation of queueing delays into locational decision-making creates a large number of new modeling and optimization opportunities. We require the specification of potentially complex rules for governing the time and space operation of the system. For instance, the queueing discipline (i.e., the set of rules indicating how the queue is depleted) may give preference to customers near a service facility over those far away. Customers too distant from the facility may be "pruned" away, never to be serviced. Other rules govern the movement of the server: for instance, whether the mobile server move sequentially from one customer to another at different locations or whether it always returns to its home base (e.g., hospital) between customers. This consideration has a great bearing on the analytical tractability of the corresponding queueing model.

The inclusion of queueing can often yield counterintuitive optimal locational decisions, for instance nonnodal locations when the corresponding deterministic model suggests nodal locations, or optimal locations which change in unusual ways as customer demand rates vary.

To illustrate the types of approaches that have been applied to "queueing/location" problems, in this chapter the authors, out of necessity, focus on their own recent research. Most of this work assumes that the server travels to the customer and back to his home base prior to initiation of service of the next customer. The ambulance application, for instance, fits much of this work. Exceptions to this general model will be pointed out as we proceed. The somewhat limited set of models considered to date should encourage others to enter this new fertile research area.

12.2.2. The General Model

We consider a system in which p mobile service units are stationed at up to p different *home locations* throughout a service region ($p = 1, 2, \ldots$). Usually the service region is modeled as a transportation network with deterministic arc lengths (i.e., travel times). Customers, assumed to be located only at nodes of the transportation network,* call by telephone (or equivalent means) into a designated switchboard, requesting on-scene service by a service unit. In response to such a service request, one of three things happens:

1. If there is at least one available service unit, a unit is immediately *dispatched* to the scene of the service request.
2. If all service units are simultaneously busy, and if it is the operating policy of the system not to enter service requests into a queue, the customer is referred to a backup system for the desired service. With this operating policy, customers who call when all units are busy are *lost* to the system.
3. If all service units are simultaneously busy and if system operating policy allows queueing, then the customer is entered into a queue with other waiting customers; the queue, having potentially unlimited capacity, is depleted in a first-in, first-out (FIFO) manner.

Associated with each serviced customer is a *service time*, which in queueing parlance, is the time dedicated solely to that customer by the responding service unit. This service time comprises the travel time from the unit's home location to the customer, on-scene service time, travel time back to the unit's home location, and, perhaps, an associated off-scene service time. Most of the models in the following sections assume that only one customer is serviced per trip by a service unit away from the unit's home location (i.e., there are no "back-to-back" assignments of the server in which the server is directly assigned to a waiting customer from the scene of a previous service request).

The service units could be ambulances, emergency repair vehicles, customer pick-up vehicles, certain types of delivery vehicles, vehicles containing sales persons, and so on. Typically, these units are housed in *facilities*

---

*Some of the results presented here extend to more general spatial distributions of customers.

such as depots, garages, business offices, retail outlets, or—in the case of some urban ambulances—designated parking spaces along a curbside.

The general system design problem for such systems entails determining the appropriate total number of service units p, the units' home locations, and their service territories. (A service territory is the set of locations to which the service unit may be dispatched, even if all other service units were available for dispatch.) The problem is made difficult by inclusion of the three major probabilistic features of systems operation:

1. the unpredictability of arrival times of calls for service;
2. the probabilistic locations of calls for service;
3. the variability of service times, due both to differing travel times to different nodal customer locations and to differing on-scene (and perhaps off-scene) service requirements.

In our modeling of the above probabilistic features, arrival times in (1) are assumed to be governed by a homogeneous Poisson process. Briefly, such a process is a "memoryless" stochastic process in which customers appear (i.e., call in) at a constant average rate (say) λ per unit time ($\lambda > 0$) and the probability that k customers appear during a fixed interval of length T is given by

$$P\{k \text{ customers in } T\} = \frac{(\lambda T)^k e^{-\lambda T}}{k!}, \qquad k = 0, 1, 2, \ldots.$$

Times between arrivals of successive customers are independent and are governed by the negative exponential probability density function with mean λ^{-1}. The process is memoryless since the future arrival times of customers do not depend on past arrival times. The operational postulates which give rise to the Poisson process (see, for example, Larson and Odoni, 1981) are often very reasonable approximations to reality. For instance, numerous researchers have validated the Poisson model for the case of spatially distributed emergency services (such as emergency medical, police, fire, and emergency repair, see Larson and Odoni, 1981).* The uncertainty of customer arrival times, as reflected by the Poisson process, is a major cause of queueing delay. The chances for queueing would be greatly diminished if each customer arrived precisely $1/\lambda$ time units after the immediately previous one; unfortunately this is not the case in service systems of the types described above. Thus, we must seek to understand the locational consequences of such temporal uncertainties.

Probabilistic feature (2) above, reflecting the uncertainty of locations of calls for service, is most often described in our models by an arbitrary

---

*In emergency services, the Poisson processes governing customer arrival times are usually found to be time-varying, or nonhomogeneous, Poisson processes.

discrete probability distribution over the nodes of the network. Briefly reviewing, if node i generates a fraction w_i of the total service demands from the entire network, then the probability that a random service demand that arrives at some time t from node i $(i = 1, 2, \ldots, m)$ is equal to w_i ($w_i \geq 0$, $\sum_{i=1}^{m} w_i = 1$). Some of the analysis presented here has been extended to the case where customers may also be distributed continuously over the arcs of the network. In one case, we have a result in which customers can even be distributed continuously over a two-dimensional space (i.e., no network restriction is required). But most often we assume strictly nodal sources of customers.

The variability of service times, (probabilistic feature (3) above) is modeled by a general probability distribution with no special properties other than finite mean and variance. Part of the service time distribution is determined by the distribution of travel times from the unit's home location to its customers. When the responding unit is located at its home location, say at point x, in the service region (most often a network), the total service time associated with a service demand from node j is

$$\tilde{S}(x \mid j) = \tilde{U}_j + (\beta/v)d(x, j),$$

where $d(x, j)$ is the minimal travel distance from x to node j, v is the unit's response speed, β is a given parameter, and $\tilde{U}_j$ is the nontravel component (i.e., on-scene plus off-scene) of service time which may depend on nodal location j. The term $(\beta/v)d(x, j)$ accounts for the *round-trip* travel time between the home location of x and the service request at node j. For example, $\beta = 2$ implies that the unit requires as much time traveling from the facility at x to node j as it does in the return trip. For modeling purposes we require that $\beta \geq 1$. Figure 12.1 shows the temporal sequence associated with a service response for a demand from node j, a sequence which occurs with probability w_i each time a random customer arrives. Again, we emphasize that the exact effects of a unit's travel times are included in the general service time distribution of $\tilde{S}(x \mid j)$.

Because of the analytical difficulties introduced by the above probabilistic phenomena, results available to date are confined to systems in which some restrictions apply. For instance, with p service units ($p > 1$), we have results only for the "loss system," but not for the system that allows queueing. For the latter, we have results only for the single server ($p = 1$) system. At key points in the development we discuss prospects for extending and generalizing the available results.

12.2.3. Loss Systems (Problem P1)

In this section we discuss systems with zero queueing capacity, that is, systems in which customers who arrive when all p service units are busy are *lost*. In Section 12.2.4 we examine systems in which queueing is allowed.

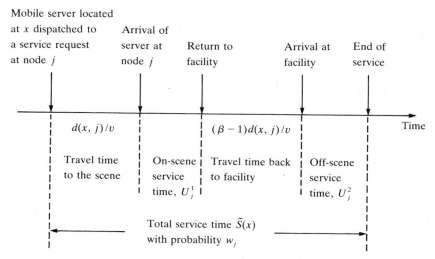

Figure 12.1. Temporal sequence comprising a service time.

In the loss system, each customer is either served immediately or lost (rejected) at a cost. In practice, a rejected customer is usually referred to some secondary or back-up service system which responds to the customer; an example would be private ambulance companies which provide back-up to public ambulance services. A reasonable objective function is to minimize the weighted sum of mean response time (travel time from the service unit's home location to the customer) and the cost of rejecting the customer from the system. (We assume here that response time and cost of rejecting will be expressed in terms of a single set of units, that is, time will be converted into "dollars" or vice versa.) The respective weights are the probabilities of immediate response (i.e., at least one free service unit) and rejection (all units busy). Our goal is to find a *single home location* at which a facility would be constructed to house *all p* mobile units, with the location chosen so as to minimize the weighted total cost. We will call such a location the p-server-single-facility-loss-median, or p-SFLM. We shall prove that this p-SFLM coincides with the deterministic 1-median, that is, the site that minimizes the average travel time. This result is valid regardless of the topological structure of the travel medium, travel distance metric, and the spatial demand distribution. Also, the only constraint on the cost of rejection is that it should be nonnegative.

We assume that the location of service requests is governed by some general probability distribution function over the region of interest, R, and that the locations of successive requests are statistically independent. All response units are assumed to be indistinguishable in terms of their service time distribution, and hence their expected service time. For a facility located at x, the objective function takes on the following form

$$z(x) = [1 - P_s(x)]\bar{t}(x) + P_s(x)Q , \qquad (12.2.1)$$

where $P_s(x)$ is the steady state probability of saturation (i.e., all service units busy), $\bar{t}(x)$ is the expected one-way travel time to a random customer, and Q is the cost per rejected customer, $Q \geq 0$.

To evaluate $z(x)$, we need to know the expression for $P_s(x)$. From a queueing point of view, the stochastic system we are considering is a queueing system with Poisson input, general independent service times, p servers, and zero queueing capacity. The standard queueing abbreviation for such a system is $M/G/p/0$ (the M represents memoryless, a property of Poisson processes). For such a system, $P_s(x)$ is given by the Erlang Loss Formula (e.g., see Larson and Odoni, 1981):

$$P_s(x) = \frac{\rho(x)^p/p!}{\displaystyle\sum_{i=0}^{p} \rho(x)^i/i!} , \qquad (12.2.2)$$

with $\rho(x) = \lambda\bar{S}(x)$, $\bar{S}(x) = \bar{U} + \beta\bar{t}(x)$ = expected service time for one service request, and $\bar{U}$ = expected non-travel related component of total service time.

Now we have an expression for $z(x)$ and our optimization problem may be stated as

$$\min_{x \in R} z(x) . \qquad (12.2.3)$$

We will first prove a weaker version of our main result equating the 1-median location with the p-SFLM.

Theorem 12.1.   *The p-SFLM coincides with the 1-median location if $Q \geq \bar{t}(x)$ for all $x \in R$.*

Proof.   Since the 1-median location minimizes $\bar{t}(x)$, we need only show that

$$\frac{dz(x)}{d\bar{t}(x)} \geq 0 , \qquad \text{for all } x \in R .$$

From (12.2.1) we have

$$\frac{dz(x)}{d\bar{t}(x)} = [1 - P_s(x)] + \lambda\beta[Q - \bar{t}(x)] \frac{dP_s(x)}{d\rho(x)} .$$

But

$$\frac{dP_s(x)}{d\rho(x)} = \left[\sum_{i=0}^{p} \frac{\rho(x)^i}{i!}\right]^{-2} \frac{\rho(x)^{p-1}}{(p-1)!} \left[\sum_{i=0}^{p} \frac{\rho(x)^i(p-i)}{i!p}\right] \geq 0 .$$

This implies that $dz(x)/d\bar{t}(x) \geq 0$ and our result follows. $\square$

We offer the following intuitive interpretation for Theorem 12.1. Since it costs more to lose a customer than to service one ($Q \geq \bar{t}(x)$), we would like to minimize the probability of saturation, $P_s(x)$. Increasing $\bar{t}(x)$ increases the expected service time, $\bar{S}(x)$, for each service request. This, in turn, will produce more work for the service units and thus increase the chance that all service units are busy. Therefore a location that minimizes $\bar{t}(x)$ also minimizes $z(x)$.

It turns out that we can relax the bound on Q and obtain the same result.

Theorem 12.2. *The p-SFLM coincides with the 1-median location for* $Q \geq 0$.

Proof. For convenience, we will suppress the argument x in $P_s(x)$, $\bar{t}(x)$, $P(x)$, and $\bar{S}(x)$. From (12.2.1) we have

$$\frac{dz}{d\bar{t}} = (1 - P_s) - \lambda\beta\bar{t}\,\frac{dP_s}{d\rho} + \lambda\beta Q\,\frac{dP_s}{d\rho}$$

$$\geq (1 - P_s) - \lambda\beta\bar{t}\,\frac{dP_s}{d\rho}$$

$$\geq (1 - P_s) - \rho\,\frac{dP_s}{d\rho}\,.$$

The first inequality follows from the proof of Theorem 12.1, the second is true because $\rho = \lambda\bar{u} + \lambda\beta\bar{t} \geq \lambda\beta\bar{t}$. Algebraic arguments then show that $[(1 - P_s) - \rho(dP_s/d\rho)]$ is nonnegative. (Since this step is algebraically involved, interested readers are referred to Chiu and Larson, 1985.) □

The above result may appear a bit counterintuitive due to the lack of any restrictions (except for nonnegativity) on the rejection penalty cost Q. However, one develops a better intuition by considering the expected system cost per unit time, say $\bar{c}$. We will do this for the case of $p = 1$ service unit. When the service unit is free the expected cost (of traveling) per unit time is zero; when the unit is busy, the expected response cost per unit time is $[\bar{t}(x)/\bar{S}(x)] + \lambda Q$. Thus,

$$\bar{c} = P_s(x)\{[\bar{t}(x)/(\bar{U} + \beta\bar{t}(x))] + \lambda Q\}\,.$$

Since $\bar{c}$ is the product of two positive functions, each monotonically increasing in $\bar{t}(x)$, $\bar{c}$ is minimized by minimizing $\bar{t}(x)$.

To sum up the key result in this section, the optimal home location for a facility to garage service units operating in a loss system is the 1-median location. Hence, congestion of the type observed in a loss system has *no effect* on optimal facility location—in the sense that one could use the 1-median model to determine the optimal location.

12.2.4. Infinite Capacity Queue (Problem P2)

We now switch from a loss system to the more difficult situation in which a potentially infinite queue of service requests is permitted. We will deal with systems having only a single service unit and our locational problem is to find that home location for the unit which minimizes its *average response time* to a random customer, where response time is the sum of the travel time and the queueing delay. The service unit's operation is restricted to a network topology. Our results include solution procedures for a general network and efficient algorithms for a tree. We later generalize the tree results to the case where, in addition to traditional nodal demands, continuous arc demands are also allowed.

Model Formulation and General Network Results
We consider a general undirected network $G(V, A)$ with node set $V(|V| = n)$ and arc set A. Service demands occur exclusively at the nodes, with each node i generating an independent Poisson stream of rate $\lambda w_i (\Sigma_i w_i = 1)$. Here, $\lambda \geq 0$ is the network-wide demand rate. Travel distance from point x on G to node i in V is $d(x, i)$ which is symmetric and equals the length of the shortest path $P[x, i]$. For each network arc the distance required to travel a fraction θ of an arc is equal to θ times the length of the arc. In all cases, travel time equals travel distance divided by a constant travel speed v. (The speed, in general, may be arc-specific, but to simplify our notation we omit this generalization.)

The location problem we are interested in is embedded in an $M/G/1/\infty$ queueing system (Poisson input, general independent service times, a single server, infinite queueing capacity). As indicated earlier, we assume a first-in-first-out (FIFO) queueing discipline. The expected response time $\overline{TR}(x, \lambda)$ is the sum of the mean queueing delay, $\bar{q}(x, \lambda)$, and the mean travel time, $\bar{t}(x)$,

$$\overline{TR}(x, \lambda) = \bar{q}(x, \lambda) + \bar{t}(x) . \tag{12.2.4}$$

The mean travel time is the usual 1-median function,

$$\bar{t}(x) = (1/v) \sum_{j \in V} w_j d(x, j) . \tag{12.2.5}$$

For the mean queueing delay, it is well known that with an $M/G/1/\infty$ queueing system (e.g., see Larson and Odoni, 1981)

$$q(x, \lambda) = \begin{cases} \dfrac{\lambda \overline{S^2}(x)}{2(1 - \lambda \bar{S}(x))} , & \text{for } \lambda \bar{S}(x) < 1 , \\ +\infty , & \text{otherwise} , \end{cases} \tag{12.2.6}$$

where $\bar{S}(x)$ is the mean service time $= \bar{U} + \beta \bar{t}(x)$, $\overline{S^2}(x)$ is the second moment of service time, $\bar{U} = \Sigma_{j \in v} w_j \bar{U}_j$, and $\bar{U}_j$ is the expectation of $\tilde{U}_j$ for each node $j \in V$.

The location problem becomes:

$P(\lambda)$: $\min_{x \in G} \overline{TR}(x, \lambda)$.

We will call an optimal solution to $P(\lambda)$, $x^*(\lambda)$, a *stochastic queue median* (SQM).

Before we engage in a search for the SQM, we can easily characterize $x^*(\lambda)$ for extreme values of λ. Any point on the network that minimizes $\bar{t}(x)$, and thus $\bar{S}(x)$, is a Hakimi (1964) 1-median, which we shall denote by HM. (In general, as discussed in Chapter 2, Hakimi 1-medians are not unique.) When the service request rate λ is very small, queueing very rarely occurs and thus $\bar{t}(x)$ dominates $\bar{q}(x, \lambda)$ (see (12.2.6)). Thus, intuitively, a HM minimizes $\overline{TR}(x, \lambda)$ for small values of λ. For large λ values, we must be careful not to increase λ so greatly that queueing saturation is guaranteed to occur; this happens whenever $\lambda \bar{S}(x) \geq 1$. if $\bar{S}(x)$ is minimized, as it is at a HM, then λ can be increased up to (but not equal to)

$$\lambda_{\max} \equiv [1/\bar{S}(\text{HM})] .$$

If there exists a unique HM on the network, then for λ values sufficiently large (but less than $\lambda_{\max}$) the HM is the SQM. If there are multiple HMs on the network, then a HM that has, as well, minimum second moment of service time (see (12.2.6)) is a SQM. These observations are summarized in the following theorem.

Theorem 12.3. *A SQM coincides with a HM when λ is sufficiently small. A SQM coincides with a HM having minimum second moment of service time when λ is sufficiently large but less than $\lambda_{\max}$.*

The proof is given by Chiu (1986a).

Example 12.1. To obtain some insight into the system's operation, consider the simple symmetric 2-node, 1-arc system shown in Figure 12.2. To avoid complexity assume $v = 1$, $\beta = 2$, $\bar{U} = 0$. Then, $\bar{S}(x) = 2\bar{d}(x) = 1$ for all $x \in [0, 1]$, that is, all points on the network are Hakimi 1-medians. Similarly, one can easily derive that $\overline{S^2}(x) = 4x^2 - 4x + 2$. Thus, the mean queueing delay is

$$\bar{q}(x, \lambda) = \frac{\lambda(4x^2 - 4x + 2)}{2(1 - \lambda)} , \qquad \text{for } 0 \leq \lambda < \lambda_{\max} = 1 ,$$

a quadratic function of x for any λ value. Here $\bar{q}(x, \lambda)$ is minimized where $\overline{S^2}(x)$ is minimized, namely at $x = 1/2$. Since $\overline{S^2}(1/2) = 1$,

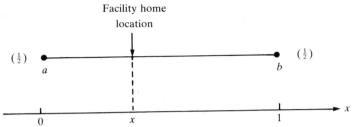

Figure 12.2. Two-node, one-arc example.

$$q(\tfrac{1}{2}, \lambda) = \min_{x \in [0,1]} \bar{q}(x, \lambda) = \lambda / [2(1 - \lambda)] \,.$$

$\overline{S^2}(x)$ is maximized at $x = 0$ and $x = 1$, at which points $\overline{S^2}(0) = \overline{S^2}(1) = 2$. Thus,

$$\bar{q}(0, \lambda) = \bar{q}(1, \lambda) = \max_{x \in [0,1]} \bar{q}(x, \lambda) = \lambda / (1 - \lambda) \,,$$

representing a *doubling* in mean queueing delay in comparison to the minimum possible. While traditional p-median location models would be indifferent to all $x \in [0, 1]$, the queueing result reveals a factor-of-two variation in the queueing component ($q(x, \lambda)$) of the objective function over $[0, 1]$. The entire response-time objective function is

$$\overline{TR}(x, \lambda) = \bar{q}(x, \lambda) + \bar{t}(x) = \frac{\lambda(4x^2 - 4x + 2)}{2(1 - \lambda)} + \frac{1}{2} \,.$$

In Figure 12.3 expected response time is plotted as a function of λ for both $x = 0$ and $x = 1/2$. As can be observed from the figure, the queueing component of the objective function becomes an arbitrarily large fraction of the total as λ increases. This demonstrates the limited value of p-median locational models for the type of stochastic systems we are examining, since such deterministic models focus on only one component of the objective function, a component that may be dominated by the stochastic component.

Applying Theorem 12.3 to the above example, $\lambda = 0$ is the only value of λ for which any $x \in [0, 1]$ is a SQM. In most networks, however, the HM is unique (at a node); in these cases, there exists a strictly positive λ value, say λ_δ, such that the HM is the SQM for all λ in the range $0 \le \lambda < \lambda_\delta$. Since point $x = 1/2$ is a HM with minimum second moment of the service time, this point is the SQM at λ values near $\lambda_{max} = 1$. In the above example it turns out that $x = 1/2$ is the SQM for all positive permissible λ values, $0 < \lambda < 1$. In most examples containing a unique HM there exists a large λ value, say $\lambda_L < \lambda_{max}$, such that the HM is the SQM for all λ, $\lambda_L < \lambda < \lambda_{max}$. For intermediate values, that is $\lambda_\delta \le \lambda \le \lambda_L$, the SQM tends to be pulled away from the HM towards points having smaller values of $\overline{S^2}(x)$.

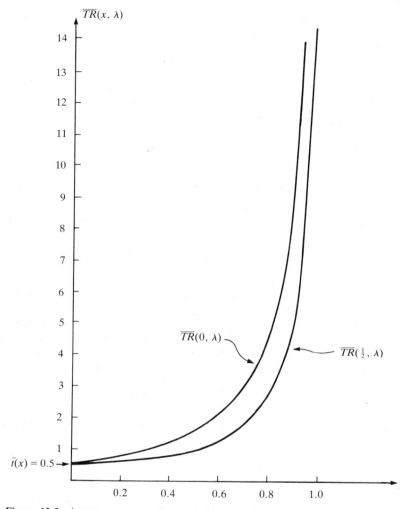

Figure 12.3. Average response time as a fraction of location and demand rate λ.

Examining the objective function ((12.2.4)–(12.2.6)), we can understand intuitively the trajectory of the optimal location for three different ranges of λ values. For small λ, queueing rarely occurs and thus the travel time component of the objective function dominates, yielding the optimal location at the HM. For large λ, one is concerned that the queue remains stable, implying finite mean queueing delay. Queue stability requires avoiding the singularity in the denominator of (12.2.6), implying adherence to the inequality $\lambda \bar{S}(x) < 1$, a condition that is eventually violated for any x other than the HM as λ increases to λ_{max}. Hence, to guarantee queue stability at λ near λ_{max}, the SQM must return to the HM. For intermediate λ values, the numerator of (12.2.6) plays an important role by pulling the SQM away from the HM (for those cases in which the minimum value of the second moment of service time is not obtained at the HM). It is this search for the SQM at intermediate λ values that is the concern in much of the remaining discussion in this section. ○

Before proceeding with the search for the general SQM, and to gain a different perspective, we will view the dependence of $\bar{q}(x)$ through the variance of service time instead of the second moment. We can write

$$\overline{S^2}(x) = \text{var}\,[S(x)] + (\bar{S}(x))^2 ,$$

where var$\,[S(x)] \equiv$ variance of the service time $= \overline{S^2}(x) - (\bar{S}(x))^2$. In general, reducing the second moment involves a trade-off between reducing the variance of the distribution of the random variable and the mean, or more precisely, the square of the mean. For x values having constant mean, such as in the simple example above, the x value having smallest variance will yield the smallest mean queueing delay. In the example, with the facility at $x = 1/2$, each customer requires precisely one time unit of service time, implying zero variance. On the other hand, at $x = 0$, 50% of the customers require 0 service time and 50% require 2 time units, implying a variance of 1. A random customer will experience a probability of the server being busy, equal to $\rho(x) = \lambda \bar{S}(x) = \lambda$, independently of the server's home location. But, since $\bar{U} = 0$, given that the server is busy in the $x = 0$ system, he must be busy on a customer requiring 2 units of service time. Therefore the mean residual time until completion of service on the customer currently being serviced is 1 time unit. Hence, if one arrives as a customer and finds oneself to be in queue, then one's conditional mean time until the queue is depleted by one is 1 time unit. On the other hand, if one arrives and joins a line for the $x = 1/2$ system, the server must be busy with a customer requiring 1 unit of service time; the conditioned mean time until the queue is depleted by one in 1/2 a time unit, 50% less than that of the $x = 0$ system.

This "mean residual service time for the customer currently being served" at the time of a random customer arrival plays a key role in determining mean queueing delay—whether the random arrival is <u>first</u> in line or tenth in line. And this mean residual time is known to be $S^2(x)/[2\bar{S}(x)] = [\text{var}\,(S(x)) + (\bar{S}(x))^2]/[2\bar{S}(x)]$ (see, for example, Larson and Odoni, 1981). The derivation rests on the fact that a Poisson arriving customer, being randomly incident on the server's state, tends to fall into a service time interval larger than average when he finds the server busy. In fact, the likelihood of falling into a service time interval of length s is directly proportional to both the relative frequency of service times of length s (as reflected by the value of the service time probability density function at s) and s itself. The service time interval being larger than average for each arriving customer in queueing implies that the queue is less likely to be depleted at the time of arrival of the next arriving customer. The resulting cascading effect can cause large queueing delays. To sum up, "everything else being constant," reducing variability in service times in queueing systems reduces queueing delays. If one cannot reduce variability without increasing the mean service time, it may be preferable to incur an increase in the mean (e.g., a move from the HM) to enjoy a decrease in the service time variability, and hopefully a decrease in the objective function value.

To locate $x^*(\lambda)$ for intermediate values of λ, one needs to evaluate $TR(x, \lambda)$. For a facility located at a point x units of distance from node a on arc $[a, b]$, which we will refer to as "x on $[a, b]$," we define the sets of vertices $V_1(x; a, b)$ and $V_2(x; a, b)$ as follows:

$$V_1(x; a, b) = \{ j: j \in V \text{ and } d(a, j) + x < (\alpha_{ab} - x) + d(b, j) \}$$

and

$$V_2(x; a, b) = N - V_1(x; a, b),$$

where α_{ab} is the length of arc $[a, b]$. In words, the shortest path between $j \in V_1(x; a, b)$ and x will pass through node a. Likewise, to nodes in $V_2(x; a, b)$, we can travel from x most quickly via node b. When the context leaves no ambiguity, we will drop the arguments and simply use the notations V_1 and V_2. We can now write $\bar{t}(x)$, $\bar{S}(x)$ and $\overline{S^2}(x)$ as follows, after some simplifications:

$$\bar{t}(x) = (1/v)(c_1 x + c_2),$$

$$\bar{S}(x) = \bar{U} + \beta \bar{t}(x),$$ (12.2.7)

$$\overline{S^2}(x) = (\beta^2/v^2)x^2 + [(2\beta^2/v^2)c_3 + (2\beta c_5/v)]x$$
$$+ [(\beta^2/v^2)c_4 + (2\beta/v)c_6 + \overline{U^2}],$$

where $\overline{U^2} = \Sigma_{j \in V} w_j \overline{U_j^2}$, $\overline{U_j^2}$ = second moment of $\tilde{U}_j$, which we assume to be finite for all $j \in V$,

$$c_1 = \sum_{j \in V_1} w_j - \sum_{j \in V_2} w_j,$$

$$c_2 = \sum_{j \in V_1} w_j d(a, j) + \sum_{j \in V_2} w_j(\alpha_{ab} + d(b, j)),$$

$$c_3 = \sum_{j \in V_1} w_j d(a, j) - \sum_{j \in V_2} w_j(\alpha_{ab} + d(b, j)),$$

$$c_4 = \sum_{j \in V_1} w_j[d(a, j)]^2 + \sum_{j \in V_2} w_j[\alpha_{ab} + d(b, j)]^2,$$ (12.2.8)

$$c_5 = \sum_{j \in V_1} w_j \bar{U}_j - \sum_{j \in V_2} w_j \bar{U}_j,$$

$$c_6 = \sum_{j \in V_1} w_j \bar{U}_j d(a, j) + \sum_{j \in V_2} w_j \bar{U}_j[\alpha_{ab} + d(b, j)].$$

As x increases, denoting movement of the facility location from node a toward node b, one notes that the set $V_1(x; a, b)$ will generally decrease in size. We will define the entire segment of an arc over which the sets V_1 and V_2 remain fixed as a *primary region*. If the triangle inequality holds for the network, any arc $[a, b]$ can be partitioned into at most $n - 2$ primary regions. A boundary point joining two adjacent primary regions will be referred to as a *breakpoint*. If x is a breakpoint on $[a, b]$ *associated with some node i*, then

$$x = \frac{d(b, i) - d(a, i) + \alpha_{ab}}{2} \tag{12.2.9}$$

implying that the two alternative routes from x to node i have equal length. All breakpoints can be computed readily using (12.2.9).

It is clear from (12.2.4)–(12.2.8) that $\bar{t}(x)$ and $\bar{S}(x)$ are linear, while $\overline{S^2}(x)$ is quadratic and convex over a primary region. From (12.2.4) and (12.2.6) one can also prove the convexity of $\overline{TR}(x, \lambda)$ over a primary region when $\overline{TR}(x, \lambda)$ is finite. The proof relies on the positivity of $\overline{S^2}(x)$ for all values of x (see Berman, Larson, and Chiu, 1985).

Lemma 12.1. $\bar{t}(x), \bar{S}(x)$ *are linear in x and* $\overline{S^2}(x)$ *and* $\overline{TR}(x, \lambda)$ *(when* $\overline{TR}(x, \lambda)$ *is finite and* $\lambda > 0$*) are strictly convex over a primary region.*

Across breakpoints, the sets V_1 and V_2, and thus the defining coefficients of (12.2.8), change. Going through a breakpoint from left to right, the derivative of $\overline{TR}(x, \lambda)$ with respect to x just to the right of the breakpoint is less than it is just to the left. Therefore, it is possible that $\overline{TR}$ has an interior local minimum in any primary region. The exact local minimum, if it exists, is found as a solution to a quadratic equation. To ensure global optimality one has to identify all primary regions and then compare the respective local minimum $\overline{TR}$ values in each primary region—a type of "brute force" operation, but one that (1) yields a precise optimum location x^* and (2) requires no more than $O(n^3)$ operations for the entire network. To reduce computational requirements, one is motivated to develop a heuristic to locate the SQM, which we present next.

A SQM Heuristic
As discussed earlier, (12.2.4)–(12.2.6) suggest that in optimizing $\overline{TR}$ there is a "tug-of-war" between minimizing $\overline{S^2}$ and $\bar{t}$ (thus $\bar{S}$). A HM does not, in general, minimize $\overline{S^2}$ over G. Thus, starting at a HM (to ensure feasibility, assuming $\underline{\lambda} < \lambda_{max}$), one seeks to direct the SQM search towards decreasing values of $\overline{S^2}$. This is the intuition behind the following heuristic which builds up a subnetwork of G and then locates the SQM over this subnetwork. Here we assume uniqueness of the HM at a node to simplify exposition.

Algorithm 12.1 *The SQM Heuristic for a General Network*

Step 1: Determine the Hakimi 1-median HM of $G(V, A)$. Calculate the second moment of the service time at HM. Set σ to be equal to that second moment and label the node where HM exists.

Step 2: For all unlabeled nodes i connected directly by an arc to a labeled node, compute $\overline{S^2}(i)$ (i.e., the second moment of the service time evaluated at node i). If $\overline{S^2}(i) > \sigma$ for all i, go to Step 3. Otherwise, determine node i^* having the smallest second moment $\overline{S^2}(i^*)$ of all eligible unlabeled nodes, set $\sigma = \overline{S^2}(i^*)$, label node i^*, and repeat Step 2.

Step 3: Call the last labeled node i^*. Define the set NL to be all the unlabeled nodes i connected directly by an arc to node i^*. Focus the search for SQM only on the subnetwork (nodes and arcs) defined by all the labeled nodes and the set NL.

In approximately 10 test problems on networks with up to 30 nodes (Berman et al., 1985), the above heuristic has successfully located the SQM.

Movement of the SQM as a Function of Demand Rate
One is often interested in the parametric behavior of the SQM $x^*(\lambda)$ as λ varies. We already know that $x^*(\varepsilon)$ and $x^*(\lambda_{max} - \varepsilon)$ (ε small) correspond to the HM. In all computational experience with general networks, one of the following has occurred as λ is increased from $\lambda = 0+$ to $\lambda = \lambda_{max} - \varepsilon$:

1. $x^*(\lambda)$ jumps from node to adjacent node, starting at the Hakimi 1-median, moving away in a direction of decreasing second moment of the service time, and eventually retracing the same path back to the Hakimi 1-median as λ nears λ_{max}. Sometimes $x^*(\lambda)$ remains fixed (zero jumps) at the Hakimi 1-median for all λ, $0 \leq \lambda < \lambda_{max}$; this occurs when the HM also minimizes the second moment of service time.

2. $x^*(\lambda)$ jumps as in (1) above, but upon reaching the farthest node in the jump sequence there exists a range of λ values for which $x^*(\lambda)$ moves continuously along a path of one or more arcs, the path emanating from that farthest node and terminating at a critical location; at this point $x^*(\lambda)$ starts moving back, revisiting each of the earlier visited points—first continuously, then discretely on the nodes. The case of zero jumps here implies continuous movement away from the HM and then back again to HM in a continuous fashion.

We will have more to say about $x^*(\lambda)$ in the next section.

Tree Network Results

As seen elsewhere in this book, finding the optimal network locations often becomes much simpler when the network is restricted to be a tree (i.e., a network with no cycles). Convexity results, which seem to be easier to obtain for a tree, and the uniqueness of paths from point to point, often provide the ammunition needed to obtain exceedingly simple procedures for finding the optimal locations.

In this section we exploit the special properties of trees to prove that the SQM heuristic becomes exact on a tree and to characterize precisely the trajectory $x^*(\lambda)$. We utilize the fact that, on trees, there are no breakpoints on any arc, and thus each arc is a single primary region. We also note that the nodal set V_1 increases in size as one moves across a node along any path—from one arc to the next. (Recall that node a in the definition of V_1 is always the node immediately to the left of the facility on the arc containing the facility.) Keeping track of the changes in the modal partitions V_1 and V_2, one can prove the following.

Lemma 12.2. $t(\bar{x})$, $S(\bar{x})$, $\overline{S^2}(x)$, and $\overline{TR}(x, \lambda)$ (when finite) are convex along any path of a tree network.

Convexity is strict for $\overline{S^2}(x)$ and $TR(x, \lambda)$ when λ is nonzero. The proof follows from observing that the directional derivative of these functions across a node along an implied path is increasing. Note that these functions are not necessarily "smooth" at a node since the defining coefficients in (12.2.8) vary with the changes in V_1 and V_2. The details of the proof are given by Chiu, Berman and Larson (1985).

Equations (12.2.4)–(12.2.6) and Lemma 12.2 imply that the SQM has to lie on the unique path connecting the minimizers of $\bar{t}(x)$ and $\overline{S^2}(x)$, which we will call the queue median path (QMP). For any point outside this path, one can find a point on the path that has smaller values of both $\bar{t}(x)$ and $\overline{S^2}(x)$. Let us illustrate this with Figure 12.4. Let node k minimize $\bar{t}(x)$ and let point y minimize $\overline{S^2}(x)$. Any path moving away from node k will result in a larger $\bar{t}(x)$. Likewise, any path leading out of point y will increase the value of $\overline{S^2}$. Both observations are direct consequences of the convexity of these functions. Therefore, any point, z, outside the QMP $P[k, y]$ will have larger S^2 and $\bar{t}$ than the point in $P[k, y]$ closest to z, namely the point defined by $P[k, z] \cap P[y, z] \cap P[k, y]$. For example, z_1 is "worse off" than node i, z_2 is "worse off" than node k, and node j is "worse off" than point y. The SQM heuristic identifies the QMP since, starting from the HM, it follows a unique (as guaranteed by the convexity of $\overline{S^2}$) path leading to the minimizer of $\overline{S^2}$. Therefore, this heuristic is exact for a tree network.

To find SQM on the QMP, one is further limited by the feasibility conditions $\lambda \bar{S} < 1$. Starting from the HM along the QMP, one searches for a

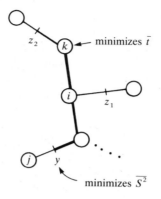

QMP contains $x^*(\lambda)$

Figure 12.4. Queue median path illustration.

point where either the derivative of $\overline{TR}(x, \lambda)$ becomes zero, or the directional derivative changes sign across a node. Convexity of $\overline{TR}$ along any path of a tree guarantees that such a point is optimal for problem $P(\lambda)$.

Trajectory[†] of $x^*(\lambda)$

Having established that the QMP contains all optimal solutions to $P(\lambda)$, we wish to characterize the exact trajectory of the SQM as a function of λ. Before presenting the trajectory, we will first introduce some notation and formally establish the optimality condition to problem $P(\lambda)$.

Along an implied directed path $i\text{-}j\text{-}k$, we define $\text{DTX}(x, \lambda) \equiv \partial \overline{TR}(x, \lambda)/\partial x$ when x is interior to an arc. Along the same directed path $i\text{-}j\text{-}k$, we define $\text{DTX}(j, \lambda)_{\text{in}}$ at node j, as the in-derivative of $\overline{TR}(x, \lambda)$ where the defining coefficients of (12.2.8) are computed with nodal partitions $V_1(x; i, j)$ and $V_2(x; i, j)$. Likewise, $\text{DTX}(j, \lambda)_{\text{out}}$ is evaluated with nodal partitions $V_1(x; j, k)$ and $V_2(x; j, k)$. The following optimality condition is the direct consequence of the convexity of $\overline{TR}(x, \lambda)$ along any path of a tree.

Optimality Condition for $P(\lambda)$

Suppose $x \in T$ and $1 - \lambda \bar{S}(x) > 0$, then the pair (x, λ) is optimal in $P(\lambda)$ if one of the following two conditions is true:

1. $\text{DTX}(x, \lambda) = 0$, if x is interior to a link or
2. if x is at a node, then $\text{DTX}(x, \lambda)_{\text{in}} \leq 0$ and $\text{DTX}(x, \lambda)_{\text{out}} \geq 0$ along *any* path through node x.

[†]The remainder of Section 12.2.4 is more technically advanced than the rest of the chapter. Without loss of continuity, the reader may proceed directly to Section 12.2.5.

The approach we will employ is to take a point on the QMP and ask: "For what value(s) of λ, if any, will x be optimal in $P(\lambda)$?" We can answer this question by utilizing the just established optimality condition: for fixed x, find the zero(s) of $DTX(x, \lambda)$ in λ (or $DTX(x, \lambda)_{in}$ or $DTX(x, \lambda)_{out}$ if x is at a node). For completeness, let us first explicitly write $DTX(x, \lambda)$ below,

$$DTX(x, \lambda) = A(x, \lambda)/[2(1 - \lambda \bar{S}(x))^2] \, ,$$

where

$$A(x, \lambda) = A_1(x)\lambda^2 + A_2(x)\lambda + A_3 \, ,$$
$$A_1(x) = (\beta/v)c_1\overline{S^2}(x) + (2/v)c_1(\bar{S}(x))^2 - \bar{S}(x)\overline{S^{2\prime}}(x) \, ,$$
$$A_2(x) = \overline{S^{2\prime}}(x) - (4c_1/v)\bar{S}(x) \, ,$$
$$A_3 = (2/v)c_1 \, ,$$

where the prime $(')$ denotes the derivative with respect to x.

Henceforth, we will restrict our attention to the directed QMP leading out of the HM, with all derivatives evaluated in this implied direction. To facilitate discussion, we assume a QMP as depicted in Figure 12.5, with i_1 being the HM and y the minimizer of $\bar{S}^2$ over our tree network, say, T. For fixed $x \in$ QMP, we plot $DTX(x, \lambda)$ as a function of λ. There are three possibilities of $DTX(x, \lambda)$ which we denote by $DTX(x_i, \lambda)$, $i = 1, 2, 3$ (see Figures 12.5 and 12.6):

1. $DTX(x, \lambda)$ crosses the λ-axis twice;
2. $DTX(x_2, \lambda)$ is tangent to the λ-axis;
3. $DTX(x_3, \lambda)$ has no zero in λ.

As expected, a singularity occurs as λ approaches $[\bar{S}(x_i)]^{-1}$ in $DTX(x_i, \lambda)$, $i = 1, 2, 3$. Furthermore, the following are always true when we restrict ourselves to the QMP:

- $DTX(x, 0) = DTX(z, 0) = c_1/v$ if x and z are on the same arc.
- $DTX(x, \lambda) \leq DTX(z, \lambda)$ if x is in the interior of path $P[\text{HM}, z]$; equality holds only when $\lambda = 0$ *and* x, z on the same arc.
- At node j, $DTX(j, \lambda)_{in} < DTX(j, \lambda)_{out}$ for all $\lambda \in [0, 1/\bar{S}(j)]$.

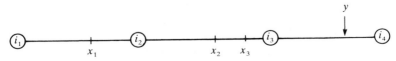

Figure 12.5. A hypothetical QMP.

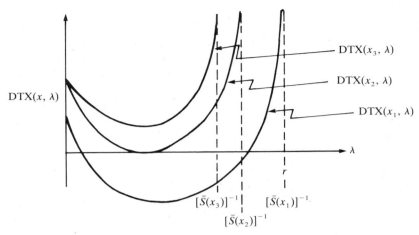

Figure 12.6. Three possible DTX(x, λ).

For rigorous proof, we refer the readers to Chiu (1985). Given the above facts, other characteristics (such as curvature) of DTX(x, λ) are unimportant in proving the following result.

Theorem 12.4. $x^*(\lambda)$ *moves continuously along the QMP from the HM (at* $\lambda = 0$*) as* λ *increases, then reaches a point of maximum distance from the HM at some* λ *value, say* λ_{crit}*, and then retreats continuously back to the* HM *upon further increase of* λ*.*

Assuming uniqueness of the HM, $x^*(\lambda)$ is uniquely defined because $\overline{TR}(x, \lambda)$ is strictly convex ($\lambda > 0$) along all paths of a tree network. Figure 12.7 is a composite picture of DTX(x, λ) and $x^*(\lambda)$ on the QMP. The reader should be able to trace $x^*(\lambda)$ in conjunction with the DTX(x, λ) plots. The intercepts λ_i represent zeros of DTX$(i_k, \lambda)_{in}$ and DTX$(i, \lambda)_{out}$, where i_k represent the nodes on the QMP. In particular, curve (1) is DTX$(i_1, \lambda)_{out}$, (2) DTX$(i_2, \lambda)_{in}$, (3) DTX$(i_2, \lambda)_{out}$, (4) DTX$(i_3, \lambda)_{in}$, and (5) DTX$(i_3, \lambda)_{out}$. With all the λ_i computed, one can easily identify $x^*(\lambda)$ for any given λ. For example, if $\lambda \in [\lambda_3, \lambda_4]$, we know $x^*(\lambda)$ is on arc $[i_2, i_3]$. This information allows us to compute the defining coefficients of (12.2.4). To exactly locate $x^*(\lambda)$, one needs only to solve DTX$(x, \lambda) = 0$, now with λ fixed. Details of the procedure are given by Berman et al. (1985) or Chiu et al. (1985).

There is a turning point on the QMP, the point at which $x^*(\lambda)$ begins its trip back to the HM. This is a point x where DTX(x, λ) is tangent to the λ-axis. When x is at a node, DTX$(x, \lambda)_{out}$ will be tangent or totally above the λ-axis, as in the case of node i_3 in Figure 12.7. Operationally, to identify this turning point, we have the following lemma.

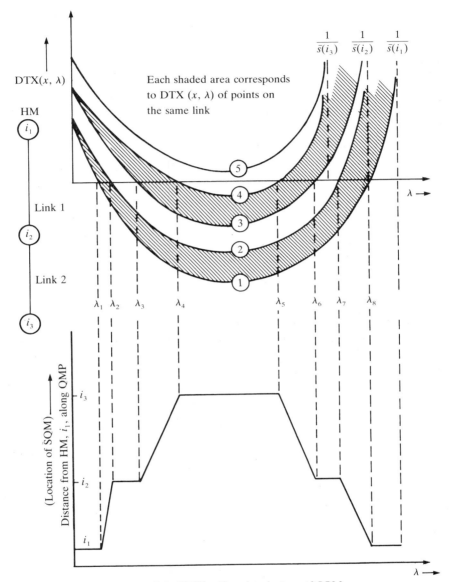

Figure 12.7. DTX(x, λ) and trajectory of SQM.

Lemma 12.3. *x on the QMP is a turning point if*

1. $(8\beta/v^2)c_1^2\overline{S^2}(x) - [\overline{S^{2'}(x)}]^2 = 0$, *or, if x is at a node,*
2. $[(8\beta/v^2)c_1^2\overline{S^2}(x) - (\overline{S^{2'}(x)})^2]_{\text{in}} \leq 0$ *and*
   $[(8\beta/v^2)c_1^2 S^2(x) - (S^{2'}(x))^2]_{\text{out}} \geq 0$,

where the [ ]$_{\text{in}}$ *and* [ ]$_{\text{out}}$ *notations are used to account for the appropriate defining coefficients of* (12.2.8).

The Case of Continuous Arc Demands

Allowing continuous arc demands necessitates additional notation. We shall just discuss informally the generalization of this queueing system. The temporal arrival process is still time-homogeneous Poisson. Given a request for service, the probability of it being from node j is w_j, $j \in V$, and from arc l is f_l, $l \in L$, $(\Sigma_j w_j + \Sigma_l f_l = 1)$. Given that it is on arc demand, the exact location of the service request is governed by some general probability distribution over the arc. The nontravel related component of service time, U, is now nodal as well as arc specific (i.e., U_j, $j \in V$ and U_l, $l \in L$). With a strong conviction and a never-dying appetite for algebra, one can rewrite (12.2.7) (12.2.8) and prove Lemmas 12.2, 12.3, and Theorem 12.4. Except for (12.2.7) and (12.2.8), other equations look surprisingly similar. Modeling, notational, and algebraic details are given by Chiu (1986b).

12.2.5. Determining Optimal Service Territories and Locations (with No Server Cooperation)

Optimal Allocation of Service Territories

Up to this point, all of our spatial analysis has focused on determining the optimal home location for one service unit (queueing option) or for p service units (loss option). Optimality is understood to imply minimization of mean response time, that is, the sum of queueing delay and travel time.

A related spatial deployment problem is as follows. Suppose p service units are already located at p distinct home locations throughout the network. each unit is allocated a *service territory* which is a distinct subset of nodes such that all customers originating from those nodes will be handled by that unit. Each node is assigned to precisely one unit. *There is no inter-territory cooperation*, so that whenever a customer requests service and his (her) designated server is busy, that service request is entered into a FIFO queue. In such a system, each service territory (with its service unit) operates as an $M/G/1/\infty$ queue, independently of the other service territories. The spatial question is as follows:

- How can one optimally design the service territories so that mean response time to a random customer is minimized?

Thus, in this formulation, locations are fixed and service territories must be found. This is analogous to the "allocation" portion of the "location-allocation" algorithm proposed to solve p-median and related problems (Cooper, 1964).

In this last section we briefly present some results on the $p = 2$ server case. The methods can be extended (with some difficulty) to $p > 2$ servers (Berman and Mandowsky, 1986).

Let $x^i \in N(V, A)$ be the home location of response unit i, $i = 1, 2$. A districting policy that determines service territories is a partition of the set V into two sets V^1 and $V^2 = V - V^1$, with V^1 being the set of nodes in the district (service territory) of unit i. The fraction of total customer demand which is from service territory i is

$$W^j = \sum w_j, \qquad j \in V^i .$$

For any given policy (V^1, V^2) the expected response time to a random customer is

$$\overline{TR} = W^1 \overline{TR}^1 + W^2 \overline{TR}^2 , \qquad (12.2.10)$$

where $\overline{TR}^i$ is the conditional mean response time in service territory i, with the travel time and queueing components determined by applying (12.2.4)–(12.2.6) to each respective service territory. (In service territory i, the conditional nodal probabilities are w_j / W^i for all $j \in V^i$.) The problem is to find an optimal policy (V^1, V^2), that is, a policy that minimizes $\overline{TR}$.

It turns out that we can categorize the optimal policy by ranges of the service request rate λ. Starting at $\lambda = 0$, we define four "λ regions,"

Region A	$0 \le \lambda \le \lambda_A$
Region B	$\lambda_A \le \lambda \le \lambda_B$
Region C	$\lambda_B \le \lambda < \lambda_{max}$
Region D	$\lambda_{max} \le \lambda$,

for constants λ_A, λ_B, and λ_{max} (yet to be specified).

Lemma 12.4. *For region* A, *the optimal policy is based on service unit proximity to customer location (i.e., each node is assigned to the closest service unit).*

This result follows from the analogous results stated earlier regarding optimal service unit locations. At small λ values, travel time dominates queueing delay, hence a service unit's closeness to customers determines the optimal policy.

As might be expected, λ_{max}, denotes the limit of feasible λ-values. For all $\lambda \ge \lambda_{max}$, there exists no partitioning (V_1, V_2) such that $\overline{TR}$ is finite. Hence, for region D, there exists no feasible solution since at least one of the two queueing subsystems is unstable.

To find the optimal policy in region C, we must compute λ_{max}. Suppose $\overline{S}^i(V^1, V^2)$ denotes the mean service time in service territory i $(i = 1, 2)$ under policy (V^1, V^2). Then, to guarantee queue stability, we must have $\lambda W^i \overline{S}^i(V^1, V^2) < 1$ for $i = 1, 2$. A moment's reflection will convince one that

$$\lambda_{max}^{-1} = \min_{\substack{\text{all policies} \\ (V^1, V^2)}} \{\max [W^1 \overline{S^1}(V^1, V^2); W^2 \overline{S^2}(V^1, V^2)]\} .$$

$$(12.2.11)$$

The policy which is the solution to the "minimax" problem of (12.2.11) is the only one that assures queue stability for λ sufficiently close to λ_{max}. Hence, in region C the optimal policy is the one found by solving (12.2.11). The problem can be formulated and solved as an integer linear programming problem. Obtaining the optimal solution is not difficult since the solution to the relaxed version of the problem (i.e., with integrality constraints removed) has at most two noninteger variables (see Berman and Larson, 1985, for details).

For region B, in general, different policies are optimal for different ranges of λ values. That is, policy $(V^1, V^2)^1$ may be optimal for $\lambda_A \leq \lambda \leq \lambda_1$, policy $(V^1, V^2)^2$ optimal for $\lambda_1 \leq \lambda \leq \lambda_2 \leq \lambda_3$, etc. Efficient heuristics for finding good (and often optimal) policies are given by Berman and Larson (1985).

A Location-Allocation Algorithm

In the above subsection, we discussed the problem of finding optimal districting policy *given* fixed home location for the servers. Here we assume that the home locations are not given and we need to look for the *simultaneous* optimal districting and location policy.

The method used to find the optimal districting location policy is a location-and-allocation improvement heuristic procedure (an idea first used by Cooper, 1964). In this procedure, we combine the method to find the optimal location of an $M/G/1$ server discussed in Section 12.2.4 and the method to find the optimal districting presented in the last section.

For the case $p = 2$, the heuristic begins with an initial location policy $(X^1, X^2)_0$ (X^i is the home location of service unit i, $i = 1, 2$). Using this initial location the best districting policy $(V^1, V^2)_0$ is then found by employing our districting method. Now in each district i the optimal home location can be found using the SQM model with V^i as the relevant set of nodes, having an arrival call rate λW^i and the probability of a call for service equal to w_j/W^j for any node j in V^i, $i = 1, 2$. This gives a new set of locations $(X^1, X^2)_1$ and again the districting method can be used to find $(V^1, V^2)_1$ and so on. The heuristic terminates when there is no change in the districting-location policy. For more details about the problem for the cases $p = 2$ and $p > 2$, the reader can refer to Berman and Mandowsky (1986).

12.2.6. Variations of the Basic SQM Model

In this section we shall briefly discuss the effect of relaxing and/or changing some of the underlying assumptions of the stochastic queue median (SQM) model, as developed in the previous sections. Specifically, we consider three factors for modifying assumptions:

1. Queueing discipline;
2. System operating characteristics;
3. Planar problem.

Queueing Discipline

One of the assumptions made in the SQM model is the use of a single priority, work conserving queueing discipline which does not depend on the service time information of calls in queue. Examples of allowable queueing disciplines include first-in-first-out (FIFO), last-in-first-out (LIFO) and service-in-random-order (SIRO).

Priority Queueing-Location (PQL) Model

In the context of urban emergency service (UES) systems there is a natural prioritization of calls for service. The fact that higher priority should be assigned to calls that endanger human life is one of the reasons that a realistic UES system model should allow for prioritization of calls for service. Motivated by this, new research (Batta, Larson, and Odoni, 1988) has led to a formulation and solution techniques for a PQL model on a network. The model allows for an arbitrary, but fixed, number of priority classes. The salient features of the formulation are:

- Use of a nonpreemptive priority queueing discipline having FIFO discipline within each priority class.
- Travel speed of the server can depend on the priority class of the customer being serviced.
- Nontravel time related service time (on-scene plus off-scene service time) distribution can be priority dependent.
- The spatial distribution of calls can be priority dependent.
- Importance weights are attached to the average response time of calls within a priority class. These are used in calculating the system-wide weighted average response time to a call.

The objective in the PQL model is to find the location of the facility which minimizes the weighted average response time to a call. The major results and observations are as follows:

- For the tree network case, strict unimodality of the average queueing delay function (when finite), for each priority class, is established. Unimodality properties are used to identify a subtree on which the optimal location must lie.
- The set of optimal locations on a general network has been characterized for extreme values of the average arrival rate of calls.

Service Time Dependent Queueing-Location (STDQL) Model
The use of service time dependent queueing disciplines can lead to a significant improvement in the average queueing delay of calls served by the system. For example, it is well known that shortest-job-first (SJF) service order has the minimum average queueing delay for calls amongst a wide class of queueing disciplines (for example, see Kleinrock, 1976). Another motivating factor for considering such models is that the system dispatcher is unlikely to adhere to a strict queueing discipline such as FIFO, but perhaps may like to utilize service time information of calls in queue when dispatching units to calls.

Motivated by this, we have recently formulated and developed solution techniques for a STDQL model which allows for the use of any queueing discipline that depends on the expected service time of calls (Batta, 1989). The system can be analyzed as an $M/G/1$ nonpreemptive priority queueing system, being FIFO within each priority class, with location dependent priorities. Based on this observation, both exact and heuristic algorithms for finding the optimal location of the facility have been developed.

The major results and observations are as follows:

- The location set for extreme values of λ has been characterized.
- Primary regions, used in the SQM model, can be subdivided into subprimary regions on which the priorities of calls do not change. This is an essential feature in developing an optimization procedure for determining the optimal location.
- Based on computational experience, it is conjectured that for a tree network with a unique Hakimi median and no nontravel time related service times, the optimal location of the facility under shortest (longest)-job-first queueing discipline is closer(further away) to(from) the Hakimi median than that obtained from using a FIFO queueing discipline.

System Operating Characteristics
There are two operating assumptions made in the SQM model which can be potentially troublesome in applications:

- All calls must eventually be served by the single server.
- The server must return directly home between successive calls.

Rejection Models
Recent progress has been made on rejection models in which calls from nodes can be probabilistically rejected from nodes, at a cost (Batta, 1988). Two models are considered. In the first model, the rejection of calls is location dependent (the cost of rejection can also depend on the specific

location of the call), but calls can be rejected from the system even if no queue exists. In the second model, calls are rejected only if a queue exists when the call arrives into the system. The remaining assumptions are similar to the first model.

The resulting queueing systems are analyzed for both models, and algorithms are developed for finding the optimal location of the facility and the corresponding optimal acceptance probabilities at nodes of the network. The objective is to minimize the system-wide average cost of serving a call, where this cost is a weighted sum of the average response time of calls served by the system, and the average rejection cost of calls not served by the system.

Traveling Server SQM Problem

Relaxing the assumption that the server must return home between successive calls for service, and permitting the server to travel directly to one of the calls in queue, results in pairwise dependent service times for calls. This model is useful for modeling repairman systems.

Batta (1984) examined the traveling server problem under two sets of assumptions. In the first model, an infinite queue capacity is permitted, with a FIFO queueing discipline. An additional assumption of infinite return speed on traveling to the home location from the server's last call in a busy cycle, permits one to use results from Coffman and Hofri (1978) to analyze the resultant queueing system. A heuristic algorithm has been developed to find the location of the server, the objective being to minimize the average response time to a call.

In the second model, a finite queue capacity is permitted, allowing general queueing discipline. The assumption of infinite return speed is dropped, and calls are admitted to the system when the server travels back to his home location (the calls are only answered once he reaches there). One can develop expressions for the average response time in a busy cycle using a standard busy cycle type analysis. This then leads to an algorithm to find the location of the facility which minimizes the average response time of calls answered by the server.

The SQM with a Permanent Facility

Another assumption of the SQM model is that the service unit returns to its home location (which may be just a designated parking space along a curbside), upon completion of an on-scene service. However, in practice the service unit may need to travel to a permanent facility following the provision of an on-scene service. When a demand occurs, the unit, if available, travels from its home location to the scene of the call, continues to the permanent facility and eventually returns to the home location. An example of such a system is an ambulance where the permanent facility is a hospital.

The optimal home location can be found using a similar analysis to that of the SQM model. However, some of the findings are different. For example, in the loss model, the optimal home location is not necessarily at a node. Also, the trajectory of the optimal solution when λ is varied from 0 to λ_{max} is not the same as in the SQM model, due to the influence of the location of the permanent facility. For more details on the analysis the reader can refer to Berman and LeBlanc (1983).

The SQM with Random Arc Length
In the SQM, it is assumed that the length of arcs of the network are deterministic. However, this is not necessarily the case as discussed in Chapter 2. An attempt to apply the SQM model with random lengths is described by Berman (1985).

Planar Problem
The SQM model operates on a network with calls for service originating from nodes of the network. In certain applications, such as for locating a tool crib in a manufacturing plant, a planar formulation may be more appropriate.

Batta, Ghose, and Palekar (1989) examine the SQM model on the plane with fixed, arbitrarily shaped, impenetrable barriers to travel, and employing the Manhattan travel metric. Developing on the results of the corresponding p-median problem (without queueing congestion) due to Larson and Sadiq (1983), they show that the planar region can be partitioned into cells and subcells. They then establish strict convexity (when finite) of the average response time function within a subcell of a cell, and use this to develop a globally convergent algorithm to find the optimal location of the facility. In the absence of barriers they establish strict convexity (when finite) of the average response time on the plane; this provides an efficient algorithm for finding the optimal location. Batta et al. give an analogy between network location problems and location problems on the plane which employ a Manhattan travel metric.

Brandeau (1985) also examines the SQM model on the plane, with the Manhattan travel metric but in the absence of barriers to travel. She considers the continuously-distributed demand case, and establishes similar convexity results for the objective function.

12.2.7. The Case of Multiple Cooperating Servers

So far our focus in this chapter has been on single server models. This is necessitated by the desire of analytical tractability: the $M/G/1$ queues can be thoroughly analyzed whereas queues of the form $M/G/p$ ($p > 1$) remain unsolved. Even the notation $M/G/p$ is too restrictive for the spatially dispersed systems we are likely to encounter, since the "G" in the standard queueing notation implies that all service times are drawn independently from a single probability distribution, independent of the server or the state of the system. In practice, for instance, in ambulance systems, each server has his "own" service time distribution, shaped by local demand and travel characteristics and by the pattern of interdistrict dispatching. Moreover, a server's service time tends to increase with increasing system congestion levels, reflecting greater likelihood of distant (interdistrict) assignments.

Ignoring Travel Time Effects on Service Times

A relatively easy to analyze situation occurs when the total service times can be approximated to be equal to the sum of the on-scene and off-scene service times (which is justified when the on-scene and off-scene service times are at least an order of magnitude greater than the travel times, so that the travel times can be ignored). In this case, Berman and Larson (1982) showed that when the service requests occur according to a general renewal process, and that there are p service units to be located, then an optimal set of locations exists solely on the nodes of the network. In addition, when the service requests are governed by a homogeneous Poisson process and the service times are exponentially distributed, the optimal locations can be analytically derived using the formulation of the "HY-PERCUBE" queueing model (Larson, 1974). For more details the reader can refer to Berman and Larson (1982).

Multiple Servers at One Location (Queueing Allowed)

Another multiple server situation arises when all p servers are housed at the same home location. In Section 12.2.2 we showed that if customers are turned away (i.e., lost) when all p servers are busy, the optimal location for the garage facility is the 1-median. A more difficult case arises when one allows queueing of customers. Using an approximation to the $M/G/p$ queue derived by Nozaki and Ross (1978), Batta and Berman (1989) recently developed some procedures for locating such a garage facility. Nozaki and Ross' approximate expression for the mean wait in an $M/G/p$ queue is based on just the first two moments of the service time, and thus the analysis follows from the techniques shown in Section 12.2.3. Many of the results are predictable: for λ near zero or λ_{max}, the optimal location is the median; the "tug of war" between the mean and the variance of the service time remains important here, with outcomes similar to those shown in Section 12.2.3.

The General p Server Problem

However, the most practical model, that is, the one most likely to arise in practice, must allow separate home locations for each of the p servers and it must allow server cooperation in the form of interservice district dispatching. For the case of general service times, this remains an analytically unsolved problem. However, recently Berman, Larson, and Parkan (1987) have developed two approximate procedures for locating the p home facilities.

The first heuristic utilizes both the "$M/G/1$" location model and the

HYPERCUBE model in a "location/allocation" iterative scheme. More precisely, given proposed locations for the p facilities, it uses the HYPERCUBE model to calculate, for each one of the servers, the fraction of dispatches to each possible customer location. This "response pattern" information is then used to improve the location of each server by "pretending" that each server behaves as an independently operating $M/G/1$ queue, as in Section 12.2.3. The iterative scheme continues until it converges to a local optimum.

The second heuristic also uses the HYPERCUBE model to predict response patterns, given p proposed locations, but then separately locates each server as in a 1-median problem (with nodal weights determined by the response pattern). Again, a "location/allocation" iterative scheme is used.

Both procedures are found to give satisfactory results. A detailed simulation model was employed to verify the accuracy of the gradients that were computed from the analytical model and the (near) optimality of the resulting locations. In both heuristics, the mean service times of the servers are recalibrated at each iteration to reflect magnitudes compatible with the HYPERCUBE-computed response patterns, This "mean service time calibration" (Jarvis, 1976) has been found to be essential in developing good locations.

This concludes our treatment of locational problems in the presence of queueing. In the final part of this chapter, we examine locational problems exhibiting another type of unpredictability, random travel times.

12.3. LOCATIONAL DECISIONS ON NETWORKS WITH RANDOM TRAVEL TIMES

12.3.1. Introduction

The type of network that we deal with now is probabilistic with respect to travel time on its arcs (see also Chapter 2). The travel time for each given arc can take any one of a finite number of values associated with that arc. As a result, the network itself at any given time instant can be in any one of a finite number of *states*, with each state differing from all others by a change in at least one arc travel time. The network makes transitions from state to state dynamically.

The way these transitions are made is one of the distinguishing features of the models in this section: we assume that there is a degree of "*predictability*" and *interdependence* with regard to the states of the network. This assumption is motivated by our concern with applications to the types of urban service systems mentioned earlier. In addition to completely random events such as road accidents, travel times on urban networks are also affected by more predictable factors, for example, time of day, weather conditions and day of week to name a few. Given the current "state" of an urban network, as described by the arc travel times, we can assign probabilities to its making a transition during the next period of time to each one of any possible number of future states. For example, the presence of heavy traffic conditions during the morning rush hour on a rainy Friday would imply a high probability of having similarly poor travel conditions throughout that day.

The Markov process is a mathematical model which is particularly convenient for the study of this type of probabilistic behavior. The basic concepts of the Markov process are those of "state" of a system and of "transitions" among states. In a Markov process, the probability of a transition to state s during the next time interval given that the system now occupies state r, is assumed to be a function only of r and s and not of any history of the system before its arrival in r. In other words we may specify a Markovian transition probability matrix P with elements p_{rs} ($r, s = 1, 2, \ldots, S$, where S is the total number of network states) indicating the probability that state r at time period k will be succeeded by state s at time period* $k + 1$. This is shown schematically in Figure 12.8 for a five-node network with $t_r(i, j)$ denoting the arc travel time between neighboring nodes i and j when the network is in state r.

To illustrate this point a little further, Figure 12.9 might be a simple depiction of the possible transitions between states of an urban transportation network. In this representation (N = night hours, M = morning peak-traffic hours (e.g., 7–10 am), D = mid-day period (e.g., 10 am–4 pm), A = afternoon peak-traffic hours (e.g., 4 pm–6 pm), E = evening hours), we can see how the Markovian transition matrix would help in describing both the dynamic behavior of the network and the interdependence among states. For instance, if M_1 stands for heavy traffic conditions during the morning peak traffic period, M_2 for average traffic conditions, and M_3 for unusually light traffic conditions, then the transition probabilities p_{NM_1}, p_{NM_2}, and p_{NM_3} would indicate the relative likelihood of each one of these conditions prevailing on a particular day. Similarly, if D_1 and D_2 represent, respectively, moderate and light traffic at mid-day, the transition probabilities $p_{M_1D_1}$ and $p_{M_2D_2}$ would indicate the relative likelihood that heavy morning traffic would be succeeded by, respectively, moderate and light mid-day traffic.

The second significant difference between usual facility location problems and those of this section is that the "facilities" to be located are *movable*, as in Section 12.1. The motivation for relocating their home locations is, naturally, provided by the fact that the network on which the server operates itself undergoes changes of state. Depending on the state of the network (and, note, on the probabilities of transition to future states) the optimal location of the servers may change. The reason is that demands for

---

*It is not necessary to assume that the network makes transitions at discrete time periods k, $k + 1$, $k + 2$, \ldots. Many of the results of this section also apply to the continuous time case. However, the discrete time assumption is particularly convenient for expository purposes.

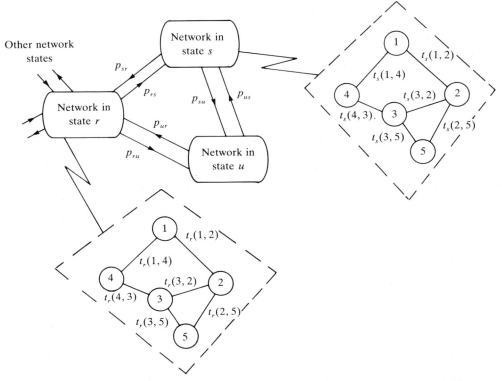

Figure 12.8. A five-node network with probabilistic travel times and Markovian transitions among states.

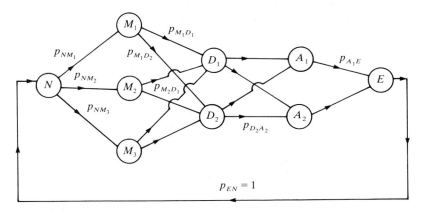

Figure 12.9. A transportation network exhibiting cyclic transition behavior.

the service in question are, as usual, assumed to be generated randomly at the nodes of the network and the servers will travel to these nodes to serve the demands.* Since travel times on the network depend on the state of the network, so will optimal locations on it.

The objective of the facility location problem in the context of the scenario of this section is to find the set of locations for the p (≥ 1) movable servers *for each and every state of the network* so as to minimize the long-term ("steady-state") total cost of offering the service. To reflect realities, we shall assume that all server relocations have a cost.† The long-term cost to be minimized is a weighted sum of total expected travel time between servers and demands and of the expected cost of all server relocations that take place per unit of time. The weights will be related to the equilibrium (steady-state) probabilities Π_r, of the markovian network, where Π_r is the probability of being in state r.

We shall examine two versions of this problem, each motivated by a different set of applications. In the first, problem P3, it is required that the *same set* of p locations must be used for the p servers every time the network is in state r, *regardless of the past history of server locations*. This requirement recognizes the fact that, for several types of urban services, deployment strategies consist of locating servers (e.g., ambulances, fire engines) at stations (e.g., ambulance stations, fire houses) whose identity depends solely on the current state of the network and not on previous server locations.

In the second version, problem P4, this restriction is removed and locational decisions take into consideration not only the current state of the network but also previous server locations which, for a markovian network, are summarized by the current and most recent network and server configurations. Problem P4 is more appropriate for cases (e.g., police cars, taxicabs, mobile libraries, "bloodmobiles") in which there are no, or few restrictions, on where a server can be located at any given time.

In Section 12.3.2 we shall review the notation and assumptions for our models. As encouragement to the reader we note that, while the notation is quite cumbersome, the underlying concepts are relatively simple. Section 12.3.3 describes problems P3 and P4 mathematically, and Section 12.3.4 presents node-optimality results for these problems. Section 12.3.5 discusses various algorithms for solving special cases of these problems and some final comments, including some examples, are given in Section 23.3.6.

In order to maximize clarity of concepts in our definitions of P3 and P4 that follow, we have ignored the possibility of cyclic Markov chain behavior that requires the specification of multiple transition probability matrices (e.g., see Figure 12.9) as well as behavior where times between successive transitions are not constant. That is, we focus on the simple case in which

---

*Conversely, we could just as well have demands traveling to the servers or two-way travel (between a demand and a server and back again) depending on the type of application.

†Note that by setting relocation costs to infinity, one can force the servers to be stationary, that is, be fixed facilities as in the classical p-median problem.

the time between successive transitions is a known constant and one transition probability matrix governs all transitions, regardless of the time of day. The more general model may be analyzed using ideas of semi-Markov processes, for random durations between successive transitions (Heyman and Sobel, 1982), and time-varying cyclic Markov processes (Howard, 1960).

12.3.2. Notation and Assumptions

Let $G(N, L)$ be an undirected network with N the set of nodes (with $|N| = n$) and L the set of links. At constantly spaced intervals ("epochs") $G(N, L)$ undergoes changes of *state*. If r and s are two distinct states of the network and if $t_r(i, j)$ indicates the travel time on arc $[i, j] \in L$ (for $i \in N$, $j \in N$) then $t_r(i, j) > 0$ and $t_r(i, j) \neq t_s(i, j)$ for at least one arc $[i, j] \in L$. Let M be the set of all possible states of G with ($|M| = S$). Networks with $S > 1$ can be characterized as "probabilistic" in the context of this section while those with $S = 1$ as "deterministic."

Transitions between network states at the epochs are governed by an ergodic Markov transition matrix P with $p_{rs} \in P$ being the probability of a transition from a state r to a state s ($r \in M, s \in M$). We also denote the steady-state probability vector of the matrix P as Π (with $\Pi P = \Pi$, $\Sigma_{r=1}^{S} \Pi_r = 1$).

A total of p *mobile servers* are to be located on the network. The servers satisfy demands which are generated exclusively at the nodes of $G(N, L)$ with w_i being the conditional probability that a demand comes from node i ($i \in N$) given that a demand was generated (w_i can be viewed as the "normalized weight" of node i).

The system operates as follows: whenever there is a demand for service, that demand is assigned and travels to the server closest to it (or vice versa) in terms of travel time. Whenever there is a change of state of the network, the operator of the service has the option of relocating one or more of the servers. A relocation of a server has an associated cost, which we shall choose to express in units of travel time. The long-term cost to be minimized will be the weighted sum of the total expected travel time of demands to the servers (under all states of the network) and of the expected cost of all server relocations.

We shall denote the shortest travel time between any two points x and y on G when the network is in state r as $d_r(x, y)$, the shortest travel time between a point x and its nearest point in a set $Y = \{y_1, y_2, \ldots, y_p\}$ of p points on G, when the network is in state r, as $D_r(x, Y)$, the shortest travel time between the αth point in a p-point set Z and the γth point in a p-point set Y with the network in state r as $D_r(Z_\alpha, Y_\gamma)$, and the cost (in units of travel time) of relocating a server from x to y with the network in state s as $f[d_s(x, y)]$.

We now state the assumptions under which the results in this section are derived.

1. All servers are available whenever a demand occurs (i.e., any queueing type congestion is ignored).

2. The network G is connected for all $r \in M$ and the travel times $t_r(i, j)$ for all $r \in M$ and all $[i, j] \in L$ are finite.

3. The time required to travel a fraction θ $(0 \le \theta \le 1)$ of any arc $[i, j] \in L$ for any state $r \in M$ is equal to $\theta \cdot t_r(i, j)$.

4. The current state of the network and the current locations of the servers are known to the service operator at all times.

5. Time intervals between changes of state are much longer than trip times on the network.

6. The relocation cost function $f(\cdot)$ is nondecreasing concave.

Assumption 1 implies, in practice, a system with low server utilization (e.g., like many ambulance and fire services but not like police patrol services which are usually characterized by utilizations in the 0.30–0.50, or higher, range). Assumption 1 also holds true in cases where each mobile server could simultaneously serve any number of demands (e.g., mobile community libraries and "bloodmobiles"). The relaxation of Assumption 1 constitutes, of course, the principal motivation for the models and results which were presented in Section 12.2.

Assumptions 2 and 3 are clearly of a technical nature; they are unlikely to cause any difficulty in practical applications (it is always possible to specify arcs in such a way that Assumption 3 is satisfied), but are essential for proving Theorems 12.5 and 12.6.

Assumption 4 allows the operator of the service to always choose the path with the shortest travel time when directing a server from its location to a demand point and to take into consideration the current server locations in deciding which servers to relocate or to dispatch to demands. Assumption 5 renders negligible the probability that arc travel times will change while a server is traveling to a demand. (Were this to happen, the server might no longer be traveling on a shortest travel time path.) Taken together, Assumptions 1, 4, and 5 guarantee that all service demands are served by the time-closest server.

Finally, Assumption 6 is necessary for Theorems 12.5 and 12.6 to hold. It implies, "economies of scale" for the cost of travel times in relocating servers, a reasonable hypothesis in most practical contexts. (Obviously, the family of acceptable functions $f(\cdot)$ also includes linear cost functions.)

12.3.3. The Two Problems

We can now define the two problems that will be discussed in this section. As already noted, the two problems, P3 and P4, are defined for two different problem scenarios.

Problem P3

Under the scenario for P3, we postulate that the same set of p locations (for the p servers) must be used every time the network is in state r, regardless of the past history of the network.

To describe P3 in mathematical terms, we must first define the concept of a strategy. Let the column vector $K(r) = \{K_1(r), K_2(r), \ldots, K_p(r)\}^T$ represent a set of p points where the p servers are located when the network is in state r $(r = 1, 2, \ldots, S)$. A *strategy* is then any $p \times S$ matrix $K = \{K(1), K(2), \ldots, K(S)\}$, where each column $K(r)$, $1 \le r \le M$, provides the set of p locations where the servers will be placed when the network is in state r. A *simple strategy* is any strategy with $K(1) = K(2) = \cdots = K(S)$, that is, a strategy in which servers remain stationary under all states of the network.

We also need to define binary variables $W_s(K_\alpha(r), K_\gamma(s))$ as follows: if the server at $K_\alpha(r)$ is relocated to the location $K_\gamma(s)$ (for $\alpha, \gamma = 1, 2, \ldots, p$) when the network makes a transition from state r to state s, $W_s(K_\alpha(r), K_\gamma(s)) = 1$; otherwise it is equal to 0.

For any given strategy K, the quantity

$$A = \sum_{r=1}^{S} \sum_{i=1}^{n} \Pi_r \, w_i \, D_r(K(r), i) \tag{12.3.1}$$

gives the long-term (steady-state) expected travel time to servers on the network per transition epoch. Similarly the quantity

$$B = \sum_{r=1}^{S} \sum_{\substack{l=1 \\ l \ne r}}^{S} \Pi_r P_{rl} \left\{ \sum_{\alpha=1}^{p} \sum_{\gamma=1}^{p} W_l(K_\alpha(r), K_\gamma(l)) f[d_l(K_\alpha(r), K_\gamma(l))] \right\} \tag{12.3.2}$$

represents the long-term expected cost of server relocations per transition epoch, taking into account all possible changes of state from any possible state and the current locations of the servers.

Our problem is to minimize

$$Z = A + B . \tag{12.3.3}$$

Two sets of constraints apply to our problem:

$$\sum_{\alpha=1}^{p} W_l(K_\alpha(r), K_\gamma(l)) = 1 , \quad \text{for } \gamma = 1, 2, \ldots, p ,$$
$$\forall r, l \in M, \quad r \ne l$$
$$\sum_{\gamma=1}^{p} W_l(K_\alpha(r), K_\gamma(l)) = 1 , \quad \text{for } \alpha = 1, 2, \ldots, p ,$$
$$\forall r, l \in M, \quad r \ne l . \tag{12.3.4}$$

Constraints (12.3.4) ensure that, following any change of state (from state r to state l, $\forall r, l \in M$), each and every one of the p servers will be assigned (by remaining stationary or relocating) to exactly one location.

Problem P4

In this second problem the scenario of P3 is relaxed: the operator of the service does *not* have to use the same set of p locations for the p servers every time the network is in a given state r. Thus, the set of p locations to be used when the system is in state r, *depends not only on the current state r but also on the entire past history of the system*. For a markovian network, this past history is of course summarized by the previous state of the network (i.e., the state from which the network reached the current state). This means that the server assignment/relocation strategy for each state must be a function of the previous state of the network *and* of the position of the servers in that previous state, a total of $S\binom{n}{p}$ combinations. Once this is recognized the formulation of P4 is analogous to that of P3 shown earlier (for details, see Berman and Rahnama, 1983).

Problems P3 and P4 are illustrated in Examples 12.2 and 12.3 at the end of this section.

12.3.4. The Solution Space

Two fundamental results that discretize the solution spaces for P3 and P4 can now be presented.

Theorem 12.5. *At least one set of optimal locations for* P3 *exists on the nodes of the network.*

Theorem 12.6. *At least one set of optimal locations for* P4 *exists on the nodes of the network.*

The proofs of Theorems 12.5 and 12.6 are given by Berman and Odoni (1978) and Berman and Rahnama (1983), respectively. Although rather long, both proofs are very similar and follow the lines of other proofs of node-optimality (Hakimi, 1964; see also Chapter 2 of this book). In the present case, one must show that (i) expected travel cost (term A in (12.3.3)) and (ii) expected server relocation cost (term B) are each a concave function over the length of any network arc $[i, j]$ on which a server is located. In view of the fact that a linear combination of concave functions is concave, (i) and (ii) together prove the theorem since one can do at least as well by moving the server from the interior of arc $[i, j]$ to either node i or node j.

As a result of Theorem 12.5, the total number of strategies that need be considered for P3 is $\binom{n}{p}^{S}$. This is because there are p nodes to be chosen out of n possible locations (the nodes of G) for each state of the network (resulting in $\binom{n}{p}$ possibilities) for each of the S states of the network. Similarly, by Theorem 12.6, there are $S\binom{n}{p}$ possible previous "histories" for P4 and $\binom{n}{p}$ choices for server locations for each of these histories. If we define $a = \binom{n}{p}$ this means that there are a^{Sa} possible combinations in the solution space.

12.3.5. Solving P3 and P4

We now provide a brief survey of various solution approaches for problems P3 and P4. We begin with a special instance of the problems, and then address questions related to the general versions.

Single Server on a Tree

For the simple case in which a *single* server is to be located on a tree network undergoing markovian state transitions, it turns out that the solutions to P3 and P4 *are always identical*. The reason is that the optimal strategy in this case is to keep the single server *stationary* at a single node, independently of the state of the tree. That node is the (single) median of the tree under *all* states of the network. This remarkably simple result is a consequence of the fact that for trees, the location of the median is independent of the arc lengths, as long as the arc lengths are positive, and is determined solely by the "weights" w_i of the tree's nodes, a property first proven by Goldman (1971) using the "majority theorem" (cf. Chapter 2). Since the weights w_i ($i = 1, 2, \ldots, n$) are, by assumption, independent of the state of the network, so is the location of the tree's median in our problem. It thus suffices to find the median of the tree for any *one* state to determine the optimal location of the server for all states! This can be accomplished in time proportional to n (and independently of S) by examining the tree in *any* one state and using Goldman's majority algorithm (cf. Algorithm 2.1 in Chapter 2).

General Network with p Servers

It is quite straightforward to formulate the general version of P3, that is, locating p servers on a general network, as a 0-1 integer linear programming (ILP) problem (see Berman and Odoni, 1978, or Berman and LeBlanc, 1984). Unfortunately, the size of the ILP grows quickly with the number of nodes, n, and the number of states, S: the number of 0-1 variables increases in proportion to $S^2 \times n^2$ and the number of constraints in proportion to $S \times n^2 + S^2 \times n$. Thus, even a modest size problem (e.g., with $n = 25$, $S = 3$) may be computationally too expensive to solve using the ILP approach.

A simple heuristic algorithm for obtaining (hopefully) good solutions to P3 has been developed by Berman and LeBlanc (1984). This algorithm is an extension of the heuristic to solve the single facility problem reported by Berman and Odoni (1982).

In somewhat simplified terms the Berman and LeBlanc algorithm belongs to the general class of "node-substitution" heuristics: one begins with an initial set of p locations for each one of the S states of the network and attempts to improve this initial solution by efficiently examining one server after another for each and every state of the network for a possible change of location that would reduce the current value of the objective function. For each such change one must, of course, also find the corresponding optimal strategy for reassinging (relocation of) servers. The algorithm terminates as soon as no improvements can be found after a complete pass through examining all the servers in all the states of the network.

This heuristic algorithm has been programmed in APL, with some modifications designed to speed up the search for possible improved locations (Berman and LeBlanc, 1984). The solutions obtained through the heuristic have been compared with those obtained through the exact solution of the ILP formulation for 21 modest-sized (due to the size limitations for solving the ILP problem no large problems were solved) sample problems. In 19 out of the 21 cases, the heuristic produced the optimal strategy; in the other two cases the suboptimal strategies found by the heuristic had a cost only 2–3% higher than that of the optimal strategies. Execution times were much smaller with the heuristic. For example, for four problems with $n = 25$ and $S = 2$, the heuristic averaged about 10 CPU-seconds of execution time on a Honeywell DPS/80 computer as compared to 820 CPU-seconds for the exact ILP solution on a CDC CYBER 175, despite the fact that the CDC computer executes approximately 5–10 times faster than the Honeywell.

P4 on a general network with p servers can be formulated as a markovian decision theory (MDT) problem and solved by using a standard MDT algorithm, for example, Howard's policy iteration approach (Howard, 1960). While a discussion of MDT and its application to problem P4 are beyond the scope of this chapter, we note here that, as Berman and Rahnama (1983) have shown, Howard's algorithm, when coupled with careful exploitation of some characteristics of P4 that give its MDT formulation a special structure, makes it possible to solve P4 problems of sufficiently large size to permit the modeling of nontrivial situations (e.g., $n = 10$, $S = 3$, $p = 2$). This is encouraging, in view of the large size of the solution space for P4 as noted in Section 2.3.

12.3.6. Numerical Examples and Comments

Two numerical examples will illustrate some of the above material.

Example 12.2. Consider a two-state network as shown in Figure 12.10, where the numbers next to the arcs represent travel times and those next to the nodes are the weights w_i. The only difference between the two states is the travel time on arc [3, 2] which is equal to 1 in state 1 and to 9 in state 2. The markovian transition matrix P that describes the statistical dependence between the two states is also shown in Figure 12.10. The steady-state probabilities that result from P are $\Pi_1 = 0.4$ and $\Pi_2 = 0.6$. We assume that $f(d) = 0.1\sqrt{d}$ is the relocation cost function, concave as required by Theorems 12.5 and 12.6.

Suppose that we wish to locate two servers on our network. If we are solving problem P3, there are $\binom{5}{2}^2 = 100$ possible strategies according to

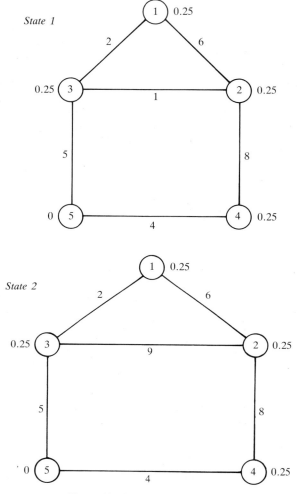

Figure 12.10. A two-state example.

Theorem 12.5. Problems of this size can be solved quite easily by hand (see Berman and Odoni, 1982). For this example the optimal strategy is $\{K(1) = (3, 4), \; K(2) = (1, 4)\}$. That is, when the network changes from state 1 to state 2, the server on node 4 should stay at its location $(W_2(4, 4) = 1)$ whereas the server on node 3 should be relocated to node 1, and vice versa when the change of states is from 2 to 1. This solution makes intuitive sense; the server at node 3 moves to node 1 in order to maintain some proximity to node 2 whenever the network undergoes a transition from state 1 to state 2. It turns out that this, in fact, is the optimal strategy as long as the relocation cost function is $f(d) = C\sqrt{d}$ and $0 \le C < 0.2357$. When $C \ge 0.2357$, the simple strategy $\{K(1) = (1, 4),\ K(2) = (1, 4)\}$ becomes optimal. This is not surprising since the relocation cost is high when C is large.

Under the scenario of P4, using Howard's policy iteration algorithm, it can be shown (Berman and Rahnama, 1983) that the optimal policy is identical to the one obtained for P3. In other words, in this example, the optimal strategy (when $f(d) = 0.1\sqrt{d}$) for problem P4 turns out to be independent of the network's "history." ○

Example 12.3. In this example, we illustrate a case where the optimal strategies for P3 and P4 are different. Consider the network of Figure 12.11 with 4 nodes and 6 arcs whose travel times are denoted by $e_1, e_2, \ldots, e_6$, as shown. Let $w_i = 1/4$ for all i and let us try to locate optimally one server. This network is assumed to have 6 states; in state r, $e_r = 2$ and all other $e = 1$. All state transition probabilities $p_{sr} = 1/6$ $(s, r = 1, 2, \ldots, 6)$, leading to steady-state probabilities $\Pi_r = 1/6$ $(r = 1, \ldots, 6)$. We will assume that $f(d) = \varepsilon > 0$, that is, the cost of moving the server is always very small.

It can be seen that in each state there are exactly two locations from which the server can optimally service demand in that state. For example, in state 1, placing the server at either node 2 or 3 is optimal, *for that state alone*. In general, placing the server at either node which is *not* adjacent to e_r is optimal for state r considered alone. Let us denote this set of two nodes by N_r. Now some thought will reveal that, if ε is sufficiently small, the optimal strategy for operating this system under the problem P4 scenario is: "move the server to either node in N_r whenever the system enters state r, unless the server is already at a node in N_r, in which case do not move the server (and save the cost of relocation)." Clearly, in this optimal strategy the location of the server is allowed to vary each time state r is entered,

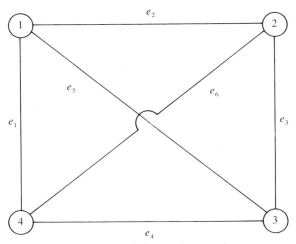

Figure 12.11. A four-node example.

depending on the previous location of the server (which obviously will depend on the state that the system leaves to enter into state r). This, of course, is not permitted under the problem P3 scenario which requires that the server be designated a single optimal location in each state $r = 1, 2, \ldots, 6$. Indeed, it can be shown without too much effort, that for problem P3 there are several optimal strategies in this example (one such strategy is $\{K(1) = 2,\ K(2) = 3,\ K(3) = 1,\ K(4) = 1,\ K(5) = 1,\ K(6) = 2\}$) and that all these strategies have an associated value of Z which exceeds by an amount $\varepsilon/9$ the value of Z achieved under the optimal strategy for problem P4. ○

Two comments are in order before concluding this section. First, note that the mobile server location problems presented here are very general ones, in the sense that many known versions of minimum facility location problems on networks can be viewed as special cases of P3 and P4. For example, the probabilistic network problem discussed by Mirchandani and Odoni (1979) (cf. Chapter 2) in which stationary facilities must be located on a network that undergoes probabilistic transitions among S states is a special case of P3 where only simple strategies (i.e., $K(1) = K(2) = \cdots = K(S)$) are permitted. If in the Mirchandani–Odoni problem we further allow the number of states S to be reduced to 1, we obtain the standard p-median problem (cf. Chapter 2).

The second comment is that, for applications in the urban context, the number of states necessary to model adequately the changes in travel times that occur on a daily basis is not very large. For example, the network state representation shown in Figure 12.9 with $S = 9$ will be more than sufficiently detailed for many purposes. It is thus possible that quite realistic applications will be carried out in the near future using (possibly extensions of) the algorithms described here.

ACKNOWLEDGMENTS

This research was principally supported by National Science Foundation Grant No. 8204318-ECS to the Operations Research Center of MIT. It was also supported in part by National Science Foundation Grant No. ECS-8307798, in part by National Science Foundation Grant No. 51496, in part by the National Science Engineering Council of Canada, Grant No. A4578, and in part by the New Faculty Development Award of the State University of New York at Buffalo.

EXERCISES

12.1 Show that feasible locations of the SQM on a tree network are connected. A location x for the SQM is feasible if the objective function value $\overline{TR}(x, \lambda)$ is finite. (A set of S on a network is connected if two points a and b belong to S, the path(s) connecting a and b also belongs to S).

12.2 Define $v(\lambda) = \min_{x \in T} \overline{TR}(x, \lambda)$, where the SQM problem is defined on a tree network. Show that $v(\lambda)$ is nondecreasing in λ.

12.3 We define the expected SQM problem on a tree T as

$$\min_{x \in T} E_\lambda[\overline{TR}(x, \lambda)],$$

where the expectation is taken over random variable λ. For the expected SQM problem to be meaningful, we require that each problem $P(\lambda)$: min $\overline{TR}(x, \lambda)$ to be feasible for those λs with nonzero probability measures. This problem arises where the total arrival rate λ is not homogeneous in time, but each λ persists for a long enough period so that the expected response time $\overline{TR}(x, \lambda)$ is realized. Show that the objective function $E_\lambda[\overline{TR}(x, \lambda)]$ is convex over any path of the tree network.

12.4 In the 1-median problem, there may be multiple optimal solutions. Show that the set of optimal 1-medians on a tree network is connected. Show, by way of an example, that multiple optimal 1-medians may not be connected on a general network.

12.5 By way of an example, show that maximum number of breakpoints on a general network can be as high as $n(n-1)(n-2)/2$, where n is the number of nodes.

12.6 Consider a rectangle with sides a and b in length. The spatial distribution of calls for service is uniform over the entire region, and total call rate is λ. Travel metric is rectilinear with travel directions parallel to the sides of the rectangle. Travel speed is V_x and V_y along the two axes. Find the SQM if the nontravel related component of total services time is independent of the locations of the incident and the facility.

12.7 What is the effect of an existing permanent facility in the network on the location of the service unit? In this case, the service unit (e.g., an ambulance) travels to the demand, performs some on-scene service, continues to the permanent facility (e.g., a hospital) where off-scene service is received and then returns to the "home" location. For more details on the problem and some results refer to Berman and LeBlanc (1983).

12.8 Develop a model that incorporates both types of uncertainty discussed in this chapter (uncertainties in the link length as well as uncertainties that are due to the limited capacity of the service units). An initial step in this direction is given by Berman (1985) where the case of a single service unit operating on a network with discrete random lengths is discussed.

12.9   Find simultaneously the optimal service territory and optimal locations for $P > 2$ servers. Refer to Berman and Mandowsky (1986) for more details.

12.10   Find the optimal location of facility that houses k servers ($M/G/k/\infty$ queueing system). For an approach that utilizes a queueing approximation, refer to Batta and Berman (1989).

REFERENCES

Batta, R. (1984). *Facility Location in the Presence of Congestion*. Ph.D. Dissertation, Operations Research Center, Massachusetts Institute of Technology, Cambridge.

Batta, R. (1988). *Single Server Queueing-Location Models with Rejection*. *Transportation Science* **22**, 209–216.

Batta, R. (1989). "A Queueing-Location Model with Service Time Dependent Queueing Disciplines." *European Journal of Operational Research* **39**, 192–205.

Batta, R., and O. Berman (1989). "A Location Model for a Facility Operating as an $M/G/k$ Queue." To appear in *Networks*.

Batta, R., R. C. Larson, and A. R. Odoni (1988). "A Single Server Priority Queueing-Location Model." *Networks* **8**, 87–103.

Batta, R., A. Ghose, and U. S. Palekar (1989). "Locating Facilities on the Manhattan Metric with Arbitrarily Shaped Barriers and Convex Forbidden Regions." *Transportation Science* **23**, 26–36.

Berman, O. (1985). "Locating a Facility on a Congested Network with Random Lengths." *Networks* **15**, 275–294.

Berman, O., and R. C. Larson (1982). "The Median Problem with Congestion." *Computers and Operations Research* **4**(2), 119–126.

Berman, O., and R. C. Larson (1985). "Optimal 2-Facility Network Districting in the Presence of Queueing." *Transportation Science* **19**(3), 207–216.

Berman, O., and B. LeBlanc (1983). *Optimal M/G/1 Server Location in the Presence of a Fixed Facility*, Working Paper WP-22-83. Faculty of Management, University of Calgary, Alberta, Canada.

Berman, O., and B. LeBlanc (1984). "Location-Relocation of N Mobile Facilities on a Stochastic Network." *Transportation Science* **18**(4), 315–330.

Berman, O., and R. R. Mandowsky (1986). "Location-Allocation on Congested Networks." *European Journal of Operational Research* **26**(2), 238–250.

Berman, O., and A. R. Odoni (1978). *Locating Mobile Servers on a Network with Markovian Properties*, Working Paper OR-083-78. Operations Research Center, Massachusetts Institute of Technology, Cambridge.

Berman, O., and A.R. Odoni (1982). "Locating Mobile Servers on a Network with Markovian Properties." *Networks* **12**, 73–86.

Berman, O., and M. R. Rahnama (1983). "Optimal Location Relocation Decisions on Stochastic Networks." *Transportation Science* **19**(3), 218–232.

Berman, O., R. C. Larson, and S. S. Chiu (1985). "Optimal Server Location on a Network Operating as an $M/G/1$ Queue." *Operations Research* **33**, 746–771.

Berman, O., R. C. Larson, and C. Parkan (1987). "The Stochastic Queue *p*-Median Problem." *Transportation Science* **21**, 207–216.

Brandeau, M. L. (1985). *Exploiting Convexity and Separability Properties of Location Problems*. Ph.D. Dissertation, Engineering-Economic Systems Department, Stanford Univeristy, Stanford, California.

Chiu, S. S. (1985). *Optimal Trajectory of the Stochastic Queue Median As Total Demand Rate Varies*. Tech. Rep., Engineering-Economic Systems Department, Stanford University, Stanford, California.

Chiu, S. S. (1986a). "A Dominance Theorem for the Stochastic Queue Median Problem." *Operations Research* **34**, 942–944.

Chiu, S. S. (1986b). "Optimal *M/G/*1 Server Location on a Tree Network with Continuous Link Demands," *Computers and Operations Research* **13**, 653–669.

Chiu, S. S., and R. C. Larson (1985). "Locating an *n*-Server Facility in a Stochastic Environment." *Computers and Operations Research* **12**, 509–516.

Chiu, S. S., O. Berman, and R. C. Larson (1985). "Locating a Mobile Server Queueing Facility on a Tree Network." *Management Science* **31**, 764–772.

Coffman, E. G., and M. Hofri (1978). "A Class of FIFO Queues Arising in Computer Systems." *Operations Research* **26**, 864–880.

Cooper, L. L. (1964). "Heuristic Methods for Location-Allocation Problems." *SIAM Review* **6**(1), 37–53.

Goldman, A. J. (1971). "Optimal Center Location on Simple Networks." *Transportation Science* **5**, 212–221.

Hakimi, S. L. (1964). "Optimal Location of Switching Centers and the Absolute Centers and Medians of a Graph." *Operations Research* **12**, 450–459.

Heyman, O. P., and M. J. Sobel (1982). *Stochastic Models in Operations Research*, Vol.2. McGraw-Hill, New York.

Howard, R. A. (1960). *Dynamic Programming and Markov Processes*. MIT Press, Cambridge, Massachusetts.

Jarvis, J. P. (1976). "A Location Model for Spatially Distributed Queueing Systems." *Proceedings of the 1976 IEEE-SMC International Conference on Cynernetics and Society*, pp. 32–35.

Kleinrock, L. (1976). *Queueing Systems*, Vol.2. Wiley, New York.

Larson, R. C. (1974). "A Hypercube Queueing Model for Facility Location and Redistricting in Urban Emergency Services." *Computers and Operations Research* **1**, 67–95.

Larson, R. C., and A. R. Odoni (1981). *Urban Operations Research*. Prentice-Hall, Englewood Cliffs, New Jersey.

Larson, R. C., and G. Sadiq (1983). "Facility Locations With the Manhattan Metric in the Presence of Barriers to Travel." *Operations Research* **31**, 652–669.

Mirchandani, P. B., and A. R. Odoni (1979). "Locations of Medians on Stochastic Networks." *Transportation Science* **13**, 85–97.

Nozaki, S. A., and S. M. Ross (1978). "Approximations in Finite-Capacity Multi-Server Queues with Poisson Arrivals." *Journal of Applied Probability* **15**, 826–834.

Index